BASIL

A Short History of the Second World War

Collins

FONTANA BOOKS

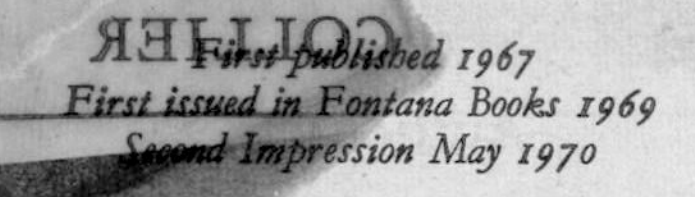

First published 1967
First issued in Fontana Books 1969
Second Impression May 1970

Maps by Edgar Holloway

Printed in Great Britain
Collins Clear-Type Press
London and Glasgow

Author's Note

The purpose of this book is to present a concise account of the Second World War in the light of the mass of material which has become available in the course of the past twenty years or so.

I have had generous help from wartime commanders, staff officers, and others who have given me the benefit of their special knowledge of particular aspects of the war. At many points guidance from leading actors in my story, or from scientific or other experts, has been invaluable.

However, with minor exceptions I have not relied for any material statement of fact on uncorroborated testimony from such sources. Unless supported by diaries or similar evidence, the reminiscences of even exceptionally observant principals or eye-witnesses do not take the place of historical studies founded on contemporary documents, or of the documents themselves. But they nearly always make the scrutiny of the written record more agreeable, and often they make it more rewarding.

Much of the help received from participants in the war was given to me before a word of the book was written. Among friends and correspondents who have helped me at a later stage I must mention in particular Lieutenant-General T. W. Corbett, who very kindly read the draft of chapter 15. I am also indebted to General Corbett for calling my attention, before the chapter was drafted, to two points mentioned in the notes.

Captain S. W. Roskill, R.N., a one-time colleague whose official history of the war at sea is an indispensable source, has been good enough to read the manuscript from the naval aspect. I am grateful to him and to other readers of the manuscript or proofs for valuable comments and suggestions.

My debt to other colleagues and fellow-writers on military history will be obvious from the bibliography.

Specific references to published authorities have been grouped in the Notes at the end of the book, except in a few instances where it seemed right to insert a footnote for the benefit of readers who may not wish to turn to the main body of the notes.

The maps have been expertly drawn by Mr. Edgar Holloway.

The method adopted in this book of designating military

commands and formations conforms generally with established practice in the Western countries; but pedantic accuracy has not been sought at the expense of clarity. In particular, the traditional use of Roman numerals to designate a corps (which presumably arose from the need to draw a self-evident distinction between corps and divisional designations in hand-written orders) has been avoided, since experience shows that such designations as 'XXXIX Corps' are sometimes puzzling to non-military readers.

For simplicity, holders of the German rank of Colonel-General (which has no exact equivalent in the British or United States Armies) have been referred to in the text as generals.

It remains for me to record my gratitude to Mrs. F. M. Brown for her patient typing of the text, appendices and tables.

B.C.

When I was twenty I knew that men were
linked together in one province.
When I was thirty I knew that they were
linked together in one nation.
When I was forty I knew that they were
linked together in one world of five
continents.

Shozan Sakuma, Japanese defence expert
(1811-64)

Contents

CONTENTS

Maps

MAPS

MAPS

Tables

CHAPTER I

PRELUDE

1918-34

Towards the end of the First World War a wave of revulsion from the slaughter and destruction of the past four years swept through Europe and beyond. Ample experience, it was felt, had shown the futility of attempts to settle disputes between civilized nations by recourse to arms. Most of the belligerents had everything to gain by cutting their losses and agreeing never to fight again.

The existence of this powerful trend of thought and feeling might have been expected to speed the coming of an armistice and ease the problem of concluding a just and stable peace. In practice it did neither. Even when the causes of the war were forgotten by everyone but a few experts, it was still possible to quarrel about ways of making peace.

In 1918 there was no more eloquent apostle of human concord than President Woodrow Wilson of the United States. Chosen by fate to lead to war the only belligerent nation in the Western World whose wealth and influence had grown as a result of Europe's preoccupation with self-destruction, he remained a man of peace and an impassioned enemy of military autocracy. When the German government became convinced in the late summer of that year, that only an immediate respite could save their army from annihilation or collapse, they decided to link their request for an armistice with an offer to make peace on the basis of fourteen tentative proposals which Wilson had put forward in a famous speech.[1] They also decided to make their request through him rather than apply in the first instance to the less pacific Marshal Foch. But the

President was in no position to commit the European Allies, and the European Allies were in no position to commit the President. If Woodrow Wilson was determined not to surrender any of the influence for good which he counted on exerting, European statesmen were equally determined that no important step should be taken without full discussion. The decision to grant an armistice had therefore to wait while a fully accredited envoy, Colonel Edward Mandell House, was despatched to Europe with instructions to threaten the Allies with the loss of American support if they failed to fall in with the President's ideas. Even when agreement was reached between House and the Allied statesmen just over a week after his arrival on October 26, time had still to be allowed for German Armistice Commissioners to receive instructions, make their way to the appointed meeting-place, and consider the terms proposed. Meanwhile the armies of the Allied and Associated Powers continued to improve their positions on the Western Front, but not to an extent which would have made it utterly impossible for anyone to claim after the war that the German Army had not suffered an overwhelming defeat.

Thus hostilities on the Western Front did not cease until five weeks after the Germans had first offered to make peace on the basis of the Fourteen Points. But it does not follow that the Allied and Associated Powers erred in not granting Germany an armistice as soon as she asked for one, or that Woodrow Wilson and his ideals were solely accountable for the deaths of men who would otherwise have lived. Nor does it follow that the President's ideals were unsound. If he seemed to depart from them a little in his handling of the pre-armistice negotiations, the reason was that he wore, beneath the morning coat of an idealist, the shining armour of a patriot. The coming of peace was delayed because he was determined to do the right thing by his country, and because he and the Allied statesmen distrusted each other a little and the Germans more.

Even so, the consequences were far-reaching. When the Germans first asked for an armistice, the empires of the Hohenzollerns and the Hapsburgs stretched from the Vosges

1 Europe in 1918

o the Carpathians and from the Baltic to the Adriatic. When their request was granted, Germany had only the semblance of a government and Austro-Hungary was an arena where Austrian Germans, Magyars, Poles, Czechs, Slovaks, Ruthenians and Yugoslavs paraded jealous claims to nationhood.

The loss of those five weeks was neither the sole nor the primary cause of these disasters. The German revolution might have occurred even if fighting had stopped in October; the collapse of the Austro-Hungarian Empire could scarcely have been averted in any case. But the doubts and hesitations with which the Wilsonian programme was accepted, the very fact that some of the belligerents accepted it largely because they feared that a rich and influential backer might desert them if they refused to do so, suggested that the consequences of linking the question of an armistice with the much bigger question of the ultimate peace terms were likely to prove harmful. In

Central Europe the delay contributed to a climate of despair and recklessness which made the break-up of a great administrative and economic unit at the heart of the civilized world more complete and more catastrophic than it might otherwise have been. The peacemakers were left with the huge task of not only trying to reconcile a whole host of divergent interests on lines inadequately sketched in the proposals to which they had agreed, but of making the attempt in conditions which forced them either to build a new system, or to acquiesce in a state of affairs which could easily slide into anarchy.

Any solution of long-standing European problems likely to be arrived at in these circumstances was bound to seem unsatisfactory to many people. The victors would therefore have been well advised, in their own interests, to share the odium of an imperfect settlement with the vanquished by associating them as closely as possible with the drafting of the peace treaties. Even if they had not pledged themselves in the pre-armistice negotiations to discuss the detailed application of the Fourteen Points with the other side, they would have had everything to gain by doing so. As it was, they spent so much time on attempts to reconcile their own differences of outlook that they found themselves obliged to cut the proceedings short. German delegates were allowed to make only written comments on the draft Treaty of Versailles, and a preliminary conference between Allied and American delegates was deemed to have taken the place of the peace conference proper.[2] This was dishonest, and hence a crime.[3] It was also likely to cause trouble in the future, and hence a blunder.

Even so, within six or seven years a great deal of the bitterness engendered at Versailles disappeared. In 1924 the Dawes Plan gilded the pill of Reparations; in 1925 the Locarno Pacts began a new era in Franco-German relations; and in 1926 Germany joined the League of Nations.* Full cultural and commercial exchanges between Germany and her former enemies were resumed to the satisfaction of all parties. Not only old scars but also those inflicted when French and Belgian troops marched into the Ruhr in 1923 seemed to have

*See Appendix 1.

healed when Gustav Stresemann's avowal that he wanted to be 'the German who makes peace with France'[4] was matched by Aristide Briand's assertion that the time had come for Frenchmen and Germans to forget their quarrels.

Yet Locarno could not undo all the consequences of four years of war and a further seven years of enmity. From the strategic point of view a great weakness of the peace settlements was that they did not satisfy the French craving for security. Aware that Germany, even when shorn of substantial territories on her Eastern and Western frontiers, would still have a big advantage in manpower and industrial potential, the French had pressed in 1919 for a frontier on the Rhine, but had settled for a demilitarized Rhineland and the theoretical safeguard of British and American guarantees which lapsed when the United States refused to ratify the Versailles Treaty. Better relations with Germany in the second half of the nineteen-twenties did not make France any less determined to compensate for her small population and limited productive capacity by linking herself with Belgium, Czechoslovakia, Poland, Rumania and Yugoslavia. Nor did they prevent her statesmen from falling back, some ten years after Locarno, on the old remedy of alliance with Russia.

Meanwhile the French maintained by far the largest army in Europe outside the Soviet Union, as well as a powerful navy and an air force strong enough on paper to give the British some anxious moments in the early twenties. In 1927, two years after Locarno, they began building the Maginot Line, a chain of fortified positions between the Swiss frontier and Lorraine.[5] Germany, on the other hand, was limited to a small professional army of seven infantry and three cavalry divisions. Insistence on voluntary recruitment was intended to prevent her from piling up reservists, but in fact helped her to build a body of picked men. Military aircraft were forbidden, but the ban did not prevent the Germans from maintaining the nucleus of an air force by sending recruits abroad for training. Restrictions on artillery kept the German Army short of guns, but encouraged officers of the Ordnance Branch to look for substitutes. As early as 1930 a book on space-travel by a Transylvanian Saxon, Hermann Oberth, put them on the path to the A-4 long-range rocket.[6]

The problem inherent in the lack of balance between French and German armaments and the reluctance of patriotic Germans to accept permanent inferiority was not solved when Germany promised at Locarno to respect her existing frontiers in the West and to press for revision of her Eastern frontiers only by means short of war. Keeping their large army and adding to their fortifications, the French pointed out when the need for such measures was questioned that their frontiers had been violated twice within a lifetime. The Germans, when assured that the French Army was essentially a defensive weapon and that they themselves could not need many troops unless they meant to go to war, replied that armies were a recognized means of exerting diplomatic pressure without war, and that the French Army had in fact invaded Germany in 1923.

If the problem remained in the background for a good many years after Locarno, the reason was not that it had been solved but that Stresemann's policy was oriented towards the future and that meanwhile Germany's energies were largely absorbed by her economic recovery. The inflation of 1923 had wiped out the savings of small investors, but not the fixed assets from which fortunes could still be made if liquid capital were forthcoming. Under the stimulus of foreign loans, industry made such rapid strides after 1924 that output was soon well above the pre-war level, despite the surrender of important centres of production under the Versailles Treaty. By 1928 wages and prices were rising at a measured pace, unemployment was falling, and a brisk demand for a wide range of consumer goods showed that Germans of all classes had money in their pockets. While such conditions lasted, hardworking citizens were not likely to go out of their way to raise awkward issues, and Stresemann did not encourage them to do so. Observers of the international scene concluded that there was not much wrong with the state of Europe which could not be put right by a judicious scaling-down of French armaments when the time came for a general settlement.

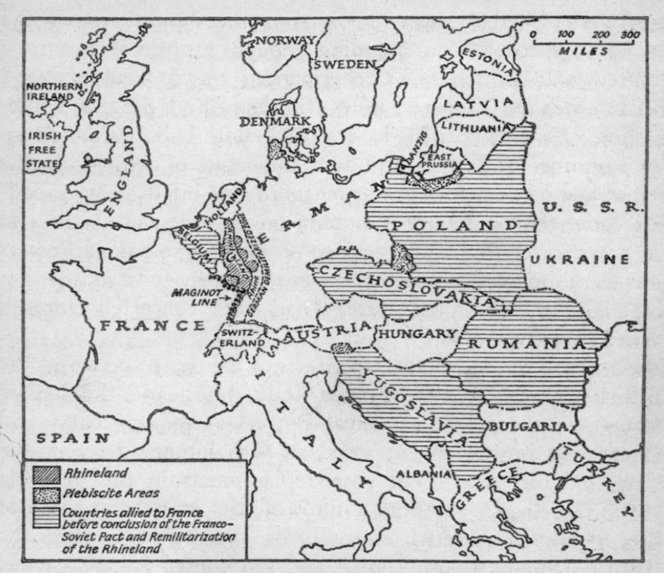

2 Versailles Europe and the Maginot Line

In the Far East, on the other hand, the war and its diplomatic aftermath had led by 1928 to a state of unstable equilibrium.[7] Two important aims of American foreign policy in recent years had been to prevent Japan from establishing hegemony over Eastern Asia, and her ally Britain from asserting naval supremacy throughout the world. At the Washington Conference in 1921 and 1922 the United States had marshalled all her diplomatic resources to persuade the Great Powers to uphold the *status quo* in the Pacific, bolster a crumbling China as a barrier against Japanese encroachment, and accept a programme of naval disarmament designed to substitute Anglo-American for British command of the sea.* Japan's dependence on imported raw materials had been expected to put Britain and the United States in a strong position to enforce these arrangements, but strategically neither

*See Appendix II and Map B.

was well placed to meet the situation that might arise if the Japanese succeeded in hoarding enough supplies for even a limited war in China. The American naval base at Pearl Harbor was five thousand miles from the China Seas, and completion of a new British base at Singapore had been held up by a number of factors, the most important of which was the reluctance of post-war governments to risk inflation by spending more than the bare minimum on armaments. At the end of the nineteen-twenties neither of the Anglo-Saxon Powers was in a position to undertake major operations in the Far East, and no common strategy had been concerted between their respective staffs.

At the London Naval Conference in 1930 between the British Commonwealth, France, Italy, Japan and the United States, the three leading naval Powers agreed to renew and extend the limitations imposed at Washington. They undertook to build no capital ship replacements in the next six years; the British accepted a limit of fifty cruisers in place of the seventy considered essential by their experts; and the British Commonwealth, Japan and the United States assented to parity in destroyers and submarines although their needs and situations differed widely. Again, no plans for joint action in the event of undesirable developments in the Far East were concerted between American and British service chiefs.

The reluctance of the Western Powers to commit themselves to staff talks did not, however, prevent the Japanese from regarding their attitude as unjust and oppressive. Almost within living memory the British and the French had staked out large claims in Africa, while the Americans had possessed themselves of extensive territories in California, New Mexico the Philippines and Texas. Still more recently the French had fought for Syria and the Greeks had been encouraged to fight for Smyrna. That the Japanese were forbidden to take as much of China as they could hope to hold seemed to some of them unfair and hypocritical. A pro-Western Japanese government had accepted the Washington agreements with good grace but confidence in the British had been shaken by England's assent to arrangements which sacrificed her naval supremacy and the interests of her ally on the altar of solidarity between the English-speaking peoples. The Chief of the Japanese Naval Staff did not lack sympathizers in his own country when he gave up his post as a protest against his government's ratification of the London Treaty.

At the same time, it did not escape observers in Japan that Anglo-American support for China was confined to the economic sphere and that the British and American fleets were in no position to intervene in the Western Pacific. Warnings that the West might find Japanese statesmen increasingly difficult to handle after the London Conference were shown to be near the mark when, on September 18, 1931, a mysterious explosion which did minor damage to the Japanese-controlled Southern Manchurian Railway was followed by an exchange of shots between Chinese troops and Japanese armed guards. Claiming that the local authorities were incapable of keeping order, the Japanese proceeded to put troops in Mukden as prelude to a military occupation of the whole of Manchuria.

The Japanese were alleged to have engineered the railway incident. In any case, their subsequent actions seemed a clear contravention of the undertaking which they had given at Washington to respect Chinese sovereignty. Refusing to withdraw their troops from Manchuria when asked to do so, they set up the puppet state of Manchukuo. The Chinese responded with a boycott, rioting broke out in the International Settlement at Shanghai, and the Japanese presented an ultimatum and landed troops in the neighbourhood after demands for compensation and the suppression of anti-Japanese associations had been rejected. Fighting stopped when the Chinese accepted the ultimatum, but meanwhile their troops had been pushed back and the rights and privileges of foreign residents had been sharply challenged.

Irrespective of responsibility for the incidents which sparked off the trouble, Japan's repudiation of the obligations she had accepted at Washington was the kind of action which might have been expected to bring a sharp response in the days of British naval supremacy. In 1932 naval supremacy was shared, in theory, between Britain and the United States; but neither country possessed the means of striking instantly at an enemy thousands of miles away, and neither British nor American statesmen were willing to threaten military action at the risk of involving themselves in a prolonged war in which the initial advantage would lie with Japan. Japanese spokesmen told their British and American friends long afterwards that economic sanctions, without war, would have been enough to bring extremists to their senses. But many statesmen feared at the time that economic sanctions might themselves lead to war, and in both English-speaking countries an embargo on trade with Japan would have been unpopular with merchants and industrialists struggling to make ends meet after a disastrous slump. The ultimate effect of an exchange of views through the usual channels was that both American and British administrators were left with the impression that more ought to have been done to convince the Japanese that aggression would be unprofitable in the long run, and that probably someone or other on the far side of the Atlantic deserved blame for not doing it.

Encouraged by the failure of Britain and the United States to stand up for their rights and those of other signatories to the Washington agreements, the Japanese responded to an adverse verdict at Geneva by leaving the League of Nations. They went on to occupy Jehol and threaten the Chinese homeland south of the Great Wall. In 1934 they exercised their right to denounce the Washington Naval Treaty; at the conference summoned in the following year to discuss renewal of the London Treaty, due to expire in 1936, they refused to negotiate unless granted parity with the strongest naval Powers. When this demand was unanimously rejected, they took no further part in the proceedings and set to work on an intensive programme of naval construction.

The Americans and the British tried to counter these moves by giving increased economic and financial support to the Chinese National Government. In addition, the United States made a bid for goodwill in the Western Pacific by promising complete independence to the Philippines by 1946. But aid to

China and an enlightened attitude towards dependent peoples were not effective substitutes for fleets and armies with secure bases. It remained a disturbing thought for the West that the end of the long naval truce between Japan and the Western world would leave Japan free to build as many ships as she could find the means of building. Moreover, the security of American communications west of Hawaii would depend henceforward on the willingness of the Japanese to observe the terms of the mandate which forbade them to fortify the Marianas and the Caroline and Marshall Islands. On the other hand, Japan would still be vulnerable to such economic pressure as her customers abroad might be able and willing to exert.

The lesson of the 'China incident' was not lost on the British Chiefs of Staff. Within a month of the Japanese landing at Shanghai they called on the government to heed 'the Writing on the Wall', discard the assumption that there would be no great war involving the British Empire for at least ten years, and start providing for defensive commitments without awaiting the outcome of the Disarmament Conference which had just assembled at Geneva.[8] The government agreed that the naval base at Singapore must be completed and equipped with fixed defences by the time the London Naval Treaty expired, but not that other commitments were almost equally important. Before long, however, developments nearer home compelled them to take a fresh look at the whole question of Britain's international obligations and the resources available to meet them.

An important aim of British foreign policy after the First World War was to foster conditions in which business could be transacted with a reasonable assurance that markets and currencies would remain stable for some time to come. In the interests of the concord which alone seemed likely to create such conditions in Continental Europe, a succession of Prime Ministers and Foreign Secretaries worked hard, if not always consistently, to restore Germany to the family of nations, calm French fears, and curb a tendency to assume that the problem would disappear if Germany were carved up. A nation with world-wide commercial interests but not, on the whole, a great producer of the raw materials for which belligerent Powers were willing to pay high prices, Britain stood to lose more than she could hope to gain by breaches of the peace. Her aims, in Europe and elsewhere, were essentially pacific. At the same time she was not willing that a single Power should dominate the Continent. A bitter awakening in 1914 had not destroyed her dream of a peace-loving Europe in which confidence in the future would provide the surest basis for sound trade and rising dividends.

In the Locarno era the British ideal seemed within measurable distance of fulfilment. Germany found in Stresemann a statesman who thought that the national welfare was not incompatible with good relations with former enemies. Frenchmen were willing to believe after their experience in 1923 that friendship with Germany might be better than enmity, although they were not yet willing to disarm.

Between 1924 and 1928 Stresemann played the leading part in negotiations which restored Germany's credit, gave her industry a fresh start with borrowed capital, and greatly lightened the burden of the Allied occupation. In 1929 he crowned his achievements by arranging that the final withdrawal of the occupation troops should begin five years ahead of time. In return, Germany was asked, under the Young Plan, to extinguish her liability for reparations by making annual payments for a further fifty-nine years at a mean rate substantially lower than that to which she had pledged herself for an indefinite period under the existing Dawes Plan.

These terms were not as good as those which Stresemann had hoped to get when the negotiations began; but he judged, correctly, that the Reichstag and President Hindenburg would accept them. A national plebiscite held about two months after his death in October showed that an overwhelming majority of voters, even if they did not altogether approve of the Young Plan, were not willing that extreme measures should be taken to resist it. Legislation adopting the Plan was duly passed in March, 1930.

In the meantime a violent campaign against the Plan was conducted by the German National Party under Alfred Hugenberg, an industrialist who had made a fortune in the inflation and had invested part of it in newspapers and other organs of publicity. Hugenberg's conviction that the government ought to think twice before pledging the earnings of Germans yet unborn was shared by men prominent in finance and industry; but that did not help him to put his case before the millions who swayed elections. Casting about for a means of widening the scope of his appeal, he found what seemed to be a good one in temporary association with an obscure figure on the fringe of Bavarian politics. This was Adolf Hitler, the leader of a party which held only twelve seats in the Reichstag, but nonetheless a compelling speaker who had the knack of suiting his discourse to his audience.[9]

Hitler was forty in 1929. Failing to qualify for orthodox training as artist or architect, he had lived on the brink of destitution for some years before joining the German Army in 1914 as an Austrian volunteer. Since the war he had found his niche as a political organizer and professional critic of democratic institutions. The gist of his doctrine was that Germany had been foolish to provoke Britain before the war by founding colonies outside Europe, and ought still to look to European Russia as a proper field for expansion; that she had not suffered a military defeat in 1918, but had been cheated and betrayed; and that effete politicians and Jewish conspirators inside and outside the Fatherland would continue to obstruct German progress until their panoply of intrigue and evasion was shattered by the power of a ruthless will. As long as trade was good and unemployment falling, the last tenet made little appeal to electors. In 1928 only 810,000 votes were cast for Hitler's National Socialist Party as compared with more than nine million for the Left Wing Social Democrats and some four million for the Right Wing National Party.

Hugenberg's brief partnership with the National Socialists in 1929 did nothing to advance his interests. A joint appeal to the nation to resist the Young Plan at all costs attracted little support not already pledged to one or other of the Right Wing parties, and Hugenberg's standing with his own supporters was no higher at the end of the campaign than at the beginning. Hitler, on the other hand, received the benefits of wide publicity for his speeches in the Right Wing press, new or renewed contacts with potential backers, and access to substantial funds. He lost nothing by the failure of an effort which made him a nationally-known figure at the very moment when an economic transformation was about to bring conditions favourable to his ideas.

Acutely sensitive to the ebb and flow of credit, German industry was affected for some months before the Wall Street crash by the tendency of American financiers to take advantage of boom conditions on the domestic market rather than lend abroad, and for many months after it by the calling in of short-term loans to meet obligations previously covered by holdings which had lost their value overnight. With the sources of credit drying up, even successful firms in Germany were forced to retrench, while some of the less successful had no choice but to close their doors. The number of registered unemployed in Germany rose from 650,000 in the summer of 1928 to roughly twice that figure in the autumn of 19[illegible]. Thereafter it continued to rise to approximately three million in the autumn of 1930, about five million by the autumn of 1931, and more than six million in the worst months of 1932 and 1933.

Meanwhile a wave of revulsion against a system which allowed such things to happen swept round the world. In Britain economic pressures bore the Left Wing Prime Minister Ramsay MacDonald from office, brought him back as leader of a coalition whose programme was rather to right than to left of centre, and widened the gap between intellectuals who claimed to know how affairs should be conducted, and statesmen who claimed to know how they could be conducted. In the United States Herbert Hoover, the moderate leader of the predominantly Right Wing Republican Party, lost ground to the Left Wing Roosevelt. In Germany, the immediate effect of the world slump was to add to the number of people willing to give a hearing to extremists on both flanks.

Notwithstanding his hostility to the Republic, the well-fed Hugenberg was hardly the man to lead a successful attack on the evils of pluto-democracy. Adolf Hitler, a Chaplinesque figure who had raised himself from the depths of poverty and degradation by his own efforts, was open to no such objection. His opportunism, his lack of principle, his incapacity for intellectual detachment, his inability or reluctance to justify his theories by close argument, were not defects in the eyes of ninety-nine per cent of the voters to whom his speeches were addressed. No appeal to reason, no parade of facts and figures, could have matched the force of his conviction that troublesome realities were obstacles to be overcome by strength and cunning.

When Germany went to the polls to choose a new Reichstag in September, 1930, some thirty million votes were cast. Hitler's National Socialist Party polled nearly six and a half million, the Communist Party more than four and a half million, Hugenberg's Nationalists rather less than two and a half million. Dr. Rudolf Brüning, the middle-of-the-road Chancellor who had hoped that an appeal to the country would make his leadership secure, could hardly feel reassured by the support given to the extreme Left and Right. In London a very experienced Chief of the Imperial General Staff, Sir George Milne, predicted in the light of the votes cast for the German extremist parties the emergence of a new bloc of revisionist Powers consisting of the ex-enemy states and Italy.

From the date of the election until his accession to power more than two years later, Hitler lost no opportunity of exploiting tension between his supporters and their Communist opponents. In this he succeeded so well that before long he was able to threaten the authorities with the choice between admitting him to office, and suffering an endless succession of disorders for which he took care to disclaim responsibility. Summoning an old associate, Ernst Röhm, to overhaul his private army, the SA, he made himself master of a para-military organization which soon outnumbered the legally-constituted forces of the Reich. At the same time, recognizing the importance of having the Regular Army on his side, he went all out to win its confidence by asserting that his aim was to gain power by legitimate means, and that National Socialism had more to offer to ambitious soldiers than could be hoped for from either a Republic shackled by the Versailles Treaty or a Communist régime in which the army would be subject to political domination.

In the summer of 1931 Germany faced the full force of the economic blizzard. One of the big German banks was forced to close when the great Austrian banking house, the Kreditanstalt, suspended payment; as a means of bolstering the mark, Brüning used emergency powers vested in the President to impose additional taxation and put through reforms which included cuts in unemployment benefit. Timely help from France, not so hard-hit by the slump as countries whose economies were less self-contained, might have softened the blow if her statesmen had been willing; but Brüning roused their suspicions by proposing his own remedy in the shape of a customs union with Austria. Not willing that the clause in the Versailles Treaty which forbade such a union should be abrogated, the French mobilized their financial and diplomatic resources to defeat the project in partnership with Czechoslovakia and Italy.

The rebuff did not help Brüning's appeal to the moderate parties to back him as a sound leader who could be trusted to see the country through its troubles. His economies were not popular. Five million Germans were out of work. From time to time avowed enemies of republicanism, representing movements with hundreds of thousands of adherents, paraded the streets of Berlin and other German cities as members of strong-arm bands. In these circumstances, the authorities were bound to ask themselves what action they should take in case of serious disorder arising either from large-scale clashes between Communist and National Socialist gangs, or from an attempt by either of the extremist parties to seize power. General Groener, the Minister of Defence, and General Erich von Hammerstein, the Commander-in-Chief, reported that the army would fire without hesitation on the SA, or any other para-military organization, in the event of an attempted *coup d'état*; but there was still the risk that street fights between Communists and National Socialists might slide into civil war. Brüning was reluctant to precipitate a crisis by banning the SA, but was forced to do so in the spring of 1932, when the Prussian state government threatened independent action on the strength of evidence that the SA had planned to seize strategic points if Hitler defeated Hindenburg in the Presidential election held in the previous year.

At that point a relatively obscure servant of the Republic intervened with shattering effect. Major-General Kurt von Schleicher was an officer with friends in high places, who had played some part in the formation of the government and whom Groener had made liaison officer between the administration and the armed services. Schleicher agreed that the army would have to open fire on Hitler's supporters if they put themselves flagrantly in the wrong by trying to seize power; but he wondered what would happen if National Socialists and Communists made simultaneous risings and if the Poles, whom many German officers suspected of designs on the Reich, chose that moment to attack. Moreover, he did not believe that the Chancellor could shelter indefinitely behind the President's special powers. Observing that the National Socialists held 107 seats in the Reichstag and were thus the second party in the state, he concluded that since the government were manifestly unable to obtain a majority by rallying all deputies of the moderate Left and Centre, their only chance of survival was to obtain one by coming to terms with National Socialism. When Brüning's ban on the SA convinced him that this had ceased to be practical politics, he used his influence in Presidential circles to get rid of Brüning by asserting that the army had lost confidence in him. At Schleicher's prompting, the octogenarian Hindenburg then invited Franz von Papen to form a government, after extracting from Hitler an assurance that he had no immediate intention of opposing such a government.

A Catholic nobleman with a good reputation as a gentleman rider, Papen could not hope to unite the moderate Left and Centre where Brüning had failed, and a sharp tussle with the

National Socialists at his first appearance before the Reichstag did not suggest, either, that he would succeed in uniting the parties of the Right. The plan he evolved after a quick look at the course was to rely on the President's power to keep him in the saddle until he could put through electoral and constitutional reforms which would make a Right Wing Chancellor's position more secure. In the meantime his influence with men who could exert the power of the purse and the credit squeeze might help to tire the opposition. Armed by the President with wide powers to dissolve the Reichstag, he was able, for a start, to put his rivals to the expense of fighting two elections in the space of a few months.

Towards the end of 1932 these tactics seemed very near success. When Papen came to office in the early summer, the National Socialist Party was forging ahead on every side. In the two elections held while he was Chancellor the number of votes cast for its candidates fell from 37.3 per cent of the total in July to 33.1 per cent in November, its representation in the Reichstag from 230 seats to 196. By December the party was not only visibly losing its hold on Right Wing voters while the Nationalists were strengthening theirs but was in desperate financial straits, having only just managed to fight the last election by scraping up all the ready cash it could muster and pledging its credit to the limit and beyond. Moreover, Hitler had been forced to confess that he was neither able to form a majority government nor willing to contribute to one by taking office as Vice-Chancellor.

The fact remained that, after two elections, Papen was still as far as ever from commanding popular support. He could rule only as long as the President continued to sign decrees, could face the Reichstag only while the President gave him power to dissolve it. Claiming that this put Papen in an untenable position, Schleicher and others urged him after the November election to step aside for a while in order to give the President one more chance of finding a Chancellor capable of forming a majority government. Papen did so, confident that none of the party leaders could form a government and that he would soon be back in office as the one man whom Hindenburg trusted to fill the delicate role of Presidential Chancellor.

This was a correct estimate of Papen's standing with the President. But it did not allow for the strength of Schleicher's convictions and the extent of his influence as an authority on the views of the armed forces. By the beginning of December attempts to find a Chancellor capable of forming a majority government had so clearly failed that Hindenburg felt justified in asking Papen to return to his post. Schleicher protested that a further spell of government by decree would be an abuse of the constitution, and an unnecessary one since he himself was quite capable of forming a parliamentary government. When he added on the following day that Papen, like Brüning before him, had forfeited the confidence of the army, the old President felt obliged to transfer the mandate to Schleicher although he would infinitely have preferred not to do so.

Schleicher began a short-lived attempt to live up to his undertaking by inviting Gregor Strasser, leader of the progressive wing of the National Socialist Party, to take office as Vice-Chancellor in a coalition extending from just left of the extreme Right to just right of the extreme Left. Instead of splitting the National Socialists, as Schleicher may have expected it to do, this move had the effect of driving Strasser into the wilderness and uniting the rest of the party more firmly than ever behind Hitler. Still confident that he could win support from the Left, Schleicher went on to announce a programme of wage stabilization and agrarian reform which alienated his following on the Right without satisfying the trade unionists to whom it was primarily addressed. Unable to face the Reichstag, Schleicher was forced to resign when the President refused him a dissolution on January 28, 1933.

The way might now have seemed clear for Papen to take up the threads again, return to office as a Presidential Chancellor, and put through the electoral and constitutional reforms which he had already outlined to Hindenburg. But meanwhile an abrupt change of tactics had carried him in a new direction. More than three weeks earlier, on January 4, he had had a long talk with Hitler at the house of a well-known banker, Kurt von Schroeder. More recently negotiations involving members of the President's intimate circle had opened between representatives of the National Party and a National Socialist Party mysteriously in funds again. By the last week in January Papen and Hindenburg were too deeply committed to a new policy to be able to revert without embarrassment to their old one, even if they had wished to do so. On January 28 they responded to Schleicher's departure by agreeing that Hitler should take office as Chancellor in a coalition government controlled in theory by nominees of the President and the National Party. This move was afterwards condemned by critics abroad as a sell-out to financial interests. At the time it was regarded by its sponsors as an astute means of muzzling Hitler and at the same time saddling him with a salutary share of responsibility for the conduct of affairs.

The men who made Hitler Chancellor had, at any rate, some grounds for their belief that they risked nothing by doing so. Of eleven ministerial posts in the new government, only three went to National Socialists. Foreign Affairs remained in the hands of the experienced Baron Konstantin von Neurath, a faithful servant of the Reich and generally regarded as a staunch Conservative. General Werner von Blomberg, a soldier whose opinion Hindenburg valued so highly that he summoned him specially from the Disarmament Conference at Geneva to pass judgment on the transaction, took the key-post of Minister of Defence. Papen himself became Vice-Chancellor, with the privilege of being present whenever the Chancellor reported to the President. In addition he held the important position of Minister-President of Prussia. He did not foresee that exceptional circumstances would put extraordinary powers into the hands of the Prussian Minister of the Interior, a post which he and Hindenburg allowed to go to a prominent National Socialist, Herman Göring.

The Hitler-Papen coalition did not command a majority of the 584 seats in the Reichstag, but could count on 196 National Socialist and 52 Nationalist deputies to support any agreed measure. At their first meeting the Cabinet decided that the Chancellor should try to obtain a majority by bringing in the Centre Party; if he failed, a new election would be held, on the understanding that the composition of the Cabinet was in any case to remain unchanged. The result was that, by declaring within twenty-four hours that negotiations had broken down and announcing before the Centre Party could issue a denial that the President had agreed to dissolve the Reichstag, Hitler was able to force an election with the resources of the state at his disposal.

In preparation for the election, Göring used his powers as Prussian Minister of the Interior to rid himself of subordinates hostile to National Socialism, recruit fifty thousand special constables of whom four-fifths were drawn from the SA and the SS, and order the police to show no mercy to demonstrators of whom he disapproved. Short of bringing about a constitutional crisis by dismissing Göring, Papen and the President could do nothing to check these abuses, and there is nothing to suggest that they seriously contemplated such drastic action at a time when co-operation with the National Socialists still seemed possible.

Barely a week before polling day, the fortunes of the National Socialists were advanced by a stroke of luck so timely that they were long suspected of engineering it, although more recent knowledge suggests that they merely turned it to good account. On February 24 the police raided the headquarters of the Communist Party in Berlin. Three nights later a Left Wing extremist, once thought to have been the tool of others but now believed to have acted independently, set fire to the Reichstag building, apparently as a protest against the link-up between Hitler and Papen. Easily persuaded that the Communists had arranged the affair as a reprisal for the raid on their headquarters, the President promptly signed a decree restricting personal liberty, the freedom of the Press, and the rights of assembly and association guaranteed by the Weimar Constitution. These powers did not enable Hitler to force electors to vote for him, but their ultimate effect was that he was able to dominate the Reichstag without obtaining a clear majority.

Despite wholesale intimidation of Left Wing candidates and their supporters, the National Socialist Party in fact gained less than 44 per cent of the votes cast on polling day. Of 647 deputies elected, only 288 were National Socialists, the National Party returning the same number as at the last election. The factor which gave Hitler effective control was the freedom to stifle opposition which Hindenburg had bestowed on him after the Reichstag fire. By the time the assembly met on March 23 to debate a measure framed to give the Chancellor dictatorial powers for four years, nearly a hundred Left Wing deputies had either been arrested or gone into hiding. Outside the building, the Storm Troopers detailed to guard it chanted threats of fire and murder if the measure were not passed. With an adequate number of opposition deputies out of the way, the National Socialists could afford to disregard Left Wing opinion and even to ride roughshod over the Centre Party. In the outcome, the Centre Party as well as the National Party voted with them. The measure was passed by 441 votes to 94, and the President accepted the situation on the strength of a worthless promise that Hitler would take no unorthodox step without further consultation.

Within the next nine months Hitler made himself supreme master of the Reich by transferring the sovereign powers of the federal states to the central government, merging the trade unions in an all-embracing German Labour Front, and suppressing all political associations except his own party. The power of the SA to oppose his will was broken by a ruthless purge in the summer of 1934, and the SS under Heinrich Himmler took its place as the Führer's personal instrument of oppression and revenge.

When Hindenburg died a few weeks later, the German Army became the only organized force in the state with power to unseat Hitler. The likelihood of its doing so in the immediate future was, however, slender. Not many officers had the means of knowing in 1934 that the Führer was a liability rather than an asset. On the eve of the June purge, Blomberg had published a fulsome declaration of the army's faith in Hitler, apparently in the belief that the crippling of such a powerful rival as the SA was well worth the price. Immediately after the President's death, all members of the armed forces were required to take an oath of loyalty to the new Head of State. A good deal was to happen before the relatively few officers who had come to suspect that Hitler was leading Germany to disaster were able to contemplate the sacrifice of their scruples. By that time they had learnt enough to know that, while a successful revolution might be the only way of saving the Fatherland, the effect of an unsuccessful one might be to extinguish for ever the power of the officer caste to intervene for good or ill.

CHAPTER 2

BREAKDOWN IN EUROPE

1931-36

At least two years before Hitler became Chancellor, studen international affairs saw the danger that Germany's econo troubles might tempt her rulers to look for a smokescree grievances shelved during the Locarno era. The Allied o pation was over, the world crisis had put an end to reparatio but there was still powder and shot in the territorial and armament clauses of the Versailles Treaty.

The prospect of a fresh bout of Franco-German recrimi tions was repugnant to British statesmen, but they conso themselves with the reflection that attitudes were sure change when a generation embittered by the war gave pla to younger men who would understand that the events 1914-18 had been disastrous for the whole of Europe a not merely for the losing side. In the meantime at least o bone of contention would be removed if the French could persuaded to concede Germany the right to rearm on an agree scale and to accept reductions in their own army. The wa might then be clear for a general settlement which woul affirm and guarantee Germany's Eastern frontiers as Locarn had affirmed and guaranteed her frontiers in the West.

No detailed British proposals on these lines were, howeve ready when the long-awaited Disarmament Conference held it first meeting on February 2, 1932. The MacDonald-Baldwi coalition were not willing, until well into 1933, to tell French men and Germans how many troops the British thought France and Germany ought to have.

Meeting in the shadow of dire events in the Far East, the

Conference was ill-fated from the start.[1] The French were willing to negotiate, but reluctant to part with their existing superiority in numbers and equipment without tangible evidence of Germany's good faith. The Germans, too, expressed their willingness to come to terms, but only on the understanding that they were not to be treated as suppliants. The substance of their case was that the surrender of the greater part of their armed strength under the armistice convention and the peace treaty had been intended as the first step towards a general scaling down of armaments. The French, however, had shown no sign of coming down to the low level imposed on Germany. If they now wanted to negotiate, they must prove their sincerity by matching their claims to Germany's real needs for the defence of her long frontiers.

How many troops and weapons Germany really needed for this purpose could, however, only be a matter of opinion. No impartial assessment could be expected where almost everyone competent to judge the issue was an interested party. Attempts to arrive at acceptable figures by negotiation seemed doomed to end in fruitless discussion of minor points. Protesting that the French seemed to want to keep the side that had lost the war in permanent subjection, the German delegates refused to take any further part in the Conference unless formal recognition were given to Germany's right to negotiate on equal terms.

The British did not aim at keeping Germany in permanent subjection, but at reviving and extending the co-operation begun at Locarno. They therefore made strenuous efforts to shepherd the Germans back into the fold. Eventually the German Foreign Minister, Baron von Neurath, consented to resume discussions after the French had agreed that Germany was entitled to equality of rights 'in a system which would provide securely for all nations'.

The system proposed by the French was that nations should contribute according to their means to an international force which the Council of the League of Nations would use to punish an aggressor. This was a bold plan, but it did not appeal to the British, who were neither willing to surrender control of their forces to an international body, nor satisfied that the system would work, especially as the Americans were specifically excluded since they were not members of the League. Additional complications arose from an attempt by the British to rule out bombing from the air except as a means of keeping order in unsettled territories. The project was dropped after critics had called attention to the difficulty of defining territories which qualified for the privilege of being bombed.

The Conference was now entering on its second year, and Hitler had come to office in Germany. His advent was disturbing to the French, already made uneasy by British criticisms of their scheme. Scenting breakdown, the British were moved to come out at last with their own plan. This proposed a peacetime strength of 200,000 men for the German Army, the same for the French Metropolitan Army, and a further 200,000 to take care of French commitments abroad. The Conference accepted the British plan as a basis for discussion, but negotiations soon broke down in face of Hitler's obvious determination to rearm at his own pace and without reference to anything decided at Geneva. In the summer of 1933 officials in Berlin openly confessed to the British Air Attaché that Germany was manufacturing aircraft, building fortifications and intensifying military training. In September Baron von Neurath defended such breaches of the Versailles Treaty on the ground that other nations had evaded the obligation to disarm. In October Germany withdrew from the Disarmament Conference and announced her intention of leaving the League of Nations.

While France, it was true, had not disarmed, the picture of a Germany so menaced by her neighbours that she had to rearm quickly did not carry much conviction outside her own frontiers. The French expressly disclaimed any intention of launching a preventive war, and were still willing to negotiate. They did not admit that their existing armaments were excessive. They argued that, while France might seem to command huge military resources, in fact these consisted largely of reservists who would need three months' training before they could hold their own against first-class troops. She had no hidden reserves in the shape of para-military or pre-military organizations. Germany, on the other hand, possessed in such organizations the means of expanding her army so rapidly that she might well be able to put more trained troops in the field at the outset of a war than France could hope to do. Later experience showed that, while there was a much bigger difference between para-military organizations and a proper army than the French assumed for the purpose of their argument, they were not far wrong in thinking that a crisis might find them incapable of doing very much without calling up reservists.

One country which could not be justly accused of failure to disarm was Britain. Since 1918 she had reduced her armaments so drastically that only a token force could have been sent across the Channel if circumstances had arisen which entitled either France or Germany to invoke her aid under the Locarno pacts. This was a dangerous situation for the British, who could not hope to stay out of a Franco-German war and were under a solemn obligation to help the side which could show that it had been attacked. Accordingly the government responded to another warning from the Chiefs of Staff in the autumn of 1933 by appointing a Defence Requirements Committee to advise them how to plug the worst gaps in the national and imperial defences.

It was not, however, until February 1934 that the Defence Requirements Committee rendered their report, and not until the summer of that year that the government were ready to consider all its implications. By that time more than two years had elapsed since the Chiefs of Staff, alarmed by the Shanghai incident, referred ominously to 'the Writing on the Wall'. During the whole of the intervening period nothing of any consequence had been done to strengthen the national or imperial defences except at Singapore. Similarly the French had done little or nothing to modernize their army or overhaul their strategic doctrines while the Disarmament Congress continued to sit. German rearmament, on the other hand, had made a flying start under the direction of men to whom the Versailles era had given leisure to review their problems, and whose efforts were regarded by their fellow-countrymen not as an evil necessity but as the highest expression of the national will.

In February, 1934, the Defence Requirements Committee advised the British government to take steps during the next five years to make ready, for prompt despatch to the Continent when it was needed, an expeditionary force of four infantry divisions and a cavalry division, with armoured and air components; complete a long-delayed scheme of air defence at home; and start looking to the coast defences, which had not been modernized for thirty years and were almost wholly out of date. The Committee had no reason to suppose that Hitler was contemplating an attack on Britain, but thought that he might be ready by 1938 or 1939 for adventures which would bring him into conflict with the French.

The government had no fault to find with these proposals on military grounds, but turned them down for reasons which reflected the proverbial reluctance of British statesmen to appear to commit the country to a European war by taking realistic steps to avert one. The Chancellor of the Exchequer, Neville Chamberlain, declared that the Committee's plan, which would have added about as much to the national expenditure on armaments during the next five years as had been spent in ten days at the height of the First World War, was beyond the nation's means.[2] He went on to argue that, if the object was to convince Germany that Britain had no intention of standing by while she made herself master of Europe, the government could achieve it more cheaply by dispensing with an expeditionary force and putting the taxpayers' money into an expanded air force. In face of his arguments the government lopped a third from the sum which the Committee had proposed to spend on refurbishing the national and imperial defences; reduced the army's share by about a half; and sanctioned the first of a series of air expansion schemes which followed each other with disconcerting rapidity during the next few years.

As a deterrent the air expansion schemes were a failure. Neither the plan sanctioned in 1934 nor the more ambitious one adopted in the following year made more than perfunctory provision for the stored reserves of aircraft which an air force would need in time of war. In the light of this omission and of repeated attempts by British statesmen to reach an understanding with Germany, Hitler had no difficulty in persuading himself that Britain did not really mean to fight and that he would be given a free hand in Eastern Europe as long as he did not directly threaten British or French territory. This was not quite the impression which British governments intended to convey, although more experienced diplomatists than Hitler might have put such an interpretation on their actions up to the last few months of 1938.

As a genuine contribution to readiness for war the expansion schemes were again unsatisfactory. Their best feature was that they helped to lay the foundations of an effective system of air defence. But that was a benefit which the government were not entitled to expect in 1934, for the radar devices which made the system effective had not yet been invented. Then and later, the strength of the schemes was supposed to be that they provided the country with a powerful striking force which, in case of need, could be used to bomb Germany into submission while the French Army held her troops at bay and the Royal Navy prevented her submarines from starving Britain out. Hardly anyone suspected that the bomber forces contemplated in the schemes were incapable of doing anything of the kind.

Meanwhile a vigorous handling of foreign affairs helped Hitler to consolidate his position at home. A pact with Poland in 1934 shook the French system of alliances in Eastern Europe and pushed the Poles towards the strategic isolation in which they stood in 1939. On the other hand an attempt to seize Austria by treachery in the summer of that year failed. On July 25 Austrian agents of the National Socialist Party broke into the Chancellery in Vienna and murdered the Chancellor, Dr. Engelbert Dollfuss; but Mussolini moved troops to the Brenner, the Austrian government soon regained control, and the Führer was made to see that he had gone too far. In Paris and at Stresa in the following March and April,

British, French and Italian statesmen rubbed in the lesson by affirming their Locarno pledges and letting it be known that they did not mean to stand aside while Germany swallowed Austria. For the first time since he came to power, Hitler found himself facing joint resistance from the three leading Western European countries.

But the Stresa front soon crumbled under pressures for which German diplomacy could claim little credit. About the time when Hitler became Chancellor, Mussolini had made up his mind to conquer Abyssinia in order to unite Italian possessions in East Africa and avenge a forty-year-old Italian defeat at Adowa. A talk with Pierre Laval, the French Foreign Minister, in January, 1935, left him satisfied that France would make no difficulties.[3] At Stresa neither Laval nor his British counterpart, Sir John Simon, mentioned Abyssinia although Simon had told a colleague before he left London that he would not fail to raise the subject.[4] Mussolini's impression that no one would stand in his way was thus confirmed. Laval claimed later to have made it clear at the January meeting that only economic penetration would be tolerated but no one told Mussolini in unmistakable terms, at a time when such advice could still have been offered as a *friendly* warning, that Italy might lose the power of making her influence felt in Europe if he committed the flower of her army to the subjugation of a country whose remoteness and poor communications had discouraged would-be conquerors since the beginning of recorded time.

In the next few months a sharp blow at the Stresa front was struck by Anglo-German negotiations to which France and Italy were not parties. A British visit to Berlin had been arranged, with French approval and Italian consent, for early March. Postponing it at the last moment on the pretext that the Führer had a cold, the Germans announced the revival of the Luftwaffe and the introduction of compulsory military service. Notwithstanding these open breaches of the Versailles Treaty, the British government decided without further reference to Paris or Rome that the visit should be made when Hitler was ready. Accordingly, Sir John Simon and Mr. Eden respectively Foreign Secretary and Lord Privy Seal, held conversations with the Führer on March 25 and 26.[5] They were assured that Germany had no aggressive intentions, and especially no intention of seizing Austria or Czechoslovakia, although Hitler confessed that he would 'like to see Austria disappear from the chessboard of European politics'. Germany, said the Führer, needed a peacetime army of 36 divisions because she had undertaken at Locarno to respect the demilitarized zone in the Rhineland and because France had 44 divisions, Poland 34 and Russia 101. In reply to a question from Simon, he said that Germany had already reached air parity with Britain, and went on to mention a figure of 2,100 aircraft.

As a statement of fact, the Führer's claim left something to be desired. Germany had not reached air parity with Britain.[6] The first-line strength of the Royal Air Force in March, 1935, [illegible]s about 900 aircraft, a figure which the Luftwaffe was not [illegible] to attain for at least nine months.* If Hitler was thinking [illegible] of the Royal Air Force as a whole but of squadrons based [illegible] home, then he was closer to the truth but still wrong. The fighting strength of the squadrons at home, including auxiliary squadrons at least equal in value to newly-formed German squadrons, was about 580 aircraft, a figure which the Luftwaffe could reasonably hope to reach by the early autumn. At the time of Hitler's interview with Simon and Eden the Luftwaffe may well have had some two thousand aircraft of all types, including transport machines and trainers; but how

*The first-line strength of an air force is a somewhat academic figure based on the sum of the establishments of its operational units and formations. It excludes stored reserves but ought logically to include immediate reserves with squadrons, although in practice these are sometimes omitted when first-line strengths are compared. The *effective* strength of an air force, on the other hand, depends not on theoretical establishments but on the numbers of aircraft actually held and fit to fly. For example, on the outbreak of the Second World War the Luftwaffe (transport squadrons excluded) had a first-line strength of 3,700 aircraft. The number of aircraft actually held by operational units and formations was 3,609, but 450 of these were grounded for overhaul, inspection or repair. Thus the effective strength was 3,159 aircraft.

EDGAR HOLLOWAY
NORWAY
SWEDEN
Oslo
Stockholm
GREAT
BRITAIN
North Sea
EIRE
DENMARK
Copenhagen
Baltic Sea
Danzig
London
HOLLAND
Berlin
Warsaw
BELGIUM
GERMANY
Paris
Prague
FRANCE
Vienna
Vichy
SWITZ-
ERLAND
AUSTRIA
Budapest
YUGO
SLAV
Belgrade
PORTUGAL
SPAIN
ITALY
Rome
ALBANIA
Mediterranean
MALTA
MOROCCO
TUNISIA
ALGERIA

EUROPE UNDER THE AXIS, 1942
Axis Powers and their Associates
Lands occupied by Axis Powers
Vichy France
Neutral States
White Sea
FINLAND
Leningrad
ESTONIA
LATVIA
Moscow
Minsk
U. S. S. R.
Brest Litovsk
Stalingrad
Kiev
Rostov
Caspian Sea
RUMANIA
Bucharest
Black Sea
Sofia
BULGARIA
TURKEY
GREECE
PERSIA
SYRIA
IRAQ
Sea
TRANS JORDAN
Persian Gulf
ARABIA
E G Y P T
0 500
MILES

many usable machines of military value it could have put into the air on that date is not known. We do know, however, that three months earlier its first-line squadrons mustered only 146 aircraft towards an establishment of 246, and that the whole number of aircraft of first-line type in Germany was then 565. The records show that many of these aircraft were without engines or other essential parts.

The British government had not seen the German records when Simon reported to the Cabinet on his return to London; but they knew the strength of their own force, and their air advisers had a good knowledge of the programmes to which the Luftwaffe was working. They might have been expected, therefore, to conclude without more ado that Hitler's claim was either fraudulent, or based on a genuine confusion between aircraft of all types, aircraft of first-line type, and aircraft of first-line type embodied in operational squadrons. On the contrary, the statesmen made a resolute attempt to show that not only their own advisers but also the German Air Staff, who seemed equally unconvinced by Hitler's figures, must be mistaken. Their attitude was based not on any special faith in the Führer's arithmetic, but on reluctance to accept the Air Ministry's figures in preference to rival calculations made at the Foreign Office and elsewhere. How far, if at all, official estimates of German strength on the eve of the war were affected by such cross-currents is never likely to be known. What we do know is that in 1939 the Air Staff, whom statesmen in and out of office had repeatedly accused during the past four years of underestimating Germany's air striking power, in fact overestimated the strength of the Luftwaffe's long-range bomber force by forty per cent, and that of its reserves by four hundred per cent.*

In the meantime the British government responded to Simon's news by following one admittedly unsound scheme of

*The figures for the Luftwaffe were:

	British Estimate (Spring 1939)	*True figure (Outbreak of War)*
Long-range bombers	1,650	1,180
Reserves	nearly 5,000	under 1,000

air expansion with another, and then hastening to conclude a naval agreement with the Führer before he could come out with fresh surprises. In the summer of 1935, without consulting the French or the Italians,[7] they entered into arrangements whose effect was to concede to Germany the right to build five battleships, two aircraft carriers, twenty-one cruisers, sixty-four destroyers and all the submarines she was likely to be able to build for a good many years to come. British spokesmen defended this bargain on the ground that the alternative was to allow Germany to take the law into her own hands. Foreigners pointed out that open condonation of breaches of the Versailles Treaty was hardly in line with Britain's attitude at Stresa.

As a logical corollary to their admission that the German Navy must be reckoned with, the British government went on to consider in broad terms the situation that might arise if Britain found herself simultaneously at war with Germany and Japan. Eventually they came to the conclusion that the right course would still be to send a fleet to Singapore. But it was, of course, impossible for them to foresee that the French fleet would be out of the reckoning when the crucial moment came.

Meanwhile a plebiscite to decide the future of the Saar had gone overwhelmingly in favour of reunion with Germany, and France had negotiated a pact with Soviet Russia which was still unratified in the early part of 1936. These two events created the right conditions for Hitler to confront the Western democracies with another hard choice between more or less orderly retreat and a bold return to the Stresa front. Germany had been forbidden at Versailles to build fortifications or maintain or assemble troops on the left bank of the Rhine or within fifty kilometres of the right bank. The Locarno agreement had perpetuated the ban with the willing agreement of the Germans. From their point of view it had the advantage of giving Germany an indisputable right to invoke the Locarno guarantees if French troops should enter the demilitarized zone and try to seize the Ruhr, as they had done in 1923. Once the Germans had helped themselves to the right to build military aircraft, however, the ban on fortifications had the disadvantage of preventing them from setting up bases near the French and Belgian frontiers. The French government recognized early in 1935 that this state of affairs might lead to trouble, but were still uncertain what to do when their Ambassador in Berlin, M. François-Poncet, warned them later in the year that German troops might march into the zone if the Franco-Soviet pact were ratified.

In January, 1936, the French and German Foreign Ministers visited London for the funeral of King George V. On January 27 Baron von Neurath assured Mr. Eden, who had succeeded Simon as Foreign Secretary, that the Saar plebiscite had left France and Germany nothing to quarrel about, that Germany intended to respect her Locarno pledges, and that she expected others to do likewise.[8] Later that day M. Pierre-Etienne Flandin, the French Foreign Minister, asked the Foreign Secretary what he thought the French government ought to do to meet the risk of German action in the Rhineland. Eden's reply, afterwards amplified in a telegram which mentioned Belgian as well as French interests, was that first the French must decide for themselves whether they wanted to make a new bargain with Germany or preserve the *status quo*.[9]

This might have seemed a misleading answer if the understanding between London and Paris had been less close. No one knew better than the Foreign Secretary that the future of the demilitarized zone could not be decided by negotiation between France and Germany alone, or merely in accordance with French and Belgian views. The question affected all the signatories to the Rhineland Pact. None the less his view was that the zone had been created primarily to give security to France and Belgium, and that therefore it was for them to decide in the first instance whether, and at what price, they wanted to preserve it.* Moreover, the decision was particularly crucial for the French, since they would have to provide all or most of the troops needed to keep or turn the Germans out of the Rhineland if force should prove to be the answer. The

*Avon, The Earl of, *The Eden Memoirs: Facing the Dictators* (London, 1962), p. 334.

British and the Italians, although nominal guarantors, were not likely to do much, for the latter were preoccupied with their Abyssinian campaign and the former were leading an attempt by fifty nations to persuade them to call it off. If the worst came to the worst, the British would doubtless make a token contribution; but they would hardly welcome trouble with Germany at a time when fear of Italian reprisals against Alexandria or Malta had led them to move to the Mediterranean the most valuable part of the Home Fleet, nearly all the anti-aircraft guns they could scrape up, and most of the material normally kept to provide local seaward defences at home ports in the event of war.

Thus everything would turn on the attitude of France. The French knew that they would not gain universal approval if, in case of flagrant aggression by Germany, they delivered a swift counter-stroke before referring the matter to the League of Nations; but such a course would be well within their rights, and it might shatter for ever the power of Hitler to lead Europe to disaster. On the other hand, if the French preferred to negotiate, then they could scarcely expect a diplomatic triumph but might at least succeed in forcing their adversary to show himself in his true colours. The one course they could not afford to take, and which none of the Locarno Powers except Germany could afford to encourage them to take, was to sit back and wait for Hitler to present them with a *fait accompli*.

Nevertheless, that was the course they took.[10] A month after Flandin's visit to London, they had still not decided whether they wanted to negotiate or keep the German Army out of the Rhineland at all costs. They had moved in the direction of negotiation by asking their military adviser, General Maurice Gamelin, what compensation he would expect if the right to keep the Rhineland demilitarized were surrendered; but they had neither opened conversations with the Germans nor asked Gamelin what he proposed to do if the right were not surrendered and the Germans challenged it.

As had long been expected, at the end of February the Chamber of Deputies adopted the Franco-Soviet pact. To meet

Hitler's probable objection that the pact was incompatible with Locarno, Flandin offered to submit the issue to the Permanent Court of International Justice at The Hague. A day or two later he instructed the French Embassy in Berlin to take up an offer of friendship which Hitler was reported to have made in an interview with a French journalist.

But the clock already stood at five to twelve for France and Britain. Far away beyond the frontier, a tussle of wills between Hitler and his generals culminated in a decision to send a force about 30,000 strong into the Rhineland but withdraw it at the first sign of opposition. To the generals, the venture seemed a desperate gamble which might lead to a crushing defeat for the Fatherland. Hitler was willing to risk not only a crushing defeat for the Fatherland but even his own deposition.

On Saturday, March 7, three battalions crossed the Rhine with orders to advance on Aachen, Trier and Saarbrücken bu to be ready to fall back at once if they were attacked. The re of the force was ordered to take up positions from which i could be swiftly extricated if the French showed signs of moving troops towards the frontier. Simultaneously the German government denounced the Rhineland Pact on the ground that France had violated it by concluding an agreement with Russia, and offered to return to the League of Nations and enter into arrangements for a new demilitarized zone which would make the whole of the French and Belgian frontier defences worthless.

In the course of the day the French government learned, if in truth they did not already know, that their General Staff had no plans to meet the situation, although it came as no surprise to them. Unable, even if they had been willing, to despatch so much as the single mobile column which might have changed the course of history, the statesmen were free to devote themselves to appeals to London and Geneva. At Hitler's prompting, a reluctant German Army had won the first battle of the Second World War without firing a shot.

CHAPTER 3

ON THE EVE

1936-39

When the German Army moved into the Rhineland in March, 1936, its whole strength consisted of a hundred thousand professional soldiers and about half a million raw recruits who had joined in the previous November after a brief period of quasi-military training without arms. By doubling the period of military service, Hitler was able within the next three years or so to raise the number of men under arms in Germany to nearly a million and a half, out of a total of roughly two-and-three-quarter million men liable for call-up and considered fit for service in the field. The question for a dictator bent on conquest was, however, not so much the extent of the available manpower as how soon it could be transformed into an efficient fighting force.

On the whole, Hitler did not believe that this could be done much before 1943. On the other hand, he wanted to be ready to seize favourable chances which might crop up in the meantime. Lashed on by his impatience, and fed from a military budget which soon rose to the equivalent of not less than a thousand million pounds a year,[1] the architects of the new German Army made such progress that by 1939 they were able to mobilize 52 first-wave and 53 reserve divisions. About two-thirds of the reserve divisions, however, consisted largely of men who had not touched a rifle for twenty years or had received only a summary training before they joined their units. Most German officers subscribed to the general professional opinion that the French Army, with its 45 first-wave and 54 reserve divisions, was still the best in Europe.

There were important differences between the French and German armies in equipment, organisation and tactical doctrine; but few informed critics believed in 1938 and 1939 that these gave Germany a marked advantage.

At sea, the numerical odds against the Germans appeared almost overwhelming. The German Navy was told in 1938 to prepare for war in 1944, was otherwise left largely to its own devices, and based its plans on the assumption that time could be found for an ambitious programme of new construction. On paper, the combined British and French fleets outnumbered the German in 1939 by eight to one in capital ships and cruisers, ten to one in destroyers, and between two and three to one in submarines. Many of the British and French ships were, however, old, and some were almost obsolete. Conversely, Germany's two battlecruisers were fast and formidable, the tonnage of all her new ships exceeded their stated displacement, and her so-called 'pocket battleships', although designed as commerce raiders rather than to fight capital ships, were fully capable of defeating cruiser escorts. Moreover, the long-term plans of the German Navy looked to a *guerre de course* for which the British and the French were not as well equipped as British naval experts thought desirable.

Even so, on balance it is fair to say that there was never a time between 1936 and 1939 when France and Britain needed to defer to Germany because of any inability to muster substantial forces on land and sea. Until Munich they could count, in the event of a war involving Czechoslovakia, not only on their own resources but also on a minimum of thirty Czech divisions, supplied from the well-equipped Skoda factories and manning an exceptionally strong defensive line. Even after Munich, they had no reason to suppose that Germany would be able to bring to bear against them a weight of attack by land or sea which they were incapable of meeting.

The situation in the air was very different. In 1934 Britain had chosen the weapon of air power for her duel with Hitler, not because the Defence Requirements Committee made that choice (for they did not), but because her statesmen did. By the autumn of 1936, however, the government were forced to recognize that the struggle for numerical parity with the Luftwaffe had been lost.[2] On the other hand, radar and the promise of the Hurricane and the Spitfire had put the country within sight of the much more important goal of command of the air over her own territory, at any rate by day. For the first time since the end of the First World War, the fighter and the anti-aircraft gun looked like gaining the advantage over the bomber within the area covered by the defensive system. This did not mean that bombers would no longer be needed, for few objectives were likely to be as well defended as the United Kingdom; but it did mean that the old argument that counter-bombardment was the principal weapon of air defence was losing its validity.

This was a new strategic factor of paramount importance for Britain; but its significance was partly lost on her statesmen until events opened their eyes in the autumn of 1938. A new scheme of air expansion introduced just before the reoccupation of the Rhineland set a target of only thirty fighter squadrons, with a first-line strength of 420 aircraft, as compared with seventy bomber squadrons with a first-line strength of 1,022 aircraft.[3] During the next two and a half years an immense amount of work went into the improvement of the air defences; but during that time no special priority was given to the production of fighters and anti-aircraft guns, which came forward very slowly.

On the other side of the Channel the position was still worse. Where Britain's air defences only needed teeth and claws to make them formidable, the French system did not promise to be very satisfactory even when completed. Belated attempts to improve it by grafting on some of the good features of the British system did not save the situation in 1938.

These deficiences made the Munich surrender predictable on military grounds, irrespective of any other reasons which France and Britain might have had for not wanting to fight for Czechoslovakia. The Luftwaffe did not really pose such a threat to the West as it was thought to do, but the fear of air attacks had become an obsession with statesmen aware that they had failed to make the air defences strong enough. At the height of the crisis Britain, Czechoslovakia and France collectively disposed of much larger forces than Germany could bring to bear on land or sea; but Germany's strength in the air appeared decisive.* The Luftwaffe had 1,040 serviceable bombers and 1,171 operational crews, of whom 744 were fully trained and the rest partly trained.[4] France was virtually defenceless in the air, while Britain could muster only about eighty first-class fighters and fifty modern anti-aircraft guns to supplement her older weapons. In view of the tendency of air advisers in most countries to magnify the menace of the bomber, the reluctance of the British and French governments to go to war would have been understandable even if none but strategic factors had entered into their calculations.

Even so, the price they paid for their tardy attention to the air defences was staggering. The thirty or more Czechos-lovakian divisions, the strong Czechoslovakian fortress l[illegible] the Skoda arms factories—all were thrown away. Moreo[illegible] while Britain was not bound by treaty to Czechoslovak[illegible] France was. The failure of France to honour her obligations struck a blow at her self-esteem from which she took a long time to recover.

Before and after Munich, numerous accounts reached London of clashes between Hitler and his service chiefs. On the whole, little attention was paid to these reports, still less to suggestions that the British government might help the opposition to seize power. Even if British statesmen had believed that a handful of German generals were capable of unseating Hitler, they were not inclined to enter into close negotiation with a class of men whom many of them blamed not only for prolonging the First World War after Germany's setback on the Marne in 1914, but also for helping Hitler to attain the position from which they now claimed to be trying to expe[illegible] him.

Nevertheless the Führer's grip on Germany, especially before Munich, was by no means as firm as many foreigners believed it to be. By 1938 the moderate Right posed a bigge[illegible]

*See Appendix III.

threat to his authority than the moderate Left had been able to offer in 1933.[5]

In November, 1937, with the reoccupation of the Rhineland safely behind him and the pace of German rearmament surpassing all peacetime records, Hitler confided to a select gathering of diplomatic and military advisers that the object of all this frenzied activity was to enable him to win living-space for the German people in Eastern Europe, and that he meant to make a start by seizing Austria and Czechoslovakia. Baron Konstantin von Neurath, Field-Marshal Werner von Blomberg and General Freiherr Werner von Fritsch, Commander-in-Chief of the German Army, all stipulated that nothing should be done to provoke a conflict with France and Britain, and all three were relieved of their posts within the next few months.

Hitler took advantage of Blomberg's dismissal to tighten his grip on the armed services by putting himself at the head of an organization which Blomberg had founded some years earlier with the intention of creating an instrument of control analogous in function to the British Chiefs of Staffs Committee. In February, 1938, the Oberkommando der Wehrmacht, or Supreme Command of the Armed Forces, became theoretically responsible under the Führer's direction for the entire shaping of German strategy. As Chief of Staff, subordinate only to himself as Supreme Commander, Hitler chose General Wilhelm Keitel, an officer described by his former chief as 'nothing but the man who runs my office'. The High Commands of the three fighting services retained their existing structure, but became subject to a varying degree of supervision from the Supreme Commander and his staff. Such intervention was most marked in the case of the army, since Hitler did not claim special knowledge of the navy or the air force, but did believe that he knew how operations on land should be conducted.

Among a number of existing organizations grafted on to the new headquarters was the Amtsgruppe Ausland/Abwehr, or Foreign Intelligence and Counter-Espionage Bureau, whose chief, Admiral Wilhelm Canaris, became theoretically answerable to Keitel although he still had direct access to the Führer. A wary spectator of the intrigue which had pushed Fritsch and Blomberg out of office, Canaris soon became convinced that Hitler would lead Germany to dishonour and defeat unless steps were taken to limit his power or get rid of him.

As befitted Germany's master-spy, Canaris was an elusive figure, a man of contradictions. A long experience of intrigue had made him a master of the indirect approach, but he retained a seaman's regard for candour and straightforwardness. He believed that the English, whom he had met and fought as a young naval officer in the First World War, possessed those qualities, and that they were also shrewd and realistic. He was sure that they would end by winning any war in which they engaged. He was also sure that they would never give Hitler a free hand in Eastern Europe. He concluded that the policy of eastward expansion to which Hitler was committed was bound to lead eventually to a collision with Britain and hence to Germany's defeat.

Canaris was not the only man in Germany who thought along such lines. Hitler's bid for undivided control of the armed forces when Blomberg was dismissed gave a new impetus to feelings of disapproval and resentment among a substantial number of serving and retired officers, civil servants, landed proprietors and devout Christians to whom the Führer's racial theories were as repellent as his open contempt for the traditional methods of diplomacy. They regarded him not as an inspired leader defending Germany's legitimate claims against would-be oppressors, but as a vulgarian hurling abuse at civilized nations which would one day rise and smite him. Since the Reich could not afford to get rid of National Socialism at the price of defeat in war, the problem for Germans determined to overthrow the régime was to choose a moment when Hitler had not yet led the country to disaster, but was so obviously heading for a smash that it would be possible to discredit him in the eyes of his millions of supporters.

Among Hitler's opponents inside Germany, one of the most influential was General Ludwig Beck, Chief of Staff of the German Army from the time when the post was revived after the Versailles era until the summer of 1938. Almost from the beginning Beck was convinced that Hitler's policies meant war with France and Britain. A European war, he told General Gamelin in 1937, would leave the Russians as sole victors. When ordered to draw up plans for a surprise attack on Czechoslovakia he tried to show his disapproval by giving up his post, and eventually was able to cut loose by absenting himself from his office after requests to be allowed to resign had gone unanswered.

When Austria succumbed to blackmail, fraud and treachery in the spring of 1938, Beck's inside knowledge was hardly needed to tell him that Czechoslovakia would be Hitler's next objective. From that moment he made it his chief aim to prevent Hitler from going to war with the Czechs and thus involving Germany with France and Britain. General Walther von Brauchitsch, who succeeded Fritsch as Commander-in-Chief, turned down a proposal from Beck that the whole of the General Staff should resign as a protest against the trend of Hitler's policy; but Beck found useful allies in his own successor, General Halder, and to some extent in Canaris, whose freedom to send agents anywhere in the world without question was an important asset. Others willing to take a hand against Hitler included the commander of the Third Military District in Berlin and Brandenburg, the commander of the Potsdam garrison and the commandant of the Berlin police and his deputy.

In the course of the summer Beck and his associates made plans to arrest Hitler if and when he gave the final order for war with Czechoslovakia. Their intention was to bring him before a People's Court, where evidence of his mental instability would be tendered. To forestall a counter-stroke by the SS, Himmler and his second-in-command would be removed from their posts, and if necessary they too would be arrested. The army would then take over the hour-to-hour administration of the Reich until a provisional government headed by some acceptable public figure could be installed in office. Brauchitsch would be told nothing until the last moment, and in any case no action would be taken unless Halder gave warning that war with Czechoslovakia was imminent.

In August the conspirators despatched an emissary, Ewald von Kleist-Schmenzin, to London to warn the British not to be deceived by Hitler's claim to be interested only in the fate of the German minority in Czechoslovakia.[6] He was to tell the government that detailed plans existed for the conquest of the whole country, that they were likely to be put into effect about the end of September, and that 'all the German generals' were against war.[7] He was also to urge the government to stiffen the French and give the plotters a helping hand by declaring in unambiguous terms that Britain would fight if Czechoslovakia were invaded. A public announcement to that effect might, it was thought, be enough to persuade Hitler to change his mind. Alternatively, Beck was prepared, on t[illegible] strength of even a private assurance from the British that th[illegible] meant business, to put Hitler out of office and 'make an end of this régime'.

Kleist succeeded in seeing a number of prominent Englishmen. Among them was Sir Robert Vansittart, nominally the government's Chief Diplomatic Adviser although his advice about matters affecting relations with Germany was seldom taken, since he was considered too pro-French. He carried back with him a reminder that Chamberlain had already given Hitler a hint by pointing out in the spring that a conflict involving Czechoslovakia was not likely to be limited to countries with direct obligations towards the Czechs; but he did not obtain either a public or a private pledge that Britain would go to war.

The absence of such a pledge was not, however, a decisive factor. The conspirators were bound to conclude that, irrespective of anything that might be said or left unsaid beforehand, France would find it impossible to stand aside if Czechoslovakia were attacked; and Canaris was confident that Britain would not leave France in the lurch. The one point which Beck and his friends had to be quite sure about before they struck was that Hitler had committed himself irretrievably

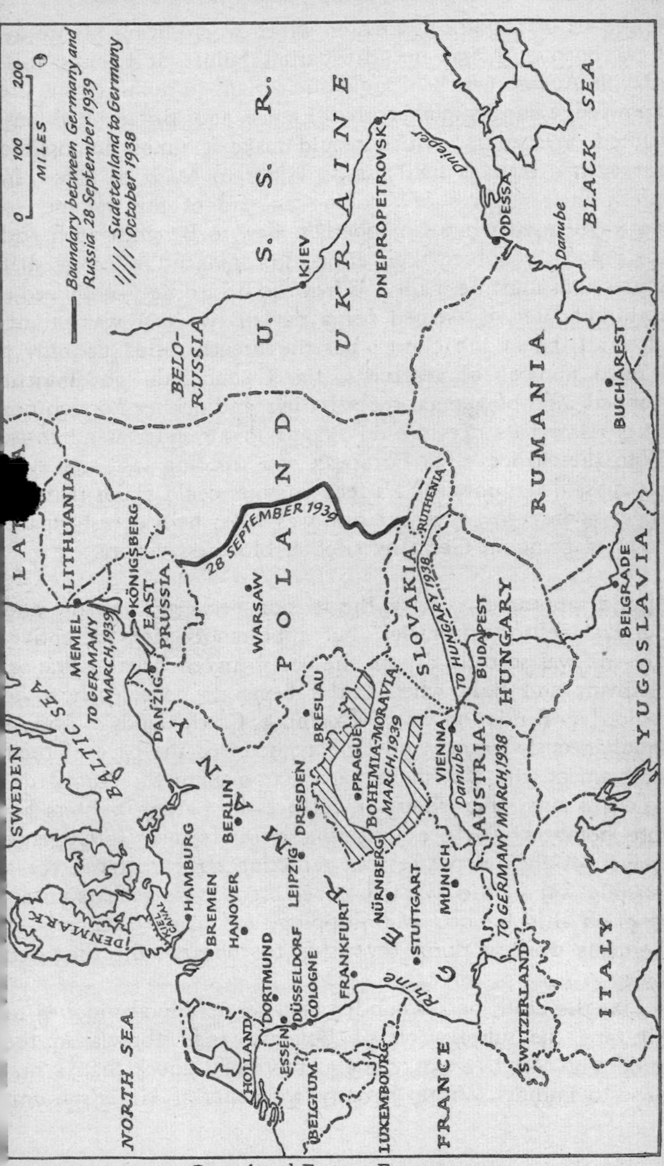

3 Central and Eastern Europe, 1939

to the act of flagrant aggression which would bring France in. Consequently it was not the partial failure of Kleist's mission in August which brought their plans to nothing, but the knowledge in September that France and Britain had embarked on a course which would make it almost impossible for even a man as bellicose as Hitler to resort to force. In effect, their chances of 'making an end of this régime' in 1938 collapsed when Chamberlain flew to Berchtesgaden and the French redoubled their efforts to convince the Czechs that concessions must be made.[8] When the British fleet mobilized a fortnight later, it seemed for a day or two that war might, after all, be in the offing; but the French called up only a limited number of reservists, the Chamberlain government stopped short of general mobilization, and neither London nor Paris relaxed its pressure on Prague to surrender at all costs. With the chances of a European war receding fast, not even the most determined of Hitler's enemies could claim that the right moment to get rid of him was when he was just on the point of bringing Germany another bloodless victory.

Munich appeared to relax the tension between Germany and the European democracies, but appearances were deceptive. The ink was scarcely dry on the pact between Britain, France, Germany and Italy when Hitler began to consider how he could lay hands on the 'remaining Czech lands'. Almost simultaneously France and Britain increased the pace of their rearmament, the British in particular making the crucial decision to strengthen their air defences by putting fighters before bombers.[9] Before long the newly-formed Intelligence Branch of the Luftwaffe was gathering target-material for a possible war in the West, bomber crews were rehearsing attacks on British ports and shipping, and many thousands of Germans were working feverishly to complete the Siegfried Line.

Like the death of a wounded man regretfully abandoned to his fate, the subjugation of Bohemia and Moravia in the middle of March, 1939, came as more of a shock than a surprise to Europe. Within seventy-two hours of Hitler's triumphant journey to Prague the British government sounded the Russians as to their attitude to further German advances. A few days later the Soviet government agreed in principle to a joint declaration by Britain, France, Poland, and Russia that they would resist any further act of aggression against a European state, although they would have preferred a preliminary meeting at Bucharest of the Powers most concerned. Both projects were defeated when the Poles, unwilling to make common cause with the Russians, protested that promptness was needed and that there was no time for multilateral discussions. Coming at the very moment when Hitler helped himself to Memel, their plea seemed all the more compelling since it also coincided fairly closely with a well-founded report that Hitler had already broached the question of an attack on Poland with his service chiefs.[10] On March 31, three days before the staff of the German Supreme Command were ready to circulate the first paper on the subject,[11] Neville Chamberlain made his fateful announcement that Britain and France would stand by Poland in the event of any action clearly threatening her independence. A fortnight later he extended his guarantee to Rumania and Greece.

As if to show that they meant business, Chamberlain and his colleagues went on to introduce a limited degree of conscription; lay the foundations of a substantial reserve by preparing to bring the twelve divisions of the Territorial Army up to strength and then doubling them; and set up a Ministry of Supply to speed production of the weapons and equipment needed for a Continental war. In addition they promised the French that four British divisions should cross the Channel within thirty-three days of mobilization, that these should be accompanied by a small Air Component intended primarily for reconnaissance but incorporating a few fighter squadrons, and that part of the British bomber force should move to France in time of war as an Advanced Air Striking Force. Eventually it was agreed that ten medium bomber squadrons should go to France, that another ten should make their contribution from bases at home, and that a German invasion of the Low Countries should be the signal for the whole of the British metropolitan bomber force to co-operate with the French as their primary task 'during any critical phase of the invasion'.[12] In the light of these undertakings the French High Command were entitled to reckon that a German attack through Belgium might be opposed by up to 100 French, Belgian and British divisions supported by 700 or more British and French bombers.

Hitler's opponents in Germany now had the clear statement of British intentions for which they had often asked; but they could not bring themselves to believe, without some further sign, that it was meant to be taken at its face value. Conversely, the British did not understand why their determination to make war on Hitler if he attacked Poland should be doubted. Such faith as they had ever had in the German generals was severely strained by their failure to do anything decisive during the months that had elapsed since Beck's resignation. Visits t London by various emissaries in 1939 were even more inc clusive than Kleist's visit in the previous summer. The Britis could only tell their guests that they had no doubt of the government's determination to go to war if Poland were in vaded; the emissaries could only point out that the circum stances in which their friends were willing to act had not ye arisen. Both sides were left with the impression that they had been put off with polite evasions, and that there was no cer tainty as to what the other side would do at the crucial moment

In Germany, preparations for war were carried a stage further in 1939 when, on May 23, the service chiefs ex pounded to Hitler their plans for a campaign against Poland.[13] Almost simultaneously, the British government took steps to guard against a surprise attack by the Luftwaffe.[14] Th radar chain was brought into operation, guns were moved to prepared positions, and Air Chief Marshal Dowding, the ai defence commander, received authority to intercept aircraf making unauthorized flights over British territory. The eleven year-old dirigible *Graf Zeppelin* was, however, allowed to g unscathed when she crossed the East Coast near the Humbe in the early summer, although she was rightly suspected o reconnoitring the radar chain.[15] Two fighters of the Royal Auxiliary Air Force were sent from Dyce to take a look at her when she repeated the experiment in August, but they found her well outside the three-mile limit. Neither sortie yielded anything of value to the German Air Staff, who remained as dangerously ignorant of their chances of defeating Fighter Command in a pitched battle as their British counterparts were of their chances of making serious inroads on German productive capacity by trying to bomb the Ruhr with the forces they expected to have during the first year or two of war.

By the second half of June it was known in London that detailed plans for the invasion of Poland had been discussed in Germany, and even that late August had been mentioned as a possible date for the invasion to begin.[16] It was also said that Hitler hoped that negotiations for a trade agreement with Russia, begun in May, might pave the way towards Poland's isolation.

Apart from any question of forestalling Hitler, a glance at the map was enough to show Chamberlain and his colleagues that their only hope of opening a safe route by which troops and supplies could be carried to Poland in time of war lay in reviving the contacts with Russia which they had initiated in March. They had, in fact, begun fresh approaches in April, but without much hope of success or much real prospect of it. Once they had given guarantees to Poland and Rumania, they had little left to offer which was likely to appeal to Stalin unless he valued the long-term advantages of friendship with Britain more highly than their past coolness had encouraged him to do. Germany, on the other hand, could offer the almost immediate benefits of a new partition of Poland and a blind eye to ideological penetration of some or all of the Baltic States.

Hitler was therefore in a fairly strong position when he made up his mind not only that negotiations for an economic pact must be resumed and pressed to a successful conclusion, but also that a political pact must be pushed through at all costs. By the middle of August he felt sure enough of at least the economic pact to tell the Italian Foreign Minister, Count Galeazzo Ciano, that he had decided to begin his Polish campaign by the end of the month and complete it by the middle of October.

In the following week he summoned all officers who were to take leading parts in the campaign to a conference at which he broke the news that the economic pact was to have a political sequel.[17] After telling them that he had decided to settle the Polish problem in the immediate future, 'even at the cost of war', he assured them that they had nothing to fear from French or British intervention. The conquest of Poland and agreement with Russia, he said, would free Germany from the consequences of an Anglo-French blockade by giving her access to rich sources of food and raw materials. In any case the democracies were not likely to become serious opponents in view of their unreadiness for war, their inability to help Poland without hurling themselves at the Siegfried Line, and their notorious love of compromise. Not altogether reassured by these arguments, which failed to shake the conviction of the General Staff that the army was not strong enough to fight on two fronts, some of the generals took comfort in the hope that a second Munich might yet bring Germany another walk-over.

Hitler had other preoccupations. Some time before 1 p.m. on August 23, many hours before the political pact was signed and a good deal earlier than the Supreme Command time-table called for a decision,[18] he gave orders that the assault on Poland should begin on August 26.

Meanwhile the democracies were stirred to action by the news that Moscow was awaiting the arrival of Joachim von Ribbentrop, Neurath's successor as Foreign Minister, to sign the pact. As the outcome of meetings between Ministers and their service advisers in London on August 22 and later, warships and reconnaissance aircraft were moved to war stations, trawlers were requisitioned, and air reconnaissance of the North Sea began on August 24. In addition, steps were taken to re affirm the government's pledge to the Poles in solemn terms and to warn Hitler that an attack on Poland would find Chamberlain and his colleagues 'resolved and prepared to employ without delay all the forces at their command'. In Paris, General Gamelin advised the Council of Ministers on August 23 that the Poles could be expected to hold out long enough to prevent Hitler from attacking in the West before the spring of 1940, and that in any case France seemed to him to have no choice but to adhere to her engagements.

These and other events made August 25 a busy day for Hitler.[19] After telling the British Ambassador, Sir Nevile Henderson, in the middle of the day that he would like to settle the Polish question without going to war with Britain and that the British would do well to take the hint, he learned towards evening that they had put the ball into his [illegible] by building their guarantee to the Poles into a formal alliance signed that afternoon. The French received a similar invitation to desert their friends in the late afternoon. But meanwhile the Italian Ambassador brought the news that his government, with whom the Führer had concluded a 'Pact of Steel' on May 22, was not prepared to go to war. Telling Göring that he must have time to sort out the political situation, Hitler countermanded the attack on Poland soon after learning that the Angio-Polish Treaty had been signed.

The attitude of German officials on the following day, however, left little doubt that the attack was regarded in circles close to the Führer as no more than postponed. Moreover, German propaganda, with its constant harping on the woes of Danzigers and Polish-domiciled Germans, its almost contemptuous falsification of facts and figures verifiable in any impartial reference-book, told its own tale. Even if no one outside Germany had known of Hitler's confession to his service chiefs that Danzig and the Polish Corridor were only pretexts, even if his plenipotentiaries had not declared in half a dozen embassies and a score of drawing-rooms that Germany must have Poland, Belorussia and the Ukraine as part of her living-space, no great perception was needed to divine that he was after something more than the liberation of fewer than a million Germans who had lived with every appearance of contentment in Poland before he came to power. The obvious inference from all this propaganda, rather exceptionally untruthful even by international standards, was not that Germany would be justified in attacking Poland, but that she meant to do so at all costs and on any pretext.

Even so, Europe was not allowed to fall into the abyss without a final struggle. The Anglo-Polish Treaty did not induce the German generals to arrest Hitler, although no pledge which they could ever have obtained in London could have been more specific; but the number of attempts at conciliation made by official and unofficial intermediaries of various nationalities surpassed all previous experience. All were defeated by Hitler's inflexible determination to use force in spite of innumerable warnings that Germany could not hope to gain any long-term advantage by plunging Europe into war.

Some of these attempts proved not merely useless but positively harmful. By August 29 the German Army was so obviously ready to cross the frontier without further warning that the Polish government told the British and French Ambassadors that afternoon that they had decided on general mobilization. Still hoping that direct negotiations between Berlin and Warsaw might break the deadlock, the Ambassadors asked that the announcement should be postponed for a few hours in order to give the British more time to bring the negotiators together.[20] But mobilization could not be postponed *for a few hours.* Either the posters calling out reservists not already notified by other means had to be put up early enough to give the men a reasonable chance of seeing them before nightfall and reporting to their mobilization centres on the following day, or the whole sequence had to be put back for an entire day. So the effect of the Ambassadors' intervention was to postpone the first day of mobilization from August 30 to August 31, with the result that the Polish Army was ten divisions short when the crucial moment came.

In the meantime Polish offers to negotiate were greeted with offers of terms which no sovereign Power could accept

On August 31 Hitler issued his 'Directive No. 1 for the Conduct of the War'. At 4 a.m. on September 1 the British Embassy in Warsaw received from London a final exhortation to urge on the Poles the importance of being reasonable. Less than an hour later German troops crossed the frontier, and at 10 a.m. the Polish Ambassador in London informed the British government that his country was at war.

CHAPTER 4

THE CAMPAIGN IN POLAND AND THE RUSSO-FINNISH WAR

1939-40

The Poland of 1939 had been created at the end of the First World War as a buffer between Germany and Russia, and had become a satellite of France at a time when fear and hatred of Communism in the capitalist countries was intense. Si Hitler's rise to power the Polish Foreign Minister, Colo Josef Beck, had tried to steer his country towards indepe ence by concluding non-aggression pacts with his neighbou on both flanks; but the Führer's aggressive contempt for the Slav peoples remained as dangerous as ever, and Polish dis-trust of Russia was undiminished. Arguing that 'with the Ger-mans we may lose our freedom, with the Russians we shoul lose our soul',* the Poles chose what proved to be the greate of two evils by refusing, even when the Germans were visibly preparing to attack them, to admit Russian troops to thei territory.[1] At the same time they did not rule out Russian hel in the air, and were willing to receive Russian munitions an raw materials.

Even before the Russo-German pact left Poland no secur link with the outside world except through Rumania, her situ-ation was perilous in the extreme. Her frontiers with Ger many and German-controlled Moravia and Slovakia were s long that even an army several times the size of hers coul not have held them. Western Poland was a promontory thrus deep into hostile territory. In the whole of this broad trac

*Marshal Edward Smigly-Rydz, quoted by Paul Reynaud in *La Franc a sauvé l'Europe* (Paris, 1947).

of country, much of it good farmland with few steep gradients to slow down an invader, there was no great natural obstacle west of the Vistula and the San. In Upper Silesia some of Poland's most vital centres of production abutted on the frontier. Further north, the western elbow of the Vistula was only forty miles from German territory, Warsaw barely eighty miles from East Prussia. In the south, the Germans could pass troops through Slovakia almost to the head-waters of the Dniester. Here the Carpathian Mountains, rising to 8,000 feet in the High Tatras and the Beskids, gave Poland her only naturally strong frontier; but even to guard the Carpathian passes might be difficult for an army stretched to meet attacks from west and north. With much of their industry concentrated in the western half of the country, the Poles would hardly dare to shorten their lines by retreating behind the chief rivers unless they could count on supplies from abroad to eke out reserves of war material which would otherwise be exhausted in three months.

When Marshal Smigly-Rydz, the Polish Commander-in-Chief, reviewed his plans for war with Germany in the early summer of 1939, he still hoped that supplies would reach him from Russia.[2] Even so, he faced a hard decision. He expected, rightly, that the enemy's forces would far outnumber his, not only on the ground but also in the air. To play for safety by giving up Western Poland and withdrawing in good order to the strong line of the Vistula and the San was therefore his obvious solution, but one which would be valid only if supplies from Russia did not fail him. On the other hand, by trying to hold on to his centres of production in the west as long as possible, he might expose his army to defeat by a superior force if he failed to pull out at the right moment.

A compromise seemed the only answer, and indeed became the only answer when the Russo-German pact was signed. Smigly-Rydz concluded that he ought not to give up the whole of his huge western salient without a struggle, but must expect to be pushed away from his forward positions within a month. Rather than fall straight back to the Vistula-San Line, he would then try to cover as much of the country as he could by holding an intermediate line of lakes and lesser rivers running roughly north and south through Bydgoszcz and Katowice. If driven from the Bydgoszcz-Katowice Line, he would still hope to hold a front somewhere in Poland until the Germans succumbed to pressure from the French and British.

How long he expected to have to wait before such pressure was applied was not made clear when this plan was outlined to British officers some months before the outbreak of war. It was, however, common ground that, without supplies from abroad, he would not be able to hold out for more than about six months even if his centres of production in Western Poland were not overrun. The British, knowing that the intention of the French High Command was to stand on the defensive during the early stages of a war with Germany, promised no early offensive on the Western Front.[3] On the other hand General Gamelin told the Polish War Minister in May, 1939, that he would open an offensive with his main forces on the sixteenth day of mobilization, but stated after the war that he expressly ruled out an attack on the Siegfried Line, and that in any case his promise was conditional on the signing of a political agreement which was not in fact signed until a good deal later.[4] The effect at the time was to give the Polish High Command the impression that Gamelin would make a push at the end of the first fortnight, although not necessarily to convince them that he could be relied upon to exert more pressure than was needed to pin down the minimum of 25 to 35 divisions which the Germans were expected to deploy on the Western Front at the beginning of the war.* In any case the Polish Commander-in-Chief could have no doubt that, irrespective of the situation in the West, the campaign in the East would call for all his skill.

At his famous conference at Berchtesgaden in August, 1939,

*'The Poles,' the British Military Attaché in Paris reported after the Polish War Minister's visit, 'were a little disappointed that the French were not prepared to go bald-headed for the Germans.' This seems to contradict the widely-held belief that they counted on Gamelin to launch an all-out assault with about that number of *French* divisions.

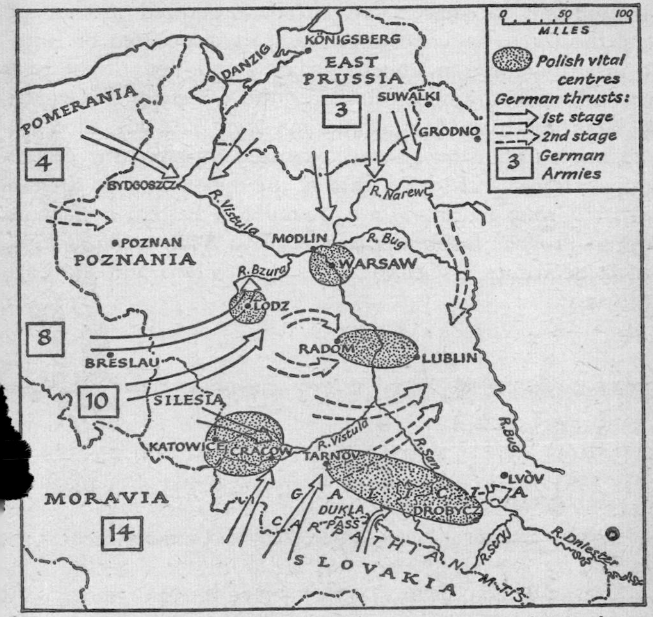

4 The German Strategic Plan for the Conquest of Poland

Hitler made it clear that the army's task in the event of war with Poland would be the 'swift and ruthless destruction' of the Polish Army.[5] The High Command of the German Army proposed to achieve this by attacking both flanks of the huge Polish salient, at the same time thrusting their centre across the Silesian frontier in great strength, forcing the enemy to accept battle west of the Vistula by making a swift dash for the crossings in his rear, and using their armoured and mechanized columns to encircle him while their infantry kept him pinned down to a defensive front. Forcing the passage of the Narew in the north and making a wide sweep through Galicia in the south, their flanking armies would then complete a second enveloping movement designed to trap any Polish troops on the far side of the river line.

In addition to some 1,600 aircraft organized in two air fleets, the forces assigned to the campaign consisted of forty-two infantry, three mountain, six armoured, four 'light' and four motorized divisions, all under the direction of General von Brauchitsch as Commander-in-Chief, and all except a small High Command reserve organized in two army groups and five armies. Just over a third of the divisions were allotted to Army Group North, with two armies in Eastern Pomerania and East Prussia; just under two-thirds to Army Group South, with three armies in Central and Upper Silesia and the Carpathians.

TABLE 1

THE POLISH CAMPAIGN: GERMAN ORGANIZATION AND STRENGTH

ORGANIZATION: THE ARMY

Army Group North (General Fedor von Bock)
- Third Army (General von Küchler), East Prussia
- Fourth Army (General Gunther von Kluge), Eastern Pomerania

Army Group South (General Karl von Rundstedt)
- Eighth Army (General Blaskowitz), Central Silesia
- Tenth Army (General Walther von Reichenau), Upper Silesia
- Fourteenth Army (General List), Upper Silesia, Eastern Moravia and Western Slovakia

ORGANIZATION: THE LUFTWAFFE

Luftflotte 1 (General Albert Kesselring), to support Third and Fourth Armies

Luftflotte 4 (General Löhr), to support Eighth, Tenth and Fourteenth Armies.

STRENGTH: THE ARMY

Allotment of First Wave, Second Wave and Reinforcing Divisions

	inf.	*armoured*	*light*	*motorized*	*mountain*	*totals*
Army Group N.	17	2	—	2	—	21
Army Group S.	23	4	4	2	3	36
OKH Reserve	2	—	—	—	—	2
Totals	42	6	4	4	3	59

STRENGTH: THE LUFTWAFFE

Approximate number of first-line aircraft: 1,600

In theory, co-ordination at the highest level was the responsibility of the Führer and Supreme Commander working through the Supreme Headquarters staff; but in practice not even Hitler considered this a workable arrangement. Effectively, Brauchitsch exercised undisputed control with the aid of his own staff and that of his subordinate commanders and their staffs, and with willing co-operation from Luftwaffe commanders at all levels.[6] Colonel Nikolaus von Vormann, the army liaison officer with the Führer, was instructed by Brauchitsch and Halder that his most important task was to prevent Hitler from interfering with the command of the army. Throughout the entire campaign Halder never once spoke on the telephone to Hitler or to either of the two senior officers of the Supreme Headquarters staff who travelled with him in his special train.*

From the moment when German troops began to stream across the frontiers of Poland on September 1, Marshal Smigly-

*Walter Warlimont, *Inside Hitler's Headquarters 1939-45* (London, 1964), p. 32.

Rydz and his staff faced problems almost unimaginably different from those which had figured in their peacetime discussions with French and British officers. Deprived by the delay in mobilization of their ten reserve divisions, they were not only forced to go into action with nothing but their regular army of 30 infantry divisions, one armoured brigade and eleven unmechanized cavalry brigades, but were also caught on the wrong foot inasmuch as even some of the regular divisions were still assembling when their constituent units were overrun or bypassed by the enemy. Their small air force, about 500 aircraft strong, was crippled in forty-eight hours by systematic bombing which destroyed much of it on the ground and forced surviving squadrons to disperse to emergency landing-grounds without reserves of fuel or where orders could not reach them. Even the weather seemed to have conspired against the Poles, for a hot, rainless summer had dri up watercourses and had baked the ground so hard that many places both tracked and wheeled vehicles could skirt road-blocks by taking to the fields. Hardly bothering about their flanks, and confident that the infantry coming up behind them would keep their rearward communications open, the enemy's armoured columns raced forward at a speed which upset all previous conceptions of what was feasible.

In these conditions, made worse after the first two days by persistent bombing of rail centres, bridges and road junctions, every instinct of a proverbially hard-fighting nation prompted the defenders to engage the enemy as far forward and as soon as possible. Nothing could have been more fatal. Above all, Marshal Smigly-Rydz needed time to study the direction of the enemy's main thrusts and to sort out essentials. This would have been possible only if he had had at his disposal a powerful counter-attack force, held well back from his frontiers. As it was, he had few reserves, and some of his strongest formations in Western Poland were so far forward that they could not be withdrawn before they were either committed to battle or left standing in the rear of an enemy not concerned to form a continuous front but only to press forward.

In the south, after stubborn fighting on the frontier which was expensive for both sides, Smigly-Rydz succeeded in pulling back his left at the cost of heavy losses during its pursuit to the San by the German Fourteenth Army. In the big bend of the Vistula south of Warsaw, however, some six or seven of his divisions assembling round Radom were caught well forward of the river by the Tenth Army, which had crossed the frontier on a fifty-mile front with the intention of clawing out his centre. At the end of a week of heavy fighting in wooded country south-west of the town, the whole of this force found its escape barred by armoured and motorized columns curling round its flanks, while further to the north the Tenth Army's left had wheeled outwards to block the approaches to Warsaw from the west.

During the second week in September, nearly all Western Poland south of a line east and west through Warsaw thus passed into German hands. In the extreme south, the Fourteenth Army was soon beyond the San; in the north, the Third and Fourth Armies were pressing south and south-east across the Narew and along both banks of the Lower Vistula. Apart from troops in Eastern Poland, the garrisons of Warsaw and Modlin and some isolated pockets of resistance, there nevertheless remained in North-West Poland some ten or twelve divisions which the invading columns had left undefeated in their wake.

On September 9 the High Command of the German Army assured General von Rundstedt, commanding Army Group South, that this force was retreating towards Warsaw with all the transport it could muster and that it was not likely to attack him.[7] Less than twenty-four hours later it fell violently on his left flank on the Bzura. Refusing to go over to the defensive, Rundstedt counter-attacked in strength from the south-east. At the same time he pushed from the south and west with relatively weak forces, and asked Army Group North to block the enemy's escape to the north. The outcome was not only the most hard-fought battle of the whole campaign, but also the biggest battle of encirclement yet fought by the remodelled German Army.

The Battle of the Bzura ended in the third week of September with the capture by Army Group South alone of more than 150,000 prisoners and large quantities of equipment; but meanwhile the skill and toughness with which the Poles held out against the best part of eighteen German divisions revived the hope that, even with Western Poland overrun, a defensive front might still be formed somewhere in the country. Encouraged by reports that some enemy formations were running out of fuel, Marshal Smigly-Rydz suggested to the Allies on September 14 that, rather than accept defeat, he should fall back with the remnants of his army to the line of the Dniester and the Stryj and should hold the extreme south-eastern corner of Poland as a bridgehead from which the whole country might eventually be reconquered with French and British help.[8] But the project collapsed when Russian troops began to cross the Eastern Frontier on September 17 and opened fire on Polish forces.

That night the Polish government and Commander-in-Chief took refuge in Rumania, leaving the Bzura pocket to cave in a few days later and Modlin and Warsaw to hold out until the end. Determined to capture Warsaw before the time came for a settlement with the Russians, Hitler ordered that it should be in German hands by the last day of the month.[9] As the German Army had no intention of fighting a house-to-house battle in city streets, and could not in any case have gained a decision by such means within the time allowed, the outcome was a savage air and artillery bombardment which forced the garrison to ask for terms after thousands of non-combatants had been killed and acres of buildings laid flat. At noon on September 27, some fifty-six hours after the beginning of the air attacks, the bombardment was called off. Next day the commander of the Warsaw garrison signed the instrument of surrender with the comment: 'A wheel always turns'.[10]

By going to war with Poland in 1939, Russia increased her population by some thirteen million former Polish subjects. She added to her domain many thousands of square miles of former Polish territory, including a substantial area in the south which former partitions of Poland had allotted not to Russia but to Austro-Hungary. Her primary object was not, however, the satisfaction of these imperialist aims but the safeguarding of her strategic situation in view of Hitler's well-publicized designs on European Russia.[11] The Russians were glad to push their frontier forward by one hundred to two hundred miles, even though the Germans also advanced theirs. At the same time, the campaign increased their influence in the Baltic states. Immediately after it Esthonia, Latvia and Lithuania were induced to accept pacts of mutual assistance which gave Russia the right to establish naval, military and air bases in all three countries.

These concessions reduced the risk of a German penetration of the southern Baltic states as prelude to a lightning attack on Leningrad. The fact remained that Leningrad was only twenty miles from the Finnish frontier, and might well be attacked from that direction if Finland should fall within the German orbit. When the Finns refused a pact on the lines of those accepted by Russia's other Baltic neighbours, the Soviet government asked that, in return for the handing over of a tract of country of no particular value to either side, the frontier should be pulled back 'a few dozen kilometres', and that they should be allowed to set up a naval base at Hangö, opposite their corresponding base at Paldiski, on the Esthonian side of the entrance to the Gulf of Finland.[12] After negotiations had dragged on for two months, the Soviet government announced that the Finns had fired on Russian troops, and on November 30, 1939, they declared war.

The Finnish Army was small and not organized for a war of conquest; but its 200,000 men were at home in any weather, had excellent small arms, and included a high proportion of ski troops trained to move so rapidly over deep snow that they could make rings round tracked vehicles. The Red Army was ten times as large, but its heavy equipment was a doubtful asset in one of the worst winters within living memory, and its troops were not trained or equipped to push home an offensive with only the weapons they could carry. A high proportion of them had not been taught to move on skis through difficult country, and had no experience of storming modern defence works even in good weather.[18]

On their extreme right the Russians succeeded by the middle of December in taking Petsamo by overwhelming its defenders with the superior fire-power of a large force based on Murmansk. Elsewhere the first month of war brought them nothing but disasters. Their few routes into Finland through the lakes and forests of the five-hundred-mile sector from Lapland to Lake Ladoga were commanded with ease by small bodies of determined men with built-in mobility and armed with hand-grenades and quick-firing automatic weapons. Thriving on hardship, moving swiftly in and out of cover, the Finns allowed the wallowing Russian columns to advance until they were hemmed in on all sides, and then annihilated them or drove them back with fearful slaughter. On their left, in the Karelian isthmus, the Russians were halted by the Mannerheim Line, a massive system of steel and concrete fortifications disposed in depth on a narrow front with both flanks on water. By the end of 1939 Russian losses were already many times heavier than those suffered by the Germans in their all-out campaign in Poland, and in Leningrad the hospitals were crammed with wounded.

Conscious that their bargain with Hitler and their attacks on Poland and Finland had outraged opinion throughout the non-Communist world and had raised doubts even in Russia the Soviet government resolved that at all costs the Finnish campaign must not be allowed to end in a fiasco. In January elaborate preparations were begun for a frontal assault on the Mannerheim Line, accompanied by an outflanking movement across the frozen inlet south-west of Viipuri. At the same time the widely-respected Marshal S. K. Timoshenko was appointed Commander-in-Chief on the Finnish front. His offensive was launched on February 11 after a tremendous artillery bombardment, but made little progress until the effect of the huge losses suffered on both sides began to be felt by the numerically weaker Finns. Breaking through on an eight-mile front, th

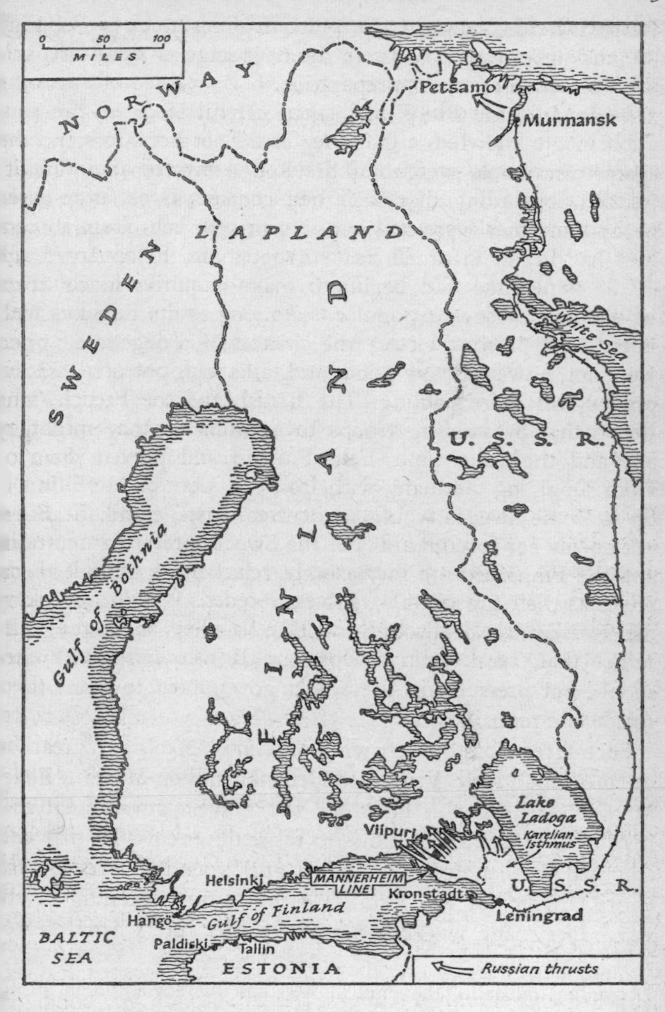

5 The Campaign in Finland

Russians held about half the width of the isthmus by February 21, and were ready to pass to the next stage of their offensive after a further week of preparation.

Meanwhile the Finns had taken careful stock of the situation in the knowledge that they could not hope to stand out against the whole weight of the Red Army for an indefinite period. Concluding that their best course was either to make peace while they were still winning or seek help from abroad, they had begun informal peace negotiations in January,[14] and at the same time had begun to make enquiries in countries where their cause was popular.[15] As long as the Russians were intent on a prestige victory the chances of a negotiated peace were not, however, very good, and talks with potential helper proved still more baffling. The British and the French, who hoped that by sending troops to Scandinavia they might, a one and the same time, help Finland and prevent Sweden from supplying Germany with iron ore, were quite willing t do so if the Swedes would grant them passage and the Finn ask openly for foreign aid; but the Swedes preferred neutralit and the Finns became increasingly reluctant to commit them selves as their prospects of success receded. Within a week o the Russian break-through in Karelia they suggested that rather than send them troops, the British and the French should put pressure on the Soviet government to grant them reasonable terms.

Soon afterwards the left wing of Timoshenko's army reache the main road from Viipuri to Helsinki, and on March 4 Field Marshal Mannerheim informed the Finnish government tha his forces could not continue to resist the enemy. By that dat admitted Russian losses in killed and wounded exceeded th entire strength of the Finnish Army at the beginning of th war.* Not many weeks earlier the Soviet rulers had referre

*According to Stalin, the Finnish War cost the Soviet Union 48,74 dead and 158,000 wounded. The Finns claim that the Red Army losses were substantially higher than these figures, and that their ow losses were considerably lower than the Russian estimate of 60,0c dead and a quarter of a million wounded.

to the Finnish government as 'the White-Finnish clique at Helsinki', 'oppressors of the Finnish people', and 'the Mannerheim-Tanner gang'.[16] Nevertheless on March 12 they signed a treaty of peace which transferred to Russia a comparatively small part of Finland near Viipuri and north of Lake Ladoga, but which left the Finns in possession of the rest.

CHAPTER 5

THE WAR IN THE WEST: THE SAAR TO NARVIK

1939-40

When reluctant British statesmen decided in the spring of 1939 that the time had come for high-level staff talks with the French, the general expectation was that the war which they still hoped to avert would be a struggle between dictatorship and democracy. Japan, it was thought, might be persuaded by patient diplomacy to stay out; the United States had publicly announced her intention of not intervening in a European quarrel; and the role of Russia was uncertain. Hence the grand design which emerged from the staff talks was essentially a design for war with Germany and Italy.[1] The result was that, when war did come, in some ways France and Britain were better prepared to fight Germany and Italy than they were to fight Germany alone.

French and British naval experts believed that spring that, in the event of war with the Axis Powers, their superiority in surface ships would give them substantial control of the Atlantic and of both ends of the Mediterranean. At the same time, they recognized that they could not hope to dominate the Baltic, and might not always be able to prevent German commerce raiders from breaking out of the Narrow Waters. In the Central Mediterranean, where the poor air defences of the British naval base at Malta were a handicap, the outlook would depend largely on whether the Italian air force proved capable of sinking warships. East of Suez, danger would threaten only if Japan decided, after all, to enter the war on the Axis side. In that case, Far Eastern hazards would have to be weighed against the disadvantage of weakening Allied control of the

Mediterranean by sending away too many ships. In effect, the British had promised the Australian government in 1937 that a fleet would be sent to Singapore if the Japanese made trouble, but they had not committed themselves as to the number of ships that they would send.

On land the European democracies, and especially Britain, did not expect to be able to deploy their full strength until at least two years after the outbreak of war. In the meantime they would face a strong German Army, backed by a powerful air force, and a weak Italian Army stretched to defend the Alpine frontier and a sprawling African empire, to say nothing of newly-conquered Albania. On the principle of tackling the weaker partner first, they concluded that their best course would be to stand on the defensive from the Swiss frontier to the North Sea throughout the early stages of the war, and to make the defeat of Italy their first objective. To begin by attacking the more powerful enemy would, the French thought in the light of their experience in the First World War, be far less rewarding than to allow him to exhaust himself by making the first move. Moreover, an argument for the Italy-first strategy which appealed strongly to the British was that success against the Italians in North Africa would remove any threat to Allied interests in the Middle East, secure the Suez Canal as a supply route for the oil on which the Allies counted for their ability to make war, and perhaps pave the way for a turning movement against Germany's southern flank.

The Italy-first strategy had, however, to be shelved when Mussolini decided in the summer of 1939 not to go to war. Italian abstention was not regarded as a handicap by the British government, who had adopted a conciliatory attitude towards Italy and had ordered their Commanders-in-Chief on the spot to do nothing provocative. Nevertheless the effect was to condemn the Allies to a purely passive approach to the war on land unless they could find some other way of asserting themselves. As they were determined not to reverse their decision to play a waiting game on the main front, this meant for practical purposes that their only alternative to inaction was an outflanking movement in the north.

In Germany, no review of grand strategy comparable
that made by the Allied staffs in the spring of 1939 wa
tempted before the outbreak of war. Theoretically the
reme Command existed partly to make such studies; in pr
its officers were seldom encouraged to look beyond the
paigns which Hitler had immediately in view. When Ger
attacked Poland and found herself at war with France
Britain, the armed services had no up-to-date plans fo
conquest of British or French territory at home or ab
Moreover, even their capacity to sustain a successful def
campaign in the West seemed doubtful. The departu
most of the German Army for the Eastern Front left
eleven first-wave and twenty-two reserve divisions, with
artillery and no armour, to face some sixty to seventy F
divisions with a huge preponderance in field guns,
thousands of siege guns and heavy howitzers, and an
wardly formidable array of well-armoured tanks. The
man Navy was greatly outnumbered by the Allied nav
warships of every class. Although capable of taking the
ative in the *guerre de course*, it had fewer than a tenth
long-range submarines considered by its experts necessa
sustained attacks on British trade. The Luftwaffe was
off, with roughly 3,600 first-line aircraft as compared wit
under 2,800 British and French in the home theatre, but
half its squadrons were committed to the campaign in P

The Allies had, however, no intention of exploitin
temporary advantage on the Western Front by taking the
sive there while the enemy was preoccupied elsewhere.
if they had not been committed by their long-term plan
defensive strategy in the main theatre, the Commander-in
of their land forces would still have been handicapped
knowledge that his heavy artillery was not yet in positio
the special projectiles which might have helped him to
the Siegfried Line had not arrived, and that, even with
700 British and French fighters more or less at his d
and indirect help from another 500 British fighters
flank, he still lacked the well-knit system of air defence
he would need if the Luftwaffe attacked objectives in h

When the British asked General Gamelin on September 4 how he proposed to help the Poles, he replied that he would 'lean against' the German fortified line to test its strength.[2] In practice, he confined himself to a cautious advance on a front of sixteen miles, followed by an equally cautious retreat which left the strength of the enemy's fortifications still untried. For six months from the end of October his armies in the main theatre made no further move, while the number of German divisions facing them grew from the original 33 to more than 80 by the end of the year and more than 130 by the spring of 1940.

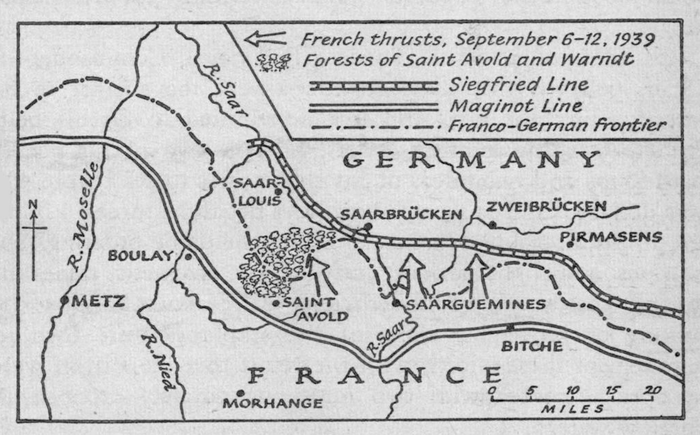

6 The French Offensive in the Saar, September 1939

As the Germans were unable to attack in the West as long as their armour was locked up in Poland, and were afterwards prevented by unfavourable weather from doing so, the outcome was the long period of inaction which neutral commentators called the phoney war. But there was no phoney war at sea. As soon as the Allies declared war on September 3 the Führer sanctioned surface and underwater attacks on British trade, stipulating only that they should be carried out in accordance with international custom. Allegedly in the belief that he was tackling an armed merchant cruiser, the commander of the submarine U30 contravened this rule on the first day by sinking the liner *Athenia* at the cost of 112 lives.[3]

The forces available to the German Navy for attacks on trade in the early stages of the war consisted of three pocket battleships (one of them out of action for long periods), twenty-six ocean-going submarines, and about thirty submarines with a restricted range. The Luftwaffe had some ninety bombers whose crews were specially trained for maritime warfare, but air attacks on merchant vessels were forbidden until the end of September. Apart from these and a few flying boats, the only German aircraft designed for a nautical role were some obsolescent seaplanes intended chiefly for reconnaissance.

Grand-Admiral Erich Raeder, the naval Commander-in-Chief, believed that these resources were too slender to be effective but was none the less determined to do his best. Anticipating the Führer's orders, he sent two of his pocke battleships and two-thirds of his submarines to sea before w was declared, and as soon as hostilities began he turned a blin eye to the illegality of undeclared minefields by ordering submarines and light surface craft to lay magnetic mines in British coastal waters under cover of darkness.[4] After the middle of November some of the seaplanes were used to supplement these efforts, with the result that the British were at once presented with two mines inaccurately dropped in shallow waters.

The British countered by electrically 'wiping' the hulls of merchant vessels so that they tended not to activate the mines, but soon produced a better answer in the shape of a specially-designed cable which enabled them to keep the shipping-lanes open by exploding mines at a safe distance. About 60,000 tons of shipping succumbed to magnetic mines in September and October; but coastal traffic continued to ply between United Kingdom ports at a rate which more than sufficed to keep the machinery of distribution working smoothly.

Orthodox attacks by submarines with torpedoes promised to be much more damaging. Sinking about ten ships a week in the first few weeks of the war, U-boats caused the Allies so much anxiety that the British decided to risk three of their six aircraft carriers in the Western Approaches in order to provide some safeguard for ocean traffic during the awkward period before full effect could be given to the system of convoy worked out before the war. On September 17, three days after an unsuccessful attack by the U36 on the *Ark Royal*, the U29 sank the *Courageous* as she was flying-on her aircraft towards dusk.

A month later Lieutenant Prien, commanding the U23, brought off a still more spectacular feat by entering Scapa Flow through a hazardous channel and sinking the battleship *Royal Oak*, at anchor about a mile from the shore. The Luftwaffe followed with attacks on fleet anchorages in the Firth of Forth and at Scapa on successive days. In the light of these experiences the British, who had already taken steps to disperse their fleet if the need arose, concluded that their only safe course was to station their most valuable ships elsewhere until they could find enough aircraft, anti-aircraft guns and other equipment to make Scapa Flow impregnable. For the next five months the bulk of the Home Fleet, when not at sea, had to make do with a temporary base on the West Coast of Scotland.

Meanwhile the pocket battleships *Admiral Graf Spee* and *Deutschland* had gained the High Seas, where they proceeded to justify Raeder's hope that their mere presence would lead to an extravagant dispersal of Allied naval resources even if they did not sink many ships.[5] Slipping out of the North Sea while British reconnaissance aircraft were grounded for a final inspection before beginning their patrols, the *Graf Spee* appeared off Pernambuco at the end of September; the *Deutschland*, starting a few days later, escaped detection in darkness and thick weather. By the end of October no less than twenty-three British and French capital ships, aircraft carriers and cruisers were hunting for the two German ships from stations between the Indian Ocean and the South Atlantic. In addition, three capital ships and two cruisers had joined the Allied escort force in the North Atlantic. The return of the *Deutschland* to Germany in November left the

Allies still carrying a heavy burden until the middle of December, when the *Graf Spee*'s captain scuttled her after a fight with British cruisers off the River Plate. By that time the pocket battleships had accounted for nearly a dozen sinkings and had cost the Allies many anxious hours.

Thus the slenderness of Raeder's resources did not prevent him from achieving remarkable results. Although heavily outnumbered, with the help of a small contribution from the Luftwaffe he succeeded, within three months of the outbreak of war, in sinking two heavy ships and a respectable total of merchant shipping; driving the better part of the British Home Fleet from its base; and causing the Allies to scatter their forces instead of concentrating them. Conversely, attempts to bomb German warships in harbours and roadsteads were so unsuccessful that the British were forced to give up the whole idea of using their heavy bombers in daylight against well-defended targets.[6] Since aircraft usable only at night would scarcely be able to provide tactical support for troops, an incidental effect of this decision was to lop some 200 to 250 bombers from the total on which General Gamelin could expect to call in case of need.

At the same time, Raeder had the satisfaction of exposing the inadequacy of the enemy's watch over the North Sea. British reconnaissance aircraft failed to spot the *Deutschland* on her homeward voyage, and in the same month the battle-cruisers *Scharnhorst* and *Gneisenau* were able to cruise for some days towards Iceland, and to sink the armed merchant cruiser *Rawalpindi* between Iceland and the Faeroes, without being brought to action by any British or French capital ship.

Raeder's problem, once he had gained this temporary advantage, was to find some way of making it permanent. A possible solution had been foreshadowed before the war by the naval strategist Admiral Wegener, who held that his superiors had missed a golden opportunity of outflanking the British between 1914 and 1918 by omitting to seize bases in Norway.* As early as October 10, Raeder pointed out to Hitler that the

*Vice-Admiral Wolfgang Wegener, *Die Seestrategie des Weltkrieges* (Berlin, 1929).

offensive against British trade would become easier if he could station submarines at Norwegian ports. Two months later he returned to the charge, this time arguing that a German occupation of Norway would not only cut off Allied supplies from Scandinavia but would have the additional advantage of forestalling any attempt by the Allies to dominate the approaches to the Baltic by themselves establishing bases in that country.

In recent years relations between Germany and the Scandinavian countries had, however, been so satisfactory that even Hitler shrank from invading Norway without some colourable pretext. At a timely interview on December 14 the leader of the small Norwegian party of National Union, Vidkun Quisling, alleged that British intervention was imminent, and on the same day the Führer sanctioned preliminary studies for a possible expedition to Norway and Denmark.[7]

It was true that the Allies were keenly interested in Scandinavia, chiefly in connection with their economic blockade. For some years before 1939 Germany had imported much greater quantities of iron ore than she produced at home, drawing approximately half her foreign supplies from sources which the Allies could deny her in time of war, and roughly three-quarters of the rest from Sweden. The Allies calculated that her capacity to make war would be greatly reduced if they could cut off her supplies from the principal Swedish orefields at Kiruna and Gällivare. As long as Germany controlled the Baltic the Allies were powerless to prevent her from receiving ore through the Swedish port of Luleaa, on the Gulf of Bothnia; but in winter, when Luleaa was ice-bound, the main outlet for the Swedish ore was Narvik, a Norwegian port linked by rail with the orefields. As traffic southward bound from Narvik could pass through Norwegian territorial waters almost to the Skagerrak by using the deep-water channel called the Leads, the question for the Allies was whether they could prevail upon the Norwegians to allow them to counter what they considered an abuse of neutral rights by mining or patrolling the Leads. The alternative was to seize Narvik, but this the Allies were not prepared to do without an invitation. Moreover, even if they controlled Narvik or the Leads, they would still be unable to prevent Germany from receiving Swedish ore for at least half the year.

When Russia followed her adherence to the Moscow Pact by attacking Finland, the British and French governments believed that they might be able to plug this huge gap in their blockade if they could persuade the Scandinavian Powers to join them in helping the Finns. Subject to Norwegian and Swedish assent, their plan was to put ashore at Narvik a force which would advance along the railway with the twofold object of opening a route to Finland and securing the orefields against German or Russian aggression. Smaller forces would land at Trondheim, Bergen and Stavanger in order to deny the vital airfield near Stavanger to an aggressor and establish bases at Trondheim and Bergen for up to 150,000 British and French troops. Thus the Allies would, at one and the same time, put themselves in a position to guarantee the integrity of Southern Scandinavia, advance their own interests by ensuring that the output of the Swedish orefields did not get into the wrong hands, and rescue themselves from the odium of conducting a passive war on land by presenting an evident threat to Germany's northern flank.

On February 5 the Allied Supreme War Council approved this plan as one to be put into effect if the Scandinavian governments were willing. The French, aware of the disadvantages of prolonged inaction, readily agreed to provide their share of troops on the understanding that the enterprise should be managed by the British.

Nine days later the German auxiliary warship *Altmark* was seen in Norwegian territorial waters. According to information in the possession of the British Admiralty, she was on her way from the South Atlantic to a German port with nearly three hundred British seamen who had been taken from merchant vessels sunk by the *Graf Spee* and illegally detained when other survivors were put ashore at Montevideo in the previous December. A British destroyer flotilla commanded by Captain Philip Vian chased her into a small fiord near Bergen, but was stopped at the entrance to the fiord by Norwegian gunboats, whose officers asserted that the *Altmark* was unarmed and that no prisoners had been seen aboard her when she was searched on the previous day.

On the night of February 16 Captain Vian, fortified by precise instructions from the Admiralty, took the destroyer *Cossack* through the ice-floes with searchlights burning, entered the fiord and approached the Norwegian gunboat *Kjell*. The *Kjell*'s captain assured Vian that two searches of the *Altmark* had revealed no sign of prisoners, refused his request that she should be taken to a Norwegian port under joint escort pending an enquiry, and claimed that she was entitled to seek sanctuary in neutral waters and must be allowed to proceed to her destination. At that stage the *Altmark* ran aground while trying to ram the *Cossack* and escape, the *Cossack* grappled her, and a boarding-party outfought her crew and released 299 British seamen locked in storerooms and elsewhere. The ship was found to carry an armament of pom-poms and machine-guns.

The consequences of the *Altmark* incident were far-reaching. Convinced that he might be forestalled if he did not act promptly, Hitler appointed Lieutenant-General Nikolaus von Falkenhorst, a corps commander who had once served as a staff officer in Finland, to take charge of the projected conquest of Norway and Denmark, fixing March 20 as the date by which preparations should be completed. At the same time the Allies became less inclined to stand on the letter of the law when dealing with neutral governments. They considered putting troops ashore at Narvik and elsewhere without waiting for an invitation, but had not secured the bare minimum of reluctant acquiescence which still seemed desirable when the Finnish surrender cut across their plan.

Although the break-up of the ice at Luleaa was not far off, they then reverted to their earlier project to mine the Leads. Expecting that this would provoke a German counterstroke and that the Norwegians, but probably not the Swedes, would then be welcome Allied intervention, they decided to hold a first echelon of six infantry battalions ready to go ashore at Narvik, Trondheim, Bergen and Stavanger, but not to organize or equip them for landings in face of serious opposition, and not to count on being able to advance further up the railway from Narvik than the Swedish frontier. Thus the basis of the Allied plan, as it stood in the early spring of 1940, was the assumption that, although the troops were not to go ashore unless and until the Germans reacted to the mine-laying operation, they would still have time to establish themselves at the principal Norwegian ports before the enemy arrived in strength.

The German plan was far more ambitious. While the conquest of Denmark was expected to be comparatively easy, it was thought that six divisions would be needed to take and hold the whole of Norway. About 500 transport aircraft would be available to carry airborne forces and some supplies, but most of the troops would have to go by sea. Surprise was deemed essential, yet the half-million tons of shipping needed to carry six divisions to Norway in one lift would stand no chance of escaping detection, even if the necessary transport could be found. Hence the essence of the plan was a lightning descent on vital objectives by fewer than nine thousand assault troops carried in fast-moving warships. Most of their equipment, with a few additional troops, would go ahead in outwardly harmless merchant vessels which were to play the part of Trojan horses. The rest of the troops would follow only when the initial assault was over and would be routed through Oslo, whence they would be distributed by the best means available at the time.

The advantages of this plan were obvious. But the burden thrown on the assault troops would be immense, and getting them to their destinations by warship would mean staking the whole of the available German surface fleet on a single venture. Furthermore, any delay in seizing Oslo might be disastrous, and even its prompt capture would not ensure the safe arrival of supplies and reinforcements at places where they were most likely to be needed. Disembarking at widely-separated points on the coast of a sparsely-inhabited country the size of Italy, the assault troops would be in an unenviable position if their equipment failed to turn up. In any case they would have to hold on for at least some days with no outside help except such supplies as might be brought by air.

Although Falkenhorst was ready on the appointed day, persistent ice in the Great Belt prevented Hitler from decreeing until April 2 that the landings should take place on the 9th. The Allies decided on March 28 to mine the Leads on April 5, but afterwards put off doing so until the 8th in consequence of last-minute objections by the French to the determination of the British to link the mining of the Leads with the sowing of mines in German rivers.

Accordingly, on the German side the first of the merchantmen carrying equipment for the assault troops set out on the day of Hitler's decision. The cruiser *Hipper* and fourteen destroyers, laden with 3,700 troops of the 3rd Mountain Division bound for Narvik and Trondheim and supported by the battlecruisers *Scharnhorst* and *Gneisenau*, were at sea by the early hours of April 7, and were followed by forces consigned to destinations in Southern Norway. On the Allied side, the battlecruiser *Renown* left on April 5 to cover the mining of the Leads, and by the morning of April 7 all the troops intended to go ashore at Narvik, Trondheim, Bergen and Stavanger if called upon had either embarked in transports or warships, or were on the point of doing so. The cruiser *Aurora* was waiting to escort the Narvik force if Hitler showed signs of responding to the mining of the Leads by invading Norway; other cruisers had been chosen to intervene at short notice; and nineteen British, French and Polish submarines were patrolling the southern part of the North Sea and the approaches to the Skagerrak. At Scapa Flow, now fully restored to service, the main part of the British Home Fleet under Admiral Sir Charles Forbes was ready to engage the enemy's heavy ships if the opportunity arose.*

Meanwhile many indications that the Germans were preparing an expedition of some kind had been noted in London. The Scandinavian capitals were seething with rumours; soon after midday on April 6 a neutral source reported that troops

* See page 91.

carried in ten ships were due at Narvik on the night of the 8th and that Denmark was also to be invaded; and British bomber crews returning from leaflet-dropping raids that night saw a stationary warship in the Jade Roads, a large ship further north, and signs of unusual activity at North German ports. Some of this information was, however, passed only tardily to Admiral Forbes, and the consensus of opinion in British naval circles was that an attempt by commerce-raiders to break into the Atlantic was the enemy's most probable course of action and would present the biggest threat to Allied interests.

A little after eight o'clock in the morning on April 7, a British aircrew on reconnaissance about 150 miles south of the southernmost tip of Norway saw a number of German warships outward bound. Receiving this news about the middle of the forenoon, Forbes made up his mind to await the results of a projected air attack on the ships before deciding what to d The outcome was a long wait before he learned, in the la afternoon, that the attack had failed and that not less than thirteen German warships, including at least one battlecruiser or pocket battleship, were now believed to be at sea.

Meanwhile the Admiralty had passed him the previous day's warning about ships bound for Narvik, adding that it was of doubtful value. Forbes concluded that the enemy was more likely to make for the High Seas than for Norway, and that a breakout must be averted at all costs, if indeed there was still time. Taking his fleet to sea at 8.15 p.m., almost exactly twelve hours after the German expedition was first sighted, he set a course designed to bring the enemy to action if he headed north-about for the Atlantic.

Almost at that moment the German warships, after passing within 300 miles of Scapa Flow in the gathering darkness turned away to starboard on the next leg of their voyage. Towards morning they again altered course to starboard on reaching the latitude of Trondheim with time to spare. By daybreak on April 8 Forbes was far behind them on an almost parallel course which took him further every moment from the less powerful German forces about to start for Norwegian ports from Oslo to Bergen.

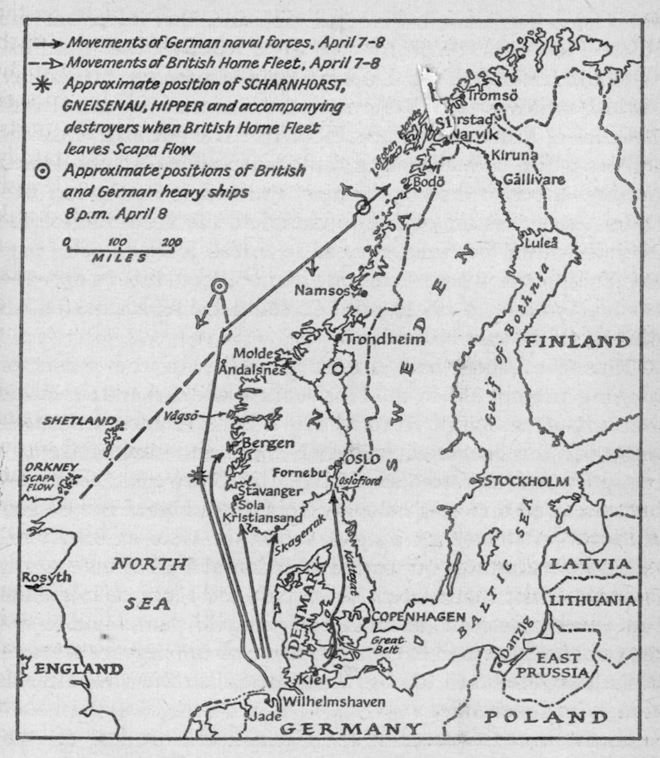

7 The Scandinavian Theatre: British and German Naval Moves, April 7-8, 1940

Soon afterwards a chance encounter between the *Hipper* and one of many British destroyers at sea in connection with the mining of the Leads suggested that part, at any rate, of the force which Forbes was seeking had slipped past him; that the warning about the ten ships bound for Narvik might, after all, be genuine; and that now or never was the time for the Allies to give effect to their plan to put troops ashore in Norway before the Germans arrived in strength. The view taken at the British Admiralty was, however, that first of all the naval situation must be cleared up, and that therefore the Home Fleet must be reinforced. Soon after midday the First Sea Lord, Admiral Sir Dudley Pound, ordered the cruiser *Aurora*, which was to have been the mainstay of the Narvik expedition, to move to Scapa Flow for that purpose, and four cruisers which had taken aboard the troops intended for Bergen and Stavanger to disembark them and put to sea within two hours. As it was impossible to complete the unloading of the cruisers within that time, they were forced to leave still carrying equipment whose removal immobilized the troops and would continue to do so until it could be replaced after an interval of at least some days.

Thus the Allies had already parted with the means of carrying prompt aid to the Norwegians when they learned, in the early afternoon of April 8, that a Polish submarine patrolling near the Skagerrak had challenged and sunk a German transport and that soldiers rescued by Norwegian fishermen had disclosed that they belonged to a force bound for Bergen. Although circulated by a news agency in Oslo at 8.30 p.m., this information was not passed to Admiral Forbes until nearly two and a half hours later. Meanwhile the Norwegian authorities alerted the coast defences, but withheld permission to sow the minefields needed to complete some of the defence schemes. No steps were taken to obstruct or demolish the vital airfields at Oslo and Stavanger.

Partly in consequence of these omissions, the loss of complete surprise made little difference to the unfolding of Falkenhorst's plan next day. As Hitler expected, Denmark succumbed within twenty-four hours and after little more than a formal struggle. At most of the principal Norwegian ports the assault troops landed punctually or were only briefly delayed by defenders who fought with exemplary courage but were handicapped by difficulties of recognition or deceived by ruses. At Narvik one of two coast defence ships, whose commander held his fire to allow a German spokesman to return to his own ship after a parley, was blown to pieces by an unexpected salvo, and the other ship did not long survive her. At Trondheim the *Hipper* and four destroyers forced the entrance to the fiord at high speed before sunrise, helped by a lucky hit on the cable which fed the coast defence batteries with current for their searchlights; while at Bergen serious damage to the cruiser *Königsberg* did not prevent the landing of enough troops to capture the town within an hour. Unfortified Stavanger, with its seaplane base and its crucial airfield eight miles from the town at Sola, fell to seaborne and airborne forces. At Kristiansand an order to the defenders not to fire on British or French ships, arriving after a force headed by the cruiser *Karlsruhe* had been twice beaten off, caused so much confusion that at the third attempt she was able to enter the harbour in time to complete her turn-round before nightfall.

Outside Oslo the defences had more scope and a longer innings. As early as the late evening of April 8 the German expedition was seen entering the [illegible] of the long Oslofiord, where a Norwegian patrol boat challenged the invaders and rammed a torpedo boat. The minefield intended as the cornerstone of the seaward defences was still unlaid, partly because the authorities feared that it might prove an obstacle to friendly as well as hostile ships; but in spite of this deficiency the coast defences went on to score a spectacular success by sinking the *Blücher*, Germany's most modern cruiser. As a result about half the troops intended for the capture of Oslo were lost, and the rest had to be put ashore on the wrong side of the fiord. Eventually six companies of airborne troops flown in by midday took the city with the aid of a stratagem which caused them to be mistaken for the vanguard of a larger force. Thus the Norwegian success was less complete than it might have been if a resolute attempt had been made to deny the main airfield at Fornebu and a smaller one at Kjeller to the enemy; but the delay gave time for King Haakon and his ministers to escape and organize resistance, and throughout the day and the following night the sea-route to Oslo remained closed to German supplies and reinforcements.

The situation at Narvik also looked unpromising for the invaders.[8] After the sinking of the two coast defence ships, ,000 troops of the German 3rd Mountain Division, including the divisional commander, disembarked from the ten destroyers which had completed th: last leg of the voyage; but they faced a cheerless prospect. Their light mountain guns, not sent with the heavy equipment but carried on the decks of the destroyers, had been washed overboard by heavy seas, and three supply ships on which they were counting had failed to arrive. One of two tankers bringing fuel for the homeward voyage was also missing, with the result that the destroyers were unable to complete their turn-round before the Allies caught them. A British destroyer flotilla commanded by Captain B. A. W. Warburton-Lee, arriving on April 10, destroyed or temporarily disabled half of them, and three days later a squadron led by the veteran battleship *Warspite* accounted for the rest. Survivors joined the troops on shore and were armed with rifles and machine-guns captured from a Norwegian depot; but the advantage of additional manpower was offset by the difficulty of feeding twice as many men as the divisional commander had bargained for.

For more than a week the situation at Narvik seemed so precarious that Hitler contemplated a desperate attempt at rescue. Attempts to fly in mountain guns and other equipment were abandoned after ten aircraft had crashed on a frozen lake outside the town. On April 19 the Swedish authorities accepted 350 tons of provisions for transit by rail, but other supplies were limited, at any rate in theory, to those which could be dropped from the air or delivered by seaplane.

Even so, the Allies were forced to recognize in the middle of April that neither their naval superiority nor the skill and determination of Norwegian coast defence gunners had prevented the Germans from carrying troops to destinations hundreds of miles from their starting-points and putting them ashore with little difficulty almost everywhere except at Oslo. The *Gneisenau* was damaged when she and the *Scharnhorst* met the *Renown* on April 9 as they began their diversionary sweep; the *Karlsruhe* was sunk by a British submarine soon after leaving Kristiansand on her homeward voyage that evening; and British naval aircraft finished off the *Königsberg* after the forts at Bergen had crippled her. But the Allies completel failed to intercept the German warships in time to forestall the landings. The assault phase ended with Denmark a conquered country and all the chief towns in Norway held by German garrisons.

The question was whether the Norwegians, still in possession of huge tracts of country in the southern and central counties and the far north, could win back what they had lost. General Ruge, appointed Commander-in-Chief on April 10 after he had helped to save the King and members of the government from capture by German patrols, believed that this might be done if he could hold out for the ten days or so which he expected to elapse before powerful British and French forces came to his assistance. His policy was to retain as much as possible of the relatively open country in the neighbourhood of Oslo, where Allied troops unaccustomed to mountain warfare might be used with good effect, but at the same time to avoid crippling losses which would prevent his army from claiming its share of success when the tide turned against the Germans.

His first aim was defeated by the slenderness of his resources, the difficulty of imposing a coherent strategy on his subordinates, and the swiftness with which the Germans were able to bring in reinforcements and equipment once their sea communications with Oslo were reopened. Mobilization ought, on paper, to have added 120,000 men to the armed forces; in practice more than half of these were swallowed up when most of the mobilization centres were overrun on the first day. In any case General Ruge's widely dispersed forces were threatened at too many points for him to be able to concentrate more than a small proportion in one corner of the country. Part of the territory he was most concerned to hold had already been surrendered by the time he was firmly in the saddle; much of the rest was lost when a substantial body of men retreating from Kristiansand gave up the struggle on the same day as about 3,000 troops near the eastern frontier were outmanœuvred and pushed across it into Sweden. By the middle of April he was no longer able to defend the neighbourhood of Oslo, but faced the problem of preventing the

Germans there from linking up with those at Trondheim by advancing up the parallel valleys of the Gudbrandsdal and Österdal. The question was whether he should shorten his lines by falling back into the valleys or stand further forward.

After consulting the local commander, he decided not to retreat into the Gudbrandsdal unless forced to do so, but to stand on a line across its mouth, some miles south of Lillehammer. If that line could be held until help arrived, a successful counter-attack would take the Allies swiftly into open country where manœuvre was possible. If it proved untenable, he might still be able to fall back to reconnoitred positions at Faaberg or further to the rear at Tretten.

Meanwhile the Allies were considering the problem of Norway in the light of their own preoccupations. Still intent on taking Narvik because of its economic significance and fo psychological reasons, they none the less recognized that the base which would suit them best if they meant sooner or late to reconquer the whole country for the Norwegians or in partnership with them was not Narvik but Trondheim, the ke to Central Norway and the main link between north and south. Chiefly because a seaborne expedition to Trondhein would expose valuable warships to air attack they decided however, to see what came of landings on either side of th port before committing themselves to a frontal attack whic they hoped not to have to make.

In the third week of April the first echelons of two Allie forces made unopposed landings in Central Norway. North o Trondheim, three British Territorial battalions without moto transport, field artillery or anti-aircraft guns went ashore a Namsos, about 130 miles by road from their objective Roughly the same distance south of Trondheim two battalion and a light anti-aircraft battery landed in two flights at Aan dalsnes and Molde. The commander of the more souther force had orders to move on Trondheim, but was first t secure Dombaas, an important communications centre whe the road and railway from Oslo through the Gudbrandsd fork left and right for Aandalsnes and Trondheim. He w also told to prevent the Germans from using the railway t reinforce their troops at Trondheim, and to avoid isolating General Ruge's forces in the south.

With the help of the Norwegian railway system and hired transport, the more northerly force advanced by April 19 to a point about sixty miles from Trondheim. Norwegian officers recommended a further advance to a position which they considered stronger, but the force commander[9] was reluctant to push his luck too far in view of his lack of air support and anti-aircraft weapons. Warships provided some degree of air protection for his base at Namsos, but some of them had duties in the North Sea which prevented them from being always present.

On April 20 the Luftwaffe bombed Namsos after an early-morning reconnaissance, destroying practically all covered storage accommodation at the quayside and delaying the unloading of transport and anti-aircraft guns for newly-arrived French mountain troops who formed the second echelon. In the course of the next two days the Germans attacked along the road from Trondheim, landed small parties behind British and Norwegian forward positions from ships which pushed through a narrow channel connecting the Trondheimsfiord with the hitherto icebound Beitstadfiord, and bombed road and rail communications in the British rear at Steinkjer. The British pulled their front back about twenty-five miles under severe pressure but without heavy losses, and the Norwegians withdrew from their forward positions in good order. The Germans then broke off their offensive while the French, who had not yet been in action, planned a counter-attack with ski-troops across snowbound country on the German right.

The Allied force commander approved of the French plan, but had given an unfavourable account of his prospects in earlier reports which stressed his lack of air support. Chiefly in consequence of reverses suffered by British and Norwegian forces further south, but also influenced by the setbacks at Namsos and Steinkjer and the hope of a counter-balancing success at Narvik, the Allies decided on April 27 to pull out of Central Norway. Accordingly the whole of the British and French troops in the Namsos areas, now some 6,000 strong,

withdrew after suffering a total of 157 casualties since the
first of them went ashore. Norwegian forces in the neighbourhood were left with no choice but to lay down their arms.

On the other side of Trondheim, the Allied commande
received on landing so grave an account of the situation in th
south as to convince him that he would have little chance of
denying the railway to the enemy without isolating the Nor
wegians unless he gave a helping hand to General Ruge. Afte
securing Dombaas, he therefore took his force 140 mile
from its base to assist in checking a German advance into th
Gudbrandsdal.

When the first flight of British troops reached the forwar
area on April 20, the Norwegians at the mouth of the valle
were facing south on a line athwart the seventy-mile-long Lak
Mjøsa, with two infantry battalions and a battery of artiller
east of the lake and a mixed force west of it. At General Ruge'
request the new arrivals were put under the orders of the loca
commander, who dispersed them to different parts of th
front in three detachments, each about two and a half com
panies strong. The Norwegians held their ground successfull
that day, but were very tired after more than a week of con
stant skirmishing.

Next morning the Germans renewed their attack east of th
lake with increased vigour. One of two British detachments i
that sector went into action only briefly; the other moved fo
ward in the afternoon to relieve a Norwegian regiment in a
awkward position on an exposed hillside, with both flanks di
appearing into woods. Unable to move except on the road
where the snow was hard, the Territorials could not preve
the enemy from pushing on their flanks, and had to be e
tricated by the troops they were supposed to be relievin
Eventually they succeeded in establishing a position furth
back, through which the Norwegians then withdrew.

While this action was in progress the local commander d
cided to withdraw his whole force behind Lillehammer duri
the night and stand next day at Faaberg with British troo
alone, in order to give his own troops a chance of recuperati
and reorganizing higher up the valley. In the outcome, ho

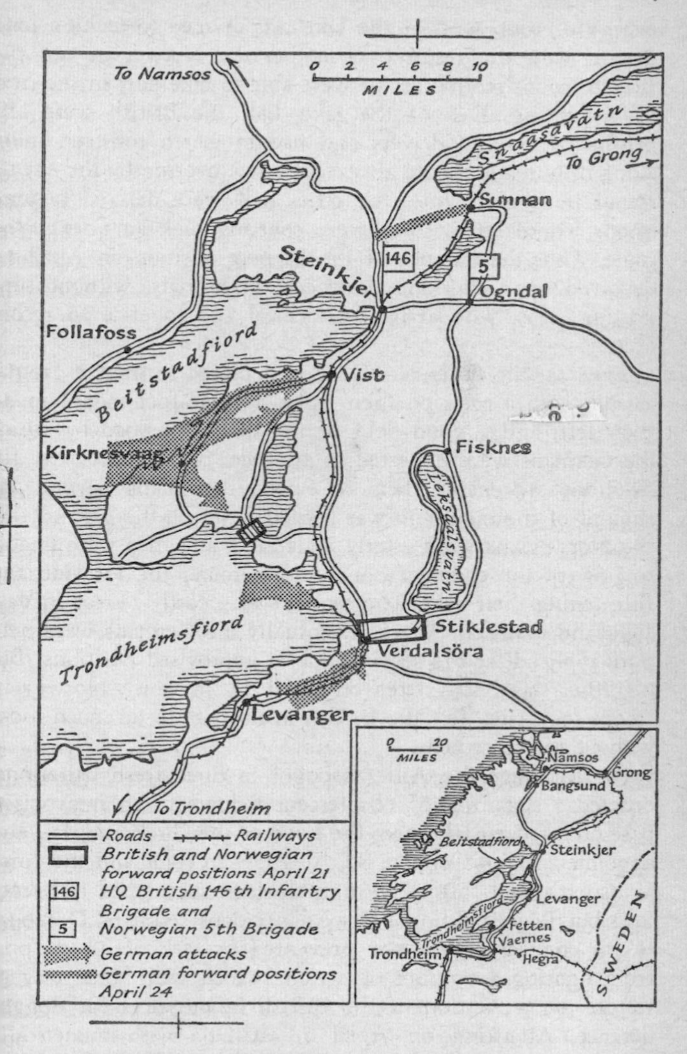

8 Namsos and the Battle of Steinkjer

ever, the group west of the lake was obliged to make a long detour, with the result that neither the Norwegian nor the British troops in that sector were able to take part in the next day's fighting. East of the lake, half the British were left behind by civilian drivers and had to march fourteen miles along hilly roads before all except a few overrun by the enemy found transport; while the other half were delayed because troops whose retreat they were covering took an unexpected route. Thus the defence of the Faaberg position on April 22 devolved upon 650 inexperienced Territorials, without supporting arms, who arrived piecemeal and too late to reconnoitre.

Even so, the defenders were well placed to meet a frontal assault, with a river on their right, a 2,000-foot mountain on their left, and a good field of fire down the road by which the Germans were expected to advance. But their request for ski troops to enable them to extend their flank beyond the summit of the mountain was turned down on the ground that the Norwegians were utterly exhausted, and they were unable to prevent the enemy from working round the far side and threatening their rear. The sequel was a costly retreat in daylight and under air attack. Eventually the Germans were held until nightfall at the second of two improvised positions. But a further stand at Tretten on April 23, in which Norwegian troops took part, left the British in no state to do much more without reinforcement.

At that stage the Allies brought in three fresh battalions, ordered a squadron of obsolescent fighters to an improvised base on a frozen lake near the head of the Gudbrandsdal, and appointed Major-General B.C.T. Paget to command the force in its expanded form. The fighters soon succumbed to bombing; but Paget, adding Norwegian troops south of Dombaas to his command, was not prevented by lack of air support from fighting a number of actions which went some way to restore the reputation of the British infantryman for dogged defence. Attacking on April 28 at Otta with numerically superior forces backed by tanks, artillery and low-flying ai

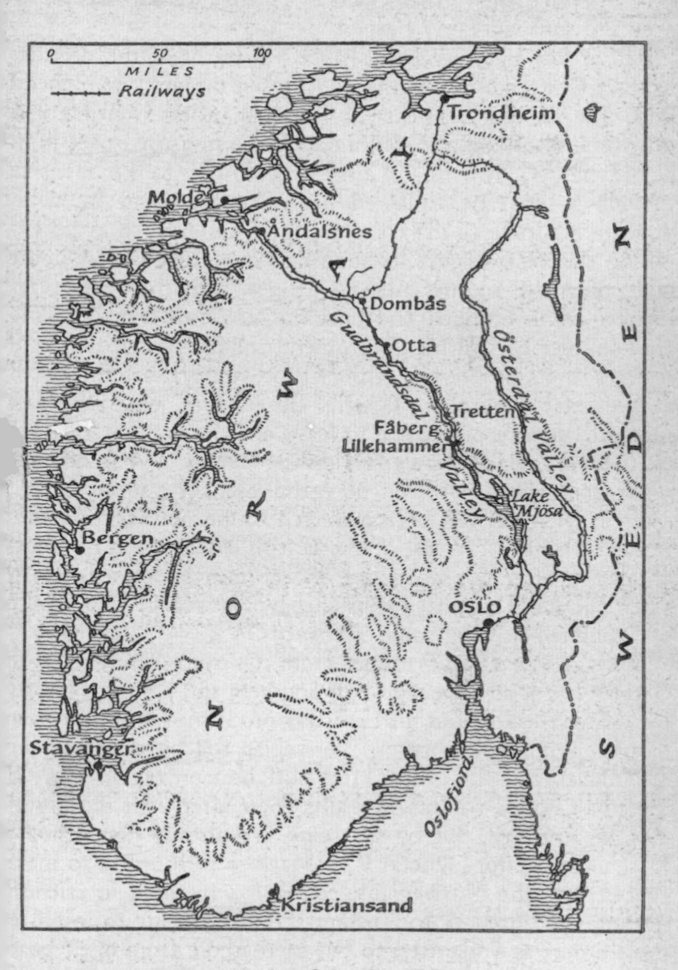

9 Central and Southern Norway

craft, the Germans under General Pellengahr met stiff resistance and suffered fairly heavily.

Earlier that day, however, Paget had learnt of the decision to leave Central Norway and had broken the news to General Ruge that the end was near. Obligated by orders from London to relinquish his plan of falling back at a measured pace until he had enough artillery and air support to pass to the offensive in both valleys, he followed his successful stand by withdrawing his force to the coast by stages designed to avoid exposing the Norwegians to annihilation in the field. On the night of April 29 the cruiser *Glasgow*, with fire-hoses playing, put in to bombed and burning Molde to take off King Haakon, members of his government, and the Norwegian gold reserves, brought overland from Oslo like the treasure-chest of a mediaeval sovereign. General Ruge, torn until the last moment between reluctance to leave and the hope of carryin on the struggle elsewhere, followed on May 2, but withou his troops, who had shown no enthusiasm for a proposal that some of them should be transferred to the northern counties in British ships. The last of the British left in the early hours of May 3, after the rearguard of 240 men had embarked in seven minutes. Organized resistance by Norwegian forces south of Trondheim ceased soon afterwards.

With the overland routes from Oslo to Trondheim in German hands and the whole of Southern and Central Norway lost, King Haakon and his ministers proclaimed their intention of prolonging resistance on Norwegian soil by disembarking at Tromso. But the Allies were still bent on taking Narvik. They had hoped for quick results there after their naval success on April 13, but by that date had already despatched a force under Major-General P. J. Mackesy with orders to make contact with the Norwegians, establish a foothold in friendly territory, and prepare for further action. Refusing to interpre these orders as a mandate to put men ashore from open boat under machine-gun fire, General Mackesy had resisted proposals for a frontal assault; but by early May he had tw battalions, with two Norwegian brigades on their left, within ten miles of the north bank of the fiord leading to the harbour and a battalion almost within sight of their objective on the south bank. Major-General Eduard Dietl, the German commander, had two battalions of mountain infantry in the north; in Narvik itself, and guarding the approaches along the south bank and the railway to the Swedish frontier, he had one battalion of mountain infantry and a naval battalion recruited from the destroyer crews. He was short of essential items of equipment, but received some help from bombers which kept Allied shipping under constant attack.

Withdrawal from Central Norway enabled the Allies to build up their forces investing Narvik to nine French and Polish battalions. On the other hand it led them to divert three British battalions, in addition to five independent companies formed specially for the purpose to an attempt to check a German advance overland from Trondheim. Although the overland route was so long and difficult that the arrival of a relieving force before Narvik fell would have been almost a miracle, the Germans went to the length of adding a seventh division to the six allocated to Norway, and despatched it to Trondheim with orders to push northwards with all speed. Making a bold use of outflanking movements to circumvent Allied and Norwegian opposition, the newcomers advanced rapidly to Bodø and beyond, where they arrived in wild and almost trackless country as events were moving to a climax further north.

Meanwhile the Allies, not reassured by the news that Hitler and the King of Sweden had exchanged letters affirming Swedish neutrality, feared that failure on their part to take Narvik promptly might not merely harm their reputation in neutral countries, but put the enemy in a position to seize the Swedish orefields. At the same time they faced a situation in France which drove them to the paradoxical conclusion that their best course was to seize Narvik as soon as they could, make sure that the port facilities were in no state to do Germany any good for at least some months, and then leave the neighbourhood as quickly as possible. Towards the end of May about half the destroyers which might be needed to repel a landing in Britain were tied up in the Narvik venture, and this knowledge weighed more heavily with the British Chiefs of Staff than the presumption that the German Navy was still worse off. The decision to come out of Northern Norway was taken in principle on May 24, and received formal assent from the Allied Supreme War Council on May 31. Informed of it next day, the Norwegians asked for a delay of twenty-four hours to enable them to consult the Swedish government about a plan, which proved abortive, to put the northern counties under neutral supervision.

In the meantime, however, the Allies had contemplated raising their forces in Northern Norway to corps strength with the object of holding on indefinitely, and had appointed Lieutenant-General C. J. E. Auchinleck commander-designate. Arriving on the spot with wide discretionary powers towards the middle of May, Auchinleck assumed command of the troops already present in place of General Mackesy, confirmed Mackesy's policy of using British troops to block the route from the south, and put the attack on Narvik in the hands of the French Général de Brigade Emile-Marie Béthouart, like Dietl an authority on mountain warfare. Béthouart was told of the decision to leave, but agreed that the attack should go forward.

At midnight on May 27 Béthouart, supported by an all-British naval bombardment and intermittent patrols by two British fighter squadrons from a reconstructed Norwegian base at Bardufoss, launched an assault southwards across the mile-wide Rombaksfiord with two battalions of the French Foreign Legion and a Norwegian battalion, carried partly in fishing vessels and partly in the first landing craft used by the Allies in the war. Simultaneously two Polish battalions, with a third in reserve and a fourth covering their rear, attacked eastward on the south bank of the fiord. By 5 p.m. the German garrison had retreated inland with heavy losses and Béthouart's three battalions from the north were in the outskirts of the town. There the French stood aside to allow the Norwegians to enter Narvik first. The quays, ore-handling plant and railway were found to be so badly knocked about that nothing more seemed necessary to prevent the Germans from making use of them when the impending withdrawal allowed Dietl's forces to return.

Meanwhile the Allies had begun to prepare in secret for their exodus. The British were out of Bodø by the end of May, a quantity of equipment not needed at Narvik was sent home before the end of the month, and elaborate plans were laid to hide the significance of the intense activity visible at and near the Allied military base at Harstad. Two convoys of store-ships left Harstad and Tromsø on June 7; thirteen merchant vessels and two warships took aboard the main Allied force of nearly 25,000 officers and men between June 4 and the morning of June 8, when the rear party, with Generals Auchinleck and Béthouart, left for Scapa Flow in the flagship of Admiral of the Fleet Lord Cork and Orrery, originally commander of the Allied naval forces but since April 21 in supreme command. King Haakon, accompanied by his ministers and representatives of the armed forces, embarked for the United Kingdom in the cruiser *Devonshire*; surviving units of the Norwegian Navy were ordered to Scottish waters; and General Ruge stayed to organize the demobilization of his remaining troops and negotiate an armistice.

General Dietl, preparing for a last stand in the mountains east of Narvik while four trains waited beyond the Swedish frontier to take his troops away if all else failed, knew nothing of all this until he learned after the departure of the Allied commanders that the Norwegians were ready to make terms. The *Scharnhorst, Gneisenau, Hipper* and four destroyers were, however, at sea for reasons not connected with the Allied withdrawal, and at 8 p.m. on June 7, when the force was cruising 300 miles west of Narvik, its commander, Admiral Marschall, received belated reconnaissance reports which led him to conclude that the enemy might be coming out of Norway. Thereupon he abandoned a plan of action which would have taken him to Harstad some thirty-six hours after the last Allied ship had left, and set out to look for the crowded transports which he hoped to find at sea.

In the early hours of June 8, soon after he had informed a

sceptical shore command of his change of plan, Admiral Marschall sighted a British tanker accompanied by an armed trawler. After sinking both ships he sent the *Hipper* to deal similarly with the 20,000-ton armed merchant vessel *Orama*, homeward bound in company with a hospital ship and carrying a hundred German prisoners, but otherwise unladen. He then ordered the *Hipper* and the destroyers to Trondheim to refuel and carry out his secondary task of protecting traffic in the Leads, while he himself took the battlecruisers northwards to search for aircraft carriers reported earlier in the day to be north-west of Narvik.

Towards four o'clock that afternoon he sighted the *Glorious*, carrying the fighter squadrons which had covered the assault on Narvik and accompanied by the destroyers *Ardent* and *Acasta*, but making the homeward voyage independently of the two main Allied convoys because she was short of fuel. A squadron and a half of her own aircraft were aboard her in addition to the landbased fighters, but none was airborne to warn her commander in good time that a superior enemy force was closing with ner. Theoretically faster than the battlecruisers although hopelessly outmatched in armament, the *Glorious* made off at high speed as soon as they were seen, but was soon engaged by the *Scharnhorst* at an opening range of nearly fifteen miles. With her bridge a wreck, and heavily damaged aft, she sank at 5.40 p.m., some twenty minutes after her commander had given the order to abandon ship.

Meanwhile the *Ardent* had gone down fighting, but the *Acasta* was still afloat. Before succumbing to a final salvo from the *Scharnhorst*, she scored a hit which damaged her attacker so severely that Admiral Marschall then withdrew with both his ships to Trondheim. As a result nearly all the fifteen hundred or more seamen and airmen aboard the *Glorious* and the two destroyers were drowned, since no British or German ship remained on the scene to pick up survivors. But the retirement of the battlecruisers had also the effect of giving undisputed passage to an Allied convoy which would have been well within Admiral Marschall's reach if the *Acasta*'s intervention had not compelled him to break off his search for it. A brief sortie from Trondheim some twenty-four hours after the best part of 10,000 Allied troops had been carried safely through the danger-area brought him no success, and at her next attempt to put to sea the *Gneisenau* was torpedoed and badly damaged by a waiting submarine.

So ended a campaign in which the Germans attained all their major objectives, while the Allies were so hampered by failure to gauge the enemy's intentions and scale of attack that they were hard put to extricate their forces without disaster. The fact remains that Hitler's success in Norway was gained by sacrificing the modest surface strength which made it possible. The state of the German Navy at the end of June was that most of its ships had been sunk or were undergoing repairs which would keep them out of action for many months, and that only one heavy cruiser, two light cruisers and four destroyers were fit to show themselves outside the Baltic.* Repairs and additions brought the effective surface strength to four cruisers and eight destroyers by September; but not even the most spectacular success in Continental Europe would make invasion of Britain feasible with such a force unless the Luftwaffe could redress the balance. There remained the possibility that extension of his flank to the North Cape might help Hitler to defeat Britain by bombing or submarine blockade; but Scandinavian airfields were too far from the United Kingdom to serve as bases for the single-seater fighters needed to give effective escort to day bombers, blockade was a slow business, and at midsummer Germany had fewer than a dozen ocean-going submarines ready for action.

The Allies, too, suffered substantial naval losses in the Norwegian campaign, but they emerged from it with an immense superiority in warships of every category. When both

*The cruisers were the *Hipper*, the *Nürnberg*, and the veteran *Emden*, recently repaired after suffering minor damage off Oslo. Both battle-cruisers and the pocket battleship *Lützow* were undergoing major repairs, so was the light cruiser *Leipzig*, and the pocket battleship *Admiral Scheer* was refitting. The light cruiser *Köln*, less seriously damaged than the *Leipzig*, was also under repair, and the *Blücher*, *Karlsruhe*, *Königsberg*, and ten destroyers had been sunk or wrecked.

their own and German surface strength were at their lowest ebb, the British alone had five capital ships, eleven cruisers and fifty-seven destroyers in Home Waters, with a further twenty-three destroyers on escort duty in the Western Approaches.

At the time, however, the problems which an expensive victory posed for Hitler were less apparent to the Allies than their own mistakes. Dissatisfaction with the British government's handling of affairs in Central Norway led to so much criticism that in May Neville Chamberlain and his colleagues resigned in favour of a coalition led by Winston Churchill, more praised for his innocence of the cardinal sin of failure to prepare for war than blamed for his shortcomings as First Lord of the Admiralty and Chairman of the Military Co-ordination Committee in Chamberlain's administration.[10]

CHAPTER 6

THE WAR IN THE WEST: THE CLIMAX

1939-40

At the end of the Polish campaign in September, 1939 the High Command of the German Army favoured a defensive strategy in the West on at least three counts. In the first place they thought, like the French, that there was a good deal to be said for letting the enemy make the first mistake. Secondly, a frontal assault on the Maginot Line seemed out of the question without overwhelming superiority in numbers and fire-power, while a turning movement through the Low Countries would conflict with Hitler's promises to respect Belgian and Dutch neutrality. Thirdly, General von Brauchitsch did not believe that, on their showing in Poland, the bulk of his troops were ready for an all-out effort against the armies of two first-class powers.

Hitler discounted such arguments. Claiming that the army was equal to all demands and that only its leaders were reluctant to fight, he insisted that a major offensive should be launched as soon as the enemy's determination to carry on the struggle became clear. Plans for his removal from office or assassination were revived, but nothing came of them. An attempt by Brauchitsch on November 5 to talk him over led only to bad feeling, and on the same day orders were given for the troops to move forward in readiness for an assault to be delivered a week later.[1]

Little or nothing, however, had been done to prepare air-fields in Western Germany for a winter campaign by providing them with runways. Moreover, wastage due to difficult conditions in Poland had not yet been made good to the extent of re-equipping mobile formations with more than the bare minimum of transport.[2] Thus a spell of wet weather threatened to ground the Luftwaffe even if the armoured columns were not halted by a combination of bad going and insufficient vehicles. In the light of unfavourable forecasts the attack was countermanded on November 7, but the troops were not recalled from positions already reached. A similar sequence of events in January left them only about half the original distance from their start-lines, even though the plan of campaign had changed radically in the meantime.

Besides helping Hitler to launch his Scandinavian campaign, these postponements gave the High Command a much-needed respite. Strict discipline was enforced throughout an army which necessarily included a high proportion of men straight from civilian life. Reservists called up in the previous summer without recent training were put through their paces. Upwards of forty new divisions were formed during the winter, although for some months shortages of weapons and other equipment made even maintenance of existing formations difficult. The mobile formations, with one division added, were reorganized as ten armoured and five motorized divisions, with no light divisions. With some difficulty, enough tracked and wheeled vehicles were found to give the armoured divisions about 2,600 tanks and to fit them and the motorized divisions for at any rate a brief campaign.[3] By the spring the High Command were able to allot to the Western Front and the OKH Reserve a total of 134 divisions, including all the armoured and motorized formations.[4]

During the winter some hundreds of modern tanks with 37-mm. armament or better came from the factories; but in general the German tanks, although fast and able to cover comparatively long distances without refuelling, remained inferior in toughness and hitting-power to French tanks of the corresponding class. By grouping the armoured divisions in four armoured corps, however, the High Command gave themselves the means of concentrating substantial bodies of armour at a number of points and of varying the incidence of their thrusts in order to make the most of any opportunity.

Still weak in heavy artillery although strong in anti-aircraft weapons, the Germans relied largely on air power to support both their armour and their infantry. Out of a first-line strength of roughly 4,500 aircraft in the spring of 1940, the Luftwaffe allotted some 3,500 to the campaign in France and the Low Countries, besides 45 gliders and about 470 transport aircraft.[5] About 1,700 of the 3,500 were bombers or dive-bombers, about 1,200 single-seater or heavy fighters. Although these were outwardly impressive figures, such forces might have had very little influence on a battle fought over a vast area if the Germans had not provided themselves with an organization and a signals network which helped them to send aircraft promptly to the sector deemed decisive at a given moment.

The Allies, too, took advantage of the long wait to build up their forces. The French were obliged to reorganize their arms production and return some reservists to industry before they could equip substantial numbers of new formations;[6] but by the spring of 1940 their output was rising sharply, and they were able to allot to their North-East Front a total of 94 divisions or their equivalent in fortress troops.[7] By that time the British had sent to France ten infantry divisions, a tank brigade and some mechanized cavalry. Some eight Dutch and twenty-two Belgian divisions gave approximate numerical equality between the two sides in terms of major formations.*

There was also approximate equality in number of armoured fighting vehicles.† The Allies had, however, no counterpart to

*There was also a Polish division forming in France.

†Apart from the British contribution, by the spring of 1940 the French had manufactured about 3,400 tanks since 1935. On the eve of the campaign about 2,300 of these were with their three armoured divisions, three light divisions, and 27 independent battalions. The newly-formed 4th Armoured Division (Colonel de Gaulle) went into action on May 17 with about 100 heavy tanks not used before, so that the number of tanks issued to formations and units on the North-East Front by that date was not less than about 2,400. Probably the tanks allotted to the 4th Armoured Division's light battalions ought

the German armoured corps. Up to the eve of the campaign the British had brought into the line no armoured formation larger than a brigade, although their 1st Armoured Division was forming in England and was ordered to France still incomplete, on May 11. As for the French, the organization as well as the design of their armour reflected the conviction of their High Command that tanks were to be regarded as partly an adjunct to mechanized cavalry, partly a means of supporting infantry advancing at a tempo dictated by the speed with which artillery could be brought forward. Even their light and medium tanks depended more on armament and armour than on speed, their heavy tanks were designed to give and withstand punishment rather than go fast and far, and more than half their armoured strength was in independent battalions widely dispersed among infantry formations or kept in reserve to be distributed later. The rest was shared between three light mechanized divisions which were essentially reconnaissance formations, and three armoured divisions, with a fourth in prospect. The armoured divisions were not grouped in a corps, but formed an armoured reserve which in practice was soon broken up. While in general the French tanks were superior to the enemy's in ruggedness and fire-power, this advantage was offset by limitations of range which restricted their mobility on and off the battlefield.

Nor could the Allies match the enemy's air support weapon. The French had studied the technique of co-operation between armoured columns and dive-bombers developed by the Germans, but had come to the conclusion that a well-defended front was unlikely to be breached by such means. They had cancelled their own order for dive-bombers, noting that the prototype seemed slow and vulnerable and believing that more could be done with fast medium bombers flying at tree-top height.[8] They had, however, failed to develop a medium bomber able to stand up to strong defences, and in any case

---

also to be added, although these battalions had been dispersed by the time the division went into the line. In addition the French had about 600 old tanks assigned to the local defence of airfields.

political and industrial strife, arising largely from dissatisfaction with the official policy of non-intervention in the Spanish Civil War, had played such havoc with production that in the spring of 1940 they had only about 100 to 150 effective bombers of all types for the North-East Front.[9] The British had sent about the same number of light and medium bombers to France, and were unable to send more for lack of airfields; but the whole of their metropolitan bomber force, amounting altogether to some 400 to 500 aircraft, was pledged to support the Franco-British armies in one way or another if the need arose. But the value of the British bomber force, for whose sake so many sacrifices had been made, was limited. The light and medium bombers were very vulnerable,[10] the heavy bombers could not be used in daylight and were inaccurate at night, and the weight of bombs needed to destroy a given objective was much greater than the British thought.

The Allies were better off for fighters. The French had some 600 or 700, of which, at the lowest estimate, more than 400 were ready for action on the North-East Front; the British some 53 effective squadrons, each with an initial equipment of fifteen or more aircraft, immediate reserves included.[11] The policy of the British was not to expose their naval bases and centres of production by sending away too high a proportion of their fighter force; but in practice their contribution included every squadron for which room could be found in France when the time came to send it.* In addition home-

*At the outset of the campaign in France and the Low Countries the British added four fighter squadrons to their six already in France. On May 13 they sent another 32 aircraft, drawn from several squadrons. M. Reynaud, the French Prime Minister, asked on May 14 and 15 for ten more squadrons. The British sent eight half-squadrons, but found that there was not enough room at the French airfields at their disposal for the remaining six squadrons. Although Air Chief Marshal Dowding, their air defence commander at home, strongly opposed any further weakening of his force, they fell in with M. Reynaud's wishes to the extent of ordering six squadrons to concentrate in Kent and work from forward bases across the Channel at a strength of three squadrons at a time. More could have been done only if preparations had been made earlier to base a larger fighter force in France.

based fighters made many sorties over French, Belgian and Dutch territory. The Allies were, however, handicapped in a Continental campaign by a lack of the weapons and equipment, other than aircraft, which go to make up a sound system of air defence. The French had only a rudimentary early-warning system, few anti-aircraft guns, and a method of allotting air support to troops which was much criticized by their own officers.[12] In these circumstances success would have been difficult even if many more fighters had been available.

The respite also gave time for momentous changes in the German plan of campaign.[13]

The original intention, as outlined by the High Command at a time when they still hoped to talk Hitler out of an offensive, was to defeat as many Allied troops as possible, and at the same time seize a tract of Dutch, Belgian and French territory as a protective belt for the Ruhr and a base for sea and air warfare against Britain. These aims they planned to fulfil by pushing eight armoured, two motorized and twenty-seven infantry divisions under General Fedor von Bock into Central Belgium and thence advancing on a forty-mile front towards the Channel coast. The obvious weakness of this plan was that it promised no decision. Even with all his armour on the right, and perhaps reinforced by one armoured division remaining in the OKH Reserve, Bock would hardly be strong enough to encircle the main mass of the Franco-British armies, which would have a good chance of saving themselves by pulling their left back to the Somme, if indeed they failed to halt Bock on the French frontier or in Belgium. Thus a likely result would be a stalemate, with all the uncertain business of defeating Britain by blockade, attrition or invasion left to do.

After a series of discussions between Hitler, Brauchitsch and others, the High Command agreed at the end of October to give Bock an additional six divisions so as to enable him to attack on a wider front and strike south-westwards towards the Upper Somme as well as westwards and north-westwards towards the coast. Even so, the plan was still open to the criticism that it reproduced the more obvious but not the more imaginative features of those propounded a generation earlier by

Schlieffen and the younger Moltke. Moreover, the effect of strengthening Bock's Army Group B was to so weaken Army Group A, on his left, that its commander, General Karl von Rundstedt, might have difficulty in making the deep thrusts needed to protect his neighbour's flank and in following up any success achieved in that sector.

Throughout the early winter General von Rundstedt and his Chief of Staff, General Erich von Manstein, pleaded with Brauchitsch to shift the centre of gravity of the attack from Bock's front to their own. If Hitler was resolved on a bold stroke at the cost of renouncing his pledges, then he ought, they argued, to make it a decisive one. Allied forces north of the Somme must be annihilated, not pushed back to a strong defensive line. The crossings of the Somme must therefore be seized before the retreating Allies reached them. In their view, this could be done only if the main thrust was delivered along the line from Sedan to Abbeville, where the distance from the Meuse to the vital area was shortest.

Partly as a sop to Rundstedt and partly because Hitler also wanted, for reasons not disclosed, to make the left wing stronger, Brauchitsch agreed in November to give Army Group A an armoured corps for the purpose of attempting a surprise crossing of the Meuse at Sedan; but he insisted that, while there might be a strong case for shifting the centre of gravity to Rundstedt's front, this could only be done after the attack had started. Hence the original plan, as modified at the end of October and in November, was still in force when Hitler ordered on January 10 that the attack should begin a week later. The news that two staff officers carrying documents which compromised the plan had made a forced landing in Belgium on that day did not lead him to order any immediate change, although bad weather did force him to call off the attack a few days later.

At the end of January Manstein was promoted and relegated to a command at Stettin. On February 17, however, he was summoned with other newly-promoted officers to report to the Führer, and was able to put his and Rundstedt's case at a private interview. In the meantime war games had suggested to the High Command that very strong forces would be needed to achieve anything worth-while at Sedan; Hitler had declared, according to Alfred Jodl, that Army Group A ought to have more armour; and Jodl himself had referred to the Sedan-Abbeville route as a 'tactical secret path' which might lead to success.[14] On the day after Manstein's visit Brauchitsch and Halder told Hitler that they had decided on a change of emphasis. Six days later the plan of campaign was issued in a new form which gave Rundstedt forty-four divisions and the task of thrusting across the Meuse in the Sedan-Dinant sector, with the Somme as his objective and the annihilation of Allied forces north of it as his strategic aim.

The French High Command formed an accurate impression of the German plan as it stood at the end of October, had ample warning of the attacks projected in November and January, and received from the Belgians the gist of the information gleaned from the partly-destroyed documents taken from the German officers who made a forced landing. On the other hand they did not learn of the radical alteration made in February. Thus they were confirmed in their belief that an attack across the Belgian plain was the enemy's most probable course of action. Early in October General Gamelin had expressed the contrary view, telling General Sir Edmund Ironside, Chief of the Imperial General Staff, that he expected the blow to fall south of Namur;[15] but later he came to the conclusion that an offensive in that sector would be too difficult to mount. The Belgian Ardennes, consisting largely of rolling country with a moderate number of steep gradients, were not an impassable barrier; but the considered opinion of Gamelin and his staff was that the Germans would not choose to make their approach march across wooded uplands where the limited capacity of the roads might prevent them from bringing up their artillery fast enough to achieve surprise or sustain the momentum of an armoured thrust. Moreover the Meuse, some sixty yards wide at Sedan and too deep to be forded, would be difficult to cross under concentrated infantry and artillery fire.

The corner-stone of the French defensive system was the Maginot Line, which gave the Allies an almost impregnable

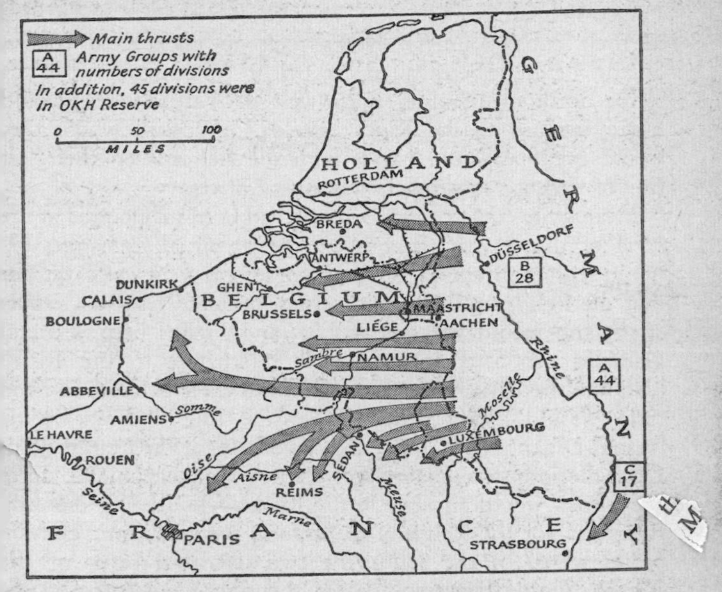

10 The German Plan for the Offensive against France and the Low Countries

front from the Swiss frontier to Longuyon. Proposals to extend the fortified line to the sea had been made on a number of occasions but had always been turned down, partly because the French were concerned to keep the battle zone away from their industrial area near Lille, and wished therefore to meet an invader approaching through Flanders or Hainault before he reached the frontier. As they were also determined to avoid an encounter battle, this would be difficult unless plans for an advance to prepared positions could be concerted with the Belgians. Thus there were political as well as military arguments against the construction of permanent defences which would leave the Belgian Army in the cold, and these were regarded as still valid even when Belgium renounced her military alliance with France after the remilitarization of the Rhineland. Only field works were constructed along the

Franco-Belgian frontier, and even these were not to b
in their entirety unless events took an unexpected
Should Belgium be invaded the British troops assigned
sector north of Maulde, north-west of Valenciennes,
move forward to the River Scheldt, or Escaut, whe
would eventually join hands with the Belgians on the
line of defence covering Ghent and Antwerp.

Meanwhile contact with Brussels had been maintained
level of the service attachés and by unofficial exchang
tween senior officers. Satisfied by the second week in Nov
that the Belgian military authorities meant to resist a G
attack and would welcome British and French help, G
Gamelin proposed as a possible alternative to the
plan that the Allied armies, if invited to enter Belgium i
time, should swing their left to the line Louvain-W
Namur-Dinant-Givet, some sixty-five miles at the nearest
from the industrial districts of French Flanders. In the
the British would advance to the River Dyle, leaving ro
their left for the Belgians to prolong the line from L
to Antwerp. In the south the two left-hand corps
French Ninth Army would join the right-hand corps
Meuse. In the centre, where there was no river lin
French First Army would go forward to hold the gap on
side of Gembloux. By this means the tides of battle wo
kept away from the neighbourhood which the French
to spare, the Allies would shorten their line, and a broa
of Belgian territory which would otherwise have to be
doned to the enemy would be saved.

The British raised no objection, although they may hav
some misgivings about an accompanying proposal to rus
French Seventh Army, hitherto in reserve, along the co
the neighbourhood of Antwerp or beyond. On Novemb
the Supreme War Council approved the plan as one to b
plemented if circumstances were favourable. Otherwis
less exacting Escaut plan would be adopted.

Thus the position at the end of the winter was tha
Allied armies might find themselves committed at short
to one or other of two alternative courses, and that thei

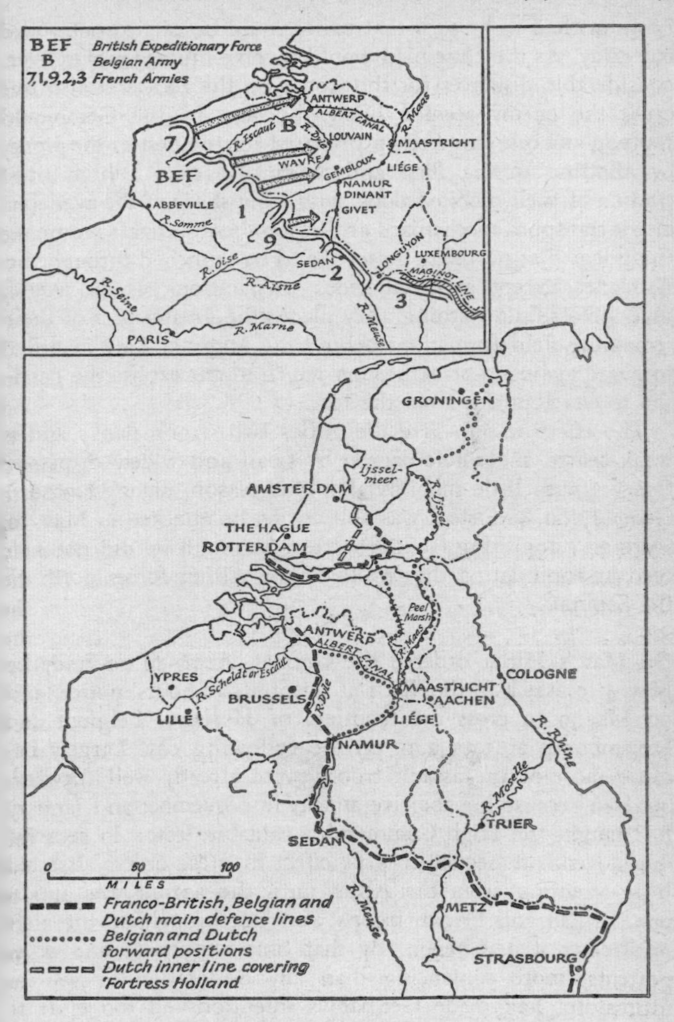

11 French, Belgian and Dutch Defence Plans

positions had to be such that either could be carried out without delay. As the Dyle plan would involve hurried moves over considerable distances for the troops on the left, and also because the enemy seemed likely to come by the Gembloux route in any case, the French prepared for the best or the worst by allotting to the First and Seventh Armies a high proportion of their mobile troops, with a big share of the available motor transport, mechanized artillery and anti-aircraft weapons. Confident that no major attack could be launched through the Ardennes except after laborious preparations which would give them ample warning, they placed the greater part of their remaining field formations behind the Maginot Line in order to guard against a breakthrough which might expose the garrison to envelopment from the rear.

The effect was to give the Allies two strong flanks and a weak centre, the whole backed by small and widely dispersed reserves with little mobility. For this reason, amongst others, General von Rundstedt was able, when he attacked in May, to score an astonishing tactical success, although he did not succeed in annihilating the whole of the Allied forces north of the Somme.

On May 1 Hitler ordered the German Army to be ready by May 4 to attack in the West at twenty-four hours' notice, and on May 9 to cross the frontiers of Holland, Belgium and Luxembourg at 5.35 a.m. on the following day. Largely because most of the assault troops were already well forward, but also because the abortive attacks in November and January had taught the High Command a valuable lesson in security, the movements needed to give effect to these orders attracted little attention from the Allies until the assault was almost due. British and French troops were not brought to the alert until after it had begun. By that time air attacks and other portents, more convincing than any declaration of war or ultimatum, had made Germany's intentions all too clear to Dutch and Belgian statesmen.

Of German objectives in Dutch territory, the most important from a purely strategic point of view were the crossings f the Lower Meuse in the Maastricht appendix. Between two nd three hours before the launching of the main assault, about ixty Germans crossed the frontier in that neighbourhood, ome dressed in fitters' or mechanics' overalls, others wearing Dutch steel helmets and greatcoats over German uniforms. The Dutch succeeded in blowing most of the bridges at which his incursion was aimed, but soon afterwards air landings urther to the west in Belgian territory, followed by a stout ush from the east, gave the Germans a substantial measure of ontrol in the crucial area. Attacking with twenty-eight divi- ions under command, General von Bock was able after a brief lelay to put the first of his three armoured divisions across he Lower Meuse.

The Dutch had called meanwhile for Allied help, but their efusal to hazard their neutrality by entering into staff talks efore the blow fell had ruled out any unified military plan. he French Seventh Army, attempting to make contact with ir forces near Breda, found German troops already in the eighbourhood, began to run short of ammunition, and with- lrew behind the Scheldt. Arrangements had, however, been nade to carry the Dutch gold reserves and stocks of diamonds o England if the need arose. These were put into effect by May 11. The Royal Family and some members of the govern- nent, narrowly escaping capture by German airborne forces, followed in the course of the next two days, and a cruiser, two lestroyers and a submarine of the Royal Netherlands Navy ook refuge in British ports. British demolition parties destroyed r otherwise made useless to the enemy large stocks of petrol- um; fighters from England flew protective sorties over Dutch erritory to the limit of their radius of action; and for five lays the Dutch Army kept up a struggle which had gone gainst them from the start.

The Dutch defensive system consisted of an inner line pro- ecting Rotterdam, The Hague and Amsterdam, an outer or nain line some twenty miles further east, and a series of overing positions intended to delay a westward advance cross the Maastricht appendix, the Peel Marshes and the orthern provinces. In theory such a system ought to have enabled the defenders to make good use of their substantial rifle strength by moving troops rapidly along interior lines to the sectors where they were most needed. In practice, the effect was to lock up a great part of the Dutch Army in static positions which proved of little value, since the enemy was able to land airborne troops behind them and could use his bombers to make rapid reinforcement of the threatened sectors extremely difficult. Moreover, the Dutch had no satisfactory system of air defence and were weak in weapons capable of dealing effectively with armoured fighting vehicles. Taking full advantage of these factors, by May 13 the invaders had a corps under Lieutenant-General Rudolf Schmidt in front of Rotterdam, which the Dutch hoped to save by declaring it an open city.

The Germans, however, contested this claim on the ground that Dutch troops were actively defending fortified positions in or on the outskirts of the city. Under orders from his superiors, General Schmidt made provisional arrangements to take the place by assault on May 14 after a preliminary bombardment by about 90 dive-bombers due over the target at 1.30 p.m.[16] At 10.30 a.m. on that day he delivered an ultimatum threatening complete destruction of the city unless the garrison undertook within two hours that resistance should cease forthwith; but on learning about twenty minutes before the time was up that his ultimatum was likely to be accepted, he despatched a signal postponing the dive-bomber attack. After receiving a non-committal answer from the Dutch a little later he went on to draw up and present the terms of surrender, which contained no threats but stipulated that negotiations should be completed by 4.30 p.m. so as to give his troops time to occupy the city before nightfall.

Meanwhile the use to be made of the Luftwaffe at Rotterdam was the subject of a long conversation on the telephone between Reichsmarschall Göring and the commander of Luftflotte 2, General Kesselring, who stated after the war that he was not aware at the time of any negotiations with the Dutch and still believed that Schmidt's corps needed air support. Presumably as a result of that conversation there appeared in the neighbourhood of Rotterdam a few minutes before 1.30

p.m. not the 90 dive-bombers which Schmidt had asked the Luftwaffe not to send, but roughly the same number of long-range bombers. About half the crews misunderstood or failed to see the warning flares which Schmidt then ordered his troops to light. They proceeded to bomb the commercial quarter of the city, dropping more than 90 tons of bombs which did a great deal of damage and killed nearly a thousand civilians.* The garrison surrendered about two hours later. Next day the rest of the Dutch Army capitulated, and almost simultaneously the British government, who had hitherto held out against the bombing of any but strictly military targets, sanctioned the first air attacks on the Ruhr.[17]

Meanwhile General von Bock's good start had enabled him not only to thrust deep into Holland, but also to advance into Belgium with the apparent intention of forcing the Gembloux gap.

The Belgian plan, as it stood when the Germans opened their attack, was to assist in countering any such move by holding covering positions on the Albert Canal and the Meuse upstream from Maastricht for at least five or six days in order to give the Allies time to come forward into Belgian territory. Thereafter the bulk of the Belgian Army would stand in the Antwerp-Louvain position, where its right would make contact with the British left if the Allies carried out their projected advance to the Dyle. Should the enemy come through the Ardennes, then so far as the Belgians were concerned he would be met forward of the Meuse only by lightly-equipped troops which would not try to do more than delay his advance with the help of road-blocks and demolitions.

The gist of this plan was already known to the Allies when, at four o'clock in the morning on May 10, the Belgian Foreign Minister called on the British Ambassador and made the first request for Allied help. But it had not been formally communicated, no government-sponsored staff talks had been held, and no Supreme Commander had been appointed to impose a

* The number of killed and injured was estimated at the time at 30,000. This appears to have been an exaggerated figure, even when allowance is made for non-fatal casualties.

common strategy on Belgian, British and French troops. Nor was a Supreme Commander appointed later. General Gamelin doubled the posts of Commander-in-Chief, Land Forces and Chief of Staff for National Defence in his own country, and also had ultimate control of the British Expeditionary Force, although this was subject to General Gort's right of appeal to his own government. But he had no power over the Belgian Army, and even where British and French forces were concerned he was reluctant to interfere with the conduct of the battle by General Alphonse Georges, who commanded on the North-East Front.[18] Consequently a tremendous burden was thrown on Georges, although he was far from possessing the authority and status of a Supreme Commander. As for Gamelin, his self-abnegation relegated him to a position in which the buoyancy and breadth of vision which were among his chief assets became of little value. As long as he refused to take matters into his own hands, he could not even do much t rectify such mistakes as his subordinates might make.

From the outset the task of the French High Command was made difficult by a partial collapse of the Belgian plan. Early on May 10 German airborne forces seized three of the main bridges across the Albert Canal immediately west of Maastricht, while paratroops landing within the perimeter of the neighbouring Fort Eben-Emael distracted the garrison from their task of covering the bridges and ultimately forced them to surrender. Although the Belgians succeeded in recapturing one bridge, the loss of the other two effectively turned the Albert Canal Line and led the Belgians to withdraw from their covering positions ahead of time.

Meanwhile Gamelin and Georges decided in consultation that the Dyle plan should be put into effect. Accordingly the British, with ten divisions less one temporarily in the Magino Line, began their advance to the Louvain-Wavre position, whil the eight infantry divisions of the French First Army on thei right moved forward behind a cavalry screen of two ligh mechanized divisions.* On reaching the line to be held b

*Contrary to expectations, the Luftwaffe made little attempt to inter fere with these moves.

he First Army the cavalry commander reported, however, that little had been done to prepare it for defence.[19] Rejecting his roposal that the High Command should revert to the less ad-venturous Escaut plan, Georges responded to the news by ccelerating the First Army's advance and reinforcing it at the expense of his scanty central reserve near Rheims. The result vas that, by the time the enemy was ready to come to grips vith the Allies in Central Belgium, not only thirteen of the est divisions in the French Army but two-thirds of its rmoured and light mechanized divisions, with roughly a third f all its first-line armoured fighting vehicles, were on or ehind the 22-mile sector from Wavre to Namur.

Along the ninety-five-mile stretch from Namur to Longuyon, n the other hand, Georges had only the twelve infantry and arrison divisions of the French Ninth and Second Armies, not ll of which were in position when the enemy arrived. In ront of them was a forward screen of four light cavalry livisions and two cavalry brigades, consisting largely of nounted troops with some mechanized elements and tank attalions.

General von Rundstedt began his advance to the Namur-Longuyon front on May 10 with forty-four divisions under ommand, of which seven were armoured and three motorized. His mobile formations, organized in three armoured corps, were rouped to form two powerful assault forces under Generals von Kleist and Hoth. On the left, General von Kleist's task vas to move in the general direction of Sedan with his two rmoured corps under Generals Guderian and Reinhardt, fol-owed by a two-division corps of motorized infantry, and to lo his best to establish bridgeheads across the Meuse at Sedan nd Monthermé. Further north General Hoth, with one rmoured corps, followed by one division of motorized in-antry, was to make a covering attack at Dinant and maintain ontact with Army Group B's left wing.

Using the full width of the roads to push their tracked and vheeled vehicles forward in two or more lanes where this vas possible, Rundstedt's mobile formations advanced rapidly hrough Luxembourg and the Belgian Ardennes, meeting little effective opposition from the Belgian and French skirmishers. They were not much hampered by demolitions and obstruc- tions which were mostly unguarded and could therefore be repaired, removed or circumvented. On May 12 forward elements of both Kleist's and Hoth's groups reached the Meuse, the French cavalry withdrew to the left bank, and the High Command of the North-East Front responded to an anxious message from the Second Army by ordering an armoured division and a motorized infantry division to move to the rear of its left flank.[20]

Nevertheless Georges and his staff still believed that the chief threat was to the First Army.[21] They also believed that if the enemy did attack the Second Army, possibly in the hope of wheeling southwards to roll up the Maginot Line, he would do so only after pausing for at least a day or two in order to bring up his artillery. They concluded that, even if the un- expected did happen, they would have time to bring up fresh formations from the south and perhaps reallocate some of the reinforcements sent to the First Army. After disposing of the three armoured divisions which formed the core of their central reserve they were, in fact, obliged to summon an in- fantry division from Lorraine in order to have something to put behind the Ninth Army in case of need.[22]

The enemy had, however, no intention of giving them such a respite. On Kleist's orders, Guderian attacked at Sedan on May 13 with only moderate artillery support, but after a pro- longed bombardment of the French infantry and artillery posi- tions by dive-bombers. For the most part well dug-in, the defenders were not seriously harmed by the bombardment, but many of them were so dazed and cowed by it that Guderian assault troops were able to cross the river in collapsible boat hurl themselves across the exposed ground between the left bank and the main defence line, and storm the French trenches and pillboxes with comparatively little loss. Wild rumours to the effect that the Germans were already across the river with tanks then caused a great part of the division whose front had been breached to disappear. The result was that on May 14 Guderian was able to start taking his armour across hastily-repaired bridge and assembling it on the left bank. A full-scale counter-attack by a corps consisting of a light cavalry division and the newly-arrived 3rd Armoured Division and 3rd Motorized Infantry Division was to have been launched by the French that afternoon; but at the last moment the corps commander, who had received contradictory orders calling on him both to counter-attack and to contain the enemy, postponed the attack and dispersed his tanks along a defensive front.[23]

Having thus lost his chance of striking a crippling blow at Guderian before he could complete a westward wheel after crossing the Meuse on a north-south axis, General Georges still hoped to intercept him by diverting the 2nd Armoured Division from the position in rear of the First Army to which he had ordered it on May 13. Its tracked vehicles were, however, travelling separately from its wheeled vehicles, and on May 15 the two columns became irretrievably separated when the spearhead of the German armour passed between them.[24] Thus two of the three French armoured divisions ceased to be capable of acting as effective counter-attack formations before either of them had gone into action.

At Monthermé, Reinhardt scored no success comparable with Guderian's at Sedan. Attempting an assault crossing of the Meuse without strong air support, his troops captured a small bridgehead, but there they were pinned down by a garrison division of the Ninth Army until events elsewhere transformed the situation.

At Dinant, on the other hand, Hoth made such good progress that his covering attack developed into a major thrust. When blowing the bridges on May 12, the French omitted to destroy a footbridge across a weir just north of the town. German motor-cyclists crossed it that night. Next day Hoth succeeded after bitter fighting in pushing troops across the river in collapsible boats, and by May 14 his engineers had completed a bridge fit for wheeled and tracked vehicles and he had substantial forces on the left bank.

After some hesitation, the commander of the French First Army Group decided on that day to transfer the 1st Armoured Division from the First Army to the Ninth in order to mount a counter-attack designed to throw Hoth back to the Meuse. But the journey south through an area thronged with retreating troops was slow and consumed much fuel. The petrol lorries were held up by congestion on the roads. The division was refuelling, and had sent most of its artillery to the rear, when at 9 a.m. on May 15, one of its half-brigades was caught by part of the more southerly of Hoth's two westward-moving columns and by-passed by the rest of the column. About five hours later Hoth's more northerly column ran into the division at a moment when it was re-grouping. Losing many of its tanks in these two actions without ever fighting as a complete formation with all its supporting weapons, the French 1st Armoured Division then retreated westwards, abandoning and destroying some of its vehicles on the way because they were too short of fuel to complete the journey.[25] By the time it reached French territory on May 16, with only 17 tanks left, practically the whole of the Ninth Army and part of the Second Army had disintegrated, leaving a gap nearly sixty miles wide through which Rundstedt's forces were pouring towards the Somme.

CHAPTER 7

THE WAR IN THE WEST: THE CLIMAX (II)

1940

'hen Rundstedt's armoured formations broke out of their
·idgeheads across the Meuse on May 14 and 15, the crumbling
the French centre left the Allies with practically no organ-
ed forces on the main axis of the enemy's advance, but with
ıbstantial armies north of the Sambre and south of the
isne.[1] As their troops north of the Sambre were fully en-
ıged with Bock's forces while those south of the Aisne were
ɔt seriously threatened, the most promising manœuvre which
mained open to them was a counter-attack northwards, de-
gned to cut Rundstedt's communications before the main body
his infantry could take a firm grip on the ground won by
is armour.

The three French armoured divisions concentrated near
heims at the outset of the battle would have been an in-
ıluable weapon for this purpose, but by May 15 they had
een dispersed. Even without them, however, General Georges
ıd many more divisions in the south than were needed to
ɔld the fortified line from Longuyon to the Swiss frontier.
hese divisions were not particularly mobile, but the railways
ere still working smoothly enough to make large troop move-
ents possible,[2] and in any case some days were bound to
apse before a counter-stroke could be delivered with full
fect.* In the event, the most favourable conditions for a

Contrary to popular belief, air attacks did little to impede Allied
ɔop movements during the first week of the assault. Thereafter their
ief effect was to enforce diversions which put a premium on good

counter-attack did not arise until some nine to twelve day after the initial assault, when the bulk of Rundstedt's armoure divisions were well forward and were providing their ow flank-guards pending the arrival of follow-up formations.[3]

Meanwhile Georges had decided to do everything he coul to halt Rundstedt's westward advance by forming a new front facing east, in the western foothills of the Ardennes or on th Oise.[4] This proved impossible since the Germans, having give much thought to the problem of refuelling, were able to pus their armoured columns forward much faster than the Frenc could rally their scattered troops in improvised positions By nightfall on May 20 Rundstedt's forward troops were on th Channel coast at the mouth of the Somme, and he had ele ments of seven armoured divisions and one motorized infantr division between the Allied troops in the north and the mai body of French divisions in the south. Moreover, his leadin formations were already across General Gort's communica tions with the bases in Normandy and Brittany on which th British relied for most of their supplies.

Barely a week after crossing the Meuse, Rundstedt' armoured formations had thus reached positions from which as soon as he gave the word, they could wheel north and north east with the intention of catching the Belgian Army, th British Expeditionary Force and the French First Army in pocket between his and Bock's forces. On the other han his long southern flank from the mouth of the Somme t Sedan was still weak.[5] As the motorized infantry corps whic was to take over the stretch from the sea to Péronne did n come forward until May 23, the first few days after Run stedt's spearheads reached the coast were an anxious time f him and the German High Command.

---

staff work, since delays had to be allowed for when movements we planned. About a dozen rail-cuts on May 17 did not prevent t large number of French units and formations in transit on that d from reaching their destinations by alternative routes, and over t whole period from the middle of May to the first few days of Ju about 25 divisions were moved from Lorraine and the Vosges to t Somme-Aisne front.

The weakness of Rundstedt's southern flank did not escape e French; but for some days after the break-through on the euse General Georges and his staff were preoccupied with cal counter-attacks and attempts to restore the situation in e centre. General Gamelin, on the other hand, had leisure to flect on the situation in the calm of his command post at incennes, and to study air reconnaissance reports which ressed the dearth of follow-up troops immediately behind the erman armour. As a comparatively young man, Gamelin had ayed a leading part in drafting Joffre's orders for the Battle the Marne. Just over a quarter of a century later he made his mind that the time had come for another saving stroke; it he feared to precipitate a crisis of confidence by superseding eorges, although he was strongly urged to do so and himself spected by May 18 that Georges was not physically equal to s task.[6] After a brief interview with Georges and others on lay 19, Gamelin went into a room by himself and drafted a ctfully-worded order calling on Georges to prepare with all s might for a counter-attack from the neighbourhood of ttigny towards the crossings of the Meuse immediately below dan. Such a counter-stroke, Gamelin thought, might be comned with an attempt by the First Army to break southwards om Douai towards the Somme.[7]

A few hours later Gamelin was relieved of his post and placed by the seventy-four-year-old General Maxime Weyind, summoned from Syria for the purpose. His order, which eorges did not regard as mandatory, became a dead letter, id for the next two days Georges and his staff continued to isy themselves with minor matters while they waited for ie new chief to make his wishes known. No preparations ere made for the all-out offensive proposed by Gamelin, and i May 19 the second of two local counter-attacks by the complete 4th Armoured Division under Colonel de Gaulle, though strikingly successful so far as it went, achieved othing decisive since it was not supported. Ultimately many ore divisions than Gamelin had thought of using for his tack near Attigny were moved to the Somme-Aisne front, it only to be committed in June to a defensive battle which

the French could not hope to win, since by that time th
Germans were able to bring to bear against them practicall
the whole weight of their field army.

General Weygand began his tenure of office on May 21 b
visiting the northern group of armies. Although one of th
main purposes of his visit was to discuss the situation wit
General Gort, he left without seeing Gort.[8] After his retur
to Paris he issued an instruction calling on the northern grou
of armies to prevent the Germans from making their way t
the sea (which they had reached two days earlier), and on th
British Expeditionary Force and part of the First Army t
counter-attack towards Cambrai and Bapaume under cover o
a withdrawal to the Yser by the Belgian Army.[9] The Britis
government also wished their Commander-in-Chief to attac
south-westwards 'with about eight divisions'. General Gor
who had already warned the War Office that he might hav
to fall back on the neighbourhood of Dunkirk,[10] was force
to explain that his troops were under severe pressure fron
Bock's fc[illegible] on the east, and could not disengage in orde
to march off in a new direction. Moreover there was, to sa
the least, no certainty that the Belgians would agree to with
draw to the Yser, that their doing so would contribute to th
safety of British and French troops moving away from them
or that the First Army would be able to find the five or si
divisions which Weygand expected them to throw into th
offensive. Gort believed that a limited sortie in the genera
direction of Cambrai and Bapaume might be possible abou
May 26, but that any major attempt to cut Rundstedt's con
munications on that axis would have to be made by th
French troops in the south.

Meanwhile he had given orders for a local counter-attack t
clear Rundstedt's troops from the neighbourhood of Arra
which he could not afford to relinquish except in his own tim
The attack was delivered on May 21 by two light infant
battalions, a battalion of motor-cyclists and two tank battalio
with 74 tanks. These were supported on the west by part of
French light mechanized cavalry division. The attack was s
successful that Major-General Erwin Rommel, commanding th

ƷGerman 7th Panzer Division, believed at the end of the day hat he had been attacked by very strong forces with hundreds of tanks.[11]

Leaving part of his armour to take care of his southern flank ınd part near Arras to guard against a further British sortie, Rundstedt began his northward thrust on May 22, but with orces substantially reduced by these precautions and the wear ınd tear of the past twelve days. In the meantime Bock had lecided to disregard instructions to make his main thrust in he direction of Lille and to push hard towards Courtrai in the ıope of driving a wedge between the Belgians and the British.[12] As a result of this move, and in the light of a capured document which revealed Bock's intention, Gort felt obliged on the evening of May 25 to renounce a push towards Bapaume and use the two divisions earmarked for the purpose to protect his eastern flank. Next day General Blanchard, commanding the French First Army Group, agreed that the Belgian Army, the British Expeditionary Force and the French First Army should withdraw to a bridgehead covering Dunkirk ınd protected on the west and south-west by the line of canals ınd canalized rivers running inland from Gravelines past Saint-Omer, Béthune and La Bassée.[13] The Belgian Army was, ıowever, unable to make its way into the bridgehead, and on May 27 surrendered unconditionally.

Meanwhile Army Group A's forward troops had reached he canal line, where Rundstedt decided on May 23 to halt his ırmoured units,[14] which had lost up to half their tanks and vould soon be needed for a southward thrust against the nain mass of the French Army. Hitler endorsed this decision on the following day, adding that any further advance by the ırmoured formations would restrict the Luftwaffe's field of ction.[15] All that was now asked of Rundstedt was that he hould prevent the enemy from escaping across the canal ine under pressure from Army Group B. Forty-eight hours ater Hitler nevertheless authorized resumption of Army Group A's advance; but General Guderian, commanding the German 19th Corps, reported after visiting his forward units n May 28 that an armoured thrust towards Dunkirk would entail needless sacrifices, and that anything further that was needed to complete the discomfiture of Allied troops in the bridgehead could safely be left to Bock's infantry.

The last word at Dunkirk was not, however, with the Luftwaffe's bombers or Bock's infantry, but with British sea power and air power. The German High Command believed until after the Belgian surrender that they could pin Gort down by denying him access to Ostend, and that they would then be able to crush him between their two army groups. They were also disconcerted by Gort's refusal to give up Arras until he chose to do so, and by unexpectedly stiff resistance from British and French garrisons at Boulogne and Calais. Largely as a result of these miscalculations, they failed to prevent him from carrying out his planned series of withdrawals and establishing himself in a position which gave him access to a commanded sea. Once he was in the bridgehead, the Germans found themselves unable to make much impression on him with the forces which they were willing to devote to the purpose in view of the further demands which would soon be made on them and of the manifest eagerness of the Luftwaffe to assume the leading role in the last act of the drama.

Contrary to expectations, the Luftwaffe proved incapable of preventing the British from embarking troops on a large scale, even after the port of Dunkirk had been severely damaged by bombing.[16] Under cover of strong though discontinuous patrols by fighters based in the United Kingdom, the British succeeded in withdrawing not merely the 40,000 to 50,000 men whom they hoped to save, but practically the whole of their Expeditionary Force, with the exception of roughly 140,000 troops who were serving with the French armies south of the German corridor, or on the lines of communication in Normandy and Brittany.* Between May 26 and June 4 a stream of British vessels took off about 225,000 British, roughly 110,000 French and some 2,000 Belgian troops. In addition about 50,000 French troops were carried in French ships. Thus the German Army and their supporting air formations failed to complete

*The bulk of these were afterwards withdrawn through ports in Western France.

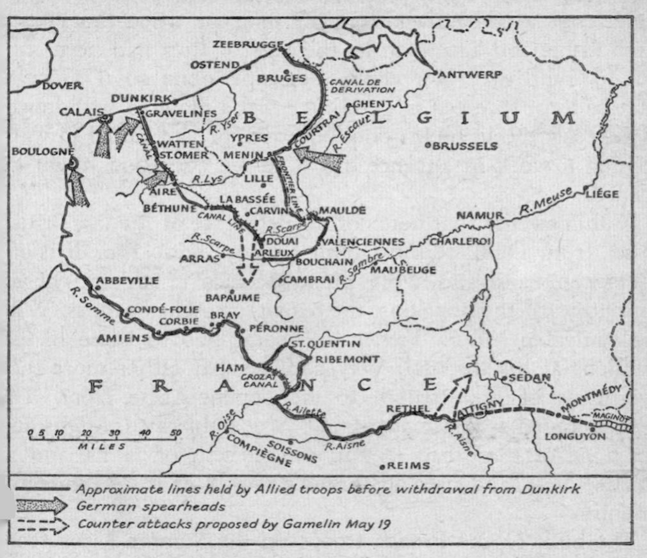

12 The Situation in France and Belgium after the Break-through on the Meuse

eir task, although they succeeded in defeating the Belgian rmy and could claim to have driven nearly 400,000 Allied oops from French soil with the loss of practically the whole f their heavy equipment and huge quantities of stores.

At the time the withdrawal from Dunkirk seemed to most e-witnesses a miracle of improvisation. In fact it was the uit of careful planning, and was organised with a thorough-ess not apparent to the thousands of men who owed their eedom to it. Commanders and staff officers continued until e end to issue detailed and written orders, embarkations hich seemed haphazard were conducted in accordance with nsidered programmes, and the Army Postal Service even elivered letters and parcels to units awaiting their turn to nbark. Calm seas and spells of cloudy weather helped the itish to get their troops away, but they could not have saved large an army, or have embarked French troops on the same terms as their own from the moment when the French High Command agreed to let them go, if they had been content to improvise. Nor could they have done so if General Gort had not foreseen in good time that a planned withdrawal to the coast might be his only salvation, or had failed to warn London a week in advance that a rescue operation might be needed.

Within twenty-four hours of the departure of the last British vessel from Dunkirk the German Army, with 140 divisions under command and a big preponderance in armour, began its southward thrust against the remaining Allied armies. With the equivalent of 62 French and some two to three British divisions at his disposal, Weygand devoted rather more than two-thirds of his strength to the Somme-Aisne front. The total included four armoured and three light cavalry divisions but none of these had its full complement of tanks, and in practice Weygand used his armour mostly as a substitute for infantry.

The bulk of the French troops on the Somme-Aisne front were posted in positions intended for all-round defence and were told to hold them at all costs, since Weygand did not believe that an orderly retreat would be possible if his front were breached.[17] In theory these strongpoints, many of them in villages and farms deserted by their peacetime occupants were mutually supporting, but in practice the system was riddled with gaps not adequately covered by artillery, so that it did not provide an effective obstacle in the absence of protective minefields and of mobile formations capable of searching dead ground and sealing off penetrations. Deprived by the very nature of Weygand's plan of practically all power of manœuvre, the defenders fought stubbornly, but some of them could not prevent their positions from being by-passed and surrounded. Consequently they could not be supplied after the first two or three days and were forced to surrender for lack of food and ammunition.

Attacking with the skill and enterprise which seldom deserted them as long as they retained the initiative, the Germans succeeded within a week in pushing their right across the Lower Seine and their left across Marne. On June 10 the French government left for Tours, with Bordeaux as their ultimate destination; on June 14 German troops entered Paris. At a Council of Ministers on June 16 the Prime Minister, Paul Reynaud, argued strongly in favour of continuing the war, if necessary from French North Africa.[18] But he received so little support that he resigned at the end of the meeting and was succeeded by the aged Marshal Philippe Pétain, who promptly asked the enemy for an armistice. Under the armistice terms German troops occupied a large part of France, but not the Mediterranean seaboard or the central and south-eastern provinces.

For the German people the collapse of France was a triumph which soothed the hurt inflicted on their self-esteem in 1918. The fact remained that Britain was still in the fight with almost overwhelming naval superiority, a fighter force which had already taken the measure of the Luftwaffe at Dunkirk, and a large industrial potential. Unless Hitler could persuade or compel the British government to make peace, he would not be able to carry out his policy of eastward expansion except at the cost of condemning Germany to a two-front war which she could not count on winning.

Meanwhile Italy had taken advantage of the misfortunes of the French to declare war on France and Britain. Although this development was a setback for the British from the naval point of view, it had the compensating advantage of at last allowing them to take up the threads of the 'Italy first' strategy which they had planned before the war.* The Italians, with some thirty divisions on the Alpine frontier, attacked on June 20 after German armour had appeared in the rear of the French, but made little progress.

When the British government had first to reckon with the possibility that France might be defeated, their estimate of their chances of survival was framed against the background of a forecast completed by their military advisers before the withdrawal from Dunkirk was fully under way or the withdrawal from Narvik begun. Fearing that the two with-

*See Chapter 5.

drawals might lead to almost crippling naval losses and also overestimating the strength and staying power of the German bomber force, the experts drew a gloomier picture than they might have drawn if they had been able to wait another week or two before committing their thoughts to paper.[19] The Chiefs of Staff knew, for example, that irrespective of the number of men brought back from Dunkirk, the Commander-in-Chief, Home Forces, was not likely to have enough tanks, field artillery and anti-tank guns before the winter to drive the Germans out if they succeeded in putting a well-equipped expeditionary force ashore in Britain. They also knew that the navy had not nearly enough destroyers to cover all vulnerable stretches of coast while continuing to protect trade. Their conclusion that more destroyers were urgently needed was unassailable in theory, but had only a limited relevance at a time when the Germans had so few warships that they could not hope to land or supply an expeditionary force unless and until the Luftwaffe succeeded in establishing such an ascendancy that British naval power could be safely disregarded.

Similarly, the Chiefs of Staff foresaw that, precisely because the Germans would count on air power to compensate for their naval weakness, the supply of fighter aircraft was likely to be a crucial factor. But their proposal that the United States government should be asked to comb through stocks of service aircraft for the benefit of the British fighter force was unrealistic, for the addition of unfamiliar types at a moment of crisis would have created awkward problems. The real answer was to increase output of the well-tried Hurricane and Spitfire. This was successfully done[20] by the British aircraft industry under the direction of a new Ministry of Aircraft Production headed by Lord Beaverbrook, whose methods were open to criticism but who helped to give the fighter force nearly seven hundred more aircraft between May and October than the Chiefs of Staff expected when they made their forecast.*

*At the beginning of the war the British were producing about 700 aircraft a month, but these were of all types, including trainers, and only about a sixth were fighters. Between September and February

About the time of Dunkirk and shortly afterwards, Winston Churchill stressed in his speeches and broadcasts the difficulties which Britain would face if she fought alone against Germany and Italy, and did not dwell to any marked extent on the difficulties which would face the other side. He adopted this approach in the light of expert guidance, but also, and perhaps most of all, because he was determined to steer clear of complacency, stir the British public to unheard-of efforts, and bring home to American statesmen the dire consequences which might follow any reluctance on their part to give full economic and financial support to the surviving champion of the European democracies.

Nevertheless the problems which confronted Hitler were substantial. In July the Führer ordered that preparations for the invasion of Britain should begin.[21] Thereupon Field-Marshal von Brauchitsch moved thirteen picked divisions to the Channel coast as the first wave of a landing force; the navy began to assemble transports, barges, tugs and motor-boats, but warned Hitler that the effects on Germany's economy might be serious; and the security authorities made plans to interrogate prominent British citizens, requisition public buildings and deport able-bodied workers. But Brauchitsch and Halder, who counted on sending thirty-nine divisions to England in four waves, wished to land on a broad front from Ramsgate to Lyme Bay.[22] They also wished to complete by the end of the third day the disembarkation of the 260,000 men, 30,000 to 40,000 vehicles and 60,000 or more horses allotted to the first-wave divisions. The naval planners, on the other hand, insisted that the initial seaborne landings must be confined to a

---

747 fighters were delivered, in March 177, and in April 256. Thereafter output of the essential types rose so sharply that in the next six months 2,679 fighters were delivered, as compared with 1,983 predicted at the time of the withdrawal from Dunkirk. Conversely, German production on the outbreak of war was roughly the same as the British for an air force twice as large, and it remained almost stationary at 700 to 800 aircraft a month during the next twelve months. Consequently the Luftwaffe suffered from a lack of depth which tended to make it a declining asset at times of stress.

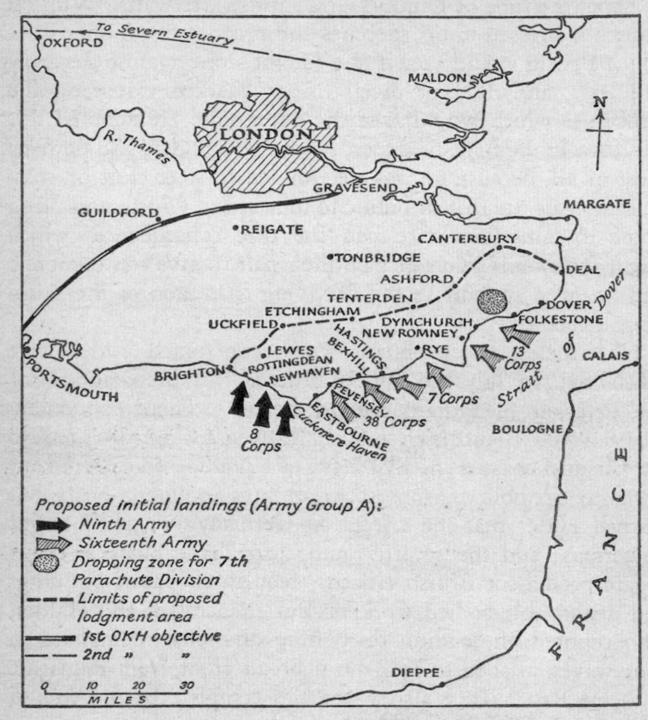

13 Operation 'Sealion'

narrow front at the eastern end of the Channel so that the flanks of the crossing could be protected by mines and aircraft. They added that lack of the shipping needed to carry the second echelons of the first-wave divisions in one lift would force them to spread the first-wave landings over about ten days instead of three, and that in any case the navy could not be ready before the middle of September, when a long spell of calm weather could not be relied upon.

Whether a landing in such circumstances would be worth attempting unless the British were already on the verge of surrender was debatable. A point on which there was, however, no

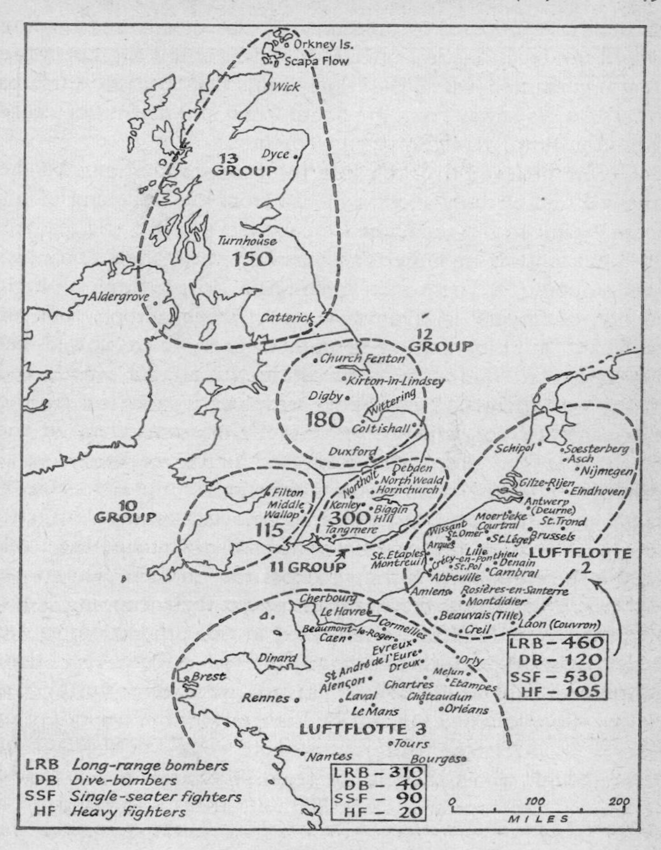

14 The Battle of Britain

Strength of British fighter force and German air striking forces on September 7, 1940

All figures are approximate. The British figures are for serviceable fighter aircraft. The German figures are for serviceable long-range bombers (LRB), dive-bombers and ground attack aircraft (DB), single-seater fighters (SSF), and heavy fighters (HF) other than night-fighters. Minelayers and reconnaissance aircraft are not shown.

substantial difference of opinion was that an opposed landing would not be a practical operation of war unless the Luftwaffe could guarantee when the time came that British warships would be kept away from the South Coast and that interference from the Royal Air Force would be minimal.

Göring believed that he could fulfil these conditions, but he allowed himself only about a month from the launching of his main assault to the time when the navy expected to be ready.[23] In the meantime he undertook a new series of attacks on ports and shipping.[24] These attacks cost the British three of their eighty destroyers in Home Waters, about 30,000 tons of merchant shipping out of a million tons which flowed between United Kingdom ports while the attacks lasted, and about 150 aircraft as compared with nearly 300 lost by the Germans. In consequence of the preliminary offensive the British changed the organization and timing of their coastal convoys, hastened existing arrangements for the diversion of ocean traffic to West Coast ports, and moved destroyers hitherto at Dover to Portsmouth, where they still threatened the flank of the force planning to move across the Channel. They were not prevented from continuing to sweep their shipping lanes, and their aircraft factories remained in full production, as did two factories[25] which supplied all the engines for their Hurricanes and Spitfires.* Thus they were able, during the weeks which divided the fall of France from the beginning of heavy air attacks on Britain, to make good the shortage of fighters with which their losses from Norway to Dunkirk had left them, take current losses in their stride, and build up a small reserve.

At the beginning of the second week in August the British fighter force, under Air Chief Marshal Sir Hugh Dowding, mustered the equivalent of fifty-five and a half operationally

*These were the Rolls-Royce factories at Derby and Crewe. Rolls-Royce had taken over a large number of factories and workshops in the neighbourhood of Derby so that production of essential components could continue in the event of damage to the main works, but additional factories near Glasgow and at Manchester were not yet ready.

fit squadrons, with a tactical strength of 666 aircraft and an actual strength of about 1,100, less some 350 temporarily grounded for overhaul, inspection or minor repairs.[26] Rather more than four-fifths of the force was equipped with Hurricanes or Spitfires, but there were also six squadrons of Blenheims, fit only to tackle unescorted bombers; two squadrons of Defiants which were credited with remarkable results at Dunkirk but did not prove so successful later; and half a squadron of obsolescent Gladiators. The Aircraft Storage Units held nearly 300 Hurricanes and Spitfires and some 80 Defiants ready for immediate delivery to squadrons.[27] Dowding was nearly 200 short of his establishment of pilots, but still had enough to man all his serviceable aircraft and provide a margin for reliefs.[28] Above all, his force was organized, equipped and trained to meet precisely such a blow as the enemy was about to deliver.

On the German side, the three air fleets assigned to the attack on Britain had, between them, about 800 single-seater and 300 heavy fighters, of which 702 and 261 respectively were serviceable on August 10.[29] The heavy fighters were, however, of little value for escorting bombers, although they achieved one or two successes as fighter-bombers or ground-attack aircraft. The striking-forces consisted of just under 1,000 serviceable long-range bombers and about 300 serviceable dive-bombers.[30] The dive-bombers were an easy prey for fighter pilots and anti-aircraft gunners; and the number of long-range bombers which could be put into the air at one time would depend in practice on the number of single-seater fighters available to escort them, each bomber needing at least two fighters to give it a good chance of survival in daylight. Reserves were scanty.

In general, the German High Command had a fair knowledge of the enemy's resources at the onset of the battle. The Luftwaffe's subsequent calculations of British strength were, however, based largely on unsound inferences from unreliable data, and at all stages the effectiveness of the British radar system was underestimated. The Luftwaffe was also handicapped to some extent by having become largely an adjunct to the army. Skilled judges of the day-to-day requirements of a land campaign, the Luftwaffe's senior commanders and staff officers had no experience of independent operations in face of a powerful and well-organized system of air defence. Yet the task before them involved not only the overthrow of such a system, but also the virtual elimination of naval forces numbering nearly a hundred warships and some seven hundred armed patrol vessels.

After a series of postponements caused by doubts about the weather, Göring chose August 13 for the launching of his all-out air offensive.[31] On the preceding day the Luftwaffe attacked radar installations on the South Coast, and brought off an exceptional feat by knocking out a station in the Isle of Wight. Unaware of this success and believing that such attacks were a waste of time, Göring ordered that no more should be made. Eleven days elapsed before the British could open a stand-by station on another site, but in general they continued to receive good warning of the enemy's approach.

The morning of August 13 was cloudy. An attempt to postpone the start until the afternoon miscarried, with the result that some bombers flew to their targets unescorted, while some fighters made aimless sweeps unaccompanied by bombers. In the course of the twenty-four hours the two air fleets in France and the Low Countries lost 45 aircraft without gaining any advantage over the opposing fighter force, which lost only thirteen aircraft and seven pilots and suffered only minor damage to one of its airfields.

After another cloudy day, a fresh start was made on August 15, when all three air fleets put into effect the programme scheduled for the second of the four days which the High Command had allowed for the subjugation of the defences south of a line from London to Gloucester.

The task which fell to General Hans-Jürgen Stumpff, commanding Luftflotte 5 in Norway and Denmark, was to attack airfields near Newcastle and in Yorkshire. The distance was much too great for single-seater fighters, and even heavy fighters could cover it only by carrying supplementary fuel-tanks. Moreover, Stumpff had only about 35 heavy fighters to take care of more than 120 bombers. Despatching his striking-force in two formations from bases far apart, he therefore devoted all the fighters to the protection of his older and slower bombers, and sent his newer bombers across the North Sea without escort.

Both forces were detected long before they reached the English coast. They were roughly handled by the defences, which destroyed sixteen bombers and seven fighters at no cost to themselves. Some crews dropped their load in the sea, and only about a quarter successfully attacked a primary objective. Further south, Luftflotten 2 and 3 scored hits on two aircraft factories and a number of fighter bases, but their losses were fairly heavy. Next day the Luftwaffe High Command calculated that Air Chief Marshal Dowding's strength must be down to about 430 aircraft, of which 300 might be serviceable.[32] In fact, he had about 1,100 aircraft of which 700 were serviceable, and more than 200 Hurricanes and Spitfires were ready for immediate despatch from the Aircraft Storage Units.[33]

In the light of this experience and of two more days of give and take over southern England on August 16 and 18, Göring decided that stronger fighter support was needed and that for the time being the main effort must be made against objectives well within reach of single-seater fighters. He believed that by this means he could force Dowding to use up his remaining fighters in the south-east and bring in squadrons from outlying sectors to replace them. When these in turn had been knocked out, the whole of the United Kingdom, with all its naval and air bases, would lie open to attack.

Accordingly, Göring put most of the single-seater fighters at the disposal of Field-Marshal Albert Kesselring, commanding Luftflotte 2 in North-East France and the Low Countries. General Stumpff was ordered to prepare for a night attack on Glasgow at some future date, but took no further part in the main battle. Field-Marshal Hugo Sperrle, commanding Luftflotte 3 on Kesselring's left, was to prepare for night attacks on Liverpool but meanwhile would keep up harassing attacks by day and especially in cloudy weather.

But Dowding and his subordinate commander in the south-east, Air Vice-Marshal Keith Park, were determined that the battle should be fought in their way, not the enemy's. Dowding refused to reinforce Park so generously as to leave three-quarters of the kingdom at Göring's mercy, Park to match his fighters against Kesselring's on terms not of his own choosing. Park's policy was to shoot down as many bombers as he could, protect his airfields from heavy damage, and engage Kesselring's fighters with forces just large enough to prevent them from playing a decisive part.[34]

The second phase of the battle, which opened on August 24 after five days of indifferent weather, went only moderately well from Göring's point of view. Park found Kesselring's bombers rather hard to reach and was unable to ward off some damaging attacks on his bases, but succeeded in keeping his force substantially intact without massive reinforcement. At the end of a fortnight he had twenty-three squadrons under command, as compared with twenty-one at the outset of the battle. Thirty-six squadrons and two detached flights guarded the rest of the United Kingdom. The British fighter force as a whole had 746 serviceable aircraft,[35] and its average daily effort was increasing while that of the Luftwaffe was declining.[36] By early September Dowding's squadrons were flying on a busy day not merely more daytime sorties than Kesselring's fighters, but more than the whole of Kesselring's and Sperrle's bombers and fighters put together.

Moreover, Kesselring's strength was running down at a time when his superiors would soon have to provide the requisite conditions for invasion, or confess their inability to do so. At that crucial stage he had fewer than 500 serviceable long-range bombers and only about 530 serviceable single-seater fighters, in addition to some sixty interchangeable between his command and Sperrle's.[37] He was told to compensate for the weakness of his escort force by making full use of his hundred or more heavy fighters, but experience had shown that these were not a match for Hurricanes and Spitfires.

Göring came to the conclusion that he must do everything he could to hasten a decision, and that his best chance of chieving one lay in attacking an objective which the enemy vould take good care to defend. He chose London as the arget, but not solely for that reason. On the night of August 4 bomber crews sent to attack two aircraft factories and an il refinery in the Home Counties had dropped bombs on a umber of London boroughs, although they had orders not to lo so. The British had retaliated by bombing Berlin. Hitler vas therefore willing to see London attacked in earnest, but nsisted that bombs should be aimed at specific targets such s docks and factories.[38] The time for indiscriminate bombing ntended to sow confusion might come later.

Accordingly, Kesselring broke off his attacks on Park's air-ields at a moment when they were causing the British a good leal of anxiety. His first raid of the new series was aimed at argets east of Tower Bridge and further down the river, and was made with rather more than 300 bombers and about 600 single-seater and heavy fighters in the late afternoon of September 7.

Earlier on that day, a committee appointed in London to study German preparations for invasion reported that large numbers of barges were concentrated in the Channel ports and that information from captured enemy agents suggested that German troops might be about to attempt a landing in the South of England.[39] The Chiefs of Staff, meeting about the time when Kesselring's bombers were approaching, concluded that the Commander-in-Chief, Home Forces, ought to bring his troops to instant readiness by issuing the code-word 'Cromwell', which meant 'Invasion imminent'; the staff of the Home Forces Command came independently to the same conclusion; and the signal was despatched that evening. On receiving it, some commanders exceeded their instructions by calling out the Local Defence Volunteers, or Home Guard. Thereupon some members of the Home Guard caused church bells to be rung, which they were not authorized to do unless paratroops were seen descending. When no German airborne and seaborne troops appeared, the government were blamed for these mistakes and were widely believed to have been stampeded by Kesselring's raid into ill-considered action.

The raid did a fair amount of damage, and was followed by a night attack which brought the number of Londoners killed or seriously injured by the early hours of September 8 to about two thousand.[40] Twenty-one British squadrons went into action, but most of the bombers were intercepted only when they had dropped their load or were so close to their objectives that even badly-aimed bombs fell on thickly-populated districts. The Germans lost forty-one aircraft which they could ill spare, the British seventeen pilots and forty-four fighters destroyed or badly damaged.

Kesselring followed with three more daylight raids on London on September 9, 11 and 14, using about 200 bombers on the first occasion and smaller numbers on the other two. On September 9 more than half the bombers were forced by the defenders to drop their loads well short of their objectives, but the later raids were more successful. Concluding on September 10 that air supremacy had not yet been won, Hitler postponed until September 14 his decision as to whether invasion should be attempted. Later he decided to wait until September 17 in order to give the Luftwaffe another chance of forcing the issue and perhaps gaining a success so complete that an opposed landing would not be necessary.

With only two clear days left, Kesselring prepared for an all-out effort on Sunday, September 15. Slender resources compelled him to deliver his attack on London in two instalments separated by an interval long enough to allow some of his aircraft to take part in both. Sperrle agreed to devote a small force to a diversionary attack on Portland, and the day would end with an attack by bomb-carrying heavy fighters on the Supermarine aircraft factory near Southampton. These diversions would not, however, prevent the British from refuelling and rearming during the interval between the two phases of the main attack.

The assembly of Kesselring's forces for the first phase was easily detected by the British radar system. By 11.30 a.m., when the leading German aircraft reached the English coast, Park had eleven of his twenty-one single seater squadrons airborne, and six squadrons contributed by his neighbours were coming east and south to reinforce him. After being harried from the coast to the Medway towns by a total of five squadrons, the attackers were met by two of six squadrons which Park had ordered up as the engagement was beginning, then by four which had assembled north-east of London, and after that by five reinforcing squadrons which had come south as a single formation. During the last two actions the Germans distributed a substantial bomb-load over London, but achieved no notable concentration. As they withdrew, Park threw in the last four of his single-seater squadrons, and two more reinforcing squadrons came from the west to join in the pursuit.

In the afternoon the radar chain gave a shorter but still ample warning. By the time the Germans approached, with their bombers and close escort in two formations supported by a forward screen of high-flying fighters, Park had nineteen and a half squadrons in the air, and once again six reinforcing squadrons were on their way Intercepted on four separate occasions between the coast and their objective, some of the bombers jettisoned their load and turned away, some were shot down, and the rest flew on.

A brisk action, involving fifteen British and Allied squadrons, then developed over London. Most of the defending fighters were caught up in fierce encounters with the German fighter screen, but some went on to engage the bombers, which scattered a big load over a wide area. Thus the fighter-to-fighter battle which Kesselring had long been seeking came at last, but brought him no favourable decision.

Meanwhile about thirty of Sperrle's bombers approached Portland, caught the sector responsible for its defence with two out of three single-seater squadrons committed to the main battle, and delivered an attack which did minor damage to the dockyard before being brought to action by the remaining squadron. Finally, Kesselring's fighter-bombers, some twenty strong, performed a remarkable feat by eluding most of the fifty or sixty aircraft sent to find them, but were hotly engaged by the Southampton guns and missed the target.

The Germans lost sixty aircraft destroyed and many damaged, Kesselring's bomber force suffering particularly heavy losses. But such losses might have been borne if they had been offset by some positive achievement. The factors which made the day's events decisive were the strength and vigour of the British effort and the failure of the German fighters to gain a clear ascendancy. These factors showed that the Luftwaffe was not within measurable distance of creating the right conditions for invasion and that its estimates of the losses inflicted on the enemy in recent weeks were not reliable. On August 16 the High Command had credited Dowding with 300 serviceable aircraft in all parts of the country; on August 29 the head of Kesselring's fighter organization had claimed 'unlimited fighter superiority'.[41] Yet on September 15 Dowding was twice able to put more than 300 aircraft over the south-eastern counties alone. In the last series of engagements over London, German aircrews who had been assured that they were not likely to meet more than about a hundred British fighters from first to last had been set upon by nearly twice that number within the space of half an hour.

Not surprisingly, Hitler concluded on September 17 that air supremacy was still lacking. On that ground and also because the immediate future held no promise of the week or more of 'flat calm' which his naval advisers considered necessary to disembark the troops, vehicles and horses of the first-wave divisions, he decided not to give the order for invasion.[42] On the following day he sanctioned partial dispersal of the invasion fleet and called a halt to the assembly of invasion craft. He continued for some time afterwards to speak of a possible landing in October; but the chances of carrying out the venture so late in the year were small, especially as the Naval Staff now needed fifteen days' notice instead of ten.

Theoretically, a landing might still be made in the spring of 1941, or even later. But Hitler himself had pointed out, when arguing for a landing in 1940, that the opposition was likely to be much stronger in 1941.[44] And indeed, there was little prospect that Germany's armed forces, even if their enthusiasm for invasion were rekindled after the March equinox and if the problem of crossing an uncommanded sea could be overcome, would be able to complete the conquest of Britain efore the bulk of the army and the air force were needed for ther purposes. Planning for an attack on Russia had begun in uly; active preparations began in October with the construction of airfields in Poland. The assault could scarcely be deayed beyond the early summer if worthwhile results were to e achieved before frost and snow put an end to profitable ampaigning. If the British could somehow be brought to sue or peace before the chestnuts were in blossom, all might yet e well from the German point of view. If not, then Germany's eet would be set on the uncertain path of a two-front war.

TABLE 2

THE BATTLE OF BRITAIN: GERMAN AND BRITISH LOSSES[48]

(Aircraft destroyed, or damaged and written off as unrepairable)

	German	*British*
Preliminary Phase (July 10-August 12)	286	150
First Phase (August 13-18)	258	103
Interim Phase (August 19-23)	32	11
Second Phase (August 24-September 6)	380	286
Third Phase (September 7-30)	433	242

CHAPTER 8

THE CROSSROADS (I)

1940-41

When Mussolini announced on June 10, 1940, that Italy was about to enter the war against France and Britain as Germany's ally, few Italians could feel much sympathy with Hitler's cause. On the other hand, French claims to leadership of the Latin races had long been resented, and the British had not been forgiven for their attitude to Mussolini's Abyssinian adventure.

From a practical standpoint, Italy was not in a position to embark on more than a brief campaign. Lack of raw materials and other economic ills would make it almost impossible for her to undergo a long war without becoming dependent on her better-endowed partner, and thus losing more than she could hope to gain.[1] In May, 1939, Mussolini had warned Hitler that he would not be ready to fight for at least three years, and in August he had refused to do so unless granted supplies of coal, petroleum, steel, timber and other commodities not likely to be forthcoming. When he decided ten months later that, after all, the time had come for Italy to join the struggle, he gambled on quick results which would enable him to claim a share in the spoils of victory before his reserves were exhausted.

Largely because of the economic factor, the state of the armed forces, with the possible exception of the navy, was unsatisfactory. Italy had an army of about seventy divisions, but lacked the means of providing them with heavy equipment and transport on a scale which would make them formidable. Her air force, regarded until about 1936 as outstanding, was equipped in 1940 with aircraft outclassed in performance by recent British and German products, although they were of excellent quality and well designed. On the other hand Admiral Domenico Cavagnari, the Naval Chief of Staff, could reckon on having in commission by July or August a total of six battleships, nineteen cruisers, about fifty destroyers and more than a hundred submarines.[2] These would include two modern battleships of advanced design. No major fleet action had, however, been fought by the Italian Navy in modern times.

In April, some two months before Italy entered the war, the Allies had agreed on a number of measures designed to improve their chances if German progress in Scandinavia or elsewhere should encourage Mussolini to go to war.[3] These included the rebuilding of their naval strength in the Eastern Mediterranean, which had diminished since 1939; defensive precautions at Gibraltar, Malta, Alexandria and Haifa; and the diversion of British merchant shipping, other than mail steamers, from the Suez Canal to the long route round the Cape.

As a result, by the date of Mussolini's announcement the Allies had in the Eastern Mediterranean four battleships, an aircraft carrier, eight cruisers and twenty destroyers under Admiral Sir Andrew Cunningham, in addition to a French squadron of one battleship, four cruisers, and three destroyers. In the Western Mediterranean the French had two battleships, two battlecruisers, ten cruisers and thirty-five destroyers based on Toulon, Bizerta, Algiers and Oran; the British one battleship, one cruiser and nine destroyers at Gibraltar. Two of Cunningham's battleships were, however, old and slow, and he had neither enough destroyers to take his fleet to sea without stopping all other activities, nor the long-range aircraft needed for reconnaissance. On the other hand the French fleet in the Western Mediterranean, with its fast modern battlecruisers and its exceptionally powerful destroyers, was very strong.

The fall of France was therefore a major setback for the British from the naval point of view. Without French warships and naval bases, any challenge to Italian control of the

Sicilian Channel would be difficult. Malta would become more vulnerable than ever, and even Gibraltar might be hard to hold. Alexandria, although the only practical alternative to Malta since Haifa had not been developed as a base for heavy ships, was itself exposed to air attack and lacked facilities for major repairs.

In the light of these and other factors, the British government considered withdrawing Cunningham's fleet to Aden and blocking the Suez Canal, or alternatively moving it to Gibraltar and concentrating on the defence of Atlantic trade. About the time when Hitler was ordering his service chiefs to prepare for the invasion of England, the British concluded, however, that abandonment of their Mediterranean and Middle Eastern strategy would be a fatal step. A strong fleet would remain at Alexandria, three thousand miles by sea from the stretch of coast where the German Army hoped to land. Egypt, the Suez Canal and British petroleum interests bordering on the Persian Gulf would be defended. Kenya, the Sudan, Iraq, Palestine and Aden would be held. Greece and Turkey would be helped to defend themselves if Germany attacked them, notwithstanding the refusal of the Turks to be bound, after the French collapse, by a promise to join the Allies if Italy entered the war against them. In general, reinforcements and supplies consigned to the Middle East from United Kingdom ports would go by the long route round the Cape, as a rule taking about six weeks to reach their destinations; but aircraft would be disembarked and uncrated at Takoradi, on the Gold Coast, and would fly to Egypt across French Equatorial Africa, some of them carrying light stores. Some urgently-needed reinforcements would, however, be sent in warships through the Straits of Gibraltar and the Sicilian Channel, and occasional fast convoys might also be sent by that route where the stake seemed to justify the risk.

At the same time, the British were acutely sensitive to the danger that Hitler might seize as much of the French fleet as came within his grasp.[4] They had asked the French, when they released France from her obligation not to make a separate peace, to put their warships out of Hitler's reach, but had

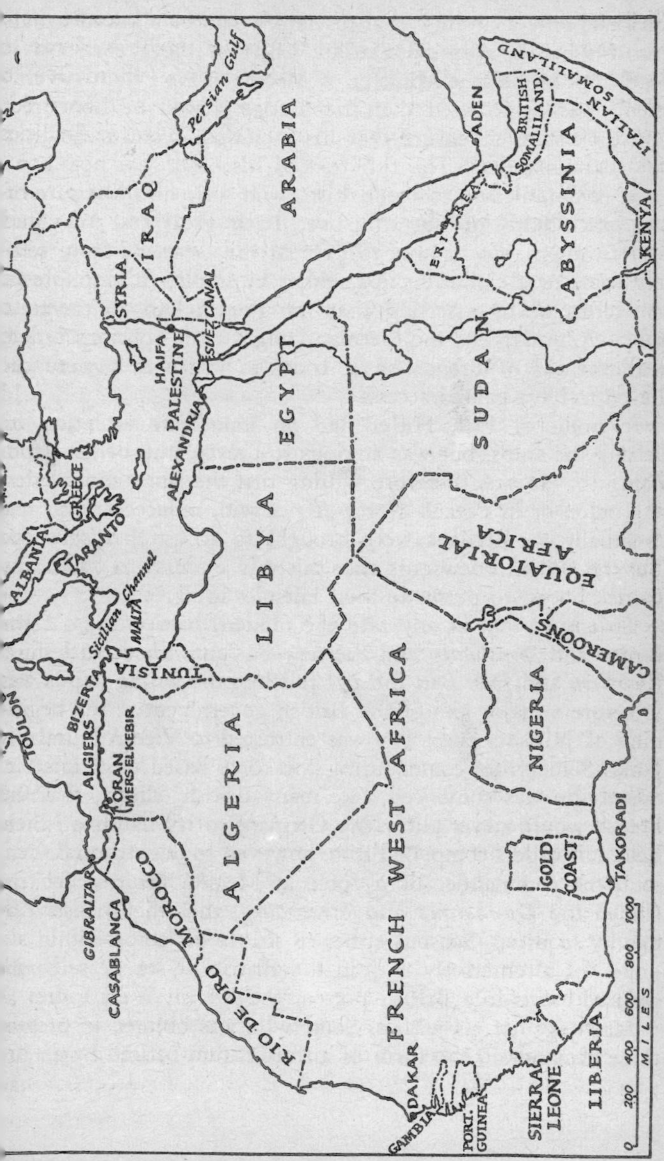

15 The Mediterranean and Middle East

obtained only a promise that no ship would be allowed to fall into his hands. Admiral Darlan, Chief of the French Naval Staff until he became Minister of Marine in the Pétain government, was determined that the pledge should be honoured, and took steps to ensure that his intentions were made clear to all commanders. The full text of his order was not, however, communicated to the British, who were also unaware of the exact terms of the armistice. Their great fear was that Darlan might not be able to prevent the Germans from seizing some or all of the ships, either by finding a loophole in the terms or by asserting that the French had contravened them. Alternatively, the Germans might issue spurious orders with the aid of French naval codes to which they were believed to have gained access.

In point of fact, Hitler had no immediate intention of seizing the ships, but was anxious to prevent the British from doing so. He was therefore willing that the ships should stay at Toulon or in French North Africa with reduced crews, and eventually the Italians were brought to accept that solution. But the British knew only that this was a course to which the French hoped to persuade their enemies to agree.

To ensure that at any rate the modern battlecruisers *Dunkerque* and *Strasbourg* and the new but unfinished battleships *Richelieu* and *Jean Bart* did not fall into the wrong hands was therefore a major aim of the British government at the beginning of July. Its execution was entrusted to Vice-Admiral Sir James Somerville, commanding the force based on Gibraltar. Somerville was convinced, like many British officers, that the French would never allow the Germans to lay hands on their fleet. His orders compelled him, however, to tell Admiral Gensoul, the commander of a force at Mers-el-Kebir which included the *Dunkerque* and *Strasbourg*, that the British Admiralty required Gensoul either to scuttle his ships within six hours, or alternatively to join the British at sea or sail with reduced crews to a British port or the French West Indies.

Much against his wishes, Somerville was obliged to present these demands in the form of an ultimatum backed by an immediate show of force. Unwilling to yield to a naked threat, Admiral Gensoul at first refused to negotiate, reported to his superiors that he had been asked to scuttle his fleet, but did not mention the alternatives that had been put to him. Later he offered to demilitarize his ships where they lay; but this solution, although one which Somerville was authorized to accept if the French suggested it, was clearly impractical within the time-limit laid down by the British Admiralty.

Accordingly, Somerville had no choice but to open fire on the French ships in the late afternoon of July 3. The *Dunkerque* was disabled, two battleships and a destroyer were sunk or otherwise put out of action, the *Strasbourg* and five destroyers escaped to Toulon, and 1,297 French lives were lost. A few days later, after a similar ultimatum had been presented at Dakar, the *Richelieu* was in turn attacked by the British, but more lightly and in less tragic circumstances. The *Jean Bart* at Casablanca was not molested, as she seemed unlikely to be ready for active service for some time to come.

These events did not improve relations between the British and the French government established at Vichy. In the main, however, Pétain and his colleagues remained faithful to a policy of collaborating with Hitler only to the extent of denying the British access to parts of the French colonial empire still under their control. Where they did offer concessions not contemplated in the armistice, they more than once succeeded in so protracting the negotiations that the Axis Powers obtained little benefit. In Syria, for example, the Germans were granted the use of French airfields and war material, but too late for them to give effective aid to an anti-British movement in Iraq which was suppressed without much difficulty.[5] Conversely, an attempt by Free French forces to land at Dakar with British support was vigorously opposed and ended in total failure.

American diplomacy played an important part in encouraging the Vichy government to evade German demands, and also in stiffening General Franco's determination not to allow passage to German troops bent on capturing Gibraltar. But this was only a small part of the American contribution to the war with Hitler and Mussolini during the long months when Britain fought alone. Ostensibly in return for fifty old destroyers, of which only nine were delivered before the end of 1940, Britain granted the United States ninety-nine-year leases of bases in the Caribbean and the Western Atlantic. In reality these sacrifices purchased not merely the destroyers, but a degree of economic and financial support without which continued resistance to the Axis Powers might have been impossible. By the second winter of the war the whole of Britain's dollar resources, and more, were hypothecated to the financing of existing contracts, so that no more orders for American war material could have been placed if support from the United States government had not been forthcoming. The Lend-Lease Bill, which became law in March, 1941, solved this problem by empowering the President to furnish the British with virtually everything they needed, and to leave the question of repayment to be decided by the President at his discretion. This arrangement was not, however, retrospective. Under contracts already made, the British continued to pay in dollars or their equivalent for most of the goods they receivec up to the time when the United States became an active belligerent.

Meanwhile Anglo-American staff talks were begun in conditions of profound secrecy.[6] These led to the conclusion tha Europe and the Atlantic were the decisive theatre. Should the United States resort to force, her main effort would be mad there, and if Japan, too, were involved a defensive strateg would be adopted in the Pacific until Germany and Italy wer defeated. The British failed, however, to convince the Ameri cans that, even for a defensive strategy, Hawaii was too remot from Japan's most probable objectives and that they would d well to move their fleet to Singapore. The Americans ha kept the fleet at Pearl Harbor after an exercise in May, 1940 as a warning to Japan. Their view was that it ought to sta there until the Japanese became more amenable, that demand for its return to the West Coast ought to be resisted, but tha a further move which would uncover the western approaches to their homeland could not be accepted. Unwilling on both political and strategic grounds to do as the British proposed, they were not shaken by the argument that Japan was unlikely to attack the United States but would go for the abundant raw materials of Indonesia and South-East Asia.

For the moment, however, the focus of strategic interest was neither Europe nor the Far East, but the Mediterranean and Middle East. America was not yet at war, and at best she would not be able to put a large army in the field for at least two years. The British, still on the defensive at home, could not hope to find the large forces needed for a frontal assault on German-occupied Northern Europe. But they were well placed to strike at the Italians, and soon did so. As early as July 9 a fleet action off the Calabrian coast showed that the Italian fleet was not invincible; on November 11 aircraft from the carriers *Illustrious* and *Eagle* put half the Italian battle-fleet out of action at Taranto and drove the other half to safer harbours.[7] In September Marshal Rodolfo Graziani attacked from Cyrenaica across the Egyptian frontier with five divisions in the line, two in reserve, and about three hundred serviceable fighters, bombers and ground-attack aircraft in support.[8] He was, however, quickly brought to a halt by poor communications, insufficient transport and lack of water. Similarly, an Italian army based on Albania which invaded Greece at the end of October was soon thrown back by the Greeks. Thus by late November the omens were favourable for a British counter-offensive designed to end Graziani's hopes of advancing further into Egypt.

Unsuccessful in the daylight battle, the Luftwaffe turned in the autumn and winter of 1940-41 to an attempt to bludgeon the British into surrender by attacking objectives in built-up areas under cover of darkness.[9] Between September and May the bomber units which had taken part in the Battle of Britain, reinforced by roughly a hundred aircraft brought from Germany made 71 major raids on London and 56 on other cities or large towns.* In the course of these attacks nearly 19,000 tons of high-explosive were aimed at objectives in London, about 12,000 tons at objectives elsewhere. Extensive use was made of radio-beams and marker-flares to guide inexperienced crews to their targets; radio beacons, blind-landing equipment and alternative landing grounds were employed on a lavish scale to reduce the hazards of the homeward flight. Notwithstanding these and other aids, losses due largely to unsuccessful take-offs and landings were so heavy that the number of bombers fit for use at one time was never much more than half the paper strength of the units which took part.

At the beginning of the night offensive the British were poorly equipped to deal with it, largely because they had intentionally given preference in their long-term preparations to the winning of the daylight battle which the more far-seeing of their strategists rightly expected to be crucial. For this reason radar devices intended wholly or mainly for use at night had received a lower priority in development and production than the early-warning system, which indeed was needed at all hours. In the autumn of 1940 air-to-air radar had been in service for many months, but had not yet been successfully married to an aircraft fast enough to make good use of it. Upward-looking radar for anti-aircraft batteries, searchlight companies and ground control of interception was still under development and coming forward only in small quantities. In September only eight and a half fighter squadrons out of sixty were specialists in night fighting; only 1,311 heavy anti-aircraft guns, including 88 at Scapa Flow, were available for home defence; and the layout of gun sites, searchlight stations and gun operation rooms east of London dated from a time when German bombers had not gained access to French airfields and were unlikely to approach from the south and west

*A major raid was defined by the Luftwaffe as one involving the despatch of aircraft carrying 100 or more tons of bombs to a single target area. Apart from London, which suffered its heaviest attack on the night of April 19 and its most memorable one on that of December 29, the places most heavily bombed were Liverpool, Birmingham, Glasgow and Plymouth.

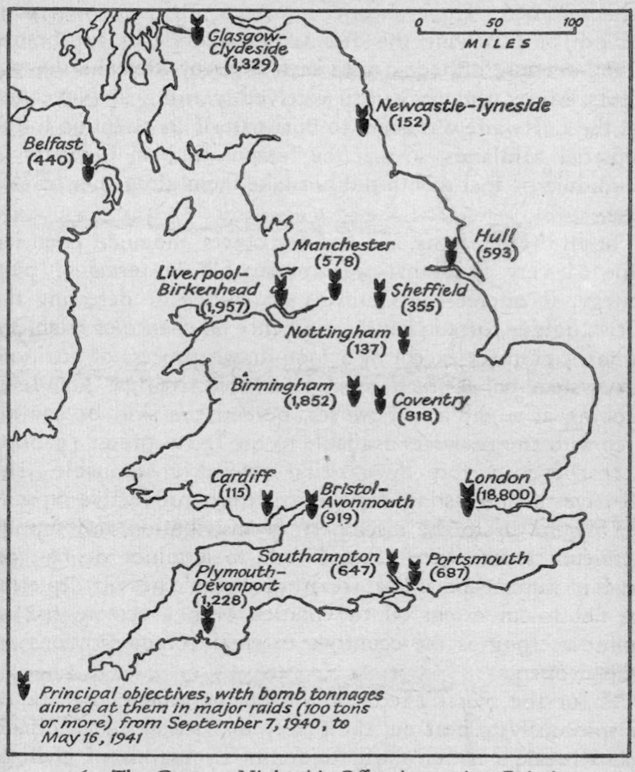

16 The German Night Air Offensive against Britain

Even so, the guns provided an effective means of keeping
ıe enemy to heights which made accurate bombing of crucial
ırgets such as aircraft factories extremely difficult. The de-
enders also had the benefit of a well organized system of in-
elligence. On many occasions the switching on of German
ıdio beams some hours before an attack enabled the British
ɔ detect the beams, predict the target, warn local authorities,
ıd be ready with radio counter-measures which they had
evised since the Germans first tried out the system in the

early summer. These counter-measures included ingenious methods of falsifying the data fed to aircrew by the beams, as well as more orthodox ruses such as decoy fires and dummy targets. Moreover, the British received warning in November that the Luftwaffe was about to turn part of its attention to the industrial Midlands, so that the famous raid on Coventry in the middle of that month did not take them altogether by surprise.

For all these reasons, and also for others, the night offensive achieved very little that was measurable in terms of pure strategy. It offered the Germans no chance of defeating the British fighter force in battle, and hence no chance of establishing air supremacy except by a long-drawn process of attrition. The systematic destruction of vital objectives by high-level bombing at night was, however, beyond the skill of any air force with the resources available to the Luftwaffe in 1940-41 so that even victory by attrition proved unattainable. The offensive did no lasting damage to British productive capacity as a whole, or to the machinery of distribution and supply. Petroleum stocks were affected only to a minor degree; reserves of human and animal foodstuffs became heavily depleted but not to an extent which entailed even a remote risk of famine as long as the country's external communications remained open.

As for the moral effects of the bombardment, they failed conspicuously to bear out the theory that sustained air attack would break a nation's will to fight. Thousands of civilians were killed and thousands of buildings destroyed or damaged. But consequent population-shifts were small and proved more beneficial than harmful, since they tended to remove the young, the old and the infirm from centres of production and hence to ease the problem of housing, feeding and providing transport for the essential workers who stayed behind. At the height of the Blitz on London the Ministry of Home Security 'had only good reports' of the spirit in which the inhabitants faced danger and discomfort.[10] Two nights after the big raid on Coventry in November the authorities provided facilities for 10,000 people who might wish to leave the centre of the city, but only about three hundred used them.[11]

In spite of the Luftwaffe's evident lack of success, and although Britain's effective bomber strength was much lower than the enemy's, the British were not discouraged from pursuing plans for their own night air offensive. The Prime Minister had expressed the opinion on September 3 that 'bombers alone provide the means of victory'.[12] This was questioned by some strategists, but not by all. On October 23 Sir Charles Portal, who was about to become Chief of the Air Staff, proposed that primary targets in populous parts of Germany should be attacked as often as possible on dark nights when precise bombing of small military objectives was difficult. The War Cabinet stipulated, when they adopted this proposal at the end of the month, that the primary targets should still be military objectives; but six weeks later, after Coventry, Birmingham and Bristol had all been heavily damaged, they sanctioned an experimental attack designed to cause the greatest possible havoc in a built-up area. The sequel was the despatch to Mannheim on the night of December 16 of 134 bombers whose crews were given no precise objectives of a strictly military kind.[13]

More attacks on built-up areas followed in 1941. Thus British and Germans alike were soon engaged in destroying cathedrals and hospitals and killing non-combatants of all ages and both sexes, either in the course of impractical attempts to bomb strictly military objectives, or in accordance with the theory that built-up areas were themselves military objectives and that any course of action which promised to shorten the war was both legitimate and sound. Tests introduced by the British later in the year, showed, however, that only a small proportion of crews sent to bomb German cities at night arrived within five miles of the target.[14] Similarly German crews, although better provided with navigational and target-finding aids, quite often dropped their bombs many miles from objectives which they afterwards claimed to have attacked.

The full extent of these shortcomings was not apparent to

either government at the time. By the early part of 1941 Hitler knew, however, that he had failed to bring Britain to the verge of surrender. On February 6 he issued a directive which stressed the importance of attacking seaborne traffic bound for the United Kingdom, and its ports of entry.[15] Although regarded as the starting-point of a phase of the war which came to be called the Battle of the Atlantic,[16] this directive was not concerned solely with ocean convoys and West Coast ports. Hitler's orders were that the Luftwaffe should attack not only 'the most vital British import harbours' but also aircraft factories and the sources of anti-aircraft weapons and ammunition. At the same time the navy and the Luftwaffe were to make a joint effort against shipping, paying special attention to merchant shipping and particularly to inbound traffic. Many of the aircraft used for the offensive against shipping were incapable of reaching the ocean convoy routes and confined themselves to minelaying or attacks on coasters.

These orders came at a time when Germany's underwater fleet was at its lowest ebb since the beginning of the war. Only 21 U-boats were fit for service in the Atlantic at the beginning of February.[17] Similarly the Luftwaffe, having sent some of its most experienced anti-shipping crews to the Mediterranean in recent weeks, was not in the best position to wage all-out war on Atlantic trade. About 80 aircraft set aside for air-sea warfare were available in the Western theatre in April; but only units equipped with the Focke-Wulf 200, or Condor, could cover the Atlantic as far to seaward as 20° West, and the number of aircraft of this type fit for service at one time was never more than about a dozen and seldom more than six or eight. Their task was to report and shadow convoys for the benefit of submarines, but bombs were carried and crews were often tempted to make kills on their own account. Other means of attacking shipping, either directly or indirectly, included some thirty or more fast patrol craft used chiefly for laying mines at night in coastal waters, about half a dozen merchantmen equipped as commerce raiders, and a small but highly resourceful surface fleet.

Although more submarines and aircraft became availabl

17 The Battle of the Atlantic: the North Sea and the Atlantic Convoy Routes

later in the year, the number of submarines, in particular, remained substantially less than the minimum which Admiral Raeder had repeatedly urged Hitler to provide. Even so, the achievements of Raeder's anti-shipping forces in the spring and early summer were spectacular. Between March and June over one and three quarter million tons of British, Allied and neutral merchant shipping were sunk in the North and South Atlantic and United Kingdom waters, as compared with roughly a million tons in the corresponding period in 1940.[18] The figure for the whole of 1941 was rather more than three and a quarter million tons, and the final total was swelled by more than another million tons sunk by various means in the Mediterranean, the Indian Ocean and the Pacific. The fact remains that the offensive failed to inflict on the British losses which they could not bear. At the beginning of the year they had reckoned on receiving 35 million tons of imports in the next twelve months; in the spring they lowered their sights to 31 million.[19] As it turned out they made do with 30.5 million, and even at that rate reached the end of the year with larger stocks of both food and raw materials than they held when France fell. On the other hand, the loss of so much carrying capacity at a time when a great deal turned on the reinforcement and supply of troops abroad was a factor of lasting consequence.

In the meantime the British succeeded in mastering the immediate situation by about midsummer of 1941. In the absence of heavy attacks on the United Kingdom in daylight, they were able to provide such massive air protection for shipping within reach of fighter bases that the bombing of inshore traffic became more and more difficult and expensive. To counter attacks by submarines and aircraft further from the coast, they relied chiefly on routing their convoys further north, stronger surface escort, better anti-aircraft protection for merchant ships, and sorties from newly-developed airfields in Northern Ireland, the Hebrides and Iceland by long-range aircraft with new or improved radar devices and depth charges. Other measures favoured either by the Air Ministry or by the Admiralty included patrols at very long ranges by the four-engined aircraft which were being delivered to the bomber force; attacks on U-boat pens; and the conversion of merchant ships and ocean boarding vessels to carry catapult-launched Hurricanes intended to shoot down German aircraft where shore-based fighters could not reach them. The first proposal was turned down by the Air Staff in favour of the second, but the attacks were unsuccessful. The last proposal was adopted, bu ghtings by catapult-launched fighters were rare, and only ne success was recorded in 1941.[20]

The broad effect of the greater degree of protection given ocean convoys in the spring and summer was to drive U-oat commanders to work further out to sea in the hope of lacing themselves beyond reach of escort vessels and patrol-ng aircraft. As this also placed them outside the radius of tion of their own aircraft, the benefit of co-operation with e Luftwaffe was lost so far as inbound convoys were con-rned, although German reconnaissance crews could still give arning that outward-bound convoys were approaching. The ritish responded by meeting inbound traffic still further to award. By the end of May they were able, in partnership ith ships of the Royal Canadian Navy based on Newfound-nd, to provide escort across the whole width of the Atlantic r such traffic, and afterwards similar protection was extended convoys outward bound. Merchant shipping sunk in the orth Atlantic fell in July to a third of the monthly average r the previous five months, and the total for the second alf of 1941 was roughly a quarter of that for the whole ear.[21]

There remained the German surface raider, always a source f anxiety to a nation whose responsibilities for the defence f trade were world-wide. As it happened, armed merchant-en achieved their most striking successes before the Battle f the Atlantic was heard of. In the ten months which preceded e issue of Hitler's directive of February 6, 1941, they sank out twice as much shipping as in the next eight months; erefore until the end of 1941 they sank no ships at all.[22] But e true measure of their value to the Germans was the effort pended by the British on attempts to catch them.

Much the same was true of the German warships, with e difference that the effectiveness of their commerce raids gan to fall off rather sooner and much more dramatically. the early winter of 1940 a surprise attack by the *Admiral heer* on an Atlantic convoy escorted only by an armed mer-ant cruiser warned the British that the German Navy was

beginning to recover from its losses in the Scandinavian cam
paign.[24] The British received a further warning on Christma
Day, when a convoy was approached by the *Hipper* off Cap
Finisterre, but escaped without loss because it was carryin
troops and was therefore more powerfully escorted than mos
convoys. The obvious inference was that the British would b
wise to divert some of their more valuable warships to th
Atlantic convoy routes; and this was confirmed when in Feb
ruary the *Scharnhorst* and *Gneisenau* succeeded in reachin
the Atlantic through the Denmark Strait, but twice refraine
from attacking ships whose escort included a battleship.[25]

On March 22 the *Scharnhorst* and *Gneisenau* put into Bres
after sinking or capturing about twenty ships from convoy
which had dispersed after seeing their escort turn for home. A
Brest they were closely watched, and in April the *Gneisena*
was seriously damaged by air attack. An excursion into th
Atlantic by the battlecruisers, the new battleship *Bismarc*
and the cruiser *Prinz Eugen*, was therefore abandoned in favou
of a sortie by the last two ships.[26]

Leaving Gdynia on May 18, the *Bismarck* and *Prinz Euge*
did not reach the North Sea undetected. On May 21 a repo
from Stockholm placed them in the Skagerrak, and that even
ing they were seen lying in a fiord near Bergen. Accordingl
Admiral Sir John Tovey, who had succeeded Sir Charl
Forbes in command of the Home Fleet, faced the problem
intercepting them before they disappeared in the vastness
the open seas. At the same time he could not afford to assun
without further evidence that the Atlantic was their destin
tion.

Admiral Tovey had more ships than the enemy, but
single ship which could both catch and sink the *Bismarc*
with her 28-knot speed and her eight 15-inch guns and oth
armament. Keeping part of his fleet in hand, he therefo
sent his two fastest ships, the battlecruiser *Hood* and th
battleship *Prince of Wales*, to support five cruisers order
to watch the routes to the Atlantic through the Denmark Stra
and the Iceland-Faeroes passage. These two had the necessa
speed, and their combined broadside was capable of sinkir

TABLE 3

THE BATTLE OF THE ATLANTIC: PHASE ONE[22]

Monthly breakdown of British, Allied and neutral merchant hipping tonnage sunk by various means, with monthly averges for earlier and later periods for comparison)

	By submarines	*By surface raiders*	*Other causes*	*Totals*
Monthly averages, eptember 1939 to December 1940	162,957	32,811	100,922	296,690
941				
anuary	126,782	97,222	96,236	320,240
ebruary	196,783	86,117	120,493	403,393
March	243,020	118,545	168,141	529,706
April	249,375	43,640	394,886	687,901
May	325,492	15,002	170,548	511,042
une	310,143	17,759	104,123	432,025
uly	94,209	5,792	20,974	120,975
Monthly averages, August to December 1941	125,190	8,855	130,610	264,655

ny ship afloat. But success by such means would, of course, e possible only if the twenty-year-old *Hood* and the newly-ommissioned *Prince of Wales* stayed together and fought ogether.

Next day poor visibility, which hampered air reconnaissance, revented the Admiral from establishing until the evening that he German ships had left the fiord. Flying his flag in the attleship *King George V* and accompanied by the battle-ruiser *Repulse* and the aircraft carrier *Victorious*, he then left capa Flow for Icelandic waters.

About 7 p.m. on May 23 the German squadron entered th Denmark Strait on a south-westerly course, with the *Bismarc* leading. The ships were soon spotted by the two Britis cruisers patrolling there, which reported their position an began to shadow them.

At that moment Admiral Tovey was still far to the south but the *Hood* and the *Prince of Wales*, with four destroyers were only about two hundred miles away. Accordingly th force commander, Vice-Admiral L. E. Holland, prepared fo action and set a course which, had he held it and maintaine his speed, would have put him in a favourable position to en gage the enemy in the early hours of May 24.

As it was, on learning about midnight that the cruisers ha lost touch with his quarry, he turned away and for two hour held northward at reduced speed while his destroyers wen ahead to reconnoitre in the night-long twilight of norther latitudes. Apparently hoping to take the enemy by surprise he did not break wireless silence to recall his destroyers whe the cruisers re-established contact at 2.47 a.m., nor did h make a radar search or use his aircraft to supplement report from the cruisers during the last stage of his approach.

As a result of this manœuvre, Admiral Holland lost bearin on the German ships. No longer able to intercept them b steaming almost at right angles to their heading, he wa obliged to make his final approach on a course almost paralle with theirs.

At 5.35 a.m. the enemy showed up fine on the *Hood*'s star board bow. Intent on bringing the greatest possible weight o fire to bear on the *Bismarck*, Holland decided to take his ship into action in close order at the cost of reducing their freedo of manœuvre. During the night the German ships had, how ever, exchanged stations, so that the *Prinz Eugen* was now leading. At a distance of some fourteen miles this fact seeme not to have been apparent to those aboard the *Hood*, althoug it was noticed from the *Prince of Wales*.

The decisive factor was the excellence of the *Bismarck*' shooting. All four ships opened fire almost simultaneously the *Hood* apparently engaging the wrong target in consequenc of the mistake in identification. With her second or third salvo the *Bismarck* hit the *Hood* so heavily that she exploded and was lost with all but three of her company of 1,419 officers and men. The *Prince of Wales*, changing course abruptly to avoid the wreckage, scored two hits which damaged some of the *Bismarck*'s fuel tanks, but herself received seven hits and was forced to turn away.

Even so, the action was not an unqualified success from the German point of view. With the *Bismarck*'s endurance reduced by leakage from her damaged tanks, the German force commander, Admiral Lütjens, decided to abandon his mission, send the *Prinz Eugen* away and make for a French port. At best, however, this would mean steaming upwards of two thousand miles through waters on which substantial British forces were converging In addition to the main body of the Home Fleet under Admiral Tovey, these included Admiral Somerville's force from Gibraltar and two capital ships, the *Rodney* and the *Ramillies*, released from escort duty.

In the course of the following night Admiral Lütjens succeeded in shaking off the shadowing cruisers and the *Prince of Wales*, but passed dangerously close to the Home Fleet, from which Admiral Tovey had detached the *Victorious* and four cruisers as a reconnaissance and striking force. Soon after midnight the *Bismarck* was attacked by torpedo-carrying aircraft from the *Victorious*, but visibility was poor and she suffered only one hit which did little damage. By 10 a.m. on May 26 Lütjens was about 700 miles due west of Land's End, heading south-east towards the Spanish coast but only about thirty hours from safety if he cared to risk a direct approach to his objective at Saint-Nazaire.

The general belief in London that morning was that the *Bismarck* would make for Brest. Sir Frederick Bowhill, the air officer responsible for maritime reconnaissance by land-based aircraft and flying boats, was none the less of the opinion that Admiral Lütjens would not head directly for so obvious a destination, but would try to make landfall at Cape Finisterre and approach one or other of the French Atlantic ports from that direction. Having served before the mast in his youth, the Air Marshal spoke with a voice understood by seamen. His recommendation was adopted by the Admiralty, who had operational control of his command, and an American-made Catalina flying-boat was despatched on a course so well calculated that the aircraft almost collided with the *Bismarck*'s superstructure.

From that moment Lütjens must have known that his chances of escape were far from good. Low cloud and rough seas helped him to ward off pursuit during the greater part of the day; but towards nightfall one of a number of torpedoes launched by aircraft from the carrier *Ark Royal* struck the *Bismarck* aft, damaging her propellers and jamming her rudder. At dawn on May 27 Admiral Tovey decided to approach her with his heavy ships as soon as the light was in his favour. The battleships *King George V* and *Rodney* opened fire shortly before 9 a.m. at 16,000 yards and by 10.15 a.m. had closed to point-blank range. Fearing that he might run out of fuel and observing that the *Bismarck*'s guns were silent, Tovey then ordered the battleships to withdraw and leave the *Bismarck* to be finished off by torpedoes launched by his cruisers. A strong ship bravely manned, the *Bismarck* held out long after most warships would have sunk; but at 10.36 a.m., after the cruiser *Dorsetshire* had put three torpedoes into her, she went down with colours flying.*

Within the next few weeks the *Lützow*, the *Prinz Eugen* and

*British and German naval historians agree that the *King George V* and *Rodney* disabled the *Bismarck* but did not sink her, possibly because they shortened the range so much that their shells entered her hull with too flat a trajectory to damage her below the waterline. Her plunge to the bottom at 10.36 a.m. has been generally attributed, therefore, to the torpedoes launched by the *Dorsetshire*. On the other hand a popular account published in Germany many years after the war, and apparently based on the evidence of the senior officer among 110 survivors of all ranks, asserts that the torpedoes were ineffective and that the *Bismarck* sank only when her engineers blew scuttling charges. No claim to that effect appears to have been made by or on behalf of German officers during or immediately after the war, allegedly because it was considered inexpedient to let the British know that their torpedoes were not as good as they were thought to be.

the *Scharnhorst* were all more or less severely damaged by air attack. During the same period nine large supply ships, despatched for the purpose of refuelling or provisioning warships, merchant cruisers and sometimes U-boats, were sunk or captured in the North and South Atlantic. In consequence of these and earlier events, by the end of July German surface raiders had ceased, at any rate for the time being, to present a serious threat to ocean trade.

CHAPTER 9

THE CROSSROADS (II)

1940-41

Against the background of repeated bombing of their cities and a struggle to maintain their external communications the British prepared, in the early winter of 1940, to take the offensive in North Africa.

After his advance across the Cyrenaican frontier into Egypt in September, Marshal Graziani disposed his forward troops in ten fortified camps about eighty miles short of the British railhead at Mersa Matruh. Two of these were on the Egyptian coast at Sidi Barrani and Maktila, four about twelve miles to the south and south-west round Tummar and Nibeiwa. The rest were some fifteen miles further inland, on the far side of the escarpment which divides the stony plateau of the Western Desert from the sandy coastal strip. By early December Graziani had the equivalent of nine divisions in Egypt or close behind the frontier, and could count on some 330 bombers, fighters and ground-attack aircraft for indirect and close support. He was under pressure from Rome to resume his advance as soon as possible, and was generally expected to do so about the middle of the month.

General Sir Archibald Wavell, commanding British land forces in the Middle East, was determined to hit Graziani hard before he moved on Mersa Matruh. But Wavell's responsibilities were far-reaching, and he might find himself committed at almost any moment to a campaign in the Balkans. Hence he could spare for an offensive in the Western Desert only one armoured and one infantry division, reinforced by a regiment of heavily-armoured infantry tanks and about 1,800 officers and men from the garrison of Mersa Matruh. Air support would be given by about 300 aircraft which Wavell's colleague, Air Chief Marshal Sir Arthur Longmore, had been able to find only at the cost of depleting his strength at Aden, in the Sudan, and at Alexandria. Four of Longmore's squadrons had already gone to Greece in consequence of the Italian attempt to invade that country from Albania.

Thoroughness and guile had therefore to take the place of numbers on the British side. To overcome the disadvantage of a long approach march and insufficient transport to lift the assault force without cutting down supplies, Wavell ordered that enough food, water, fuel and ammunition to last for five days should be accumulated over a period of three weeks at two dumps midway between Mersa Matruh and the Italian camps. Those of the camps which were to be attacked on the first day were carefully simulated at rehearsals disguised as routine exercises. Rumours were spread in Cairo and elsewhere to the effect that substantial British forces were about to move to Greece, and visible preparations were explained away as defensive counter-measures to the long-awaited Italian offensive.

The tactical plan adopted with Wavell's approval by Major-General R. N. O'Connor, commanding the Western Desert Force, was to make his final approach in darkness, pass his infantry and heavy tanks through the gap between the central group of camps and the escarpment, and take Nibeiwa and Tummar from the rear before pushing on to invest Sidi Barrani.[1] Meanwhile the troops from the Matruh garrison would watch Maktila; the armoured division would form a protective screen on the west; and the camps south of the escarpment would be left alone until their rearward communications were so disorganized that they became an easy prey.

The first phase of the assault was timed for the morning of December 9. On December 6 the infantry division moved to a position forty miles south-west of Matruh, where the troops halted, well dispersed, for thirty-six hours before continuing their advance to a rendezvous fifteen miles from Nibeiwa.

About midday on December 8 their columns were seen from an Italian reconnaissance aircraft, whose crew estimated that there were 400 vehicles between thirty and forty miles from Nibeiwa; but the Italian Tenth Army remained convinced that the British were deploying for defence. Two squadrons of infantry tanks, supported on the flanks by Bren gun carriers firing as they advanced, reached the Nibeiwa camp next morning without meeting any opposition until they crossed the perimeter.

At Nibeiwa and elsewhere some of the defenders fought gallantly; but the odds were loaded against them, especially on the first day, by the unexpectedness of the attack, the lack of a plan to meet it, and the sudden appearance of well-armoured tanks of a type whose existence was not suspected. Although much more numerous than the British and equipped with many more field guns and light and medium tanks, the Italian forces in Egypt and Cyrenaica had no major armoured formations within a hundred miles of the front, and their armoured units in the forward area were not tactically disposed. In three days General O'Connor's troops captured 38,300 prisoners and large quantities of equipment and stores for the loss of 624 officers and men killed, wounded or missing. As the booty included enough large lorries to equip a newly-arrived transport company whose vehicles had not yet arrived, they were then able to press on with the intention of seizing the enemy's forward bases at Bardia and Tobruk. With Tobruk in O'Connor's hands, the administrative problem promised to become so much easier that a decisive victory might fall within his grasp.

After ordering that both places should be held, Marshal Graziani saw that there was a strong case for giving up Bardia in order to concentrate on the defence of Tobruk. Mussolini insisted, however, that a prolonged stand should be attempted at Bardia as a means of delaying and exhausting the enemy.

This ruling proved disastrous. In the outcome Bardia held out for less than three days at the cost of 400 guns lost and 40,000 of all ranks killed or captured. Tobruk, defended by little more than half the troops sacrificed at Bardia, fell even more swiftly. With its capture the British gained possession

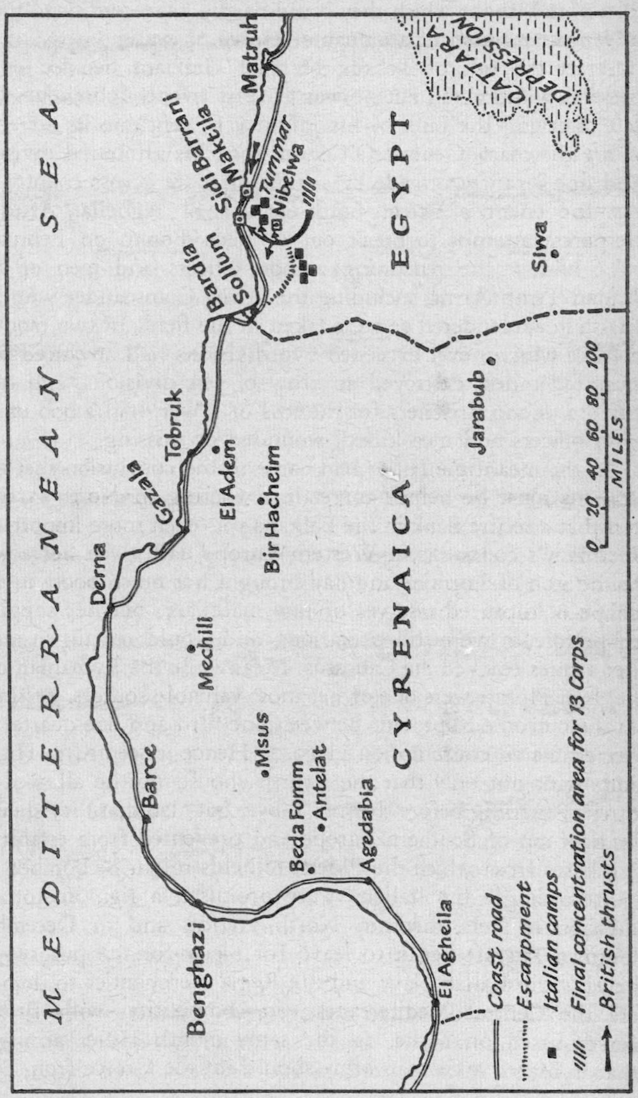

18 Cyrenaica and the British Offensive at Sidi Barrani December 1940

of a port without which they could hardly have continued their advance, and also of a valuable reserve of water.

After the fall of Tobruk Marshal Graziani decided on a general withdrawal, but he was at least twenty-four hours too late. Leaving the bulk of his infantry to continue its advance along the coast, General O'Connor took his armoured division and one infantry brigade by a difficult route across country to cut the enemy's retreat north-east of El Agheila. After a desperate attempt to break out at Beda Fomm on February 5, 6 and 7, the remaining 25,000 officers and men of the Italian Tenth Army, including the Army Commander with all his staff, surrendered or were taken in the field. In two months a force which never exceeded two divisions had advanced five hundred miles, destroyed an army of ten divisions, and captured 130,000 prisoners for the loss of fewer than 2,000 of its own officers and men killed, wounded or missing.

In the meantime Hitler had come to the conclusion that the Italians must be helped to retain a footing in North Africa, but that a secure flank in the Balkans was even more important. Germany's conquests in Western Europe had given her access to the iron of Lorraine and had brought her much booty in the shape of captured reserves of raw materials; but her supplies of petroleum were still precarious, and would remain so until her armies reached the Caucasus. Meanwhile the Rumanian oilfields at Ploesti were one of her most valuable sources, destined in the outcome to provide between one-fifth and one-quarter of her estimated consumption in 1941. Hence it seemed to Hitler important not only that the British should not be allowed to carry everything before them in Libya, but also that they should be kept out of Southern Europe and prevented from establishing bases from which the Ploesti oilfields might be bombed.

Accordingly the Italians were promised a light motorized division to help them in North Africa, and in December German aircraft began to leave for Sicily for the purpose of helping the Italian Navy and the Regia Aeronautica to dominate the Central Mediterranean in competition with British forces based on Malta. In the same month Hitler arranged that in March a German army should invade Greece from Bul garia. Deciding later that this was not enough, he undertook on the first day of the crucial battle at Beda Fomm to add an armoured division to the forces in North Africa if the Italians agreed to stand well forward of Tripoli. Mussolini was willing, Marshal Graziani relinquished command of the Italian forces in Tripolitania to General Gariboldi, and on February 12 Lieutenant-General Erwin Rommel landed at Tripoli as commander-designate of a corps despatched for the purpose of co-operating with Gariboldi in a bold and aggressive stand near Sirte.[2]

The Luftwaffe contingent in Sicily, which amounted to the best part of two hundred aircraft by the middle of January, soon made its presence felt by severely damaging the carrier *Illustrious* at the eastern end of the Sicilian Channel.[3] Malta, an island smaller than the Isle of Wight with a population of about 300,000, was repeatedly attacked during the next four and a half months by German and Italian aircraft which could reach their objectives in less than twenty minutes from Sicilian bases. Many buildings were damaged and 375 civilians were killed or seriously injured, as compared with 189 in the preceding seven months when the island was attacked by Italian aircraft only; but shelters dug in the easily-worked limestone saved many lives, and the Luftwaffe's losses were fairly heavy. Starting with only a single squadron of Hurricanes and about a hundred anti-aircraft guns, but afterwards reinforced by additional Hurricanes flown from Egypt and brought through the Mediterranean from Gibraltar, the defenders destroyed sixty German and sixteen Italian aircraft in the air and about a dozen on the ground for the loss of thirty-three fighters in combat out of a grand total of seventy-eight British aircraft destroyed in one way or another.[4] Attacks on Malta by German aircraft ceased for the time being in the first week of June, when a redistribution of the Luftwaffe's resources in preparation for the campaign in Russia left no operational units in Sicily.

In the meantime German aircraft based in the Central Mediterranean but refuelling at Rhodes were able to drop mines in the Suez Canal and thus threaten interference with

British plans to reinforce the Middle East by way of the Cape and from India and beyond. The British responded by unloading as many ships as they could at Suez and ports further south, laying a pipeline from the head of the Gulf of Suez to Port Said so that tankers could discharge fuel oil for Admiral Cunningham's fleet without entering the Canal, and doubling the railway from Suez to Ismailia. At the same time they made a bid to reduce congestion of the Suez route by opening road and rail links between Aqaba and Palestine.

With the help of such expedients, the British succeeded in carrying to Egypt during the first seven months of 1941 about 239,000 soldiers, sailors and airmen and more than a million tons of equipment and supplies.* On the other hand, they failed to prevent the safe arrival at Tripoli in February and March of some 25,000 German troops with 8,500 vehicles and 26,000 tons of stores, although they did succeed in sinking about 100,000 tons of German and Italian shipping in the Central Mediterranean during the first five months of the year.[5]

Meanwhile General Wavell opened a series of offensives designed to drive the Italians from their East African possessions, restore the Emperor Haile Selassie to his throne, and end any threat to Kenya and the Sudan.[6] These moves raised acute problems for the Italian Commander-in-Chief, the Duke of Aosta. Already responsible for the defence of Abyssinia, Eritrea and Italian Somaliland, in the previous August the Duke had added the strategically valueless British Somaliland to his cares by annexing it after defeating a small British force at Tug Argan. Numerically his forces were much stronger than any likely to be used against them, but more than two-thirds of his rank and file consisted of native troops whose first loyalty was to their own kin. He was also handicapped, particularly in Abyssinia, by an organization designed for internal security

*The first figure excludes troops transferred from one part of the Middle East Command to another. Roughly 144,000 officers and men made the long voyage round the Cape from the United Kingdom, about 60,000 travelled from Australia or New Zealand, and the rest came from India or South Africa.

rather than external defence. To add to his difficulties, many Abyssinians had never become reconciled to Italian rule and sided secretly or openly with Haile Selassie. As he could not hope to be reinforced on a substantial scale as long as the British controlled the Red Sea, and was under orders to hold on in the hope that events elsewhere might turn the scale in his favour, he faced the uncongenial prospect of a purely defensive campaign fought with troops whose power of manœuvre and acquaintance with tactical withdrawals were very small.

The Duke concluded that his chances of escaping ultimate defeat were slender. He was none the less determined to fight to the end and especially to maintain his grip on Eritrea, where two British divisions from the Sudan were advancing on Asmara with the evident intention of breaking through to the Red Sea at Massawa.

The key to the defence of Asmara lay some fifty miles north-west of the town at Keren, where natural obstacles improved by field works and a massive road-block dominated the only route by which a substantial force could approach from that direction. Unwilling on psychological grounds to fall back so far before attempting a firm stand, the Duke did his best to halt the enemy further forward but was unsuccessful, with the result that the decisive action was fought, after all, at Keren. There the attackers were held up for eight weeks; but on March 25 and 26, after probing vainly for weak spots on the flanks, the British thrust at the Italian centre with two brigades on a narrow front, cleared the road-block under heavy fire, and at last burst through in pursuit of a beaten enemy. On April 1 they entered Asmara, a week later they were in Massawa. On April 11 President Roosevelt set the seal on their success by declaring the Red Sea no longer a combat area and hence open to American shipping.

Meanwhile resistance in Abyssinia and the Somalilands had collapsed or was collapsing. By the middle of March the Duke of Aosta's forces in the south were no longer capable of protecting civilian life and property against assaults by native rebels, so that the arrival of British troops was not an unmixed evil from the Italian point of view. On April 6 the civil authorities at Addis Ababa made formal submission after an official had asked the British to enter the city without delay in order to prevent looting; a month later the Emperor Haile Selassie's return to his capital marked the end of a troubled chapter in Italian history.

Apart from widely separated bodies of troops which had still to be rounded up, there remained the force which had retreated southwards after the Battle of Keren and the fall of Asmara. On April 3 the Duke, with his reserve troops, joined this force at Amba Alagi, a fortified position commanding a pass nearly 10,000 feet above sea level on the road from Asmara to Addis Ababa. As this was the route by which General Wavell intended to withdraw troops and vehicles needed elsewhere, the effect of his orders in the early part of April was to pin the Italians between two forces advancing along the road in opposite directions for the purpose of clearing it. Established in an almost impregnable stronghold, wit[h] no hope of breaking out but with food for three months and a fairly good supply of water, the survivors of the Army of Eritrea made a spirited defence, but at last agreed that further resistance was useless. On May 19 they laid down their arms after marching past a guard of honour, and next day the Duke made his formal surrender.

In the north, on the other hand, events did not shape so well for the British.

Expecting in February that the Germans might be ready to invade Greece through Bulgaria about the middle of March, the authorities in London instructed General Wavell to concentrate all available forces in Egypt and prepare them for despatch to the Balkans at short notice. Cyrenaica was to be held as a secure flank for Egypt with the smallest force that would suffice.

To decide how many troops were needed to hold Cyrenaica was not easy. On the assumption that the newly-arrived German contingent in Tripolitania would not be ready for a major offensive before the summer, Wavell calculated, however, that one infantry division and one armoured division less one

19 Eritrea Abyssinia and the Somalilands

rigade should be enough to give a reasonable degree of ecurity pending the arrival of further troops from East Africa r elsewhere. The infantry division was incompletely trained nd equipped, the armoured element of the armoured division n urgent need of re-equipment or at any rate a major overaul; but both formations, it was hoped, would be in better hape by the time the enemy was ready.

As things turned out, the respite was shorter than Wavell xpected, and the fitting out of an expeditionary force for the alkans made such demands on his resources that the dangers nvolved in leaving units in Cyrenaica with worn-out tanks and nsufficient wheeled vehicles had to be accepted. Not only inxperienced but deficient in transport and hence far from obile, the infantry division could not be risked in the forward area, and towards the end of March was withdrawn about 150 miles to the rear. In front of it there was only the incomplete armoured division, consisting of one weak brigade and a support group.

Then and later, the decision to send troops to the Balkans at the cost of weakening the North African front was much criticized, not least on the ground that the three or four divisions thus made available for Greece were not, in any case, enough to ensure success or even make it probable. But the view which prevailed was that failure to help a hard-pressed ally when the collapse of the Italian Tenth Army must be presumed to have freed troops for the purpose would create a deplorable impression even if it could be justified in theory. Not dissenting from this argument, Wavell became committed to simultaneous offensives in East Africa and defensive operations in North Africa and the Balkans.

On reaching Tripoli, General Rommel found the Italians, with one incomplete armoured division and four infantry divisions mostly without artillery, preparing for a stand at Sirte. He therefore moved elements of his light division there as they arrived from Germany, but afterwards pushed forward to a stronger position about twenty miles west of El Agheila. Satisfied by the middle of March that there was no immediate threat to Tripoli, he went on to propose an ambitious offensive for early May, but was warned against outrunning his supplies and to attempt nothing big until his armoured division reached him about the middle of that month.

Returning to his headquarters on March 23 after visiting Rome and Berlin to explain his proposals at first hand, Rommel at once ordered his troops to seize El Agheila and sanctioned a reconnaissance in force with the British forward position at Mersa Brega as its objective. After taking El Agheila without difficulty he pushed on with plans for the reconnaissance in force, but gave neither the Italians nor his own staff any hint that he was contemplating more than a limited advance.

Rommel's attack at Mersa Brega began on March 31 and was supported by some fifty German dive-bombers which had

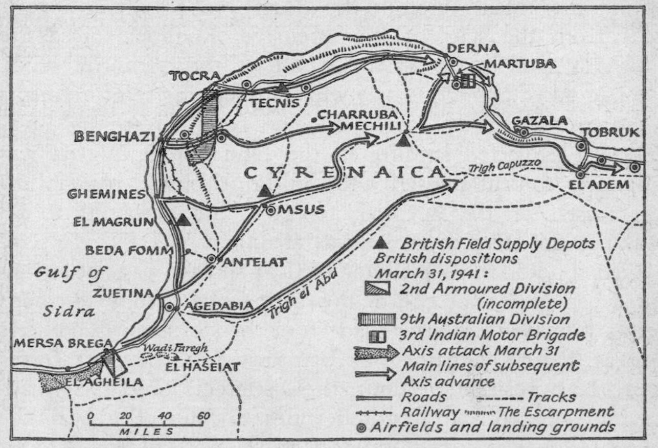

20 The Axis Offensive in Cyrenaica, March-April 1941

reached North Africa from Sicily. It fell on a front held by the support group of the one British armoured division in the forward area. After holding his positions through the forenoon and the early afternoon, the British commander on the spot asked that the armoured brigade in rear of his left flank should attack the German right; but the divisional commander was unwilling to commit his armour at a time when there were only a few hours of daylight left. Facing heavier pressure from the enemy towards the end of the day, the support group eventually fell back along the coast road to escape being cut off.

As it happened, the failure of the British to stop Rommel on he first day proved fatal to their chances.[7] Conforming with he withdrawal of the support group, the armoured brigade began a retreat which cost it such heavy losses from mechanical breakdowns that it soon became incapable of fighting. With no fully mobile formation to take its place, the defenders could not prevent a substantial body of German and Italian troops from pushing up the coast of the Gulf of Sidra, fanning out to the north-east, and threatening them with a wide turning movement through the desert. In less than a fortnight from the start of his offensive, Rommel forced the British to give up almost the whole of the territories which they had taken two months to win. Summoning reinforcements at the cost of withholding a division from Greece and postponing a projected landing in the Dodecanese, Wavell was obliged to content himself with holding Tobruk, re-establishing himself on the Egyptian frontier, and preparing to resume the initiative when he was stronger.

Even so, Rommel's brilliant tactical success was not an unmixed benefit. At the end of the campaign his forward troops were a thousand miles by road from their base at Tripoli. As long as Tobruk remained in British hands the Axis forces were in no position to attain their strategic objective by advancing another four hundred miles to Suez. Benghazi, the only intermediate port of military value, was vulnerable to air attack and at times unusable, and in any case had been so thoroughly damaged by the British before they left that it could handle only coastal traffic incapable of carrying much more than half the supplies needed to meet current consumption and build up a reserve for future Axis operations. After twice failing to take Tobruk by assault in April and early May, Rommel had no choice but to wait until his disgruntled superiors saw fit to reinforce him or could hit upon a way of cutting off the supplies which the British were pouring into the port at the rate of nearly a hundred tons a day.[8]

In contrast with the war in the desert, which offered Hitler the prospect of driving the British from the Middle East but was generally regarded in Berlin as a sideshow of little interest except to the Italians, the campaign in the Balkans was preceded by elaborate political and military preparations.

On March 1 Bulgaria publicly threw in her lot with the Axis Powers. Next day German troops which had been assembling in Rumania since December began to cross the Danube with the object of invading Greece on April 1. On March 27 a *coup d'état* by Yugoslav officers unwilling that their country should follow Bulgaria's lead seemed to threaten a serious setback to the German programme, but in fact delayed it for less than a week. In a few days enough troops and aircraft were found to invade Yugoslavia as well as Greece, and on April 6 both countries found themselves at war with Germany. In the meantime an encounter with Admiral Cunningham's fleet off Cape Matapan cost the Italians three cruisers and two destroyers, but this setback had no immediate effect on the situation ashore.[9]

The essence of the plan for the defence of the Greek mainland to which the British and the Greeks had agreed after prolonged discussion in early March was that a force intended to consist of three Greek and three or four British divisions, with seven additional Greek battalions, should give battle to the Germans on a line running from the mouth of the River Aliakmon to the Yugoslav frontier north-west of Edessa. Three Greek divisions, with some garrison troops, were to stand further forward in order to delay an advance on Salonika, and fourteen would continue to contain about twenty-eight Italian divisions in Albania. Between the right of the Albanian front at Pogredatz and the left of the Aliakmon Line there was, however, a gap some sixty miles wide, barred at its western extremity by natural features but providing a back-door into Greece for an invader able to gain access to Southern Yugoslavia and push southwards through Prilep and Monastir.

The German plan, as modified at the end of March, laid down the axiom that Yugoslavia must be destroyed, even if she declared herself favourable to Germany. Belgrade would be bombed; the country would be cut in two by simultaneous advances south-east from Styria and north-west from Sofia; and from Blagoevgrad three divisions would advance to Skoplje for the twofold purpose of opening the southward route through Prilep and joining hands with the Italians in Albania. About the same time, strong forces from Southern Bulgaria would move into Greece with Salonika and Edessa as their first objectives.

Thus the importance of the Monastir gap was fully apparent to the Germans. It was also apparent to the British and the Greeks. The difference was that, whereas the Germans had the physical means of exploiting their opportunity and meant to use them, the British and the Greeks could see no solution but to ask the Yugoslavs to do what they could to keep the enemy away.[10]

In the circumstances in which the Yugoslavs soon found themselves, this proved to be very little. At any rate on paper, the rifle-strength of their army far exceeded that of the forces used against them; but they were short of field, anti-tank and anti-aircraft guns, their air force was strong by Balkan but weak by German standards, and inevitably their attention was focused on the north. The Germans were at Skoplje by the evening of April 7, and next day they arrived at Prilep with the obvious intention of pushing on through Monastir and turning the inner flank of the Aliakmon Line.

Instead of giving battle on that line the defenders thereupon withdrew to a position with their right on the coast near Mount Olympus and their centre south-east of Kozani. In theory, a series of positions covering the Siatista and Klisoura passes prolonged their new line to Lake Prespa, near Pogredatz; but in practice their left was in the air and the gap between the armies wider than ever. Only if the highly successful but battle-weary force in Albania pulled back its right some ninety miles to the neighbourhood of Grevena would there be a solid front across the whole width of Greece.

This was in fact the intention of the Allied Commander-in-Chief, General Alexandros Papagos; but the moral effect of withdrawing a victorious army seemed so likely to be calamitous that he withheld the crucial order until too late. Consequently he was obliged on April 16 to safeguard the left of the force retreating from the Aliakmon Line by sanctioning a further withdrawal to a shorter line running inland from Thermopylae.[11] At the same time he suggested that, if only to spare the country by cutting short a struggle whose outcome seemed inevitable, the British might like to consider removing their troops and leaving the remnant of his army to fight on without hope of victory. Five days later, after receiving direct reports from the west, British and Greek representatives agreed that the end was near and that the long-term interests of both

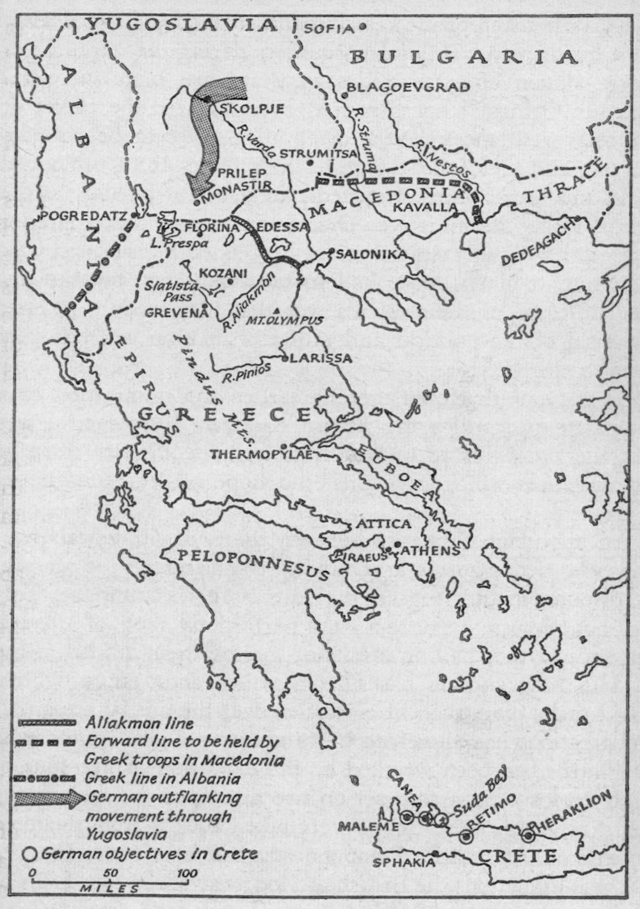

21 Greece and Crete

ountries would be best served if the British formations withdrew while they were still intact. Soon afterwards the King, he Prime Minister and the British Minister left for Crete, where the British still hoped to retain a naval refuelling base t Suda Bay.

Thus command of the Greek mainland changed hands without a major battle. In local encounters during the retreat from the Aliakmon Line the Allies were at times more successful than the Germans; but they had overestimated the effects of Yugoslav resistance, they allowed themselves to be outmanœuvred, and they failed to unite their forces for a prolonged stand and thus compel the enemy to fight for territory at the risk of losing the initiative. The Germans, moving on interior lines and with an ample number of trained divisions and air squadrons to draw upon, had many advantages, but the immediate cause of their success was that they made a realistic appraisal of the political and military situation and left very little to chance.

As at Dunkirk eleven months earlier, the culmination of a campaign over which the British had very little control was that they were forced to withdraw an expeditionary force in circumstances which gave them no hope of saving its heavy equipment.

An important difference between the two withdrawals was, however, that whereas at Dunkirk command of the air was in dispute, in the Aegean the Luftwaffe was supreme. This was not because the British were particularly short of aircraft, but because they had no means of getting them quickly to the Middle East, and no bases from which short-range fighters could make more than brief sorties over the crucial areas. All embarkations had therefore to be made at night. As the port of Piraeus had been wrecked by the explosion of 250 tons of high explosive in a ship set on fire during an air raid on the night of April 6, the troops were taken aboard from sheltered beaches in Attica, the Peloponnesus and elsewhere. In spite of these limitations the British carried away about four-fifths of their troops, leaving behind 8,000 lorries and many guns.*

*Four-fifths is a rough estimate. About 62,500 British troops ha[d] been carried to the Greek mainland by the time the withdraw[al] began. Altogether 50,732 men were brought away in the last wee[k] of April, but this figure included a number of Greeks and Yugoslav[s]. In addition a good many stragglers made their way to safety by u[n]orthodox routes.

)riginally all except a few were to have been taken straight o Alexandria, more than 400 miles away; but the final de- ision was that cruisers and transports should go only as far as ;rete in order to shorten their turn-round and reduce demands n escort vessels.

Less than twenty-four hours after the beginning of the with- lrawal, the Führer sanctioned preparations for a landing in ;rete by airborne forces backed by a small seaborne expedi- ion.[12] This was intended by General Kurt Student, com- nander of the newly-created air landing corps and chief spon- or of the project, as the first of a series of 'island-hopping' entures with Suez as their ultimate objective. The expedition vas planned, however, as a self-contained operation involving bout 13,000 airborne troops, 9,000 mountain troops with more t call, 500 serviceable first-line aircraft, more than 500 trans- ort aircraft and 72 gliders. General Alexander Löhr, com- nanding the air fleet responsible for the Balkan theatre, was ppointed to the chief command, with General Student as his rincipal subordinate. The airborne troops were given as their rimary objectives the island's three airfields at Heraklion, Retimo and Maleme, all of which Student hoped to capture on he first day, in addition to Canea and the naval base at Suda Bay. At a conference in Athens a few days before the start, attalion commanders were told that the British strength in ;rete was equivalent to about one division, that there were lso remnants of two or three Greek divisions, and that some f the inhabitants would welcome the invaders and even give hem active help.[13]

In point of fact, the permanent British garrison in Crete onsisted of one infantry brigade; but arrivals from the Greek nainland, and the issue of rifles to troops normally assigned to on-combatant duties, had brought the total of British and Greek forces to about 40,000 fighting men. The defenders vere, however, very weak in air support for their land forces nd air protection for their ships, partly because the nearest irfields in Egypt were 300 miles away but also because the Royal Air Force in the Middle East had suffered heavy losses n recent months. On the other hand, they had the advantage of good warning, for the enemy's preparations left them in no doubt that either he meant to land in their midst, or was willing to go to extraordinary lengths to give that impression. Major-General B. C. Freyberg, V.C., who had been appointed to command the reinforced garrison at the end of April, believed that he had a good chance of repelling an airborne invasion, but doubted whether he could cope with a combination of airborne and seaborne landings.

Largely because the German planners had only a sketchy knowledge of the enemy's dispositions, the airborne assault on May 20 nearly ended in disaster. The intention was that most of the paratroops and glider-borne troops should land in quiet areas where they could sort themselves out before going into action. In practice, many of them were put down in the midst of the defences and came under fire from the outset. Little progress was made on the first day at Heraklion or Retimo or on the approaches to Canea. At Maleme three battalions of paratroops and one incomplete battalion of glider-borne troops were held up until dusk by a battalion of New Zealanders supported by two tanks, but succeeded by the following morning in pushing the defenders off the landing-area, which became a no-man's-land swept by fire from both sides. Transport aircraft with reinforcements and supplies were therefore unable to land early on the second day, as had been planned. Ammunition was dropped by parachute from the first day; but only a limited volume of supplies could be delivered by such means, and fetching more than bare essentials from relatively distant dropping areas or distribution centres would in any case have been difficult for units without transport and in close contact with the enemy.

The problem of supply was made still more difficult by the utter failure of the seaborne expedition. The German plan was that two convoys, one of 25 and the other of 38 small ships, should land 6,300 troops at Maleme and Heraklion on May 21 and 22, and that two steamship flotillas should carry guns and tanks. The first convoy was delayed by reports that British warships were about, entered Cretan waters some hours after the troops were due to disembark, and was intercepted by three cruisers and four destroyers which had held off until nightfall to escape air attack. Ten ships were sunk, an Italian torpedo-boat acting as escort was damaged, and the rest of the convoy dispersed or turned for home without putting any troops ashore. The second convoy was then recalled, escaped with the loss of one ship, but also failed to carry out its mission. None of the guns or tanks reached Crete in time to be of use.

In the meantime General Student, facing the collapse of his whole project, had decided to stake everything on an attempt to take Maleme at all costs. On May 21 he ordered his last two companies of paratroops to join his forces there, and asked that transport aircraft carrying a first instalment of mountain troops should start landing with the least possible delay. The paratroops were soon pinned to the ground a mile from their objective, but the arrival of the mountain troops, daringly landed under artillery fire on the still disputed airfield, proved the turning point. By the late afternoon the airfield, littered with the wrecks of transport aircraft but still usable, was effectively in German hands and could be used to fly in supplies and light equipment. Even so, it was not until several days later that the troops at Maleme finally established contact with those south-west of Canea, and not until May 27 that the municipal authorities at Canea surrendered the town to a dishevelled paratroop commander whose men had drawn no rations during their first five days in Crete.[14]

In the meantime German air supremacy had put such a strain on Admiral Cunningham's ships that the British were earnestly considering whether to pull out rather than risk the crippling of the Admiral's fleet. The collapse of the Canea front and the inability of the British to bring in reinforcements under air attack decided the issue. On the night of May 8 warships took aboard the 4,000 troops at Heraklion, and mbarkation was begun at Sphakia, on the south coast, of as many of the rest of the garrison as could get away. Largely because the island's poor communications made Sphakia hard to reach, only about 18,000 British troops were saved, as compared with roughly 12,000 left behind. In addition to 11,835 of all ranks captured by the enemy, the British lost 3,479 soldiers and 2,011 seamen killed or wounded, the Germans about 6,000 soldiers and airmen killed, wounded or missing. On the naval side, the battle for Crete left Admiral Cunningham with only two battleships and three cruisers fit to engage the four battleships and eleven cruisers which the Italians could bring to bear against him.

The capture of Crete by airborne forces alone excited intense interest and was regarded in many countries as an example likely to be followed on an increasing scale. Even in Germany few people knew that disaster had been narrowly averted and that only the timely landing of the mountain troops on May 21 had turned the scale. But the experience was decisive. No more was heard of airborne landings in Cyprus and then Egypt, and throughout the rest of the war no further expedition on such ambitious lines was attempted by the Wehrmacht

Meanwhile the use made by the Luftwaffe of French airfields and war material in connection with events in Iraq had led the British government to conclude that Hitler might have designs on Syria and that they would do well to get their blow in first.* The Führer had, in fact, decided against intervention but General Wavell's reluctance to commit himself on yet another front did not shake his political chiefs. On June 8 a mixed force which included Free French troops entered Syria from Palestine with orders to capture Beirut, Rayak and Damascus and afterwards advance on Palmyra, Homs and Lebanese Tripoli. The force made good progress for the first few days, but was then stoutly opposed by the French, who particularly resented the use of Free French troops against them On June 21, however, Damascus fell, and on July 14 agreement was reached on terms which allowed the Allies to occupy Syria and the Lebanon but gave French troops the right to retain their arms.

The closing stages of this brief campaign coincided with an ambitious attempt by the British to drive Rommel back from the Egyptian frontier and relieve Tobruk. To make it possible, a convoy carrying 82 cruiser, 135 infantry and 2

*See page 165.

ght tanks was brought through the Mediterranean instead of oing by the Cape, and reached Alexandria on May 12.

The plan adopted by the British after anxious thought was) advance on a twenty-mile front between Sollum and Sidi)mar, with their infantry and a brigade of infantry tanks on ıe right, and a brigade of cruiser tanks and the support group f their armoured division left of centre. By this means they oped to bring the enemy's armour to battle, destroy it, and ress on to Tobruk or further.

An obvious disadvantage of this plan was that the cruiser anks were likely to bump into the enemy's frontier defences ıstead of using their speed and range to sweep round them; ut that limitation had to be accepted for two reasons. On dministrative grounds it was necessary that the infantry tanks hould stay near the coast until they reached Sollum, and on actical grounds it was necessary that the cruiser tanks should e close at hand so that the two brigades could join forces at moment to be determined later. Only if he used his whole orce, Wavell felt, could he expect to bring on a major battle, nd only if he kept it together could he expect to win one.

The offensive was due to begin on June 15. A week before ıat date Rommel had in the forward area his armoured divi- ion, with the addition of a weak Italian division partly in ıe frontier zone and partly at Bardia. In the course of the next ew days, however, intercepted wireless traffic and other indi- ations led Rommel to think that he might be attacked in the ear future. Accordingly he took steps to guard against a sortie om Tobruk, and to bring part or all of his light division for- ard at short notice.

Apart from his tactical insight, one of Rommel's strongest oints was that he was well supplied with anti-tank weapons, ıcluding about a dozen 88 millimetre anti-aircraft guns which ould be used in a dual role and were capable of stopping ny British tank at a distance of a mile or more. On the first ay of the offensive he committed only a small part of his rmour but made good use of his guns to pin down the enemy n the flanks and inflict substantial losses; on the second day e launched two counter-attacks designed to drive in the enemy's centre and out-flank or cut up his left. Neither object was attained, but the combined effect was to prevent the British from uniting their forces and cripple a good many of their tanks, whose two-pounder armament was almost useless at ranges much exceeding half a mile.

Towards the end of the day the British believed that they might still be able to bring their cruiser and infantry tanks together in the morning. Rommel, on the other hand, was confident that the situation was shaping well from his point of view, and said so to the commander of his armoured division. He was proved right early on the third day when the British, with only twenty-two cruiser and seventeen infantry tanks still fit to fight, decided to call off their offensive.

Thus the state of the war in the European and Middle Eastern theatres in the late summer of 1941 was that neither side had established a clear lead but that time was fighting against Germany and Italy. At home the British, sustained since the spring by the promise of increasing American aid, had beaten off the threat of imminent invasion, survived the night air offensive and kept their sea communications open. In the Balkans and the Aegean the Axis Powers were in the ascendant; but their adversary still had a fleet at Alexandria, while further to the east and south the British had tightened their grip on the Red Sea and the Persian Gulf by defeating the Italians in East Africa and pro-Axis elements in Iraq and Syria. In North Africa Rommel was on the Egyptian frontier but had failed to take Tobruk and was fighting a difficult battle with his superiors for the reinforcements needed for a decisive effort.

CHAPTER 10

GERMANY AND RUSSIA

October 1939- March 1942

A natural consequence of the partition of Poland in 1939 was that the Soviet authorities were driven to conclude that the strongly fortified Stalin Line, constructed since 1936 along the old Russo-Polish frontier, had become redundant and that new defensive positions would have to be built near the Demarcation Line in Central Poland. Completion of the new line was not, however, regarded as an urgent task.[1] Until the summer of 1940 the general opinion in Moscow was that war with Germany could not be ruled out, if only because Hitler had made it clear before the Moscow Pact was signed that he would like to win living-space for the German people in European Russia, but that the German Army would be fully occupied in the West until 1941 or later. At the same time there was a tendency among Soviet strategists to question the value of fixed defences.[2] Access by Soviet forces to strategic bases in Finland and the consolidation of Soviet influence in the Baltic States and the Balkans would, it was hoped, so limit the courses of action open to Germany in the event of a clash that the Red Army would be able to give a good account of itself without tying up a great part of its strength in static lines.

Although the failure of the Red Army to turn the Mannerheim Line in the early winter of 1939 did not throw a very favourable light on its capacity to defend Russian soil by taking the offensive, Soviet military doctrine was still unchanged when the swift collapse of the French Army showed that Germany's striking-power had been underestimated. Immediately after the collapse of France the Soviet rulers took steps to strengthen their hold on the Baltic States; they also renewed their pressure on the Finns. At the same time they gave Russian industry a new tempo by introducing a forty-eight-hour week, forbidding migration of labour and threatening severe penalties for absentees.[3] Almost simultaneously they made a practical demonstration of their declared interest in the Balkans by moving troops into Bessarabia and part of Bukovina after presenting an ultimatum which Berlin advised the Rumanians to accept. The immediate consequence was that Hungary and Bulgaria hastened to make claims of their own in Transylvania and the province of Dobrudja.

A point to which Stalin and his colleagues seem, however, to have failed to give as much weight as they might have done was that, although the Moscow Pact appeared to recognize Russia's right to an undisputed sphere of influence in South-Eastern Europe, Hitler was not a man who would allow himself to be easily outwitted. Profiting by the Hungarian and Bulgarian claims, he stepped in with a solution of the Balkan problem which forced the Rumanians to make substantial concessions to both countries as the price of German support against any further demands which the Russians might make on them. By this means Hitler greatly increased his influence in a corner of Europe which the Kremlin had hoped to take under its own protection.

An inevitable consequence was that the Russians became highly suspicious of German intentions. They were, however extremely reluctant to precipitate a crisis, since their armed forces had just emerged from a drastic purge and had scarcely begun an ambitious programme of re-equipment. New weapons which were on the way but had not yet appeared in substantial numbers, or in some cases not at all, when France fell, included the KV and the T-34 tank, the Mig-3 and the Yak-fighter, the Il-2 and the P-2 bomber, the Katyusha mortar and the first Russian-made anti-tank rifle.[4] The Red Army was also short of mechanized transport.[5] Hence the Soviet rulers had good grounds for wishing to postpone a conflict at least until the 1940 and 1941 campaigning seasons were over.

22 The Balkans

In these circumstances Russia took refuge in a policy of qualified appeasement. On the one hand, the Soviet rulers showed their disapproval of Hitler's encroachments by making diplomatic gestures which did not prevent him from subjugating Yugoslavia and Greece and reducing Bulgaria and Rumania as well as Hungary to vassalage; on the other hand, they offered him tempting rewards for future good behaviour. The paradoxical outcome was that, although by the end of

1940 relations between Berlin and Moscow could scarcely be described as friendly, Russian deliveries of grain and raw materials to Germany were maintained, and even increased, at a time when the Germans had fallen seriously behind with reciprocal deliveries of manufactured goods.[6] As part of a new bargain negotiated early in 1941, Germany also received generous compensation for a strip of Lithuanian territory occupied by Russian troops in defiance of her prior but equally oppressive claim.

If Stalin hoped to convince Hitler as late as 1941 that the Kremlin would not yield to force and that war with Russia would bring Germany no economic benefit which she could not obtain more easily by trade or barter, then he miscalculated. From the moment in the summer of 1940 when the Führer's dormant suspicions were aroused by the Kremlin's prompt reaction to his successes in Western Europe, no economic argument could convince him that he would be able to breathe freely as long as Russia retained the power to cut off supplies from her own territory and perhaps undermine his influence in adjacent countries. Moreover, another factor was at work besides the clash of interests in the Balkans. In spite of the Moscow Pact, Hitler could not afford to allow the Russians to dominate South-East Europe, if only for fear that the oilfields of Ploesti might be lost to him before those of the Caucasus became his by right of conquest. But he also had preoccupations in the far north, where he was anxious to prevent the Soviet leaders from establishing unchallenged supremacy in Finland and perhaps threatening his supplies of iron ore from Sweden. On the very day in November when the Soviet Foreign Minister, Vyacheslav Molotov, arrived in Berlin to present the Kremlin's case and listen to German proposals for partition of the still unconquered British Empire, Hitler decreed that preparations for war with Russia should continue without intermission. A month later he ordered that preparations needing more than eight weeks for completion, if not already begun, should be put in hand at once and completed by the middle of May. In September Admiral Raeder had argued that Britain was the real enemy, and British oil in the

Middle East a more valuable prize than Russian oil in the Caucasus.[7] Although momentarily attracted by the idea of substituting a Middle Eastern for a Russian campaign, Hitler soon became convinced that his first thoughts were best. Neither Franco nor Pétain, he found, would co-operate wholeheartedly in an attempt to place North-West Africa under Axis control as the prelude to an eastward thrust towards the Suez Canal and beyond. The alternative was an advance through Syria and Palestine, which threatened to be still more hazardous.

Thus Germany became committed, by almost insensible degrees, to the grandiose project on which the army had been working since July. Surprised by the *coup d'état* in Yugoslavia at the end of March, Hitler agreed that the attack on Russia must be put back until June 22 in order to give the armed forces time to settle accounts in the Balkans once for all. Even so, he remained deaf to suggestions that the entire project was misconceived and would merely give Britain an ally without doing anything to improve Germany's economic position. The chief consequences of the postponement were that troops moving into Russia in June found rather better going than they could have expected in May after an exceptionally wet spring, but were left with barely five months in which to break the back of their task before ice and snow made active campaigning almost impossible for units not trained or equipped for such conditions.

The German plan was based on the assumption that the Russians would be unable to offer effective resistance if they lost their chief European centres of production in the Ukraine, the Donetz basin and the industrial areas of Leningrad and Moscow.[8] It seemed to follow that the Russians would make a resolute attempt to defend these objectives, and would also try to hold the Baltic States not merely because of their economic importance but as a means of barring the approaches to Leningrad by land and sea. At the same time, it was obvious to the German planners that the largest force which they could hope to maintain on Russian soil would soon be greatly outnumbered if the Russians were given time to mobilize their vast manpower and bring up fresh formations. Dividing their armies into three main groups, the Germans sought to gain a sweeping ascendancy at the outset by defeating the greatest possible number of Russian troops on the approaches to Leningrad and Moscow and south of the Pripet Marshes.

In its final form, the plan allotted 50 divisions to Army Group Centre, under Field-Marshal Fedor von Bock, for the purpose of making a two-pronged thrust on either side of the main route to Moscow through Minsk and Smolensk. On his left, 29 divisions under Army Group North, commanded by Field-Marshal Wilhelm Ritter von Leeb, were to advance from East Prussia in the general direction of Leningrad. On the other flank the task of capturing Kiev as the first step towards the occupation of the Donetz basin and the Black Sea coast was entrusted to Army Group South, under Field-Marshal Karl von Rundstedt. To enable Rundstedt to deal with the whole of the Russian armies south of the Pripet Marshes, he would have some 42 German divisions under command, and would also issue directives to a mixed force of German, Hungarian, Italian and Rumanian divisions moving on his extreme right.

How the opening battles would turn out was, of course, uncertain. The Germans believed, however, that the superior fighting value of their well-organized and powerfully-equipped formations would give them a big advantage even if they were outnumbered from the start. By the thirtieth day Army Group North would, they thought, have gained the high ground east of the Latvian frontier after seizing the crossings of the Dvina before the less mobile enemy could reach them in strength; about the same date the two wings of Army Group Centre might be expected to complete a double enveloping movement by joining hands beyond Smolensk; and meanwhile Army Group South would have taken Kiev and have wheeled southwards to encircle a substantial body of Russian troops before sweeping on to the south-east. At that stage a number of armoured formations would be transferred to Army Group North from Army Group Centre so as to enable the former to complete the conquest of the Baltic States while

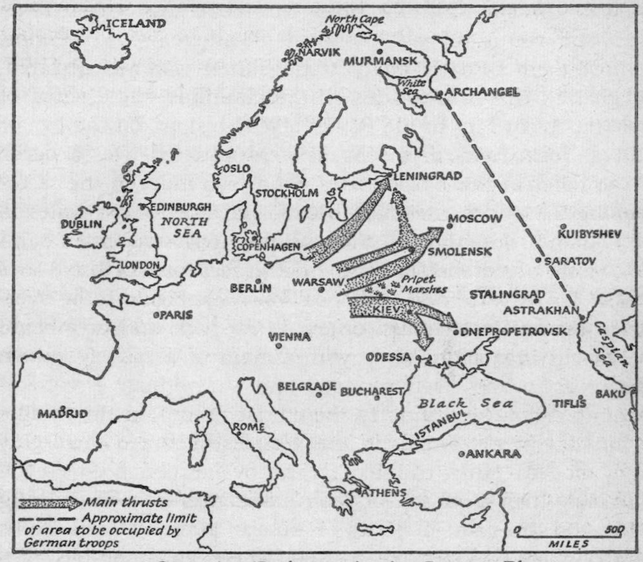

23 Operation 'Barbarossa': the German Plan

the latter rounded up the forces in its rear before continuing its advance to Moscow. Thereafter a further series of actions, culminating in a vast mopping-up operation, would pave the way for the occupation of practically the whole of European Russia west of a line from Archangel to Astrakhan.

So far as the British were concerned, the details of this plan did not become known until the war was over. Even so, from the end of March a good deal of information was received in London which pointed to the likelihood of a German attack on Russia in the spring or early summer. The gist of it was passed on to the Soviet government, who responded by publicly accusing 'the forces arrayed against the Soviet Union and Germany' of trying to embroil them with the Germans.

Nevertheless the Russians moved large numbers of divisions to the western provinces and the Baltic States. These were not, however, disposed in accordance with any systematic plan of defence.[9] In choosing locations for them, the Soviet High Command seems to have assumed that there would be time to move them to their final positions after war was declared, and that all that was needed in the meantime was a show of strength. According to the Soviet official history, on the eve of the war formations in the West were scattered over a depth of 190 miles in the Baltic States, 60 to 190 miles in the sector covering the approaches to Moscow, and 250 to 380 miles in the Ukraine. Superficially these dispositions conformed with the concept of defence in depth; but in fact some of the troops were so far forward that their positions were bound to be overrun in the first few hours, others so far back that they could be brought into action only with the aid of a railway system which was to find itself plunged into war without a word of warning. Again according to the official history, in the middle of June the Soviet armies in the West had between them only 1,475 modern tanks manned largely by inexperienced crews; little more than a quarter of their older tanks were in working order; and the great majority of Russian aircraft on all fronts were obsolete.[10] To make matters worse, an ambitious programme of airfield construction was still unfinished. All the fighter aircraft in the West had therefore to be concentrated at a limited number of bases, where they could not be adequately dispersed for lack of space.[11]

As the day of reckoning approached, the Soviet rulers, who cannot have been unaware of these shortcomings but were either unable to remedy them or unwilling to do so for fear of precipitating an attack, redoubled their efforts to conciliate Hitler. Reports which suggested that the Germans might be about to launch an offensive were received with outward incredulity, or dismissed as 'provocation', even when they came from Russian sources. Up to the time when the Germans began to shell their positions and bomb objectives in their rear, commanders of formations in the forward areas received no warning from Moscow that an attack was imminent, and were forbidden to push patrols into German-held territory or open fire on the scores of German aircraft which violated Soviet air space. As late as June 21, long after the Germans opposite the Grodno sector had begun to take down their wire with the obvious intention of crossing the Demarcation Line in the immediate future, Molotov made a final desperate attempt at appeasement by begging the German Ambassador to tell him what had gone wrong with Russo-German relations.

At four o'clock next morning Hitler launched his assault on Russia with a panoply of war which dwarfed Napoleon's Grand Army, yet was still almost puny in relation to the vastness of the territories he hoped to conquer. Attacking on a front from the Baltic to the Black Sea, and with an eye not only to the spires and domes of Leningrad and Moscow but also to the treeless Kalmuk steppes a thousand miles from the start-line, the Germans began with forces not so very much stronger on the ground, and considerably weaker in the air,[12] than those used in the previous summer against France and the Low Countries.

Even so, it did not seem unlikely that Hitler might succeed where Napoleon had failed. By 1941 the technique of lightning war had been brought to such a high pitch in the Wehrmacht that the Red Army's primitive organization, poor strategic disposition and limited power of manœuvre were sure to tell heavily against the Russians at the outset. Furthermore, these limitations might prove decisive if the Soviet authorities failed to rally their forces for a series of determined counter-attacks at the crucial moment when the enemy's lines of communication became stretched and the momentum of his onslaught began to flag. Whether a Communist state would be capable of such a recovery seemed doubtful to observers brought up in the capitalist tradition. Partly for that reason, and also because a country which had executed or dismissed a high proportion of its senior officers a few years earlier was bound to be short of experienced tacticians, the staying-power of the Soviet Union in a war with Germany was not rated very highly. In the middle of June the strongly pro-Russian British Ambassador, Sir Stafford Cripps, reported that diplomatic circles in Moscow did not expect the Red Army to stand up to a German attack for more than three or four weeks.[13] A week later the general belief in London and Washington was that the campaign just beginning would be over in a few months at the most.[14]

The view taken in the Kremlin on a day of almost unrelieved disaster may not have been very different. In the extreme south the Russians successfully defended their positions on the Pruth against attacks by the Rumanian Third and Fourth Armies and the German Eleventh Army. Almost everywhere else troops in the immediate neighbourhood of the frontier were quickly overwhelmed or by-passed, and formations committed later in the day as they arrived piecemeal from the rear suffered appalling casualties. In twenty-four hours the Germans took 10,000 prisoners, destroyed at least 800 and possibly as many as 1,200 or more Russian aircraft, and advanced up to fifty miles.[15] Unable to form a clear impression of what was happening,[16] but determined not to show a lack of the offensive spirit, the Soviet General Staff issued orders which were uniformly unrealistic and impractical. Against this background of calamity it was noticeable that Stalin spoke no word of comfort or reassurance to the Russian people for many days, and that the broadcast speech in which Molotov announced that Russia had been invaded was hardly that of a man confident of victory.[17]

For the next three weeks the Germans continued to make spectacular progress.[18] By the middle of July the spearheads of Army Group North were probing difficult country between Lake Peipus and Lake Ilmen after cutting through some twelve to fifteen Russian divisions, while Army Group Centre had encircled a force about twice as large between Bialystok and Minsk and had thrust its armour almost to Smolensk. Army Group South, delayed by heavy rain and the failure of the troops on its extreme right to make any headway before the beginning of the month, was not yet at Kiev but was shaping for a gigantic battle of annihilation which promised to knock out half the remaining strength of the Red Army. In a message to the British Prime Minister on July 19, Stalin admitted that the situation was tense and that the worst had yet to come.[19]

Even so, by that date the Germans had begun to discover that the conquest of Russia was not following the pattern of past campaigns. In the armies of the West it was usually taken for granted that a commander who found himself in a position untenable by textbook standards would do his best to extricate himself, not only to avoid unnecessary suffering but also because no one would thank him for allowing himself to be defeated unless he had received express orders to hold on at all costs. This was not altogether so in the Red Army, where an officer who proposed to shift his ground because the local situation seemed unpromising was more likely to be accused of treason or cowardice than commended for his tactical insight. Moreover, in the early stages of the campaign tactical withdrawals were often out of the question for the Russians because their communications were so poor that no one in the forward area knew enough about the general situation to say whether a retreat was either necessary or feasible. Similarly, small bodies of men who became separated from their units often chose to fight where they stood, even against hopeless odds, rather than try to save themselves at the risk of being shot by their own side for attempting an unauthorized withdrawal.

The proverbial doggedness of the Slav in face of adversity also contributed to the reluctance of the Russians to give ground. After the first day or two of dismay and confusion they did not willingly surrender, even when wounded. If this was partly because the Russian fighting man was temperamentally inclined to hold life cheap and honour dear, an additional motive was a well-founded suspicion that any Russian who survived a spell in a German prison camp would be doubly lucky if he escaped trial as a deserter at the end of the war.

This attitude cost the Soviet Union losses in killed and wounded which would have been suicidal for a country without almost unlimited manpower, but it also had its disadvantages from the German point of view. Russian troops surrounded or by-passed could not be relied upon to lay down their arms when resistance had become pointless by orthodox standards; consequently mopping-up and the guarding of lines of communication were difficult and sometimes costly. At some places, too, salients, re-entrants and pockets of resistance became so inextricably confused that the Germans had difficulty in knowing whether they were outflanking the Russians or the Russians outflanking them.

Meanwhile the masters of the Kremlin were recovering from a shaky start. Although at some places in Belorussia and the Western Ukraine the Germans were welcomed at the outset as liberators from Communist oppression, Hitler's declared hope that the Soviet edifice would crumble into ruin as soon as the door was kicked open was soon dashed. On July 3 Stalin, at last breaking silence, strengthened his hold on the masses with a broadcast which marked the beginning of a new phase in his relations with the Soviet people and his country's relations with the outside world.[20] Abstaining from the usual diatribes against the capitalist States, and addressing his hearers for the first time not merely as comrades but as friends, he announced a 'scorched earth' policy and appealed to every Soviet citizen to uphold the struggle against the invaders both from patriotic motives and for the sake of all victims of National Socialism. Where the Red Army was forced to retreat, he said, not a loaf of bread or a pint of oil, not a railway engine or a truck, must be left to fall into the enemy's hands. Livestock must be driven away, stocks of grain must be handed over to the State, and property which could not be removed must be destroyed.

In the same speech Stalin called for the formation of partisan groups throughout occupied territory. In point of fact, little was done to organize such activities on a large scale until nearly a year later, and the movement did not approach its full momentum much before 1943. On the other hand, in 1941 a substantial number of Russian troops who had become separated from their parent formations were at large behind the enemy's lines. Although handicapped by the absence of a central authority responsible for distributing supplies and information, some of these undertook subversive activities similar to those afterwards undertaken by the partisan units which many of them joined.

Almost simultaneously the chain of command of the Soviet armies in the West was modified by the formation of three chief commands under the supreme direction of a defence committee headed by Stalin and with Molotov, Voroshilov, Malenkov and Beria as members. At the same time political commissars attached to army formations were given back their old status after some years of partial eclipse and were supplemented by many thousands of political soldiers recruited from the Communist Party; in addition each of the three Commanders-in-Chief was provided with a war council headed by the local Party Leader. Above all, a start was made with the removal of industrial plant, equipment and key workers to safe areas. More than fifteen hundred enterprises, most of them large, were moved between July and November to the banks of the Volga, the Urals, Siberia, Kazakhstan and Central Asia, mainly from the Ukraine, the Donetz basin, Leningrad and Moscow.[21] Thus the German assumption that the industrial areas of European Russia were indispensable to the Russians was invalidated.

Even so, a great deal of plant had to be abandoned, and time was needed for enterprises to settle down in new surroundings, and in some cases to find new sources of raw material and recruit new workers to replace those left behind. By the end of the year, output in general had fallen since June by about a half, and reserves of some types of ammunition were exhausted. Government agencies reported serious shortages of many raw materials, foodstuffs and manufactured products, including aluminium, copper, pig iron and rolled iron, steel, tin, coal, grain, sugar, cattle, pigs, aircraft, guns and tanks.[22]

In the summer, aluminium was the raw material in most demand. 'Give us that,' Stalin told President Roosevelt's emissary, Harry Hopkins, at the end of July, 'and we can fight for three or four years.' Just over a month later he asked the British for 30,000 tons of aluminium by the beginning of

October, 400 aircraft and 500 medium and light tanks a month for an indefinite period, and a second front in France or the Balkans. Without these, he added, Russia would be either defeated, or crippled for a long time to come.[23]

When this request was received, the aircraft carrier *Argus* and seven merchantmen were on their way to Arctic waters with aircraft and munitions for the Russians.[24] Six weeks earlier Britain had signed a diplomatic agreement with the Soviet Union and had promised to send all possible help and make no difficulties about payment. In effect, a second front in France already existed, and would go on existing as long as the forces in the United Kingdom were watched by thirty to forty German divisions. In addition, the British were maintaining a third front in North Africa, a fourth front in German skies, and a fifth front in the shape of a specially-augmented air offensive over Northern France. In view of the urgency of Stalin's appeal the War Cabinet decided, however, not to administer a rebuff by reminding him of the slenderness of their resources and the difficulty of doing more than they had already undertaken to do, but on the contrary to give him some positive encouragement even at the cost of delaying the expansion of their own forces.[25] They promised to send him 5,000 tons of aluminium from Canada at the earliest possible moment and 2,000 tons a month thereafter, and to find each month from United Kingdom production half the tanks and aircraft he had asked for. The other half would, they hoped, be forthcoming from the United States.

The assumption that the Americans were able and willing to give almost unlimited aid to Hitler's enemies, was not, however, well founded. President Roosevelt had declared himself in favour of making the United States the great arsenal of democracy, and Congress had voted huge sums for the purpose. But the country was not at war. Her output of war material was small and would remain smaller than that of the United Kingdom until well into 1942; her raw materials were still being used largely to make consumer goods. Moreover, the President's foreign aid programme was hard to reconcile with tentative plans to raise and equip an American army of two hundred divisions. Arriving in London in the middle of September to prepare for a three-Power conference on supply which was to be held in Moscow later in the month, a mission headed by Averell Harriman made it clear that deliveries of American war-material in the next nine months would come far short of the quantities which the British had been led in the spring to expect that they might receive.[26]

Whether the Americans, still outwardly at peace with the whole world, were wise to retain in their own country weapons which the British or the Russians could have used in active theatres was a question which even the best-informed of their strategists found hard to answer. Not surprisingly, Harriman and his colleagues were not prepared to discuss it with the British. Consequently the London talks revolved chiefly round the allocation of such supplies as were available. The American delegates proposed to allot to the Russians, largely at the expense of allocations already promised to the British, a total of 1,524 tanks in the next nine months. As this would leave Stalin with 726 fewer than he had asked for even after he had received the 2,250 promised from United Kingdom production, the British felt bound to ask that the deficiency should be made good at the cost of still further reducing their own share and holding up their plans for the equipment of new armoured formations at home and in the Middle East. Much the same difficulty arose in regard to aircraft, and it was solved, or left unsolved, in roughly the same fashion. So far as the British were concerned, the effect was to leave them with 1,613 fewer tanks and about 1,800 fewer aircraft than they had counted on receiving.

In consequence of these decisions the British and American delegates were able to tell the Russians at the Moscow Conference that, so far as medium and light tanks were concerned, the requirements stated by Stalin at the beginning of the month would be met.[27] In addition the British promised 250 Bren gun carriers a month from United Kingdom production, the Americans some scout cars and anti-aircraft and anti-tank guns. Most of the raw materials and partly manufactured goods for which the Russians asked would also be forthcoming. The British undertook to meet the whole of Russia's demands for cobalt, cocoa beans, copper, diamonds, jute, lead, rubber, tin, wool and zinc, and reaffirmed their offer of 2,000 tons of aluminium a month from Canada. The Americans agreed to meet demands for barbed wire, graphitized electrodes, molybdenum, nickel-chrome wire and phosphorous, provide some armour plate, rolled brass and toluol, and look into the possibility of finding some aluminium. Apart from these, the Russians proposed to buy in the open market large quantities of food, including North American wheat and sugar from the Netherlands East Indies.

Whether all these goods would reach their destinations was another matter. The Americans and the British did not promise that they would do so, but only that the quantities specified would be made available and that the Russians would be helped to ship them to the ports of their choice. As the Soviet Union had only a small merchant fleet and few warships in European waters outside the Baltic and the Black Sea, it was obvious that a substantial volume of shipping would have to be found by the Western democracies. Moreover, traffic to and from North Russia, where the Soviet delegates wished most of the war material to be sent, would have to be escorted wholly or mainly by British warships. The first of eight convoys organized by the Commander-in-Chief, Home Fleet, before the end of the year was in fact already on its way to Archangel when the Moscow Conference broke up.* As alternatives to Archangel or Murmansk, the Americans and the British suggested Vladivostok and one or more routes through Persia; but the Russians wished to keep Vladivostok for consignments consisting mainly of food for their Far Eastern provinces. Obviously reluctant to see foreign influences at work in territories bordering on the Caspian, they were not attracted by the other proposal, but eventually agreed that some

*Archangel was the port chosen by the Russians, who were confident that they could keep it open with icebreakers even in the worst weather. By November their inability to do so was apparent, and thereafter most traffic was routed to Murmansk, although Archangel was still used occasionally in the summer.

goods might be sent through Persia on condition that all traffic north of Kasvin came under their control.

Meanwhile the Red Army had suffered appalling setbacks but was showing remarkable resilience. Absolute power, a big intake of recruits, and a stock of weapons accumulated over the years all helped the Soviet leaders to spring surprises on the enemy by bringing up fresh formations when their resources were supposedly exhausted. Many of these were crudely equipped by Western standards, but that was not always a disadvantage. In densely wooded or marshy country with few roads, cavalry trained to fight in an alternative role as mounted infantry could move faster, had more freedom of manœuvre, and could be more easily supplied than mechanized formations. Although generally defeated in the long run because of their lack of artillery and all-round inferiority in fire-power, these troops served the purpose of the Soviet Supreme Command by slowing down the enemy's advance and bringing him nearer and nearer to the day when his offensive capacity could no longer be sustained by an adequate flow of fuel, tyres, spare parts, and replacements for worn-out vehicles.

Conversely, brilliant tactical successes did not save the German High Command from nagging doubts as to the soundness of the assumption that the Red Army could be defeated in a single campaign.[28] Jubilant at the beginning of July, the General Staff grew much less so as the difficulty of forcing a decision before the winter became more and more apparent.

On the German left, the situation in the third week of the campaign was that Army Group North had cleared the Russians from all but a small part of the Baltic States with unexpected swiftness. Its two armoured corps were in the neighbourhood of Ostrov, awaiting orders for the culminating stroke which would, it was hoped, complete the destruction of the Soviet forces in the North-Western Sector, under Marshal Voroshilov.[29] In the outskirts of Leningrad, thousands of impressed workers and local defence troops were digging trenches and anti-tank ditches, laying minefields, and erecting strongpoints in the knowledge that the Germans were on their way, that the Finns were also militant, and that nothing had been done before the war to bar the approaches to the city from the south. To buy time for these activities, seven weak divisions had moved to an improvised line along the Luga River, with their right on the Gulf of Finland and their left abutting on a region of thickly wooded and almost roadless country near Lake Ilmen. But with two armoured corps at the enemy's disposal, these hastily-constructed outpost positions seemed unlikely to hold out for more than a few days.

To commit the whole of Army Group North's armour to a frontal assault on the Luga position at the risk of pushing the enemy back without finally defeating him was not, however, a course which appealed to the Germans. Moreover, it would have had the disadvantage of leaving an awkward gap on their right, in which Russian troops were known to be at large and from which counter-attacks might be launched on both sides of the junction between Army Group North and Army Group Centre. Accordingly, one armoured corps was ordered to advance up the Luga road and to the west of it, the other to pull out to the east and then wheel northwards with the object of clearing up the situation on the flank, cutting communications between Leningrad and Moscow at Chudovo, and drawing a net round the whole of the Soviet forces on the Leningrad front.

The immediate consequences of this move were that the corps on the right, under General von Manstein, was forced to give battle in unfavourable country and fight its way back to the west after being cut off for three days, and that the corps on the left, under General Reinhardt, soon found itself with more to do than it could comfortably undertake. Both corps were then ordered to attack the Luga position, but at widely separated points and with the proviso that Manstein's corps should first share in a further attempt to turn the flank. Only in the middle of August, a month after German troops first closed up to the Luga, were the two armoured corps at last brought together for a concerted attack near the western extremity of the Russian Line.

24 The Advance on Leningrad, July-August 1941

Almost at that moment a substantial Russian force, nominally of eight divisions with some tanks and mounted troops, emerged from the marshes south of Lake Ilmen and fell on the extreme right of Army Group North. The result was that Manstein's corps had no sooner reached its new position in the north-west than it was ordered to turn about and hasten to the rescue. A counter-attack launched on August 19 restored the situation, but left the two armoured corps separated by 150 miles. Even so, Leningrad was virtually cut off by the end of the month; but by that time the garrison had had a full two months in which to prepare defensive positions and accumulate supplies.

In the central sector Marshal Timoshenko, with five armoured corps advancing on his front to threaten Moscow, was unable to save Smolensk but managed by the third week in

July to establish a line some twenty-five miles further east.[80] In the meantime the Soviet Fifth Army, with other troops bypassed in the early stages of the invasion, had withdrawn to the Pripet Marshes, where they seemed well placed not only to threaten Army Group Centre's communications with its forward troops on the Smolensk front, but also to strike at the northern flank of Army Group South's forces advancing on Kiev.

Thus the state of affairs immediately before the day on which, according to the original plan, part of Army Group Centre's armour was to have moved north to strengthen Army Group North, was that resistance in the Baltic States had almost ceased. On the other hand, both Army Group Centre and Army Group South were momentarily checked, and there was a deep re-entrant along the dividing-line between them. Moreover, a Russian salient south of Lake Ilmen threatened Army Group Centre's other flank and also the southern flank of Army Group North, where Manstein's corps had just run into trouble. In these circumstances, the crucial question which the Germans had to answer was how they could best use Army Group Centre's armour to save themselves from becoming so bogged down on all three fronts as to lose their chance of scoring a decisive success before the end of the campaigning season.

The solution favoured by the Army High Command and many commanders in the field was to disregard the situation on the flanks, leave the armour with Army Group Centre, and use it for a gigantic two-pronged thrust which would, at one and the same time, capture Moscow and envelop the whole of Timoshenko's forces on the Smolensk front. In this way, it was argued, a great many of the enemy's remaining formations would be destroyed, and not merely his capital but the focus of his lateral communications would pass into German hands. With Moscow gone, effective resistance in the north and south would soon become impossible, and his forces there could be rounded up at leisure.

Hitler did not agree. Moscow, he thought, was only 'a geographical expression'. In his view the essential aim was to cripple the enemy's war economy by investing Leningrad, seizing the Ukraine and the Donetz basin, and capturing Rostov as a vital point on the route by which the enemy drew his oil from the Caucasus. Moreover, by invading Russia and thus depriving himself of the grain and raw materials which she had been supplying, he had taken a risk which he would continue to run until her richly productive areas in the south were safely in his hands. This in itself was enough to make him reluctant to concentrate on the capture of Moscow at the cost of leaving the conquest of the Ukraine and the Donetz basin until later.

Accordingly, on July 19 the Supreme Command, at that time still reasonably confident that Army Group South could defeat Marshal Budienny's forces in the South-Western Sector with its existing resources if helped to overcome the threat to its left from the Soviet Fifth Army, ordered Army Group Centre to divert its armour from the advance on Moscow and use it to clear up the situation on its flanks in the interest of all three army groups. At the same time Army Group South, besides co-operating with Army Group Centre against the Fifth Army, was to envelop Budienny's armies, and Army Group North to continue its advance on Leningrad after making sure that its right was secure and that there were no gaps along its front.

The controversy which followed was important not only because it profoundly affected Hitler's relations with his generals and even led to an abortive plot to depose him when he visited Army Group Centre at Novy Borisov early in August, but also because his failure to cut the discussion short allowed the situation to drift for the best part of five weeks. During those five weeks critics of the Supreme Command's proposals lost no opportunity of decrying them, and much ingenuity was expended on the planning of operations which conformed outwardly with the Supreme Command's directive but left Army Group Centre's troops in a favourable position to continue the advance on Moscow. Both Brauchitsch and Halder thought of resigning as a protest against the go-slow in the central sector, but decided not to do so when Brauchitsch became convinced that their resignations would not be accepted and that the gesture would change nothing.

On August 21 Hitler at last ruled in unequivocal terms that 'the most important aim before the onset of winter' was not the capture of Moscow but the conquest of the Crimea and the Donetz basin and the severance of Russia's oil route from the Caucasus. Not even this pronouncement silenced criticism, but thereafter he was able to rout objectors by asserting that his decision was based primarily on economic grounds and that soldiers notoriously did not understand such matters.

In its final form, the operation on which the Führer insisted was no mere turning inward of the flanks of the three army groups to eliminate pockets of resistance, but a double enveloping movement on a mammoth scale. The better part of Army Group Centre's armour, under General Guderian, was to strike southwards at an angle of ninety degrees to the main axis of the advance on Moscow, break through the almost unguarded tract of wild country between Timoshenko's main front and the remnants of the Soviet forces in the Pripet Marshes and about Gomel, and sweep on past Konotop. Meanwhile Army Group South's armour under General von Kleist, already entering the bend of the Dnieper by the third week in August, would cross the river in strength and wheel to the north. Unless Budienny moved with unexpected swiftness, practically the whole of the troops which he was still pouring into Kiev would be surrounded when Kleist and Guderian met on the open plateau a hundred miles in his rear.[31]

In the last weeks of summer this manœuvre was carried out with dazzling success. Pushing his leading division across the Desna at Novgorod-Seversk on the third day of his advance, Guderian was threatening by September 9 to cut the more northerly of the two main routes from Kiev to the east. Two days later Budienny and his political mentor, Nikolai Khrushchev, warned the Soviet Supreme Command that the time had come to pull out of the Kiev salient. Stalin, apparently convinced that every day devoted by Army Group Centre to its southward thrust increased the chances of saving Moscow, insisted that, on the contrary, the salient must be held. Twenty-four hours later Kleist burst out of the bridgehead across the Middle Dnieper which he had established at Kremenchug, and on September 16 he and Guderian joined hands at Lokhvitsa.

According to the Soviet official history, 527,044 officers and men of the Red Army were encircled in the Kiev pocket. How many of these were killed in desperate attempts to break out in the course of the next few days, how many escaped and how many were captured no one knows.* But the broad outcome was that Stalin paid for his determination to detain Guderian in the south for as long as possible with the loss of four armies and a monstrous tally of human suffering.

Whether Hitler was justified in pausing to clear the Kiev re-entrant and the Pripet Marshes at a crucial stage in his eastward drive is another matter. The double enveloping movement scored a brilliant tactical success but brought Germany no decision. Guderian's dash to the south held up the advance on Moscow for many weeks and exposed his vehicles to heavy wear and tear at a time when many of them were in poor shape after weeks of difficult going on poor roads. By the time it began, Army Group South's own armour had already cut through most of the Soviet forces in its path and was across the Lower Dnieper, with nothing but a rather remote threat to its flank to prevent it from pressing on to the Donetz basin or beyond as fast as its supplies could follow it. As for the economic arguments with which Hitler bolstered his case, the facts were that no territorial gains as late as September could do much to improve Germany's economic position before the winter; that the loss of Rostov would not prevent the Russians from drawing oil from the Caucasus through Astrakhan; and that German experts were beginning to suspect as early as July that Russia would not be fatally handicapped even if she lost the whole of her productive capacity in the south and much else besides.

*The Germans claimed 665,000 prisoners. Russian historians assert that this was more than the entire strength of the troops in the salient, and that not more than about a third of the men encircled were captured.

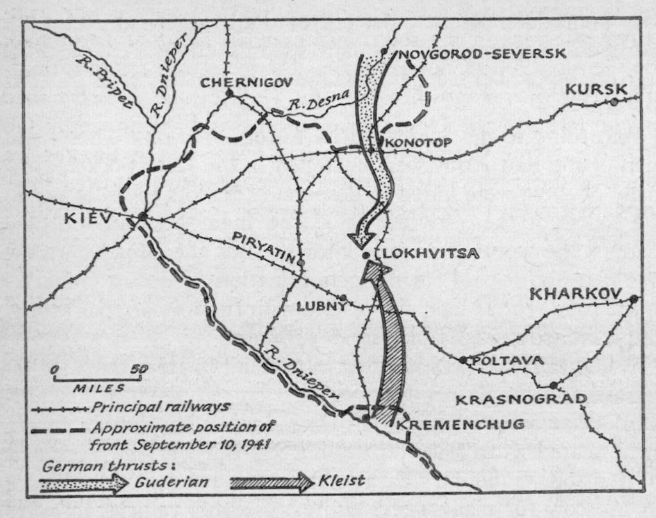

25 The Kiev Pocket

Irrespective of where the truth lay in this controversy, it was clear by the third week in September that the Red Army was still undefeated, that only a decisive victory within the next few weeks could save the Wehrmacht from a winter campaign for which it was ill prepared, and that further progress in the south, although desirable, was not likely to lead to any significant decline in the enemy's fighting strength. Leningrad was almost completely invested and was destined not to be relieved until nearly a third of its three million inhabitants had died of starvation;[32] but its fall would not be decisive and in any case was not in sight. In these circumstances Hitler agreed to resume the offensive in the central sector at the end of the month. But winter was approaching, and little time was left in which to score a decisive success with mobile formations whose vehicles had been driven almost to the limit.

On the other hand, the weight of attack which the Germans could mount was impressive. On paper, the number of divisions on the Eastern Front had increased by more than forty since the beginning of the campaign. By leaving only a few armoured divisions in the south and none in front of Leningrad, the German High Command was able to concentrate a formidable array of strength between the Velikie Luki-Moscow road on the left and the Desna River on the right. Conversely the Soviet Supreme Command, who had every reason to expect a renewed thrust towards Moscow but once again allowed their forward troops to be taken by surprise, could muster only a numerically strong but far from homogeneous force consisting largely of raw recruits with a stiffening of more seasoned troops. In Central Asia and the Far East, however, there was still a substantial reserve of fresh divisions which were to make important contributions to the battle when the Defence Committee at last decided that they could safely be moved westwards.

The offensive began well for the Germans, with advances of up to forty miles on the first day.[38] Orel fell on October 2, so suddenly that its captors found the trams still running and wagon-loads of dismantled industrial equipment standing in sidings ready for despatch to the east. Vast numbers of Soviet troops were caught too far forward near Viazma and Bryansk, and only a series of covering actions by units hastily brought from the rear and flanks made it possible for some of them to escape encirclement and fall back to a prepared line running roughly north and south through Mozhaisk.

Deciding that the time had come for heroic measures, the Soviet rulers then made the crucial decision to weaken their Far Eastern garrisons for the sake of the threatened front. Gathering the threads into their own hands, they appointed General G. K. Zhukov to command the Central Sector in place of Timoshenko, who was given the task of saving something from the wreck of Budienny's armies in the south. An outstanding strategist who resented political interference with the army and had fallen foul of the régime in 1937, Zhukov was regarded as a lukewarm Communist but was credited with saving Leningrad when he was sent to the North-West Sector in September.

Zhukov had, however, barely had time to settle into his

new job when the Germans captured Kaluga and thereby turned the southern flank of his line through Mozhaisk. By the middle of October they had not only turned the northern flank as well by seizing Kalinin, but had also broken through the defences in the neighbourhood of the Velikie Luki-Moscow road at Volokolamsk. With the enemy only fifty to sixty miles from Moscow, the Soviet authorities began on October 12 to prepare the city for a siege. On the same day arrangements were completed for the removal of many government agencies and the whole of the diplomatic corps to Kuibyshev, on the Middle Volga. Their departure was the signal for an unofficial exodus which passed into Muscovite legend as 'the great skedaddle'.[34] Railway stations were besieged, privileged officials filled the tanks of their cars with petrol and sped eastwards on doubtful pretexts, and an appeal to the masses to join 'workers' battalions' attracted only 12,000 volunteers out of a peacetime population of about four million. Not unwilling to rid the city of 'useless mouths' but determined to preserve their authority and stamp out looting, the masters of the Kremlin responded by letting it be known on October 17 that Stalin was still in Moscow, and adding two days later that a state of emergency existed and that deviationists would be shot.

Nevertheless the Red Army fought on stubbornly, and in conditions which were becoming daily less favourable for their opponents. The German Army's faith in the superiority of its armour took a sharp jolt when, on October 6 and 11, an armoured division was twice outfought between Orel and Tula by a brigade equipped with the T-34 tank.[35] Soon afterwards heavy rain, sleet and snow, alternating with spells of relatively mild weather, covered the roads with a coating of mud and slush which reduced the speed of tracked vehicles to a fast walk and sometimes immobilized wheeled vehicles for hours at a time. Such bad going was disagreeable for both sides but particularly inconvenient for the attackers, with their long lines of communication and their high degree of dependence on mechanized transport. At times unable to reinforce and supply their forward troops except by air, the Germans tried to mend matters by laboriously building corduroy roads in the

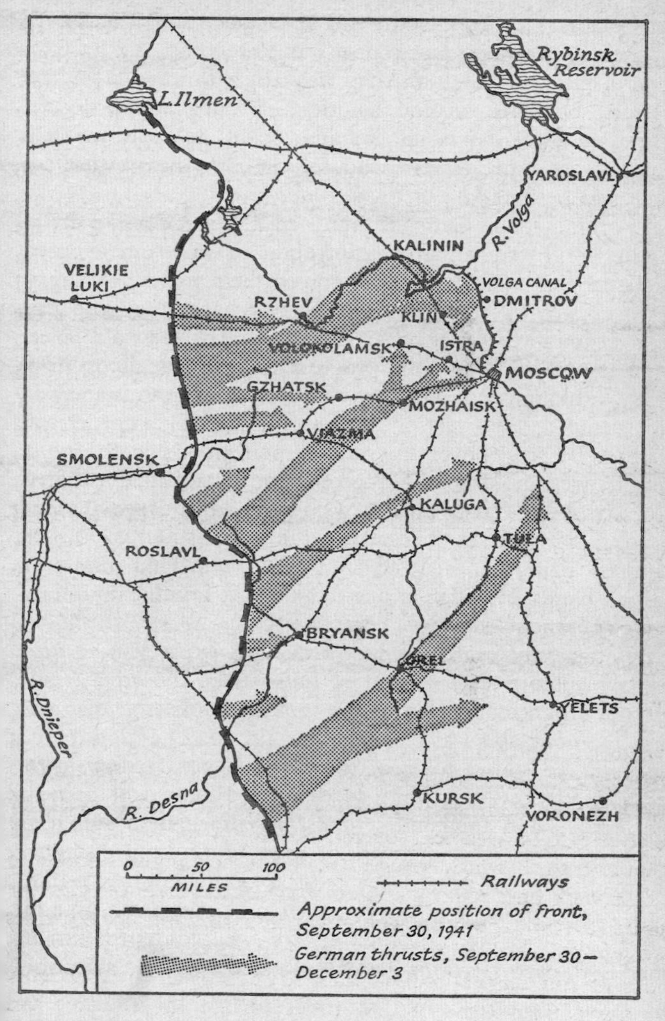

26 The Advance on Moscow, September 30-December 3, 1941

worst places. However, by the end of October they were driven to conclude that their best course was to regroup and wait for a hard frost. The alternative was to withdraw to winter quarters, but this classical solution did not appeal to the Führer, and there was no unanimous will to insist upon it among those army officers who felt in their hearts that too much was being asked of tired troops.

Accordingly, the Germans launched a new offensive in the middle of November after a fortnight's pause and a public admission that bad weather had forced them to break off their advance. Moving for the first time over hard snow and firm ice, they found that they had regained some of their old power of manœuvre and that rapid progress was possible along roads which, although still poor by Western European standards, had ceased to be rivers of mud surrounded by impenetrable swamps. By the end of the month their troops in the north and due west of Moscow had taken Klin, established a bridgehead across the Volga canal at Dmitrov, and pushed forward to Istra, only fifteen miles from the outer suburbs. On the southern flank of their advance Tula remained firmly in Russian hands, although at one stage it was imminently threatened with encirclement.

But these successes, impressive enough when viewed on a map of suitable scale a hundred miles from the front, could not hide from commanders on the spot the knowledge that their men had gone about as far as they could go. The capture of a few hundred square miles of snowbound country deep in the heart of Russia did nothing to ease the problem of carrying fuel, rations and ammunition across vast tracts of hostile territory served by a sparse network of roads and a limited number of broad-gauge railways incapable of accepting German rolling-stock except after laborious conversion. At the same time the bitter cold was more debilitating for well-equipped but unsuitably dressed Germans than for Russians with less sophisticated weapons but warmer clothing. Petrol was precious, but shivering men could not be prevented from using it to make fires when they halted. To guard against night attacks, mobile units were compelled to warm up the engines of their vehicles very few hours. Perhaps for the very reason that German utomatic weapons were made to specifications which called or careful machining to narrow tolerances, they tended to jam n very cold weather and were sometimes hard to load. All this nade progress difficult and aggravated the problem of main-aining a force whose communications were stretched to the imit or beyond.

Moreover, the fortnight's respite at the beginning of Nov-mber gave time for Russian as well as German commanders o take stock of the situation and adjust their dispositions. By he middle of the month the October panic in Moscow was a ning of the past, about half the population had left for the ast with the government's blessing, and immense pains had een taken to put the defences of the city in good shape. Besides deploying large numbers of anti-aircraft guns and arrage balloons, the authorities had given a good deal of hought to the problem of the incendiary bomb in the light of ritish experience in London and elsewhere.[36] By the same ate substantial numbers of troops were beginning to arrive rom the Far East and were being directed to strategic positions n the rear. By thrusting forward his left and centre, Field-Marshal von Bock was in danger of butting his head against ne strong defences immediately west of Moscow and exposing is flank to a counter-attack from the newly-arrived formations ssembling north of the city.

As events turned out, at the end of November Bock's left altered to a standstill beyond Dmitrov under the weight of ocal counter-attacks which Zhukov was able to make without ommitting his whole strength. Further south, one division of ne German Fourth Army made contact in the afternoon of December 2 with the outer ring of Moscow's last-ditch de-ences; but the weather was atrocious, the light fading, and the ay ended with both sides claiming successes which neither ould follow up. Still further to the German right, elements of uderian's armoured group succeeded next day in isolating ula for some hours by cutting both the railway and the main oad to Moscow, but were unable to go further for lack of sup-lies. The Russians under Zhukov then counter-attacked and

pushed Guderian's forces off the road after a sharp tussl
which proved expensive for the Germans.[37]

These efforts left Bock's troops so spent that the questio
was no longer whether they could maintain their advance, bu
how they were to meet the ambitious counter-offensive whic
Zhukov launched some forty-eight hours after his success a
Tula.[38] Should Bock fall back on his whole front, thereb
shortening his communications but committing himself to a
awkward disengagement which might end in a running fight
Or should he try to hold his positions at the risk of exposin
his centre to envelopment by Soviet forces converging o
Smolensk?

Always reluctant to give ground, Hitler ruled against
general withdrawal. The outcome was that Bock succeeded i
holding a salient round Rzhev and Gzhatsk which put hi
still within a hundred miles of Moscow; but deep re-entran
opened on his flanks, the German front became extremely lon
and the hardships of the winter campaign taxed the enduranc
of the toughest troops. By Christmas the Russian adventu
had cost the German Army three-quarters of a million cas
alties;[39] the unremitting pressure of day-to-day events on
force with insufficient reserves had permanently blunted th
striking-power of the German long-range bomber arm; ar
hopes of turning the occupied territories to good account we
fading because such attempts as were made to establish a wor
able system of government and a healthy economy were frus
rated by the National Socialist policy of murder and repressio

On the other hand, Hitler's strategic insight proved sour
inasmuch as the Red Army failed to bite off the Rzhev salie
Trying to do too much with forces inadequately trained ar
equipped for a major offensive, the Russians advanced at
cost in human and material losses which made success pr
gressively harder. Moreover, as their communications leng
ened they came up against much the same difficulties of supp
as had slowed down the German advance a few months earli
In March the spring thaw and a mounting tally of casualt
and losses in material finally brought them to a halt. By th
time the Russians had pushed nearly to Velikie Luki and

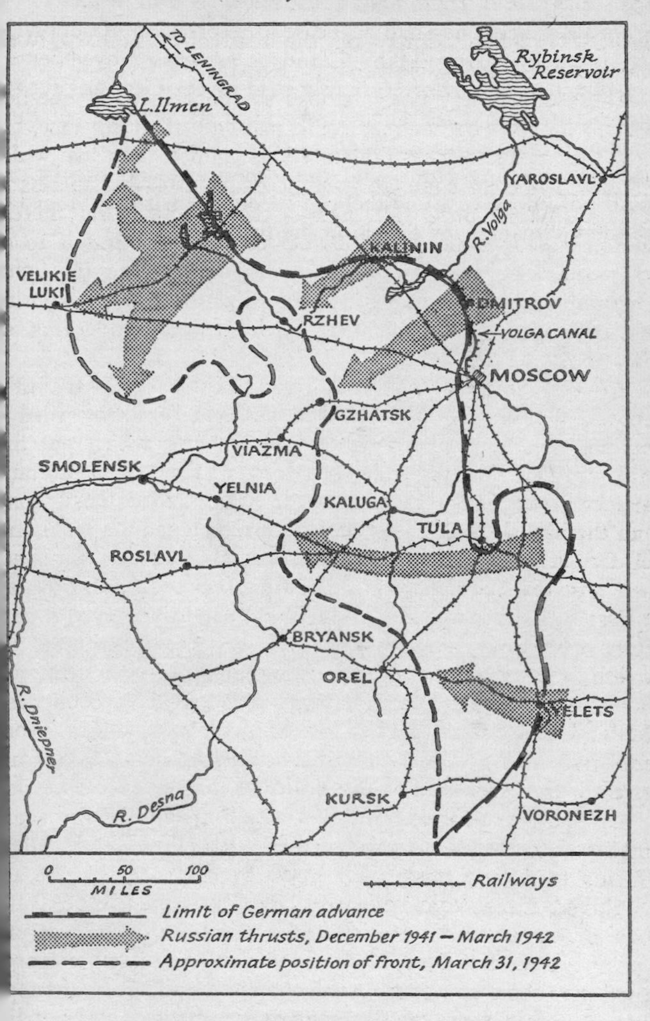

27 The Soviet Counter-Offensive, December 1941-March 1942

beyond Kaluga. They had also eased the problem of supplying Leningrad by taking Tikhvin, and as early as November 29 had liberated Rostov, precariously held by the Germans for ten days before that date. Their losses were staggering; but their manpower was immense, their factories were at full blast far from the fighting front, and the Americans and the British could not afford to allow them to be defeated if they hoped to see the German Army beaten in the field.

CHAPTER 11

THE DESERT WAR

May 1941 - February 1942

In the summer of 1941 the British government, puzzled by large discrepancies between the numbers of troops and aircraft sent to Egypt and the numbers used in battle, decided that the time had come for a drastic overhaul of administrative arrangements in the Middle East. The proportion of serviceable aircraft began to rise when a Chief Maintenance and Supply Officer, directly responsible to the Air Officer Commanding-in-Chief, was installed in Cairo; but the army's difficulties were not solved by the appointment of an Intendant-General with special powers. The government then appointed a Resident Minister of State in Cairo and made him a member of the War Cabinet.

This reform was intended not only to promote efficiency, but also to lighten the burden thrown on General Wavell, who had repeatedly called for some such change, and on his air force colleague, Air Chief Marshal Sir Arthur Longmore. In the outcome, neither stayed to receive the benefit. Called to London for consultation on the eve of the battle for Crete, Longmore learned to his surprise that he was not to return and would be succeeded by his deputy, Air Marshal A. W. Tedder. A month later it was Wavell's turn. Beyond question a man of exceptional insight and an outstanding strategist, he had notched up an impressive tally of success since he first took the offensive against the Italians in the Western Desert and East Africa. But he seemed to the government to have been slow off the mark in Iraq and Syria. The failure of his limited offensive in the spring was also held against him, although the attempt had cost the enemy such substantial losses that it might almost have been reckoned a success.

Concluding that Wavell was tiring and that they were in danger of riding a willing horse to a standstill, the authorities decided to replace him by General Auchinleck, whose services at Narvik and elsewhere had led him to the important post of Commander-in-Chief in India. Wavell, characteristically remarking that he had taken some wickets but had had some sixes scored off him, stepped good humouredly into the position vacated by his successor. By early July only Admiral Cunningham remained of the three-man team which had turned the Italians out of East Africa and asserted British control over the vast area from the Western Desert to the Persian Gulf and from the equator almost to the borders of Anatolia.

When Auchinleck arived in Cairo to take up his new appointment, Hitler's Russian campaign was less than a fortnight old. Three German army groups, each far stronger than any force which the Commander-in-Chief in the Middle East could hope to put into the field, were thrusting deep into Soviet territor and were expected to conquer European Russia within thre months.[1] By the end of the year, or perhaps earlier, victoriou German armies might be ready to cross the Caucasus and push southwards towards the Suez Canal and the Persian Gulf.

Auchinleck concluded that his first concern must be for hi northern flank. On July 4 he signalled to London that he ha no intention of taking the offensive in the Western Desert unti Syria was firmly in his hands and Cyprus secure against sea borne and airborne assault, and that even then he would nee at least two armoured divisions and a strong air componen before he could think of tackling Rommel. Rejecting the argu ment that it would pay him to attack before the enemy wa ready even though his own preparations might be incomplet he went on to make it clear that he would rather lose his po than commit himself to a premature offensive which migh so weaken him as to expose him to certain defeat if the Ge mans crossed the Caucasus later in the year.

Without necessarily accepting all Auchinleck's assumption

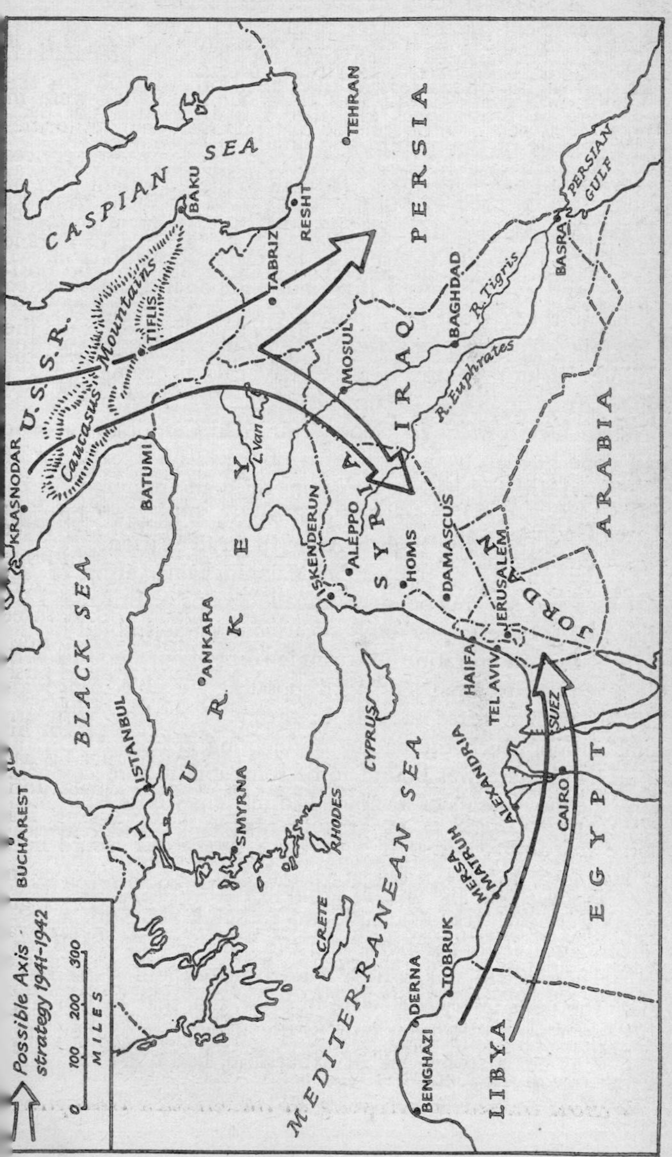

28 The Caucasus and the Middle East

the government agreed, after calling him home for consultation, that he must be given time for thorough preparation. The start of his offensive was then fixed provisionally for the beginning of November. The date was afterwards put back to the middle of the month, and finally to November 18.

As Rommel was at least equally unready, the outcome was a long respite, used by both sides to build up their resources as best they could in face of difficulties of supply. Auchinleck took the opportunity to organize his major formations in two armies, and again showed how much importance he attached to the northern front by choosing General Maitland Wilson, a seasoned commander whose all-round knowledge of the Middle Eastern theatre was exceptional, to command the Ninth Army in Syria. Command of the Eighth Army in the Western Desert went to General Sir Alan Cunningham, who had done brilliantly in East Africa but had no experience of desert warfare and had never commanded an armoured force.[2] These appointments were not challenged, although Churchill would have liked the Eighth Army to go to Wilson.

By the middle of November Cunningham's army of six divisions and six independent brigade groups or brigades contained by far the largest body of armour yet assembled by the British. By concentrating in a single corps about two-thirds of the seven hundred tanks at his disposal he was able to provide himself with a force capable in theory of dealing with any combination which the enemy could bring against it. On the other hand there was bound to be some difficulty in co-ordinating the movements of armoured formations whose equipment included fast cruiser tanks, slow infantry tanks, and American Stuart tanks which were even faster across country than the cruisers but could not go far without refuelling. Other weaknesses were the lack of a tank and anti-tank gun with a good performance at long ranges, and the flimsiness of the British four-gallon petrol tins, which tended to leak and waste much fuel. The next few weeks were to show, too, that British commanders, handicapped not only by the inadequacy of their anti-tank guns but also by lack of experience, had not overcome tendency to disperse their effort in the belief that any threat from the enemy's armour must be countered by tanks.

TABLE 4

BRITISH LAND FORCES FOR OPERATION 'CRUSADER,' NOVEMBER 1941

Eighth Army (General Sir Alan Cunningham)
- 30th Corps (Lieutenant-General C. W. M. Norrie)
  - 7th Armoured Division
  - 4th Armoured Brigade Group
  - 1st South African Division
  - 22nd Guards Brigade
- 13th Corps (Lieutenant-General A. R. Godwin-Austen)
  - New Zealand Division
  - 4th Indian Division
  - 1st Army Tank Brigade
- Tobruk Garrison (Major-General R. M. Scobie)
  - 70th Division
  - Polish Carpathian Infantry Brigade Group
  - 32nd Army Tank Brigade
- Oasis Force (Brigadier D. W. Reid)
  - 29th Indian Infantry Brigade Group
  - 6th South African Armoured Car Regiment
- Army Reserve
  - 2nd South African Division

NOTES. The 7th Armoured Division consisted of the 7th and 22nd Armoured Brigades, divisional troops, and a Support Group made up of two motorized infantry battalions, an anti-tank regiment, and a field artillery regiment with one additional battery. A brigade group consisted of a brigade with attached troops.

DISTRIBUTION OF TANKS

	Cruiser	Infantry	Light	Total
30th Corps				
7th Armoured Brigade	141	—	—	141
22nd Armoured Brigade	155	—	—	155
HQ 7th Armoured Division	8	—	—	8
4th Armoured Brigade	—	—	165	165
HQ 30th Corps	—	—	8	8
Totals with 30th Corps	304	—	173	477
13th Corps				
1st Army Tank Brigade	3	132	—	135
Tobruk Garrison				
32nd Army Tank Brigade	32	69	25	126
Totals with active formations	339	201	198	738
Reserves				
In forward area	—	—	(*a few*)	—
In workshops	92	77	90	259
In transit, due late November	124	52	60	236
Totals	216	129	150+	495+

Much hampered by air and submarine attacks on their seaward communications but unable to do much about them, the Germans and Italians also found time to forge a new chain of command. At the end of July they formed an armoured group of three German and five Italian divisions under General Rommel, complemented by a mobile corps of two Italian divisions under General Gastone Gambara. Of the German divisions, two were armoured and the third was in effect, and later in name also, a light division consisting mainly of lorried infantry. All the Italian divisions were infantry divisions with the exception of the two in the mobile corps, one of which was armoured and the other motorized. Together the armoured group and the mobile corps formed the North Africa Command under the Italian General Ettore Bastico. By the middle of November the North Africa Command disposed of roughly 550 tanks, with few or no reserves, but of these about 160 were Italian light tanks of little value.

TABLE 5

AXIS LAND FORCES IN NORTH AFRICA, NOVEMBER 1941

North Africa Command (General Ettore Bastico)
  Armoured Group Africa (General Erwin Rommel)
    German Africa Corps (Lieutenant-General Ludwig Crüwell)
      15th Panzer Division
      21st Panzer Division
      Africa Division (later 90th Light Division)
      Savona Division (Italian)
    Italian 21st Corps (General Enea Navarrini)
      Bologna Division
      Brescia Division
      Pavia Division
      Trento Division
  Italian Mobile (20th) Corps (General Gastone Gambara)
      Ariete Armoured Division
      Trieste Motorized Division

NOTES. Each of the German armoured divisions consisted of one tank regiment (two battalions); one motorized infantry regiment (two battalions); one reconnaissance unit; one anti-tank unit; one machine-gun battalion; one engineer battalion; and one artillery regiment (three batteries). The Africa Division consisted of seven battalions of motorized infantry with divisional troops and details.

Reserves. Few or no replacements, apart from tanks recovered and repaired expected before December.

DISTRIBUTION OF TANKS

	German (PzKw. II, III, IV)	*Italian M13/40*	*Italian light*	*Totals*
15th Panzer Division	133	—	—	133
21st Panzer Division	111	—	—	111
Ariete Division	—	146	52	198
Other divisions	—	—	110	110
Totals with active formations	244	146	162	552

Throughout the summer, supply was Bastico's abiding problem, and hence Rommel's. After the departure of the Luftwaffe contingent from Sicily in the first half of the year, Rommel repeatedly urged that the enemy should be prevented from using Malta as a base for attacks on Axis convoys; but his superiors, unwilling to risk another Crete, argued that the protection of shipping in the Central Mediterranean was a job for the Italians. It was not until late October, when the British moved a naval surface force to Malta, that Hitler agreed that the German underwater fleet in Mediterranean waters should be strongly reinforced and that the Luftwaffe must take a new grip of the situation.

Even so, and in spite of the sinking of ships carrying substantial quantities of fuel and other stores, by the end of September it was common ground between the Germans and the Italians that a fresh attempt must be made to take Tobruk as the prelude to an advance into Egypt. A month later Rommel felt strong enough to contemplate an attack about the middle of November, and to make light of warnings from Bastico and others that the British, too, were preparing an offensive. On November 14, however, he was obliged to fly to Rome for a conference with the Italian Chief of Staff. He had not yet returned to his headquarters when, on November 18, the British forestalled him.

So far as the Axis forces were concerned, the situation in the Western Desert on the eve of the British offensive was that preparations for the attack on Tobruk had reached an advanced stage. Four of the five Italian divisions of Rommel's armoured group, in addition to the Africa Division, stood in a ring round the perimeter, and the German 15th Panzer Division, with 133 tanks, was in their rear and to the east of them. Bardia, Sollum, and the frontier as far south of Sidi Omar were guarded only by Rommel's remaining Italian division, augmented by Italian militia and some German infantry; but the German 21st Panzer Division, with 111 tanks, was astride and to the south of the Trigh Capuzzo west of Sidi Azeiz, ready to move towards the frontier if a threat developed in that direction. The southern flank of the troops investing Tobruk was covered by General Gambara's Italian mobile corps, which had taken up defensive positions at Bir el Gubi and Bir Hacheim. Its armoured component, the Ariete Division, had 146 medium and 52 light tanks, all Italian.

General Cunningham had a good knowledge of these dispositions, for the British had local air superiority and had been able to reconnoitre freely. His aims were to defeat the enemy's armour and relieve Tobruk; and he hoped to achieve them by using his 13th Corps, consisting mainly of infantry with an army tank brigade of 135 tanks, to pin down the enemy in the forward area while passing his highly mobile 30th Corps, with 477 tanks, across the undefended frontier south of Sidi Omar. After crossing the frontier the 30th Corps would either move towards Tobruk by way of Sidi Rezegh, or wheel to the right towards Bardia. The corps commander, Lieutenant-General C. W. M. Norrie, favoured the first course, arguing that it would force the enemy to fight for his communications south of Tobruk and was therefore the best way of bringing him to battle. On the other hand, there was a risk that Rommel might move his armour towards the frontier and that Norrie would find himself too far to the west. In order to give himself time to weigh up the enemy's response Cunningham decided to wait until the 30th Corps reached Gabr Saleh, about thirty miles west of Sidi Omar, before committing himself one way or the other. Meanwhile he ordered the 30th Corps to protect the left flank of the 13th Corps, under Lieutenant-General A. R. Godwin-Austen.

Neither Norrie nor Godwin-Austen liked this method of protecting Godwin-Austen's flank; but to put part of Norrie's armour temporarily under Godwin-Austen, or alternatively to leave the 13th Corps to fend for itself, seemed to Cunningham even more objectionable. Norrie felt, too, that a mere advance to Gabr Saleh might not be enough to stir the enemy to action, and that Cunningham was in danger of surrendering the initiative by not deciding at once in which direction the 13th Corps should move. But Cunningham was confident that he would lose nothing by waiting, especially as he proposed to go forward with Norrie and would be able to give his decision on the spot.

The 30th Corps duly crossed the frontier at dawn on November 18 and advanced to Gabr Saleh by the evening, meeting nothing more formidable on the way than two reconnaissance units but losing more than forty tanks through mechanical breakdowns. Meanwhile Rommel returned from Rome, came to the conclusion that reports of British movements pointed to a reconnaissance in force rather than a full-scale offensive, and made no change in his dispositions.

On reaching Gabr Saleh Cunningham was therefore still in the dark as to the enemy's intentions, and hence still unwilling to send the whole of the 30th Corps to Sidi Rezegh for fear that the German armour might fall on Godwin-Austen's flank. Accordingly the 4th Armoured Brigade Group, with more than a third of Norrie's armour, was held back next day to watch the gap between the 30th and 13th Corps. The advance was resumed by the 7th Armoured Division, consisting of the 7th and 22nd Armoured Brigades and a Support Group.

As it happened, the success achieved by all three armoured brigades in the next two days was in proportion to the boldness with which they were pushed forward. The 7th, moving on Sidi

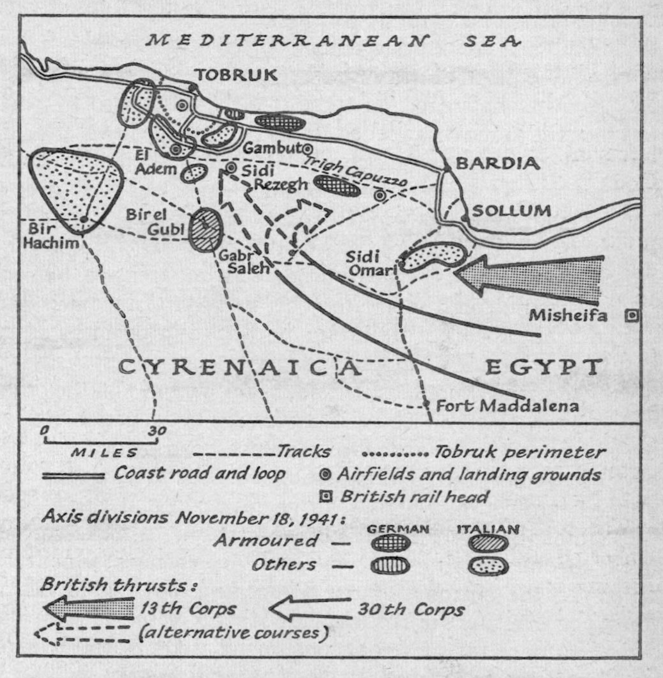

29 Operation 'Crusader', November 1941-January 1942

Rezegh, reached the neighbourhood without meeting any Germans, took the airfield by surprise, and captured 19 aircraft. The 22nd, with orders to reconnoitre towards El Gubi, paused to attack the Ariete Division in its prepared positions and lost 25 tanks. The 4th, confining itself to patrols round Gabr Saleh, was attacked at 4 p.m. on November 19 by a battle group from the German 21st Armoured Division, and twenty-four hours later by the whole of the 15th Armoured Division. Thus the broad effect of the moves made by both sides on November 19 and 20 was to split Norrie's armour into three widely separated formations, each with about 100 to 120 fit tanks at the end of the second day's fighting, while the German armoured divisions, with up to 240 tanks between them, tended to close up and concentrate on one objective at a time.

The subsequent course of events was shaped, however, not only by what happened on those two days, but also by what was thought to have happened. In its two engagements at Gabr Saleh the 4th Armoured Brigade Group lost about fifty tanks destroyed or damaged. Not knowing that it had well over a hundred left, the Germans regarded it after the second engagement as a spent force. When Rommel at last became convinced that the British had launched a major offensive, he concluded that he could safely turn his back on Gabr Saleh and continue the process of defeating the British in detail by sending both German armoured divisions north-westwards to destroy the 7th Armoured Brigade at Sidi Rezegh. On the other hand Cunningham and Norrie, reviewing the situation just as the 4th Armoured Brigade Group's second engagement was beginning, were so far from expecting a serious reverse that they ordered the Tobruk garrison to begin a sortie at dawn next day, although originally they had not meant to make such a move before bringing the whole of the enemy's armour to action. As the outcome of the engagement was not in fact a serious reverse for the British, they saw no reason later in the day to postpone the sortie or countermand arrangements to support it.

Consequently the struggle which began on November 21 at Sidi Rezegh and south of Tobruk turned out not to be the short, sharp bout between two German armoured divisions and a British armoured brigade which Rommel was expecting. Nor did it become the decisive encounter between the whole of the German armour and a superior British armoured force which Cunningham had hoped to bring about when he planned his offensive. On the contrary, it developed into one of the most extraordinarily complex battles ever fought. For three days infantry, tanks, guns and armoured cars coming south from Tobruk were opposed by the German and Italian forces watching the perimeter, which in turn were attacked not only from that direction but also on a front facing south by the British 7th Armoured Brigade and the Support Group, pressing northvards to support the break-out. The 7th Armoured Brigade ınd the Support Group were likewise in action on two fronts rom the moment when the German armoured divisions, vheeling northwards after completing their move from Gabr saleh, attacked them from the south and south-east. Chasing he German armour northwards, but too far behind to intervene effectively on the first day, came the 22nd Armoured Brigade ınd the 4th Armoured Brigade Group, followed by the rest of he 30th Corps, including the hitherto uncommitted 1st South African Division. To add to the confusion, there were times vhen parts of the battlefield, which extended over a depth of ıbout twenty miles from the Tobruk perimeter to the open lesert, were obscured by clouds of dust and smoke so dense that ınits under orders to join the fight had to hold back because it vas utterly impossible to see what was happening or distinguish friend from foe.

These conditions did not prevent the German armour from establishing a clear ascendancy over the more loosely handled British formations. At the end of the first day the 30th Corps was still in good shape, with its infantry intact and 209 fit tanks at its disposal; at the end of the second day the 7th Armoured Brigade had ten tanks left, the 22nd had thirty-four, and the 4th had been temporarily knocked out by a chance blow delivered by the German 15th Panzer Division at a moment when all three brigades had just withdrawn from an inconclusive engagement with the 21st. Conversely, the Germans still ıad 173 tanks fit for action at nightfall on November 22. They made such good use of them that in the course of the next lay the 15th Panzer Division, joined by the Ariete Division and the 21st Panzer Division's tank regiment, was able to smash through a position held by one brigade of the South African Division south of Benghazi, destroy a third of the 22nd Armoured Brigade's remaining tanks, and complete an enveloping movement by meeting the rest of the 21st Panzer Division coming south from the Trigh Capuzzo. In the light of this setback, which left Norrie far from ready to accept defeat but with ıis force much battered, Cunningham felt bound to suggest to Auchinleck that he might like to consider breaking off the

offensive while there was still some armour left for the defenc
of Egypt.

Meanwhile the British 13th Corps had succeeded not merely
in pinning down the enemy on the frontier but in getting be
hind him and advancing westwards along his supply routes. In
spite of his gains at Sidi Rezegh, Rommel was thus in dange
of losing the whole of his forward troops unless he could re
open their communications before their stocks ran out. More
over his path to Tobruk was still blocked, the 30th Corps wa
still in the fight, and the British were in a better position tha
the Germans or the Italians to bring up reinforcements and
re-equip their armoured formations from reserves. Concluding
that victory was still possible, Auchinleck responded to Cun
ningham's suggestion on November 23 by ordering him to
keep up relentless pressure even if it cost him his last tank
Two days later Auchinleck relieved Cunningham of his com
mand with the comment that he had done extremely well bu
was beginning to think defensively. Lieutenant-General N. M
Ritchie, hitherto Auchinleck's Deputy Chief of Staff, then
assumed command of the Eighth Army.

Rommel, too, was of the opinion that the battle was not ye
lost and won. From the moment when he was first persuaded
to take the British offensive seriously, he had recognized tha
the loss of his frontier positions might put his whole force in
jeopardy. Learning early on November 24 that the enemy had
suffered a staggering blow at Sidi Rezegh on the previous day
he decided that the time had come to relieve the pressure on
his forward troops by shifting his armour eastwards with th
object of encircling and destroying the British forces on and
near the frontier. His plan was that the 21st Panzer Division
should cross the frontier south of Sidi Omar, wheel through
180 degrees and attack westwards; that the 15th Panzer Divi
sion should straddle the frontier and attack from south to
north; and that the Italian mobile corps, which Mussolini had
agreed on November 23 to put at his disposal, should block th
enemy's escape to the west by moving to Fort Capuzzo.

For various reasons, none of these formations was able t

omplete its task. Of the two divisions of the Italian corps, one
eems never to have received the order to move eastwards,
vhile the other made such a slow start that early on November
5 Rommel decided to recast his plan on the assumption that
e would have to do without it. He then ordered the 15th
'anzer Division to abandon its projected advance from south
o north and attack eastwards between Sidi Omar and Sidi
zeiz; but the division was so short of supplies that, instead
f attacking, it was obliged to make for Bardia in search of
mmunition, fuel and water. On the other hand the 21st
'anzer Division succeeded in crossing the frontier south of
idi Omar. But it did so without its tank regiment, which had
een lent to the 15th Panzer Division on November 23. As a
esult the tank regiment started too late to go forward with
he rest of the division, and it was twice driven back by artillery
re when it tried to follow. Giving up the idea of attacking
vestwards, the German divisional commander then held to the
orth and finished up at Bardia after breaking through a lightly-
eld position between Fort Capuzzo and Sollum. Meanwhile
he British forces south of Tobruk were making such good
rogress that on November 27 and 28 Rommel was forced to
ring back his armour in order to prevent them from seizing
he whole of the area for which both sides had fought so
tubbornly a few days earlier.

The eastward dash of Rommel's armour was thus an ex-
ensive failure. It caused some alarm in the British rear, but
lid nothing to ease the lot of the Axis troops in the forward
rea, and indeed reduced their chances of survival by robbing
them of fuel and ammunition. After losing a third of their
anks to no purpose the Panzer divisions found, too, that the
British had profited by Rommel's absence to tighten their grip
on Tobruk, reorganize their forces, and give their armour a
new lease of life.* In the next few days the Germans succeeded

*The German Panzer divisions returned with 74 tanks between
hem. On November 27 the British 4th and 22nd Armoured Brigades
ad 122, drawn partly from the 7th Armoured Brigade, which had
eturned to Egypt to refit.

in winning back much of the ground lost since their departure but only at the cost of still further depleting their resources a a moment when the British were preparing to resume th offensive with renewed vigour.* The outlook, Rommel tol Bastico after learning on December 4 that he could expect littl help from home before the end of the month, was so unpromis ing that he might have to give up the whole of Cyrenaica. Afte a stormy discussion he agreed that Cyrenaica should b abandoned only as a last resort and that a stand should b made at Gazala, but warned the Italians not to expect to much.

On December 15 the 13th Corps, reinforced at Norrie's ex pense, attacked at Gazala with the intention of pinning th enemy to his prepared positions, cutting the coast road in hi rear, and making a wide sweep round his flank. Rommel, wit the surviving elements of nine German and Italian division in hand or already sent to the rear, took prompt steps to sav his force, and succeeded in doing so partly because Godwin Austen's Stuart tanks, with their limited range, were unabl to complete their turning movement in time to prevent hin from pulling out. But he was powerless to rescue the 15,00 Axis troops at Bardia and further forward, the last of whon surrendered a month later. Meanwhile he continued to with draw his main force in good order, paused at the end o December to make a vigorous stand at Agedabia, and early i the New Year was back in the position near El Agheila fron which he had leapt forward ten months earlier. Thus the out come of Auchinleck's decision not to break off his offensive o November 23 was that within two months the Axis forces wer driven from the whole of Cyrenaica with the loss of roughl a third of their strength.

*The 1st Armoured Division, bringing the 2nd Armoured Brigad with 166 new tanks, had arrived from England in the second half o November, and was due to relieve the 7th Armoured Division a soon as the 2nd Armoured Brigade completed its desert training Meanwhile its divisional artillery and other troops would be availabl as reinforcements for the Eighth Army. In addition substantial rein forcements were about to come forward from Egypt, Cyprus, Palestin and Syria.

TABLE 6

BRITISH AND AXIS CASUALTIES IN OPERATION 'CRUSADER,' NOVEMBER 1941-JANUARY 1942

(In round figures)

	Total force	*Killed*	*Wounded*	*Missing*	*Total Casualties*
British	118,000	2,900	7,300	7,500	17,700
German	65,000	1,100	3,400	10,100	14,600
Italian	54,000	1,200	2,700	19,800	23,700
Axis totals	119,000	2,300	6,100	29,900	38,300

Even so, the Eighth Army's failure to destroy the Axis armies was a setback for the British. Auchinleck knew that his hold on Western Cyrenaica would be insecure until Rommel was driven so far back that the counter-stroke which had robbed Wavell of the fruits of victory in 1941 could not be repeated. He was therefore anxious that Ritchie should push on without delay. It soon became clear, however, that further progress was out of the question until Benghazi could be put into full working order as a supply base, that this would take some weeks, and that meanwhile not more than one and a half to two divisions could be maintained in the forward area. Such a force might find itself in trouble if Rommel counter-attacked before the end of February; but to give up hundreds of square miles of conquered territory, even as a temporary expedient, was not an acceptable alternative. At the time the risk appeared to Auchinleck and Ritchie very slight, for the Axis forces were believed to have been so severely punished that Rommel seemed unlikely to be able to take the offensive for some time to come.

But in war the unexpected nearly always happens. A month before Rommel's retreating armies reached El Agheila, the Japanese had landed in Malaya and shattered the American Pacific Fleet at Pearl Harbor. These events did not directly affect the situation in Cyrenaica; but consequent diversions of land and air forces to the Far East sharpened Auchinleck's anxieties for his northern front, and demands on British naval resources made it impossible for the government to do much to remedy a state of affairs in the Central and Eastern Mediterranean which had suddenly become unfavourable. On December 19 the battleships *Queen Elizabeth* and *Valiant*, lying at Alexandria, were holed by explosive charges clamped to their hulls by Italian under-water swimmers; on the same day the small but important surface force based at Malta since October ran into a newly-laid Italian minefield and was crippled. These reverses, coming on top of the sinking of the carrier *Ark Royal* and the battleship *Barham* by German submarines in November, and almost coinciding with the return of a powerful Luftwaffe detachment to Sicily, tipped the scales so markedly against the British that by the end of the year Axis convoys were running to Tripolitania with little risk of loss.

On January 5 a convoy reached Tripoli carrying 54 German tanks, their crews, a supply of fuel, and other much-needed equipment and stores. This modest access of strength encouraged Rommel's staff to press for a spoiling attack which might help to make the Axis position less vulnerable. Rommel agreed that there was something to be said for attacking the British before they could concentrate their forces for the coming offensive. On January 18, with 84 German and 89 Italian tanks at his disposal and ten weak divisions under command,* he gave preliminary orders for an advance towards Agedabia and through the difficult country stretching inland from the coast to the Wadi Faregh and beyond.

On that date the Eighth Army had practically nothing within

*These were the 15th and 21st Armoured Divisions and the 90th Light Division, forming the Africa Corps; the Ariete and Trieste Divisions, forming the 20th Corps; and the Bologna, Brescia, Pavia Sabratha and Trento Divisions, of which the first two formed the 10th Corps and the others the 21st Corps. All were so much reduced in manpower that their combined strength did not exceed that of three full-scale British infantry divisions. The new organization became effective on January 22, when Rommel's command was renamed *Panzeramee Afrika*.

a hundred miles of the enemy except one infantry brigade group and the incomplete 1st Armoured Division, consisting of the 2nd Armoured Brigade and the 1st Support Group. The 2nd Armoured Brigade, with about 130 cruiser and light tanks, was at Antelat, roughly seventy miles from the front.* The infantry brigade group and the 1st Support Group, the latter with 24 light tanks in addition to the usual complement of motorized infantry and supporting arms, were well forward, and had been given the task of keeping the enemy under constant threat of attack by harassing his outposts. If attacked in strength, they were to fall back to a line through Agedabia and El Haseiat, where a stand would be made should the unexpected happen. Foreseeing that it might not be easy to man a defensive line in such conditions, the commander of the 1st Armoured Division, Major-General F. W. Messervy, had suggested that an infantry division should come forward to Agedabia and that he should move his armoured brigade closer to El Haseiat, but the proposal had been turned down because of the difficulty of keeping the additional troops supplied.

Rommel began his advance on January 21, with strong air support and after a day or two of sandstorms which hampered observation from the air. The British forward troops fell back more or less as planned, but next day a mixed group of German lorried infantry and German and Italian artillery slipped past their flank at a moment when General Messervy was preoccupied with a supposed threat to his centre. Reaching Agedabia before midday, they effectively turned the Agedabia-El Haseiat position while the British were still wondering how to hold it. Seeing a chance of drawing a net round the enemy and forcing him away from his lines of communication, Rommel then ordered his troops to push on towards Antelat and spread out widely. After a series of confused actions which cost both sides fairly heavy losses but were particularly expensive for the British, most of the 1st Armoured Division and the infantry brigade group succeeded in uniting their forces and retreating to Charruba, where they

*The territory in which the events described in the next few paragraphs took place is shown in Maps 18 and 20.

arrived late on January 25 with about forty tanks still fit to fight.

Meanwhile General Godwin-Austen, whose corps was responsible for the whole of the threatened area, was weighing the chances of stopping the enemy before he reached Benghazi and Msus. They seemed to him so uncertain that on January 24 he asked for discretion to order a general withdrawal towards Mechili. General Ritchie granted it and sanctioned preliminary steps, but insisted that Msus should be defended and Benghazi covered. After conferring with Auchinleck and Tedder on the following day he cancelled the withdrawal of an infantry division from Benghazi, ordered Godwin-Austen to use it in an offensive role, and countered an appeal to Auchinleck by taking it under his own command. He also ruled that the 1st Armoured Division, instead of retreating to Mechili, should defend Charruba and protect the infantry division's flank.

Ritchie's confidence was based on a feeling that the enemy was exploiting an unexpected success and must be in danger of outrunning his supplies. After chasing the 1st Armoured Division northwards Rommel did, in fact, halt his armour at Msus on January 25 because he was short of fuel; but he was soon on the move again after pausing to replenish his stocks and weigh up the situation. On January 26 he decided to make a feint towards Mechili, send a small force from Msus towards and north of Benghazi by a difficult cross-country route, and bring up the 90th Light Division and the 20th Corps on the left.

On January 27 unfavourable conditions for Tedder's aircraft helped to conceal the preliminary stages of these movements; but the feint towards Mechili was seen, and by the evening Ritchie knew that the enemy was thrusting both in that direction and towards Benghazi. Still full of confidence, he ordered the 13th Corps to counter both moves, adding that the enemy was weaker than the British in both areas and that probably the thrust towards Mechili was his main effort; but next day the news that German and Italian mobile formations were approaching Benghazi convinced him at last that he must pull out without delay. About 4,000 of his troops who remained in the town after the demolitions were blown were cut off by Rommel's encircling movement to the north, but managed to escape that night by marching through the enemy's back areas. By the end of the first week in February the Eighth Army, its bluff called, had retreated to a line from Gazala to Bir Hacheim. Thus the British lost the airfields of Western Cyrenaica, without which they could hardly hope to regain control of the Sicilian Channel or carry supplies to Malta.

CHAPTER 12

THE FAR EAST

December 1935 - May 1942

At the London Naval Conference towards the end of 1935 the Italians, already inclined to resent the attitude of the democracies towards their projected conquest of Abyssinia, refused to take an active part in the proceedings. When Japan withdrew from the conference Britain, France and the United States were left, therefore, to conclude a treaty which would become significant only if the Japanese, and perhaps also the Italians, could be induced to sign it later.[1] But the chances of world-wide agreement began to seem remote when trouble in Abyssinia, the Rhineland, Spain and Central Europe was accompanied by signs of growing accord between Rome, Berlin and Tokyo and by fresh disturbances in China.

On July 7, 1937, Japanese troops stationed near Peking with the consent of the Chinese government clashed with Chinese forces near the Marco Polo bridge.[2] For a time both sides seemed willing to adjust the quarrel, but further incidents followed, and the gap grew wider. Thereafter Japan refused to attend a conference of signatories to the Nine-Power Treaty and other nations with Far Eastern interests; General Chiang Kai-shek made peace with his Communist opponents in face of a new threat to his authority; and soon Japan and China were fighting with a startling disregard on the part of the Japanese for the interests of non-combatants. In August the British Ambassador in China was seriously wounded when his car was attacked by Japanese aircraft; in December the United States gunboat *Panay* was sunk in the Yangtze River and

British gunboats were fired upon by Japanese shore-batteries while rescuing survivors.

As in 1932, an Anglo-American embargo on trade with Japan was suggested as a means of halting aggression; but this time it was the British Foreign Office which pressed for action and the American State Department, abetted by the British Prime Minister, which held back.* President Roosevelt then proposed that he should summon all foreign plenipotentiaries in Washington to a meeting and, through them, advise the nations to reduce their armaments and abide by international conventions in return for the prospect of equal access to raw materials for all. Although welcomed by some members of the British government as a sign that Roosevelt was determined to do everything he could to avert a general war, this offer was greeted with a marked lack of enthusiasm by Neville Chamberlain, who feared that the President's message might cut across his own attempts to reach agreement with Germany and Italy. Chamberlain agreed that *effective* intervention by the United States would be extremely valuable, but believed that in practice the American tradition of noninvolvement would prevent Roosevelt from going beyond vague threats which might do more harm than good.

Apparently concluding that there was no immediate prospect of whole-hearted co-operation with the British and that he must think first of defending the Western Hemisphere, the President abandoned his project, went on to sanction the largest programme of naval construction permitted by treaty, and in effect fell back on a policy of avoiding a head-on collision with Japan until he was ready for it. From the point of view of the European democracies, a great disadvantage of this policy was that legislation intended by Congress to prevent the United States from sliding insensibly into war, as had happened in 1917, threatened to make the purchase of American war material as difficult for France and Britain as for Germany, Japan and Italy.

Meanwhile the Japanese, not very effectively opposed by Chiang Kai-shek's well-subsidized armies, continued to make

*The Earl of Avon, *Facing the Dictators* (London, 1962), pp. 531-45.

rapid progress. In the early summer of 1938 they put a substantial force ashore at Amoy, more than a thousand miles south of their starting-point at Peking, and in October landed troops still further south in Bias Bay. As a result Hong Kong, whose population included nearly a million British subjects of Chinese origin, became cut off from all that was left of Nationalist China after the Japanese had overrun a great part of the northern provinces and had seized a strip of territory running down the coast past Amoy and Canton. An attempt by the invaders to push northwards and eastwards into Mongolia was, however, checked by Soviet troops which were strongly reinforced as the threat to Soviet interests became apparent.[3] In the autumn of 1939 the Russians at last succeeded, after many months of inconclusive fighting, in winning at Halkin Gol a victory which brought an uneasy peace, but which left both sides reluctant to remove troops even when they were urgently needed elsewhere.*

For some time after the outbreak of war in Europe the Far Eastern policy of both Britain and the United States was still to do as much as they could for Chiang Kai-shek without precipitating a war with Japan for which neither of them was likely to be ready much before the spring of 1942.[4] The British also aimed at preventing Japan from sending war material to Germany, and at keeping Malayan industry in a flourishing state as an indispensable source of rubber, tin and dollars.†

British and American views of Far Eastern strategy, however, were not identical. The British believed that, if the Japanese did decide to risk war with the British Empire and the

*For the site of this battle see Map 65.

†Malaya, about the size of England and Wales and inhabited by roughly two million Malays, two million Chinese, small numbers of Indians and Japanese and some 18,000 Europeans, of whom four fifths were British, produced nearly two-fifths of the world's rubber and more than half the world's tin. In 1940 and 1941 between two thirds and three-quarters of all Malayan exports went to the United States and Canada. Without the dollars thus earned, the British could not have paid for American goods ordered before Lend-Lease took effect.

United States, they would try to overrun South-East Asia and Indonesia, that they would be unable to do so without capturing a base on the east coast of the Kra Isthmus or the Malay peninsula, and that therefore the best defence was to station at Singapore a fleet strong enough to dominate the Gulf of Siam and the South China Sea. The Americans were more concerned with the threat to the Philippines than with that to Malaya or the Netherlands East Indies, and they were unwilling, on political as well as strategic grounds, to send their powerful Pacific Fleet to Singapore. In the spring of 1940 they decided that the fleet, hitherto on the West Coast of the United States, should stay at Pearl Harbor on the conclusion of an exercise held in May.[5]* The move was intended chiefly as a warning to Japan, but it had the practical advantage of putting the fleet in a rather better position to intercept the Japanese Navy in the neighbourhood of the Philippine Sea if American possessions should be directly threatened. In the opinion of the British, on the other hand, the fleet was still too far from the probable scene of action to be able to intervene effectively. Apart from Pearl Harbor the Americans had an advanced base in Manila Bay, where their small Asiatic Fleet was stationed; but it had not been developed as a base for the main fleet and was within easy reach of Japanese air bases in Formosa. The United States government hoped, however, that by the spring of 1942, or perhaps earlier, they would be able to station enough heavy bombers in the Philippines to make the Japanese think twice before attacking them.

Within the next few weeks the fall of France and Italy's entry into the war made it impossible for the British to contemplate sending a strong fleet of their own to Singapore in the near future. The Americans, who had received discouraging reports from their Ambassador in London, Mr. Joseph Kennedy, were not prepared to reverse their decision to keep their main fleet at Pearl Harbor, and indeed were not yet ready to give Britain the full support in her struggle with Germany and Italy which they gave later. After consulting the United

*See Chapter 8.

States government the British decided that, as a gesture of appeasement which might help to give themselves and the Americans a respite in the Far East and the Pacific, the so-called Burma Road should be closed to supplies for the Chinese Nationalist forces for three months during the coming monsoon season, when the weather would in any case reduce traffic to a minimum.[6]

The next few months brought a striking improvement in Britain's prospects of survival; but they also brought developments which made it seem more likely than ever that Japan might strike in the near future at territories teeming with the raw materials she needed. Soon after the fall of France the Japanese asked the Governor-General of French Indo-China for permission to station troops in the country and for access to air bases.[7] In September the Vichy government gave way to the extent of allowing access to the northern provinces, and almost simultaneously Japan pledged herself, under a Tripartite Pact with Germany and Italy, to give Germany full military support if the United States entered the war against the European Axis.[8] On the other hand, the British victory over the Luftwaffe in August and September helped to strengthen President Roosevelt's conviction that, nothwithstanding the adverse comments of his Ambassador, Britain was still worth backing. Besides responding to the Japanese move in Indo-China by giving Chiang Kai-shek credits to the value of another hundred million dollars, promising him a supply of modern fighter aircraft, arranging to issue passports to American citizens willing to serve in China as pilots or instructors and putting a virtual embargo on the export of scrap iron and steel to Japan, the United States government thereupon pushed through the Lend-Lease Bill and sanctioned staff talks with the British.[9]

These talks, followed by further conversations at the Atlantic Meeting between Roosevelt and Churchill in August 1941 showed that there was full agreement between the Americans and the British as to the importance of defeating Germany first in the event of simultaneous war with the European Axis and Japan; but they also showed that the Americans had very little armed strength at their disposal apart from the Pacific and Asiatic Fleets, were not prepared to share control of any part of it with a foreign government or to adopt any course which might appear to commit the country to the support of British imperialism, and were still unwilling to send their main fleet to a British base. American, British and Dutch commanders and staff officers in the Far East recommended in April 1941 that, if the possessions or interests of any of the three countries were attacked, the United States Pacific and Asiatic Fleets should attack Japanese communications, and that the Asiatic Fleet should use Hong Kong as an advanced base and should move if necessary to Singapore. But these recommendations were not endorsed by the United States government, and the British Chiefs of Staff were against using Hong Kong as an advanced base because they could not promise that Hong Kong would be held.[10]

In the same month the Japanese decided that they must prepare for war, but would resort to arms against the Americans, the British and the Dutch only if Japan's existence were threatened by embargoes or encirclement.[11] On May 12 they asked that normal commercial relations with the United States should be resumed, and that the Americans should put pressure on Chiang Kai-shek to make peace with them and should help them to gain access by way of trade to the oil, nickel, tin and rubber of the South-West Pacific.[12] On the other hand, they did not break off attempts which they had begun in January to persuade the Vichy French to allow their armed forces into the southern provinces of Indo-China.

Accepting these proposals as a basis for negotiations, the Americans made a counter-offer on June 21. On the previous day, however, they banned the export of oil from their eastern seaboard, except to the British Empire and the Western Hemisphere; and on June 22 Germany contravened the spirit of the Tripartite Pact by invading Russia, thus presenting the Japanese with a pretext to escape their obligations under the pact if they felt inclined to do so.

These events threw the Japanese into a state of some perplexity.[13] They still wished to avoid war with the West. With the notable exception of the Foreign Minister, Yosuke Matsuoka, their leading statesmen had no desire to fight the Russians, with whom they had recently concluded a Neutrality Pact after many months of strained relations. Against these considerations they had to balance the real or fancied risk that any sign of weakness on their part might encourage the Americans to exert economic pressure which, unless offset by increased supplies from territories controlled by the British and the Dutch, would confront them with the choice between war and abject surrender to any demands that might be made on them. After prolonged debate they decided, therefore, to compromise between Matsuoka's policy of whole-hearted collaboration with Germany, and the inclination of most of Matsuoka's colleagues to avoid war with Russia but to maintain a firm grip on Indo-China as an insurance against the breakdown of negotiations with the Americans. The government's reluctance to go the whole way with Matsuoka was reinforced by the growing conviction of the Prime Minister, Prince Konoye, that his country's only hope of an honourable solution lay in making peace with China and the West on almost any terms which did not sacrifice everything won since 1937.

Accordingly the Japanese reinforced their troops in Manchuria, maintained their pressure on the Vichy French, and continued their efforts to end the war in China and come to terms with the United States. But these decisions were not much more than a fortnight old when a reconstruction of the Cabinet eliminated Matsuoka and left Konoye more than ever determined to impose a peaceful solution on his colleagues if he could retain his leadership and if the Americans were willing to come to terms with him.

In the meantime American cryptographers had broken the Japanese diplomatic cipher.[14] Besides intercepting a great deal of traffic not intended for their eyes, officials of the State Department were therefore able, on some occasions, to read communications from the Japanese government before the Embassy in Washington had time to deliver them.

Not surprisingly, the Japanese found Vichy more amenable

than Washington. On July 21 the French government gave way, and by the end of the month Japanese troops were in Saigon and had gained control of the important naval base at Camranh Bay. The Americans, who had told the British on July 10 that they would impose financial and economic embargoes if Japan went ahead in Indo-China, at once froze all Japanese assets in the United States, thus bringing trade with Japan to a standstill except by special licence.

This move was regarded with mixed feelings by the British and the Dutch, who feared that the effect might be to hasten preparations by the Japanese to invade Malaya and the Netherlands East Indies in search of raw materials more urgently needed than ever; but they followed suit because they could not hope to defend their possessions except in partnership with the United States.[15] For the Dutch there was the added complication that their trade with Japan was conducted entirely in dollars.

Thus Japan was placed in the position most dreaded by those of her statesmen who wished to avoid war with the West. Not only three-quarters of her foreign trade but nine-tenths of her entire supply of oil were cut off, with the result that she was obliged to start drawing on reserves. Extremists were soon urging the government to make war while they still had the means of doing so. Forced by pressure from his colleagues to draft his formal proposals to Washington in terms not likely to be accepted, Prince Konoye decided to make a supreme bid for peace by asking President Roosevelt to meet him at some convenient point in the Pacific.[16] According to the account which he afterwards gave, his plan was to make the best bargain he could with Roosevelt, and then persuade the Emperor to accept it before extremists bent on war could intervene.

Meanwhile the President had left Washington for the Atlantic Meeting at Placentia in Newfoundland. There Churchill invited him to try the experiment of warning the Japanese in unmistakable terms that any further encroachment in South-East Asia might lead to war between Japan and the United States.[17] With some reluctance, he agreed to do so on the understanding that precisely similar warnings would be given simultaneously by the British and the Dutch. On returning to Washington he was, however, persuaded by Mr. Cordell Hull, the Secretary of State, to change his mind. A warning of sorts was handed on August 17 to Admiral Kichisaburo Nomura, the Japanese Ambassador in Washington; but it differed markedly from the text discussed at Placentia, and it did not mention war.

There remained Konoye's proposal that he and the President should meet. At first attracted by the idea, Roosevelt tentatively suggested a rendezvous at Juneau in Alaska; but this project, too, was vetoed by Cordell Hull, who persuaded the President that a meeting would be harmful unless it were preceded by an agreement reached through diplomatic channels.[18] The result was a rebuff for Konoye, which contributed to his fall and replacement in October by General Hideki Tojo. On becoming Prime Minister Tojo retained his existing post as Minister of War, and also assumed responsibility for Home Affairs.

Although reckoned a militarist, Tojo had no mandate to break off negotiations with the West. Early in November the civil government and the military authorities agreed that one more attempt should be made to persuade the United States to accept a permanent settlement on terms which would give Japan a commanding position in China and undisputed access to the raw materials she needed. If the attempt failed, then an interim agreement on terms more likely to appeal to the Americans would be proposed. But the authorities also agreed that negotiations must not be allowed to drag on while stocks of oil dwindled. Preparations for war would be completed by the beginning of December, and hostilities would follow on a date to be decided by the Chiefs of Staff if agreement were not reached by the last week in November.

While this policy was being hammered out in Tokyo, the United States government was warned by its Ambassador that economic sanctions seemed to be pushing Japan towards war.[1] Almost simultaneously its military advisers recorded the opinion that the Pacific Fleet was not strong enough for a major offensive and would become so only if all units were withdrawn from the Atlantic, but added that American naval and air forces in the Philippines were expected to attain within the next few months a strength which might enable them to present a substantial threat to Japanese interests and especially to Formosa.* Even a brief respite would tend, therefore, to put the United States in a stronger position to make war or negotiate a final settlement.

From this point the position reached about the end of the third week in November was that both the United States and Japan were prepared to consider an interim agreement; that a special envoy, M. Saburo Kurusu, had joined Admiral Nomura in Washington; and that the State Department knew, from intercepted messages, that the Japanese government had set a time-limit for the negotiations.[20] In essence, the terms to which the Japanese were willing to agree were that they should be relieved of economic pressure and should have a free hand to make peace with China; that both sides should abstain from movements of armed forces in South-East Asia and the South Pacific outside Indo-China; and that the Japanese forces in Indo-China should withdraw from south to north on the signing of the interim agreement, and from the whole country on the conclusion of peace with China or an equitable settlement in the Pacific area. Counter-proposals drafted by the State Department were broadly similar, except that the Americans wished the Japanese to bind themselves to cross no international frontier unless attacked and to reduce their total forces in Indo-China to 25,000 men. The State Department also had in mind provisos intended to prevent the Japanese from interpreting the lifting of economic restrictions as a licence to pile up war materials or flood the American market with unwanted goods.†

On November 22 the Japanese proposals and a draft of the American reply were shown to Australian, British, Chinese and Dutch diplomatic representatives in Washington, whose re-

*Memorandum circulated by Joint Board, November 5, 1941. The Joint Board were the precursors of the Joint Chiefs of Staff.
†The Japanese and American proposals are summarized in Appendix V.

sponse to the American draft was afterwards described by the Secretary of State as generally favourable. In the course of the next two days the State Department learned that the American proposals were acceptable to the Dutch, that the Australian, Chinese and United Kingdom representatives were still awaiting definite instructions, and that a favourable response from the Chinese was highly improbable. However, on November 25, or at any rate by the early hours of November 26, it became clear that the Chinese disliked the proposals but that the British, although reluctant to see Japan appeased at the expense of China, were anxious to avoid war and were willing to give the President and the State Department a free hand.

At that stage events took an unexpected turn. On November 26 Hull told the President that the Australians, the British, the Chinese and the Dutch were all either actively opposed to the American proposals or lukewarm about them, and that in his opinion the time had come to drop all proposals for an interim agreement. On the same day Nomura and Kurusu were handed proposals for a final settlement on terms which included the withdrawal of all Japanese forces from the whole of China and Indo-China.

The Japanese could hardly be expected to accept such an ultimatum. At a series of meetings between November 27 and 29 they decided that Japan had no choice but to fight, and on December 1 the Emperor ratified the government's decision at a formal conference. Nomura and Kurusu stayed in Washington. On December 7 they received the last instalment of a long message breaking off negotiations, but were unable to deliver it until after hostilities had begun.

Thus the United States exchanged the status of a country which had declared an 'unlimited national emergency', but was not at war, for that of an active belligerent. On December 11, after Japan had received formal declarations of war from the Americans and the British, Germany and Italy declared war on the United States.

In December 1941 Japan had an army of 51 divisions, an army

air force about 1,500 aircraft strong, and a navy roughly equivalent to the combined American, British and Dutch fleets in the Far East and the Pacific, except that the Japanese had more aircraft carriers and more carrier-borne aircraft. Twenty-one divisions of the Japanese Army were in China and thirteen were watching the Russians on the Manchurian Front. These preoccupations and the needs of home defence left as the only land-based forces immediately available for operations in

TABLE 7

JAPANESE, BRITISH, DUTCH AND UNITED STATES NAVAL FORCES IN PACIFIC AND FAR EASTERN WATERS, DECEMBER 1941[22]

	Capital Ships	*Aircraft Carriers*	*Cruisers*	*Destroyers*	*Submarines*
Japanese	10	10	36	113	63
British (including Dominions and Free French)					
Singapore	2	—	3	8	—
Hong Kong	—	—	—	3	—
Australia	—	—	4	2	—
New Zealand	—	—	2	—	—
Dutch					
Java	—	—	3	7	13
United States					
West Coast	1	1	—	67 (West Coast and Pearl Harbor)	—
Pearl Harbor	8	2	21		27
Manila and Balikpapan	—	—	3	13	29
Allied totals	11	3	36	100	69

NOTES. Of the ten Japanese aircraft carriers, six were fleet carriers and four light fleet carriers. In addition the Japanese had six seaplane carriers. The Japanese naval air force numbered rather more than 1,000 aircraft, about half of them carrier-borne.

South-East Asia and the South-West Pacific eleven divisions of well-trained troops, about 700 aircraft of the army air force, and some 450 aircraft belonging to the navy but not embarked.[21]

The Japanese could not hope to defeat the United States and the British Empire with such forces, and they had no thought of doing so. They aimed merely at taking advantage of the war in Europe and the Middle East to seize an expanse of land and sea which would make them economically self-sufficient and give them so strong a defensive perimeter that their opponents would concede their claim to a generous share of the world's sources of raw materials rather than go to the trouble of dislodging them.

To attain even this comparatively modest aim with so few troops would however, be impossible unless the same formations could be used at different places in succession. Accordingly, the Japanese planned their advance in four phases.[23] In the first phase, six of the ten divisions immediately available after one had been set aside as a reserve for the second phase would move into Malaya, Siam and South Burma; one reinforced division would deal with Hong Kong; some two-and-a-half divisions would overrun the Philippines: and a small force under naval control would seize the American staging-posts at Guam and Wake. Thereafter much the same forces, supplemented by additional troops as occasion served, would complete the conquest of the British and Dutch possessions in South-East Asia and Indonesia and the establishment of the prescribed perimeter. At the end of the fourth phase, which the Japanese High Command expected to reach after a campaign of not less than three to four months, the line to be held would run from the Kurile Islands through Wake and the Marshall and Gilbert Islands to the Bismarck Archipelago, thence by way of Timor, Java and Sumatra to the Nicobar and Andaman Islands, and along the Indian frontier to the Naga Hills.*

*See Map B.

TABLE 8

OUTLINE OF JAPANESE PLAN OF CONQUEST, 1941-42[24]

PHASE ONE

A Four divisions of Twenty-fifth Army from South China and Indo-China to advance on Singapore after initial landings astride frontier between Siam and Malaya.
B Two divisions of Fifteenth Army from Indo-China to occupy Siam and advance into Southern Burma.
C One reinforced division of Twenty-third Army from South China to take Hong Kong.
D Two-and-a-half divisions of Fourteenth Army from Formosa and Palau to take Philippines.
E Small force under naval control to take Guam, Wake and Makin Islands.
F About 350 naval aircraft in four fleet carriers and two light fleet carriers, with destroyer flotilla, to attack Pearl Harbor and Oahu. Escort and support by two fast battleships, two cruisers, eight tankers and advanced warning force of submarines.
G Army air force to support (A) to (D) with two air divisions about 700 aircraft strong.
H Navy, besides undertaking (E) and (F), to support (A) to (D) with two battleships, two light fleet carriers, eighteen cruisers, fifty-two destroyers, about sixteen submarines, about 100 carrier-based aircraft and about 450 land-based aircraft.

PHASE TWO

A Sixteenth Army, formed from elements of Fourteenth and Twenty-third Armies with one division from reserve, to advance from Philippines towards Southern Sumatra, seizing objectives in Borneo, Celebes, Amboina and Timor.
B Small force under naval control, having completed capture

of Phase One objectives, to prolong eastern perimeter to Bismarck Archipelago and New Guinea.

PHASE THREE

Twenty-fifth Army and Sixteenth Army to converge on Java and Sumatra.

PHASE FOUR

A Reinforced Fifteenth Army to complete conquest of Burma.
B Other forces to complete western perimeter by taking Andaman and Nicobar Islands.

To achieve all this would, however, be impossible without a degree of naval superiority which the Japanese did not possess, and which they could not count on winning if they risked a major fleet action between approximately equal forces. Such local superiority as they could assert in the South China Sea would soon disappear if the Americans moved strong forces to Singapore or Manila; while even at Pearl Harbor the United States Pacific Fleet would present at least a potential threat to Japanese communications. All the plans of the High Command would therefore be in vain unless American naval power could be crippled by a bold and unorthodox stroke delivered at the outset of the war.

In the light of the British success against the Italians at Taranto in November 1940, the Japanese Naval Staff came to the conclusion that they might be able to deliver such a stroke by using carrier-borne aircraft. A plan of attack was tried out at war games in Tokyo in September and approved on November 5.[25] Accordingly, in the third week of November four fleet carriers and two light fleet carriers, accompanied by a destroyer flotilla and supported by two fast battleships, two cruisers, eight tankers and an advanced warning force of submarines, left the Kurile Islands on a course which would take them by unfrequented routes to a point between two hundred and three hundred miles north of Pearl Harbor. Arrangements were made to recall the force if it were detected or if the negotiations in Washington took a favourable turn.

In the last few weeks of peace the American authorities intercepted a number of messages which hinted that war was imminent, but none of them pointed unmistakably to Pearl Harbor. On November 27, twenty-four hours after Cordell Hull's refusal to consider an interim agreement, the United States Navy Department warned the Commanders-in-Chief of the Atlantic, Pacific and Asiatic Fleets that an aggressive move by Japan, which the department thought might be directed against the Philippines, Siam or Borneo, was likely within the next few days. Admiral Thomas C. Hart, commanding the Asiatic Fleet at Manila, thereupon took the precaution of moving some of his ships to Balikpapan, in Borneo; he also made tentative arrangements to send them to Singapore on the outbreak of war and to co-operate with the British and the Dutch in attempts to challenge Japanese control of the South China Sea, prevent a break-out to the west and south, and protect traffic in the Indian Ocean and the Java Sea. Similarly Admiral Husband Kimmel, commanding the Pacific Fleet at Pearl Harbor, prepared to take the offensive against Japanese communications; but he made few defensive preparations apart from routine precautions. He had no special reason to suppose that his base was threatened, he did not believe that the Japanese would use air-launched torpedoes in shallow waters, and he was under the impression that the shore-based defences of Oahu, which included a radar watch not under his control, were fully manned.

The time by Hawaiian clocks was roughly 6 a.m. on Sunday, December 7, when the Japanese striking force under Vice-Admiral Chuichi Nagumo reached its flying-off position about 275 miles from Admiral Kimmel's base. In Washington, where Admiral Nomura and M. Kurusu had orders to break off negotiations with the United States before Nagumo's aircraft could bomb Pearl Harbor but were destined not to reach the State Department until too late, the middle of the forenoon had arrived. In England it was tea-time. In Malaya an anxious Sunday was drawing to a close, a new day was approaching, and before the first bomb fell at Pearl Harbor Japanese troops would have begun to step ashore at Kota Bahru.

As soon as the carriers were in position Admiral Nagumo despatched a first wave of forty torpedo-bombers, fifty high-level bombers and roughly the same number of dive-bombers, with an escort of some fifty fighters.[26] These were followed by a second wave of thirty high-level bombers and eighty dive-bombers, also escorted by fighters. Flying above a layer of cloud at 9,000 feet, the first wave reached Oahu without opposition a little before 8 a.m. Officially the radar watch on shore had closed down at 7 a.m., and two operators who had stayed on against orders were not believed when they reported a few minutes later that they had detected a large number of aircraft at a range of 132 miles. A dozen American bombers on a delivery flight were expected at Oahu, and the inexperienced officer to whom the report was passed assumed that these were the aircraft which had been detected.

At Pearl Harbor eight battleships, in addition to many lesser craft, were in positions accurately charted by Japanese infor mants. More than a third of the officers serving with the fleet were on shore leave, aboard the warships ratings were returning cleaning-gear or awaiting the hoisting of the colours, and only one anti-aircraft gun in four was manned. There were no naval anti-aircraft batteries ashore; at the military airfields on Oahu aircraft were parked wing-tip to wing-tip as a precaution against sabotage; and pilots of shore-based aircraft were at four hours' notice. In an hour and a half the Japanese destroyed four battleships, crippled two, sank half a dozen cruisers and destroyers, destroyed or damaged well over two hundred air craft, and killed or wounded 3,581 soldiers, sailors, airmen and civilians. After a delay of about half an hour the defenders succeeded in putting up some fighters; but the loss of twenty nine Japanese aircraft in action seemed a small price to pay fo a victory compared by some naval historians with Nelson's destruction of the French fleet at Aboukir Bay in 1798.

Even so, Nagumo's success was not as sweeping as it might have been. At the time of the attack the battleship *Colorado* and the carrier *Saratoga* were on the West Coast of the United States or on passage; the carriers *Enterprise* and *Lexington* had been ordered to deliver aircraft to Wake and Midway Islands and were at sea with a number of cruisers and destroyers; and the battleships *Maryland* and *Pennsylvania* escaped serious damage. Thus the Americans were left with a substantial striking force of three battleships, three aircraft carriers and some eighteen cruisers in their Pacific Fleet, apart from any ships which could be brought in from elsewhere. As little damage was done to workshops, docks and other installations at Pearl Harbor, they were also left with a first-class naval base not too remote from the defensive perimeter which the enemy was trying to establish.

The essence of the Japanese plan for the first phase was that strong forces on the right should push southwards in Malaya while relatively weak forces took Hong Kong, the Philippines, Siam and part of Burma in order to clear the flanks and rear of the advance and help to prepare the ground for a converging attack on the Netherlands East Indies. On the left, Admiral Nagumo's attack on the Pacific Fleet was to be followed by the capture of Guam and Wake.

All the subsidiary operations contemplated in this plan were carried out without much difficulty, although not without minor setbacks.

In the Philippines, bomber crews whose softening-up attack on Luzon was delayed by fog expected heavy opposition, but found American aircraft still parked in neat rows, although some hours had elapsed since the garrison received news of the disaster at Pearl Harbor.[27] General Douglas MacArthur, commanding the land and air forces of the United States Army in the Far Eastern theatre, lost half his heavy bombers and more than a third of his fighters in the first few hours, and was unable to prevent the Japanese from wrecking the naval base in Manila Bay. Without command of the air or effective naval support he was obliged, when the enemy landed in strength towards the end of December, to give up Manila and put into effect a plan to save his force by withdrawing to the Bataan Peninsula and the island fortress of Corregidor. But the plan assumed that eventually a relieving force would reach Luzon, and no such force could be sent across an uncommanded sea. In spite of dogged stands which prolonged the fighting for many weeks, effectively the Philippines were lost when the chief towns in the northern and southern islands fell to the invaders at a comparatively early stage.

On the ocean flank, the forces ordered to take Guam and Wake reached their first-phase objectives by the end of 1941, after unexpectedly stiff resistance by the small garrison of United States Marines at Wake had led the Japanese High Command to reinforce them with carriers and cruisers returning from the attack on Pearl Harbor. Going on to the next phase, the Japanese then seized vital points in New Britain and New Ireland, and by early March had reached Lae and Salamaua in New Guinea.[28]

At Hong Kong the position was that the British government had decided long before hostilities began that the colony, consisting of the island of Hong Kong and a tract of mainland about seventeen miles deep, was ultimately indefensible but must be held for as long as possible. The Governor, Sir Mark Young, and the garrison commander, Major-General C. M. Maltby, had thus to do the best they could in the knowledge that they could not expect substantial reinforcements and that, even if they did succeed in holding a numerically superior enemy in check, they might have to ask themselves whether they were justified in subjecting the population to a prolonged siege without hope of relief.[29]

With only two weak brigades at his disposal, Maltby was obliged, in order not to make his front too wide, to place his main defensive position on the mainland so far back that there was no room for a second line behind it. Partly for that reason, but chiefly because of the risk of seaborne landings, about half the garrison had to be kept on the island, so that only three battalions, with little artillery and no air support, were available for the main position and to man outposts. Even so, General Maltby hoped, when the Japanese attacked at 8 a.m. on December 8, to hold the main position for seven to ten days. The Chinese National Government at Chungking announced their intention of taking the Japanese in the rear with the equivalent of six British divisions after a delay of about three weeks; but nothing more was heard of this move, which in any case would have come too late.

On the second night the Japanese, well trained to move under cover of darkness and in silence, launched a surprise attack which scored an important local success. Facing a whole division supported by about eighty aircraft based on Canton, Maltby held out on the mainland for a few more days before completing his withdrawal to the island on December 13. The Japanese, calling on the garrison to surrender, then paused for forty-eight hours before beginning a prolonged artillery and air bombardment interrupted only by a second summons to surrender. Late on December 18, under cover of darkness and the smoke from burning oil tanks, they crossed the strip of sheltered water between the Kowloon Peninsula and the north shore of the island. The defenders put up a fair volume of fire, but the need to cover the whole coastline and a shortage of experienced officers had prevented them from making the defences on the north shore as dense and as well sited as was desirable.

The situation at dawn next morning was that the British had lost the heights in the north-east corner of the island but still held the rest, including an important centre of communications known as the Wong Nei Chong Gap. Their troops in the threatened sector were, however, rather scattered, and the commander on the spot received permission to withdraw to the south and regroup before counter-attacking. As a result of misunderstandings he lost most of his artillery during the withdrawal. Thereafter the Wong Nei Chong Gap was also lost, and the Japanese were able to push southwards and westwards, driving a wedge through the defences and capturing or damaging the reservoirs on which the island had become dependent since its severance from the mainland. Concluding on December 25 that further resistance was useless, the Governor formally surrendered the Crown Colony to Lieutenant-General T. Sakai, commanding the Japanese Twenty-third Army.

Meanwhile the Japanese had made a good start with their main offensive in Malaya, where their opening moves were precisely those which the British had long expected them to make.[30]

From the time when the fixed defences of the naval base at Singapore were completed, it was recognized in British military circles that these gave protection only against ships at sea. Between 1936 and 1941 a good deal of attention was paid, therefore, to the problem of defending Malaya as a whole.[31] Broadly, the conclusions reached were that the conquest of Malaya would be difficult unless the invaders captured a port in Siamese territory at an early stage; that Singora, Patani and Kota Bahru were likely landing-places; and that the only completely reliable means of defence was to station at Singapore a fleet strong enough to rule out successful landings there or elsewhere on the east coast of the Malay Peninsula and the Kra Isthmus. In the absence of such a fleet, a strong air force might suffice to destroy a landing-force or sever its communications; but the planners estimated that in that case at least 336 aircraft would be needed.[32]

When the summer of 1941 brought an imminent threat to Malaya the British government were, however, unwilling to send substantial numbers of aircraft to the Far East.[33] They feared that the Germans might resume heavy air attacks on the United Kingdom; they were reluctant to scale down their air offensives over Germany and Northern France; finally, they felt that they might not be able to find the necessary shipping without trenching on the needs of the Middle East Command or reducing supplies to Russia. The consequences were that in December there were not 336 aircraft in Malay but fewer than half that number, and that many of these were old or obsolete.

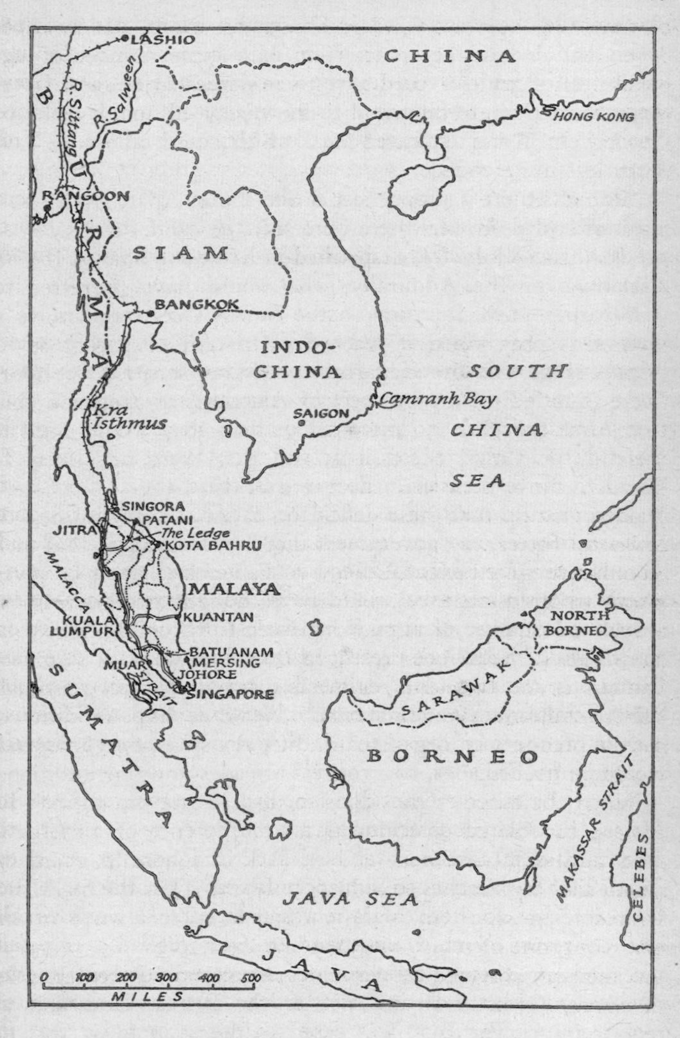

30 The Malay Peninsula and the Kra Isthmus

Meanwhile the emphasis laid on control of the air in paper plans had led to the construction of a large number of airfields, all of which would have to be defended by land forces because they might be useful to the enemy, although many of them were in unfrequented areas which could otherwise have been left undefended.

Nor was there a strong fleet at Singapore. Apart from a few cruisers and destroyers there were only the capital ships *Prince of Wales* and *Repulse*, despatched in haste and against the inclinations of the Admiralty, who would have preferred to build up a powerful force in the Indian Ocean and move it eastwards only when it reached a strength of six or seven capital ships, one aircraft carrier and ten cruisers.[34] Great hopes were founded on the prospect of American co-operation; but the Americans had no more troops than they would need to defend their own possessions, and they were not likely to agree to move their main fleet to a British base.

Recognizing that these deficiences threw a heavy burden on the land forces, the government did, however, agree that their commander, Lieutenant-General A. E. Percival, must be given more troops than they would have thought necessary if the stipulated number of aircraft had been forthcoming. The total of thirty-one battalions present in December was still seventeen battalions and two tank regiments short of Percival's estimate of his minimum requirements,[35] but gave him an army of nearly 90,000 men organized in three divisions, two independent infantry brigades, two fortress brigades and one additional infantry battalion. One division had, however, to be dispersed in isolated detachments for the defence of airfields in the north-east, and one was held back in Johore to guard the immediate approaches to Singapore Island. Thus the field force available in Northern Malaya was reduced to a corps of two divisions, one of which was tied to a static role.[36]

The plan accepted by Air Chief Marshal Sir Robert Brooke-Popham, Commander-in-Chief of the British land and air forces in the Far East, was based on the assumption that the enemy would make his main thrust across the Siamese frontier even though part of his force might land south of the frontier in Malayan territory.[37] If circumstances were favourable the mobile troops in the north would advance into Siam, seize the ports of Singora and Patani, and establish a defensive front across the narrow neck of the Kra Isthmus. But this forestalling movement, known as 'Matador', would be feasible only if the troops were ordered to start at least thirty-six hours before the enemy could reach Singora and Patani. If that condition could not be met, or if circumstances were otherwise unfavourable for 'Matador', then the main body on the left would block the road and railway from Singora on Malayan territory at Jitra, while on the right a detached column of two battalions would advance about thirty miles into Siamese territory in order to block the lesser road from Patani at a position called The Ledge.

Thus neither 'Matador' nor the Jitra alternative could be put into effect without at least a technical infringement of Siamese sovereignty. Towards the end of November Air Chief Marshal Brooke-Popham was none the less anxious to receive from the Chiefs of Staff a definition of the circumstances in which he could order the more serious trespass involved in 'Matador' without being stamped as an aggressor and thereby forfeiting American support.[38] It was not, however, until December 5, after the British Ambassador in Washington had asked both the State Department and the President to comment on the warning issued by the Navy Department, that the Chiefs of Staff were able to tell him that he could safely order 'Matador' as soon as he had reliable information that the Japanese were about to seize the Kra Isthmus or had already entered some other part of Siam.

Meanwhile Brooke-Popham had received reports of doubtful provenance to the effect that the Japanese intended to confine their initial landings to Kota Bahru, in Malayan territory, with the object of putting the British in a bad light if they entered Siam. These made him reluctant, even after he had heard from the Chiefs of Staff on December 5, to undertake 'Matador' without orders expressly covering the case of aggression against Malaya alone. When air reconnaissance on December 6 confirmed reports that Japanese convoys had sailed from Saigon and Camranh Bay, he therefore declined to order 'Matador', but issued a general alert.[39] As things turned out, this decision not only cost him his only chance of giving effect to 'Matador', but caused the troops in Northern Malaya to stand by for the next forty-two hours in pouring rain.

Further reconnaissance on December 7 showed that Japanese ships were at sea in positions from which they could reach Singora and Patani before the British, even if 'Matador' were ordered forthwith. On the other hand, 'Matador' might still have some value if the ships were not going to Singora or Patani, but were bound for Kota Bahru as precursors of a force to be sent to Singora and Patani later. Accordingly, Brooke-Popham decided not to commit himself to either 'Matador' or the Jitra alternative without further information. The troops in Northern Malaya were told that they might have to undertake 'Matador' next day, but were warned to make no move until the results of an early-morning reconnaissance of Singora were known.[40]

Again an excess of caution proved more dangerous than boldness. At 8 a.m. on December 8 Brooke-Popham received from the Chiefs of Staff a free hand to order 'Matador' in the event of landings at Kota Bahru alone. Still without news from Singora but aware that Japanese troops had landed at Kota Bahru in the small hours, he thereupon turned down a request from the troops in the north to be allowed to send a column into Siamese territory for the purpose of occupying The Ledge. At 9.45 a.m., however, he learned belatedly that the Japanese were pouring ashore at Singora and Patani, so that clearly 'Matador' was useless and the Jitra alternative the only possible course of action.[41] Meanwhile the diversionary landing at Kota Bahru had drawn off the whole of his available air striking force, leaving nothing for attacks on transports off Singora and Patani; the Japanese had begun to bomb his airfields so effectively that more than half his aircraft in Northern Malaya were lost on the first day; and some bombs intended for airfields near Singapore had fallen in built-up areas, causing about 200 casualties. Moreover, by the time the order for the Jitra alternative could be issued General Percival had left his headquarters to attend a meeting of the Legislative Assembly, with the result that it did not reach him until the middle of the forenoon. In consequence of delays for which Percival was not responsible, another four hours then elapsed before the column which the commander on the spot had wished to send to The Ledge that morning reached the frontier. As the troops had then to deal with Siamese guards who had received no orders to admit them, the final outcome was that they reached their objective only to find the enemy in possession, and were obliged to fall back to a less favourable position which they were too weak to hold.[42]

Meanwhile the main body on the left had reached Jitra after a delay due to the switch from readiness for 'Matador'. On December 12 the Japanese attacked in vain along the main road from Singora, but were more successful east of the road, where attempts by one of two brigades on the British front to drive them back were repulsed with heavy losses. Finding that the reserves of both brigades had been committed to these attempts and fearing that the Japanese might get behind him, the British divisional commander then asked permission to withdraw, was ordered to stand and fight, but eventually received authority to fall back at his discretion. The sequel was a difficult withdrawal which led to much confusion and the loss of much equipment, although only the rearguard was attacked.

As the troops in North-East Malaya had also received permission to withdraw in consequence of the abandonment by a depleted air force of the airfields which they were guarding, the situation in the middle of December was that the British were retreating on all fronts although they had yet to fight a major action. Moreover, they had suffered a disaster at sea when Japanese naval aircraft from Indo-China sank the *Prince of Wales* and the *Repulse* off Kuantan on December 10.[43] Admiral Sir T. S. V. Phillips, the newly-appointed Commander-in-Chief of the Eastern Fleet, had taken the ships to sea on December 8 with the intention of interfering with the landings at Singora, but had turned back when Japanese aircraft approached him after he had learned that fighter cover off Singora would not be forthcoming. On receiving news of a supposed landing at Kuantan he had, however, altered course in that direction, apparently in the hope that the originators of the message would divine his intention and arrange for fighters to meet him there. For the loss of three aircraft, the Japanese sank both ships within two hours of dropping their first bomb.

In spite of these setbacks, the British government continued to believe that the 'fortress of Singapore' and the 'Malay barrier' would be held. Troops and aircraft were diverted from the Middle to the Far East, and one of the consequences of a meeting between Churchill and Roosevelt in Washington was that General Wavell was appointed, at the request of the Americans, to command Australian, Dutch, United Kingdom and United States forces in South-East Asia and the South-West Pacific.[44]

But the chain of British and Dutch possessions which the statesmen called a barrier was itself the enemy's main objective, and there was no fortress of Singapore. Singapore was an island separated from the mainland by a narrow channel fringed with mangrove swamps which made observation of the surface of the water difficult and restricted the field of fire of short-range weapons. Most of its airfields and other vital installations could be swept by artillery fire from the mainland.[45] The naval base was impregnable only in the sense that its fixed defences protected it from long-range bombardment by ships and that a strong fleet based there could, at any rate in theory, have prevented an enemy from disembarking or maintaining troops at places from which they could advance to threaten the island at close quarters.

It followed that, with the Japanese already ashore in Malaya, Wavell's only chance of saving Singapore lay in winning a decisive battle on the mainland. Visiting Malaya early in January, when he was on his way to set up his new headquarters in Java, he announced his intention of fighting such a battle on the North-West frontier of Johore.[46] But he added that the two divisions retreating from the north were in poor shape and that he would rely largely on the uncommitted Australian division already in Johore and on such reinforcements as might reach him in time. In the outcome only two brigades, with some anti-aircraft and anti-tank troops, fifty-one crated Hurricanes and twenty-four pilots, arrived before the battle began.

In the second week of January the Japanese continued to make rapid progress. By the middle of the month they had swept through Central Malaya, overrun British Borneo, and seized valuable objectives on both sides of the northern approaches to the Makassar Strait. Wavell concluded that his aims must be to maintain his grip on Johore until he was strong enough to counter-attack, and to hold a line of naval and air bases from Singapore through Southern Sumatra, Java and Timor to Darwin. For the present all land reinforcements would be directed to Singapore; escort of reinforcement convoys would have the first claim on his naval resources; and aircraft would be used chiefly to protect convoys, watch Japanese shipping and support the troops in Malaya.

On January 15 the Japanese, with two divisions and some reserve troops in the forward area, attacked on a forty-mile front in North-West Johore. In consequence of Wavell's verdict on the retreating divisions responsibility for the front attacked, which ran roughly along the line of a river from Batu Anam in the east to Muar in the west, had been allotted not to the corps formerly in Northern Malaya but to an improvised force of four brigades, consisting of part of the Australian division already in Johore and the remnant of one of the retreating divisions, reinforced by a newly-arrived brigade. Three brigades were covering the main road to Singapore on the force commander's right, leaving only the newly-arrived brigade on a rather long front covering alternative routes along and near the coast.

The Japanese attack was successfully countered on the right. On the left, however, the newly-arrived brigade was overwhelmed, allowed the enemy to cross the river, and eventually was forced to destroy its heavy equipment and take to the jungle, leaving its wounded in the care of volunteers.* The force commander, with no first-hand knowledge of Japanese methods, no corps staff and inadequate resources, was not well

*Most of the wounded, with their attendants, were massacred by the Japanese. A few escaped by feigning death.

placed to restore the situation on the left; but General Percival was reluctant to order him to shorten his line by pulling back his right, believing that this would have a depressing effect on men who were fighting well. Accordingly, he arranged to plug the gap and give more depth to the whole position by moving troops from right to left and bringing in a second reinforcing brigade and other troops not hitherto committed. At the same time, another improvised force was set up to counter a threat from Japanese troops on the East Coast in the neighbourhood of Mersing.

These moves divided the Australian division between three fronts, but they did not halt the enemy. The sequel was a difficult retreat by forces too widely separated to be mutually supporting. In the course of it yet more troops were obliged to take to the jungle after parting with guns and vehicles, and the equivalent of roughly another two brigades was lost. The rest of the force successfully withdrew to Singapore Island by the end of January.

Thus what proved to be the decisive battle for Singapore was lost and won without a general engagement. At the time, however, the plight of the men who crossed the causeway connecting the island with the mainland before it was blown on January 31 was not regarded as altogether hopeless. Reinforcements disembarked in the last ten days went some way to offset losses suffered in the recent fighting, so that roughly 70,000 combatant troops[47] were still in hand.* These men, many of them untrained or only partly trained, could not be expected to hold the island indefinitely without command of the sea and with very little air support; but Wavell hoped that they might be able to hang on until substantial reinforcements reached Burma, Singapore and the Netherlands East Indies at the end of February or early in March, and that soon afterwards he

*They were organized in 38 infantry battalions, of which 13 were from the United Kingdom, 6 from Australia, 17 from British India and 2 raised locally; and 11 miscellaneous battalions. The miscellaneous battalions consisted of 3 machine-gun battalions, 1 reconnaissance battalion, 3 volunteer battalions and 4 airfield defence battalions.

might be strong enough in the air to start pushing the enemy back. As there was no room on the island for a set battle success was not, however, to be expected unless the garrison could either prevent the Japanese from landing, or pin them down before they began to thrust inland along roads, creeks and rivers.

In the event they were able to do neither. The troops guarding the beaches had been told not to use their searchlights without express orders.[48] They had also been told that, if the enemy did get ashore, they must fall back quickly and form defensive perimeters. By the time the Japanese were ready to make their attempt on the night of February 8 their preliminary bombardment had done so much damage to landline communications on the island that orders varying these instructions could not be passed. Still covered by artillery fire, and also by mortar fire from the shore and from moored landing-craft, the first wave of assault troops crossed the narrow channel in the darkness with only moderate opposition. Machine-gun fire took a heavy toll of them as they scrambled ashore, but the full weight of the three divisions now in Johore was behind them. Once they gained a foothold, there was little to prevent the army commander from reinforcing them at his own speed.

Conversely, the garrison had scarcely anything to draw upon once their attempt to contain the landings had failed. The territory they had to defend was neither a true fortress, like Gibraltar or Corregidor, nor a position of great natural strength like the Bataan Peninsula, but a populous island some thirteen miles long and up to seven miles wide, nowhere rising to more than 600 feet above sea-level. Assuming that the main effort in the event of a land battle for the naval base would be made on the mainland, authorities with limited funds and a limited labour force had done little to prepare such vital objectives as the reservoirs for defence. With no tanks, few aircraft and a central reserve of only one brigade, the garrison were not in a position to drive the invaders back into the sea, and the presence of roughly a million non-combatants effectively ruled out a last-ditch stand.[49]

In these circumstances the defenders could do no more than hold on until a point was reached at which the military advantages of continued resistance were outweighed by the moral and poltical disadvantages of exposing the civil population to undue hardship. That point was deemed to have been reached when an imminent shortage of water threatened to lead to an uncontrollable situation.[50] Accordingly the garrison surrendered on February 15. About 80,000 survivors went into captivity, and Wavell was led to reflect that his hope of holding the Singapore-Java-Darwin line might have been justified if only General Percival had been able to stem the flood for another month.

At the same time it was clear that the offensive capacity of the Japanese armed forces had been seriously under-estimated on both sides of the Atlantic. Just as the Americans had founded their long-term plans for the defence of the Philippines on the assumption that they would have a powerful fleet in the Pacific when the time came to do battle with Japan, so the British had assumed, when they asked themselves how British and Dutch possessions in South-East Asia and the South-West Pacific could be saved, that the naval base at Singapore would still be theirs when they were ready to make full use of it. Yet the situation which faced the Allies ten weeks after the start of the war was that the Japanese had command of the sea and that Singapore, Manila and Davao were all in their hands. Meanwhile they had occupied the whole of British Borneo, were reaching out to seize the Netherlands East Indies and in Burma had crossed the Salween River and were driving the British back to the Sittang.

The effect was to drive a wedge through the vast area for which Wavell had reluctantly assumed responsibility* and to make his position untenable. At the end of February he relinquished his appointment, and no successor was appointed. In March the Allies agreed that henceforward the British should be directly responsible for the area westward from Singapore

*On receiving the appointment Wavell had said that he had heard of a man being asked to hold the baby, but that this was twins.

to the Mediterranean, the Americans for the whole of the Pacific, and Britain and the United States jointly for the North and South Atlantic and the European theatre.[51] They also agreed that commanders in all areas should conform to a common strategy to be framed by the Anglo-American Combined Chiefs of Staff under the direction of the President and the Prime Minister; that China should rank as an independent theatre not included in any of the three areas of responsibility; and that advisory councils in London and Washington should receive guidance from Australian, Chinese, Dutch and New Zealand representatives. The South-West Pacific Area, which included Australia, fell to General MacArthur, while Admiral Chester W. Nimitz took command of the South Pacific Area, which included New Zealand, New Caledonia, the New Hebrides, and the islands south of the equator as far east as those of the Pitcairn group. Both men proved themselves capable and energetic commanders, but neither was particularly amenable to instructions from the Combined Chiefs of Staff. In practice the British Chiefs of Staff were often left in the dark as to what was being done in the Pacific.[52]

By the time these arrangements took effect the Japanese had made still further progress. On March 8 the Allied forces in the Netherlands East Indies surrendered after Rear-Admiral K. W. F. M. Doorman, the Dutch commander of an Allied naval force, had lost five cruisers in a gallant but vain attempt to dispute command of the Java Sea.[53] On the same day the Japanese Fifteenth Army entered Rangoon, forcing the British to fall back to the north. General Sir Harold Alexander, commanding the Burma Army, had then to choose between taking his force to China, where it would be cut off from British-held bases as soon as the Japanese took Lashio, and attempting a difficult retreat across the hills into Assam. After consulting Chiang Kai-shek and his American adviser, Lieutenant-General Joseph W. Stilwell, he decided not to make for China and withdrew his troops across the Indian frontier at the cost of exposing them to great hardships and the loss of practically the whole of their heavy equipment.

Meanwhile the Australian government, arguing that Burma was already as good as lost and that troops would soon be needed to fight the Japanese on Australian soil, had refused to divert to Rangoon one of two divisions on their way from the Middle East to the Netherlands East Indies.[54] An attack on Darwin by carrier-borne and land-based aircraft on February 19 seemed to confirm their fears, but in the end the British government's prediction that the enemy would stop short of landing in Australia proved correct. A plan for the invasion of Australia was in fact considered by the Japanese Imperial General Headquarters, but was turned down on the ground that there was no prospect of finding either the ten divisions needed for the purpose, or enough shipping to maintain them.[55]

On the western flank, Japanese forces occupied the Andaman Islands on March 23. Four days later Admiral Somerville took command of a British Eastern Fleet based on Ceylon and consisting of five old battleships, three aircraft carriers, seven cruisers, sixteen destroyers and seven submarines. Believing that any attempt to invade Ceylon would be preceded by air attacks on his bases at Colombo and Trincomalee, he decided to rely largely on a secret base at Addu Atoll, in the Maldive Islands, and to keep most of his ships at sea at times when information from secret sources suggested that attacks were imminent. The soundness of this policy was shown on April 5 and 9, when carrier-borne forces under the redoubtable Admiral Nagumo did attack Colombo and Trincomalee, but failed to discover Addu Atoll or come up with any major units of Somerville's fleet. Nevertheless a good deal of damage was done on shore, two cruisers and a light carrier detached from the main fleet were sunk, and in the same week the Japanese sank more than 100,000 tons of shipping in the Bay of Bengal[56] and dropped bombs on Indian soil near Vizagapatam in the Madras Presidency.

Concluding that Colombo, Trincomalee and even Addu Atoll were unsafe locations for their only fleet in Far Eastern Waters, the British government agreed soon afterwards that Kilindini, on the coast of Kenya, should become Somerville's main base until a strengthened fleet could return to Ceylon,[57] and that Diego Suarez, in Madagascar, should be occupied by British troops in order to deny it to the enemy as a base for attacks on merchant shipping. At the end of April a landing-force which had left the United Kingdom on March 23 was given final authority to carry out its mission, and by May 7 the port was in British hands.[58]

CHAPTER 13

A RING ROUND GERMANY: THE NORTH AND WEST

December 1941 - August 1943

At the so-called Arcadia Conference held at Washington in December 1941 and January 1942, Britain and the United States reaffirmed their intention of making the defeat of Germany their first aim in the simultaneous war with Japan and the European Axis to which they were now committed. They adopted as one of their main strategic aims the drawing of a ring round Germany.[1] In order to establish such a ring, they proposed to sustain Russian attempts to hold a line from Archangel to the Black Sea; arm and support Turkey; strengthen the British hold on the Middle East; gain possession of the whole of North Africa; and extend the line along the western seaboard of Continental Europe by reasserting control of the Atlantic. In addition they proposed to safeguard vital centres of production where these seemed vulnerable, as in the United Kingdom and on the West coast of the United States; to wea Germany down by bombing, economic pressure and subversion and to maintain a defensive posture in the Pacific theatre with the dual object of checking further encroachments and holding points of vantage for an eventual offensive against Japan.

What offensive action should follow when the ring round Germany was complete was not decided at the Arcadia Conference. Accordingly the memorandum in which the British and United States Chiefs of Staff recorded their conclusions left open the choice between an assault across the Mediterranear an advance through Turkey and the Balkans, and landings i Western Europe. But General George C. Marshall and Genera Dwight D. Eisenhower, respectively Chief of Staff of th

United States Army and Chief of the War Plans Division in the United States Department of War, were both strongly of the opinion that a landing in Western Europe was by far the best course; and after the conference was over they succeeded in persuading President Roosevelt and his confidential adviser, Harry Hopkins, that they were right. Accordingly it was with Roosevelt's approval that in April Marshall and Hopkins travelled to London to urge on the British that in the spring of 1943 some eighteen British and thirty American divisions, supported by the best part of six thousand first-line aircraft, should land between Le Havre and Boulogne, advance to the Oise, and seize Antwerp and Boulogne before pushing on to Germany.[2]

The British, with their long and bitter experience of Continental wars, might have been expected to object that the Western Allies would sacrifice one of the greatest advantages which their naval power could give them if they committed themselves twelve months in advance to a landing where the German forces in the West were strongest. Nevertheless they agreed within less than a week of Marshall's arrival in London that plans should be prepared for operations on the lines of his proposal, although they continued to think that landings elsewhere than in Northern France might also have some value.

General Marshall was not, however, solely concerned to recommend a landing in France in 1943. Proposals for a small-scale landing in 1942 had already been discussed in Washington and London under the code-name 'Sledgehammer', and one of the objects of his mission was to persuade his hosts that such an enterprise ought to be undertaken if the plight of the Russians became desperate, or alternatively if Germany showed signs of cracking. The British, who would have to provide most of the forces for 'Sledgehammer', agreed that a favourable opportunity of landing in France in 1942 ought not to be missed; but detailed examination of the tactical and logistic implications showed that, because of a shortage of landing-craft, the Allies could not hope to put ashore a larger force than the Germans, unless much weakened in the meantime, would be able to hold at bay without recalling a single division from the Eastern Front. As a means of relieving pressure on the Russians, 'Sledgehammer' would therefore be useless. On the other hand it might have some value if the German Army began to break up before the Allies were ready to mount a full-scale invasion.

Even so General Marshall was reluctant to abandon 'Sledgehammer', not least because he feared that failure to take some positive action in the West in 1942 might encourage American critics of the Germany-first strategy to press for a policy of leaving Europe to stew in its own juice and concentrating on the war in the Pacific. Towards the middle of June, however, the British War Cabinet recorded the firm opinion that 'Sledgehammer' would prove a useless sacrifice unless the Germans were demoralized by failure in Russia before it was launched. Almost simultaneously a talk with Admiral Mountbatten, the British Chief of Combined Operations, went some way to convince President Roosevelt that this was a just verdict.[8] Meanwhile the German armies on the Eastern Front had opened a new campaigning season with spectacular victories in the Kerch Peninsula and at Kharkov, and had begun a massive onslaught on Sebastopol. Hence it was not necessary to await the launching of Hitler's main offensive at the end of June before concluding that the Germans were far from breaking-point and that the circumstances in which 'Sledgehammer' could be undertaken were not likely to occur.

In default of 'Sledgehammer', and in accordance with a policy adopted in principle before the United States entered the war, the British did, however, carry out a number of seaborne and airborne raids on German-occupied Europe between the last week of 1941 and the late summer of 1942. In the first of these a small force landed at Vaagsö, off the Norwegian coast, and returned after a brief stay with ninety prisoners and thirty-six Norwegian loyalists; in the second a mixed party of combatant troops and technicians obtained eagerly-awaited information from a German radar station at Bruneval on the French coast, and blew up the station after they had dismantled its equipment and carried vital parts away; and in the third a seaborne expedition sailed up the estuary of the Loire and destroyed the gates of the lock at Saint-Nazaire in order to make it impossible for the new German battleship *Tirpitz* to dock at the only French Atlantic port where she could have done so.[4]

The fourth raid was a more ambitious one, carried out with the twofold object of bringing on a successful air battle and providing data for the planning of large-scale landings. On August 19 more than six thousand troops, of whom nearly five thousand were Canadian, were carried across the Channel and put ashore at and near Dieppe under heavy fire. Tactically the Dieppe raid was a failure inasmuch as casualties were severe except on the extreme western flank, where a coast defence battery was captured and destroyed at a comparatively small cost; strategically it was again a failure inasmuch as the air battle went in favour of the enemy, but a success inasmuch as the information brought back did prove valuable.[5]

Even though some fifty United States Rangers took part in the Dieppe raid, such ventures could not be expected to figure in American eyes as effective substitutes for 'Sledgehammer'. President Roosevelt was eager that American troops should make a substantial contribution to the war against the European Axis in 1942, and indeed had given the Russians reason to expect a large-scale Anglo-American landing in Europe before the year was out. The British could not promise such a landing, and told the Russians so; but it occurred to the Prime Minister, when he visited the United States in June, to give a new direction to the President's enthusiasm by reviving his interest in an earlier project which envisaged a landing in North-West Africa.[6]

Neither General Marshall nor his British counterpart, General Sir Alan Brooke, was at first attracted by this proposal, for both feared that its adoption might cut across their plans for 1943. But Operation 'Torch', as it was afterwards called, was in line with the Arcadia decision to gain control of the whole of North Africa, and Marshall's and Brooke's objections lost much of their force when it became apparent that the Western Allies might not in any case be strong enough for a full-scale landing in Northern France before 1944. By late July it was common ground between the American and British Chiefs of Staff that preparations to carry out 'Torch' before the end of October must be pressed forward, irrespective of what might or might not be possible in the following spring or summer.

But the long-drawn negotiations which led to this conclusion were not conducted in a vacuum. While the Americans and the British were discussing what they should do when they had drawn a ring round Germany, the Germans were doing their best to ensure that the ring should not be drawn. For German commanders and staff officers concerned with the Western Front there was, however, always the difficulty of foreseeing how far their plans might be frustrated by Hitler's continuing dream of conquest in the East. In broad terms the situation at the beginning of 1942 was that the German Army had 33 divisions in France, Belgium and Holland as compared with 163 on the Eastern Front and five in Finland;[7] and that Admiral Raeder had 249 submarines in commission and 91 ready for action. In addition he had a small but valuable surface fleet whose major units were the immensely powerful *Tirpitz*, the battlecruisers *Scharnhorst* and *Gneisenau*, the pocket battleship *Scheer* and her damaged but repairable sister-ship the *Lützow*, and the heavy cruisers *Hipper* and *Prince Eugen*.[8] The greater part of the Luftwaffe was on the Eastern and Southern fronts, but the small fighter force in the West consisted of exceptionally well trained formations and could be quickly reinforced.

In the early part of 1942 German naval strategy was strongly influenced by Hitler's belief that the British might follow up their minor success at Vaagsö by landing a substantial force in Northern Norway, as indeed they thought of doing. In the middle of January the *Tirpitz* moved from the Baltic to Trondheim, and almost simultaneously Raeder received a peremptory order from the Führer to return the *Scharnhorst*, the *Gneisenau* and the *Prinz Eugen* from Brest to their North Sea bases as the prelude to further moves.[9]

By early February the British were aware that the warships

vhich had long been idle and under repair at Brest were likely
o put to sea in the near future. They concluded that the
Germans, if they decided to move the ships to Germany or
Norway, might well prefer a swift dash up-Channel to a long
vesterly voyage, although this was far from certain. Un-
villing to risk their own heavy ships in narrow waters where
ir attacks were probable, they therefore redoubled their watch
n Brest, laid about a thousand mines between Ushant and
Boulogne and another hundred or so between Terschelling and
he Elbe, and prepared to go into action with light naval forces,
orpedo-bombers and heavy bombers. In general the disposi-
ion of their torpedo-bombers and light naval forces was
ounded on the expectation that the German commander would
o time his entry into the Channel as to reach the Dover Strait
n darkness; the role allotted to their heavy bombers on the
ssumption that the weather would be good enough for high-
evel bombing. At low altitudes crews would be unable to use
rmour-piercing bombs with any prospect of success and
vould have to rely on high explosive bombs of little value
gainst armoured ships.

But the Germans did not intend to force the Dover Strait
n darkness. Their plan was that the ships should leave Brest
n a moonless night towards the middle of February, take
dvantage of a favourable tide to reach a position half-way up
he Channel before dawn, and pass through the narrows in day-
ght but at a season when the weather might be expected to
amper bombing without precluding fighter cover. Elaborate
lans were made to provide such cover, and reinforcements
ere brought specially from Germany and Norway.

Late on February 11 air photographs of Brest showed the
arships lying at their usual berths, with anti-torpedo booms
ill in position. Nothing, therefore, suggested to the British
at by midnight they would have left port and be rounding
shant. Three British reconnaissance aircraft were patrolling
ntiguous stretches of off-shore water between the Pointe de
enmarch and Paimpol; but the first just missed the German
ips, the second returned early to base because its air-to-
rface-vessel radar was not working properly, while the third

seems also to have had a defective radar set and was recalle
a little ahead of time for fear that early-morning fog migh
prevent it from landing safely. The fighter screen which joine
the ships at first light was detected by the British early-warn
ing chain in spite of exceptional attempts at jamming; but th
significance of these portents was not understood, partly be
cause two aircraft sent to investigate ran into thick weathe
and saw nothing of importance, partly because the nav
authorities were not told until too late that the airborne rad
watch had broken down. Hence they had no reason to suspe
that the ships could have reached the Channel without the
knowledge. Thus it was purely by chance that soon aft
10.30 a.m. a fighter pilot on an offensive sweep near th
mouth of the Somme saw the German heavy ships steamin
north-east with an escort of destroyers and fast motor-boats.

By the time action could be taken on the report broug
back from this sortie, the best part of the short winter's d
had gone and the ships were a long way east of the area
which the British had hoped to engage them. The only strikin
forces immediately at hand were six slow and vulnerable to
pedo-bombers near the North Foreland, five motor torped
boats at Dover, and six destroyers at Harwich. The torped
bombers, gallantly taken into action by their leader before t
whole of their escort was in position, were all shot down; t
motor torpedo-boats were unable to cut through the enem
protective screen; and the German heavy ships successfu
dodged torpedoes launched by the destroyers. Later mo
torpedo-bombers and some heavy fighters and bomber-rec
naissance aircraft were brought forward from more dista
bases; but when most of them arrived the light was beginni
to fade, a heavy drizzle had set in, and the ships were mask
by murk and gloom. Meanwhile 242 heavy bombers w
ordered to attack; but thick clouds down to 600 feet made
necessary to exchange their armour-piercing bombs for hi
explosive, the first wave did not reach the target area un
3 p.m., and visibility was so poor that only a sixth of
whole force saw anything worth bombing. Unhit by bom
but severely damaged by contact with two mines, the *Scha*

orst limped into Wilhelmshaven next morning. The *Gneis-au* and the *Prinz Eugen*, the former slightly damaged by ntact with one mine, went on to the Elbe.

The break-out of the Brest squadron was a feat of seaman-ip which reflected great credit on the German commander, ice-Admiral Otto Ciliax. Nevertheless it proved a Pyrrhic ctory. The *Scharnhorst* was under repair for a long time ter her arrival at Wilhelmshaven; less than a fortnight later e *Prinz Eugen* was torpedoed and badly damaged by a sub-arine while on her way to join the *Tirpitz*; and before the d of the month an air attack on the *Gneisenau* at Kiel put er out of action for the rest of the war.

Even so, Admiral Raeder was able to assemble in Norwegian aters a substantial force consisting by the late spring of the *irpitz*, the *Hipper*, the two pocket battleships and ten large estroyers. With excellent bases at Trondheim and Narvik d another at Altenfiord in the far north, he was thus in a osition to confront the Western Allies, at a time when their sources were severely strained by setbacks in the Mediter-nean and the Far East, with the double threat of an Atlantic ray by the *Tirpitz* and attacks by surface ships on Arctic nvoys.[10]

To meet this situation the United States battleship *Washing-n* reinforced the British Home Fleet at Scapa from April to ly. Plans were made for American warships on the far side the Atlantic to intercept the *Tirpitz* if she broke out to the est, and Admiral Tovey arranged to take his main fleet to a whenever Arctic convoys were on passage. From March itward-bound and homeward-bound convoys on the Arctic ute were synchronized so that they passed simultaneously rough the danger-area.

On the first occasion on which the new time-table went into rce, the *Tirpitz* duly put to sea. Warned by a patrolling sub-arine, Tovey chased her with three capital ships and a fleet rrier, despatched carrier-borne torpedo-bombers with the in-ntion of sinking her near the Lofoten Islands, and so nar-wly missed doing so that thenceforward Hitler refused to ow Raeder's heavy ships to be used except in the most

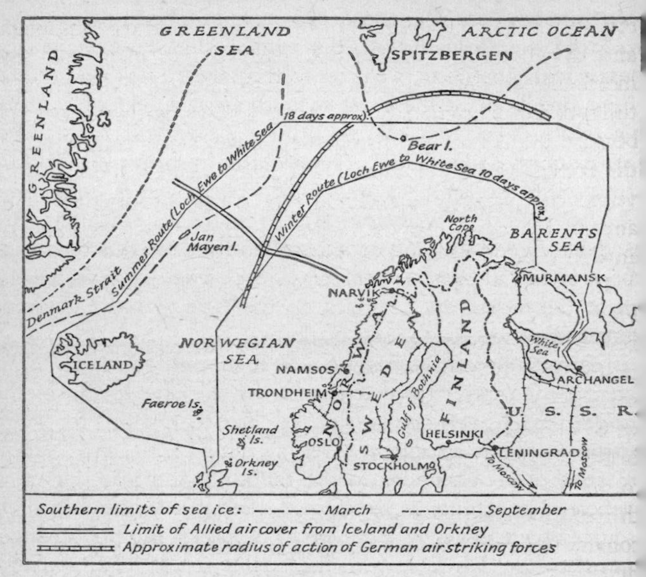

31 The Arctic Convoy Routes

favourable circumstances. When the *Lützow*, the *Hipper* a
six destroyers attempted a similar sortie nine months later, th
were engaged in the Barents Sea by five destroyers and t
light cruisers which forced them to withdraw without sinki
a single merchantman. Notwithstanding his previous cauti
Hitler was so angered by their lack of success that he heap
reproaches on Raeder, who eventually resigned and was s
ceeded by Admiral Karl Dönitz, hitherto commander of
U-boat fleet.

During the intervening period the Germans relied chie
on submarines and land-based aircraft to wage an offens
which soon began to cost the Allies heavy losses. Unable
stand far to the north because of pack-ice, convoys and th
escorts on passage between the United Kingdom or Icela
and the Kola Inlet or the White Sea became an easy p
during the season when there was no night to bring th

respite. In May Convoy PQ 16, attacked by torpedo-bombers and dive-bombers for the best part of five days, lost seven merchantmen out of fifteen; a month later only eleven of the thirty-six in Convoy PQ 17 reached their destination, largely because the Admiralty disregarded Tovey's advice and ordered the convoy to scatter when the *Tirpitz* seemed about to intervene. This disaster underlined the danger of divided control and the loss of so many Allied ships and cargoes aroused much anger in the United States.

In August a number of ships were detached from the Home Fleet to fight an important convoy through to Malta, with the result that the sailing of the next Arctic convoy, PQ 18, was postponed until September. Profiting by the respite, Tovey made arrangements to reinforce PQ 18 at the critical stage with a 'fighting destroyer escort' of sixteen fleet destroyers, bring up an escort carrier, and stand with the rest of his fleet to the north-east of Iceland. In a long-drawn battle PQ 18 lost thirteen merchantmen and the corresponding homeward-bound convoy three; but the greater part of both convoys reached their destinations, and the loss of forty-one aircraft and three submarines was a severe blow to the attackers. Thereafter the passage of convoys to and from Russia remained difficult and hazardous, but Allied losses were no longer crippling.

Meanwhile the battle which would decide whether Anglo-American plans for the invasion of Continental Europe could ever be carried out was being fought in the Atlantic and showed every sign of going in favour of the Germans. The entry of the United States into the war created golden opportunites for U-boats in North American waters and the Caribbean; in spite of the lessons of experience the Americans were slow to adopt the convoy system; and for a long time Allied losses were very heavy.[11] In the first half of 1942 the tonnage of merchant shipping sunk in the North Atlantic exceeded the total for the first half of 1941 by nearly a million tons, the tonnage sunk in all theatres was well over four million, and roughly three-quarters of all sinkings were by submarines.

In the light of such figures, one of the most difficult questions the Allied leaders had to face was whether their shipyards should give priority to cargo-ships and tankers needed to replace those sunk; escort vessels needed to keep down losses in the future; or assault craft needed for offensive operations. At a meeting at the White House on June 23 they agreed that the first essential was to speed deliveries of escort vessels; but they robbed their decision of much of its force by adding that the output of merchant ships must not be allowed to suffer.[12] In any case the American war machine had not reached a degree of development at which anyone could make sure that such broad declarations of policy would be faithfully translated into action.

As experience showed that ships sailing in convoy with both surface and air escort were seldom sunk, heavy losses also brought demands for increased numbers of very-long-range aircraft capable of covering convoys in mid-Atlantic, as well as for more long-range aircraft to be used for hunting U-boats on passage to and from their bases. But the British Air Staff, while admitting that past attempts at bombing German industrial centres had not been very profitable, rejected the conclusion that the time had come to disband or reduce the heavy-bomber force in order to make more aircraft available for maritime co-operation. Their view was that shore-based aircraft could do more to win the Battle of the Atlantic by bombing Germany than by escorting convoys or hunting U-boats, that in any case the means of equipping more than a limited number of aircraft for such duties did not exist, and that new navigational methods would soon make the bombing of Germany well worth while.

The Air Staff's claim that they could make a substantial contribution to the war at sea in the near future by bombing industrial targets and the like was not, however, borne out by events. The effect on U-boat construction of the bombing of Germany in 1942 was negligible.* Shore-based aircraft working over the sea, on the other hand, sank at least 35 U-boats

*J. R. M. Butler, *Grand Strategy, Volume III, Part II* (London, 1964), p. 543; Sir Charles Webster and Noble Frankland, *The Strategic Air Offensive against Germany* (London, 1961), Volume [illegible] pp. 473-92.

n 1942, and often contributed materially to the safety of convoys even when they sank none. As for the argument that arge numbers of aircraft could not be devoted to maritime cooperation because of a shortage of suitable equipment, according to naval strategists the shortage existed precisely because he Air Ministry preferred to order equipment suitable for ombing Germany.

The claim that new navigational aids would make night ombing less inaccurate in 1942 than in 1940 and 1941 proved etter founded. Even so, the standard commonly attained was till so low that the bomber force was considered to have done vell if, in good weather, forty crews out of a hundred dropped heir load within five miles of the point of aim. Moreover, he effect of the bombing on Germany's war economy continued o fall short of the Air Staff's expectations, largely because the Germans were able to draw to a greater extent than was foreeen on sources of productive effort not hitherto harnessed to heir war machine. A week after the first of a new series of eavy attacks on German cities severely damaged part of Lübeck, production there reached something between fourifths and nine-tenths of normal, and in 1942 Germany's inlustrial output rose by eighty per cent in spite of repeated ombing.[18]

Hitler was determined to avenge the destruction of Lübeck's nediaeval buildings, but aware that the small German bomber orce in the West could make little impression on well-deended targets. He therefore retaliated by ordering a series of o-called terror attacks, or Baedeker raids, on British cathedral ities, and afterwards sanctioned the development of pilotless ircraft and long-range rockets as alternatives to the manned omber.* Between April and June about two thousand tons of

Lübeck was attacked on the night of March 28; the directive for e Baedeker raids was issued on April 14; and development and roduction of the FZG 76 pilotless aircraft were sanctioned by Field-Iarshal Erhard Milch of the German Air Ministry on June 19. evelopment of the A-4 long-range rocket (as distinct from rearch) began about the same time, and a decree authorizing producon of the A-4 on the largest possible scale followed on July 25, 943. Hitler ruled in the same year that both weapons should be bombs were aimed at roughly a dozen objectives more or less in the Baedeker category. In addition a few attacks were made between March and September on ports and industrial areas and the end of October brought a postscript to the Baedeker raids in the shape of a fighter-bomber attack on Canterbury followed by a two-phase night attack. To bolster an effort which could not conceivably affect the issue of the war, aircraft were diverted from minelaying and other anti-shipping operations, and a small reinforcement was brought from Sicily at a time when the reduction of Malta was a far more important strategic aim than the bombing of Britain.[14]

Throughout these months the real war in the West was being fought at sea. In the second half of 1942, as in the first it seemed to go in favour of the Axis Powers. In the whole year nearly eight million tons of British, Allied and neutra merchant shipping went to the bottom, losses in the North Atlantic were nearly eight times as heavy as in the India Ocean and about ten times as heavy as in the South Atlanti or the Pacific, and submarines continued to account for th great majority of sinkings.[15] At the end of the year the Germa Navy, having lost 87 submarines through enemy action in th past twelve months and received 238 from new production was believed to have the best part of 400 in commission an at least 200 fit to go to sea.[16]

Recognizing that continued sinkings at that rate would mak havoc of their plans, the leaders of the Western Allianc agreed at Casablanca in January 1943 that attempts to beat th U-boat must have first claim on their resources.[17] Accordingl in the next five months British and American bombers aime nearly 20,000 tons of high-explosive and incendiary bombs U-boat bases and building yards without putting a single U boat out of action or appreciably affecting the German buil ing programme.[18] On the other hand, no immediately effecti steps were taken to increase the number of very-long-ran aircraft in the Atlantic theatre by drawing either on the Briti

---

adopted, and detailed plans for their employment against the Unit Kingdom were drawn up in the autumn.

bomber force or on the 71 aircraft of that type in the Pacific theatre.[19]

Even so, the outlook for the West improved considerably as more and more escort vessels ordered earlier in the war were delivered and fitted with short-wave radar. In the spring of 1943 a falling-off in the demand for special escorts for troop convoys freed more ships for normal duty, and at the same time sailings to North Russia were temporarily suspended so as to avoid unacceptable losses during the season of perpetual daylight. Consequently a number of fleet destroyers became available for the North Atlantic routes. By April 1 the Royal Navy and the Royal Canadian Navy, although still far short of the number of escort vessels needed in theory, were judged strong enough to assume sole responsibility for North Atlantic convoys, leaving the United States Navy to take care of tanker traffic between the European theatre and the Gulf of Mexico.[20] At a critical stage the burden of the battle in the North Atlantic fell, therefore, on Admiral Sir Max Horton, who had succeeded Admiral Sir Percy Noble at the Western Approaches command some weeks before Admiral Karl Dönitz succeeded Admiral Raeder as head of the German Navy.

Admiral Horton's plan, based on a method outlined by his predecessor and foreshadowed in Admiral Tovey's use of a 'fighting destroyer escort' for Convoy PQ 18 in the Arctic, was not to accept an evasive role, but to allow or even encourage the enemy to commit his U-boats in substantial numbers, and then fall on them with powerful counter-attack forces unhampered by defensive pre-occupations. As soon as he had enough escort vessels he organized some of them in escort groups whose task was primarily defensive; others went to form offensive support groups; and about a dozen destroyers were sent across the Atlantic so that similar arrangements could be made on the Canadian side.

Introduced towards the end of March, the new tactics first achieved some degree of success when, in April, the intervention of a support group helped a Halifax-bound convoy, intentionally sent through waters where a strong concentration of U-boats was known to be waiting, to escape with the loss of only one ship. In that month merchant-ship losses declined sharply after rising to a perilously high level in March, and by the end of it the enemy's losses were beginning to show an upward trend.

A more spectacular trial of strength followed early in May. On April 29 one of forty U-boats waiting south of Greenland made contact in stormy weather with a westbound convoy off Cape Farewell, and its sighting report was picked up in England. The Admiralty ordered a support group from Newfoundland to join the escort group, Horton called out a second support group from the same base when gales which dispersed the convoy prevented the first from refuelling at sea, and calmer weather late on May 4 brought the beginning of a three-day battle in which twelve merchantmen and sever U-boats were sunk.

Thereafter the climax came with astonishing swiftness. Ir the second and third weeks of May the U-boat force in the North Atlantic attacked four convoys at a heavy cost and with little gain, and in one crucial engagement with a support group and a few very-long-range aircraft from Iceland lost five boats without sinking a single merchantman. Unable to stand such losses, Dönitz conceded the match on May 22 by ordering hi surviving U-boats to withdraw. No merchant ships were sunk on the main convoy routes in June, and subsequent attempts by the Germans to revive the U-boat offensive in the North Atlantic were unsuccessful.

Thus the decisive victory which made it possible for larg numbers of American troops to fight in Europe in 1944 and 1945 was won in a few weeks in the late spring of 1943 by th destroyers and other light naval forces of the North Atlanti escort and support groups, one squadron of very-long-rang aircraft, and two escort carriers with their small complemen of carrier-borne aircraft, the whole backed by the patrc vessels, minesweepers, and general reconnaissance and fighte aircraft which kept watch over off-shore waters and the narrov seas. But towards the end of April Dönitz, misled by report which suggested that his crews had ceased to be able to detec pproaching aircraft but were capable of dealing with them vhen they came in sight, had ordered U-boats in transit through he Bay of Biscay to remain on the surface and fight it out with heir attackers. As U-boats bound for remote destinations con- inued to pass through the Bay of Biscay even when operations n the North Atlantic were suspended, the outcome was a eries of hard-fought actions in which shore-based aircraft both nflicted and suffered substantial losses.

At the beginning of August Dönitz rescinded the order; but neanwhile an escort group from the United Kingdom and hore-based aircraft from Gibraltar had joined the hunt, more ery-long-range aircraft were at last coming into service, and J-boats surfacing to replenish at sea, with their underwater ankers and supply vessels, continued to make rewarding targets or these forces and for escort carriers of the United States Navy which had begun to cover the route from New York to Gibraltar. In general, attempts by the U-boat force to find ew areas in which to work with relative impunity were not ery successful. Broadly, the situation at the end of August was hat German submarines had ceased, at any rate for the time eing, to present a grave threat to the Allies anywhere in the North or South Atlantic, but that a number were still working n the Mediterranean, while a few had reached the Indian Ocean and joined forces there with the Japanese. Thus the Western Allies reached, in the late summer of 1943, a point at which they were almost ready to tighten the ring round Fort- ess Europe in the sector from the North Cape to the Pillars of Hercules.

CHAPTER 14

A RING ROUND GERMANY: THE EAST

March 1942 - September 1943

At the close of the Russian counter-offensive in the winter o 1941-42, the state of the war on the Eastern Front was tha both sides were battered but undefeated. In the north, th Germans had been turned out of Tikhvin but were still so clos to Leningrad that on clear days they could see its rooftop glittering in the sun.[1] In the centre they were more or les firmly established in a huge salient round Rhzov and along line well forward of Roslavl and Bryansk. In the south the held Kharkov and most of the Crimea, but not Rostov, th Kerch Peninsula or Sebastopol. The Russians, holding a equally large salient east of Velikie Luki and north c Smolensk, had advanced about as far as they could hope to g on any part of the front, but their leaders were not yet full alive to the danger of trying to do too much.

Meanwhile Hitler had parted with Brauchitsch and assume direct control of the German Army. As he was temperamentall inclined to busy himself with detail, the result was that for th rest of his life he was saddled with the immense task of supe vising events at the front far more closely than a profession Commander-in-Chief would have done, while still trying exercise the supreme direction of the war on land, at sea, in th air and in the diplomatic and economic spheres.

On April 5 the Führer confided to his staff that his inte tions regarding the Eastern Front in 1942 were to take Leni grad, stand firm in front of Moscow, and aim at an overwheln ing victory in the south in order to gain access to the oilfiel of the Caucasus.[2] Although open to the criticism that more might be gained by threatening Moscow and letting the conquest of the Caucasus come in its own time, this was an understandable choice since Germany had been forced to draw on her oil reserves to the extent of more than a million tons.[3] Moreover, Hitler had in mind the possibility of inflicting a severe reverse on the Western Allies by continuing his advance through Persia and Iraq, seizing the British-controlled oilfields in the Middle East, and perhaps linking up with German and Italian forces advancing through Egypt.

No more was heard for the moment of an attack on Leningrad; but plans for the offensive in the south envisaged preliminary operations to clear the Kerch Peninsula and Sebastopol, followed by a thrust to Voronezh. Forces moving south-east from Voronezh and north-east from Taganrog would then aim at encircling the enemy in the bend of the Don and opening a way to the Volga at Stalingrad. Once Stalingrad was captured or neutralized by bombardment, the main force would wheel south to the Caucasus, seize the oilfields, and push on into Transcaucasia.

The preliminary phase began on May 8. Strongly supported from the air, German and Rumanian forces under General Erich von Manstein launched an assault on a very narrow front at the south-western extremity of the Kerch Peninsula. Enveloping the enemy's strong but dangerously exposed right after shattering his weak left, in eleven days they captured the whole peninsula and practically the entire heavy equipment of two Soviet armies.[4] Manstein's forces then turned westwards to storm Sebastopol, which fell early in July after a desperate struggle. Both sides fought stubbornly, but the Russians had little air support while the Germans were able to call on roughly six hundred bombers, fighters and reconnaissance aircraft to supplement a formidable array of field and siege artillery.

In the meantime the Soviet Supreme Command, abandoning a far-reaching plan for the reconquest of the whole of the Eastern Ukraine, had launched a limited offensive designed to free Kharkov and forestall a German advance in that sector.[5]

The Germans counter-attacked strongly, the Russians were slow to pull back, and three Soviet armies were encircled.*

Thus the situation when the Germans launched their main offensive on June 28 was that the Russians had already sustained important defeats at Kerch and Kharkov, and were on the point of sustaining a third at Sebastopol. Not surprisingly, Hitler looked forward to a resounding success and quickly succumbed to the temptation to seek a short cut to his objectives.

Conversely, the effect of these reverses on the Soviet leaders was to convince them that they could not afford many more mistakes. Clearly, the Germans were likely to go for the Volga at its nearest point, and might well disrupt waterborne traffic between Moscow and the Caspian by seizing Stalingrad. If they also took Voronezh and went on to cut the Astrakhan-Saratov-Tambov-Moscow line, in all probability the whole of European Russia would be lost. Accordingly, the Soviet Supreme Command took steps to defend Voronezh to the last, and also to bar the direct route to Stalingrad in the Rostov sector.[6] Elsewhere little could be done, or at any rate was done, to stop the Germans until events showed which of their two probable objectives was the more imminently threatened.

Irrespective of the motives which may have impelled the Soviet Supreme Command to put most of their strength on the flanks, the enemy's rapid advance in the centre can hardly have come as a surprise to them. Even so, the Russians seemed genuinely taken aback when Rostov fell on July 23, allegedly at a time when the troops there had received no orders to withdraw.[7] Nevertheless the prompt abandonment of practically all their key positions in the Don bend could scarcely have served their interests better than it did if the whole sequence of events had been planned as a master-stroke of strategy. Almost everywhere south of Voronezh, except at a few places where a weak follow-up allowed them to retain or

*According to the Soviet official history and to statements made by Khrushchev in the course of his famous indictment of Stalin in 1956, this disaster could have been averted if Stalin had not refused to allow the troops to withdraw.

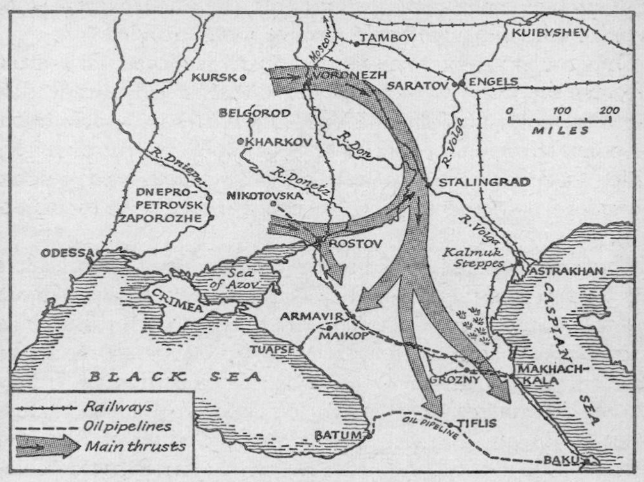

32 The German Advance to the Caucasus (as Planned)

recapture bridgeheads, their troops fell back across the river with comparatively light losses. Even at Rostov there was no great round-up of Soviet forces such as had occurred at Kiev and on a smaller scale at Kharkov.

At the same time the grand total of Russian losses in men and equipment on all parts of the southern front since May was rightly thought by the High Command of the German Army to be substantial. Altogether the retreat seemed so significant from the German point of view that by the third week in July Hitler came to believe that, as he expressed it to Halder, the Russians were 'finished'.[8] Concluding that his forces in the south no longer needed to cover their outer flank by capturing or masking Stalingrad before starting to wheel towards the Caucasus, the Führer directed that Army Group B, under the relatively inexperienced General Freiherr Maximilian von Weichs, should form a defensive front along the Middle Don and at the same time push forward a spearhead to Stalingrad. Meanwhile Army Group A, commanded by Field-Marshal Wilhelm List, was to cross the Lower Don, defeat the Soviet

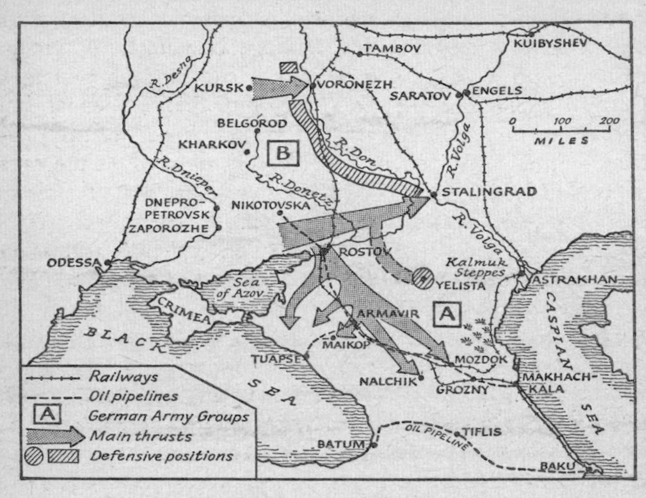

33 The German Advance to the Caucasus (as Carried Out)

forces south of the river, and enter the Kuban and th
Caucasus. To ensure speedy capture of the oil-producing region
one group of Army Group A's formations was to advance alon
the Black Sea coast, another was to occupy the Maikop
Armavir plateau while a third took Grozny, and finally a
advance would be made along the Caspian to Baku.

An obvious weakness of this plan was that Army Group A'
advance would expose a long north-easterly flank which woul
remain almost uncovered until the capture of Stalingrad re
leased troops for the purpose. Eventually a motorized divisio
from Army Group B was despatched as flank guard to Yelist
180 miles north-east of Armavir; but it could hardly be ex
pected to ward off a serious attack. The substantial force whic
remained in the Crimea after the fall of Sebastopol might hav
helped to plug the gap; but in August its formations wer
dispersed and its commander was sent with four divisions t
take part in an abortive assault on Leningrad.

Furthermore, the plan left a good deal to be desired on th
side of administration, organization and chain of command

Army Group A, although it proved incapable of reaching all its objectives, was a reasonably homogeneous body of troops. Army Group B, on the other hand, consisted of two good German armies and one weak one, with the addition of four Rumanian, Hungarian or Italian armies, none of them particularly well equipped or unreservedly devoted to the cause of Teuton *versus* Slav. Thus the army group was, at one and the same time, too large to be efficiently controlled from a single headquarters, yet too deficient in first-class formations to make a thoroughly reliable fighting force. Other weaknesses were that the rear communications not only of Army Group A but also of Army Group B's forces south-west of Stalingrad ran through a bottleneck at Rostov, and that all rail-borne supplies and reinforcements for both army groups depended on a single bridge across the Dnieper at Dnepropetrovsk.[10] An alternative route crossed the Dnieper at Zaporozhe, but the railway bridge there had been destroyed by the Russians in 1941. As late as February 1943 supplies sent by that route had to be unloaded on the west bank and reloaded on the other side.

Another factor which told against the Germans was Hitler's tendency to quarrel with subordinates and either assume their functions or replace them by men of lesser calibre. Rundstedt, Bock, List and Halder were all cast temporarily or permanently into limbo within little more than nine months of the dismissal of Brauchitsch in December 1941. By the autumn of 1942 Hitler was not only trying to double the posts of Supreme Commander of the Armed Forces and Commander-in-Chief of the German Army, but also doing his best to command Army Group A on a part-time basis while immersing himself in a mass of tactical and administrative detail. About the time of Halder's dismissal he began to shun intercourse with his staff, quarrelled temporarily with Jodl, and grew reluctant to leave his living-quarters even to attend conferences. Not surprisingly, his health suffered and his judgment became increasingly unreliable and capricious.

For some weeks after Hitler issued his new directive, formations on both flanks continued to press forward so swiftly that for the time being the hardships and setbacks of the previous winter were forgotten. Thereafter the advance slowed down, troubles multiplied, and before long the disadvantages of dividing their forces on a mammoth scale became abundantly clear to the German leaders.

On the right, comparatively little opposition was met in the early stages, so that it was not until many miles of rapid progress towards the beckoning heights of the Kabardino and Osetia lay behind them that all ranks in Army Group A began to suspect that they had bought a return ticket. Crossing the Lower Don towards the end of July, forward elements of the army group had no great difficulty in reaching Stravropol, Armavir and Maikop during the first half of August. Meanwhile the Russians were hastily preparing stop-lines in naturally strong positions on the routes to the main oil-centres.[11] Successfully but unprofitably thrusting his centre to the foothills of the Caucasus Mountains and beyond in the second half of the month, List was brought to a standstill on the left at Mozdok, well short of Grozny; failed on the right to force a way through difficult country to Tuapse; and was then dismissed for venturing to suggest that he might have been able to get to Grozny if the plan approved by Hitler had not called upon him to advance simultaneously on three fronts. As winter approached an attempt to turn the Mozdok position was decisively defeated. Thereafter the question which Hitler had to face was not whether Army Group A's forces could complete their task before the end of the year, but whether he would risk more by trying to withdraw them through the Rostov bottleneck than by leaving them where they were in the hope that the outlook might improve in 1943.

On the other flank the forces now comprising Army Group B continued after the new directive was issued to fight their way into the bend of the Middle Don and across the river, with the German Sixth Army doing most of the work and the Fourth Panzer Army coming up on its right after despatching a division to Yelista.[12] By August 19 General Friedrich Paulus commanding the Sixth Army and with the Fourth Panzer Army temporarily under command, was ready to storm Stalingrad. But the Russians had retained a number of bridgeheads on the right bank of the Don, notably some seventy miles north-west of Stalingrad at Kletskaya, and later they won a valuable foothold further west at Serafimovich. As Paulus did not pause to wipe out such pockets of resistance before continuing his advance, at most points the relatively weak formations which followed him merely closed up to the enemy's forces without attempting to push them back across the river. Thus the Sixth Army's flanks were not as strong as the Supreme Command believed them to be.

Even so, the attack on Stalingrad began reasonably well. Advancing on a broad front, Paulus succeeded by the evening of August 23 in driving his left through the northern outskirts to the right bank of the Volga. Just under a fortnight later the Fourth Panzer Army cut a path to the river through the southern outskirts. Thereupon the Führer impressed on Weichs and Paulus the importance of capturing the whole of the intervening built-up area.

Meanwhile a heavy air bombardment had destroyed a great part of the city, killed thousands of civilians, and interposed between the Sixth Army and its objectives a wilderness of shattered masonry and gutted buildings honeycombed with lurking-places for Russian infantrymen equipped with small arms, grenades and automatic weapons. Almost nightly until the middle of November, when the Volga became jammed with ice-floes, the Russians ferried supplies and reinforcements across the river. Soon masters of a branch of warfare in which gains and losses were measured by the width of a street or the thickness of a wall, the garrison defended their heap of ruins with dogged resolution.

Dismayed by the failure of more than one attempt to storm the remnant of Stalingrad still in Russian hands, many Germans took comfort in the thought that their troops were fighting a successful battle of attrition and must be containing so large a force that the enemy could have few reserves. But they were wrong. During the weeks when the Sixth Army was thought to be wearing down so many Soviet divisions that

Hitler repeatedly brushed aside warnings of the danger to the weak armies on its flanks, the Russians were keeping the reinforcement of Stalingrad within strict limits. At the same time they were concentrating more than a million men and about nine hundred tanks in two groups of armies which moved when their training was completed to strategic positions south of Stalingrad and in and behind the bridgeheads at Kletskaya and Serafimovich.[13] From October the arrival of new formations in these areas was reported by the Sixth Army's intelligence officers, who predicted attacks on the Rumanian Third Army and the Fourth Panzer Army, adding about the middle of November that the Russians had eight armies on the Don-Volga front.[14] But these warnings led to so much controversy and so little agreement at the higher levels that the few weak formations despatched in consequence set out too late to affect the issue.

Before dawn on November 19 a prolonged artillery bombardment in the Kletskaya-Serafimovich sector sounded the death-knell of Hitler's hopes of hegemony over European Russia. On that day and the next Russian assault troops backed by the weight of six Soviet armies fell in the north on the Rumanian Third Army and the left of the Sixth Army, in the south on the intermingled Fourth Panzer Army and Rumanian Fourth Army. In both sectors the poorly-equipped Rumanian formations succumbed quickly, opening gaps through which the Soviet armour raced towards the Sixth Army's rear. Passing athwart Army Group B's rail-links with the Kuban and the Donetz basin, the Russians captured by a ruse the bridge at Kalach across which passed every pound of supplies despatched by road to the Sixth Army. In less than five days the Soviet forces trapped a quarter of a million men amidst and immediately to the west of the ruins which Hitler's lust for conquest had made of Stalingrad.[15] In addition to the entire fighting strength of the Sixth Army, this total included elements of the Fourth Panzer Army and the Rumanian Fourth Army squeezed into the Stalingrad pocket from the south.

On the collapse of the Rumanian armies the Sixth Army became the only component of Army Group B which its com

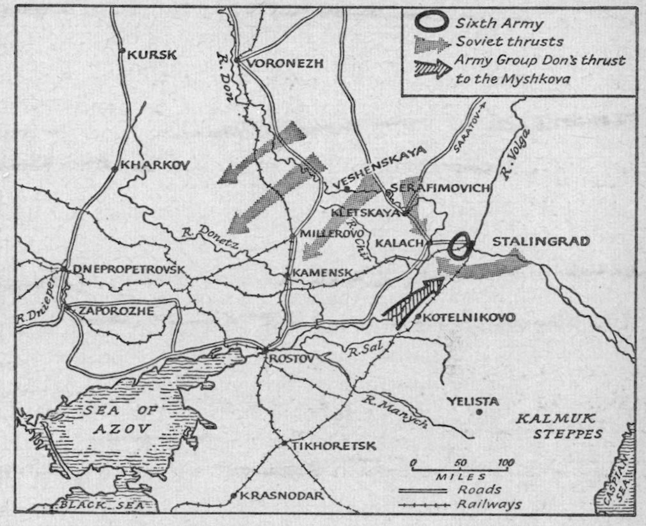

34 The Encirclement of the German Sixth Army

mander could count upon to inflict serious damage on the Russians. Concluding that failure to extricate it from the pocket might be fatal not only to his own group but also to Army Group A, General von Weichs was about to order Paulus to turn his back on Stalingrad and fight his way out to the south-west when Hitler reached a different conclusion. Deceived by a promise from Göring to deliver up to 500 tons of supplies a day to Stalingrad by air, the Führer ruled that Paulus should stay where he was.[16] At the same time he ordered the recently-promoted Field-Marshal von Manstein to set up a new headquarters on the Don front, reopen the Sixth Army's communications, and win back the territory lost since November 19.

In theory Manstein's command, known as Army Group Don, comprised the Sixth Army and all that was left of the Fourth Panzer Army and the Rumanian Third and Fourth Armies. Manstein was also promised eleven reinforcing divisions drawn from various fronts. In practice Hitler had his own radio link and liaison officer in the Stalingrad pocket, so that Manstein's control of the Sixth Army was never much more than nominal.

Manstein had no means of knowing whether the Luftwaffe was in fact capable of carrying 500 tons of supplies a day to Stalingrad; but only 25 tons were delivered on the day when he assumed command,[17] and in the next eleven days the total exceeded 150 tons on only one day, when the weather was exceptionally good and 300 tons arrived.[18] According to the account which he gave after the war, he soon became convinced that nothing could be more fatal than to leave the Sixth Army to wither away amidst the ruins of Stalingrad or on the open steppe, and that he must aim at bringing it back in fighting trim to a position in which it could help to cover the left of the armies in the Caucasus.* On the other side of the account, it could be said that the Sixth Army was already contributing to the safety of the armies in the Caucasus by holding down the forces investing it; but the weakness of that argument was that, unless supplied on a more generous scale than was possible by air, it would soon cease to make such a contribution because before long its troops would either run out of ammunition or starve or freeze to death.

Meanwhile Weichs and Paulus had missed their chance of pulling the army out while the encircling Russians were still relatively weak. Manstein concluded that the time had passed when it could hope to break out without a helping hand, and that therefore Army Group Don's first task must be to open a corridor through which supplies could be rushed into the pocket. On December 1 he ordered a reinforced Fourth Panzer Army on the right to advance towards the pocket on a date to be decided later, a small force on the left to make a supporting thrust from the confluence of the Don and the Chir, and the Sixth Army to hold itself in readiness to make a sortie towards the Donskaya Tsaritsa River as soon as he gave the word. Paulus would not be able to make a sortie without con-

*Field-Marshal Erich von Manstein, *Lost Victories* (London, 1958), pp. 304-6, 311, 316, 320.

tracting his northern front; but according to Manstein this was intentionally not stated in his written instructions, for fear that any hint of withdrawal might cause Hitler to countermand the order.*

Soft going delayed Manstein's reinforcements, and strong pressure from the enemy in the Chir sector ruled out a thrust on the left. But on December 12 the Fourth Panzer Army began to advance from Kotelnikovo with about 200 tanks. By December 18 its forward elements were across the Aksai River, some fifty miles from the south-western extremity of the Stalingrad pocket. In the rear an immense transport column stood waiting to rush 3,000 tons of supplies into the pocket as soon as a corridor was opened, and to bring up enough tractors to rescue some of the Sixth Army's field guns.

On that day Manstein appealed to the High Command to give its blessing to a break-out, at the same time sending his Chief Intelligence Officer into the pocket to impress on Paulus and his staff the importance of preparing without delay to push to the Donskaya Tsaritsa, and perhaps beyond it.[19] But the mission was not successful. Both the Quartermaster-General and the Chief of Operations thought a break-out feasible, though difficult; but Major-General Arthur Schmidt, the Sixth Army's Chief of Staff, was a man of massive courage to whom the very idea of withdrawal was abhorrent. He declared that the army would still be holding its positions at Easter, and that all Army Group Don had to do was to supply it better. Finally, Paulus himself pointed out that he could not loosen his grip on Stalingrad without disobeying an order from the Führer.

Ironically, it happened that while all this was going on at Stalingrad, the prospects of a successful breakout were being transformed by events elsewhere. On December 19 the Fourth Panzer Army's leading corps swept the enemy from the area south of the Myshkova River, and at nightfall established

*Manstein, *op. cit.*, pp. 323-4. In a later document meant for the Führer's eyes Manstein went so far as to put the case for leaving the Sixth Army at Stalingrad after relief, but in terms intended, according to his subsequent account of his motives, to bring home to Hitler the high cost of doing so.

a bridgehead on the north bank. Gazing northwards across the steppes that evening, troops of the 6th Panzer Division could see flares going up from the Sixth Army's perimeter, just over thirty miles away.

But Paulus had made up his mind while the Fourth Panzer Army was believed to be still fifty miles from the pocket that a break-out was not feasible, and he did not conceal from the Führer's liaison officer his conviction that it would be impossible for him to link up with the relief column as long as he had too little fuel to take the remnant of his armour the whole way to its front. The consequence was that Hitler, without positively forbidding a sortie, was able to counter Manstein's plea that withdrawal from Stalingrad should be sanctioned by pointing out that Paulus himself had said that he was not ready to move.

There remained the hope that Paulus might be induced to act by a formal order freeing him of responsibility not only for the decision to attempt a sortie, but also for the decision to cut loose from Stalingrad. At 6 p.m. on December 19, after telling General Kurt Zeitzler, Halder's successor as Chief of Staff of the German Army, that a break-out was the only means of saving the Sixth Army, Manstein ordered Paulus to start moving at the earliest possible moment towards the Donskaya Tsaritsa.[20] On receiving the signal 'Thunderclap' he was to continue his advance to the Myshkova, at the same time withdrawing step by step from the pocket.

But Paulus was still unwilling.[21] Hitler's insistence that Stalingrad should not be given up, although embarrassing, was not an insuperable obstacle; for Paulus was not bound to attempt an impossible task, or one whose accomplishment would have defeated the intentions of his superiors, and on that ground he would have been justified in disobeying Hitler's order and obeying Manstein's if he had been convinced that Stalingrad could not be held and that the choice lay between losing his army and saving it. But apparently he was not convinced that Stalingrad could not be held, and certainly he was not convinced that a break-out could succeed. He argued that he could not even make a start towards the Donskaya

Tsaritsa without spending six days on preliminary moves; that disengagement would be difficult or impossible in face of such attacks as were already being made on him; that his lack of mobility and the weakness of his troops after nearly three months on short rations were against success. Above all, he insisted that he needed more fuel for his tanks.*

These were powerful arguments; and whether they justified Paulus in rejecting what proved to be his last chance of saving his army could only be a matter of opinion at a time when there was no certainty that the outcome would be untold suffering and irreparable defeat. Manstein did not insist that his order should be obeyed, and was in no position to do so in view of the manifest impossibility of replacing Paulus at short notice by an equally experienced but more amenable commander. For a full week the Fourth Panzer Army's troops hung on to the Myshkova bridgehead; but they waited in vain for the sortie which might have eased the pressure on their front and helped them to move a little closer to the pocket.

Meanwhile the Russians were still attacking on the Chir and had massed substantial forces near the border-line between Army Group Don and Army Group B. On December 20 their troops emerged from an icy fog to rout the Italian Eighth Army west of Veshenskaya. Manstein's armour on the Chir front had to be rushed westwards to prevent a disastrous breakthrough towards Rostov, and on December 23 he was forced to take a division from the Fourth Panzer Army in order to avert a catastrophe on the Chir. Immediately after Christmas

*The Sixth Army is believed to have had about a hundred serviceable tanks. Paulus had, on his own showing, enough fuel to take them eighteen or twenty miles. He would therefore have had to leave some of them behind in order to give himself a reasonable chance of taking the rest to the Myshkova. Presumably no fuel would have been available for any other mechanically-propelled vehicles still fit for use, but these cannot have been numerous. Of the twenty-two divisions in the pocket, fifteen were infantry or rifle divisions which would have had to go on foot in any case. As few horses were still fit for work or likely to survive the conditions of a break-out, heavy equipment other than tanks could have been saved only if a corridor from Stalingrad to the Myshkova were held long enough for the relief column to make the double journey with its tractors.

the Russians redoubled their attacks on the Myshkova bridgehead, and on December 27 they pushed the Fourth Panzer Army back across the Aksai.

Nevertheless Manstein believed in the last week of December that he might still be able to send the Fourth Panzer Army forward to relieve the Sixth Army if it were reinforced within six days by three divisions from Army Group A, and if meanwhile a thousand tons of fuel and five hundred tons of food were flown into the Stalingrad pocket.[22] But those conditions were not met. Hitler decided on December 29 to start pulling the left of Army Group A northwards, but he sanctioned a methodical withdrawal which threatened to tie up its forces for the best part of a month. By January 8, when the Russians first called on Paulus to surrender, the Fourth Panzer Army was fighting on the defensive a good fifty miles behind Kotelnikovo, and on Army Group Don's left the collapse of the Italians had left a gap through which the Russians seemed all too likely to pour into the Donetz basin as soon as the elimination of the Sixth Army released nearly half a million troops still investing Stalingrad.

Not surprisingly, Manstein did not dissent from Hitler's ruling that the Sixth Army must fight on. After a day or two when few shots were exchanged, the Russians went on to redouble their attacks on the pocket. In just over a fortnight they captured one of the two airfields on which the air lift depended, crossed the most easterly line held by the Germans in the summer, and split the starving survivors of the Sixth Army into two groups near the centre of the built-up area and a third group further north. About 30,000 wounded had been flown out before transport aircraft were reduced to dropping their loads by parachute;[23] according to an official estimate, another 18,000 were lying in unheated cellars without drugs or dressings.[24]

Paulus reported on January 24 that he had lost touch with more than two-thirds of his army,[25] but in another message sent on that day spoke of ordering a break-out to the south-west by organized groups.[26] Nothing more was heard of this proposal after Hitler had insisted that he should be consulted before anything was done; but a few men, alone or in small parties, did take to the steppes on their own initiative, some hoping to reach the Fourth Panzer Army far away beyond Kotelnikovo, others to make contact with outposts of Army Group Don or Army Group A in the Kalmuk Steppes or further south.

On January 30 the Russians broke into the centre of Stalingrad from the north-west and west, at some points withholding their fire when they saw that the men they were approaching had obeyed orders to fight to the last round and were defenceless, or that they had put aside their arms because they were willing to surrender or unwilling to risk drawing fire on the wounded. Resistance ceased in the two more southerly pockets on that day and the next. On January 31 the newly-promoted Field-Marshal Paulus, by that time on the verge of nervous collapse, surrendered with his staff after a brief parley in which he played a passive role. The northern pocket held out until February 2, when the remnant of six divisions laid down arms which lack of ammunition had made useless. On the same day the meteorological station which had provided data for the Luftwaffe signed off with the message: 'Fog and red haze over Stalingrad'.[27]

After the Fourth Panzer Army's failure to relieve the Sixth Army in December, the situation of all the German armies from Voronezh on the Don to Nalchik in the Caucasus became perilous. On the left, the collapse of the Italian Eighth Army had torn a gap in Army Group B's front which was insecurely plugged by *ad hoc* formations and was soon to be widened by a similar disaster to the Hungarian Second Army further north. On the right, Army Group A's armies were in good shape, but the whole of its communications were threatened by the Soviet forces which were pushing the Fourth Panzer Army back on Rostov. Only Army Group Don in the centre was in a position to stem the enemy's advance, but its formations were too weak and too hard-pressed to do so without reinforcement. Moreover, even if the Fourth Panzer Army succeeded with the help of two or three divisions from Army Group A in holding

Rostov, the Russians might still be strong enough to exploit the weakness of Army Group B's front, thrust their right wing quickly to the Sea of Azov, and win a decisive victory by cutting off not only Army Group A but Army Group Don as well.

The course favoured by Manstein when the loss of the Sixth Army became inevitable was to lure the Russians to their doom by a show of weakness. His plan was to withdraw the whole of his own army group and Army Group A behind the Lower Dnieper so as to encourage the enemy to advance along the coast, and then win a decisive victory by falling on the Soviet flank and rear with forces to be assembled round the nucleus of a mobile corps which Hitler was thinking of moving from the West to the neighbourhood of Kharkov.[28] If these proposals were adopted, a logical corollary would be that Manstein should assume responsibility for the whole of the southern front, or at any rate for everything south of his existing boundary with Army Group B.

Manstein's plan showed a correct insight into the enemy's views, inasmuch as the Soviet Supreme Command did regard success at Stalingrad as the first stage of an advance which they hoped would take them to the Dnieper by the spring.[29] But it did not appeal to the Führer. Claiming that the oil which he hoped to extract from Maikop was indispensable and that he could starve Russian heavy industry of coal for its coking-ovens by holding on to the Donetz basin, he refused to give up so much territory even as a temporary expedient.[30] Manstein then relinquished his hope of winning a major battle by going the whole way to the Dnieper, but continued to insist that a big withdrawal was necessary to avert disaster.

Before long events forced Hitler to agree. In January the First Panzer Army fell back from the Caucasus with little time to spare, leaving in the Kuban as much of Army Group A as could be supplied across the Straits of Kerch. On February 2 the Russians captured a bridgehead on the south bank of the Donetz south-west of Millerovo, and by February 5 five Soviet armies were attacking the Fourth Panzer Army in front of Rostov. On February 6 Manstein was summoned to a conference with the Führer. Forewarned of Hitler's habit of countering a strategic argument with an economic one, and primed with the knowledge that a leading expert had pronounced the coal of the eastern Donetz basin useless for coking, he succeeded in showing that the choice for the Supreme Command lay between losing the whole of the Donetz basin and two army groups, and giving up the eastern half of it in order to preserve their forces intact.[31]

Next day Manstein arranged to withdraw his right to a line facing east along the Mius River, where the old Army Group South had set up defensive positions late in 1941, and started to shift the Fourth Panzer Army to the left of his L-shaped front, where it would have the First Panzer Army on its right. Allowing a fortnight for these moves, and assuming that the Mius Line remained unbreached, he could reckon on being ready by the beginning of the last week in February to bring the whole of his armour to bear against the strong Soviet forces which he expected to cross the Middle Donetz and try to pin him down in the angle between the Mius and the Sea of Azov.

At that stage the High Command extended Army Group Don's front to Belgorod, renamed it Army Group South, and took the headquarters of Army Group B out of the line so far as the Eastern Front was concerned. The ultimate effect of these changes was to give Manstein a total of thirty-two divisions on a front of 470 miles;[32] the immediate sequel was that Kharkov was lost to two Soviet armies advancing from Voronezh before he could assume effective command of the new sector and the formations assigned to it. These included the fresh and exceptionally well equipped SS Panzer Korps, with two divisions up and a third not yet in the line.

Meanwhile substantial bodies of Russian cavalry and mechanized or armoured troops had crossed the frozen Donetz on the First Panzer Army's front, thrust far to the rear under cover of darkness or by using supposedly impassable routes, and reached the main east-west railway at points from 25 to 150 miles east of the crucial railway bridge at Dnepropetrovsk. Pushing further to the south, one armoured column arrived within thirty or forty miles of Manstein's new headquarters at Zaporozhe, where Hitler had arrived on a three-day visit.[33] Eventually the Russian column ran out of fuel after passing within tank-gun range of the airfield used by the Führer's aircraft.

Undismayed by these incursions and by Hitler's fear that he would lose his chance of recapturing Kharkov before the spring thaw, Manstein bided his time until his armour was in position and the Russians were in imminent danger of outrunning their supplies, or in some cases had already done so. When all was ready, Manstein attacked northwards with the Fourth Panzer Army and the left of the First Panzer Army, followed with the SS Panzer Korps on the north-west flank, and in a ten-day battle from February 21 to March 2 defeated practically the whole of the Soviet forces between the Donetz basin and the Dnieper as far west as the Berestovaya.[34] On March 5 he went on to drive the Soviet Third Tank Army from his path; on March 7 he continued his advance with all three divisions of the SS Panzer Korps now in hand; and on March 14 he took Kharkov with ease by converging movements after restraining the SS Panzer Korps from entering the city prematurely at the risk of dissipating its strength in street fighting.

In this series of actions Manstein's performance as a master of strategy and major tactics reached its zenith. His shrewd judgment of Russian intentions, his preliminary dispositions, his refusal to be diverted by Hitler's impatience or the zeal of subordinates from what proved to be the right course, all stamped him as a master craftsman whom few rivals either in Germany or in Russia could surpass. What would have happened if he had been allowed to make his projected withdrawal behind the Dnieper, with Army Group A's infantry as well as its armour at his disposal, can only be a matter of conjecture. As it was, his achievement was to regain for the German Army, on the morrow of Stalingrad, a moral ascendancy which was not destined to last long.

Except that the Seventeenth Army was still in the Kuban, the winter campaigns of 1942-43 left the German Armies in South Russia standing more or less on the line which they had held

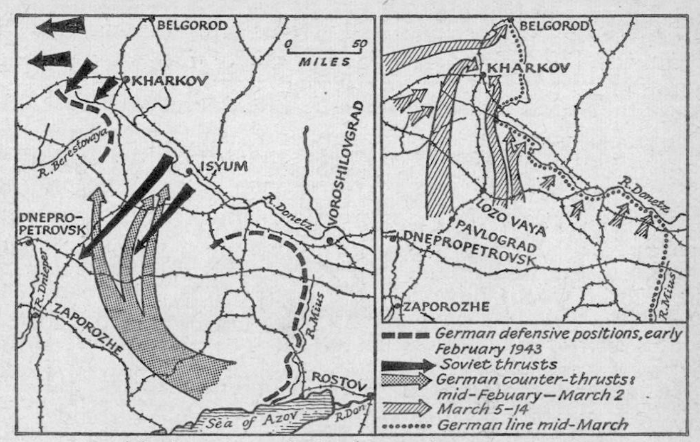

35 The Recapture of Kharkov, February-March 1943

on the eve of the summer offensive. On their left, the troops of Army Group Centre and Army Group North had settled down in timbered dugouts, apparently reconciled to the long spells of boredom, punctuated by moments of acute danger, with which survivors of the trench warfare of 1914-1918 were familiar.

When the spring thaw brought a respite for both sides, the Germans had therefore to ask themselves whether they should remain on the defensive when the ground was once again hard enough to make campaigning possible, or should try to win back the territory gained in the previous summer and since lost.

One course which they could not take, attractive though it seemed to some of them, was to make peace with the Western Allies on terms which pledged the major Western European Powers to return to the *status quo* and combine to restrain the Russians from crossing the old Polish frontier or entering the Balkans and the Baltic States. If accompanied by a change of government in Germany, and if Munich could be conveniently forgotten, such a peace might have been held to satisfy the aims with which France and Britain had entered the war; but since 1939 Britain had allied herself with the United States and Russia, and had pledged herself not to enter into negotiations with the enemy without consulting them. Moreover, at the Casablanca Conference President Roosevelt had disclosed to the world's press that the Western Allies meant to impose unconditional surrender on Germany and Italy.[35] An attempt by a group of army officers to assassinate Hitler on his way back from a visit to Army Group Centre at Smolensk on March 13 miscarried because a bomb placed in his aircraft failed to explode;[36] but even if it had succeeded, the mere extinction of the Führer would have left the conspirators with many obstacles to overcome if their ultimate aim was a negotiated peace.

In general, opinion in German military circles did not favour a purely defensive attitude which would surrender the initiative to the Russians and allow them to build up a massive numerical superiority in men and tanks. On the other hand, after losing the Sixth Army and four satellite armies, Germany no longer had the forces needed for an offensive on the scale of 1941 and 1942. On the assumption that outright victory had ceased to be within Hitler's scope, the problem was to find a cheap way of hitting the enemy so hard that it would also cease to be within Stalin's, and thus to force a draw.

With this aim in view, Manstein revived his plan of a retreat behind the Lower Dnieper. He argued that his salient along the Donetz and the Mius was sure to be attacked, and that the proper response was a planned withdrawal which would bring the enemy forward on a restricted front and expose him to a shattering counter-stroke from the north. But Hitler was not prepared to give up the western half of the Donetz basin even temporarily, and after a long debate his choice fell on a localized offensive against the Russian salient at Kursk. The proposal was that the salient, up to a hundred miles wide and eighty miles deep, should be attacked from the south by Manstein's army group, from the north by Army Group Centre under Field-Marshal Gunther von Kluge.

This project known as 'Citadel', was warmly championed by Zeitzler and Kluge, vigorously opposed by Jodl and Gud-

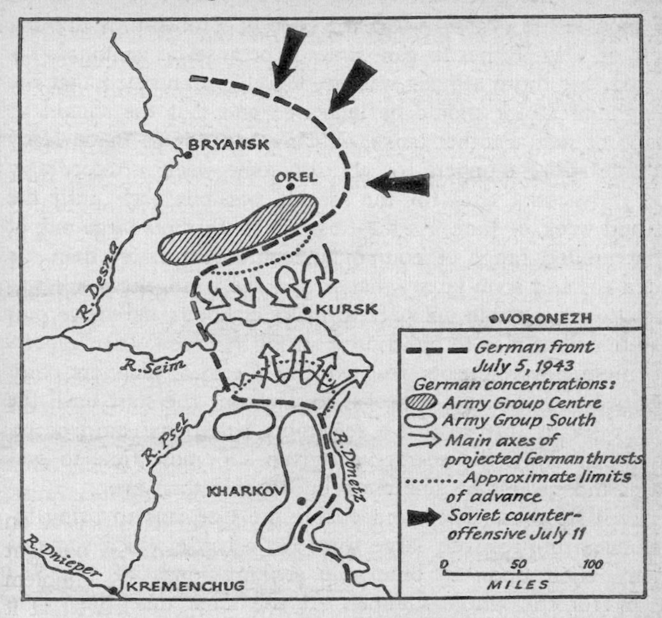

36 Operation 'Citadel', July 1943

erian, and endorsed by Manstein with the proviso that a great deal would depend on its being put into effect before the Russians recovered from the battering they had received in February and March.[37] As Jodl still had some influence at Supreme Headquarters, while Guderian was not only a leading authority on tank warfare but had been chosen by Hitler in person for the key post of Inspector-General of Armoured Troops, an understandable consequence of their disapproval was that for many weeks the Führer was more inclined to linger over the details of 'Citadel' than to take the crucial decision to put it into practice.

The original intention, as outlined by Zeitzler in April, was that 'Citadel' should be undertaken by ten or twelve armoured divisions, with supporting infantry, and should be carried out as soon as the ground was hard enough, probably in the first half of May. Either to gain time or because he genuinely believed that more armour was needed, Hitler insisted that the weight of attack should be increased and that use should be made of new Panther tanks, which could not be made ready in substantial numbers for at least some weeks. Accordingly the provisional date for the assault was put back until the second week in June. As the Russians, with their large output of a limited range of equipment, could refit faster than the Germans and soon knew what was in the wind, the result was that they were able not only to make elaborate defensive preparations but also to build up a strong reserve. When reports of these developments reached the German planners, they decided with Hitler's approval to postpone the start until the first week in July so that a few more battalions could be re-equipped. Thus the enemy was given still more time to prepare, and success became more improbable than ever.

Even so, these delays did enable the Germans to bring together an impressively large force for a battle which some of them relied upon to blunt the striking-power of the Red Army for the whole summer. At the same time they were able to increase the firepower of their tank units by using, in addition to the well-tried PzKw IV and the Tiger, which had proved its worth at Kharkov, both the Panther and the Ferdinand or Elephant, a thickly-armoured heavy tank or glorified gun-carrier with no secondary armament. By early July they had assembled north and south of the salient the formidable total of seventeen armoured or motorized divisions, backed by ten infantry divisions and equipped with roughly the same number of tanks as the entire German Army had possessed at the beginning of the campaign in the West in 1940. To provide air support about a thousand aircraft, or roughly half the first-line strength of the Luftwaffe on the Eastern Front from Murmansk to the Crimea, were concentrated at neighbouring airfields, where their presence helped to confirm the accuracy of predictions which Soviet intelligence officers had been making ever since the Germans began to show an interest in the Kursk salient in the early spring.

But if the Germans were strong, the Russians were stronger still.[38] In and about the salient they had more men, more major formations, more tanks and more guns than the enemy, and for once they were not inferior in the air. Moreover, they were forewarned, and they did not repeat their old mistake of allowing the troops in the front line to be taken by surprise. Throughout the German build-up they kept themselves informed of its progress by patrols and air reconnaissance, and they were not deceived by attempts to convince them that the main blow would fall on the western face of the salient. Above all, the postponement of the offensive from May to July gave them time not only to bring up large numbers of weapons but also to make well-thought-out dispositions, study in minute detail every scrap of ground to be defended, rehearse their actions, and in general make their preparations as thorough as possible. By July 2 the northern and southern faces of the salient were guarded by dense minefields backed by deep defensive zones in which every man knew exactly what he had to do, and in which was assembled the biggest array of anti-tank weapons yet brought together for a single battle.

The Germans opened their offensive on July 5 with the usual attempt to soften-up the defences by means of a brief artillery bombardment followed by dive-bombing. As the defenders were well provided with trenches and shelters and had an immense number of strongpoints and gun-sites, largely in positions unknown to the Germans, neither bombing nor gunfire had much effect. The assault forces then moved off in wedge-shaped formations, with the heaviest tanks leading, the light tanks spread out behind them, and infantry in tracked carriers bringing up the rear. A number of tanks were blown up by mines soon after leaving their start-lines, others were brought to a halt with damaged tracks and became sitting targets, and some of the Panthers broke down and were soon finished off. Too thickly armoured to be knocked out by the standard Russian anti-tank gun except at close ranges, those of the heavy tanks which had come safely through the minefields then began to break into the first of a series of defended zones with fair success; but many of the lighter tanks behind them were disabled or held up, and at some points these were overtaken by the infantry. Thus cohesion was soon lost, the pattern of the assault was broken up, and a good many tank units lost the power to support the infantry and had themselves to be supported.[39]

At the end of the first day the Russians claimed to have repelled all attacks with heavy losses, adding that 586 German tanks had been destroyed.[40] The Germans did not admit that they had scored so little success or had lost so many tanks, but recognized that the effectiveness of the defences had been seriously under-estimated by their planners. Even so, they had reckoned on a battle lasting several days, and they were not prepared to abandon hope after only one. Accordingly the Fourth Panzer Army, in Army Group South's sector, battered its way by July 11 to the rear of the enemy's main defensive zone, some thirty miles from its start-line, at a heavy cost in killed and wounded. In Army Group Centre's sector the situation was still more unpromising. Handicapped by dependence for part of its hitting power on some ninety Ferdinands, whose narrow field of fire and lack of secondary armament made them death-traps when isolated and hemmed in by infantry, the Ninth Army became stuck on an unfavourable slope after advancing about twelve miles.

At that stage the anxieties of the Germans were further increased by the difficulty of supplying the forward troops, who had gone into action with rations for five days. Nevertheless Hitler waited until July 13 before countermanding the offensive on the ground that the Axis front in Sicily was collapsing and that reinforcements were urgently needed in Italy.[41] Manstein, whose armour had been badly mauled by the Russian mobile reserve on the previous day, pleaded for one more chance to finish the enemy off, but in fact stood no chance of success.[42] A few days later all surviving elements of the assault forces on both fronts were back on their start-lines, and such reinforcements as Army Group South could spare were hastening round the western face of the salient to bolster Army Group Centre's attempts to deal with a counter-

37 The Red Army on the Offensive, August-September 1943

ffensive which the Russians had launched on July 11 in the)rel sector.

Almost simultaneously the Red Army pushed on with plans or converging attacks across the Mius and the Middle Donetz, ɔ that once again a planned withdrawal to the Dnieper had lmost everything to recommend it from the German point of iew. But the means of winning a decisive battle by counter-ttacking from the north had been squandered in ten days at ..ursk, and in any case Hitler insisted that the existing line long the Donetz and the Mius should be held. With his hoice thus fettered, and over-estimating the enemy's losses in ıe salient, Manstein then made what he afterwards called the isastrous decision to weaken his left in order to be able to hold fast on the right.* The consequences were that he gained a striking tactical success on the Mius at the end of July, but was hopelessly outmatched when the Russians attacked in the sector west of Belgorod a few days later. By September the whole of his forces were falling back towards the Dnieper on a five-hundred-mile front. So far as the Eastern Front was concerned, a ring round Germany was not merely in existence but was being tightened.

*Manstein, *op. cit.*, p. 452.

CHAPTER 15

A RING ROUND GERMANY: THE SOUTH (I)

February - September 1942

fter Rommel's recapture of Western Cyrenaica and the crip-
ling of the *Queen Elizabeth* and the *Valiant* at Alexandria,
e German naval authorities neglected no opportunity of im-
ressing upon the Supreme Command that for the time being
e Axis Powers were masters of the sea and the air in the
entral Mediterranean, that such an opportunity of driving
e British out of Egypt might never recur, and that Malta,
o, seemed ripe for conquest. Hitler was sceptical, but agreed
fter consulting Mussolini that Rommel should aim at cap-
ring Tobruk before the beginning of the last week in June.
n attempt would then be made to deal with Malta before he
ntinued his advance to the Suez Canal.

How Malta should be tackled was a controversial question.
he Italians were willing to find two airborne and five sea-
orne divisions as their contribution to an invasion force if the
ermans would contribute one airborne division and some
ree hundred transport aircraft; but whether they could make
success of the venture even with the help of German planners
as debatable. On the other hand a substantial force of German
mber, fighter and reconnaissance aircraft, supplemented by
alian aircraft and backed by the Italian surface fleet and
erman and Italian submarines, might succeed in gaining such
ascendancy over the island and its approaches that an
posed landing would not be necessary.

Accordingly, the Luftwaffe built up its strength in Sicily
om roughly 200 aircraft at the beginning of 1942 to more
an twice as many at the end of March. At the same time it

intensified its attacks on Malta for the twofold purpose of starving the inhabitants and making the island unusable as a base for attacks on convoys carrying supplies to Rommel. In February Axis bombers did so much damage to all three ships of the only convoy sent to Malta that none completed the voyage;[1] in March two out of four ships, also in convoy, entered the Grand Harbour safely after their escort and covering forces had held off a greatly superior Italian surface fleet, but were sunk by bombing before unloading could be completed;[2] and in April the British did not succeed either in supplying Malta or in preventing the Axis forces in North Africa from receiving nearly 50,000 tons of fuel and more than 100,000 tons of other stores. By early May the island was not only in danger of succumbing to a prolonged blockade, but so beset by more immediate dangers as to be no longer a safe point of departure for air and naval striking forces. Stocks of flour and unmilled grain were expected to last until July if the mills were not put out of action; but rations were meagre. The approaches to the Grand Harbour could not be kept clear because there were not enough minesweepers to deal with the mines laid almost nightly by the enemy's fast surface craft, and most bombers, surface ships and submarines were under orders to leave or had already left.

The remedy which suggested itself to the Maltese and the English alike was not surrender but victory in the air. The Chiefs of Staff were asked to send to the Middle East Command enough heavy bombers to smash the enemy's airfields in Sicily. This, however, they refused to do. They proposed, as an alternative more in line with the Air Staff's policy, to strengthen the island's air defences by sending through the Straits of Gibraltar aircraft carriers laden with Spitfires equipped for the occasion with supplementary fuel-tanks. These would make the long hop to Malta from positions outside the area in which interference from German and Italian bombers was probable.

This had been tried in March, when thirty-one Spitfires flew from the British carrier *Eagle*, and again in April when the United States carrier *Wasp* brought forty-seven; but on both ccasions practically all the new arrivals had been put out of ction, mainly by bombing, before they could make their resence felt. A fresh attempt was now made, after preparaions so thorough that some of the sixty Spitfires which arrived rom the *Wasp* and the *Eagle* on May 9 were ready for ction within six minutes. An hour later roughly half the orce was actively defending its new bases.

Next day the fast minelayer *Welshman*, carrying 340 tons of mmunition and other stores, entered the Grand Harbour after hazardous voyage from Gibraltar, and on May 18 the *Eagle* eturned to make safe delivery of seventeen more Spitfires. Almost simultaneously the Luftwaffe moved about sixty airraft from Sicily to the Eastern Front and some eighty-five o Africa, leaving roughly 150 serviceable bombers and fighters o continue the assault on Malta. No longer obliged to make lo with half a dozen serviceable fighters, the island's air lefences destroyed about forty German and Italian aircraft in May for the loss of twenty-five of their own in the air and six n the ground. The number of serviceable German bombers nd fighters in Sicily fell by the end of the month to less than ighty. At that stage it was, however, common ground between London and Malta that air superiority would prove an empty ain unless a substantial convoy reached the island before the nd of June.

Throughout the crucial months it was also accepted that asting control of the Central Mediterranean would be reained only when the airfields of Western Cyrenaica were once nore in British hands. Consequently a great deal of pressure vas put on General Auchinleck to drive the Axis forces back o Tripolitania without delay. But Auchinleck had been made esponsible in January for Iraq and Persia as well as Syria, and e still feared that the Germans might catch him on the wrong oot by coming through the Caucasus. In any case he was etermined not to move until he was ready. On February 27 e reported that a premature offensive in Cyrenaica might ose him his army and Egypt too. Just over a week later he efused to return home for consultation, although well-wishers n London believed that he would be wise to do so. His view was that nothing could make him change his mind, but that attempts to talk him over might sap reserves of mental and moral energy which he needed in Cairo.

Angered by Auchinleck's boldness, the Prime Minister contemplated replacing him, but changed his mind when General Brooke, the Chief of the Imperial General Staff, suggested that Auchinleck and Wavell should once again exchange jobs. Churchill then asked Sir Stafford Cripps, who was about to visit India in the hope of reconciling Hindu and Moslem aspirations, to stop in Cairo and confer with Auchinleck, and the Vice-Chief of the Imperial General Staff, General A. E. Nye, to put a long list of questions to the Middle East Command. Both reported in due course that Auchinleck's views were sound. Cripps added, after consulting the Air Commander-in-Chief, the senior naval officer on the spot and the acting Minister of State, Sir Walter Monckton, that like Auchinleck he felt that to attack before the middle of May would be to take 'an unwarrantable risk'. Cripps also thought that there was a strong case for sending heavy bombers to the Middle East, where they could be used to better purpose than against Germany.*

In face of such unanimity among men so diverse in temperament as Auchinleck, Cripps and Monckton, Churchill swallowed his impatience; but the decision not to press for an offensive before May 15 cost the government some anxious moments in view of Malta's plight. Although the Commanders-in-Chief in the Middle East were careful to add that they could not promise to start on any particular day, the Prime Minister was correspondingly put out when they signalled on May 6 that, in the light of a detailed comparison between Auchinleck's probable future strength and Rommel's, a beginning did not now seem possible until June 15, and that in certain circumstances the offensive might even have to be put off until August. The upshot was that on May 10, after earnest debate in London and a further exchange of signals with Cairo, the Prime Minister despatched in the names of the

*J. R. M. Butler, *Grand Strategy, Volume III, Part III* (London 1964), p. 453.

Chiefs of Staff, the Defence Committee and the War Cabinet a telegram which gave Auchinleck no choice but to resign or agree to fight a major battle in time to distract the enemy's attention from a convoy which the government hoped to send to Malta about the middle of June.

Auchinleck accepted this ultimatum on May 19. By that date he had been aware for more than a week of indications that Rommel was preparing to do something big.* Thus it was highly probable that the enemy would absolve him of the obligation to attack by himself taking the offensive. In that case the major battle to which Auchinleck was pledged would be fought on ground of the Eighth Army's choosing and within easy reach of its railhead at Belhamed, while the enemy's communications would be stretched. In view of all that had been done since the winter to strengthen the army and prepare its positions for defence, from the standpoint of Cairo it would be surprising if, in such circumstances, the Eighth Army failed to win.

In London the outcome of the promised battle, irrespective of where it might be fought, was awaited with confidence, even though the Prime Minister conceded that there were 'no safe battles'.[3] Auchinleck's postponements, and still more his refusal to come home for consultation, had given the impression that he was obstinate and inclined to exaggerate his difficulties from motives of caution; but no one doubted his gifts as a strategist and a leader of men. Churchill would have been happier if he had gone forward to take direct command of the Eighth Army, but this Auchinleck declined to do.[4] The claims of the desert front might have to be weighed against those of Iraq or Syria, and to make impartial decisions would, he felt, be difficult if he left Cairo. Earlier, General Brooke had suggested that a seasoned commander, other than Auchinleck himself, should replace the relatively junior Ritchie; but here, too, Auchinleck was unresponsive. Admitting that Ritchie was inexperienced, that he had been sent to command the Eighth Army only as a temporary expedient, and

* Major-General I. S. O. Playfair, *The Mediterranean and Middle East*, Volume III (London, 1960), p. 216.

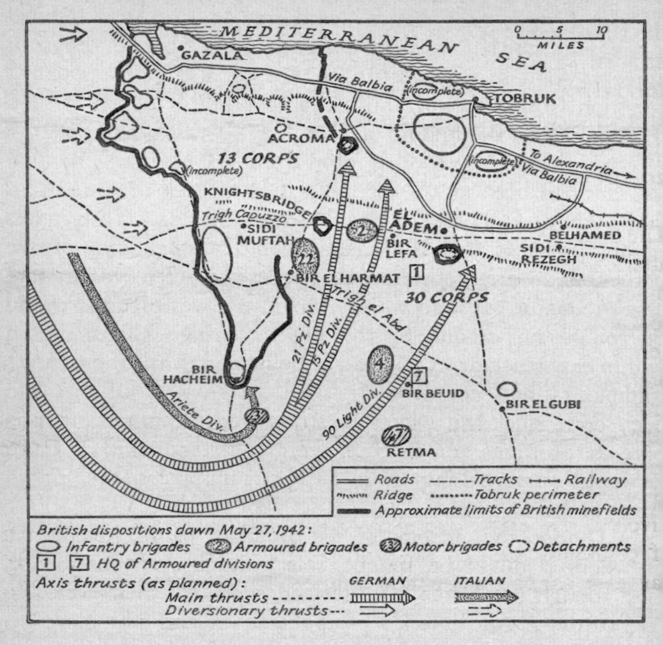

38 The Battle of Gazala, May-June 1942

that his dispute with Godwin-Austen during the retreat fron
Agedabia had been unfortunate, Auchinleck was none the les
unwilling to see him go. Mistakenly, the government and th
press had led the public to believe that Ritchie was not
mere stop-gap but the inspired leader for whom the army ha
been waiting, and Auchinleck felt that to supersede him s
soon after Cunningham's departure might undermine the con
fidence not only of the man in the street, but also of th
troops.

Thus Ritchie, an able staff officer whose only fault wa
that he had been pitchforked into a highly responsible posi
tion at a time when it was necessary to find for the Eight
Army a temporary commander who knew how Auchinlec
viewed the situation at Sidi Rezegh, was still in command whe

he time came for the army to fight a battle on which the gov-
:rnment counted for a spectacular victory. It was Ritchie who
.nnounced on May 16 that he intended 'to destroy the enemy's
ırmoured forces in the battle of the Gazala-Bir Hacheim posi-
ion'. And it was to Ritchie that Auchinleck confided, on May
:o, his views as to how that might be done.

Che position which Rommel was rightly thought to be about to
.ttack consisted essentially of a belt of minefields about forty
niles long and up to ten miles wide, extending from the coast
o Bir Hacheim and commanded for part of its length by a
eries of wired 'boxes' prepared for all-round defence. Each
ox was garrisoned by a brigade group with its own artillery,
mple ammunition, and supplies for about a week. The whole
ront was screened by a system of patrols by armoured cars and
mall mobile columns, and behind the minefields a number
f widely-separated rear positions had been set up to serve as
ivots of manœuvre and to block the principal tracks and centres
f communication as far south as the Trigh Capuzzo and as
ar east as El Adem, about fifteen miles from the Eighth
ırmy's railhead.

The Gazala-Bir Hacheim position, in common with almost
very other position astride the coast road west of El Alamein,
ould be turned by an outflanking movement through the
esert. It could also be breached by an enemy equipped to
ear a way through the minefields, either in the thirteen-mile-
ide gap between the right of the 1st Free French Brigade
roup's box at Bir Hacheim and the left of the 150th Infantry
rigade Group's box at Sidi Muftah, or more probably in the
ırrower gap immediately north of the Trigh Capuzzo, where
e minefield was not so broad. But these weaknesses were
ore apparent than real. Auchinleck's intention was not that
e Eighth Army should present an impenetrable front to the
emy, but that it should destroy him. Before the battle there
ıs a good deal of speculation among senior commanders as
whether the attack would be made south of the minefields or
one or other of the central gaps; but much of it was beside
e point. No matter which way Rommel came, he would not

be able to reach Tobruk, which was rightly assumed to be his objective, without wheeling northwards and passing diagon-ally across the rear of the defended belt. If all went well from the British point of view, he would thus expose himself to a devastating counter-attack from the two armoured divisions of Norrie's 30th Corps, with not less than 500 tanks. At the same time his escape to the west would be blocked by the 13th Corps under Lieutenant-General W. H. E. Gott, whose three infantry divisions and two army tank brigades, with 276 tanks, would meanwhile have sealed any breach made in the Gazala-Bir Hacheim front.*

If these hopes were to be realized it was, however, essentia that the armoured divisions should be held in a strategic posi tion, preferably to the east of the enemy's probable line o advance, that they should not be prematurely committed, an above all that they should not be dispersed and made to fight i small detachments with little or no support from artillery an anti-tank guns. A week before the battle Auchinleck advise Ritchie to put both armoured divisions astride the Trig Capuzzo west of El Adem, adding that it was 'of the highes importance' that their organization should not be broken up The two divisions, he wrote, must fight as divisions an Norrie must handle them 'as a corps commander'.

The Eighth Army's dispositions at the outset of the batt were startlingly at variance with this concept. At one tim inclined to believe that the attack would be made throug one of the central gaps, Ritchie had come round to the vie that an attempt to turn his southern flank was probable, b that nothing was certain. The upshot was that, instead of co centrating the whole of Norrie's armour near El Adem so th

*The distribution of the Eighth Army's tanks on the eve of the batt was: 30th Corps (1st Armoured and 7th Armoured Divisions) a reserves, 573; 1st and 32nd Army Tank Brigades (in 13th Cor with 50th, 1st South African and 2nd South African Divisions), 27 1st Armoured Brigade (under orders to join from Egypt), 145; tot 994 tanks of which 242 were Grants, 219 Stuarts, 257 Crusade 166 Valentines and 110 Matildas. Rommel had roughly 332 Germ and 228 Italian tanks, about half of them qualitively superior to a of the Eighth Army's tanks except the Grant.

could strike westwards or north-westwards at a force coming
om either direction, as Auchinleck urged him to do, he put
e 1st Armoured Division more or less on the path which
ommel would take if he approached from the west, and the
ree mobile brigades of the 7th Armoured Division more or
ss on the route which he seemed likely to follow if he skirted
e minefields on the south.* Ritchie intended to use the 7th
rmoured Division's mobile brigades to delay the enemy's
lvance (which would tend towards dispersal), but hoped
ventually to be able to assemble them for a counter-attack
which would call for concentration).

Rommel's plan, in its final form, was to give the impression
at he was about to make a heavy attack north of the Trigh
apuzzo by sending two Italian corps with some German lor-
ed infantry towards that sector in daylight, and after night-
ll to take his German mobile formations round the southern
tremity of the minefields while the Ariete Division of the
alian mobile corps on his immediate left captured Bir
acheim. Closely followed by columns carrying enough fuel
r about 300 miles and the balance of four days' supplies of
od and water, on May 27 the two German armoured divions would make for Acroma and the 90th Light Division for
Adem and Belhamed. Formations of the 13th Corps in the
rward area and in support would then be attacked from the
st and west; their rear communications would be cut by a
rce to be landed from the sea; and in four days Tobruk
ould fall.

Late on May 26 the Italians on Rommel's left duly closed up
General Gott's front and began to dig in to the accompani-

he 1st Armoured Division consisted of the 2nd and 22nd Armoured
igade Groups and the 201st (Guards) Motor Brigade; the 7th
moured Division of the 4th Armoured Brigade Group, the 7th
tor Brigade Group and the 3rd Indian Motor Brigade Group, in
lition to the 1st Free French Brigade Group and the 29th Indian
antry Brigade Group at Bir Hacheim and Bir el Gubi. Auchin-
k intended to reorganize his armour so that each division con-
ted of one armoured and one motorized infantry brigade, with
porting troops, but had not had time to make these changes when
mmel opened his offensive.

ment of an intense artillery bombardment; but their activities did not distract attention from the mobile columns on the right, which were seen and shadowed by British patrols in bright moonlight. In accordance with Ritchie's policy of trying to delay the enemy, no steps were taken to remove the 7th Armoured Division's mobile formations from exposed positions south-west of the Trigh el Abd and concentrate them for a counter-attack under the corps commander's hand. The consequences were that the 3rd Indian Motor Brigade south of Bir Hacheim was overrun early on May 27 by the Ariete Division and had to go right back to the Egyptian frontier to reform; that the 7th Motor Brigade at Retima was attacked about an hour and a half later by the 90th Light Division and withdrew eastwards to El Gubi; and that the divisional commander General Messervy, was captured with three of his staff when his advanced headquarters at Bir Beuid was in turn overrun towards the middle of the forenoon. In the meantime Messerv (who escaped a few days later) had ordered the 4th Armoure Brigade to go to the help of the 3rd Indian Motor Brigade but the brigade was attacked by the 15th Panzer Division whil moving to its assembly area, suffered but also inflicted substantial losses, and eventually withdrew towards Belhamed.

General Norrie, not yet fully aware of the setback to th 7th Armoured Division and in any case with only one of h divisions at hand for an immediate counter-stroke, then ordere the 1st Armoured Division to be ready to go south and giv battle. The immediate outcome was a headlong clash betwee the two Panzer divisions and the 22nd Armoured Brigad which moved off without waiting for the 2nd Armoure Brigade to join it; but the 22nd managed to extricate itself aft losing about thirty tanks, and the divisional commander the succeeded in delivering concerted attacks with both brigad from the north-west and the east. As the British 1st Arn Tank Brigade attacked almost simultaneously, also from th north-west, the forces on both sides were soon so closely inte mingled that British bomber crews and fighter-bomber pilc had great difficulty in finding good targets except on the fring of the battle zone. Heavily outnumbered, and with all fighters outmatched by the Messerschmitt 109F, the Western Desert Air Force could not in any case give as much help to the Eighth Army as Rommel received from the Luftwaffe and the Regia Aeronautica. But this may not have been clear to Ritchie. It was certainly not clear to Auchinleck, who seems to have believed throughout the battle that his side was 'definitely superior in the air'.*

Even so, the situation on the ground at the end of the first day's fighting seemed much more favourable to the British than to the Germans and Italians. By dusk on May 27 the French at Bir Hacheim had driven off the whole of the Ariete Division, the German supply columns were in difficulties well to the rear of the forward troops, and the 15th Panzer Division was already short of fuel and ammunition. Admittedly the German armoured divisions had reached positions within fifteen miles or less of their immediate objective at Acroma; but they had lost a third of their tanks, they were out of touch with the 90th Light Division on their right, and the 15th Panzer Division would be more of a liability than an asset until it could be supplied. Conversely, the British had no problems of supply, they had the advantage of an unbreached front against which to press the enemy in their midst, and their three armoured brigades, though battered, were still intact.

On the other hand, the Eighth Army's freedom of manœuvre was limited by the need to defend huge quantities of stores accumulated at Belhamed and Tobruk in preparation for an offensive. Moreover, the disruption of the 7th Armoured Division did not help Army Headquarters to build up a clear picture of events. The consequences were that Ritchie and his corps commanders did not at once become aware of the strength of the case for risking everything in order to destroy the two Panzer divisions before Rommel could concentrate and supply them, and that no comprehensive and flexible plan of action

*The approximate numbers of serviceable aircraft on each side on May 26 were: Luftwaffe and Regia Aeronautica in North Africa 500; Western Desert Air Force, 190. The Spitfire VB, comparable in performance with the Messerschmitt 109F, made its first appearance as a fighter in the Western Desert on June 1.

was drawn up for the second day. The commander of the 1st Armoured Division, expecting both Panzer divisions to resume their advance on May 28, intended to take them in the flank as they moved northwards; but as the 15th Panzer Division remained immobile at Bir Lefa, all that in fact happened was that the 22nd Armoured Brigade stayed to watch it, the 21st Panzer Division moved off without it, and the 2nd Armoured Brigade joined the 1st Army Tank Brigade in engaging the Ariete Division, which could safely have been rounded up at leisure if the German armoured divisions had been destroyed. Meanwhile the British 4th Armoured Brigade chased the German 90th Light Division away from El Adem, thereby removing any immediate threat to Belhamed but making no direct contribution to the defeat of the formations which mattered most. Thus the British failed to grasp an opportunity which began to wither when, early next morning, Rommel gave his Panzer divisions a new lease of life by personally leading the supply vehicles up to them.

On May 29 Rommel abandoned any immediate intention of continuing his advance, countermanded the landing from the sea, and decided to concentrate his mobile formation behind a thick anti-tank screen west of the point called Knightsbridge and to open a supply route and possible way of escape through the minefields in his rear. Attacked all day by the British 2nd Armoured Brigade and part of the 22nd, but helped by a rising dust-storm which prevented the 4th Armoured Brigade from reaching the battlefield, Rommel succeeded by the early hours of May 30 in uniting practically the whole of his three German divisions and the Italian mobile corps in the area afterwards known as the Cauldron. He then discovered that the sector immediately to the south and west of him was not a mere minefield but an armed camp held by the 150th Infantry Brigade Corps, reinforced on the previous day by part of the 1st Army Tank Brigade. Strongly supported by dive-bombers and profiting by the failure of the British to send further reinforcements while there was still time, he none the less managed on June 1 to secure his route to the west by overwhelming the 150th Infantry Brigade Group after it had beaten off attacks on May 30 and 31.

With only 130 fit tanks left, but comforted by the knowledge that the Trigh Capuzzo was now a two-way route along which he could not only be supplied and reinforced but could retreat westwards if all else failed, Rommel decided on the following day to hold the Cauldron for the time being with his one Italian and two German armoured divisions, and to send the 90th Light Division and the Trieste Motorized Division southwards to take Bir Hacheim. In spite of heavy shelling, repeated attacks by bombers and dive-bombers, and the eventual arrival of the 15th Panzer Division to join the investing force, the French under General M.-P. Koenig held out against tremendous pressure until the night of June 10, when 2,700 survivors of the original garrison of 3,600 broke out on Ritchie's orders and made rendezvous with the 7th Motor Brigade outside the perimeter.

Meanwhile the Eighth Army had at last delivered its crucial attack on the German and Italian armour in the Cauldron.

The British plan for the attack on the Cauldron was to lead off with a heavy artillery bombardment during the night of June 4. Under cover of darkness the 10th Indian Infantry Brigade of the 5th Indian Division, formerly in the Army Reserve, would then seize objectives up to a mile or more inside the Ariete Division's perimeter on the east. At dawn the 32nd Army Tank Brigade, with 70 infantry tanks and a battalion of infantry under command, would come from the north to occupy a ridge about the same distance inside the 21st Panzer Division's sector. With the ground thus prepared for it the 22nd Armoured Brigade, now in the 7th Armoured Division, would pass through the left of the 10th Indian Infantry Brigade's position and make a righthanded sweep through the Cauldron, destroying the enemy's armour as it went. During this phase the 9th Indian Infantry Brigade, also from the 5th Indian Division but temporarily under command of the 7th Armoured Division, was to complete the capture of the ground swept by the armour by occupying positions near the centre of the Cauldron and in the 15th Panzer Division's sector in the south. Meanwhile the 1st Armoured Division, well north of the Trigh Capuzzo, would stand by to intercept the enemy if he broke out to the north and east, and to follow up to the west if he retreated and left the British in possession of the battlefield.

In spite of the importance attached to this operation, which Ritchie regarded as an essential preliminary to any westward thrust by the four or five intact divisions still at his disposal, the system of command adopted for it was extraordinarily defective. With the exception of the army commander, who was not likely to be in a position to exercise tactical control, no single officer was authorized to co-ordinate the attacks on the eastern and northern fronts, although these involved formations belonging to two different corps. Even on the eastern front, where all the troops belonged to the 30th Corps, there was no co-ordinator, for Norrie's decision was that Major-General R. Briggs, commanding the 5th Indian Division, should take command during the first phase when the 10th Indian Infantry Brigade was opening a way for the armour, but that General Messervy, commanding the 7th Armoured Division, should take over when the 22nd Armoured Brigade began its sweep. The placing of the 9th Indian Infantry Brigade under Messervy instead of Briggs was intended to emphasize the distinction and help Messervy; but a further complication arose from orders which ruled that the brigade must not hamper the movements of the 22nd Armoured Brigade and added that infantry co-operating with armour must be self-protecting. This ruling was not meant to debar the 22nd Armoured Brigade from helping the 9th Indian Infantry Brigade to reach its objectives should help be needed, and that was made clear in the order; what was not made clear was that the armoured brigade would be free to go to the aid of any infantry which might find itself in difficulties if the offensive sweep should fail.

Largely on account of these shortcomings, the attack on the Cauldron was not only unsuccessful but needlessly expensive.

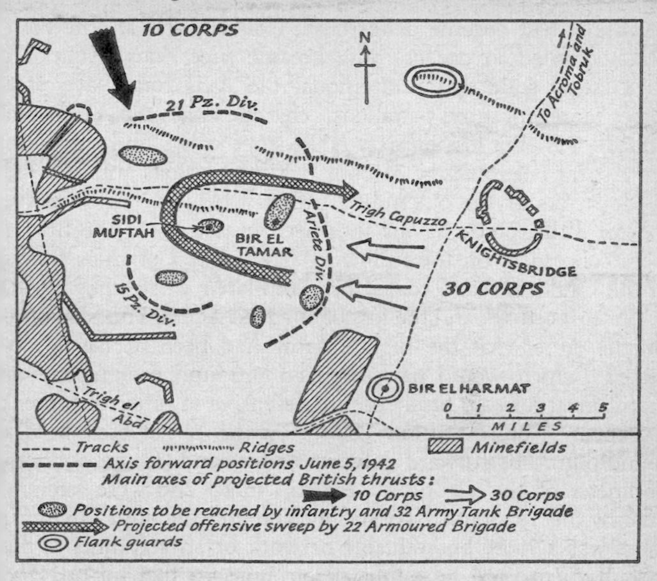

39 The Cauldron

The 10th Indian Infantry Brigade reached its objectives in the arly hours of June 5 with trifling losses; but the 32nd Army Tank Brigade came under heavy fire from anti-tank guns, ran nto an unsuspected minefield, and withdrew after losing fifty anks. The 22nd Armoured Brigade had only just begun its ffensive sweep when it was met by concentrated fire from most f Rommel's artillery, which was sited well to the rear and ad come through the preliminary bombardment more or less nscathed. It then wheeled back to a position on the left of one f the 10th Indian Infantry Brigade's battalions. Wrongly supposing, however, that the order which called on the infantry to ok after itself while the enemy's armour was being destroyed eld good even though the offensive sweep had failed, the rmoured brigade gave no help to the battalion beside it when e enemy counter-attacked at noon. Consequently the battalion as forced back, another infantry battalion was withdrawn because it had become dangerously isolated, and all the positions occupied in the morning became precarious. Attacking on a larger scale in the afternoon, the Axis forces overcame three more infantry battalions, chased away the armoured brigade with the loss of sixty tanks since dawn, and dispersed the tactical headquarters of both British divisions and also the headquarters of the 9th Indian Infantry Brigade. All effective control of the battle having thus been lost so far as the British were concerned, on the following day the rest of their troops in the Cauldron were routed or annihilated where they stood.

But this setback and the loss of Bir Hacheim did not convince Ritchie either that the Eighth Army had been decisively defeated (which would have been an unsound conclusion), or that it must now go firmly on the defensive in order to prevent the enemy from capturing Tobruk (which might have been a sound one). His forward defences as far south as the northern perimeter of the Cauldron were still intact and were strongly held by the 1st South African Division and the 50th Division; there was a loose but valuable network of strongpoints to the east of them; and he estimated on June 10 that he had 250 cruiser and 80 infantry tanks still fit to fight.* He concluded that there was a good chance that one more armoured battle might exhaust the enemy and put the Eighth Army in a position to advance.

But Rommel was quicker to seize an opportunity than the British, he had a firmer grip on his armoured formations, and generally his tank and anti-tank units still had the advantage of far better guns and ammunition. On June 11 he began a sortie from the Cauldron with the intention of reaching the coast and cutting off the 1st South African and 50th Divisions. General Norrie hoped to smash him by counter-attacking

*The true figures on that day appear to have been 185 and 63 respectively. On June 12 they were: 2nd Armoured Brigade, 4[illegible] cruiser tanks; 4th Armoured Brigade, 95; 22nd Armoured Brigade, 66; 7th Motor Brigade, 16; 32nd Army Tank Brigade, 63 infantry tanks; totals, 63 infantry and 222 cruiser tanks, of which 83 were Grants. Rommel had (on June 11) 124 good and 25 less good German and about 60 Italian tanks, or a total of 209 tanks of all classes.

wiftly with the 2nd and 4th Armoured Brigades; but a amiliar sequence of mishaps and hesitations made both rigades slow off the mark, and Rommel was encouraged to aise the stakes. Committing practically the whole of his nobile force and taking advantage of dust-storms to push his nti-tank guns boldly forward, in a two-day battle near the Knightsbridge crossing on June 12 and 13 he decisively de-eated Ritchie's armour and drove it from the battlefield. With nly fifty cruiser and twenty infantry tanks left in the for-vard area, Ritchie arranged on June 14 to remove all stores rom Belhamed and withdraw the 1st South African and 50th Divisions to the Egyptian frontier.

But withdrawal to the frontier meant either that Tobruk nust be abandoned, or that an attempt must be made to hold it s an outpost. Neither course was acceptable to Auchinleck. Knowing that Rommel's superiors were unlikely to sanction n advance into Egypt as long as Tobruk remained in British ands, Auchinleck had no intention of abandoning the place. As early as January, however, he had made it clear that he vould not accept a siege there, and in consequence the peri-neter defences had not been kept up. When he learned almost mmediately after returning from a visit to the front that Ritchie's armour had been defeated and that there was talk f a general withdrawal, he therefore sent his Chief of Staff, Lieutenant-General T. W. Corbett, to Army Headquarters with rders to insist that Ritchie should rally his forces for a defen-ive battle on the line Acroma-El Adem-Bir el Gubi, where his urviving tanks would be able to fight under cover of artillery nassed on high ground to the north.[5] As Ritchie had no in-ention of fighting on that line or of recalling the 1st South African and 50th Divisions, the interview was stormy. After number of signals had gone back and forth between Ritchie, uchinleck and the Prime Minister it was agreed, however, that ne Eighth Army should do its best to keep the enemy west f Auchinleck's line. If the attempt failed, then a temporary nvestment of Tobruk would, after all, be accepted, but itchie would aim at relieving the garrison as soon as possible.

But Ritchie proved incapable of keeping the enemy at arm's

length with the forces which he was willing to risk west of the Egyptian frontier. The 2nd South African Division, locked up in Tobruk with no British short-range fighters within reach and under an inexperienced commander, was equally incapable of holding off five or six weak Axis divisions supported by some 300 serviceable aircraft, most of them working from bases so close at hand that they were able to make repeated sorties. Rommel launched his assault on Tobruk about 7 a.m. on June 20 after a heavy bombardment by bombers and dive-bombers, a breach was opened in the outer defences within an hour, and by nightfall most of the town was in his hands. Early next morning the garrison commander capitulated in order to avoid useless slaughter. About 33,000 of all ranks passed into captivity, and in spite of eleventh hour attempts at demolition and destruction the Axis forces claimed the capture of 1,400 tons of fuel, 5,000 tons of provisions and 2,000 serviceable vehicles.

Meanwhile a convoy of eleven ships from Alexandria and one of six ships from Gibraltar had taken the place of the much-discussed June convoy to Malta, but the attempt to supply the island by taking two bites at the cherry had failed. The Italian Navy and bombers from Crete had turned back the ships bound from Alexandria; of those sent from Gibraltar only two had reached their destination. Concluding when Tobruk fell that there was no need to spend time and effort on risky airborne and seaborne landings, Hitler had little difficulty in persuading Mussolini that the Axis troops in North Africa ought to go straight on to Egypt, leaving the subjugation of Malta to the Luftwaffe and the Regia Aeronautica.[6] Eventually it was agreed that Rommel should aim at seizing Ismailia and Cairo, but must first occupy the El Alamein-Qattara position as a jumping-off place for further operations whose timing would depend on the state of his supplies. To pursue a beaten enemy, the Führer argued, was always the right policy.

But Auchinleck did not regard himself as beaten. Assuming direct command of the Eighth Army in place of Ritchie, he announced his intention of keeping the army in being as a mobile fighting force, even if ground had to be given up. On receiving news of the fall of Tobruk, Churchill had persuaded the United States government to take from their own armoured formations 300 Sherman tanks and 100 self-propelled guns which Auchinleck could expect to receive about the end of August;[7] in the last week of June the army began to feel the benefit of steps taken about the time of the Gazala battles to provide more air support in future. New landing-grounds in Egypt were made ready for use at short notice, training-units parted with some of their equipment for the benefit of first-line squadrons, and the authorities in London agreed to find more aircraft for the Middle East by diverting reinforcements from India and Australia. By the last week in June the Western Desert Air Force had more than 460 aircraft fit to fly, while the Luftwaffe had roughly 180 serviceable aircraft in North Africa, and the Regia Aeronautica about 240. Thus the British, proverbially better at winning the last battle than the first, provided themselves with the means of constantly harrying Rommel's forces at the very moment when his communications became so stretched that air cover for his forward troops and transport columns would in any case have been hard to find.

When Auchinleck assumed command of the Eighth Army on June 25, Ritchie was preparing to fight a decisive battle 120 miles east of the Egyptian frontier, with his right on the sea at Matruh and his left in the open desert some forty miles to the south-west. Although this policy had the blessing of the Middle East Defence Committee and therefore of the Commander-in-Chief,[8] a survey of the tactical situation from his new standpoint as army commander soon convinced Auchinleck that it would not do. As he had neither enough armour to counter an outflanking movement nor enough artillery to safeguard a weak centre protected by little more than a thin minefield, the probable consequence of an attempt to fight a decisive battle at Matruh would, he felt, be defeat in detail.

Shortly before midnight on June 25, Auchinleck therefore told his corps commanders that he could not afford to risk being pinned down where he stood, and would fight the enemy over

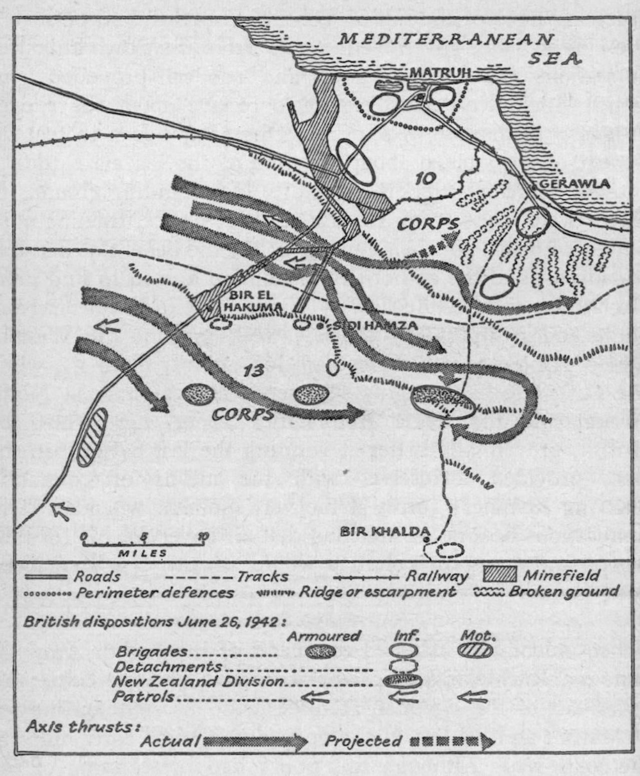

40 The Matruh Position

the whole stretch between Matruh and the Alamein-Qattar position. They were not to commit their armour except in th most favourable conditions, and each non-armoured divisio was to divide itself into two components, so that part of its in fantry and all its artillery could be used in the forward are while the rest of the infantry prepared to take up positions i the rear. This pronouncement, which contradicted the accepte principle of organization by divisions and cut clean across th orthodox doctrine that a retreating army should avoid a rur

ing fight, aroused lasting controversy; but these disadvant-
ges seemed to Auchinleck acceptable if the new arrangement
elped him to save the immediate situation and prepare for a
najor stand at El Alamein without too blatantly advertising his
eadiness to cede a large tract of Egyptian territory to the
enemy.

Late on June 26 the Axis forces came forward to the
Matruh position after a trying advance through waterless
ountry where they were constantly under air attack. By night-
all Rommel succeeded in pushing the 90th Light Division
hrough Auchinleck's centre with the intention of sending it
on to cut the coast road east of Matruh while his Panzer divi-
ions held off the British armour; but next morning it came
under heavy artillery fire and made little progress. During
he forenoon, however, Auchinleck followed up the broad
nstructions which he had issued before the battle by telling
his two corps commanders where they were to go if they
eceived orders to withdraw. The outcome was that when
General Gott, still commanding the 13th Corps and responsible for the southern half of the front, became aware some
hours later of a threat to one of his formations from the weak
21st Panzer Division, which had only 21 fit tanks, he set the
withdrawal in motion without waiting for express authority to
do so. When he reported what he had done, Army Headquarters had no choice but to order the other corps to withdraw, which it eventually did by breaking out of a rather
ramped position at a heavy cost. Thus Auchinleck's first battle
ince he superseded Ritchie resulted in his abandoning the
Matruh position without even fighting a prolonged delaying
ction, and Rommel was presented with an easy victory which
urned out to be his last.

Bewildered but not demoralized, the six weak divisions
withdrawn from Matruh then fell back to join the equivalent
f rather more than one division already in the desert belt be-
ween the coast at El Alamein and the rocky hills on the north-
rn edge of the virtually impassable Qattara depression. As this
was about the only position on the coast road between Alex-
ndria and Tripoli which could not be easily turned, it had been

regarded since 1939 or earlier as a good place at which to stop an invader from the west, and Auchinleck had given orders soon after his arrival in the Middle East that it should be prepared for defence. The state of affairs at the time of the fighting at Matruh was that a water pipe had been laid the whole way from the railway station at El Alamein to the Naqb Abu Dweis depression, some thirty-eight miles to the south-west, and that incomplete works existed at both ends of this line and near the centre at Bab el Qattara. As a result of three days of back-breaking toil by troops recently withdrawn from the Egyptian frontier or brought up from the rear, the defences were, however, in considerably better shape by the time the bulk of the Eighth Army arrived at the very end of June.

In accordance with his theory of 'fluid defence', Auchinleck made only a limited use of the prepared positions other than that at El Alamein itself. At first he put a brigade in each of them and one in each of the gaps between them; but the Bab el Qattara and Naqb Abu Dweis positions seemed to him to invite encirclement. He soon gave up using them except as pivots of manœuvre for mobile troops, and towards the end of July he adopted the concept of an L-shaped line running almost due south from El Alamein to Alam Nayil, about fifteen miles away, and thence eastwards along the Alam el Halfa ridge. By that time experience had shown that the enemy could make no impression on the strongly-held position on the British right. He would therefore, Auchinleck argued, attack south of Alam Nayil with the intention of wheeling northwards to cut the coast road.[9] In that case Auchinleck would aim at drawing him towards the Alam el Halfa ridge, and there fighting the defensive armoured battle, with tanks well covered by artillery and anti-tank guns, which he and Corbett had vainly urged Ritchie to fight near the Trigh Capuzzo when Tobruk was threatened.

However, at the end of June it was still not certain that the enemy could be stopped at all. Accordingly Auchinleck ordered that preparations should be made for a possible retreat to the Suez Canal, and that everyone and everything not needed at the front should be sent away. These were precautions which any prudent commander might have taken on the eve of a crucial action; but their combined effect was to give rise to rumours of impending calamity at the very moment when the Eighth Army's back areas were thronged with camp followers who had nothing better to do than listen to them. Moreover, the hasty departure of the Mediterranean Fleet from Alexandria did not help to create confidence.

The Axis forces advanced to the Alamein-Qattara position on June 30, skirmishing with belated elements of the Eighth Army on the way. Under almost continous air attack and often short of water, the troops were on the verge of exhaustion and the two Panzer divisions had only 55 fit tanks between them. Moreover, the unexpected decision to push straight on from Tobruk had caused such dislocation that the move would have been impossible without captured vehicles and stores. But the world was waiting for the Panzer Army Africa to conquer Egypt, and Mussolini in particular had flown to Cyrenaica on the previous day in the hope of making a triumphal entry into Alexandria or Cairo.[10]

Rommel was not a man to be influenced by such considerations; but he was so deficient in striking-power that he could hardly hope to go further without the aid of bluff, and it did occur to him that there was a good case for giving the enemy no rest. Without waiting to make a thorough reconnaissance or gain accurate knowledge of Auchinleck's dispositions, he attacked early on July 1 with the intention of repeating the tactics which had brought him such astonishing success at Matruh. His plan was that the three German divisions, followed by the Italian mobile corps, should break through the enemy's forward defence line immediately south of the defended zone at El Alamein, and that the 90th Light Division should then go on to cut the coast road while the rest of the mobile formations wheeled south and south-west to take the Bab el Qattara and Naqb Abu Dweis positions in the rear and hold off any counter-attack from the east. Meanwhile the Italian 21st Corps, less one division sent to follow the 90th Light Division, was to attack the Alamein defences from the west.

Fatigue, bad going, a sandstorm, air attacks and inadequate preparation played havoc with these arrangements. The 90th Light Division started punctually, but turned north too soon, was held up by the Alamein defences until midday, and in the afternoon came under artillery fire so intense that the troops, almost staggering with exhaustion in the grilling heat, were persuaded with some difficulty to rally round their officers and dig in as best they could. The 15th and 21st Panzer Divisions fared no better. Reaching their assembly areas more than three hours late, they took ten hours to dislodge an inexperienced infantry brigade from a hastily-prepared position at Deir el Shein, and were then driven off by the 4th and 22nd Armoured Brigades with the loss of eighteen tanks since morning. The Italians made no progress in the north, and elsewhere they could do nothing as long as their allies failed to push forward.

Next morning the 90th Light Division was again held up. Facing imminent shortages of fuel and ammunition, Rommel then cancelled the southward drive and ordered the Panzer divisions to support the Light Division's attempt to reach the coast. Almost at the same moment Auchinleck ordered his armour to attack westwards and part of his infantry to cut the enemy's line of retreat between the Alamein defences and Deir el Shein. The outcome of these attempts by both sides to force a decision was that on July 2 the 4th and 22nd Armoured Brigades, this time supported by the 7th Motor Brigade as well as the whole of the 1st Armoured Division's artillery, again drove off the 15th and 21st Panzer Division, which ended the day with only 26 fit tanks between them; that the British armoured brigades began the third day's fighting with 119 fit tanks, of which 38 were Grants; but that Rommel succeeded, on that day and the next, in extricating the remnant of his mobile formations under cover of an improvised anti-tank screen. With his divisions allegedly down to 1,200 to 1,500 men apiece, he warned his superiors that he expected to remain on the defensive for at least a fortnight.

The escape of the mobile formations was disappointing to Auchinleck, who had hoped until the last moment that his weak infantry columns would be able to pin them down while

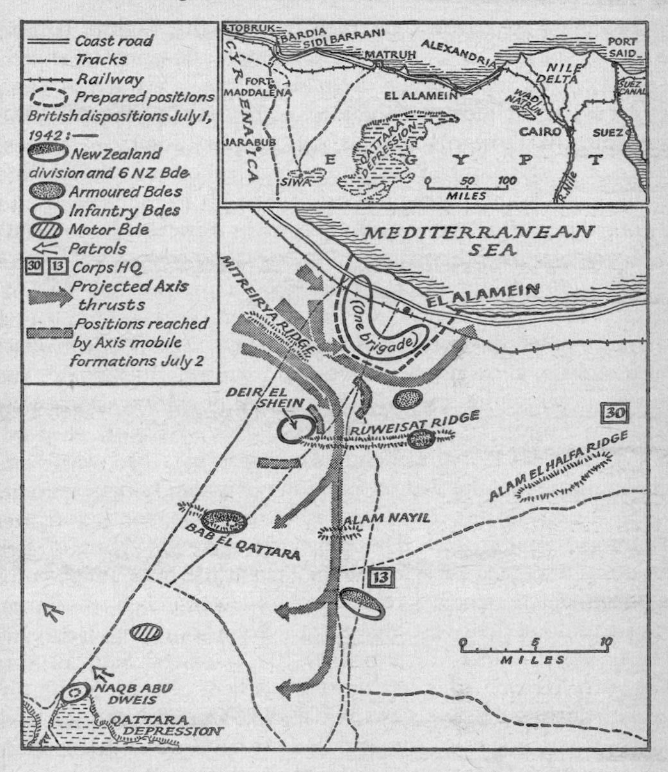

41 The Alamein-Qattara Position: First Alamein

his armour completed their destruction. Only later did it become apparent that his defensive stand had robbed the enemy of his last chance of presenting a threat to Egypt which the Eighth Army could not meet with greatly superior forces, and that in that sense Auchinleck had, after all, fought and won a decisive battle. During the next few weeks both sides tried without success to end what seemed to be a deadlock; but the difference between the two sides was that, whereas substantial reinforcements and large quantities of new and improved equipment were already on their way to the Eighth Army, Rommel could expect little help from home and depended largely on his repair shops. Even so, by the last week in July it seemed from the standpoint of Army Headquarters highly probable that towards the end of August Rommel, having rested and re-equipped his forces to the best of his ability, might make a final attempt to break through to the Nile Delta before the Eighth Army could absorb its new equipment and itself pass to the offensive.

From the standpoint of London the picture did not look so clear. The Prime Minister was so far from understanding the significance of the battle afterwards called First Alamein that even eight or nine years later he could write of July 1942 as a month in which he was 'without a gleam of military success'.* Early in August he spent just over a week in Egypt, received the impression that the Eighth Army was in a bad way, and grew angry when he was told that the Sherman tanks expected about the end of the month could not go into action before the middle of September.[11] The sequel was that the Army of the Nile was rewarded for winning the First Battle of Alamein with a purge which removed from their posts a number of officers who had done their best to prevent it from losing the Battle of Gazala. Auchinleck, described by the Chief of Staff of the German Africa Corps as 'the best Allied general in North Africa during the war', was replaced as Commander-in-Chief of the Land Forces in the Middle East by General Alexander, until recently Commander-in-Chief in Burma; his Chief and Deputy Chief of Staff, both of whom had made notable attempts to save Ritchie from mistakes which led to the loss of Tobruk, were also replaced; and command of the Eighth Army was rather reluctantly accepted by General Gott, who felt that he had been long enough in the desert and might not be the best man for the job. On August 7, however, Gott was killed when an aircraft in which he was travelling to Cairo was forced down by the enemy. The choice then fell on Lieutenant-General

*Winston S. Churchill, *The Second World War*, volume IV: *The Hinge of Fat* (Dondon, 1951), p. 390.

B. L. Montgomery, who had seen no fighting since 1940 but was known to possess unbounded confidence in his ability to do anything that might be asked of him.

General Alexander soon came to the conclusion that the Eighth Army did not lack resolution, and that the chief cause of the discouragement noticed during the retreat from Gazala was that the troops had lost faith in their equipment. Aware that this defect was about to be made good, he let it be understood that there would be no more retreats, but did not countermand arrangements for the defence of Cairo and the Nile Delta in the event of a forced withdrawal from the Alamein-Qattara position. Both he and Montgomery believed, however, that within the next few weeks Rommel would attack south of Alam Nayil, as Auchinleck's advisers had predicted in July, and that it would be possible to stop him at the Alam el Halfa ridge. In the light of growing evidence that that was, in fact, what the enemy was about to do, Montgomery completed the defence works begun by Auchinleck, posted the newly-arrived 44th Division on the ridge, and added the 22nd Armoured Brigade in dug-in positions at its western end. When the enemy came forward the 7th Armoured Division, deployed on a wide front south of Alam Nayil, would delay and harass him, but the general intention would be to draw him towards the 22nd Armoured Brigade's tanks and anti-tank guns and the 44th Division's artillery.

Meanwhile Rommel had fallen ill, had asked for a relief, but in view of the difficulty of finding one had undertaken to carry on under medical supervision until the offensive which he proposed to launch on August 30 was over. Briefly, his plan was that the whole of his mobile formations, Italian as well as German, should pass under cover of night through the thinly-held British front south of Alam Nayil, and at 6 a.m. on August 31 should deploy south of the Alam el Halfa ridge after advancing up to thirty miles through mined and almost entirely unreconnoitred country. As difficulties of supply made it vitally necessary that no fuel should be wasted, they would then try to reach the coast road by the shortest route.

For this extraordinarily difficult and hazardous undertaking, Rommel had at his disposal just over 200 battleworthy German tanks, in addition to a number of obsolete PzKw IIs and about 240 Italian medium tanks in poor condition. The Eighth Army had well over 700 tanks, of which 164 were Grants, and its anti-tank guns now included 6-pounders capable of dealing with even the most heavily-armoured of Rommel's tanks at ranges up to 1,000 yards. In air power there was approximate numerical equality between the two sides, but the British had the advantage of more convenient and better-supplied bases.*

Late on August 30 British reconnaissance aircraft reported that the Axis forces were making final preparations for the expected advance, and at last light Wellington bombers supported by flare-dropping naval aircraft went in to attack them. Hampered by minefields and bad going, Rommel's mobile divisions made such poor progress during the night that at nine o'clock next morning he wondered whether to call a halt. Eventually he decided not to do so, ordered the Panzer divisions to attack towards the Alam el Halfa ridge about six hours later than the time specified in the original programme and, in order to save fuel,[12] directed them to the western end of the ridge instead of allowing them to go further east before beginning their northward wheel. The outcome was that, after still more mishaps and delays, the 21st Panzer Division was drawn by the 22nd Armoured Brigade into a ding-dong fight which left it incapable of going much further without replenishment, and that the 15th Panzer Division on its right was still working its way forward when the acting commander of the Africa Corps called off the attack for fear of outrunning his supplies. In the course of a renewed attack next

*The Western Desert Air Force had roughly 400 serviceable aircraft, and could call on formations not under its command to provide up to about 100 medium and heavy bombers at a time for attacks on targets of special importance. The Luftwaffe and the Regia Aeronautica had about 450 serviceable aircraft in North Africa, supplemented by roughly 120 serviceable long-range bombers in Crete. With the exception of three squadrons of Spitfires VB and VC, the British fighters were still inferior in performance to the Messerschmitt 109F

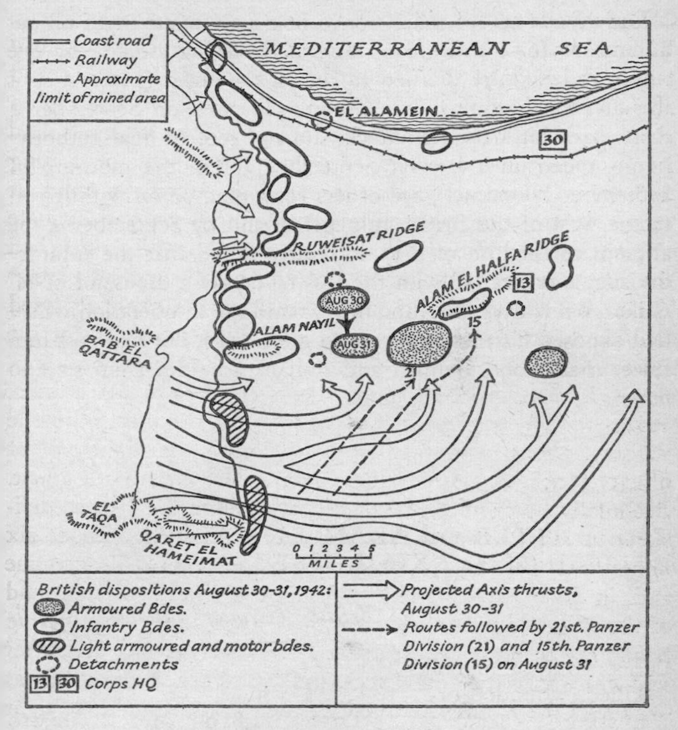

42 The Battle of Alam el Halfa, August-September 1942

morning the 15th Panzer Division successfully held off the 8th Armoured Brigade, with 84 tanks of which 72 were Grants; but towards midday the chances of bringing up enough fuel to sustain a further advance seemed to Rommel so slender that he announced his intention of going over to the defensive where he stood.

As at Gazala on May 27, Rommel was now in a situation which seemed to make his defeat within the next forty-eight hours almost certain. But Montgomery's eyes were fixed on the offensive which he hoped to launch in October, and he had already made up his mind not to risk his armour in an all-out attempt to force a decision. He sanctioned an attempt by one reinforced infantry division to cut off the enemy's retreat; but the divisional commander, although warned on September 1 to prepare for a counter-attack, did not receive final authority to go ahead until late on September 3. On the morning of September 2 Rommel gave orders for a methodical withdrawal to the west of the British minefields, and by September 4 the attempt to cut him off had so clearly failed that the infantry division was recalled with the loss of nearly a thousand of all ranks. A few days later Rommel wound up an operation which had exposed his mobile forces to great risks, but had cost him fewer than 3,000 German and Italian casualties from start to finish.

TABLE 9

THE BATTLE OF ALAM EL HALFA: BRITISH AND AXIS LOSSES

	British	*German*	*Italian*	*Axis Totals*
Officers and other ranks killed, wounded or missing	1,750	1,859	1,051	2,910
Tanks destroyed or put out of action	67	38	11	49
Other vehicles destroyed	...	298	97	395
Aircraft lost	68	36	5	41

NOTES

1. The British figure for tanks includes a number put out of action but afterwards repaired; the Axis figures for tanks and other vehicles include only those destroyed.
2. According to the British official history, 15 British anti-tank guns were put out of action, and 33 German and 22 Italian guns of unstated calibre were destroyed.

Thus the position at the end of the first week in September was that Rommel had shot his bolt, but that once more the British had failed to seize an opportunity of destroying him. So far as the Southern Front was concerned, the drawing of a ring round Germany would have to wait until Anglo-American forces landed in North-West Africa, or until Montgomery was ready to attack.

CHAPTER 16

A RING ROUND GERMANY: THE SOUTH (I)

July 1942 - June 1944

When the Western Allies agreed after the First Battle of Alamein to send an expedition to North-West Africa in October, only about three months were left in which to plan and mount the operation and settle the problem of command.[1] As the territory which the Allies proposed to occupy abutted on the British area of responsibility, command of the expedition might in the ordinary way have gone to a British officer; but President Roosevelt believed that the French were less likely to fire on the American than on the British flag, and that hence there was a strong case for representing the venture as primarily an American one. Accordingly it was arranged that only about a quarter of the troops put ashore at the outset should be British, and that the American General Eisenhower should take the chief command. The British Admiral Cunningham would, however, be in charge of the naval side, and a British officer responsible to Eisenhower would assume direct command of the land forces once they had established themselves firmly in French territory.

General Alexander was first choice for the post of commander of the land forces, General Montgomery second choice. As the Cairo purge took both to the Middle East, the officer finally selected was Lieutenant-General Sir K. A. N. Anderson.

At the planning stage, neither the United States Navy nor the United States Army showed much enthusiasm for Operation 'Torch'.* In England, too, there was at first a tendency among

*Samuel Eliot Morison, *History of United States Naval Operations in World War II*, volume II (Boston, 1957), p. 16.

senior officers to regard 'Torch' as a scheme concocted by Roosevelt and Churchill without due regard to its tactical and logistic implications.* Later, however, the British not only became firm adherents of the project but were inclined to take credit for pushing it through in spite of American objections.

Partly in consequence of these misgivings, the planners had some difficulty in arriving at proposals acceptable to their superiors on both sides of the Atlantic. As the immediate aim was to secure the whole of French Morocco, Algeria and Tunisia, there was much to be said for putting troops ashore at widely-separated points so that vital objectives in all three countries could be occupied without delay; but the objection to this course was that only limited forces would be available for the initial landings, chiefly because of a lack of shipping. At the same time, the American authorities were not willing to forgo landings in Western Morocco, although these seemed to some British officers a doubtful benefit because of the difficulty of disembarking troops on beaches exposed to the Atlantic swell. Moreover the railway linking Western Morocco with Algeria ran within twenty miles of the frontier between French and Spanish Morocco. The Americans were not alone, however, in thinking the early capture of Casablanca desirable because of its value as a port of entry.

Since something had to be sacrificed, the Allies cut initial landings in eastern Algeria out of the scheme, thus greatly reducing their chances of capturing Tunis and Bizerta at an early stage. The final plan for the initial assault was that 24,500 American troops embarked in the United States should land north and south of Casablanca and near Port Lyautey unless Admiral Cunningham decided at the last moment that unfavourable weather made it necessary to divert them to Moroccan beaches inside the Straits of Gibraltar; that 18,500 American and a few British troops embarked in the United Kingdom should land near Oran; and that 10,000 British and 10,000 American troops also embarked in the United Kingdom should land near Algiers.[2] Behind these would come some 31,000 American and 13,000 British troops in follow-up formations.

* Arthur Bryant, *The Turn of the Tide* (London, 1957), p. 403.

Immediate responsibility for the naval side of the expedition to Western Morocco was delegated to Rear-Admiral H. Kent Hewitt of the United States Navy, and D-day was put back from the middle of October to November 4, and ultimately to November 8, so as to give time for the forces assembling in the United States to complete their preparations.

Meanwhile the British were preparing for an offensive in the Western Desert. Auchinleck had asked for a minimum of two to three weeks to absorb his new equipment; Alexander was compelled to wait much longer, since Montgomery wished to attack at night and could not be ready in time for the September moon.[3] Ultimately the start was fixed, therefore, for October 23. The delay enabled General Georg Stumme, who had replaced the absent Rommel, to build up his strength a little, but he was much hampered by air attacks on his supply ships and overland communications. By the third week in September the British, with 530 serviceable aircraft in the forward area and another 650 elsewhere in the Mediterranean theatre, had such an ascendancy in the air that they were able to fly continuous patrols in daylight in order to keep Axis reconnaissance aircraft at a distance and thus hide the final assembly of their forces.

On the eve of the battle Stumme had a fighting force of some 100,000 Germans and Italians,[4] organized in four armoured and eight infantry or motorized infantry divisions, all much under strength and with only about 200 good and some 300 to 350 inferior tanks.[5] His defensive zone, afterwards described by Churchill as a 'deep system of minefields and defences', was not noticeably deeper than Ritchie's at Gazala,[6] and only about one-fifth as deep as the Soviet defences in the Kursk salient; but the minefields were dense and the defences were continuous. Not knowing where the blow would fall,[7] Stumme distributed his infantry fairly evenly over the whole front, putting the German 164th Infantry Division and the Trento and Bologna divisions in the north and the Brescia Folgore and Pavia divisions in the south, with a German reconnaissance group on the extreme right. A corresponding dis

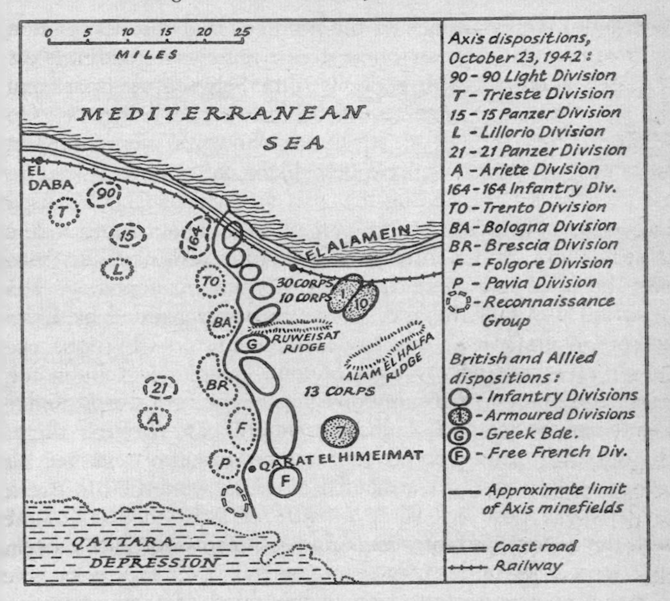

43 Second Alamein, October-November 1942

position of his armour brought the 15th Panzer and Littorio divisions behind the northern half of the front and the 21st Panzer and Ariete divisions behind the southern half; but his two light motorized divisions, the 90th and the Trieste, were in the north. Because he was short of petrol,[8] he put all his mobile formations rather closer to the front than he might have done if he had been guided solely by tactical considerations.

On the British side, Montgomery had the equivalent of approximately four armoured and seven infantry divisions, with a fighting strength of roughly 200,000 of all ranks.[9] Of his 1,100 tanks, about 400 were Shermans or Grants. He had nearly a thousand field or medium guns, about eight hundred 6-pounder anti-tank guns and some five hundred 2-pounder anti-tank guns, in addition to a small number of self-propelled guns whose value was debatable. He believed, as Auchinleck had done, that an attack in the north offered the best chance of breaking through an unturnable position. Accordingly he disposed about two-thirds of his force between the coast and the Ruweisat ridge or in reserve behind that sector.

Montgomery's plan of attack was, however, very different from any which would have been likely to commend itself to his predecessor. Reckoning that past setbacks had been caused largely by a tendency on the part of subordinate commanders to send their armour into action with little or no artillery support, he ruled that there should be 'no more manœuvre'.[10] His intention was that the 30th Corps, now commanded by Lieutenant-General Sir Oliver Leese and with four divisions up, should clear corridors through Stumme's defended zone in the north and that two armoured divisions of the 10th Corps, under Lieutenant-General H. Lumsden, should pass through them. Instead of pushing on in the fashion hitherto regarded as orthodox, however, the armoured divisions were then to pause in defensive positions while a battle of attrition was fought with the enemy's infantry and armour. Meanwhile in the south the 13th Corps, under Lieutenant-General B. G. Horrocks, was to make diversionary attacks with the object of convincing the enemy that the main attack was coming in that sector.

An offensive on these lines was duly launched on the scheduled date. At 9.40 p.m. on October 23 the Eighth Army's artillery opened its preliminary bombardment, to which the enemy did not at first reply. The infantry then advanced to the assault; but the four divisions of the 30th Corps, jammed on a narrow front in the sector held by the Trento Division, did not derive as much benefit as was expected from their superior fire-power, and great difficulty was experienced in clearing mines amidst the din of battle.[11] The result was that tanks piled up behind the infantry in the minefields, where at first light on October 24 they came under fire from the enemy's artillery. Attempting none the less to carry out its orders to drive on in spite of losses,[12] the 10th Corps succeeded at one point in getting clear of the minefields though not of the defences beyond them, but elsewhere made little progress throughout the day and the early part of the following night.

In the early hours of October 25 General Lumsden suggested withdrawing his tanks and regrouping them behind a neighbouring ridge while the corridors were being cleared, but was ordered to fight his way out to the west.[13] As this proved impossible,[14] the situation at the end of another four or five days of slaughter and confusion was that the Eighth Army had lost about 10,000 of all ranks without getting clear of the enemy's defensive zone.[15] Hundreds of tanks had been knocked out by the Axis guns, but many had been recovered and found repairable.[16]

Even so, the outlook for the Germans and Italians was not encouraging. General Stumme had died of heart failure on the first day of the battle. Rommel had left hospital to resume command, and on reaching the front had moved the 21st Panzer Division to the northern sector; but a counter-attack ordered before he arrived had been beaten off by concentrated fire from anti-tank guns, and a renewed attempt on the following day had been forestalled by air attacks while the Axis forces were still assembling. Moreover, on October 29 Montgomery succeeded in drawing attention away from the vital sector by pushing the Australian 9th Division northwards across the coast road.

In any case, the British were so deeply committed that they were not likely to call off their offensive as long as they retained their superiority in numbers and fire-power. Before the battle Montgomery had spoken of his prospects in glowing terms; on October 28 Churchill had assured the Prime Ministers of Canada, Australia and New Zealand that the offensive had begun well.[17] Twenty-four hours later the War Cabinet authorized Alexander to carry on without counting the cost.[18] Meanwhile Montgomery had begun to reorganize his forces, and at a.m. on November 2 he delivered a fresh assault on the lines of his opening gambit.

This time the British succeeded by sheer weight of numbers and equipment in breaking through the enemy's defended zone.

But the 10th Corps, earmarked for the pursuit in Montgomery's master-plan, had taken such a battering in the first week that no large-scale follow-up was possible before November 5. Rommel began to disengage on November 3, was then held up for thirty-six hours by a standfast order from the Führer, but succeeded under cover of a skilful rearguard action in extricating the greater part of his surviving troops at the cost of leaving many damaged but repairable vehicles behind him.[19]

So ended the Second Battle of Alamein. Claiming about 30,000 prisoners and a big bag of captured tanks and transport, the British counted it as the 'absolute victory' which Montgomery seemed convinced that he had won.[20] On the other hand, Rommel still had an army in being, and he continued to show an agility which his opponent could not match. During the first few days of the pursuit the Eighth Army repeatedly tried to trap him by making tight turns towards the coast, but on each occasion found that neither good weather nor bad had prevented him from moving too fast for them. Rommel then received news of the Anglo-American landings in North-West Africa, recognized that his best course was to join the Axis forces which were beginning to pour into Tunisia, and went on to complete a spectacular retreat of fifteen hundred miles. Early in February he crossed the Tunisian frontier after twice pausing for a fortnight or more to rest and reorganize his forces under the noses of his pursuers.

Meanwhile American and British troops landed in Morocco and Algeria on the appointed day, but not without opposition from the French.[21] The veteran General Henri-Honoré Giraud, whom they took with them in the hope that he would rally the local garrisons and officials to their side, proved to have no following. On the other hand Admiral Darlan, who happened to be on the spot because he was visiting a son ill in hospital in Algiers, was found to command the loyalty of the vast majority of French officers and civil servants, not so much on account of any political views which he might be supposed to hold as because he represented the legally con-

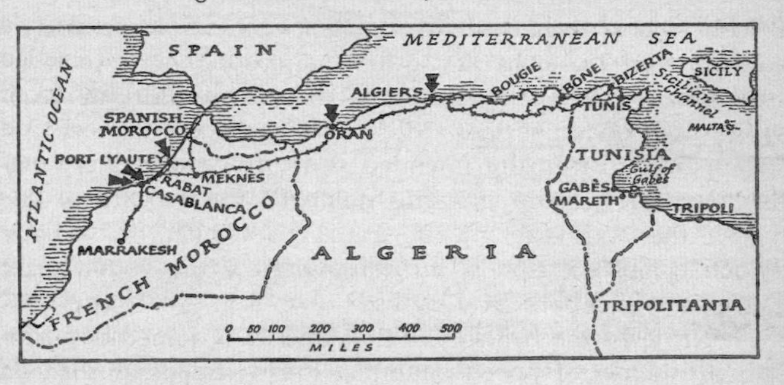

44 Operation 'Torch'

stituted government.* As the lesser of two evils the American emissaries who had been entrusted with the diplomatic side of the undertaking decided, therefore, to deal with Darlan. On grounds of expediency, and also because they had no choice, the British reluctantly acquiesced in this arrangement. They were relieved of their perplexities when Darlan was assassinated on December 24 by a young French extremist.

Under pressure from the Americans, Darlan agreed on November 10 to order a cease-fire throughout French North Africa, and on the following day to tell Admiral Jean-Pierre Esteva, Resident-General at Tunis, that it was his duty to resist the Germans, whose troops had just begun to cross the demarcation line into Unoccupied France. But meanwhile the Vichy government, apparently at the instigation of Laval and allegedly against Pétain's inclinations, despatched a signal calling on all concerned to disregard Darlan's order and treat the Americans as enemies. As a result of the Anglo-American decision not to land troops in Eastern Algeria on the first day, there was no Allied force within striking distance of Tunis when Esteva received this message, and consequently the Allies were in no position to give him a convincing assurance of support if he decided to throw in his lot with them. A few

*It has been alleged that Darlan's presence was not fortuitous.

British troops, embarked at Algiers, went ashore at Bougie and Bône on November 11 and 12, and others were dropped from the air; but by that time the Luftwaffe had already taken over at least one important airfield in Tunisia, and German and Italian troops originally intended as reinforcements for Rommel were arriving in growing numbers. By the end of the month the Axis strength in Tunisia amounted to roughly 17,000 combatant troops, including part of the 10th Panzer Division with about fifty tanks.[22]

Nevertheless the British and the Americans, joined by a substantial number of poorly-equipped French troops, pushed on to the east, made contact with the enemy about the middle of November, and by November 28 were within fifteen miles of Tunis. But a limited amount of shipping made their build-up slow, and their communications ran through mountainous country very different from the flat coastal plain in which the Axis forces were established. In the third week of December torrential rain made General Anderson's forward landing-grounds unusable and threatened to bog down any tracked or wheeled vehicle which left the roads. Recognizing that he had little chance of mounting a successful offensive in such conditions, Eisenhower decided on Christmas Eve to remain on the defensive until the rainy season was over.

Thus the Western Allies lost the race for Tunis. By the end of the year the Axis Powers had nearly 50,000 troops in Tunisia, and were still reinforcing them by making good use of all-weather airfields to supplement a limited flow of seaborne traffic. Consequently, they were able to add to the force which Rommel brought across the frontier from Tripolitania in February a substantial number of fresh and well-equipped formations, predominantly German. By the middle of the month they had at their disposal no less than four armoured and ten infantry or motorized infantry divisions, many of them much under strength and nearly all weak in artillery, but stiffened by a high proportion of seasoned troops who had fought in the Western Desert or in Russia.

On the Allied side, General Eisenhower could muster in the forward area only three and a half British divisions, three

American divisions of which one was incomplete and one still assembling, and two French divisions very lightly equipped by American and British standards. To defeat this rather loosely organized force and then turn with renewed vigour against the Eighth Army was an undertaking which might not be altogether beyond Rommel's powers.

In the middle of February General Anderson's army was standing near the western edge of the belt of high country which covers about two-thirds of Tunisia as far south as the Gulf of Gabès. As most of the objectives which General Anderson hoped to take when Eisenhower sanctioned a renewed offensive were in the north, his strongest formations were near the centre of his front or further to the left. In the south, where his troops were not in close contact with the enemy and seemed unlikely to be attacked, he had only a thin screen with no substantial reserve behind it.[23] Moreover, that part of his front was not naturally strong. On the right his line ceased to hug the heights and ran for some distance through open country with no marked features apart from occasional clumps of stunted trees and low outcrops of bare rock.

On February 14 Axis forces with about 150 tanks and strong air support attacked at two points between the Faid Pass and the desert flank, overwhelmed widely dispersed elements of the inexperienced United States 1st Armoured Division, and found little else to bar their path to Anderson's rear. By February 17 German armoured formations were up to thirty miles behind the Allied forward defence line, with every prospect of fanning out widely to overrun advanced landing grounds and centres of communication.

Alexander, newly arrived in Tunisia and henceforward responsible to Eisenhower for all Allied land forces in North-West Africa, believed that the enemy would not stream westwards with his whole force, as was widely feared, but would turn towards the coast with the intention of rolling up Anderson's line from south to north.[24] Within the next few days the 21st Panzer Division, advancing in a north-westerly direction from the Kasserine Pass, did in fact reach a point of vantage at

Thala, where it halted while the Axis commanders considered their next step. But on February 22 it was driven back by a mixed force of British armour and American and British artillery and infantry hastily assembled for this purpose. Next day the Axis offensive was called off.

In the meantime the Eighth Army was preparing to move against Rommel's main position south-east of Gabès. Recognizing that the enemy might get his blow in first, Montgomery also made preparations to fight a defensive battle at Medenine.[25] On March 6 Rommel did attack, was induced by a simple stratagem to throw all three of his armoured divisions against positions defended by nearly five hundred anti-tank guns, and was pushed back with heavy losses. The Eighth Army did not lose a single tank, and its casualties were very light. As if recognizing that his star had waned, Rommel returned soon afterwards to Germany, where he resumed his interrupted spell of sick-leave. He was succeeded by General Hans-Jürgen von Arnim, hitherto commanding the Axis forces which had been rushed to Tunisia by air and sea.

Reorganized and regrouped, the First Army then went on to win back its old positions and draw off a substantial part of the Axis forces while the Eighth Army pushed forward to attack the Mareth Line. Built by the French before the war to keep the Italians out of Tunisia, this was a system of fortifications extending from the coast, where it abutted on a steep-sided gully, to a belt of hilly country long believed to be impassable except on foot. A reconnaissance by the Eighth Army's Long Range Desert Group had shown that the hills could, in fact, be crossed by vehicles at a point about fifty miles south-west of Medenine; but a force going by that route would be able to rejoin the coast road only by passing through a narrow defile between the Djebel Tebaga and the Djebel Melab, forty miles behind the Mareth Line. There it would have to run the gauntlet of a strong force posted to defend the exit from the defile and protect the Axis flank and rear.

Montgomery's plan was to use the 30th Corps to attack the seaward end of the Mareth Line a little before midnight on March 20, and meanwhile to send at least one division through

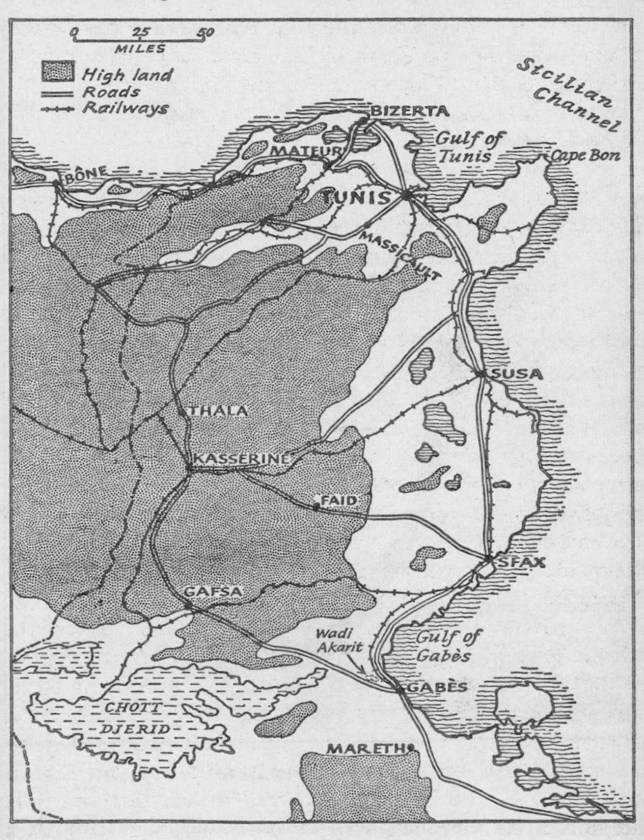

45 Eastern Tunisia

he hills with orders to approach the defile on the same vening.[26] The broken ground on the Eighth Army's right nade this a formidable undertaking. In the event the attack in hat sector led nowhere, since cruiser tanks and anti-tank guns ould not be taken over the gully even when the leading divi-ion of the 30th Corps had scrambled across it and established tself precariously on the far side. Recalling his troops from

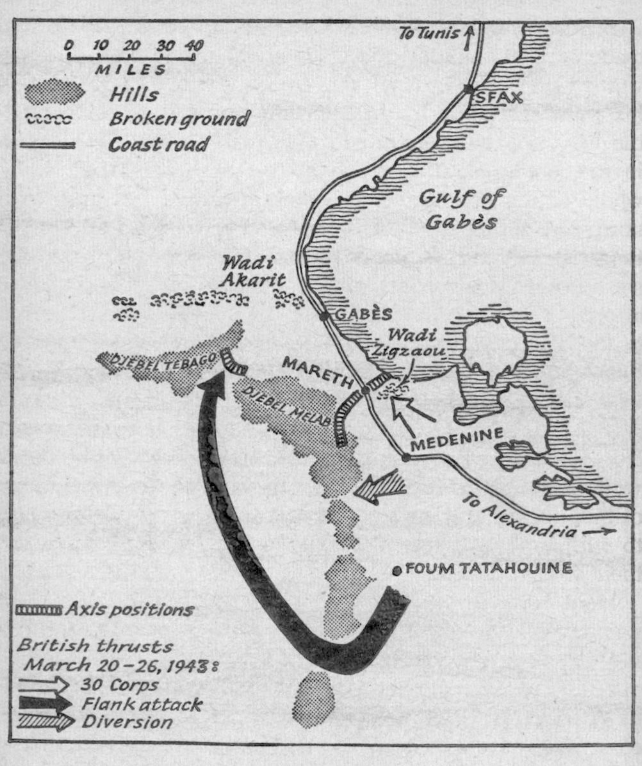

46 The Mareth Line

the gully after they had been fiercely attacked on March 22 Montgomery therefore strongly reinforced his troops at the defile, put in a diversionary attack in an intermediate position and late on March 26 succeeded in pushing upwards of two divisions through the defile after relays of bombers and dive bombers had pounded the defences in that sector throughout the afternoon. Dangerously outflanked and threatened with encirclement, most of the Axis forces then made a fighting retreat to the Wadi Akarit. But large numbers of all ranks failed to pull out in time and were cut off.

A few days later United States forces of the First Army made such a vigorous attack along the road from Gafsa towards Gabès that General von Arnim was forced to look over his right shoulder. In these circumstances three divisions of the Eighth Army, supported by 450 guns, tore a gaping hole in the Wadi Akarit position on the night of April 6. The whole of the Axis forces in the theatre then fell back to the north-east corner of Tunisia, where they took up strong positions but no longer had enough airfields for the short-range aircraft needed for tactical support and to cover the transport aircraft which the Luftwaffe had been using since November to fly in reinforcements and supplies. Meanwhile the German long-range bomber force, weakened by its efforts during the winter and its lack of reserves, had become so ineffective that British submarines and surface forces could not be prevented from re-asserting control of the Sicilian Narrows. By the last week in April the Axis High Command, having lost command of both the air and the sea, had ceased to be in a position either to withdraw its forces from Tunisia, or to supply them once their stocks ran out.

Henceforward the obvious strategy for the Western Allies was to push the enemy northwards until he reached Tunis or the Cap Bon Peninsula, where no further retreat would be open to him and he would have no choice but to surrender or be annihilated in the field. As the Axis positions on the east coast were strongly held and hard to reach, Alexander decided to do this by shifting some of the Eighth Army's most experienced formations to the First Army's sector.[27] On May 6 the British 9th Corps attacked with overwhelming air and artillery support on a narrow front commanding the main road through Massicault to Tunis, while further west the United States 2nd Corps advanced on Mateur and Bizerta. The Axis defences, stoutly manned but with little depth, collapsed in a few hours, and on May 7 Tunis fell so swiftly that hundreds of German and Italian soldiers off duty were caught unarmed in shops and cafés or strolling in the streets. Within the next week General von Arnim and his staff were captured, organized resistance ceased, and about a quarter of a million Axis troops laid down their arms. On May 17 the first through convoy to complete the passage to Alexandria since 1941 left Gibraltar, and on May 26 it reached its destination.

Even so, in one sense the fall of Tunis came six months too late. The Western Allies had undertaken 'Torch' in the hope of occupying French North Africa without too much difficulty, and preferably in time for them to launch in 1943 the full-scale assault on Fortress Europe which they had been unable to deliver in 1942. By the time Tunisia was in their hands, they had nine American and thirty-one British, British-controlled or French divisions in the Mediterranean theatre,[28] and could no longer hope to assemble before the spring of 1944 the great mass of shipping which they would need in United Kingdom waters if they were to land in Northern France. Moreover, so much had happened in the meantime that arguments and assumptions valid in 1942 did not necessarily hold good in 1943. In 1942 the British and the Americans had agreed that sooner or later their troops must land in Northern France because that was the only mutually acceptable course of action which seemed to them likely to lead to Germany's defeat. But was it still true after Stalingrad that Germany would not be defeated unless British and American troops landed in Northern France? With forty seasoned divisions at their disposal in the Mediterranean theatre, was it really necessary that, in order to claim a share in the victory, the Western Allies should wait until 1944 to make a fresh start by putting a few divisions ashore in Normandy, where they would be roughly twice as far from the Ruhr as a force landed at the head of the Adriatic would be from Vienna?

But for British and American statesmen unstinted enthusiasm for 'Overlord', as the projected landings in Northern France were called, had become by 1943 an article of faith, a test by which they measured the sincerity of their conduct not only towards the Russians but towards each other. For that reason, rather than on strategic grounds, they accepted almost without question the need to land in Northern France in 1944 when it became apparent that they could not do so in 1943. When the veteran Field-Marshal Smuts suggested that 'Overlord' might be put into cold storage and that an advance through Yugoslavia to the Danube and the Sava should be considered, he was called to order by the Prime Minister not on the ground that a force advancing by that route could not be supplied (which might have been a sound objection), but because, according to Churchill, 'Overlord' was 'the keystone of the arch of Anglo-American co-operation'.[29] Churchill himself showed repeatedly that he was attracted in 1943 by the idea of a campaign in the Balkans. But he also showed repeatedly that he was not prepared to argue the point at the risk of bringing about a serious disagreement with President Roosevelt and the United States Chiefs of Staff.*

Thus the situation of the Western Allies immediately after the conquest of North Africa was that they regarded themselves as morally committed to 'Overlord'; that they could not hope to launch 'Overlord' for at least twelve months; and that they were not willing to give serious consideration to any case which might be made for replacing 'Overlord' by an operation which could be carried out more promptly. In the meantime they had no plans except that they had decided at Casablanca in January to go on bombing Germany and to invade Sicily when they judged that they could safely do so. They agreed, however, that seven of their forty divisions in the Mediterranean theatre should go to the United Kingdom in the near future in order to start preparing for 'Overlord', and in June they came to the conclusion that the bombing of Germany might become impossible unless fighter opposition were reduced. Accordingly Operation 'Pointblank', which envisaged the wearing down of the German fighter force in combat and by the bombing of airfields and factories, was added to the Allied programme. But 'Pointblank', although not altogether unsuccessful, did not prevent the Germans from maintaining such a respectable output that in 1943 the Luftwaffe increased the first-line strength of its fighter force by seven hundred aircraft, in spite of heavy losses on the Eastern and Southern fronts.[30]

*John Ehrman, *Grand Strategy*, volume V (London, 1956), p. 112 and appendix VI.

Besides making unsuccessful attempts to bring Turkey into the war on the Allied side, the British pressed strongly in the summer of 1943 for an early offensive on the Italian mainland; the capture of the Dodecanese and especially Rhodes; and increased support for subversive movements in South-East Europe. At the same time they were at pains to point out that they regarded such ventures not as alternatives to 'Overlord' but as diversions which might help to make the success of 'Overlord' more certain. Nevertheless the Americans were unable to rid themselves of a deep-rooted suspicion that 'Overlord' was in jeopardy. Unlike the Germans, who believed that control of the Balkans was 'decisive from the point of view of winning the war',[31] they looked upon South-East Europe as a blind alley which they would enter at their peril. Moreover, they did not agree with the British that invasion of the Italian mainland should at all costs swiftly follow, or even overlap, the conquest of Sicily. Their view was that no decision to invade the Italian mainland ought to be made until the invasion of Sicily was clearly seen to be going well.

The outcome was that on July 10, when the Allies at last invaded Sicily after a pause which seemed to the British unduly long, they had gone no further with their Italian project than to draw up a tentative plan which envisaged landings in Calabria, Corsica and Sardinia in September and October. On July 24 the Fascist Grand Council in Rome passed a resolution unfavourable to Mussolini, and next day he was arrested and succeeded as head of the government by Marshal Pietro Badoglio. Thereupon the Allied commanders in the Mediterranean theatre asked General Mark Clark, commanding the newly-constituted United States Fifth Army in North Africa, to draw up a more ambitious plan than any yet considered. But Clark's plan had yet to be approved when, on August 15, Badoglio asked in secret for a negotiated peace.[32] The Allied commanders then gave the plan their blessing, and the Combined Chiefs of Staff followed suit on August 18, after organized resistance in Sicily had ceased. But meanwhile the Germans had begun to prepare for the worst by arranging to reinforce their troops in Italy on a massive scale at the first sign of trouble.

Aware that the Germans might turn against them, the Italian authorities were anxious to know how far the troops which the Allies proposed to put ashore would suffice to protect the country from Hitler's wrath. But the Allies were unwilling to disclose their plan, not only on grounds of security but also because it might fall short of Italian expectations.[33] Negotiations dragged on until September 3, and no public announcement of the agreement reached between Badoglio and the Allies on that day was made until late on September 8.[34] As large German forces were in Italy by that time and the British and the Americans only just beginning to arrive in strength, the result was that, while the Italian Navy duly submitted to the Allies, most home-based units of the army and the air force had no chance of doing so before they were overpowered and disarmed by the Germans.

The Allied plan, as approved by the Combined Chiefs of Staff on August 18, was that three infantry divisions of the British 10th and the United States 6th Corps, followed after three days by one armoured and two more infantry divisions, should go ashore in the Gulf of Salerno; that two divisions of the British 13th Corps should land at Reggio di Calabria; and that the British 5th Corps should be held in reserve as a follow-up formation. At the last moment, however, the Allies saw a chance of seizing the heel of Italy without a fight while the Germans were preoccupied elsewhere. Accordingly, on September 2 an airborne division conveyed by sea landed without opposition at Taranto, where it was afterwards joined by two more divisions. The landings at Reggio and Salerno followed on September 3 and 9 respectively. Four German divisions opposed the Allies at Salerno, but withdrew when they found themselves outnumbered by the troops which had landed there and at Reggio.[35]

The Allied formations on the Italian mainland then sorted themselves into two groups, consisting of American and British divisions under the United States Fifth Army in the west, and

47 The Invasion of Italy

British divisions under the British Eighth Army in the east. Both armies were responsible to General Alexander as Commander-in-Chief of the land forces comprising the Anglo-American Fifteenth Army Group, and Alexander in turn was responsible to General Eisenhower as Commander-in-Chief of the Allied Expeditionary Forces in the Mediterranean theatre.

This arrangement held good until the end of 1943, when Eisenhower left for the United Kingdom to supervise the final preparations for 'Overlord', taking General Montgomery with him to command the 'Overlord' land forces. Eisenhower was then succeeded by the British General Maitland Wilson, with the new title of Supreme Commander, Mediterranean Command. Thereupon command of the Eighth Army went to General Sir Oliver Leese.

In spite of last-minute changes of plan and diplomatic complications, the Allies thus succeeded by the second half of September in establishing themselves in some strength on the Italian mainland. On October 1 the Fifth Army entered Naples, and by that date the Eighth Army had taken Foggia, the centre of an important group of airfields. In Italy as a whole the Allies were outnumbered; but that scarcely seemed to matter, for they did not aim at conquering the whole country. Their objects were to capture airfields needed for the bombing of targets which could not be reached from the United Kingdom or North Africa, and to hold down as many as possible of the divisions which the enemy might otherwise use to counter 'Overlord'.

On the other hand, lack of agreement between American and British strategists ruled out energetic action in the Eastern Mediterranean, which Churchill rightly judged to be a development much feared by the Germans.[36] On September 9 the British put a few troops into Rhodes in the hope that the Italians might be induced to disarm the German garrison, and later small parties landed at Cos, Leros and elsewhere in the Aegean. But the Italians were unable to decide on their course of action before the Germans gained the upper hand, the smaller islands could not be held indefinitely unless the Allies were prepared to occupy Rhodes in strength, and entreaties from London failed to persuade President Roosevelt that the attempt was worth making.[37] So far as Yugoslavia was concerned, the Allies had agreed in the summer not to do more for the time being than set aside a few British aircraft, capable in theory of carrying up to 150 tons of supplies a month to the Serbian Cetniks under Mihailovic and the Communist Partisans under Tito. Later the British supplemented these efforts by sending about 2,000 tons of supplies by sea.

That this was all that the Allies were going to do in South-East Europe seemed, however, incredible to the Germans, who argued that they would not have gone to the trouble of landing in Italy unless they meant to seize some objective of vital interest to Germany.[38] The question, according to Hitler, was whether they would strike across the Adriatic from Southern Italy, or push further north before entering the Balkans by way of Northern Croatia and Istria. Between July and October the Supreme Command raised the number of German divisions in Italy from six to twenty-five, but they also raised the number in South-East Europe from twelve to twenty-four.[39] To check the Allied advance on Rome, they agreed that Field Marshal Kesselring, who became responsible in November for all their forces in Italy, should stand through the winter in prepared positions from the mouth of the Garigliano past Monte Cassino to the River Sangro.

Thus the Allies could claim by the early winter to have attracted to Germany's southern front a good many more divisions than might have been expected. Their problem was to keep up the pressure long enough to ensure the success of 'Overlord'. Alexander's intention was to capture Rome before the end of the year and afterwards push on to Tuscany. But whether he could give effect to such a plan would depend largely on the support which his superiors were willing to give him. Some of his formations were due to go to the United Kingdom in the near future as part of the force assembling for 'Overlord', and he calculated in October that the planned build-up from North Africa would give him not more than fourteen or fifteen divisions by December and perhaps sixteen or seventeen by February.[40] At the same time his plan for the capture of Rome, which envisaged at least one seaborne landing behind the enemy's lines, was threatened by transfers of assault vessels for the benefit of 'Overlord' formations which would not be going into action before the late spring or early summer. Between them the Americans and the British, who had solemnly undertaken to give priority to the war in Europe, were producing landing ships and landing craft at the rate of about 1,500 a month.[41] Yet their plans for the only part of the European theatre in which their land forces were actively engaged with the enemy seemed likely to collapse for lack of a mere seventy or eighty assault vessels of a particular category.

The sequel was a long-drawn Anglo-American dispute about priorities; but eventually it was agreed that enough landing ships for an attempt to take Rome in January could be found if transfers to the United Kingdom were slowed down and if renewed proposals for an attack on Rhodes were abandoned. Accordingly, on January 17 the Fifth Army opened a heavy attack on the German positions between the mouth of the Garigliano and the southern approaches to Monte Cassino, and on January 22 and 23 about 50,000 Allied troops, with some 5,000 vehicles, went ashore in the neighbourhood of Anzio, more than sixty miles behind the enemy's front and only about thirty-five miles from Rome. The landing caught Kesselring with few troops close at hand; but the Allied force commander had no instructions to exploit an unexpected success, paused to consolidate his beach-head before trying to break out of it, and by the end of January found himself hemmed in by reinforcements brought up in haste. Meanwhile Hitler had decreed that Kesselring's positions in the south should be held at all costs. Repeated attempts by the Fifth Army to break through them in February and March were unsuccessful, in spite of a heavy bombardment of Monte Cassino which Alexander sanctioned after advising the monks in the monastery on the summit to leave. At Anzio, however, the Allies succeeded in holding their beach-head in face of counter-attacks which threatened at one stage to split their force in two.

Alexander then decided to thin out his line on the right, bring most of the Eighth Army to the west for a renewed attack on the Monte Cassino position, and continue to supply and reinforce the troops at Anzio for as long as might be necessary. General Maitland Wilson approved of this programme, but warned his superiors that it was hard to reconcile with his obligations to send assault vessels to the United Kingdom and to carry out a landing in the South of France (Operation 'Anvil') for which he had been ordered to prepare. As the Americans set great store by 'Anvil' as a diversion for 'Overlord', while the British doubted whether it would draw off any troops from Northern France and would have been glad to see the last of it, another far-reaching controversy followed before the British were brought to agree that 'Anvil' should not be cancelled, although it would necessarily be postponed and might in certain circumstances be replaced by some other diversion, such as a landing in the Gulf of Genoa.[42] Only on that condition were the United States Chiefs of Staff prepared to send to the Mediterranean a small but crucial allotment of assault vessels which they would otherwise retain in the Pacific.

Meanwhile it had become clear that 'Overlord' could not be launched with any prospect of success before the first week in June, that Alexander would be able to open his renewed offensive by the second week in May, and that nothing said or done in London or Washington could make 'Anvil' feasible until long after the assault phase of 'Overlord' was over. Accordingly it was agreed that Alexander should attack when he was ready, and should aim at linking the main body of his troops with the six divisions in the Anzio beach-head about the time when Eisenhower's forces were going ashore in Normandy. In effect, Alexander's offensive thus came to play the diversionary role at one time assigned to 'Anvil', although that did not mean that there might not still be a case for 'Anvil' on other grounds.

The situation in Italy on the eve of the Allied offensive was that Alexander's troops had a local superiority of more than two to one on the Monte Cassino front, and could call on almost overwhelming air support.[43] As the Germans were known to have constructed strong positions well to the rear of their forward defence line, Alexander decided to launch a surprise attack with the object of compelling Kesselring to commit practically the whole of his available troops in the forward area, and thus achieving a quick break-through as soon as the enemy's forward defence line crumbled.[44] Steps were taken to convince Kesselring that the Allies were about to rein force the Anzio beach-head or make a fresh landing in his rear rather than deliver a frontal assault, and meanwhile heavy bombing of his back areas helped to isolate his forces in the intended battle zone.

On the night of May 11 the Fifth and Eighth Armies attacked after an intense artillery bombardment, achieved tactical surprise, and at first made rapid progress. As Alexander intended, Kesselring then made strenuous attempts to prop up his forward line. For a time it seemed that he was about to bring the Allies to a standstill; but he was unable in the long run to overcome the handicap of inferior numbers and firepower. By the third day the two Allied armies were closing on the main road to Rome below Monte Cassino, and early on May 18 Polish troops under British control cleared the flank by storming the last of the German positions near the summit. Weakened by his heavy commitment in the forward area, and with his rear threatened by the troops in the Anzio beach-head, Kesselring could do no more than fight a brief delaying action at his intermediate position north of Cassino before falling back to his last line of defence in the Alban Hills. On May 25 the Fifth Army made contact with the force from Anzio, and on June 4 the Allies entered Rome.

Repeatedly hampered by high-level controversies which made long-term planning difficult, Alexander's force thus fought its way at last to the objective which he had hoped to reach in the previous December. Nearly eleven months had passed since the Allies landed in Sicily, nearly nineteen months since the first of their troops set foot in North-West Africa. Yet their main offensive in the European theatre had not even begun.

CHAPTER 17

THE CONQUEST OF GERMANY (I)

August 1943 - August 1944

After the failure of the Kursk offensive and Manstein's setback on the Middle Donetz in the late summer of 1943, the High Command of the German Army recognized that their troops on the Eastern Front were no longer capable of inflicting a decisive defeat on the Red Army. The question was whether they could hold a defensive line in the hope that Hitler's talent for wriggling out of awkward situations might yet save something from the wreck of Operation 'Barbarossa'.

To find such a line was difficult in the absence of strong positions prepared well in advance. Regarding defensive preparations as out of step with an offensive strategy, the Führer had never taken kindly to the idea of an Eastern counterpart to the Atlantic Wall.[1] Since the early part of the year a certain amount of work had been done on the principa crossings of the Dnieper at Zaporozhe, Dnepropetrovsk Kremenchug and Kiev; elsewhere the armies which fell bac from the Donetz in August and September could not count o more than hastily-constructed field works to offset their lac of manpower.[2] As Army Group South, when it completed it withdrawal to the Dnieper at the end of September, faced th problem of defending a four hundred and forty-mile front wit thirty-seven weak infantry divisions and seventeen armoured c motorized divisions which had lost most of their hitting power,[3] there could be little doubt that the Dnieper front woul soon crumble unless substantial reinforcements were moved i from other fronts.

Moreover, the lavish use which the Russians had made

artillery and armour in recent weeks showed all too clearly how formidable an attack they were capable of mounting. Thanks to the Soviet policy of concentrating production on a limited range of weapons, and also to the large number of wheeled, tracked and half-tracked vehicles contributed by the Western Allies,[4] by 1943 the Red Army had become to a great extent the generously-equipped and highly mobile fighting force which Hitler, with his loose control of German industry and his obstinate belief that new formations could be created overnight, had never quite succeeded in making of the German Army.

Not surprisingly, a determined attempt to force the crossings of the Dnieper and clear the approaches to Moscow before the winter was highly successful. By the end of October Smolensk, Chernigov, Kremenchug, Dnepropetrovsk and Zaporozhe were all in Russian hands. The Russians then attacked south-westwards into the bend of the Lower Dnieper. They were held up by a counter-attack south-east of Kirovgrad; but they followed with sharp thrusts in the Kiev sector and across the Nogaisk Steppes. At the risk of losing the whole of his forces south of the Desna River, Hitler ruled that the iron, steel and manganese of Krivoi Rog and Nikopol should not be given up without a struggle, and that the Crimea should be denied to the enemy as a base from which the Ploesti oilfields might be bombed.[5] In the outcome the Germans managed to hold all three localities throughout November and December, but by the end of the year had lost about two-thirds of the territories occupied since 1941.[6]

The Russian advance uncovered gruesome evidence of the wholesale slaughter of Jews and other persons obnoxious to the rulers of the Third Reich.[7] On the other side of the account, the Russians themselves were suspected, on the evidence of mass graves discovered earlier by the Germans at Katyn, near Smolensk, of either shooting about 12,000 Polish officers and N.C.O.s who had fallen into their hands in 1939, or alternatively of leaving them to their fate and concealing from the Polish authorities the fact that they had done so.[8] Already on bad terms with the allegedly reactionary Polish government in

48 The Soviet Offensive 1943-1944

London when the Katyn discoveries were announced in April, the Soviet authorities had responded to the news by suspending diplomatic relations on the pretext that the Polish Minister of Information approved of a German proposal that the affair should be investigated by the International Red Cross. Since that time the Soviet press had conducted an active campaign on behalf of the Union of Polish patriots, a body of Left Wing Russian-domiciled Poles whose president was the Communist writer Wanda Wassilewska, wife of the Soviet Vice-Commissar for Foreign Affairs and herself a member of the Supreme Soviet.

Thus the long-heralded meeting between Stalin, Roosevelt and Churchill at Teheran at the end of November took place against a background of Soviet victories, but under the shadow of a well-founded suspicion that the Russians were preparing to defy the West by setting up a puppet government in Poland when the opportunity arose.[9]

Whether the Western Allies could and should have avoided such a disastrous outcome of their struggle to liberate Poland remained long afterwards a controversial question. At the time of the Teheran Conference Britain and the United States disposed of powerful forces on land, at sea and in the air, and they had not committed themselves irrevocably to 'Overlord' or 'Anvil'. At any rate in theory, it was open to them to remind Stalin that one of their principal war aims was to undo some of the harm done by his alliance with Hitler in 1939, and to leave him in no doubt that the price of their continued collaboration with him or any Soviet ruler was that there should be no Russian intervention in countries whose independence they were pledged to restore. But Roosevelt and his advisers had little knowledge or understanding of Soviet aims, they believed that the Russians were, on the whole, rather more desirable allies than the British, and the President was anxious not to alarm Stalin by appearing to make common cause with Churchill against him. At the same time Churchill, no less than Roosevelt, was impressed by a welcome offer from Stalin to join the war in the Far East once Germany was defeated. The consequences were that the American delegates at Teheran openly confided to the Russians their disapproval of Britain's concern with the sphere of influence claimed by the Kremlin in the Balkans; that the Russians joined them in urging the British to concentrate on 'Overlord' and 'Anvil' to the exclusion of other interests; and that Stalin was left with some reason to suppose that the Americans were prepared to give him a free hand in Eastern Europe as the price of his help against the Japanese.

In the early part of 1944 the Russians continued to make rapid progress. They sprang few tactical surprises, but used prodigious quantities of artillery and flouted custom by maintaining their advance during the spring thaw, when their wide-tracked tanks were able to move in conditions which brought most mechanically-propelled vehicles to a standstill. In January they relieved Leningrad and drove the Germans back to the Esthonian frontier near Pskov. In February they encircled about 50,000 troops of Army Group South on the Dnieper front at Korsun, near Cherkassy;[10] in March and April they swept on past Odessa, crossed the Dniester on a three-hundred-mile front and threw out a salient on both banks of the Pruth round Czernowitz and Botosani. The German Seventeenth Army, cut off in the Crimea, made a desperate attempt to escape across the Black Sea in the first half of May, but lost at least 60,000 of all ranks captured, killed on land, or drowned in ships sunk by the Red Air Force.[11]

The Russians, having agreed at Teheran that plans for the summer should be concerted with the Western Allies, then waited for the British and the Americans to show their hand before committing themselves deeply in Eastern Europe. Meanwhile Finland, Hungary and Rumania, led by signs of growing accord between Moscow and Washington to hope that the teeth of the communist ogre had been drawn, all prepared to make peace with Russia at the first opportunity.

Thus the Soviet rulers could claim by the spring of 1944 that the Red Army had inflicted immense damage on the German war-machine. Even so, there was no ground for the popular belief that Russia was still shouldering almost the entire burden of the war with Germany. On the eve of 'Overlord' there were 165 weak German divisions on the Eastern Front, 131 divisions of varying quality on the Western and Southern fronts.[12]* Before the Western Allies put a man ashore in Northern France, their armed forces were either actively engaged or holding down on two fronts and for the

*The figures in January and June (a small number of divisions in Finland and formations working up in Germany excluded) were:

	January 1944	*June 6, 1944*
Eastern Front	179	165
Italy and South-East Europe	48	54
France and the Low Countries	53	59
Norway and Denmark	16	18
Totals in West and South	117	131

air defence of the Reich about two-fifths of Germany's field army, at least two-thirds of her air force, and very nearly the whole of her effective naval strength.

To follow the development of the 'Overlord' plan, it is necessary to go back to August 1943. In that month the British Lieutenant-General Sir Frederick Morgan, nominal Chief of Staff to a non-existent Supreme Allied Commander, produced on the instructions of the Combined Chiefs of Staff proposals for what the Combined Chiefs called 'a full-scale assault against Continental Europe'.[13] As Morgan had been warned that he could not count on more than about 3,300 assault ships and landing-craft, he proposed initial landings in Normandy by three seaborne and two airborne divisions, but pointed out that an assault on such a limited scale was not likely to succeed unless the enemy had no more than twelve reserve divisions of good quality in France and the Low Countries on D-day. Even with that proviso it would have only a 'reasonable' prospect of success.

In spite of this broad hint, Morgan's outline plan was accepted by both the Americans and the British at the 'Quadrant' Conference at Quebec in the same month, but with the significant comment from Churchill that the forces to be employed should be strengthened by at least a quarter.[14] Churchill also recommended that the seaborne landings should not be confined to the neighbourhood of Caen, as was proposed in the plan, but should be extended to the east coast of the Cotentin Peninsula.

Nevertheless the Combined Chiefs of Staff made no immediate increase in the allocation of assault vessels to the European theatre. This was not because they did not believe in 'Overlord', which indeed they regarded as the cornerstone of their European strategy. The reasons were partly that Morgan's estimates of carrying-capacity were challenged in some quarters, partly that the Combined Chiefs of Staff in their corporate role had only a nominal responsibility for the allocation of assault shipping. At an early stage the British had played a leading part in designing the landing-ships and landing-craft needed by both American and British forces, but by 1943 both countries relied largely on American shipyards for the larger ships. Any additional assault vessels for 'Overlord' would therefore have to come mainly, if not entirely, from resources controlled by Admiral Ernest J. King, the United States Chief of Naval Operations. King was himself a member of the Combined Chiefs of Staff Committee, but was particularly interested in the Pacific theatre.

In the autumn General Morgan visited Washington, where he put the case for more assault shipping for 'Overlord' but received no more than a sympathetic hearing. Nevertheless he and his team pressed on with their detailed planning in the hope that before long the appointment of an American Supreme Commander might improve the outlook. However, no Supreme Commander had been appointed when the British and American delegates left for Teheran, chiefly because President Roosevelt could not make up his mind whether to nominate General Marshall or General Eisenhower, either of whom would have been acceptable to the British.[15]

At that stage help came from an unexpected quarter. At Teheran Stalin asked who was to command 'Overlord' and urged that the assault should be launched not later than the end of May.[16] The Western Allies then agreed amongst themselves that they would be justified in postponing D-day from the beginning until the end of that month or even until the first week in June; Admiral King undertook to allocate to the European theatre all assault vessels completed in American shipyards between March 1 and April 1; and President Roosevelt decided that General Marshall could not be spared from Washington and that General Eisenhower should be Supreme Commander.

Meanwhile two British officers, Admiral Sir Bertram Ramsay and Air Marshal Sir Trafford Leigh-Mallory, had been chosen to command the naval and air forces assigned to 'Overlord'. General Sir Bernard Paget, who had made himself the leading Anglo-American authority on the problems of an opposed landing in Continental Europe, was to have commanded the British land forces, and also to have co-ordinated

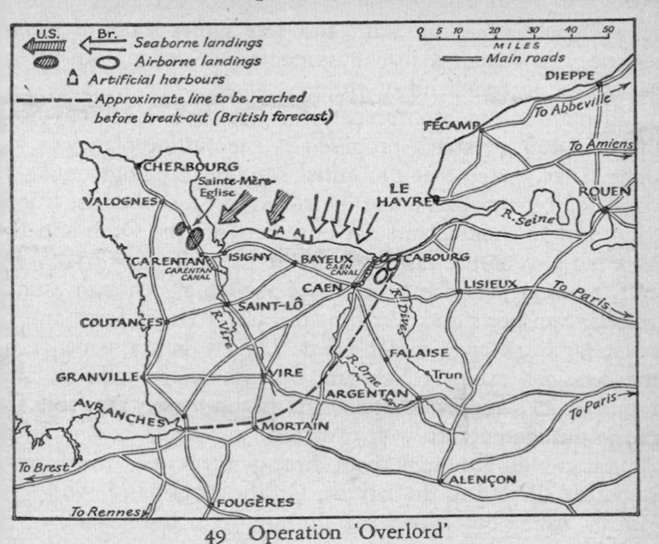

49 Operation 'Overlord'

he operations of British and American land forces during the arly stages of the invasion. Paget was, however, replaced by General Montgomery when the long-term consequences of the Cairo purge took him to an important but less crucial post in he Mediterranean theatre. Leigh-Mallory failed to gain control of the British and American strategic bomber forces, whose ommanders argued that success in the air depended on their etaining 'complete freedom of action and control over all of heir resources'.* Another British airman, Air Chief Marshal Sir Arthur Tedder, was then brought in to concert the operaions of the strategic bomber forces with those of the tactical air forces under Leigh-Mallory, and was given the post of Deputy Supreme Commander. As General Eisenhower wished o have a Chief of Staff well versed in American staff proedure, he chose the American Lieutenant-General W. Bedell Smith. The result was that the Supreme Headquarters staff inluded no British Army officer with a higher status than that

John Ehrman, *Grand Strategy, Volume V* (London, 1956) p. 290.

of a Deputy Chief of Staff, and was rather short of senior
officers who combined broad strategic knowledge with recent
experience in command of troops.

Eisenhower and Montgomery did not need to be convinced
that the scale of attack proposed in the outline plan was too
light. They agreed that the initial seaborne landings ought, if
possible, to be made by five divisions, and that the first troops
to go ashore should land not only between the Orne and the
Vire but also on the east coast of the Cotentin.

There remained the problem of assembling enough assault
vessels, transports and warships to carry a larger force and to
cover landings on a wider front. Largely in consequence of
the decisions made at Teheran, no insuperable difficulty was
found in increasing the number of assault vessels available for
the initial landings to well over four thousand, most of them
American-built although about three-quarters were drawn from
resources allotted to the British. On the other hand, while the
British Admiralty succeeded in finding a large number of
additional transports at the cost of diverting roughly half the
merchant ships normally used to carry coal and other essential
commodities between United Kingdom ports, they were unable to find all the warships needed to subdue the enemy's
fixed defences on a stretch of coast which he had been steadily
fortifying since 1940. It was characteristic of the relations between London and Washington that Admiral King refused to
believe until the middle of April that an American contribution to the bombardment forces was essential, but that he
then responded to Eisenhower's appeal by offering more ships
than he was asked to send.[17] With little time to spare, the
Admiralty finally brought together an invasion fleet of nearly
seven thousand craft, including more than twelve hundred combatant vessels of which about one-sixth were contributed by
the United States Navy, about four-fifths by the Royal Navy
and the Royal Canadian Navy, and between one-twentieth and
one-twenty-fifth by Britain's European Allies.

Another consequence of the postponement accepted at
Teheran was that more transport aircraft and gliders became

available than were expected when the outline plan was made. Accordingly, arrangements were made to use three airborne divisions instead of two. Thus the weight of the assault was raised from five to eight divisions, and if all went well the addition of nine follow-up divisions would give a total of seventeen divisions on French soil by the end of the fifth day. To ease the problem of unloading equipment and stores before a first-class port was captured, large ferro-concrete caissons, supplemented by block-ships and floating piers, would be towed across the Channel and placed off the coast to form two artificial harbours linked to the shore by articulated steel roadways. These were known as 'Mulberries'.

Even with overwhelming naval and air superiority, the Allies expected to find all this a formidable undertaking. The seaward approaches to the two American and three British landing-areas were mined and guarded by powerful coast-defence guns. Multiple lines of massive obstacles, wholly or partly submerged at high tide, had been placed off-shore to bar the beaches to landing-craft. The beaches themselves were obstructed by mines, posts, and steel 'hedgehogs' consisting of angled girders riveted together. They would be swept by fire from infantry and artillery in prepared positions, and the exits from them were blocked by more minefields, and by a variety of obstructions which included belts of wire, fences, concrete walls and anti-tank ditches. Immediately behind the foreshore was a defended zone some four to six miles deep, with strongpoints at intervals of a thousand yards or so along its forward edge.

However, the Allies believed that air attacks and naval bombardment would help to keep down fire from the coast defences, and that naval parties and engineers with special equipment which included armoured bulldozers, mine-clearance tanks and bridging vehicles would be able to deal with obstructions as long as the landings were begun in daylight and not at high water. They felt, too, that a combination of bombing with sabotage by French and Belgian sympathizers would disrupt the enemy's communications to such an extent that he

TABLE 10

FORCES UNDER ANGLO-AMERICAN COMMAND OR CONTROL FOR THE ASSAULT PHASE OF OPERATION 'OVERLORD[18]'

Naval forces	
Combatant vessels	1,213
Landing-ships and landing-craft	4,126
Transports, store-ships, etc.	864
Ancillary vessels, including tugs	736
Total	6,939

Air forces	*American*	*British or British-controlled*	*Totals*
Heavy bombers	1,970	1,470	3,440
Medium and light bombers	700	230	930
Fighters and fighter-bombers	2,300	1,890	4,190
Reconnaissance and maritime co-operation aircraft	210	1,380	1,590
First-line totals	5,180	4,970	10,150
Transport aircraft	900	470	1,370
Gliders	2,400	1,120	3,520
Land Forces			
Airborne Divisions	2	1	[illegible]
Seaborne divisions			
Assault divisions	2	3	
Follow-up divisions	6	3	[illegible]
Totals	10	7	1[illegible]

NOTE. Two British airborne divisions were available, but onl[illegible] one was used.

ould have difficulty in moving reinforcements to the crucial
ea. Even so, nothing could stop the Germans from opposing
e landings in great strength if they knew what to expect.

Accordingly, the Allies went to great lengths to achieve surrise. Since their preparations could not be entirely concealed,
ey aimed at giving the impression that they were about to
ake diversionary landings in Scandinavia and possibly in
ormandy or Brittany, but that their main effort would be
ade in the Pas de Calais and would be launched about the
iddle of July. The headquarters of a fictitious Fourth Army
onducted a brisk signals traffic with real and imaginary forations in Scotland; calculated indiscretions revealed intense
ilitary activity in the south-eastern counties; and the enemy
as fed through diplomatic and secret service channels with
mours to the effect that the Fourth Army was preparing a
rce for despatch to Norway and that the troops in the southst were the nucleus of twelve divisions due to land in the
as de Calais as the first wave of an expeditionary force of fifty
ivisions. Dummy craft were assembled in south-eastern ports
d harbours, and for every objective in Western Normandy
hich the Western Allies bombed, they bombed two elsehere.

Partly as a result of these efforts, partly because a landing
the Pas de Calais seemed inherently probable, the Germans
ad great difficulty in deciding what the Allies would do.
ield-Marshal von Rundstedt, called from retirement to fill the
ost of Commander-in-Chief, West, thought that they might
ell land in Normandy; but he also thought as late as June 5
at the outlook was obscure and that there was no immediate
rospect of invasion.[19] Hitler agreed that landings in Norandy were likely,[20] and might therefore have been expected to
pport Rundstedt; but in fact there was a weakness in Rundtedt's position which made his authority little more than
ominal. All Rundstedt's major formations in Northern France
nd the Low Countries were in Army Group B, none under his
irect control. Field-Marshal Rommel, a powerful subordinate
o whom Rundstedt was forbidden to give a firm directive, not
nly commanded Army Group B but also held the post of

Inspector of Coast Defences, with direct access to the Suprem
Command. By order of the Führer the six armoured division
in Northern France and Belgium, which Runstedt wished t
weld into a strategic reserve under a commander of his ow
choosing, were divided between an Army Group B Reserv
under Rommel and an OKW Reserve which no one coul
touch unless Hitler gave the word.

For Rundstedt this was a particularly unsatisfactory state c
affairs since he held strong views which neither Rommel nc
Hitler shared. Rommel, the great apostle of armoured wa
fare, had lost faith in mobile operations with armoured force
at any rate where the enemy had command of the air and coul
interfere with the assembly of such forces, as the British ha
done at Second Alamein. His view, which was also Hitler'
was that the only way to defeat the Western Allies was t
fight them as they came ashore or immediately after they ha
done so.[21] Rundstedt, on the other hand, was convinced th
local defences could never be made strong enough at all poin
to halt a determined enemy, that the Atlantic Wall would soc
crumble, and that everything would depend on his being abl
to counter-attack with a strong mobile reserve held ready t
move to the right place at the right moment. But he had n
such reserve, and no hope of getting one. Even if Hitler r
lented and put the three divisions of the OKW Reserve
his disposal, he would still need the three in the Army Grou
B Reserve, which his impetuous subordinate might we
commit to local counter-attacks before he could intervene.

On the naval and air sides the situation was equally u
satisfactory. Powerless in face of Allied air superiority to r
connoitre except on the most restricted scale, the Luftwaf
could throw only a fitful and uncertain light on the enemy
preparations. The navy was blind without the air, and in ar
case its resources were meagre and widely scattered. Admir
Theodore Krancke, the naval commander in the West, reporte
on June 4 that air reconnaissance in May had been insufficie
to give a clear picture, but ventured the opinion that it w
doubtful whether the enemy had yet assembled his invasic

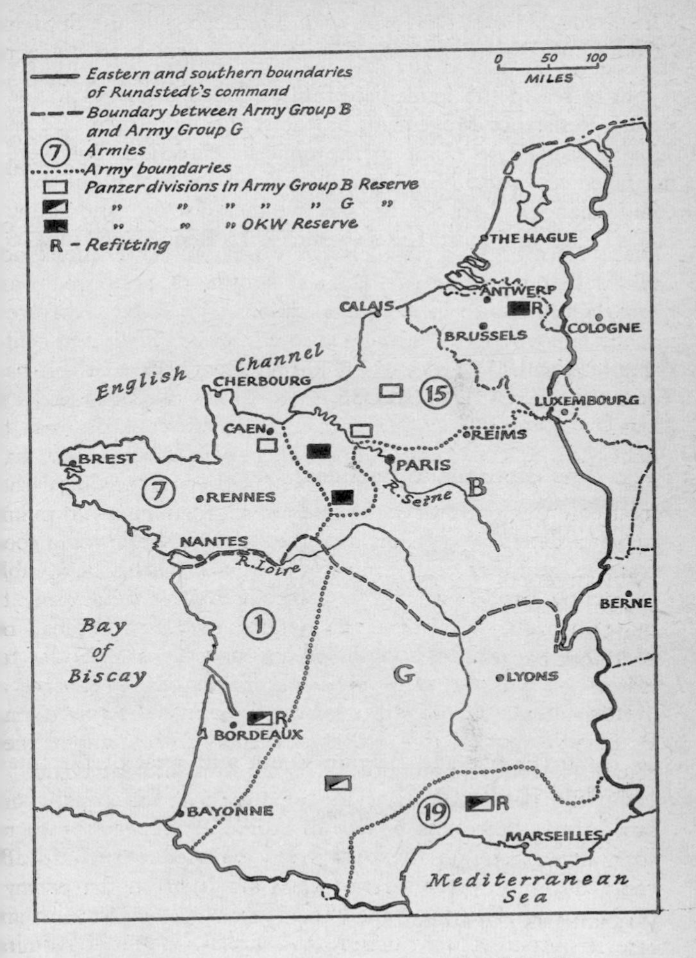

50 Organisation of the German Armies in the West, June 1944

fleet in the required strength.[22] To make matters worse, forecasts of unfavourable weather during the next few days led to the conclusion that in any case the invasion fleet was unlikely to put to sea in the immediate future. Coded messages to the French Resistance Movement, broadcast and monitored late on June 5, seemed to point in the opposite direction, but were not taken seriously. Naval patrols ordered for that night were countermanded because of the weather factor, and army officers due to report for an exercise at Rennes on June 6

TABLE 11

GERMAN FORCES IN FRANCE AND THE LOW COUNTRIES, JUNE 6, 1944[25]

Naval forces (Bayonne to Ijmuiden)

Destroyers	5
Torpedo-boats	6
Motor torpedo-boats	34
Minesweepers	309
Patrol vessels	116
Submarines	49
Artillery barges	42
Total	561

Air Forces (France and Belgium south and west of the line Brussels-Trier-Mulhouse)

	On strength	*Serviceable*
Bombers and torpedo-bombers	402	200
Fighters	336	220
Reconnaissance aircraft	89	46
First-line totals	827	466
Transport aircraft	64	31

(In addition large numbers of fighters were based in Germany, and some of these would be available as reinforcements.)

	Armoured Divisions	*Motorized Divisions*	*Other Divisions*	*Totals*
and forces				
Army Group B:				
Holland	—	—	3	3
Belgium and NE France	—	—	19	19
NW France	—	—	14	14
Army Group Reserve	3	—	—	3
Army Group G:				
SW France	—	—	4	4
SE France	—	—	7	7
Central France	—	—	2	2
Army Group Reserve	3 (2 refitting)	—	—	3
OKW Reserve	3	1	—	4
otals	9	1	49	59

ceived no contrary instructions.[23] Meanwhile Rommel, after porting earlier in the day that the pattern of Allied bombing emed to point to a landing in the Pas de Calais, had left his eadquarters to spend a night at home on his way to visit itler.

General Eisenhower also received unfavourable weather recasts. Early on June 4, when part of the assault force had ready sailed, he postponed the landings due next morning, ominally for twenty-four hours although he knew that a rther postponement might be necessary and that he risked aving to wait another fortnight for a suitable tide.[24] But ter in the day he learned that conditions over the Atlantic ad changed unexpectedly, that the storm predicted for that fternoon was likely to blow itself out during the night, and at in all probability a spell of relatively calm, clear weather as at hand. About half-past nine that evening, with half a ale blowing and thick rainclouds overhead, he ruled that verything should go forward on the assumption that D-day as June 6, and promised a firm decision in the morning. At a.m. on June 5 the omens were favourable, and at 4.30 a.m.

he took the irrevocable step which put 156,000 Allied troop in France by nightfall on the following day.*

The first to leave were the airborne troops. About twent minutes after midnight on June 6 leading elements of th British 6th Airborne Division landed in gliders on the Allie left, and within fifteen minutes seized two vital bridges acro the Caen Canal and the Orne. By daybreak the division held valuable bridgehead east of the river, had cut bridges acro the Dives to keep the enemy away, and had captured and de stroyed a battery commanding the beach on which the 3r Infantry Division was to land from the sea. On the other flan the United States 82nd and 101st Airborne Divisions ha further to go, were rather inaccurately dropped, and were ab to work only in isolated groups until daylight and the arriv of the seaborne forces gave units a chance to come togeth and act in concert.

Meanwhile more than a thousand heavy bombers of th British Bomber Command were aiming about 5,000 tons c bombs at ten coast defence batteries, while miscellaneous forc took steps to confuse and distract the enemy. Two squadro of Bomber Command with special equipment jammed th enemy's radar in order to mask the approach of the invasic fleet; four squadrons dropped dummy parachutists, strips metallized paper and fireworks so as to give the impressic that airborne landings were being made on a wide front Normandy; and aircraft and light naval craft simulated th approach of a large force to the Pas de Calais. Under cov of these diversions nearly a hundred and forty warships of t bombardment forces, including seven battleships, ranged ther

*The numbers of seaborne and airborne troops successfully carri across the Channel on D-day were approximately as follows:[26]

	American	*British (including Canadian)*	*Totals*
Seaborne	57,500	75,000	132,500
Airborne	15,500	8,000	23,500
	73,000	83,000	156,000

selves off the French coast and opened a devastating fire on the coast defences. About 7.30 a.m. in the British sector, and an hour earlier in the American sector, the first seaborne troops and vehicles went ashore after further air attacks and the firing of nearly forty thousand rockets from assault craft.

All through June 5 the Germans remained unaware that the invasion fleet was at sea.[27] In the early hours of June 6 the Seventh and Fifteenth Armies, responsible under Army Group B for the defence of Northern France and Belgium, learned that airborne troops were landing; but commanders and staffs at the higher levels were slow to believe that a crisis was at hand. Admiral Krancke ordered his command to readiness but was not convinced that a major landing was imminent, and it was not until enemy ships were reported near the Cotentin Peninsula that he sent his torpedo-boats and patrol craft to sweep the Baie de la Seine and took steps to bring up his destroyers and submarines from the Bay of Biscay. The outcome was a brief engagement with Allied bombardment forces off the mouth of the Orne, in the course of which a Norwegian destroyer was sunk. Similarly, for many hours the Luftwaffe took no action beyond sending night-fighters to investigate mysterious happenings off the mouth of the Somme.[28]

At Rundstedt's and Rommel's headquarters the state of affairs a little after 2 a.m. was that neither Rundstedt nor Rommel's Chief of Staff believed that the enemy was about to come ashore in strength, but that no objection was made to a proposal from the Seventh Army to use the 21st Panzer Division, hitherto in the Army Group Reserve, to clear up the situation arising from the airborne landings east of Caen. Between two and three hours later, when Allied assault craft were known to be approaching, Rundstedt contemplated taking the 12th SS Panzer Division and the Panzer Lehr Division from the OKW Reserve and allotting them to Army Group B; but this was soon stopped by the Supreme Command, who insisted that neither division should be committed without their prior sanction. When the ban was lifted in the afternoon Rundstedt ordered both divisions to join forces with the 21st Panzer Division and an infantry division, counter-attack from Caen, and 'drive the British into the sea'. But the 21st Panzer Division was already in action on the Orne, where it helped to prevent the British from seizing Caen on the first day as they had hoped to do, and the other two armoured divisions were not yet in position. Notwithstanding the Supreme Command's insistence that the Allied bridgehead should be destroyed by the evening because of the danger of further landings, no concerted attack by all three armoured divisions would be possible before June 8.

In the outcome the counter-attack was not delivered even on that day. By June 8 both the 21st Panzer Division and the 12th SS Panzer Division were being used defensively to prevent the British from thrusting far to the south across the Caen-Bayeux road and further east, and the Panzer Lehr Division was about to be committed in a similar role after moving forward with great difficulty under constant air attack. For the German commanders almost the only grain of comfort was the knowledge that they no longer had much reason to differ about strategy or major tactics. Rommel's hope of defeating the Allies on the coast had crumbled, but his prediction that there would be great difficulty in assembling forces for large-scale counter-attacks had been amply fulfilled. At a meeting on June 11 Rundstedt agreed with him that his only possible course of action was to remain on the defensive between the Orne and the Vire and concentrate on driving the enemy away from Cherbourg. If the American forces in the Cotentin could be defeated by thrusts from the west and north, then it might be possible to turn later against the main body of the Allied forces further east.

Hitler responded to these proposals by ordering two armoured divisions from the Eastern Front to Normandy, insisting that the Allied bridgehead between the Orne and the Vire should be destroyed, and promising that infantry divisions from Norway and elsewhere should free the armoured divisions on the Orne-Vire front for an offensive role. At the same time he pressed on with long-delayed attacks on London with FZG76 pilotless aircraft, or flying bombs, also known as V.1. In 1943 a start had been made with the construction of nearly a hundred launching-sites for such missiles, largely in the Pas de Calais; but Allied bombing had led Lieutenant-General Erich Heinemann, the officer responsible for operations in the field, to switch to simpler sites less likely to attract attention.[29] The Allies had become aware of the existence of the new sites but had decided not to bomb them, partly because they made poor targets and partly because the threat which they presented was under-estimated.[30]

By putting pressure on the commander of the launching-regiment, Heinemann succeeded in beginning his offensive from the new sites about the middle of June. The Allies countered by bombing launching-sites and other installations, but their effort was distributed over too wide a range of targets to be effective, although some highly successful attacks on storage depots showed that a more concentrated effort might have yielded good results.[31] On the other hand the missiles proved less accurate and more vulnerable to defensive counter-measures than early experiments had led Hitler to expect. Up to the middle of July well over 4,000 flying bombs were launched, but many fell short or wide, only 1,270 reached the huge area covered by the London Civil Defence Region, and 1,241 were destroyed by the air defences under Air Marshal Sir Roderic Hill. At that stage Hill, aware that most of his successes had been gained by fighters and that the anti-aircraft guns were not doing very well, took the bold decision to mass the guns on the coast at the cost of imposing more stringent conditions on fighter-pilots. In the next seven weeks the defences destroyed 2,222 missiles out of 3,791 seen or detected, and on their best day they destroyed 90 out of 97. By early September, when the launching-regiment withdrew from the Pas de Calais to escape capture by the advancing Allied armies, about 20,000 people had been killed or seriously injured by the missiles, but the offensive had brought Hitler no clear strategic gain.

TABLE 12

THE V.1. OFFENSIVE: MAIN PHASE[32]
(June 12—September 5, 1944)

1. The numbers of missiles launched, seen or detected by the defences, destroyed by the defences, and reaching the London Civil Defence Region before and after the redeployment of the anti-aircraft guns were:

	June 12 *to* *July* 15	*July* 16 *to* *Sept.* 5	*Totals*
Missiles launched:			
from sites in France	4,271	4,346	8,617
from aircraft (about)	90	310	400
Totals	4,361	4,656	9,017
Missiles seen or detected by defences	2,934	3,791	6,725
Missiles presumed to have miscarried or not accounted for	1,427	865	2,292
Missiles destroyed:			
by fighters	924	847	1,771
by guns	261	1,198	1,459
by balloon barrage	55	176	231
by joint action	1	1	2
Missiles destroyed by all arms	1,241	2.222	3,463
Missiles reaching London Civil Defence Region	1,270	1,070	2,340

NOTES

1. Of the 9,017 missiles launched, all were aimed at London except about 150 aimed at Portsmouth or Southampton and 21 aimed at Gloucester.

2. Between June 12 and September 5 roughly 20,000 people were killed or seriously injured by flying bombs. Many

buildings were destroyed, and many more damaged, but no important military objective was affected.

3. The bomb-tonnage dropped by Allied aircraft in the course of attempts to destroy launching-sites and other installations before and after the offensive began were:

December 5, 1943 to June 12, 1944	23,489 tons
June 13, 1944 to September 1, 1944	74,349 tons
Total	97,838 tons

4. The numbers of heavy and light anti-aircraft guns, rocket-barrels and barrage balloons deployed to counter flying bombs on July 19, 1944, and approximately one month later were:

	July	*August*
Heavy guns	412	800
Light guns	1,184	(1,800)
Rocket-barrels	(200)	(700)
Barrage balloons	1,750	1,750

NOTES

A The figures in brackets are rough estimates.

B Of the 412 heavy guns in position on July 19, 16 were contributed by the United States Army, the rest by the Royal Artillery. By August the American contribution rose to 80 guns.

C Of the 1,184 light guns in position on July 19, 572 were contributed by the Royal Artillery, 584 by the Royal Air Force Regiment and 28 by the Royal Armoured Corps.

D The figures for August include 208 heavy and 578 light guns sited to deal with air-launched flying bombs approaching from the east.

Meanwhile the Allied build-up in Normandy, although brought almost to a standstill for three days in June by a storm which damaged both artificial harbours and made one of them unusable, continued with comparatively little interference from the enemy. By the end of June, when the assault phase of 'Overlord' was deemed to have ended, more than 850,000 men, nearly 150,000 vehicles and well over half a million tons of stores had been disembarked on French soil.

General Eisenhower's strategic aim was to bring to battle and destroy the main body of the enemy's forces in the West. His plan, afterwards criticized in England as a characteristically American conception but in fact drawn up by three British members of his staff, was to advance to the Ruhr on two mutually supporting axes, making his main thrust along a line through Amiens and Maubeuge and a subsidiary thrust south of the Ardennes through Verdun and Metz.* An advance by the northern route alone was rejected by the planners on the ground that it would tend to put his forces in headlong collision with the enemy's on a narrow front where Eisenhower would have no room for manœuvre and no chance of concealing his intentions.

In the early stages, however, the immediate aims of the Allied armies, as outlined by General Montgomery's staff about two months before D-day, were to seize Cherbourg and establish themselves roughly on the line Avranches-Mortain-Cabourg before thrusting into Brittany and towards the Sarthe and Seine.† As this meant that the United States First Army, besides taking Cherbourg, would have to occupy more than twice as much territory as the British Second Army before joining in a general offensive, the essence of Montgomery's plan for the period immediately after D-day was that the Second Army should help the First by drawing the largest possible number of German formations to the British sector.

From the moment on D-day when the 21st Panzer Division first opposed the British advance on Caen, this policy was outstandingly successful. At the cost of disappointing members of the public who hoped for spectacular gains in the British sector, Montgomery succeeded by the last week in June in attracting to the Second Army's front not only all the German armoured divisions in France and Belgium on D-day except two in the south and one near Paris, but also the two withdrawn from the Eastern Front. In accordance with a directive issued

*Major L. F. Ellis, *Victory in the West*, volume 1, pp. 82-3.
†Ellis, *op. cit.*, p. 357, diagram I.

by Montgomery about the middle of the month, the First Army was thus able to capture Cherbourg and consolidate its bridgehead without meeting any of Rundstedt's armour.

In the light of this setback and after an unsatisfactory interview with the Führer at Berchtesgaden on June 29, Rundstedt proposed that he should be given a free hand to withdraw from Caen to positions out of range of the enemy's naval guns. He was promptly superseded by Field-Marshal Gunther von Kluge, who arrived in a blustering mood but was in no position to challenge Rommel's sombre assertion that his forces were being steadily worn down and that the enemy might thrust deep into France at any moment. On July 17, almost immediately after reporting to the Führer that the 'unequal struggle' was 'nearing its end', Rommel was seriously injured when his car was attacked by Allied aircraft.

Deceived by the strength of the Second Army's front and the false reports which the Allies had been circulating for months past, the Germans believed that the break-through would come in the British sector, probably about the time when fresh forces might be expected to land in the Pas de Calais. As a result of the long-promised arrival of infantry formations to relieve some of the armour opposing the Second Army, elements of the Panzer Lehr Division were nevertheless ordered to the First Army's front in the early part of July. About the same time the 2nd SS Panzer Division, which had come north from Toulouse, took up a position in rear of that sector. Thus the Americans found themselves facing German armour for the first time at the moment when their advance on Saint-Lô was about to be held up by a long spell of cloudy weather which hampered their supporting aircraft. On July 9 the Second Army entered Caen after a frontal assault supported by naval, air and artillery bombardments in which British heavy bombers were used for the first time in a tactical role; but further west the First Army made slow progress and lost more men in just over a fortnight than in the whole of the fighting in the American sector from D-day to the end of June.*

*In round figures, Allied battle casualties during the assault phase of 'Overlord' and in the operations mentioned were:

Accordingly, Montgomery decided immediately after the capture of Caen on a twofold operation designed to speed the progress of the First Army to the start-line for a general advance, continue the process of wearing down the enemy's forces on the Second Army's front, and discourage Kluge from shifting his armour westwards, by giving the impression that the British intended to launch a major offensive without waiting for the Americans to come forward. After consulting the army commanders on July 10 he directed that on July 19 General Omar Bradley, commanding the First Army, should press on rapidly towards Avranches as the prelude to a break-out in that sector, and that twenty-four hours earlier Lieutenant-General Sir Miles Dempsey, commanding the Second Army, should thrust in great strength towards the Caen-Falaise road thus gaining a favourable position from which to fight the German armour on the eastern flank. Telling Dempsey that, while every opportunity should be taken of destroying the enemy, the Second Army must think first of maintaining a firm flank, he took the additional precaution of sending an emissary to the War Office to explain that the real object of Dempsey's thrust was to 'muck up and write off enemy troops', and that he had no intention of committing the Second Army to a break-out before the Americans were ready. The emissary was to make it clear that everything about to be done by the Second Army was designed to help the Americans to come forward in the west while the British preserved a strong bastion in the east.

In spite of these warnings, Montgomery's aims were widely misunderstood. As the First Army did not enter Saint-Lô until July 18, General Bradley could not begin his offensive on the scheduled day. Indeed he was prevented, chiefly by bad weather which hampered his supporting aircraft, from start-

	American	*British and Canadian*
'Overlord' assault phase, June 6 to 30	37,000	25,000
Capture of Caen, July 8-9		3,500
Advance to Saint-Lô, July 3 to 19	40,000	

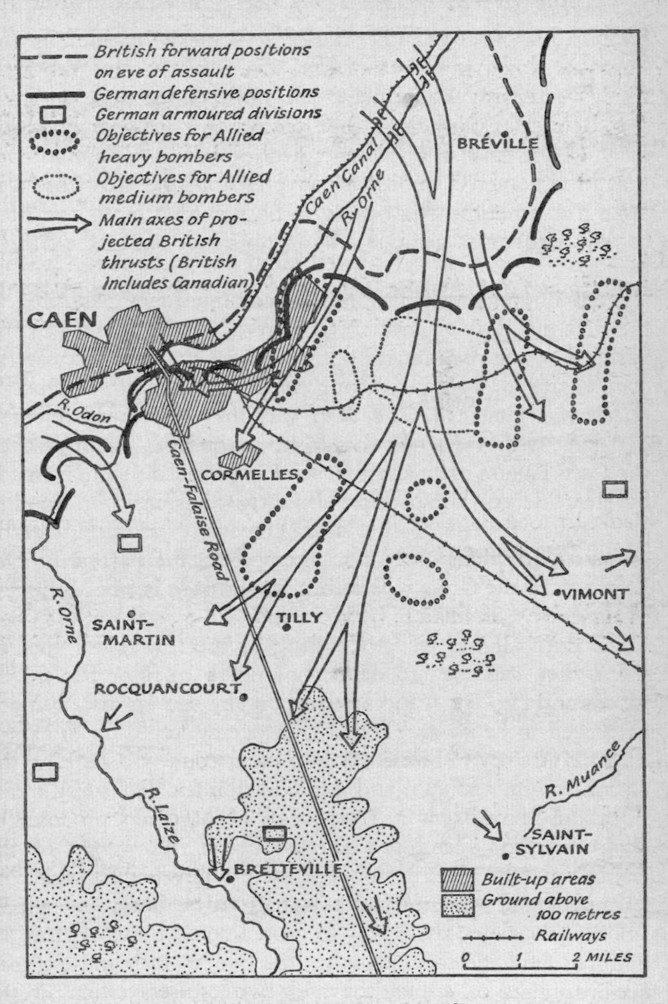
British forward positions on eve of assault
German defensive positions
German armoured divisions
Objectives for Allied heavy bombers
Objectives for Allied medium bombers
Main axes of projected British thrusts (British includes Canadian)
CAEN
Caen Canal
R. Orne
BRÉVILLE
R. Odon
CORMELLES
Caen-Falaise Road
R. Orne
SAINT-MARTIN
TILLY
VIMONT
ROCQUANCOURT
R. Laize
BRETTEVILLE
R. Muance
SAINT-SYLVAIN
Built-up areas
Ground above 100 metres
Railways
0 1 2 MILES

51 Operation 'Goodwood'

ing before July 25. Consequently General Dempsey's contribution took on added importance as a means of pinning the Germans down both before and after the start of the First Army's offensive. Nevertheless an effect of the delay in starting Bradley's attack was that Dempsey's massive diversion assumed the guise of an independent operation. The result was that Montgomery's ambitious move to hold the Germans away from the American front came to be regarded by some Allied commentators as a genuine attempt to break out in the British sector.

That impression, which official communiqués published at the time did little or nothing to correct, was heightened by the vastness of the preliminary bombardment thought necessary to compensate for the unpromising conditions in which Dempsey's attack was launched. The plan was that his three armoured divisions, with 750 tanks, should make the main thrust towards the Caen-Falaise road, and that flanking attacks should be made by elements of four or more infantry divisions with another 350 tanks. The lie of the land, however, was such that the armoured divisions could not assemble in the narrow bridgehead east of the Orne, where they would have been in full view of the enemy, and had to be kept behind the river and the Caen Canal until all was ready. Crossing by the few routes open to them, they had then to debouch from a corridor flanked by woods and buildings, and advance one by one against positions organized in depth and held by an enemy keyed up to expect a major attempt to break out into open country. Crediting the Germans with 300 guns and 230 tanks on the flanks of the corridor and immediately in front of it, Montgomery proposed to avoid exposing Dempsey's troops to the full weight of the enemy's fire by putting down a preliminary bombardment of unprecedented violence. As this had to be heavy enough to smother the defences, it was to be delivered by more than six hundred field and medium guns, the two 15-inch and eighteen six-inch guns of a monitor and two cruisers lying off the coast, and more than four times as many aircraft as the Germans had assembled for their ill-fated attack on the Kursk salient in 1943.

As things turned out, this multiplicity of weapons proved something of a handicap. More than a thousand heavy bombers of the British Bomber Command opened the air assault by plastering selected patches of ground with large bombs; but they and the American heavy bombers which came later covered only a small part of the defended area. Furthermore, they were on their way home long before most of the enemy's troops were called upon to fight, and they left behind them a cloud of dust and smoke which made the subsequent bombing of specific targets by medium bombers difficult. Going forward under cover of an artillery barrage, the leading armoured formations made a good beginning; but their advance slowed down as soon as they passed out of range of the field guns and reached areas not effectively bombed, with the result that troops and vehicles waiting to get forward piled up behind them. Hampered almost as much by traffic-jams as by the enemy, the Second Army succeeded in enlarging the bridgehead east of the Orne, but not in capturing the high ground south of the Caen-Falaise road which the three armoured divisions had been ordered to 'dominate'.

It was therefore understandable that commentators hostile to Montgomery or imperfectly aware of his intentions should conclude after a day or two that the attack had failed. Air Chief Marshal Tedder, who did not believe that the Second Army could help the First to come forward quickly by inducing the enemy to build up his strength on the eastern flank, went so far as to propose to the Supreme Commander that Montgomery should be relieved of responsibility for co-ordinating the operations of the two armies. But the facts were that the Second Army was pinning down nearly all the German armour in Northern France and most of the infantry brought in since D-day, and that since July 3 four fresh infantry divisions had moved to its front while only one weak armoured division, one infantry division and part of a second infantry division had reached the First Army's front during the same period. Undismayed by Dempsey's failure to win more territory, Montgomery concluded that he was doing what he was meant to do by attracting most of the enemy's attention, and that Bradley would soon succeed in fighting his way forward once the weather in his sector became good enough for him to be given the necessary air support.

He was soon proved right. On July 23 the Canadian First Army, under Lieutenant-General H. D. G. Crerar, set up its headquarters in Normandy, but left the Canadian 2nd Corps under command of the British Second Army, which thereupon extended its front westwards by taking over the Caumont sector from the United States First Army. On the same day General Bradley decided in the light of a favourable weather forecast to begin his advance towards Avranches on July 24. To prevent the Germans from responding to it by moving their armour from the eastern flank, the Canadian 2nd Corps, with two British armoured divisions added to its own armoured brigade and two infantry divisions, would attack along the Caen-Falaise road at dawn on July 25.

As things turned out, the skies did not clear in Bradley's sector until late on July 24, so that his offensive was postponed for twenty-four hours and began some hours later than the complementary thrust in the east. Strongly opposed by the 1st and 9th SS Panzer Divisions, the Canadians failed to open a gap for the armoured divisions and lost about 1,500 of all ranks, but attained their aim by keeping the enemy heavily engaged.

In the west the situation at first light on July 25 was that General Bradley had four armoured and eight infantry divisions up or in reserve in the sector from Saint-Lô to Lessay. Facing these were the 2nd SS Panzer Division and the Panzer Lehr Division with 109 tanks, the weak 5th Parachute Division, and four infantry divisions mustering twenty-three battalions of which seventeen were described by the Seventh Army as exhausted or weak. Bradley's intention was that, after a heavy air bombardment, three infantry divisions should attack on a narrow front a little west of Saint-Lô with the object of opening a gap through which two armoured divisions and a motorized infantry division were to press on towards Coutances, Villedieu and Brécey.

Between 9.40 a.m. and 11 a.m. nearly three thousand

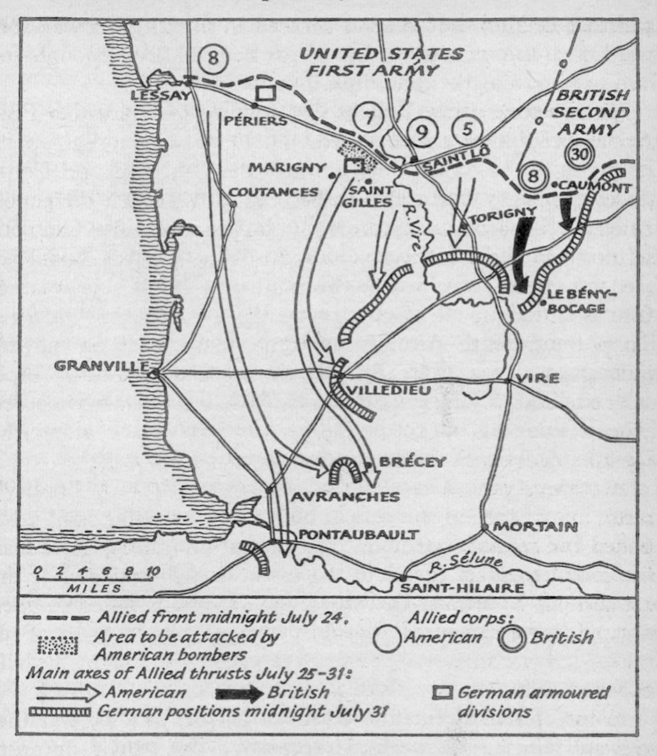

52 Operation 'Cobra'

bombers and fighter bombers of the United States Eighth Air Force and Ninth Air Force attacked the enemy's positions, dropping many thousands of high-explosive and fragmentation bombs and some hundreds of napalm incendiary bombs filled with jellied petrol. Although some crews bombed so inaccurately that roughly six hundred American troops held well back from the German lines were killed or injured, the bombardment had a devastating effect on the enemy and notably on the Panzer Lehr Division, which lost all its thirty or forty tanks in the forward area and had very heavy casualties.

About 11 a.m. the assault formations of the three American infantry divisions went forward on a front of about 6,000 yards. In spite of the pounding they had received, the German troops in front of them fought desperately to avoid uncovering the flank of the weak formations on their left; but in the course of the next thirty-six hours the Germans were gradually pushed back by relentless thrusts in which the Americans made good use of their armour to exploit small gains by the infantry. As little had been done on the German side to prepare for an orderly withdrawal on an extended front, the result was that a well-timed push by Bradley's right-hand corps forced the Seventh Army to swing back its left with a haste which proved disastrous. By July 29 the retreat had become a rout, on July 30 Kluge hastened to Army Headquarters in the hope of stopping the rot by taking direct control, and on that day the Americans swept into Avranches while the British came forward from Caumont with orders to 'step on the gas for Vire'. Except that re-entrants in both the American and British sectors had yet to be cleared, the Allied armies stood by August 1 approximately on the line from which Montgomery's planners had proposed in April that they should wheel into Brittany and towards the Sarthe and Seine.

The launching of 'Overlord' was followed by unwonted expressions of regard for the West on the part of Soviet statesmen and officials. A week after D-day Stalin paid a glowing tribute to the Allies for their forcing of the Channel, a feat which he described as without precedent in military history and contrasted with the contemptible efforts of 'invincible Napoleon' and 'Hitler the hysteric'.* Almost simultaneously the Soviet press published, on the authority of the Commissariat for Foreign Trade, an impressive list of raw materials and manufactured goods received from the United States and the British Empire since 1941, mentioning such items as 3,734 American and 5,480 British or Canadian tanks, 6,430 Ameri-

*Alexander Werth, *Russia at War 1941-45* (London, 1964), p. 855, citing *Pravda.*

can and 5,800 British aircraft, many thousands of motor vehicles and huge quantities of ammunition.[33]

Meanwhile it seemed to the British that something ought to be done to ensure that the withdrawal of German forces from the Balkans did not create a political vacuum which the Russians, if left to themselves, were all too likely to fill without consulting either the Western Allies or the inhabitants.[34] As a practical alternative to a free-for-all which might lead to anarchy or worse, they suggested that, pending agreement on peace-terms, the Russians should take control in Rumania, where Britain was under no obligation to support any particular régime, and that they themselves should look after Greece, where they did regard themselves as bound to uphold the existing government until the wishes of the majority could be made known by a plebiscite. The American State Department recoiled from a bargain which hinted at spheres of influence, but President Roosevelt agreed that the arrangement was worth trying for three months. The Russians then refused to commit themselves on the ground that American approval was half-hearted, and early in August they threw the British proposal overboard by secretly sending a mission to Communist sympathizers in Northern Greece. In Rumania their declared policy was to make no change in the social order, but what that would mean in practice was still not clear when their troops began to overrun the country a few weeks later.

In any case the era of apparent accord between East and West did not long survive a fresh bout of Soviet successes on the battlefield. On June 23 the Red Army opened a vast offensive on a four hundred and fifty mile front in Belorussia with forces estimated by Soviet writers at more than a hundred and sixty divisions, about thirty thousand guns and large mortars, well over five thousand tanks and about six thousand aircraft.[35] Overwhelmed by superior fire-power and hampered by conflicting orders, inadequate transport and attacks on their rear communications by thousands of partisans, Army Group Centre fell back too slowly to escape huge encircling movements which cost the German Army the equivalent of twenty-five divisions in little more than a month.[36]

An important aspect of this offensive was that it carried the Russians well outside their own territory at a time when the armies of the Western Allies had made no spectacular territorial gains since they first set foot in France. On July 18, when the Red Army entered Polish territory near Chelm after taking Vitebsk, Minsk and Baranovichi in Belorussia and Vilno in Lithuania, the Allies were still waiting for the United States First Army to come forward to the start-line fixed for the breakout which they hoped might give them victory by the end of 1944.

A week later the Soviet government, still on bad terms with the Polish government in London, announced that it had entered into relations with the Polish Committee of National Liberation, an organization first heard of on that day although it purported to have been set up at Chelm on July 22.[37] The President of the National Committee was a Socialist named Osóbka-Morawski, who also held the post of Chief of the Foreign Affairs Department. But the roles assigned to Wanda Wassilewska and other prominent Communists suggested that Osóbka-Morawski was little more than a convenient figurehead.

A few days later spearheads of the First Belorussian 'Front' (or Army Group), under General K. K. Rokossovsky, approached Praga, the suburb of Warsaw on the right bank of the Vistula, and further south established two small bridgeheads across the river at Magnuszew and Pulawa. On July 29 Moscow broadcast an appeal to the people of Warsaw to rise against the Germans. Without communicating directly with Rokossovsky or the Soviet General Staff, General T. Bor-Komorowski, the commander of the underground Home Army in Warsaw, then ordered his followers to attack the German garrison and break out towards the Soviet troops which he believed to be only a few miles away.[38]

The Polish attack opened on August 1, and was supported by practically the entire able-bodied population. Almost simul taneously the Germans outside Warsaw launched a counter-attack with four armoured divisions and drove the Russians back. After receiving an appeal from Bor-Komorowski through the Polish government in London, the British government asked the Russians to send help to the Poles in Warsaw by air or otherwise; but the Soviet authorities proved unhelpful, and Stalin afterwards referred in scathing terms to 'the handful of power-seeking criminals who launched the Warsaw adventure'.[39] Until the second week in September, when the Red Army at last reached Praga but had still to fight its way across the Vistula, he refused to allow Allied aircraft from England to land in Russia after flying over Warsaw, so that throughout the crucial period the only supplies received by the insurgents were those carried in a few aircraft which succeeded in making the long and difficult flight from Italy. The outcome was that, after a struggle believed to have cost the lives of 200,000 Polish men, women and children, the Home Army laid down its arms. 'May God, who is just,' its leader signalled to London, 'pass judgment on the terrible injustice suffered by the Polish nation.'[40]

Not surprisingly, Soviet spokesmen denied that Rokossovsky's advance on Warsaw was halted in order that the uprising should fail, the Polish government be discredited, and the Polish nation be so weakened by the partial destruction of its capital and the slaughter of many of its leading citizens that it would be unable to resist the onward march of Communism. Rokossovsky himself alleged that Bor-Komorowski's action was hopelessly mistimed, dismissed the Moscow broadcast of July 29 as 'routine stuff', and added that even in the most favourable circumstances Soviet troops could not have entered Warsaw before the middle of August.* But he did not explain why the Red Air Force carried no supplies to the insurgents between August 4 and September 13, except by saying when questioned on August 26 that the Soviet forces were doing their best and that high altitude drops were of little value.

Meanwhile it had become apparent to the well-informed that

*Werth, *op. cit.*, pp. 876-8.

the German Army was not strong enough to continue the struggle indefinitely on three fronts. Some Germans favoured an armistice with the Russians as the prelude to a striking victory in the West or South which would re-establish Germany's position as a great military Power; others an understanding with the Western Allies and a crusade against Communism. Hitler, as usual, took an independent line. His policy, so far as he had one, was to play a waiting game, patch up all three fronts as best he could, and make no overtures to either the Russians or the Western Allies until dissension in the enemy's camp created an opportunity which he would know how to use when the moment came.

But this was little better than a policy of despair. Relations between Russia and the West were seldom good and sometimes bad; but they were not so bad that either the Soviet Union or the Western Alliance was likely to make terms with Germany as long as Hitler was in power. Nor was there any real prospect of an irreparable breach between Britain and the United States. In the summer of 1944 the British keenly resented the insistence of the Americans on giving effect to 'Anvil' (renamed 'Dragoon') in the teeth of their argument that the diversion of troops from Italy to the South of France would weaken Alexander without helping Eisenhower. But even when their dissatisfaction was at its height they did not contemplate breaking up the alliance, and indeed were willing to contribute nearly half the naval forces needed for the enterprise.

Thus the outcome of the dispute was not a rupture between the British and the Americans, but the landing between Hyères and Cannes on August 15 of three American divisions, preceded by American and British airborne forces and followed by seven French divisions. As the British foresaw, this did not result in any diversion of German forces from Northern France, but on the contrary enabled Hitler to withdraw a number of divisions from Alexander's front and send two of them to reinforce Kluge's armies.[41] Moreover, by the time the Americans landed on the Côte d'Azur the situation in Normandy had become so threatening that on August 17 the Supreme Command ordered practically the whole of Army Group G's forces in the South of France, amounting on that date to some eleven divisions, to fall back to the north and join Army Group B. 'Dragoon' had, therefore, no immediate effect on 'Overlord', and its ultimate effect was to give Eisenhower ten additional divisions which reached him by a roundabout route, while some thirteen weak divisions were added to the forces opposing him.

Among German opponents of Hitler's policy of holding on everywhere at the risk of dragging Germany into the abyss, the most resolute were those who accepted the leadership of General Beck and Dr. Karl Goerdeler, two men of principle who had given up important posts rather than support measures which they believed to be contrary to the national interest and morally objectionable.* By the early summer of 1944, and indeed much earlier, Beck and Goerdeler were satisfied that Germany must come to terms with the Western Allies, that there could be no negotiated peace as long as Hitler was in power, and that he must be removed for that reason and also to release the German Army from its oath of loyalty. Colonel Klaus von Stauffenberg, a devout Catholic nobleman who had distinguished himself in the Polish, French and North African campaigns and had been badly wounded, was prepared to remove him; and in June it was agreed that he should place a time-bomb in Hitler's concrete bunker at Berchtesgaden on the next occasion when he was summoned in his capacity as a staff officer of the Replacement Army to a meeting at which Hitler, Göring and Himmler were all present.[42] As soon as they were dead the code-word 'Valkyrie' would be passed to the principal military headquarters in Germany and the occupied terri-

*For Beck's background and removal from office, see p. 61. Dr. Goerdeler had been Price Controller in the National Socialist government and *Oberburgermeister* (or Lord Mayor) of Leipzig, but had resigned both offices in 1935 and 1936 as a protest against the persecution of the Jews.

tories, and the army would seize power and set up a provisional government with Goerdeler as Chancellor.

For various reasons the attempt was not made until July 20. By that time Hitler had moved his headquarters to Rastenburg, in East Prussia; and on that particular day the meeting was held not in the usual bunker but in a large hut with all its windows open. Moreover, Göring and Himmler were not present. But Stauffenberg had carried his bomb to two previous meetings without using it; with the Russians only fifty miles from Rastenburg and the British attacking east of Caen, he could wait no longer. After setting the fuse he returned the bomb to the despatch case in which he had brought it, put the despatch case under the table at which Hitler was conferring with Keitel and others, and left the room. As soon as he heard the bomb explode he hastened to join the leading conspirators in Berlin, leaving Hitler's Chief Signals Officer, who was in the secret, to tell them that Hitler was dead and then block communications between Rastenburg and the outside world.

Hitler was lucky. The table helped to shield him from the explosion, the effects of blast were diminished by the open windows and the comparative flimsiness of the building. Seeing him come out of the ruins alive and able to walk, the Chief Signals Officer took no action. The result was that 'Valkyrie' messages were despatched to the appropriate headquarters when Stauffenberg reported on reaching Berlin that the bomb had gone off within a few feet of the Führer, but were overtaken by telephone calls from Rastenburg to the effect that the Führer was alive and that prompt measures were to be taken to suppress the conspiracy. Troops ordered to Berlin to arrest National Socialist officials and agents of the Gestapo were used to round up the plotters. Stauffenberg and three of his associates were shot by a firing squad within a few hours, Beck was allowed to take his own life, and thousands of men, women and children implicated in the plot or merely related to the ringleaders were arrested and executed in the course of the next nine months, in some cases after prolonged torture and in circumstances of revolting cruelty. Henceforth

German commanders in the field, conscious that they belonged to a suspect caste and that one false step might bring an invitation to choose between arrest and suicide, depended for reinforcements on Heinrich Himmler, who added command of the Replacement Army to control of the SS and the Gestapo.

CHAPTER 18

THE CONQUEST OF GERMANY (II)

July - November 1944

In the late summer of 1944 Germany faced the threat of a simultaneous collapse on three fronts. So far as the Western Front was concerned, the Supreme Command was beginning to suspect by the second half of July that there would, after all, be no landing in the Pas de Calais, that a great part of the Fifteenth Army had been withheld to no purpose from the fighting in Normandy, that the Allies were preparing without more ado to break out of their vast lodgement area.[1] In the South, General Alexander was pushing Field-Marshal Kesselring northwards in Tuscany, and indeed was confident that, if only the Americans could be persuaded to forgo a landing in the South of France, he would be ready by August to break through the so-called Gothic Line and threaten Hungary and Austria by forcing the Lubljana gap.[2] In the East, the German armies had been driven back since June on a front extending from the Baltic States to Tarnopol in the Ukraine, and might soon be forced to fight alone.

Moreover, Germany's troubles were not confined to the strategic sphere. In recent months attempts to harness more of industry to the National Socialist war-chariot while keeping a large army in the field had brought a manpower crisis but had not averted a shrinkage of supplies which threatened to become more serious as more territory was lost. Largely in consequence of Allied bombing the output of high-octane aviation spirit, in particular, had declined from 175,000 tons in April to 29,000 tons in July, and production was still falling.[3]

Hitler, much shaken by the attempt on his life but by no

neans cowed, summed up his conclusions in a midnight har-
ıngue to his advisers at the end of July.[4] The most important
ask, he said, was to prop up the Eastern Front, for failure
here would bring a direct threat to the homeland. At the same
ime Hungary must be kept in the fight for both economic and
trategic reasons; on that account Allied incursions into Istria
ır the Balkans would be highly dangerous; and it followed that
he Southern Front must be made secure even though it went
.gainst the grain to lock up a substantial force in Italy. As for
he West, to lose France would mean losing 'the starting point
ıf the U-boat war'. The Supreme Command must prepare in
ecret for a withdrawal to rear positions, but Kluge must be
old nothing except that he was to hold on everywhere.

To a great extent these intentions were fulfilled. In August
he German armies in the East succeeded in setting up a
elatively stable line almost everywhere except in the extreme
outh, where the Russians broke out of their bridgehead across
he Pruth and soon reached the Yugoslav frontier near Turnu
ieverin, forcing the Rumanians to change sides, the Bulgarians
o court Moscow, and the Hungarians to give up hope of a
ıegotiated settlement and prepare for a final desperate stand.
)n the Southern Front any immediate danger of an Allied
ıreak-through towards Vienna disappeared when President
Roosevelt declared that not more than six divisions could be
naintained through the Lubljana Gap and that General Eisen-
ıower must have Marseilles to support his advance to the
Ruhr.[5] On these grounds the President insisted that 'Dragoon'
hould be carried out at the cost of depriving Alexander of a
uarter of his strength. Almost at the same time the Wehr-
nacht overcame some of its recruiting difficulties by calling up
ıoys of sixteen and men in reserved occupations; and as winter
pproached the output of aviation spirit and other petroleum
ıroducts picked up a little, largely because the Allies made
ewer attacks on oil targets as a result of bad weather and
heir inability to frame a programme of strategic bombing to
vhich the commanders of their heavy bomber forces could be
ersuaded to conform.

There remained the problem of the Western Front, where much more than 'the starting-point of the U-boat war' might be lost if the Supreme Command allowed their forces to be defeated by refusing to shorten their lines while there was still time to do so.

On August 1 the United States land forces in Normandy were welded into the Twelfth Army Group, commanded by General Bradley and consisting of the First Army under General Courtney H. Hodges and the Third Army under General George S. Patton Jr. Besides commanding the Twenty-first Army Group, which comprised the British Second Army under General Dempsey and the Canadian First Army under General Crerar, General Montgomery continued for the time being to co-ordinate the operations of all the land forces.[6]

General Bradley's intention when he took up his new command was that the Third Army, on his right, should drive towards Rennes and then turn westwards into the Breton Peninsula, and that the First Army, on his left, should establish itself round Vire and Mortain. After a talk with Montgomery on August 1 he agreed, however, that only one corps of the Third Army should go westwards and that the rest of the Allied armies should pivot on Caen in order to force the enemy back against the Seine. On August 3 he issued fresh instructions which called for a wide sweep to the south and east by the greater part of the Third Army and a strong thrust towards Mayenne and Domfront by the First Army. The British and Canadian armies would also thrust southwards and eastwards from their more restricted lodgement area, but would take care that the hinge on their extreme left did not become unpinned until the door was fully open.

Meanwhile Kluge was worried by growing pressure from the British in the Caumont sector. He had just made up hi mind to reinforce that sector at the cost of weakening hi front near Caen when he received from Hitler a peremptor order to hold the front between the Orne and the Vire chiefl with infantry formations, assemble at least four armoure

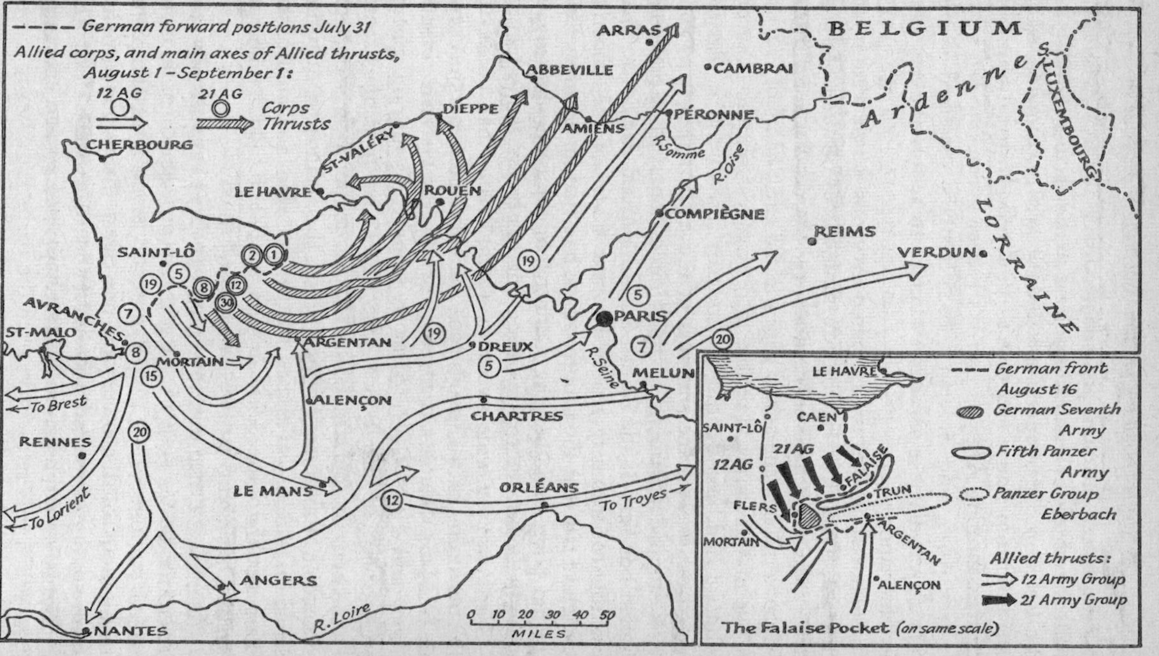

53 Normandy: the Allied Break-out and the Advance to the Seine and Beyond

divisions near Mortain, and counter-attack towards Avranches with the object of establishing a new front across the base of the Cotentin. Thereupon he withdrew in the Caumont sector to a line from Thury Harcourt to Vire, reorganized his armour by transforming Army Group B's Panzer group into the Fifth Panzer Army, and ordered a counter-attack described in his official war-diary as a decisive attempt to restore the situation in Normandy.

But the four German armoured divisions which were given the task of annihilating the American forces between Mortain and Avranches had only about 145 tanks between them. Moreover, when the attack began in the early hours of August 7 one of the four was unable to disengage from the front on which it had been fighting for the past few days. The remaining three made some progress in the early stages, but were soon stopped by troops of the United States 7th Corps and fighter-bombers of the British Second Tactical Air Force. That evening Montgomery reported to the Chief of the Imperial General Staff that the counter-attack had had no adverse effect on his plans and that the Germans might be unable to get away if they stayed to fight for a few more days at Mortain.

Next day the wide sweep to which Bradley had agreed at the beginning of the month took the United States 15th Corps to Le Mans. Seeing a chance of catching the German Seventh Army and Fifth Panzer Army in a pocket by making contact with troops of the Twenty-first Army Group coming south from Caen, Bradley swung the 15th Corps northwards through Alençon. Montgomery approved of this manœuvre, but insisted that the Allied armies must still be ready to complete the 'long hook' to the Seine in case the 'short hook' failed to destroy the enemy's forces where they stood.

As events turned out, the 15th Corps met unexpectedly stiff resistance on August 13, largely in consequence of a move which put one of its two leading divisions across the communications of the other and prevented the second division from continuing its advance until the roads were clear. The Germans were thus given time to improvise a stand at Argentan. When this setback occurred the corps had already moved further north than Bradley had expected it to go when he decided to send it in that direction, and he was not sure that it was strong enough to withstand a counter-attack even if it did succeed in getting beyond Argentan. Also he had begun to doubt the wisdom of allowing two Allied armies to meet head-on in the field. Furthermore, according to his subsequent recollection he believed at the time that the Germans had already begun to pull out of the pocket in which he and Montgomery had hoped to catch them.* Abandoning any immediate intention of continuing his northward advance, he ordered the French 2nd Armoured Division and the United States 90th Infantry Division to hold the positions reached that day, and sent the rest of the 15th Corps to Dreux as a contribution to the 'long hook'.

The result was that, when the Canadian First Army entered Falaise on August 16, a gap about twenty miles wide still separated its leading troops from Bradley's. In the quadrilateral Falaise-Condé-Flers-Argentan the remnants of some twenty divisions of the Seventh Army and the Fifth Panzer Army, mostly with little or no artillery, were holding a corridor some twenty miles long and up to fifteen miles wide against Allied armies which encompassed them on three sides. But they still had access to the main road connecting Argentan with Vimoutiers by way of Trun, and also to a road leading in the same direction through Chambois.

Montgomery concluded that an attempt to bring off the 'short hook' by closing the gap with the three or four divisions immediately at hand was still worth making. On August 16 he ordered the Canadian 2nd Corps, which already had a Canadian and a Polish armoured division moving in the right direction, to make all speed to Trun, hold the place in strength, and go on to meet the United States 90th Infantry Division, which was asked to come forward a few miles to Chambois.

The outcome of these orders was that the Canadian 4th Armoured Division took Trun on August 18 after a stiff fight with elements of three Panzer divisions. However, its leading

*General Omar H. Bradley, *A Soldier's Story* (London, 1951), p. 377.

troops were then held up at Saint-Lambert, a village about halfway between Trun and Chambois. Meanwhile the Polish 1st Armoured Division, advancing by a roundabout route, managed to put a small force into Chambois late on August 19, but by that time had outrun its supplies and was short of fuel. Elements of the United States 90th Infantry Division, which was transferred on August 17 from the Third to the First Army and delayed by a consequent reshuffle of corps commanders, arrived at Chambois only just before the Poles. Thus the Allies succeeded by the evening of August 19 in reaching both escape roads, but could scarcely be said to have closed the gap since the Germans were still fighting at Saint-Lambert and held about half the village.

Meanwhile Kluge had left his headquarters early on August 15 to visit formations in the field, and nothing more had been heard of him for many hours. On his return he explained that he had been caught in air attacks and traffic jams and that all his wireless equipment had been put out of action. On August 16 he ordered SS General P. Hausser, commanding the Seventh Army, to take command of all troops in the corridor and start withdrawing them across the Orne at nightfall. Suspected by Hitler of trying to go over to the enemy during the hours when he was out of touch with his staff, he was relieved next day by Field-Marshal Walter Model, who had just distinguished himself by organizing the successful counter-attack outside Warsaw. Kluge then left to report to Hitler, but took his own life on the way after writing a letter in which he defended his actions and proclaimed his loyalty.

Model had left the Eastern Front only about forty-eight hours earlier, and had no first-hand knowledge of the situation in Normandy. Nevertheless he judged, correctly, that the Allies had not yet had time to close the Falaise gap in strength. Encouraged by the promise of a counter-attack from outside the corridor, Hausser succeeded on August 20 and 21 in extricating nearly half the survivors of his force, many of whom escaped on foot along lanes and byways on either side of Saint-Lambert. But the cost in casualties and abandoned vehicles was heavy. The Allies took at least 30,000 prisoners in the immediate neighbourhood of the corridor between August 16 and 21, and at the end of the withdrawal Model reported that the Seventh Army had ceased to be an effective fighting force.

Meanwhile three American corps were advancing almost unopposed towards the Seine. On August 15 the leading division of the United States 15th Corps motored sixty miles from the Sarthe to the Eure without seeing any Germans, and on August 19 the same division reached the river at Mantes-Gassicourt to find a footbridge still intact and the Germans gone. That night one of its regiments filed across the bridge in pouring rain while another made the crossing in assault boats and on rafts. In the meantime the United States 12th and 20th Corps, making a wider sweep with the Marne as their objective, had reached Orléans and Chartres, while on the left the Canadian 1st Corps was working eastwards between the sea and Lisieux. With every important bridge downstream from Paris destroyed or severely damaged by bombing, the Allies seemed well placed to complete the destruction of Hausser's force before the survivors could ferry themselves across the river to join the Fifteenth Army in North-East France and Belgium.

As events turned out, the 'long hook' was only partially successful. On August 19 Montgomery decided in consultation with Bradley that the United States 15th and 19th Corps should swing northwards across the Twenty-first Army Group's front in order to deny the retreating Germans access to the ferries, and if possible should establish bridgeheads on the right bank. The two American corps succeeded in capturing a number of ferries. But they gained no bridgeheads below Mantes-Gassicourt, and one effect of their move was to force many survivors of the Seventh Army into the two big loops of the Seine south and south-east of Rouen, where the Fifth Panzer Army was able to cover their retreat by fighting a stiff rearguard action on a relatively narrow front. Between August 20 and 24, while the Americans were crossing the British front and the Allied air forces were hampered by bad weather,

Model succeeded in withdrawing to the right bank not only a large number of troops but also some thousands of vehicles which the Allies had expected to capture or destroy.

Meanwhile Hitler had ordered Model to prevent the Allies from thrusting their right between the Loire and the Seine towards Dijon, and if necessary to organize a defensive line along the Seine and the Yonne and fight a battle in and about Paris. As the forces at the disposal of General D. von Choltitz, the Military Governor of Paris, consisted of little more than one low-grade security regiment and some anti-aircraft batteries, and as he already faced a rising by French insurgents who had seized a number of public buildings, he was in no position to make an effective contribution to this programme. Indeed, he had agreed some hours before he received a copy of Hitler's order to take no action against the insurgents as long as their leaders helped him to prevent rioting and bloodshed. Fearing, however, that some act of lawlessness by extremists might lead Choltitz to denounce the agreement and order reprisals, the Resistance leaders urged General Eisenhower on August 22 to send troops into the city without delay. Accordingly, American and French formations of the United States First Army fought their way through the outlying defences on August 23, and on August 25 Choltitz surrendered to General Leclerc, commanding the French 2nd Armoured Division.

Thus the broad situation on the Western Front at the beginning of the last week in August was that the Anglo-American armies under Eisenhower held almost the whole of North-West France as far east as the Seine and Yonne and as far south as the Loire; that the Fifth Panzer Army was fighting a series of rearguard actions on the left bank of the Seine before completing its withdrawal to the right bank on August 29; and that the Allied troops put ashore in Provence had pushed up the valley of the Rhône as far as Avignon and were about to complete the capture of Marseilles and Toulon. On the other hand the Germans still held Brest and Lorient, and their forces in the West, although much weakened by ten weeks of unprofitable fighting, had escaped destruction and might still give a good account of themselves if they were lowed time to reorganize and refit. The question for the Vestern Allies was whether they could follow up their adntage by striking a decisive blow while the enemy was still f balance and the weather favourable enough to allow them make full use of their air superiority.

Believing that this could be done if Eisenhower's two army roups stayed together as 'a solid mass of some forty divions which would be so strong that it need fear nothing', Iontgomery proposed to Bradley as early as August 17 that, ter crossing the Seine, substantially the whole of the Allied mies should advance towards the Ruhr on a front of about fty miles, with their left directed on Antwerp and their right n Brussels, Aachen and Cologne. Bradley accepted the prinple of a concentrated thrust, although according to his subquent account he favoured a move south of the Ardennes toards Frankfurt rather than north of the Ardennes towards the uhr. But on August 19 Montgomery learned from Bradley at apparently Eisenhower meant to 'split the force and send alf of it eastwards towards Nancy'.

The outcome was a difference of opinion between Montomery and Eisenhower which no amount of goodwill on the art of either could ever adjust, since their attitudes were funamentally irreconcileable. Montgomery was convinced that othing mattered except victory and that he was offering his hief a chance of ending the war in the West by Christmas. e urged Eisenhower either to place the whole of the land orces at his disposal for a thrust north of the Ardennes, or ternatively to place them at Bradley's disposal for a comarable thrust south of the Ardennes. Eisenhower, not satisd that a single thrust would be decisive, and in any case coniving it to be his duty not merely to beat the Germans but hold an equitable balance between his subordinate comanders, refused to do either. In accordance with the broad rategic plan which he had accepted before D-day, he ruled at the Twenty-first Army Group, supported for the time eing by the United States First Army, should advance toards Antwerp and eventually towards the Ruhr, and that e United States Third Army should push eastwards through

Metz and Nancy.* Recognizing that the left-hand thrust must have priority at any rate until Antwerp was in his hands he agreed that Montgomery should co-ordinate the movements of the armies north of the Ardennes, but added that on September 1 he, the Supreme Commander, would assume direct responsibility for co-ordinating the operations of the land forces as a whole.

Convinced that Eisenhower was wrong, but determined to make the most of his opportunity, Montgomery began on August 29 a spectacular advance which swept the V.1 launching regiment from the Pas de Calais and carried the leading troops of the British Second Army from the Seine to Antwerp in five days. As the United States Third Army in the south continued to move forward with little opposition, the result was that by September 6 the Allied armies stood on a line from Antwerp through a point east of Brussels to Namur, thence roughly southwards to a point between Verdun and Nancy and back to Orleans and along the Loire to Nantes. The Germans, however, still commanded the seaward approaches to Antwerp from positions north and south of the Scheldt, and their garrisons had yet to be turned out of Brest and Lorient. Meanwhile they were working feverishly to close the gap between the coast and the northern extremity of the Siegfried Line north-east of Aachen, largely with improvised formations recruited from parachute regiments and other Luftwaffe units grounded for lack of fuel. On September 4 Hitler reinstated Rundstedt as Commander-in-Chief, West, but retained the energetic Model as his deputy in the crucial northern sector.

The British success touched off a train of confident predictions by highly-placed Allied spokesmen. Londoners were given to understand that the danger from long-range weapons was almost over;[7] the Chief of the Imperial General Staff thought the Germans unlikely to last through another winter; and Eisenhower spoke of seizing both the Ruhr and Frankfurt. Montgomery, on the other hand, was still convinced that his chief was heading for stagnation by trying to move both north and south of the Ardennes without the means of supporting

*See p. 413.

two advances. On September 4 he renewed his plea for a single thrust. Given even twenty divisions and a share of the seven thousand tons of supplies a day which were going to the United States First and Third Armies he could, he believed, cut through the thinly-held line on the British Second Army's front, turn the Siegfried Line, and open a way not merely to the Ruhr but across the North German Plain to Berlin.

On that date, Eisenhower was immobilized by a wrenched knee at his headquarters three hundred miles behind the lines. In the absence of a secure signals network he could communicate with the forward area only by courier or wireless telegraphy, and he depended for his knowledge of the tactical situation largely on subordinate commanders who inevitably presented matters in the light of their own preconceptions. Only a few days earlier he had assumed direct responsibility for co-ordinating the operations of the land forces, in accordance with the decision of which he had given Montgomery notice soon after the middle of August. Having shouldered the burden, Eisenhower was determined to carry it without stumbling; he was also determined to be fair. Yet he was ill-placed to make a decision which would have taxed the abilities of a far more experienced commander. His reply to Montgomery, so much delayed in transmission that the prospects of success were already receding by the time it reached its destination, was to the effect that he would welcome a strong thrust in the north but was not prepared to call a halt to progress in the south. Although he continued to assert that in principle the armies north of the Ardennes must have priority, in practice he did not prevent Bradley from diverting supplies from the First Army to the Third or from ordering Patton to cross the Moselle and force the Siegfried Line.

On September 8, however, the Germans gave the Allies something new to think about by initiating attacks on London with long-range rockets launched from Holland. Just over a week later they followed with a fresh bout of attacks with air-launched flying-bombs. On September 12 the Combined Chiefs of Staff, meeting in Quebec on the first day of the Second Quebec Conference, undertook to remind Eisenhower of the advantages of entering Germany by the northern route. On the same day Montgomery received the Supreme Commander's permission to force the Lower Rhine if he could do so with his own resources, supplemented by three airborne divisions and an additional thousand tons of supplies a day for a limited period.

TABLE 13

THE V.2 OFFENSIVE AGAINST THE UNITED KINGDOM, SEPTEMBER 1944 TO MARCH 1945[9]

1. Soon after 6.30 p.m. on September 8, 1944, two batteries of a mobile rocket-launching Abteilung, Art. Abt. (mot) 485, opened fire on London from the outskirts of The Hague, about 200 miles from the target area. On September 14 they were joined by an experimental battery, Lehr und Versuchs Batterie 444, which had moved to the island of Walcheren after firing a few rounds at Paris from the neighbourhood of Euskirchen; but soon after the middle of the month all three batteries were withdrawn in consequence of Allied airborne landings between Eindhoven and the right bank of the Lower Rhine (Operation 'Market Garden'). According to British and German sources the numbers of rockets launched and reaching the London Civil Defence Region between September 8 and September 18 were:

Launched	35
Reaching London C.D.R.	27

2. After its withdrawal from Walcheren Lehr und Versuchs Batterie 444 was ordered to open fire from the neighbourhood of Staveren, in Friesland, on Norwich and Ipswich, as these were the only English towns of even minor importance which could still be reached. Between September 25 and October 12 the battery aimed 43 rounds at Norwich and one round at Ipswich. No hits were scored, but 35 rounds fell on British soil and two were seen to fall into the sea.

. One battery of Art. Abt. (mot) 485 was ordered on Sep-
ember 30 to return to The Hague, reopened attacks on London
n October 3, and just over a fornight later was reinforced by
art of a newly-formed battery belonging to its own Abteilung
nd also by Lehr und Versuchs Batterie 444. The offensive
gainst London was maintained by the equivalent of some two
two-and-a-half batteries until March 27, 1945, when the
aunching-troops were withdrawn to Germany. According to
he best estimates available, the numbers of rockets launched
nd reaching the London Civil Defence Region during this
hase were:

Launched	1,324
Reaching London C.D.R.	501

.. The following table summarizes the figures for the whole
eriod from September 8, 1944 to March 27, 1945:

Rockets launched	1,403
On target (London C.D.R.)	517
On land or close off-shore but not on target	598
Abortive or not observed	288

. In the whole course of the campaign about 9,000 civilians
vere killed or seriously injured by long-range rockets. Many
uildings were destroyed or damaged, but no objective of out-
tanding military importance was affected.

. Before September 8, 1944, the Western Allies aimed 20,126
ons of bombs at objectives suspected of a connection with the
ong-range rocket. After that date they aimed about 1,200
ons of bombs at objectives associated with troops believed to
e concerned with long-range rocket attacks on the United
Kingdom.

TABLE 14

THE V.1. OFFENSIVE AGAINST THE UNITED KINGDOM: PHASES TWO AND THREE

1. The numbers of flying bombs launched, seen or detecte by the defences, destroyed by the defences, and reaching th London Civil Defence Region after the departure of th launching-regiment from the Pas de Calais early in September 1944, were:

	Sept. 14 *to* *Jan.* 12	*March* 3 *to* *March* 29	*Total*
Missiles launched:			
from aircraft	1,200	—	1 20
from sites in Holland (modified missile)	—	275	27
Missiles seen or detected by defences	638	125	76
Missiles presumed to have mis-carried, or not accounted for	562	150	71
Missiles destroyed:			
by fighters	71	4	7
by guns	331	87	41
by joint action	1	—	1
Missiles destroyed by all arms	403	91	49
Missiles reaching London Civil Defence Region	66	13	7

NOTE: Of the 1,475 missiles launched, all were aimed a London except about 50 aimed at Manchester. One missil reached Manchester.

Thus the final outcome of Eisenhower's determination to tak no risks and do nothing controversial was something of paradox. He had rejected in turn a massive advance by hi whole force, and what Montgomery called a 'full-blooded' thrust by twenty divisions. Yet ultimately he staked his chances of turning the Siegfried Line before the winter on a limited offensive in which the initial assault would be made by three airborne divisions, supplemented by one corps of three divisions moving on a front so narrow that even a temporary hold-up might make the difference between success and failure. In its final form, the plan proposed by Montgomery and accepted by Eisenhower envisaged the capture of nine bridges over three major rivers and five minor waterways by the one British and two American divisions of the Allied Airborne Army. The British 30th Corps, with the Guards Armoured Division leading, was to exploit the capture of the bridges by advancing to the Lower Rhine and crossing it. After the 30th Corps had crossed the Lower Rhine, part of it was to wheel westwards to cut off the Germans in Western Holland. The whole of the British Second Army was then to establish itself on a line from Zwolle through Deventer to Arnhem, throw out a deep salient east of the Ijssel, and prepare to thrust eastwards into Germany.

The strength of this plan was that, if the airborne assault succeeded, the Second Army would stand a good chance of forcing the Maas, the Waal and the Lower Rhine without fighting a major battle for each crossing. Its weakness, apart from the risks inherent in any major operation with airborne troops, was that the initial advance would be made along a single road leading from the Maas-Escaut Canal to Eindhoven.

As the airborne assault on September 17 achieved tactical surprise, this proved a justifiable risk. The United States 101st Airborne Division, ordered to capture five bridges beyond Eindhoven, took all of them on the first day, only one of them was blown, and the Guards Armoured Division joined forces with the Americans on the second day and was able to repair the damaged bridge within twelve hours. The United States 82nd Airborne Division, whose task included the capture of two bridges across the Maas and one across the Waal, seized both bridges across the Maas before nightfall on September 17. The paratroopers had to fight hard to maintain their posi-

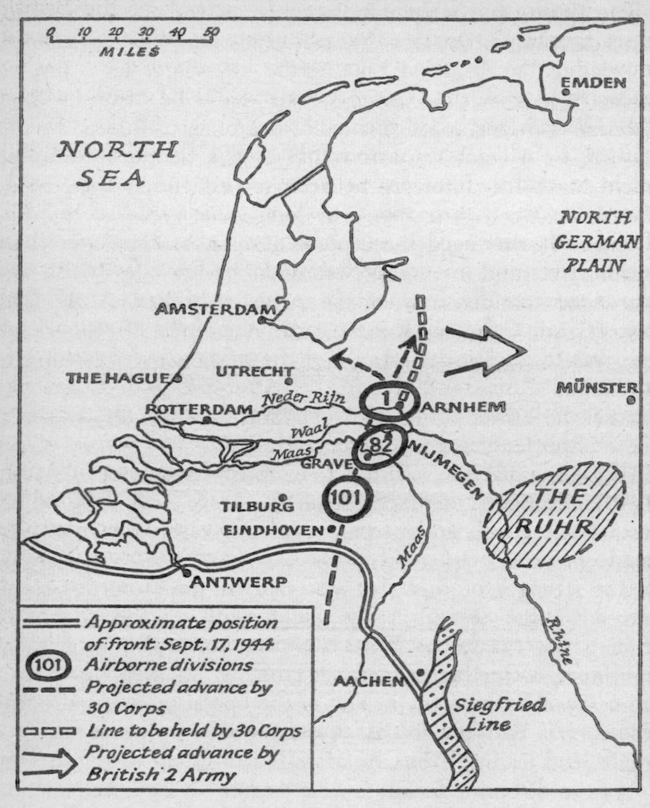

54 Operation 'Market Garden'

tions on the next two days; but on September 20 they crossed the Waal downstream from the still untaken bridge under heavy fire, and approached the northern end of the Waal bridge as the leading tanks of the Guards Armoured Division were racing across the river from the south. With the exception of the great steel road-bridge spanning the Lower Rhine at Arnhem, all the bridges needed by the 30th Corps for its advance were thus in Allied hands by the end of the fourth day.

To capture the Arnhem bridge was the task of the British 1st Airborne Division. After consulting advisers with local knowledge, the divisional commander had decided to land on the north bank of the river, about seven miles from his objective. The outcome was that he succeeded on the first day in sending a small force to the northern end of the bridge, but not in preventing the Germans from seizing the southern end. Moreover, the division was so unlucky as to land in full view of Field-Marshal Model, who hastened from his headquarters outside the town to organize a counter-stroke. Consequently the situation at Arnhem early on September 18 was that roughly six hundred British parachutists, ably commanded and well posted at improvized strong-points, were guarding the northern end of the bridge; that some miles to the west of them two more parachute battalions were being held off by Model's counter-stroke; and that still further to the west the air-landing brigade of the 1st Airborne Division was defending the divisional landing-area and awaiting reinforcements due from England at 10 a.m. But a blanket of cloud had descended over the airfields from which the reinforcements were to start. They did not arrive until the afternoon, and by that time an attempt to relieve the troops at the bridge had been repulsed with such heavy losses that the survivors, even when reinforced, were too weak to do more than join the air-landing brigade in holding a patch of territory outside the town. Not merely the detachment at the bridge but practically the whole division was thus likely to succumb unless the 30th Corps could reach Arnhem within the next few days.

But surprise had gone, resistance was stiffening, the offensive was slowing down. Elements of the 9th Panzer Division withdrawn from France and sent to the neighbourhood some ten days earlier were already engaging the British at Arnhem, and elements of the 10th SS Panzer Division were being ferried across the Lower Rhine to oppose the advance from the south. On September 20 the Guards Armoured Division was still fighting at Nijmegen, and the first of the infantry divisions coming up behind it had not yet crossed the Maas. On that day the troops at the bridge, now only 140 strong, were driven

from their positions and could not prevent the enemy fron
passing armoured elements across the river from the north t
south without making a detour to the ferries. Held up nortl
of the Waal on the following day, the 30th Corps reached th
Lower Rhine in time to bring away some two thousand sur
vivors of the 1st Airborne Division before daybreak on Sep
tember 26, but too late to force a crossing.

Thus the Arnhem operation ended with the British Secon
Army standing in a salient some sixty miles deep on the soutl
bank of the Lower Rhine, but with the Germans still holdin
the north bank, still commanding the seaward approaches t
Antwerp, and still in a position to bombard London witl
long-range rockets. Meanwhile Bradley's armies, attemptin
to thrust eastwards towards the Middle and Upper Rhine, ha
been checked at Aachen, in the Ardennes, before Metz an
south of Nancy. Too late to divert to the northern sector th
resources consumed in these eastward thrusts, Eisenhower re
sponded to the ruling of the Combined Chiefs of Staff b
affirming that his aim was to envelop the Ruhr from th
north, but added that no deep drive into Germany would nov
be possible until Antwerp could be used as a port of supply
Almost simultaneously Alexander reported from Italy that hi
forces, reduced to some twenty divisions by the landings i
the South of France, were making steady progress but wer
too weak for a decisive blow.[10]

From the German point of view the outlook at the end o
September was thus far more favourable than had seemed likel
a few weeks earlier. In the South the Western Allies had chose
to divide their forces at the very moment when Alexande
appeared to be on the point of bursting through the Gothi
Line and turning eastwards to force the Lubljana gap; in th
West they had dispersed their effort when, according to th
opinion afterwards expressed by Rundstedt, a concentrate
thrust in the north would have 'torn the German front t
pieces' and carried them into the Rhineland at one bound.

*Chester Wilmot, *The Struggle for Europe* (London, 1965 edition
p. 539 (citing Rundstedt's reply to a written question).

On the Eastern Front the Russians had made great strides in the Balkans since the summer and had induced the Finns to come to terms, but elsewhere appeared to have been checked. Moreover, as a result of the recruiting-drive some forty new or refurbished divisions were due by December.[11]

Concluding that he could afford to gamble on holding his existing line in the West for at least some weeks to come, Hitler proceeded to make ready for a counter-offensive on which he relied to change the whole complexion of the war. On October 12 he ruled that meanwhile the V.2 launching-organization, since August under Himmler, should devote itself to attacks on London and Antwerp, leaving attacks on Brussels and Liége to the V.1 launching-regiment withdrawn from Northern France to Western Germany.[12] And by that date the Western Allies, if not exactly reconciled to the prospect of a long wait before they crossed the Rhine, were at any rate aware that they could not afford to base their plans for the Far East on the assumption that they would be able to move substantial forces from Europe to South-East Asia within the next few months.[13]

In September Eisenhower added to his command the Sixth Army Group, formed from troops which had landed in the South of France. In the following month he brought forward from Brittany the newly-formed United States Ninth Army and interposed it between the British Second Army and the United States First Army. By the end of October his forces in the forward area thus consisted from left to right of the Canadian First Army and the British Second Army, comprising the Twenty-first Army Group under Field-Marshal Montgomery; the United States Ninth, First and Third Armies, comprising the Twelfth Army Group under General Bradley; and the United States Seventh and the French First Armies, comprising the Sixth Army Group under General J. L. Devers. Altogether Eisenhower had fifty-six divisions, but eight of these were immobilized in Normandy or the South of France by lack of transport. The remaining forty-eight were spread over a six-hundred-mile front, not all were up to strength, and there were shortages of certain types of ammunition made in the United States.

Undeterred by those shortcomings, Eisenhower decided that early in November the Twelfth Army Group should attack on a wide front with the threefold object of defeating the enemy west of the Rhine, securing bridgeheads on the right bank, and seizing the Ruhr and the Saar as the first step towards an advance deep into Germany. On the left the Twenty-first Army Group was to support Bradley's flank by advancing through Holland, while on the right the Sixth Army Group was to 'act aggressively with the initial object of overwhelming the enemy west of the Rhine and subsequently of advancing into Germany'.

In accordance with the strategic plan approved in the previous May and the recent ruling of the Combined Chiefs of Staff that the northern route into Germany was to be preferred, Eisenhower added to this far-reaching statement of intentions a saving clause to the effect that the thrust north of the Ardennes was to be regarded as the main effort. But the offensive in that sector was delayed by a spoiling attack on the British front, and on November 2 Bradley authorized Patton to attack towards the Saar as soon as the weather was suitable. A push in that direction would, he argued, assist the main effort by drawing German troops from the north.

As things turned out, the weather in the early part of November was consistently bad. But Patton was determined not to lose his opportunity. He believed that the German First Army defending a front of some seventy-five miles with eight or nine weak divisions, would soon crumble and that he would have no difficulty in crashing through the Siegfried Line. On November 8, after three days of heavy rain, he launched his offensive in a down-pour. Swollen rivers and sodden ground did not prevent his infantry from making a spectacular advance on the first day, but they made it impossible for him to follow up his advantage by pushing his armour forward at high speed. Consequently the Third Army's offensive neither fulfilled Patton's hopes by carrying him well into the Saar, nor attained its strategic aim by inducing Rundstedt to reinforce the First Army at the expense of his northern sectors. When Bradley's left-hand armies attacked just over a week later across country ideally suited for defence, the enemy had little difficulty in halting them without committing the major part of his reserves. The only big prize won by the Western Allies throughout the month was in the Vosges, where the United States Seventh Army captured Strasbourg after the French First Army had broken through the Belfort gap to reach the Upper Rhine near Mulhouse. Even in that sector, however, the Germans scored an unexpected success by retaining a valuable bridgehead at Colmar.

CHAPTER 19

THE CONQUEST OF GERMANY (III)

December 1944 - May 1945

The failure of the November offensive seemed to Montgomery to prove, if proof were needed, that his chief was still trying to do too much and would never get far unless he either learned to concentrate his forces for a decisive stroke, or appointed a co-ordinator who would do so.

As a candidate for the post of co-ordinator, Montgomery was not an impartial critic. But that did not mean that his arguments were worthless. It did not escape the British Chiefs of Staff that Eisenhower's avowed policy of making his main thrust in the north and a subsidiary thrust in the south had not worked well in practice, or that the Supreme Commander seemed to have a weakness for directives so broadly framed as to be open to almost any interpretation which Bradley cared to put upon them. The Chiefs of Staff concluded that their American colleagues must be asked to join them in insisting on a detailed statement of Eisenhower's intentions.[1] However, they had yet to approach the United States Chiefs of Staff when the Germans gave a new twist to the kaleidoscope.

As early as August 19 General Jodl, Chief of the Operations Staff at German Supreme Headquarters, jotted down a reminder to himself to make plans for 'going over to the offensive in November when the enemy cannot operate in the air'.[2] Early in October he produced a detailed plan for an offensive in the Ardennes, and in due course an amended version was accepted by the Führer.[3]

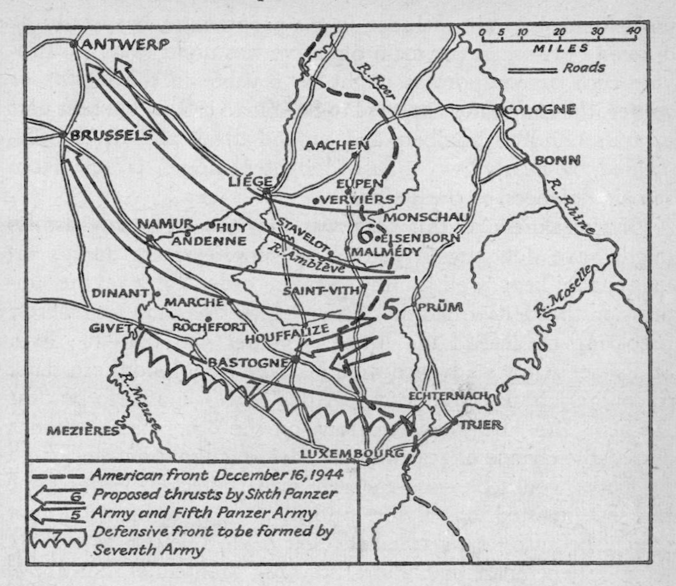

55 The Ardennes: the German Plan

In its final form, the plan provided for an attack in mid-December by some twenty-eight divisions on a front from Monschau to Echternach. On the right the Sixth SS Panzer Army, under SS General Sepp Dietrich, was to thrust westwards and north-westwards through Eupen and Verviers. Dietrich's army was to cross the Meuse between Liége and Namur, using bridges seized in advance by troops dressed in American or British uniforms, and swing towards Antwerp with the twofold aim of denying the port to the Allies and cutting off the whole of Eisenhower's forces in the north. In the centre the Fifth Panzer Army, under General Hasso von Manteuffel, was to cross the Meuse south of Namur and paralyse the nerve-centre of the British and Canadian armies by seizing Brussels. In the south the Seventh Army, under General Erich Brandenberger, would cover Manteuffel's left by throwing out a defensive screen from Echternach to Givet. Supporting attacks on both flanks were included in the programme, but would be ordered only when the main offensive was under way. To provide such air support as might be feasible in the depths of winter, the Luftwaffe expected to be able to call on the best part of four hundred bombers and ground-attack aircraft, supplemented by nearly two thousand fighters drawn largely from the air defences of the Reich.

One weakness of this plan was that the advancing armies might have difficulty in getting up supplies from dumps intentionally kept well to the rear in order to give the impression that Hitler had no offensive intentions and was merely preparing to defend the Rhine. Another was that the Sixth SS Panzer Army's advance would expose a long northern flank to counter-attacks from strong Allied forces known to be near Aachen. The Fifth Panzer Army, on the other hand, stood a reasonable chance of reaching the Meuse without disaster, since its flanks would be comparatively well protected. Hitler none the less insisted on giving priority to the right wing, not merely because he regarded the self-made Dietrich as a more reliable henchman than the aristocratic Manteuffel, but above all because only the capture of Antwerp promised him a decisive success. He believed that the Sixth SS Panzer Army, with three infantry divisions and a parachute battalion ready to take up blocking positions on its right, and with two Panzer divisions in reserve to counter any threat from that direction, should be able to push forward so swiftly that it would be over the Meuse and in good tank country almost before the Allies knew what was happening. A supporting thrust from the Roer would then cut off the Allied forces near Aachen and relieve Dietrich of all anxiety for his communications.

Thus the Germans expected to achieve surprise; and they were not disappointed. The Western Allies knew that by early December the enemy had built up a substantial armoured reserve, but they assumed that its constituent formations must be under-equipped and fit only for a spoiling attack or a defensive role. They received many scraps of information which pointed to an offensive in the Ardennes, but discounted them in the light of counter-indications which chimed better with their preconceptions. Above all, they were deceived by Hitler's insistence on keeping the Sixth SS Panzer Army well to the north until the last moment. They believed, too, that the veteran Rundstedt, who had handled his forces with notable restraint since his reinstatement in September, was unlikely to stake his reserves on a hazardous adventure. They did not know that his objections had been overruled and that his copy of the operations plan had been handed to him marked in the Führer's handwriting: 'Not to be altered'.

Thus the situation on the eve of the German offensive was that the Allies had no immediate intention of attacking in the Ardennes, and believed the enemy to be too weak to attack anywhere. Consequently there was a tendency throughout the Twelfth Army Group to regard the wooded hills between the Amblève and the Moselle as a quiet sector to which inexperienced or tired formations could safely be sent for a gentle indoctrination or a rest.*

Bradley's dispositions reflected that tendency. In early December he had some thirty-one divisions. Ten of these were facing the Saar, where the Third Army was preparing for a fresh attack which Eisenhower had authorized after a meeting with Montgomery and Bradley on December 7. With the exception of one corps which was to capture the Roer dams in order to prevent the enemy from holding up a subsequent advance by opening the floodgates, the rest were not needed for any attack which could be launched before the second week in January. In accordance with Bradley's policy of concentrating his forces for a future offensive, the majority were, however, disposed on a relatively narrow front near Aachen and along the Roer, where they were waiting to go forward as soon as the dams were safely in their hands. Consequently, General Hodges of the United States First Army, with some fourteen divisions under command, had only one corps of four divisions in the sector which was about to bear the brunt of an offensive delivered by some twenty-eight divisions organized in three armies.

*Robert E. Merriam, *The Battle of the Ardennes* (London, 1958), Chapter 3.

In the darkness before dawn on December 16, the Germans opened their assault with the leading troops of seventeen first-wave divisions. In the north the extreme right of the Sixth SS Panzer Army was held near Monschau and Elsenborn by two divisions of the United States 5th Corps advancing towards the Roer dams; but further south the United States 8th Corps, with its one armoured and three infantry divisions spread over a wide front, was too thin on the ground to do more than fight a delaying action while reserve formations were brought forward to prepared positions covering the crossings of the Meuse. Yet no steps had been taken to prepare such positions or accumulate reserves for such a purpose. Commanders and staff officers at the higher levels, deceived by the meagreness of the reports which reached them from a fast-disappearing front, believed at first that they were faced with nothing worse than a spoiling attack designed to hold up the Third Army's offensive in the Saar. Later they concluded that they could hold the flanks of the stricken sector and contain the enemy on the west with formations already committed or thrown in piecemeal to plug gaps. The situation would then be restored by a counter-attack from the south by the Third Army.

For a time a well-founded belief in the enterprise and fortitude of hard-pressed local commanders and their troops made this plan seem feasible. Towards nightfall on December 19, however, Eisenhower came to the conclusion that it would not work.[4] By the late afternoon the spearheads of the Sixth SS Panzer Army were barely fifteen miles from Liége, while the Fifth Panzer Army had entered Houffalize. Substantial bodies of American troops on the enemy's flanks and in his rear were rightly believed to be fighting well after a difficult start, but some had been out of touch with the corps and army network since the first or second day, and in general they could be assumed to be too widely dispersed to stand much chance of closing the gaps through which the enemy could bring up supplies and reinforcements. On the west there was little in front of the enemy which could be relied upon to stop him in the absence of a coherent plan to deny him the crossings of the Meuse; in the south the Third Army's counter-attack was not due to start until December 22. Apart from the threat to Liége, which Eisenhower expected Dietrich to attack within the next day or two although in fact he had orders to by-pass it, there was every likelihood that the German armour would be across the Meuse and in open country long before Patton could intervene. At the same time it was obvious that Bradley, who had not visited Hodges since the start of the offensive and whose communications with the First Army were precarious, was in no position to control the battle from his headquarters at Luxembourg.

Eisenhower knew that the loss of Antwerp and Brussels would be fatal to his plans for an offensive north of the Ardennes. He also knew that, even if he did not lose Antwerp and Brussels and was not immediately turned out of Liége, the severance of his supply-lines running southwards from Antwerp and passing east of Brussels would make his positions near Aachen and on the Roer untenable. Concluding that one man must be made responsible for seeing that the enemy did not cross the Meuse, he authorized his Chief of Staff to take preliminary steps that evening. Next morning he ordered Montgomery to assume control of all Allied land forces north of a line from Givet to Prüm, including the United States First and Ninth Armies, and Bradley to take charge of all land forces south of that line, including the Sixth Army Group.

While Bradley arranged to further Patton's counter-attack by bringing in elements of the Seventh Army and the French First Army, if necessary at the cost of shortening his line in the Vosges, Montgomery prepared to fight a defensive battle in the north. Montgomery had four Allied armies at his disposal. Even so, apart from the British 30th Corps he could count on few reserves apart from those which he might be able to create by persuading the Americans to re-group at the height of a desperate struggle for survival.

The Germans were known to be giving priority to Dietrich's army, and recent intelligence told Montgomery that Dietrich hoped to cross the Meuse between Liége and Namur, where the bridges at Huy and Andenne were obvious objectives. Accordingly, the essence of his plan was that the First Army should continue to hold the enemy on the northern flank between Monschau and Malmédy but should also defend the vital crossings by extending its line westwards beyond Marche, and that British troops should cover its right by guarding the crossings between Namur and Givet. To give General Hodges a chance of creating the reserve which Montgomery wished him to station on the right as a counter-attack formation, Montgomery arranged that the Ninth Army, strengthened by a British division, should take over the First Army's sector on the Roer. This would release the United States 7th Corps. As an additional safeguard against a turning movement round the First Army's flank, and to provide more troops for a counter-attack, the British 30th Corps would take up positions west of the Meuse. A British division would be stationed south of Liége, but in principle British troops would cross the Meuse in substantial numbers only as and when they could do so without hampering the First Army by clogging its lines of communication.

General Hodges still believed that the enemy would attack Liége.[5] Even so, he was in favour of extending his flank, and had already ordered the 18th Airborne Corps, which Eisenhower had given him as a reinforcement, to take up positions on the right of the 5th Corps. The 5th Corps in turn had broken off its attack on the Roer dams and was holding the front from Monschau to a point beyond the left bank of the Amblève. Hodges was also willing to bring in the 7th Corps on the right of the 18th Corps. But meanwhile the tides of battle had engulfed the 8th Corps, whose headquarters had moved south of the Prüm-Givet Line and whose troops were widely scattered. Hence it was apparent to Hodges that, if he were to extend his right while putting the 7th Corps into reserve, he must clean up his centre in order to save men. Unwilling to give up positions which his troops had made great sacrifices to hold, he wished to do so by attacking across the River Salm towards Saint-Vith, where elements of four American divisions were clinging to an exposed salient between the corridors driven through his original front by the Sixth SS Panzer Army and the Fifth Panzer Army.

His attack, launched with Montgomery's assent on December 21, coincided with an attempt by both Panzer armies to force a decision while the Allies were still off balance. The outcome was a series of hard-fought battles in which Montgomery more than once intervened to overcome the reluctance of the Americans to make tactical withdrawals. In the north the Germans, stoutly opposed by the 5th Corps and unable, according to Dietrich, to use their armour effectively because of the nature of the country, made no progress. In the centre they wiped out the Saint-Vith salient, drove north-westwards towards the vital stretch of the Meuse, but were brought to a halt a good twenty miles short of the crucial bridges after a desperate struggle which forced Hodges to throw in almost everything he had.

In the south the situation when Montgomery took control north of the Prüm-Givet Line was that the commander of the United States 8th Corps, by that time out of touch with Hodges, had decided after consulting Bradley to commit about 18,000 American troops to the defence of Bastogne and the important road-junction there. On December 20 Manteuffel's left-hand corps approached Bastogne, with orders to press on to the Meuse between Givet and Namur but with permission to make a limited attack on Bastogne if circumstances were favourable. Finding the place strongly held, the German corps commander sent one of his two armoured divisions towards Dinant on December 21, but waited for the garrison to reject an ultimatum on December 22 before sending the other towards Givet. Only lightly opposed, the 2nd Panzer Division pushed its forward troops to a point about four miles from Dinant by the evening of December 23, but could go no further without fresh supplies. By that time the British held the bridges from Givet to Namur in strength and had armoured patrols on the east bank. Snow had fallen after a long spell of dismal weather, and clear skies brought Allied aircraft out in force for the first time since December 12.

On the same day the United States 7th Corps took over a sector on the extreme right of the First Army's line. Montgomery was reluctant to see his only substantial American reserve committed in a defensive role unless the vital stretch of the Meuse were directly threatened, and felt sure that the enemy would not succeed in crossing the river between Givet and Namur. He therefore suggested to Hodges that, instead of using the 7th Corps to fill the gap between the right of the 18th Airborne Corps and the British, he should pivot on Marche and rest his right on the Meuse at a point downstream from Namur, perhaps even as far east as Andenne. Hodges complied to the extent of telling the corps commander to 'roll with the punch', but did not expressly order him to refuse his flank. The outcome was that on December 25 and 26 the United States 2nd Armoured Division, with British troops co-operating, engaged Manteuffel's left and drove it back to Rochefort with substantial losses.

This tactical success had the disadvantage of leaving only the British 30th Corps uncommitted and immediately available for the counter-attack which Eisenhower then pressed Montgomery to make. Montgomery and Hodges agreed that, to avoid entangling British and American lines of communication by passing the 30th Corps across the First Army's rear, they should use the British corps to free the 7th Corps for its intended role as a counter-attack formation. Accordingly, at the end of December the 30th Corps crossed the Meuse and took over the First Army's right-hand sector. Montgomery believed that the best time to strike would be when the enemy had exhausted himself by making one more attempt to force a crossing between Namur and Liége, but promised Eisenhower that he would pass to the offensive early in the New Year if no such attempt were made in the meantime.

Meanwhile Manteuffel's movements in the south had left one infantry division and one Panzer regiment investing Bastogne. Patton duly launched his counter-attack on December 22, but soon found that he had underestimated the difficulty of cutting through the German Seventh Army. He had hoped to reach Saint-Vith with three divisions in four days, relieve Bastogne on the way, and send another three divisions towards Bonn. As it was, his leading troops raised the siege of Basɔgne on December 26, after the garrison had been supplied rom the air and had beaten off heavy attacks. Thereafter all ix of his divisions, and more, were needed on the Bastogne ront.

At that stage Hitler had to choose between three courses. The first was to make a fresh attempt to cross the Meuse and arry out his original plan of cutting off the whole of the Allied forces in the north. The second was to stay on the right ank and aim at a more limited objective, such as the encirclement of the Ninth Army. The third was to dig in where he tood, withdraw his armour, and content himself with having lready compelled the Allies to postpone their offensive in the aar and the capture of the Roer dams. After hearing the views f his principal commanders, none of whom was wholeheartdly in favour of the first course, he decided that eventually a ew attempt to force a crossing must be made, but that meanwhile his troops should consolidate their gains and attack the alient created by Patton's arrival at Bastogne. At the same time diversionary attack in Alsace, foreshadowed in the original lan, would go forward in order to 'bring about the collapse f the threat to the left of the main offensive'.

Accordingly, on January 1 the leading troops of eight German divisions attacked southwards from the Saar and westwards from the Colmar pocket. In the course of the next few ays they made some progress, but their strategic aim was not ttained. Eisenhower was willing to make sacrifices in the Vosges rather than weaken his forces in the Ardennes, and vould even have reconciled himself to the loss of Strasbourg f the French had not insisted that the political consequences vould be disastrous. Tactical withdrawals, skilfully carried out, eft the attackers with little to show for their efforts but a strip f territory north of the Maginot Line and a small bridgehead cross the Rhine between Strasbourg and Karlsruhe. On the pening day about eight hundred fighters attacked Allied airelds and destroyed more than a hundred and thirty aircraft, ut well over two hundred German aircraft failed to return.

In the Ardennes the Fifth Panzer Army, with its left wing

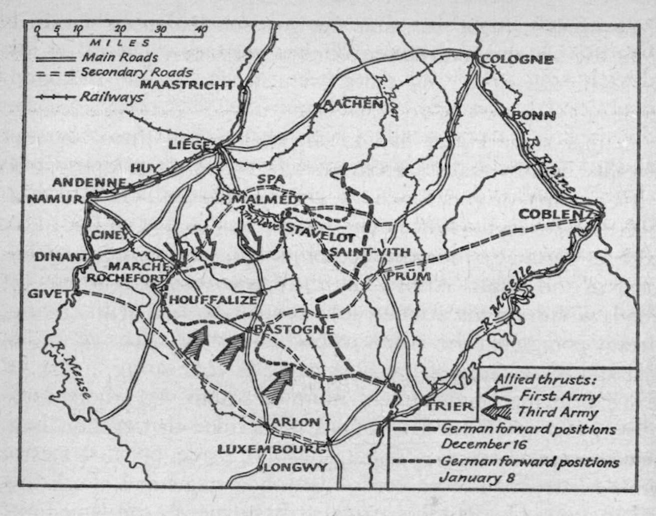

56 The Ardennes: the Allied Counter-Attack

reinforced, began the New Year with heavy attacks on the Bastogne salient. To ease the pressure Patton, adding the reconstituted 8th Corps to his command, kept up his offensive west of the town. Fighting in bitter weather, his troops made slow progress; but Bastogne did not fall.

On January 3 the First Army opened the offensive promised by Montgomery, attacking towards Houffalize with the 7th Corps leading, the 18th Airborne Corps on the left and the British on the right. Deep snow-drifts, icebound roads and mines laid in the snow ruled out a rapid advance, and again low clouds prevented the Allies from asserting their air superiority. But the Germans, too, found the going difficult. Their railheads had been heavily bombed during the brief spell of open weather in December, and they depended on a sparse network of roads not only for supplies but also for their power of manœuvre. Thus the contest took the form of a tortoise race, in which an advance of five miles in five days by the attackers was enough to put the defenders in jeopardy. At the end of the first week in January Model, who received his orders directly from the Führer since Rundstedt held aloof and would doubtless have been by-passed in any case, had seven armoured divisions in a narrow salient west of the Bastogne-Liége road, and no means of extricating them except through a bottleneck already under artillery fire and likely to become a death-trap if the skies cleared. Between Rochefort and the Amblève the First Army was grinding away at the northern face of the salient; west of Bastogne the Third Army was pushing at the southern face against resistance growing daily weaker.

Recognizing his danger, on January 8 Hitler authorized Model to pull back to the neck of the salient. Still moving too slowly to cut him off, the United States First Army continued during the next week to edge forward on a broad front, and from January 9 the United States Third Army made some progress east and north-east of Bastogne. On January 16 the two armies met at Houffalize, and the Battle of the Ardennes was over. Since December 16 each side had lost about 80,000 of all ranks killed, wounded or missing.[6] The Allies had suffered a setback to their plans and had lost more armoured fighting vehicles than the Germans,[7] but Hitler had shot his bolt so far as the Western Front was concerned.

Moreover, for the sake of a prize which slipped from his grasp when Dietrich failed to cross the Meuse or capture the First Army's fuel dumps near Spa and Stavelot on the first or second day, he had opened the back door to calamity by starving the Eastern Front of men and weapons. Of forty divisions newly formed or completely refurbished between the beginning of September and the middle of December, the best as well as the most had gone to build up the Sixth SS and Fifth Panzer Armies. In November and December Rundstedt had received more than twice as many tanks and assault guns as reached the Eastern Front.[8] Finally, in January the Western Allies were containing nearly as many German divisions as faced the whole of the Red Army on a front from the Baltic to the Danube and beyond.[9]* Notwithstanding the excellent fighting qualities of her troops, and in spite of the stoicism with which her people faced the relentless bombing of her cities, for Germany the coming year held nothing but the certain prospect of defeat.

As soon as the crisis in the Ardennes was over, the British Chiefs of Staff returned to the question of future strategy on the Western Front. On January 6 they instructed their representatives in Washington to ask the Americans to join them in calling for an account of Eisenhower's plans; to add that in their opinion the conduct of the campaign had suffered since September from a lack of proper co-ordination at the top; and to propose that a single commander should be made responsible for the main thrust north of the Ardennes.[10]

The United States Chiefs of Staff accepted the first suggestion. Accordingly, on January 10 the Combined Chiefs asked the Supreme Commander to state his intentions.[11]

In the meantime Eisenhower had reported that he found it difficult to make plans for current or future operations without knowing what the Russians were going to do.[12] His deputy, Air Chief Marshal Tedder, left for Moscow at the end of December to seek enlightenment from the Soviet Supreme Command, but announced soon afterwards that he was weatherbound at Cairo. Thereupon Churchill sent Stalin a telegram to the effect that the fighting in the West was very heavy, and that he would be glad to know whether the Western Allies could count on a major offensive by the Red Army in January. Stalin replied that his troops had meant to wait for good flying

*The figures in January were approximately as follows:

Western Front (Scandinavia excluded)	76
Italy and South-East Europe	34
Scandinavia	17
	127
Eastern Front	133
	260

weather before attacking, but that in view of Churchill's message they would launch a major offensive on the Central Front not later than the second half of January, irrespective of the weather.[13]

Thus, contrary to popular belief, the Western Allies were not at all surprised by the offensive launched by the Red Army on January 12, and neither the British nor the Americans regarded it at the time as an attempt by the Russians to win a race for Berlin by starting while they were still tied up in the Ardennes. But Stalin's subsequent claim that the Red Army 'thwarted the German winter offensive in the West' was equally unfounded. The Russian offensive did not start until four days after Hitler had tacitly admitted defeat in the Ardennes by authorizing Model to withdraw from the Houffalize salient, and it was not until January 22, when the Western Allies had pushed the Germans almost back to their start-lines, that Hitler agreed to move the Sixth SS Panzer Army to the Eastern Front. Thus the true relation between events in East and West was not that the Russian offensive prevented Hitler from crossing the Meuse, but that his attempt to do so helped to create the right conditions for the Russians to attack.

Soon after the Red Army had opened its offensive, the Combined Chiefs of Staff received Eisenhower's answer to their enquiry. This was not the concise statement of intentions which might have been expected, but a lengthy rehearsal of the case for an advance from the Middle Rhine to Frankfurt and Kassel as compared with an advance north of the Ardennes to the Ruhr and the North German Plain.[14] In the light of this examination Eisenhower concluded that his operations west of the Rhine must be so designed as to enable him to close the Rhine throughout its length. He added that his plan was to begin by trying to destroy the enemy's forces north of Düsseldorf and closing the Rhine in that sector while remaining on the defensive south of the Moselle. His next aim would be to destroy any of the enemy's forces still west of the Rhine both in the north and in the south. Finally he would concentrate east of the Rhine and north of the Ruhr the thirty-five divisions considered at that time to be the largest force which could be maintained there. With a view to drawing enemy forces away from the north by capturing objectives in the south, Eisenhower proposed to deploy east of the Rhine on the axis Frankfurt-Kassel 'such forces, if adequate, as may be available after providing 35 divisions for the north and essential security elsewhere'.

The impression made by this document on the British was that Eisenhower was willing to pay lip-service to the principle of a major thrust in the north but hankered after the southern route, and that he had not made up his mind whether he ought to close the Rhine throughout its length before crossing it in force.[15] In the last week of January, however, the British Chiefs of Staff flew to Malta to meet the United States Chiefs of Staff on the eve of a full-dress conference with the Russians at Yalta. There they exchanged views with Eisenhower's Chief of Staff, Lieutenant-General Walter Bedell Smith. Prolonged anc vehement discussion showed that the Americans were unalterably opposed to any radical change in the system of command but that Eisenhower's intentions, as expounded by Bedell Smith, were more in line with the agreed strategy thar appeared from his written account.[16] At the beginning of February the Combined Chiefs of Staff adopted Eisenhower' plan with verbal amendments drafted by Bedell Smith and th British.[17] The new version was thereupon accepted by all concerned, and Eisenhower announced that he would go ahead ir the north without waiting to close the Rhine throughout it length. In the meantime the United States First Army ha reverted to Bradley's control. However, Eisenhower agreed t leave the Ninth Army with Montgomery for the purpose o the offensive in the north, and the British to move up to fiv divisions from Italy to the Western Front.

Meanwhile the situation on the Eastern Front was such tha even if attempts to reconcile conflicting strategies should lea the Western Allies astray, the conquest of Germany could nc be long delayed. Failure to end the European war in 1944 wa none the less a serious setback for the British, who were threa ened with insupportable demands on their manpower and productive capacity at a time when they had scraped the bottom of the barrel by mobilizing well over half their employable population in direct support of their war effort.*

In January the Soviet armies between the Baltic and Belgrade were organized in eight groups, or 'fronts'.[18] In Latvia and Lithuania the First Baltic Front, under General I. K. Bagramyan, was containing two distinct German forces on the Baltic coast; on Bagramyan's left the Third Belorussian Front, under Marshal I. Chernyakovsky, was on the borders of East Prussia. Marshal Rokossovsky, who had failed by a narrow margin to take Warsaw in the previous summer, commanded the Second Belorussian Front and had his left on the Vistula just north of the city; Marshal G. K. Zhukov, commanding the First Belorussian Front, had crossed the river at a number of points and held a line along both banks to the neighbourhood of Sandomierz. On Zhukov's left the armies of the First Ukrainian Front, under Marshal I. S. Koniev, were astride the river some thirty miles east of Cracow; to the south of Koniev's armies General Petrov, commanding the Fourth Ukrainian Front, stood guard over the passes through which the German Fourteenth Army had swung northwards to outflank the Poles

*In round figures, the United Kingdom had a total population of 50,000,000 and an employable population which can be broadly estimated at 22,000,000. About 5,000,000 men and women were serving with the armed forces; about 7,000,000 were directly engaged in war production. The United States (population 150,000,000) had roughly 12,000,000 men under arms; Germany (population 80,000,000) about 7,000,000 in the army and SS and some 2,500,000 in the other fighting services. In both countries the proportion of the theoretically available civilian labour force directly engaged in war production was substantially lower than in Britain. The Soviet Union, with a peacetime population of some 200,000,000, is believed to have had an army of about 12,000,000 (with a higher ratio of combatant to noncombatant troops than in Western armies); but so many Soviet citizens had been killed, deported, or driven into hiding by the end of 1944 that probably any attempt to compare her war-effort with that of other countries on a statistical basis would be misleading. More than half the workers in Soviet factories at the end of the war are said to have been women.

57 The Soviet Offensive, January 1945

in 1939. South of the Carpathians were the armies of the Second and Third Ukrainian Fronts under Marshals R. Y. Malinovsky and F. Tolbukhin.

As Stalin had told Churchill, the Soviet Supreme Command intended to make their main effort in the centre. A great part of their strength was concentrated, therefore, under Zhukov and Koniev. According to the Soviet official history, the armies of the First Belorussian and First Ukrainian Fronts mustered more than 160 divisions, with nearly 6,500 tanks and self-propelled guns, and were supported by the best part of 5,000 aircraft.

The disposition of the German armies on the Eastern Front was on very different lines. Hitler was encouraged by the adoption of air-masts, or 'snorts', which allowed U-boats to recharge their batteries without surfacing, to believe that a new age would dawn when the German Navy took delivery of improved boats which combined this advantage with a high underwater speed made possible by exceptionally capacious batteries. He concluded that he must, at all costs, retain his U-boat bases and training areas in the Eastern Baltic.[19] Accordingly he refused a chance of withdrawing by sea at least some of the thirty divisions which Bagramyan had succeeded in pinning down in Courland and at Memel. As he was already fighting Malinovsky and Tolbukhin for the oil and bauxite of Hungary and needed twenty-eight divisions for that purpose, only seventy-five divisions remained to guard the long front from the Nemen to the San. To shorten his lines by giving up East Prussia and withdrawing behind the Vistula might have seemed an obvious step for Hitler to take; but he declined to budge, asserting that past retreats had proved disastrous. The enemy, he declared on January 9, did not possess the threefold superiority needed for a breakthrough.[20]

This may have been true in the sense that the Russians could not deploy three times as many troops as the Germans on the whole front from the Baltic to the Carpathians or beyond. It was not true of the front on which they chose to open their attack. On January 12 Koniev, and two days later Zhukov, launched a mighty offensive with a local superiority estimated by Soviet historians at 5.5 to 1 in men, 7.8 to 1 in guns, 5.7 to 1 in tanks, and 17.6 to 1 in aircraft. Followed by all the army groups north of the Carpathians except Bagramyan's, they advanced up to 250 miles in three weeks. By midnight on February 2, when the British and American delegates to the Yalta Conference left Malta to join the Russians in the Crimea, Chernyakovsky was investing Königsberg after taking Tilsit, Rokossovsky was threatening Danzig, Koniev had taken Breslau and Zhukov was forty miles from Berlin. The German armies from Schneidemühl on the old Polish frontier to Katowice in Galicia were in full retreat on German soil. The roads leading westwards from Kuestrin and Frankfurt-on-Oder were thronged with refugees,[21] and Hitler could find little comfort save the hope that Britain and the United States might make peace with Germany rather than let the Russians into Western Europe.

But the Americans and the British did not grudge the Russians their victories. The British, if asked, would not have agreed with the ailing President Roosevelt that Stalin was 'not an Imperialist'. But fate had given them allies, and they were willing to make the best of them. In any case the Western Allies, with eighty-one divisions west of the Rhine, were in no position to stem the Russian advance, even if they had wished to do so and had been willing to throw in their lot with a Germany whose power to maintain her armies in the field was collapsing before their eyes. As it was, they had no wish to quarrel with the Soviet Union.[22] On the contrary, they were eager to ensure the ratification of a plan, drawn up at a series of meetings in London between representatives of all three countries, for the partition of Germany between American, British and Soviet armies of occupation; to reach agreement about the occupation of Austria, for which the London plan did not provide; and generally to work towards a settlement which would allow the Americans to withdraw their army of occupation not more than two years after the end of the war in Europe. Remembering that the League of Nations had been crippled from birth because the United States refused to join it although her statesmen had helped to bring it into being, the Americans and the British wished to shepherd the Russians into the proposed partnership of the United Nations on terms which everyone would recognize as fair.

Nor did the Russians themselves seem inclined to break up the alliance. By the second day of the conference their troops on the Oder were beginning to outrun their supplies, and they had yet to drive the Germans out of the whole of Hungary. On February 5 their military spokesman, General Antonov, spoke of the problems of a continuous offensive in terms which recalled a proposal, made by Stalin in October, that the Anglo-American armies in Italy should, after all, lend a hand in South-East Europe by threatening Vienna.[28] The Russians raised no objection to the plan for the occupation of Germany. They accepted a British proposal that France should be represented on the Allied Control Commission and should be allotted an occupation zone carved from the American and British zones. They affirmed their intention of entering the war against Japan on terms which did not seem to President Roosevelt unacceptable.* Moreover, their attitude to the question of procedure in the Assembly of the United Nations was much more reasonable than on earlier occasions, when they had insisted that all sixteen republics of the Soviet Union should be allowed to vote.

In other respects the Russians were not so amenable. Some months earlier Mr. Henry J. Morgenthau Jnr., of the United States Treasury, had proposed that after the war Germany should be transformed into a predominantly agricultural and pastoral country. Roosevelt and Churchill had begun by endorsing the Morgenthau Plan, but had ended by shelving it as impractical, inhumane and unlikely to command popular support in their respective countries. At Yalta Stalin insisted on resurrecting this embarrassing phantom by proposing that Germany should be dismembered, stripped of four-fifths of her heavy industry, and made to pay punitive damages in the guise of reparations. On the military side, the Russians refused to disclose details of their future operations or to consider proposals for liaison between Anglo-American and Soviet commanders in the field; on the political side they remained hostile to the exiled Polish government, continued to uphold the Communist-controlled Committee of National Liberation, or Lublin Committee, and promised only that the basis of the Lublin Committee should be broadened. They did, however, accept the principle that liberated countries should be free to set up democratic institutions of their own choosing.

When the conference ended the Western delegates felt that on the whole they had succeeded in establishing a fairly good relationship with their enigmatic partner. The Russians had asked to be informed of Anglo-American strategic plans but

*See Chapter 21.

had been reticent about their own. They seemed unlikely to relax their grip on at any rate the part of Poland which they had occupied in 1939, and spoke of compensating the Poles at Germany's expense. Moreover, they showed an unforgiving spirit towards Germany, perhaps not unnaturally since millions of Soviet citizens were rightly thought to have died in German extermination centres, labour camps and prisoner-of-war cages. But they had also shown that they were not unwilling to discuss controversial questions where there was any prospect of agreement. They had made some concessions, they had not prevented the British from bringing about a truce between Communist and non-Communist elements in Greece after the departure of the Germans in October, and their attitude in Yugoslavia did not seem to rule out the possibility of an eventual settlement between Tito, the Royalist government, and themselves. Taking a broad view, British as well as American statesmen concluded that Stalin wished to co-operate with the West and that there was a good chance that Soviet promises not to alter the social structure in Rumania and to hold free elections in liberated countries would be honoured.

These illusions were soon shattered.[24] The Yalta Conference ended on February 11. On February 27 the Soviet authorities presented King Michael of Rumania with an ultimatum calling upon him to dismiss the all-Party government which he had set up with their approval in the previous August. A few days later they forced him, by similar means, to install a Communist administration. Soon afterwards the Americans were refused access to aerodromes near Budapest which Stalin had promised Roosevelt that they could use for shuttle bombing. In the course of the next few weeks the Russians declined to broaden the basis of the Lublin Committee in accordance with the procedure to which they had agreed at Yalta. They also refused to allow British and American officials to visit prisoner-of-war camps in Eastern Europe, as they had pledged themselves to do in return for facilities granted to Soviet officials in the West. They obstructed attempts to arrive at an agreed procedure for the occupation of Austria. They announced that their Foreign Minister would not head the Soviet delegation to the inaugural meeting of the United Nations at San Francisco in April. Finally, the Russians accused the Western Allies of trying to make a separate peace with Germany because the Combined Chiefs of Staff had agreed that, before Alexander invited a Soviet emissary to witness the surrender of a million German and Italian troops in Italy, members of his staff should satisfy themselves that German officers who had undertaken to negotiate the surrender were authorized to do so.

These incidents did not lead the Western Allies to conclude that Russia was a potential enemy or that they would be unable to come to terms with the Soviet authorities in the long run. They did, however, help to convince the British government that Eisenhower would do well to press deep into Germany, and especially towards Berlin, so that the West would be in a position to negotiate from strength when the time came to discuss questions which had not been broached at Yalta or had been left unsettled.[25]

At the beginning of the second week in February, when the Yalta Conference was still sitting, Eisenhower was ready to begin his promised offensive in the north. His immediate intentions were that first the British Second, the Canadian First and the United States Ninth Army, controlled by Montgomery, should seize the west bank of the Rhine from Emmerich to Düsseldorf.[26] Next the United States First and Third Armies, controlled by Bradley, would secure the west bank from Düsseldorf to Coblenz. The Third and Seventh Armies would then clear the Saar and the Palatinate while Montgomery crossed the Rhine at Wesel. This plan was in accordance with the agreed strategy, and its only disadvantages were that Bradley was dissatisfied with what he regarded as a secondary role, and that an opposed crossing of the Rhine at Wesel was likely to be the most critical operation undertaken by the Allied armies since the D-day landings. On the other hand, success would put the Ruhr at Eisenhower's mercy and might soon end Germany's capacity to make war.

When Montgomery launched his attack on February 8, the Germans had flooded a broad tract of low-lying country south and west of the Rhine, so that from Nijmegen to Cleve and beyond the corridor between the Rhine and the Maas was impassable for roughly half its width. Montgomery's plan was to drive the British 30th Corps, under command of the Canadian First Army, south-eastwards through the remaining bottleneck, pass the Ninth Army across the Roer north-east and east of Aachen, and thus give Model's forces in the immediate neighbourhood the choice between withdrawing across the Rhine and fighting an unequal battle on the west bank.

However, events took a different course. Destruction caused by over-zealous bombing prevented the leading division of the 30th Corps from getting clear of Cleve on February 9, and a premature follow-up made the congestion still worse. On the same day the Germans forced the Ninth Army to postpone the crossing of the Roer for a fortnight by destroying the discharge-valves of the one dam still in their hands. Moreover Hitler, having lost most of Upper Silesia to the Russians, ordered Rundstedt to hold the left bank of the Rhine at all costs in order to safeguard his remaining heavy industries and the great inland waterway which served them. The result was that the British Second and Canadian First Armies found themselves locked in a bitter struggle with reserves which the enemy had been expected to throw in only after they had joined forces with the Ninth Army. In just over four weeks the British and the Canadians suffered more than 15,000 casualties; but they took 65,000 prisoners and cleared the triangle between the Maas and the Rhine from Emmerich in the north to Venlo and Wesel in the south.

When the Americans were at last free to advance, opposition south of Venlo and Wesel was correspondingly lighter. On February 23 the Ninth Army, accompanied by the United States First Army on its right, moved forward across the Roer. On February 26 its right reached the Rhine near Düsseldorf, and on March 3 its left made contact with the British north of Venlo, where the Germans fought hard for another week before the last of them fell back across the Rhine. Believing that nothing would be gained by pressing on until he had everything needed to take him to the Ruhr and beyond, Mont-

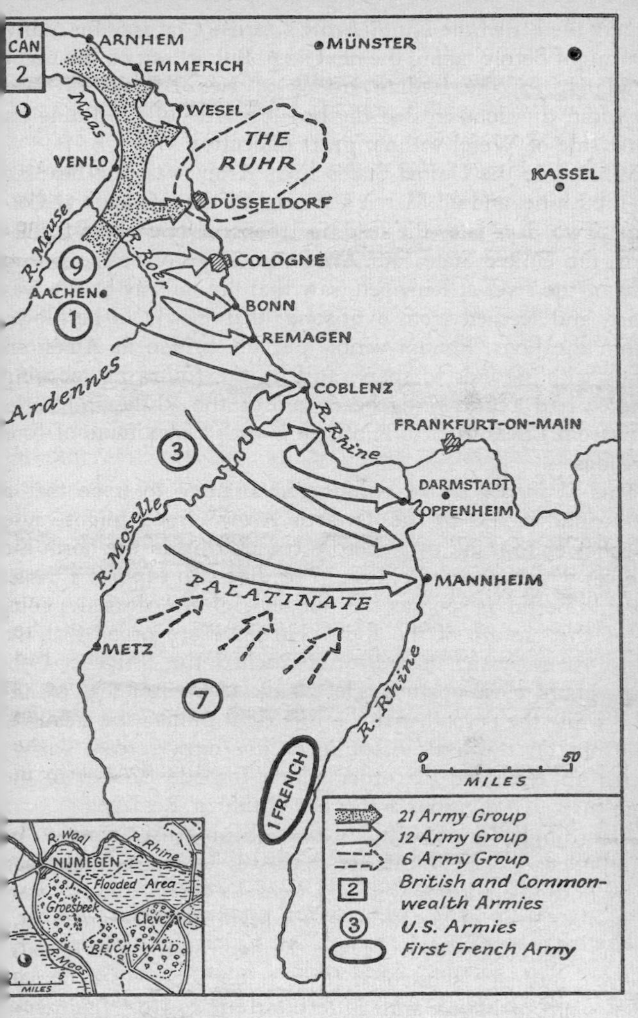

58 The Approach to the Rhine, February-March 1945

gomery then tried the Ninth Army's patience by waiting nearly a fortnight before taking the next step. But at last, on the night of March 23, the leading troops of two British and two American divisions crossed the broad barrier of the Rhine on either side of Wesel without great difficulty.

Meanwhile the United States First Army was also heading for the Rhine, and on March 5 it reached the left bank at Cologne. Two days later the leading troops of one of its formations, the United States 9th Armoured Division, came within sight of the river at Remagen, saw that the railway bridge was intact, and learned from a prisoner that it was to be blown within the hour. Prompt action put the bridge in American hands with seconds to spare, and by the following morning Bradley had a firm bridgehead east of the Rhine and authority from Eisenhower to reinforce it with a maximum of four divisions.

This fortunate stroke encouraged Bradley to hope that a spectacular success by the Twelfth Army Group might cause Eisenhower to think twice before committing in the north the reserves which he was holding in readiness to support a thrust towards Berlin as soon as the northern group of armies completed the capture of the Ruhr. He therefore urged that the Third Army, which had already reached the Rhine at Coblenz, should close up to the left bank as far south as Mannheim while the Seventh Army on its right pinned the enemy to his front on the Saar. Eisenhower not only agreed, but on March 17 rescinded the order which forbade Bradley to put more than five divisions across the Rhine at Remagen.[27]

Accordingly, on March 14 the Third Army crossed the Moselle, heading south-east across the rear of the German First Army in the Palatinate. Within a week its forward troops were on the left bank of the Rhine from Mainz to Mannheim, and on the night of March 22 the United States 5th Infantry Division pushed a substantial force across the river at Oppenheim, south of Mainz, with little interference from the enemy. Like Hodges of the First Army, Patton then proceeded to lessen the risk of losing divisions to support a thrust in the north by passing his troops to the east bank as rapidly as possible.

Thus the situation on the Allied side at the end of the fourth
'eek in March was that, in the north, the British Second
rmy and the United States Ninth Army held a bridge-
ead about twenty miles wide and thirty-five miles deep on
ither side of Wesel, and were about to envelop the Ruhr from
nat direction while the Canadian First Army cleared the enemy
ut of Holland. In the centre the whole of the United States
'irst Army was east of the Rhine and was about to envelop
ne Ruhr from the south, with support from the Third Army.
Meanwhile the Third Army had greatly enlarged its bridge-
ead and had taken Darmstadt. On the German side, the
rmies of the West had yielded 290,000 prisoners since Feb-
uary 8, Kesselring had succeeded Rundstedt after the setback
t Remagen, and Model was on the point of being trapped in
he Ruhr with 325,000 soldiers and airmen of whom about
hree-quarters were under his command. Elsewhere than on the
Western Front, the broad situation was that in Italy the Allies
vere about to launch the offensive which culminated a month
ater in the unconditional surrender of the enemy's entire force,
nd that on the Eastern Front the Russians had made little
rogress in the central sector since early February.

Until late on March 28 few people outside the close circle
f Eisenhower's intimates had any reason to doubt that the
ext few days or weeks would see the end of organized re-
istance in the Ruhr and the beginning of a massive thrust from
he Ruhr towards Berlin. That evening, however, the Com-
ined Chiefs of Staff received, 'for information', a copy of a
elegram despatched that afternoon to Moscow, in which Eisen-
ower asked the Allied Military Missions to deliver to Stalin a
personal message' to the effect that he proposed to make his
nain thrust along the axis Erfurt-Leipzig-Dresden, and a
econdary advance towards Regensburg and Linz.[28] These pro-
osals were not supported by a reasoned case, although some
eference was made to reported movements of government de-
artments to the south and possible attempts to prolong resist-
nce in Southern Germany. The Allied Military Missions found
he message so baffling that they felt bound to ask for further
nformation before delivering it. Soon afterwards, but before

receiving any communication on the subject from Eisenhower or Tedder, the British Chiefs of Staff learned that Eisenhower also proposed to take the Ninth Army away from Montgomery and use it to support Bradley's advance to Dresden.[29]

By delivering this bombshell Eisenhower exposed himself to a charge of usurping the functions of the British and United States governments by communicating with the head of a foreign government without express authority from the Combined Chiefs of Staff, and also of violating an implied promise to make his main thrust in the direction of Berlin. The United States Chiefs of Staff defended him on the first count by suggesting that operational necessity had compelled him to address himself to Stalin in his capacity as Commander-in-Chief of the Soviet Armed Forces. On the second count Eisenhower defended himself by claiming that he had never promised to march to Berlin but only to give priority to the northern route to the Ruhr, and that he had not departed from the 'overall strategic plan'. But both arguments were weak. Eisenhower lost at least as much time by using a questionable channel of communication as he would have been likely to lose if he had approached the Combined Chiefs of Staff in the first instance; and the strategic plan to which he appealed had in fact been drawn up on the assumption that Berlin was the ultimate objective.*

However, as Eisenhower's good faith was not in doubt what mattered was not so much whether he was entitled to decide a question of major strategy without reference to his superiors and to communicate his decision to a foreign government, as whether he had made the right decision.

On this question, and on others which flowed from it, the Western Allies were divided not merely by differences of opinion, but by the absence of a common understanding of the nature of the problem.

The view taken by the British government (and not merely by the Prime Minister) was that no strategic argument which

*Major L. F. Ellis, *Victory in the West*, Volume 1 (London, 1962), p. 82.

Eisenhower might adduce in favour of an advance on Dresden could outweigh the political disadvantages for the Western Allies of delaying their advance on Berlin.[30] The Soviet authorities, it was agreed on both sides of the Atlantic, had shown themselves in an unfavourable light in recent weeks. Nothing in the Yalta agreements debarred any of the signatories from entering the occupation zone of another signatory before Germany surrendered; but no one could say what the political consequences might be if Russian troops not only took Berlin but pushed deep into North-West Germany and perhaps even into Denmark. Hence, the British argued, the Western Allies had everything to gain, and nothing to lose, by exploiting their success in the north while the Russians were still held up on the Oder.

Whether American statesmen would have reached the same conclusion if they had addressed themselves to the problem in the same way will never be known, for they did not address themselves to the problem in the same way. When it came to a head President Roosevelt was suffering from severe overstrain, he died on April 12, and for some time before his death he was unable, although the British did not know it, to do a full day's work.[31] In the absence of a strong lead from any other quarter, there was nothing to focus the attention of the competent authorities on the political side of the question. It was therefore regarded as essentially a military one. At the President's wish, the British case was remitted to General Marshall,[32] who was not qualified to assess the importance of the political aspect, and who took pride in confining himself to purely strategic considerations. Marshall was also handicapped by a tendency to regard any criticism of American generals as a slight.

The result was that the United States Chiefs of Staff, impressed by Marshall's defence of the Supreme Commander's strategy, rejected a British proposal that the Combined Chiefs of Staff should warn him of the danger of advancing on Dresden at the cost of delaying his progress in the north.[33] Eisenhower, as always eager to reconcile conflicting views and be fair to everyone, assured the British that he had every intention of thrusting his left at least as far as Lübeck, and that Montgomery (although he was still to lose the Ninth Army) would be reinforced 'as necessary' by American troops. But he still refused to give up his advance on Dresden,[34] and he still attached importance to reports that the enemy was preparing a 'national redoubt' in the Bavarian Alps. On April 2 he committed himself to simultaneous advances in three directions. On April 14 he was forced, however, to confess to the Combined Chiefs of Staff that he was in danger of outrunning his supplies and must, after all, withhold his centre while he cleaned up his flanks.[35] On the following day the Soviet authorities, who had told Eisenhower a fortnight earlier that they did not expect to resume their main offensive before the second half of May, informed the American Ambassador in Moscow that they now proposed to advance in the central sector without delay.[36]

Thus the situation in the middle of April was that Eisenhower's armies were dispersed over an immensely wide front whose most conspicuous features were a deep re-entrant in the neighbourhood of the Harz Mountains and two long flanks stretching the whole way back to Rotterdam in the north and the Black Forest in the south. Meanwhile the main mass of the Soviet armies was concentrated in a broad, deep salient pointing towards the heart of Germany. At a point between Wittenberge and Brunswick, where the Ninth Army had established a small bridgehead beyond the Elbe, the Americans were roughly the same distance as the Russians from Berlin; but Eisenhower's report to the Combined Chiefs of Staff made it clear that he had no immediate intention of advancing further in that direction. On the other hand, in the north the British still had a good chance of reaching Schleswig-Holstein before the Red Army was across their routes to Denmark, while in the south the Third Army was well placed to ensure, by liberating Prague, that Czechoslovakia did not go the way of Rumania and Poland.

In the meantime Eisenhower had suggested that on making contact with the Russians his troops should withdraw to their occupation zones, either voluntarily or on request.[37] Alarmed

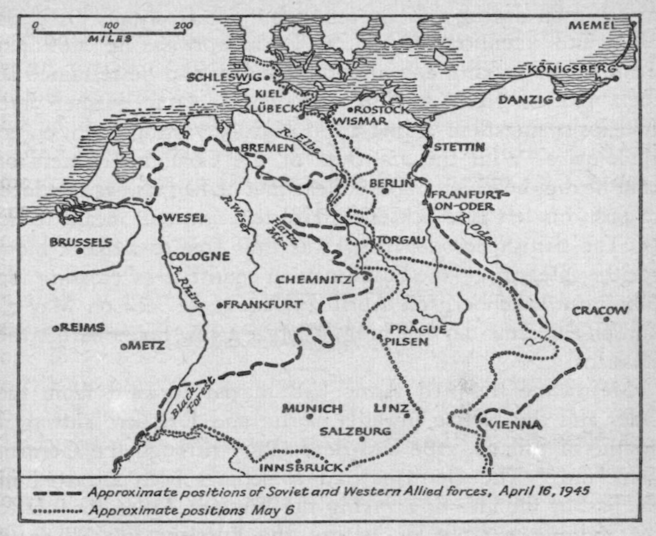

59 Approximate Lines reached by Soviet and Western Allied Forces, April-May 1945

by this proposal, the British persuaded the Combined Chiefs of Staff to assert their authority. On April 20 they instructed Eisenhower that, in principle, his forces should halt where they stood when they made contact with the Red Army, and that thereafter he should dispose them in accordance with military requirements and without reference to the boundaries of the occupation zones. Subject to that proviso, he was free to negotiate with the Soviet General Staff; but he must consult the Combined Chiefs of Staff before making any major change or raising any important issue with the Soviet authorities.[38]

But Eisenhower was still not convinced of the importance of making no concessions to the Russians. Advised by Marshall that he could safely disregard political considerations, he took full advantage of a clause in his instructions which allowed him to act on his own responsibility if he considered it essential to do so on urgent military grounds.[39] He freely disclosed his plans and intentions to the Soviet authorities, he consulted them before making any important move, and he refrained at their request from sending the Third Army further into Czechoslovakia than a line from Karslbad through Pilsen to Budejovice. With the approval of the Combined Chiefs of Staff he did, however, make it clear that he had always intended to push his left into Schleswig-Holstein and still meant to do so. The British Second Army was thus free to strike a blow for the integrity of the Scandinavian countries by crossing the Elbe near Lauenberg on April 29, taking Lübeck on May 2, and on the same day reaching Wismar a few hours before the Russians.

Meanwhile the Red Army had moved forward from the Oder and the Neisse towards Berlin and Dresden, cutting a swathe of pillage, rape and devastation through the German homeland.[40] The Germans had sometimes been attracted in the past by the idea of bringing the Western Allies hot-foot to the conference table by 'letting the Russians in'. When it came to the point, however, the handful of cornered despots who still ruled Germany made frantic efforts to stem the invasion.[41] But Army Group Vistula, responsible since January for guarding the eastern approaches to Berlin, had been weakened by the failure of a well-conceived but poorly managed counter-offensive in February. The Sixth SS Panzer Army would have been invaluable but had been sent south of the Carpathians to fight Malinovsky. Furthermore, attempts on Hitler's part to tighten his grip on the armed forces by putting the army at loggerheads with the SS did not make for confident generalship and smooth staff work. After twelve years of National Socialist rule and nearly six years of war self-tortured Germany, proverbially skilled in arms and with at least six million men still in uniform and still prepared to do their duty, was in such straits that little could be done to defend the capital against the 'half-Asiatic hordes' whom many Germans had been taught to regard as ripe for enslavement.

Celebrating his fifty-sixth birthday in Berlin on April 20

the Führer predicted that a counter-attack planned for April 22 would drive the Russians back to the Oder and beyond. But no counter-attack was launched, for the troops who were to have launched it were too weak and too disorganized to do more than try to cling to their positions. On April 25 Zhukov's and Koniev's armies completed a double enveloping movement by joining hands beyond Berlin, and on the same day Russian troops reached the Elbe between Wittenberge and Dresden to make contact with the Americans at Torgau.

Himmler and Göring, still cherishing hopes of an agreement with the West, had left Berlin with Hitler's approval on April 20. But a proposal from Göring that he should assume the leadership of the Reich as soon as it was clear that Hitler had lost the power to act was not well received, and Himmler's attempts to open negotiations with the British through the Swedish Red Cross brought a prompt refusal from Churchill to consider any offer short of unconditional surrender to the three major Powers. Convinced at last that all was lost and that Germany had proved unworthy of his leadership, Hitler stayed in Berlin to draw up a political testament nominating Dönitz as his successor, marry his devoted companion Eva Braun, and accomplish his destiny amidst the ruins of the liberal-humanist Europe which he had made it his life's work to destroy.

According to the best evidence available, the last act, which conferred a kind of immortality on Hitler by stamping him as a man who was at least faithful to his convictions, was played out on April 30, when he rang down the curtain on the astonishing drama of his existence by shooting himself after giving instructions that his body should be burnt. Dönitz received the news of his appointment in a telegram from Goebbels on May 1. On May 4 his envoy, Admiral Hans von Friedeburg, surrendered the whole of the German forces in Holland, North-West Germany, the German islands, Schleswig-Holstein and Denmark at Montgomery's headquarters near Lüneburg; on May 7 Jodl surrendered on behalf of the Supreme Command at Rheims; and on May 9 the general surrender was formally ratified in Berlin. Thus ended a war which was to have rid Europe of the curse of despotism, but which left half the Continent more or less under the Communist yoke, and the other half free to escape the same fate by coming to terms with a new imperialism whose portents were the time-and-motion study and the atomic bomb.

CHAPTER 20

THE CONQUEST OF JAPAN (I)

April 1942 - January 1945

When the Japanese went to war in 1941, their intention was to defend the territories which they hoped to conquer in South-East Asia and the South-West Pacific by holding a line of outposts running roughly southwards from the Kurile Islands to the Gilbert Islands, and thence to the mainland by way of the Bismarck Archipelago, New Guinea, the Netherlands East Indies and the Nicobar and Andaman Islands.* After their failure to destroy the whole of the United States Pacific Fleet at Pearl Harbor the Japanese saw, however, that such a strategy would not prevent the Western Allies from striking back from bases in Australia and New Zealand. Accordingly they decided in the spring of 1942 to put themselves across the lines of communication between the United States and the Antipodes by extending their perimeter southwards and westwards, and in particular to begin by establishing bases in the Solomon Islands and Papua as stepping-stones to New Caledonia, Fiji and Samoa.[1]† At the same time they made up their minds to invade Midway Island and the Western Aleutians with the object of bringing the remnant of the United States Pacific Fleet to battle and defeating it.

Admiral Nimitz, who had succeeded Admiral Kimmel in command of the Pacific Fleet, received warning of these moves from the Navy Department's intelligence sources. To meet the threat to the Solomons and Papua he assembled in the Coral Sea two striking forces built round the fleet carriers *Lexington*

* See Chapter 12.
† See Map B.

and *Yorktown*, in addition to a small cruiser force. The outcome was that the Japanese succeeded on May 3 in landing a few troops on the island of Tulagi, in the Lower Solomons, but were then swept into a naval battle in which all the damage on both sides was done by carrier-borne aircraft. The naval battle ended when the Japanese withdrew without disembarking the forces which they were to have put ashore at Port Moresby, in Papua. The Americans lost the *Lexington*, but won a substantial victory by sinking the light carrier *Shoho*, damaging the flight-deck of the fleet carrier *Shokaku*, and thus forcing the Japanese commander to turn back for fear that his fleet might be crippled by air attack.

The lesson was not lost on Admiral Nimitz. For the battle which he knew he would have to fight in the Central Pacific he relied largely on the *Yorktown*, which had been damaged in the Coral Sea but repaired, and on his two other carriers, the *Enterprise* and the *Hornet*. Admiral of the Fleet Isoroku Yamamoto, the Japanese Commander-in-Chief, would have nine battleships at his disposal in addition to four of the six fleet carriers which Admiral Nagumo had used at Pearl Harbor. Thus Yamamoto would have a big advantage in an engagement between capital ships. An encounter between four Japanese and three American carriers would be less one-sided, especially as Nimitz would be able to call on about a hundred land-based aircraft if the battle took place within range of Midway Island.

In essence, Yamamoto's plan was to draw the Americans to the north by sending four transports, with a cruiser escort, to disembark troops in the Western Aleutians while aircraft from light carriers attacked the Eastern Aleutians, and in particular the American naval base at Dutch Harbor. Meanwhile Nagumo's large carriers, preceded by an advanced warning screen of sixteen submarines and followed by the rest of the fleet, would steam towards Midway Island. After covering the disembarkation of five thousand troops who were to seize the island, the carriers and battleships, with their accompanying cruisers and destroyers, would await the return of the American fleet and choose a suitable moment to engage it. The outcome, Yamamoto hoped, would be the final extinction of American naval power in the Pacific.

But Nimitz refused to be drawn. On the contrary, he himself set a trap for his opponent. Leaving the defence of the Aleutians to his North Pacific Force of cruisers and destroyers, and counting on land-based reconnaissance aircraft to give him warning of the enemy's final approach, he ordered his carriers to take up positions well to the north-east of Midway Island, where scouting submarines and aircraft would least expect to find them.

The sequel was a spectacular success for the Americans in the Central Pacific, offset to only a minor degree by a setback in the north. The commander of the North Pacific Force, refusing to believe that the Western Aleutians were the main objective and anxious to defend the more valuable Dutch Harbor, stood too far to the east and was unable to close with the enemy in the thick weather which was common in such high latitudes. Consequently the remote islands of Attu and Kiska were lost to the Americans until they were recaptured a year later.

Meanwhile Nagumo, with his four carriers escorted by two battleships and three cruisers and with the rest of Yamamoto's fleet in his wake, was steaming confidently towards Midway Island. Believing that the American fleet was far away to the north and was unlikely to return for several days, he learned only after he had sent more than half his bombers to attack the island early on June 4 that a hostile carrier force was approaching from the north-east. Within the space of a few hours accurate attacks by dive-bombers from the *Enterprise* and *Yorktown* cost him all four of his carriers and their entire complement of aircraft. Early on June 5 Admiral Yamamoto, with his air-striking power gone, abandoned his attempt on Midway Island and turned away.

The Americans lost the *Yorktown* in this action; but they turned their victory to good account by bringing new and repaired ships into commission with a speed which left their competitors far behind. By the early summer of 1943 their naval strength in the Pacific substantially exceeded that of the Japanese in battleships and carriers, although not in cruisers.

TABLE 15

AMERICAN AND JAPANESE NAVAL STRENGTH IN THE PACIFIC, MAY 1943[1]

	American	*Japanese*
Battleships	15	9
Fleet carriers	3	3
Light carriers	5	4
Escort carriers	11	3
Heavy cruisers	10	14
Light cruisers	17	20
Destroyers	134	87
Submarines	104	69

For the time being, however, the Japanese still held the lead, with two large and three light carriers in commission. In spite of their setback at Midway Island they decided to renew their attempt to dominate the South Seas, and this time to begin by establishing a first-class air base on Guadalcanal, in the Solomons, at the same time pushing overland towards Port Moresby from their bases on the Huon Gulf.[3] Again forewarned by their code and cypher experts, the Americans disembarked about 19,000 Marines on Guadalcanal and elsewhere in the Solomons in the early part of August 1942, and in September seized Milne Bay in Papua. The outcome was a long struggle for the sea approaches to Guadalcanal, in which neither side was able to establish a clear ascendancy before the end of 1942, but which ended with the withdrawal of the Japanese garrison in February 1943.[4] By that time Australian troops disembarked at Milne Bay had ended the threat to Port Moresby by fighting their way through a fever-ridden jungle towards the Huon Gulf.[5] American and Australian bombers followed on March 3 with a devastating attack on a convoy carrying reinforcements to the Japanese base at Lae. The Japanese retaliated by using naval aircraft to attack Allied bases, thus exposing themselves to losses which reduced the effectiveness of their carrier force during the few months that remained before the Americans achieved numerical superiority

Although for a time so hard-pressed that they were obliged o borrow the British carrier *Victorious* and re-equip her with heir own aircraft, the Americans and their Commonwealth upporters were thus able in the second half of 1942 and the arly part of 1943 to put the Japanese permanently on the lefensive in the South-West Pacific. From these beginnings prang an offensive strategy whose aims were far-reaching, lthough not always clearly defined. The plan which emerged n 1943, and which the Combined Chiefs of Staff accepted in ugust of that year as part of a wider programme yet to be greed upon, envisaged two main thrusts in the Pacific.[6] On he right Admiral Nimitz, with relatively small land forces upported by an immensely powerful fleet, would advance by vay of the Gilbert and Marshall Islands and the Marianas owards the Bonin Islands. On the left substantially larger and forces, supported by two lesser fleets, would take a firm grip on the Solomons, New Guinea and the Bismarck Archi-elago as the prelude to an advance by General MacArthur to-vards the Philippines or perhaps Formosa.

From the point of view of the United States Joint Chiefs of Staff, who were its chief sponsors, this plan had the great dvantage of being flexible. It left them at liberty to decide n their own time which of the two main thrusts should be ollowed up, and meanwhile it gave them a certain freedom to huttle forces from one command to another. Nevertheless the lan had serious shortcomings. Even if some islands could be y-passed, a stage-by-stage advance across the Pacific to Japan vas bound to be a lengthy business, and because of the dis-ances involved any such advance would make extravagant lemands on the merchant shipping and assault shipping in vhich the Western Allies were deficient. Moreover, the plan ffered the Allies little hope of defeating any substantial part of the enemy's land forces at an early stage. In August 1943 he Japanese Army mustered some seventy divisions, but the ulk of these were on the mainland of Asia or in Japan. In he Central Pacific there were only garrison units; in the Philippines, the Netherlands East Indies, New Guinea and the Solomons not more than about eight to ten divisions.

TABLE 16

DISTRIBUTION OF THE JAPANESE ARMY, AUGUST 1943[7]

(major formations only)

	Divisions	*Army Air Divisions*
Japan, Sakhalin and Kurile Islands	6	1
Manchuria and Korea	19	2
China	26	1
Indo-China, Siam, Malaya and Sumatra	3	—
Burma	6	1
Philippines	2	—
Celebes, Amboina, Timor and Western New Guinea	2	—
Eastern New Guinea, Solomons and South Pacific	6	2
	70	[illegible]

How to shorten their line of approach to Japan, and how t come to grips with the main body of the Japanese Army o favourable terms, were therefore important questions for th Western Allies.[8]

One possibility was an advance from the Aleutians by wa of the Kurile Islands. Stalin's offer to fight Japan whe Germany was defeated, first made in October 1943 and repeated at the Teheran Conference a month later, was welcomed by the Allied governments partly because partnershi with Russia might make such a project feasible.[9] An eve greater attraction was that Russian participation promised to pu Japan within reach of Allied bombers. In the following yea the Soviet authorities told the Americans that the United State Army Air Corps would be allowed to station a thousan bombers in Siberia after the end of the war in Europe. Th Russians went on to build a number of new airfields nea Vladivostok, and at the same time proposed that the Americans should not only send their own bombers to Russia bu should also train and equip a Soviet strategic air force. Later they revealed by successive stages that they no longer wished the Americans to train their airmen, that they were thinking in terms of a Soviet land offensive for which they expected the Western Allies to provide over a million tons of supplies, and finally that the Americans would not be granted access to air bases closer to Japan than Komsomolsk, well over a thousand miles from Tokyo.

Another project which appealed particularly to the Americans was an offensive in China, to be delivered either by Chinese troops trained and equipped by the Western Allies, or by Chinese troops not specially trained or equipped but supported by Allied tactical air forces. But the Burma road was held by the Japanese; the Western Allies could not hope to deliver by air or pack-trail across the Himalayas the means of re-equipping any substantial part of the Chinese Army; and subsequent experience showed that the ill-armed, ill-clothed and half-starved troops who formed the bulk of the Chinese Nationalist forces were incapable of maintaining an offensive for any length of time, even when given a fair amount of air support. Chiang Kai-shek wished to go on drawing subsidies from the West and to play his part in Allied strategy. But by 1943 the Chungking government was powerless to guide output or check inflation, depended for its revenues on corrupt or inefficient local administrators even where its authority was not openly flouted, and could equip and supply its armed forces only on the most rudimentary scale.

Even so, the Western Allies were determined on political, moral and strategic grounds not to withdraw their support from Chiang Kai-shek and to keep his country in the war. After a good deal of controversy the American authorities came to the conclusion that, until land communications could be re-opened, their best course was to use China as a base for air attacks on Japan.[10] An air force built by the American Major-General C. L. Chennault round a volunteer force which had arrived in China long before Pearl Harbor was already on the spot; but its bombers could not reach Japan and were used chiefly against Japanese communications. After discussing various plans the Western Allies agreed that a substantial number of B29 very-long-range bombers should be sent to the Far East in the late spring or early summer of 1944, and that they should be supplied from Calcutta independently of the existing air-lift to Chungking, which the Allies were struggling to expand. Special facilities were installed at Calcutta, five all-weather airfields linked with the port by a pipeline were made ready some sixty-five miles to the west, and advanced bases were built under Chennault's direction near Chengtu in the province of Szechwan.* A wing of about a hundred B29s reached Bengal between April 30 and the end of May, and on June 15, 1944, sixty-eight of these aircraft made the first air attack on the Japanese homeland since the famous carrier-borne raid of April 1942.

On the same day United States Marines landed on Saipan, in the Marianas. This meant that, if all went well, very-long-range bombers would soon be able to reach Japan from bases securely held by American troops. American bases at Chengtu and elsewhere in China, on the other hand, were guarded only by unreliable Chinese troops, and some of them were already threatened by a Japanese offensive launched in April. This led President Roosevelt to wonder in July whether the effort which had gone into the Chengtu venture might not, after all, have been better devoted to the re-equipment of the Chinese Army.[11] Then and thereafter he urged Chiang Kai-shek, without success, to put his entire force under an American commander. As it turned out, the Chengtu bases did not fall, and for some months the Americans continued to use them, although infrequently because of the difficulty of bringing up fuel, bombs and ammunition. Early in 1945 the B29s were withdrawn to Bengal on the ground that their upkeep in China was uneconomic, and the Chengtu bases then closed down.

Meanwhile the only front outside the Pacific on which the Western Allies were in contact with the enemy was in Burma and Assam. There the British had halted the Japanese on the

*For Chengtu see Map 61.

threshold of India in 1942. But the country in rear of the Burma-Assam front proved highly unsuitable for the support of large-scale military operations. The failure of an attempt by the British to recapture Akyab late in 1942 and early in 1943 showed that a great deal of work would have to be done on communications and base areas before a major offensive could be launched. The defences of India had been designed to meet the attacks from the North-West, not from the North-East. There were no through roads in Bengal.[12] Supplies and reinforcements from Calcutta and North-West India had to be carried by rail to the right bank of the unbridged Brahmaputra, ferried across the river, and transported along narrow-gauge railways and roads designed to serve the seasonal needs of the tea-planting and jute industries. East and south of the Brahmaputra the terrain consisted largely of tropical rain-forest and tree-clad or scrub-covered hills rising to 11,000 feet in places, and the climate was such that campaigning was almost impossible except from November to May.

Nevertheless the Combined Chiefs of Staff recommended at the Casablanca Conference in January 1943 that a full-scale offensive, to be called 'Anakim', should be launched at the beginning of the dry season in November. This was to consist of simultaneous advances towards Mandalay by the British from Assam and the Chinese from Yunnan, and a thrust towards Myitkyina by two Chinese divisions which had withdrawn to India with the British in 1942 and were based near Ledo. The Chinese divisions were under the American General Stilwell, who also commanded the American China-Burma-India theatre and was Chief of Staff to Chiang Kai-shek. Further advances would follow in December, and would be accompanied by landings on the Arakan coast and at Rangoon.

By the end of April, however, it was clear that 'Anakim' could not be launched in 1943. Reasons given at the time included sickness among the troops and the difficulty of completing work on the lines of communication during the rainy season. But a factor which would in any case have been decisive was that the Western Allies did not have enough shipping in 1943 to carry American troops to Britain in readiness for

'Overlord' and also mount major offensives in the Pacific, the Mediterranean and South-East Asia. Field-Marshal Wavell, Commander-in-Chief in India until June, estimated the requirements for 'Anakim' at 183,000 tons of supplies a month from March. In that month, and again in April, the India Command received only some 60,000 to 70,000 tons.[13]

The question which then arose was what, if anything, should be done instead of 'Anakim'. Here there were several schools of thought. The British looked forward to the recapture of Malaya and the Netherlands East Indies. They recognized that the airlift to China must be maintained in order to keep Chiang Kai-shek in the war, but were inclined to think that in other respects the Western Allies should husband their resources until they were strong enough to take Singapore and Sumatra and break into the China Seas. The Americans, on the other hand, while they differed among themselves as to the relative importance of increasing the air-lift and reopening land communications, took the view that the liberation of China must take precedence over the restoration to the British and the Dutch of colonial territories of which many Americans would not be sorry to see them deprived. Moreover, Chungking was on the direct route from Assam to Tokyo, and Singapore was not.

The outcome was a compromise. The Combined Chiefs of Staff agreed at the 'Trident' Conference, held in Washington in May, that everything must be done to increase the air-lift from a few thousand tons of supplies a month to a minimum of 10,000 tons a month by September.[14] At the same time they went some way to meet demands for the reopening of land communications by recommending that, as a first step, an advance by the Chinese from Yunnan should be matched by vigorous thrusts into Burma from Assam. In addition, they proposed a tentative thrust towards the south-east in the shape of minor expeditions to Akyab and Ramree Island.

Meanwhile the reluctance of the India Command to launch 'Anakim' in 1943 had not gone unnoticed in London. Churchill concluded that new blood was needed in India. The sequel was that, when Lord Linlithgow retired from the post of Viceroy in the summer, Wavell succeeded him and Auchinleck returned to his old post of Commander-in-Chief, with a mission to develop communications and base installations in Bengal and Assam as energetically as he had prepared the Alamein position for defence when Cairo was threatened. In August a new South-East Asia Command was set up. After prolonged discussion the Western Allies agreed that the British Admiral Mountbatten should be Supreme Allied Commander in an essentially British theatre, and that General Stilwell should be Deputy Supreme Commander but should retain his existing posts, including that of Chief of Staff to Chiang Kai-shek.[15] Notoriously truculent, censorious and excitable, Stilwell seemed an odd choice for a position in which tact and forbearance would be at a premium. But he knew China, he had influential backers in the United States, and from the American point of view the fear that Mountbatten's attention might be drawn away from China made it essential that the new organization should include a reliable watch-dog of both American and Chinese interests.

By the time these arrangements were completed, it was apparent that once again the Combined Chiefs of Staff had set their sights too high. At the 'Quadrant' Conference at Quebec in August 1943 the combined Chiefs recognized that administrative difficulties would not allow the 'Trident' proposals to be carried out in full. They confessed their inability to give a firm directive, but agreed that the main effort in South-East Asia should go into 'offensive operations with the object of establishing land communications with China and improving and securing the air route'.[16]

About the same time eminent men on both sides of the Atlantic conceived the hope that success in Burma might be reached by a short cut. Earlier in the year the British Brigadier O. C. Wingate had launched an operation which carried his lightly equipped troops far behind the enemy's lines with the help of airborne supplies. At Wingate's suggestion, and with the backing of the Prime Minister and the Chiefs of Staff, his two brigades, hitherto called the Chindits, were transformed during the autumn and early winter into an enlarged

Special Force of six brigades.[17] His backers hoped that this expansion of his resources would enable Wingate to do great things; in fact it led him to promise himself and others more than he could perform, and sometimes to commit his formations to tasks for which they were not equipped.

Another factor which had to be taken into account towards the end of 1943 was that Chiang Kai-shek was clearly reluctant to take the offensive in Yunnan. In October he and Madame Chiang Kai-shek complained, with reason, that the air-lift had not reached the promised figure of 10,000 tons a month.* At the 'Sextant' Conference which began in Cairo in November he refused to march unless a land campaign in Burma were linked with operations at sea.[18] President Roosevelt then promised that an operation across the Bay of Bengal would be begun within the next few months, but had to confess early in December that the necessary resources could not be found. Finally, the Combined Chiefs of Staff agreed at the close of the 'Sextant' Conference that the main effort against Japan should be made in the Pacific, that landing-craft intended for an attack on the Andaman Islands should be diverted to 'Anvil' and 'Overlord', and that the chances of mounting an offensive in South-East Asia should be reviewed after further discussion with Mountbatten and Chiang Kai-shek. Both the President and the Prime Minister initialled the report embodying these decisions, but Churchill afterwards protested that he was not a party to any plan which provided no outlet in 1944 for the forces in South-East Asia.[19]

Thus all the plans discussed in 1943 for the recapture of Burma seemed at the close of the 'Sextant' Conference to have ended in frustration. The outlook was, however, less bleak than it appeared. The success of Wingate's first Chindit operation convinced the Japanese that their front east of the Chindwin

*The monthly tonnage reached five figures for the first time in December (13,450 tons). Except in March 1944, when a number of aircraft were diverted from the China route to the Fourteenth Army's front in Burma, the monthly total climbed fairly steadily thereafter to a peak of well over 50,000 tons in 1945.

River was too weak to withstand the offensive which they expected the Western Allies to launch during the dry season of 1943-44. After high-level discussion they decided to undertake a forestalling operation.[20] In its final form, their plan was that in February 1944 one division of their Twenty-eighth Army, under Lieutenant-General H. Sakurai, should open a diversionary attack in Arakan, and that in March their Fifteenth Army, under Lieutenant-General R. Mutaguchi, should attack on the Chindwin front with three divisions and seize the base at Imphal from which any British offensive would have to be launched.

Meanwhile Mountbatten had come to the conclusion that nothing he could do in Upper Burma would make it possible to open a worth-while land route to China before success in the Pacific enabled the Americans to deliver much larger quantities of supplies by sea. On the other hand, his existing directive seemed to him to call for limited offensives designed to secure the air-lift and encourage the Chinese. On January 14 he issued orders calling on Stilwell to push his American-trained Chinese force towards Myitkyina, and on General Sir George Giffard, commanding the British Eleventh Army Group, to put pressure on the Japanese in the Chindwin River area and to advance on the Arakan front with Akyab as his ultimate objective.[21] Wingate's Special Force would be used to harass the enemy in the neighbourhood of the Mandalay-Myitkyina railway, primarily with the object of helping Stilwell.

Giffard had already ordered preliminary moves on the assumption that any programme approved at a higher level would include action on such lines, and on December 21 Stilwell had assumed direct control of operations in the north with the intention of getting the drive to Myitkyina under way. Hence there was no delay in giving effect to the plan. The British 15th Corps in Arakan began its advance on the night of January 14. West of the Chindwin the 4th Corps was already in vigorous contact with the enemy. In the north Stilwell's forces advanced some thirty miles by early February. Largely in consequence of their prompt start, the British soon knew from captured documents and other evidence that the Japanese were contemplating an offensive, that the 4th Corps would almost certainly be attacked, and that probably an attempt would be made to outflank the 15th Corps.

In the light of this information the commander of the 4th Corps revised his orders to divisional commanders; Giffard reviewed the disposition of his reserves; and Lieutenant-General W. J. Slim, commanding the Fourteenth Army, told his principal administrative officer to organize day and night packing of supplies to be delivered to the 15th Corps by air. Slim had given much thought to the methods of infiltration and encirclement practised by the Japanese, and had come to the conclusion that they could be countered. Recognizing that it was impossible, on such a front as his, to set up defensive positions which could not be turned, he made it clear that formations and units by-passed or surrounded were to stand fast unless ordered to withdraw. Supplied by air, they would then form an anvil against which his mobile reserves would hammer the enemy to destruction.[22]

Slim's tactics proved outstandingly successful. The Japanese began their offensive in Arakan on February 4. Early on that day about 5,000 troops of the Japanese 55th Division passed through the front of the 7th Indian Division near the Ngakyedauk Pass under cover of darkness and mist.[23] In the course of the next few days they appeared at a number of points behind the British lines, threatened the communications of the 7th Indian Division, overran its headquarters, and attacked its formations from the rear while more troops of the same Japanese division came forward from the south. By February 7 the Ngakyedauk Pass was blocked and the Japanese were on the road to Bawli Bazar some miles to the north. In spite of Japanese fighters and an awkward approach route, the 7th Indian Division was supplied by air from February 8, and within a few days transport aircraft were making regular daily deliveries not only of food and ammunition but also of rum, cigarettes, mail and newspapers. By February 19 it was the besiegers, not the besieged, who were hungry and short of ammunition. By February 21 the Japanese were beginning to collapse, two days later they were driven from the Ngakyedauk Pass, and on February 24 General Sakurai called off his offensive.

The number of troops involved in this action was not very large, and the sector attacked was not of cardinal importance. None the less the Battle of the Ngakyedauk Pass was a turning-point in the war in South-East Asia. It showed that the tactics which had carried the enemy to success in Malaya and Burma could be countered and turned to his disadvantage by a commander able to call on reserves and transport aircraft. At the same time it threw a disturbing light on a known weakness in the structure of the South-East Asia Command.[24] The American transport aircraft used for the air-lift to China were not under Mountbatten's command, although he was responsible for the security of the air-lift, but were under Stilwell as Commanding General of the China-Burma-India theatre. In 1943 Mountbatten had been given limited powers to divert aircraft from the air-lift in an emergency. But the operations then contemplated were not those which he was conducting in February, and he wished to make sure of his position before taking any action which might otherwise lead to misunderstanding. After trying to get in touch with Stilwell, he asked the Combined Chiefs of Staff on February 18 to concur in his diverting thirty-eight Dakotas from the air-lift until the emergency in Arakan was over. No reply reached him until February 24. By that time he had surmounted the crisis with his own resources. Even so, the experience suggested that on a future occasion he might have to take the risk of acting first and asking permission afterwards.

Meanwhile Slim had ordered the 15th Corps to resume the offensive in Arakan without waiting for the Japanese to give up the Ngakyedauk Pass. At the same time signs of a coming attack on the 4th Corps were accumulating. The corps commander knew that the whole future of the campaign in Burma, the continuance of the air-lift to China, even the fate of China itself, might depend on his holding his base area at Imphal. He concluded that, if the need arose, he would have to adopt a variant of Slim's standfast tactics by concentrating his three divisions in the Imphal plain, holding vital points with minimum forces, and assembling the largest possible reserve for a counter-attack.[25] Slim agreed, but stipulated that permission to withdraw should be given by the corps commander in person and only when he was satisfied that a major offensive had begun.

General Mutaguchi's plan was to start with a diversion in the south by pushing the Japanese 33rd Division in the general direction of Tiddim at the end of the first week in March, and afterwards to swing the greater part of it in a northerly direction towards Imphal.[26] In the centre the 15th Division, starting a week later, was to advance westwards, cut the enemy's main supply route from Bengal by blocking the Dimapur-Imphal road, and then attack southwards from the high ground at the northern edge of the Imphal plain. Meanwhile the 31st Division was to capture the gateway to the Assam Valley by driving the British from Kohima. About 7,000 men of the 1st Division of the so-called Indian National Army, recruited from adherents of the 'Free India' Movement, were to move with the 15th and 31st Divisions. All formations would carry supplies for three weeks.

From an orthodox standpoint a great weakness of this plan was that all but a small part of the force would be obliged to make its approach march along jungle tracks over high mountain ranges. Normal methods of supply would be impractical for most formations, which would have to depend on capturing the enemy's dumps before their stocks ran out. Another unfortunate circumstance from Mutaguchi's point of view was that he could not start without the Japanese 15th Division, which was held back in Siam to meet the threat of an Allied landing and then made a slow journey to Burma along routes subject to Allied bombing. The delay meant that Mutaguchi would derive little or no benefit from the diversion in Arakan which in fact ended in failure before the date eventually fixed for the main offensive.

However, as Mutaguchi could not build roads for his supply columns or prevent General Sakurai from launching his diversion on the earliest date permitted by his instructions, he had no choice but to put up with these disadvantages and carry on

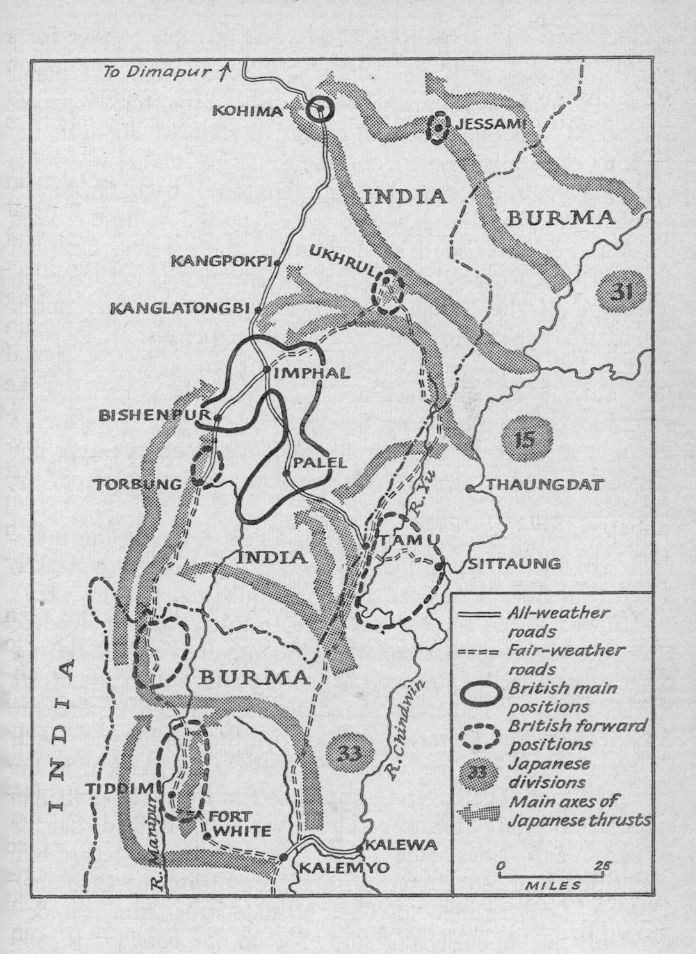

60 Burma: the Japanese Offensive on the Central Front, March-July 1944

with his plan. By March 7 his left was approaching positions held by the 17th Indian Light Division astride the Manipur River north-west of Kalemyo. On that day Lieutenant-General G. A. P. Scoones, commanding the 4th Corps, took the precaution of ordering his administrative staff to organize the stocking of supply points along the routes to Imphal which his divisions would use if he ordered them to fall back. On March 9 about two thousand Japanese were reported to have crossed the Manipur River south of Tiddim on the previous day, and on March 12 Scoones learned that the enemy was in the neighbourhood of the Indian frontier some miles further north. On March 13 he gave the 17th Division permission to withdraw.[27] But the division waited until 5 p.m. on March 14 before moving off, and had not gone far when it found its route blocked by the enemy. Scoones was obliged, therefore, to rescue it at the cost of committing all his reserves except one brigade needed to guard the approaches to Imphal from the east.

In order to provide Scoones with a new reserve, Slim thereupon arranged to bring the 5th Indian Division from Arakan by air, but first ascertained from Mountbatten that he would be allowed to use some twenty-five to thirty aircraft diverted from the China air-lift and that Mountbatten would arrange covering approval.[28] Between March 19 and 29 aircraft of the British No. 194 Transport Squadron, supplemented by twenty American transport aircraft, duly carried the 5th Division, with its guns, mules and jeeps, the 260 miles from Arakan to the Central Front. The covering approval for which Mountbatten asked after telling Slim to go ahead was not withheld; but the American authorities made it clear that they did not regard him as entitled to divert aircraft without consulting the Combined Chiefs of Staff beforehand. Their attitude struck him as understandable but militarily unsound; for no one outside his command could judge whether diversion was or was not justified in a particular case, and no one inside it ought to be put in a position to override the opinion of the Supreme Allied Commander.

Meanwhile the Japanese 33rd Division maintained its pres-

ıre in the Manipur River sector, and the 15th and 31st Divions pressed on towards Imphal and Kohima. At the same
me the British 4th Corps continued to withdraw its outlying
ɔrmations to the Imphal plain but kept a garrison at Kohima.
n March 29 the 15th Division reached the Dimapur-
ohima-Imphal road north of Imphal, as both sides expected
to do. About 155,000 men and 11,000 animals within the
nphal perimeter were then cut off from their main bases in
engal. But they had enough food and ammunition to hold out
ɔr five weeks, even if not a round or a ration reached them
air within that time, and all roads and tracks leading to the
nphal plain were securely guarded. Supplies could not, in
ıct, be flown to Imphal for some time to come, since all avail-
ɔle transport aircraft would be fully occupied for the next
ɔrtnight in bringing up reinforcements and supplying Kohima
ıd other outposts. But arrangements were made to start on
pril 18, and thus prevent stocks from falling below a level
hich would suffice for a long siege and also nourish a strong
ɔunter-offensive.

Thereafter the story of the Ngakyedauk Pass was repeated
n a vast scale, but with the difference that this time no im-
ɔrtant objective had been overrun. On April 5 Scoones, re-
eved of responsibility for Kohima and with formations from
rakan and the Army Reserve in India arriving on his left,
gan to re-group for a counter-attack. On April 18 the newly-
rived 33rd Corps raised the siege of Kohima after the garrison
ıd held off the enemy for a fortnight, and on the following
ıy the Japanese 15th Division's troops on the Kohima-Imphal
ad abandoned their attempt to take Imphal from that direction
d went over to the defensive. Mutaguchi's intention was that
e 31st Division should then send a force southwards to en-
le the 15th Division to renew its attack. But Lieutenant-
eneral K. Sato, commanding the 31st Division, counter-
ınded the order when he saw that his positions near Kohima
ere threatened.

Thus the situation at the end of the third week in April was
at the Japanese advance had come to a standstill in all sectors.
ıe 31st Division had received no supplies since the begin-

EDGAR HOLLOWAY
Lake Baikal
MONGOLIA
MANCHURIA
SAKHALIN
JEHOL
Paotou
Peking
Tientsin
Liulin
Yellow R.
Port Arthur
KOREA
Tungkwan
Kaifeng
Tokyo
CHINA
JAPAN
Hankow
Shanghai
Chungking
Yangtze R.
Nanchang
Ryukyu Is.
Okinawa
Bonin Is.
BURMA ROAD
Kweiyang
West R.
Lashio
Canton
Formosa
Mandalay
Hong Kong (Br.)
BURMA
INDO-CHINA
Hanoi
Hainan
SIAM
SOUTH CHINA SEA
Luzon
Mariana Is.
Saipan
Tinian
Guam
Rangoon
Bangkok
Manila
PHILIPPINE ISLANDS
Saigon
Leyte
Mindanao
Yap
Davao
Palau Is.
Caroline
Kota Bahru
MALAYA
SARAWAK
SUMATRA
Singapore
BORNEO
Halmahera
Biak
Admiralty Is.
CELEBES
Aitape
Hollandia
NEW GUINEA
Batavia
JAVA
Timor Sea
Darwin
0 200 400 600 800 1000
MILES
AUSTRALIA

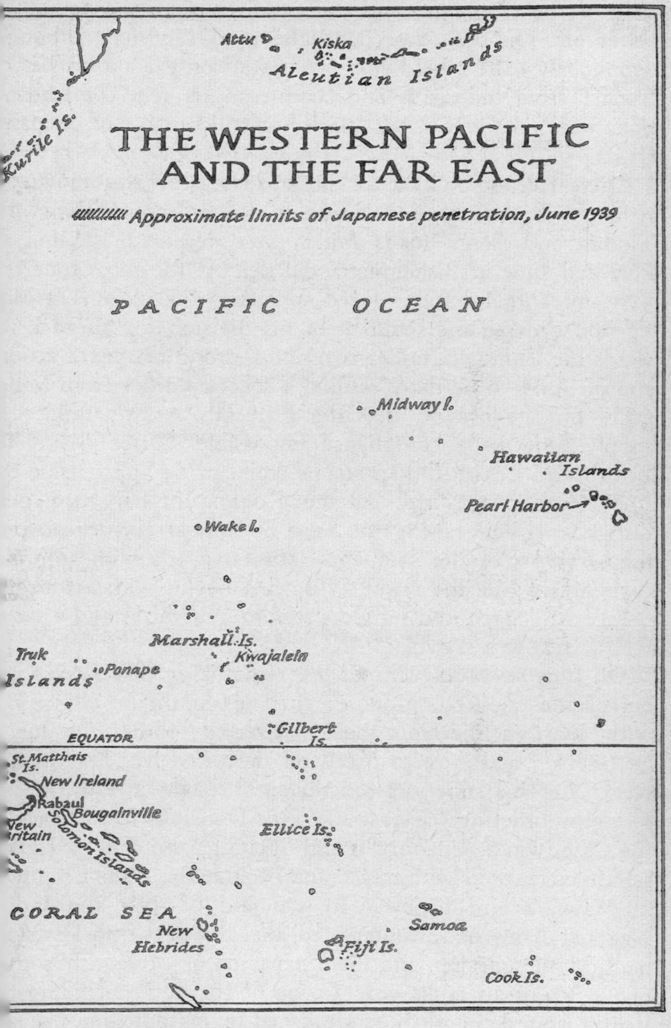

THE WESTERN PACIFIC AND THE FAR EAST

////////// Approximate limits of Japanese penetration, June 1939

Attu
Kiska
Aleutian Islands
Kurile Is.
PACIFIC OCEAN
Midway I.
Hawaiian Islands
Pearl Harbor
Wake I.
Marshall Is.
Kwajalein
Truk Islands
Ponape
Gilbert Is.
EQUATOR
St. Matthais Is.
New Ireland
Rabaul
Bougainville
New Britain
Solomon Islands
Ellice Is.
CORAL SEA
New Hebrides
Samoa
Fiji Is.
Cook Is.

ning of the campaign, and the 15th Division was not mucl
better off. On the other hand the 33rd Division, althougl
temporarily halted, held strong positions on the approaches t
Imphal from the south and south-east. Its rear communica
tions were relatively good, and it was still capable of offensiv
action.

Thereafter the outlook for the Japanese grew steadily wors
Attempts by the 33rd Division to reach Imphal along th
Tiddim and Tamu roads failed after desperate fighting i
May and June at Bishenpur and Palel. At the same time th
31st and 15th Divisions faced appalling difficulties. On Ma
31 Sato ordered the remnant of his division to fall back tc
wards the Chindwin under cover of a strong rearguard actior
and on June 19 he flatly refused a contrary order from Mut
guchi on the ground that the Fifteenth Army's failure t
supply him made compliance impossible. Three days lat
British and British-Indian troops from inside and outside tl
Imphal perimeter met on the Kohima-Imphal road ne
Kangkokpi, thus raising the siege of Imphal and threatenir
the survivors of the 31st and 15th Divisions with annihil
tion. Meanwhile the rainy season had begun with a four-d
deluge which reduced jungle tracks to quagmires and a hea
long retreat to a crawl.

On June 26 Mutaguchi, at last recognizing that success w
out of the question, proposed that he should be allowed
withdraw to a line from the Yu River to Tiddim. On July
he received authority to break off the offensive. Less than
week later his superiors sanctioned a retreat already in f
swing by ordering the 31st and 15th Divisions to fall back
the Chindwin at Thaungdut and Sittaung, and the 33rd Di
sion to cover their withdrawal and itself retire to the Chindw
at Mawlaik and Kalewa. By the end of July the Indi
National Army had disintegrated, the 31st and 15th Divisio
had lost all cohesion, and there remained of Mutaguchi's ar
of 84,280 of all ranks only 30,775 fit for duty, including t
lightly wounded and those weakened by malnutrition but st
able to march.*[29]

*The Japanese Fifteenth Army's 53,505 casualties included 30,5

Meanwhile the Northern Combat Area Command was making slow progress towards Myitkyina and the Burma road. In February Stilwell's two American-trained Chinese divisions were reinforced by a Chinese tank unit and by Merrill's Marauders, an American counterpart of Wingate's Special Force. In early March Stilwell secured the Hukawng Valley, about half-way between the Assam-Burma frontier and his objective, and on March 3 he told Slim that he hoped to take Myitkyina by a sudden dash.[30] But thereafter the threat to Kohima and Imphal, reports of a coming attack on the Peking-Hankow railway, and the growing power of the Communists in North China all made Chiang Kai-shek reluctant to see any part of his resources committed far outside his frontiers.[31] For many weeks Stilwell had great difficulty in urging his Chinese divisions forward. He was therefore tempted, both then and later, to make up for lost time by using lightly-equipped special forces for tasks which would normally have been undertaken by orthodox infantry formations with supporting artillery.

In February the 16th (Long Range Penetration) Brigade of Wingate's Special Force began a march of about 360 miles through wild country on the borders of Assam and Burma to the neighbourhood of Indaw, immediately west of the Mandalay-Myitkyina railway. It was followed by the 77th and 111th Brigades, both conveyed by air, and later two more brigades were committed. Wingate's orders were to help Stilwell's advance on the Northern Front by harassing the enemy's communications. But he hoped that his brigades might become the spearhead of an advance to the Irrawaddy and beyond by orthodox formations, and after the operation had begun he also conceived the idea of contributing to the defence of Kohima and Imphal by cutting the communications of the

---

dead or missing. The British lost 16,667 killed, wounded or missing between the opening of the battles of Kohima and Imphal and the end of July (battle casualties only). The Japanese 55th Division (Twenty-eighth Army) recorded 5,335 casualties between January and July; the British 3,560 in the Battle of the Ngakyedauk Pass and 3,362 battle casualties elsewhere on the Arakan front from March to July.

Japanese 15th and 31st Divisions on the Central Front. Consequently Wingate's death in a flying accident on March 24 left his successor, Brigadier W. D. A. Lentaigne, in some doubt as to what was expected of him. However, in April it was agreed that the primary task of Special Force was still to help Stilwell, that eventually part of the force should move towards Stilwell's line of advance in the north while part stayed further south, and that the force should go under Stilwell's command on the night of May 16.

When that date arrived, Stilwell was still separated by many miles of difficult country from his objectives. His immediate aim was to take Myitkyina as a vital link between a new Burma road to be driven southwards from Ledo and the old Burma road through Wanting and Chefang. But he had not reached Myitkyina, and indeed had yet to sweep the enemy from his path at Kamaing and Mogaung. On May 17, however, a column of Merrill's Marauders, augmented by Chinese infantry, raised his hopes by capturing the Myitkyina airstrip about four miles from the town. Confident that Myitkyina would fall within the next few days, Stilwell thereupon refused an offer from Lentaigne to send in that direction a detachment commanded by Lieutenant-Colonel J. R. Morris.[32] But the Japanese garrison of roughly seven hundred men stood firm in face of repeated attacks by his Chinese troops. Stilwell then called for reinforcements from India, urged the hospital authorities to send back to their units all men capable of pressing a trigger, and on May 25 directed that Morris's detachment (called Morrisforce) should be sent to Waingmaw, on the left bank of the Irrawaddy opposite Myitkyina.[33]

Meanwhile Morrisforce, with an effective strength of roughly one battalion, had gone into action at a point some fifteen to twenty miles from Waingmaw and separated from it by a river. Floods and broken bridges compelled the troops to make a long detour, with the result that they did not reach Waingmaw until May 29. On May 30, and again on June 2, Morrisforce broke into the Japanese positions, but on both occasions was driven out for lack of artillery support. Meanwhile Stilwell's forces outside Myitkyina on

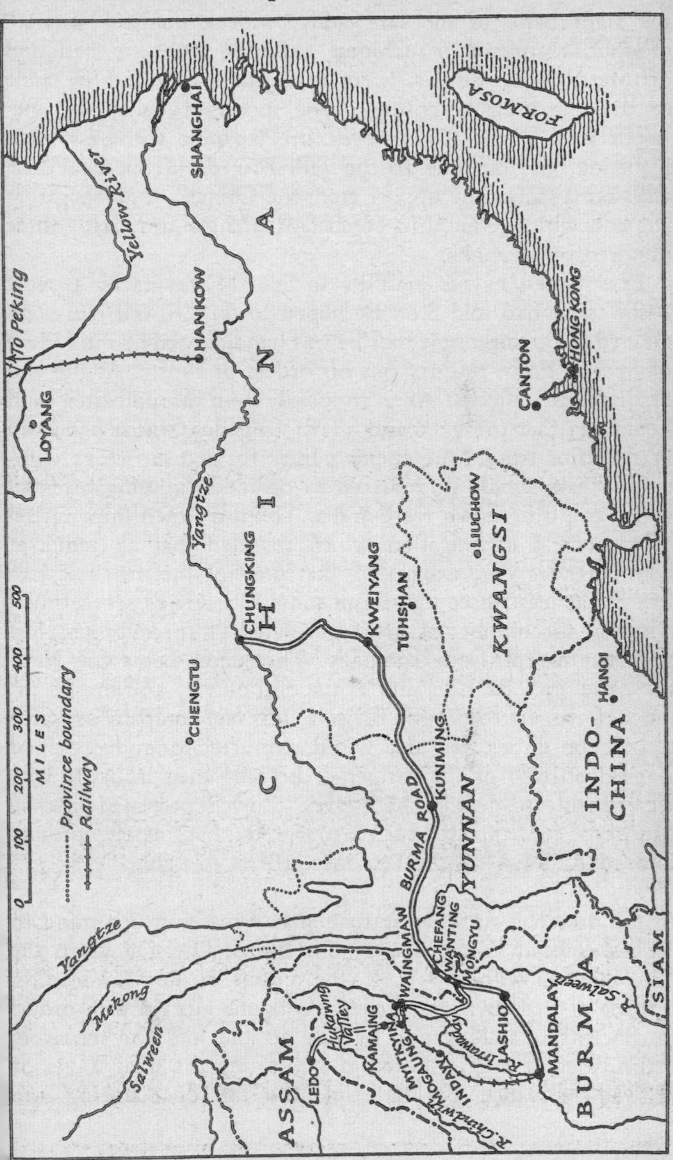

61 Burma: the Northern Front and the Burma Road

the right bank of the Irrawaddy, with a nominal strength of four regiments of Chinese infantry and one battalion of Merrill's Marauders, were at a standstill, and by June 6 the Japanese garrisons had increased fourfold. Between June 7 and 16, however, the Japanese withdrew from Kamaing, and on June 26 the 77th Brigade of Special Force, with rather leisurely support from the Chinese, took Mogaung at a cost which reduced its combatant strength to roughly three hundred of all ranks.

Exasperated by his inability to take Myitkyina by a swift dash, as he had told Slim he hoped to do, Stilwell had complained in the meantime that he was handicapped by the failure of Special Force to carry out his orders promptly. At the end of June he objected to a proposal from Mountbatten and Lentaigne that the 77th and 111th Brigades, which had been in action or behind the enemy's lines for sixteen weeks without a break, should be replaced by orthodox infantry brigades which could be flown from India. The three men then agreed to a medical investigation which revealed that all ranks in both brigades were exhausted, that most of the men had had malaria at least three times and some as many as seven times, and that the number of men considered fit for duty was just sufficient to form one company. Thereupon Lentaigne withdrew the 77th Brigade, and at the end of July and the beginning of August the 111th Brigade, less one company assigned to garrison duties, was also withdrawn after Mountbatten had warned Stilwell of the danger of keeping men in battle who were unable to defend themselves. Stilwell protested that he had never contemplated such a course, but had merely objected to the withdrawal of the few men still fit to fight.

In the previous April Mountbatten had made up his mind to replace Special Force by the 36th Indian Division when the time came to withdraw it. In the middle of July the leading brigade of that division reached Myitkyina airstrip with orders to concentrate at Mogaung by July 28 and join two relatively fit brigades of Special Force in supporting the final stages of Stilwell's advance. By that time the fall of Kamaing and

Mogaung had made the Japanese positions on the Upper Irrawaddy untenable. On August 1 the commander of the Myitkyina garrison committed suicide after ordering the regimental commander to withdraw the remnant of his troops, and on August 3 Stilwell's international force entered the town to find only 187 Japanese still there. Stilwell continued to hold his appointments until October, when he was relieved at Chiang Kai-shek's request of his duties as Chief of Staff to the Chinese Supreme Command and left for the United States. The American Lieutenant-General A. C. Wedemeyer, who had little experience of command in the field but had been Deputy Chief of Staff in the South-East Asia Command since its inception, was then appointed Chief of Staff to Chiang Kai-shek, and the American China-Burma-India Theatre was divided into two theatres separated by the frontier between China and Burma. Later a British officer, General Sir Oliver Leese, was appointed to command all the land forces under Mountbatten's control.

In the meantime the Japanese had begun their expected offensive in China. On April 17, 1944, some five divisions crossed the Yellow River from east to west, and by May 21 the Japanese held the southern portion of the Peking-Hankow railway and had captured Loyang. The Japanese Eleventh Army, with eight divisions under command, then launched a series of attacks designed to capture the railway running south and south-east from Hankow to Canton and Liuchow and the American airfields in Southern China. But difficulties of supply made progress slow, the Chinese Tenth Army resisted stoutly, and in December the Eleventh Army was ordered by its superior formation not to push further west than Tuhshan and to be content with consolidating its gains and opening a route through Kwangsi province into Indo-China.

The Chinese armies in Yunnan also took the offensive in the late spring of 1944, although not until after the Americans had threatened to cut off supplies if they failed to do so. On May 10 some twelve weak divisions, strongly supported by the Fourteenth United States Army Air Force, crossed the Salween with the object of establishing themselves in the neighbourhood of the old Burma road and making contact with the force which Stilwell was expected to push southwards through Myitkyina. Ill-supplied and under-nourished, the 72,000 men of the Chinese Eleventh and Twelfth Army Groups were soon brought to a halt by 10,000 troops of the Japanese 56th Division, but succeeded in pinning down part of the 56th Division's forces in isolated garrisons.

Early in September Lieutenant-General M. Honda, commanding the Japanese Thirty-third Army, launched a counter-offensive with two incomplete divisions. Almost simultaneously the Chinese took two of the first-stage objectives which they had been investing since the early summer, and on September 15 Honda decided to call off his offensive and concentrate on rescuing the remnant of the 56th Division's beleagured troops and blocking the Burma road. A few days later Imperial General Headquarters, recognizing that failure on the Central and Northern Fronts called for drastic measures, advised Lieutenant-General H. Kimura, commanding the Burma Area Army, that severance of land communications between Burma and China was of secondary importance but that the oil-producing and rice-growing regions of Southern Burma must be held. Thereupon Kimura, with only ten divisions to share between the Thirty-third, Fifteenth and Twenty-eighth Armies and a strategic reserve, arranged to defend a line from Lashio through Mandalay to the Irrawaddy delta, and to guard his exposed flank in the north by holding a deep series of positions in the neighbourhood of Mongmit.

On October 2 Mountbatten issued a directive which called upon the Northern Combat Area Command to clear the enemy from the mountainous country near the Chinese frontier without losing sight of its responsibility for the security of the air route and the opening of land communications.[34] Accordingly, on October 16 the command began a southward push from Myitkyina, directing the British on its right towards Mongmit, and the Chinese on its left towards the junction of the Ledo road and the Burma road at Mongyu. Just under a fortnight later the Chinese in Yunnan resumed their drive along the Burma road with orders to make contact with the Northern Combat Area Command in the frontier area.

General Honda, with barely two divisions in hand, thus faced convergent advances by two forces, each greatly superior in numbers to his own. Nevertheless the Chinese in Yunnan came forward so slowly, and with so little regard for security, that he was able to deal them some smart blows with his right while using his left to secure his line of retreat and fight a series of rear-guard actions with the British, the Americans, and the American-trained Chinese. Towards the middle of January, however, he learned that the enemy was about to close on his right-hand division in overwhelming strength. Recognizing that only a brisk withdrawal could avert disaster, Honda told the divisional commander that he must on no account allow himself to be surrounded.[35] On January 20 troops of the Northern Combat Area Command's First Chinese New Army reached the Burma road at Wanting to find that the enemy had gone. Land communications with China were open at last.

CHAPTER 21

THE CONQUEST OF JAPAN (II)

September 1943 - September 1945

In September 1943 the rulers of Japan reviewed their problems in the light of Mussolini's fall from power. Hitler's growing difficulties in Russia, and their own setbacks in the past eighteen months.[1] These included their naval defeat at Midway Island; losses in the South Pacific; minor but ominous penetrations of their front in Burma; and the dwindling of their merchant fleet at a rate which had risen fairly steadily since the beginning of the war.

They concluded that they could expect no more help from Europe, that sooner or later their existing line in the Pacific would become untenable, and that eventually they would have to be content with a shorter line running from the Kurile Islands through the Caroline Islands and Western New Guinea to Timor. The greater part of the conquered territories in South-East Asia and the South-West Pacific must, however, be held both on strategic grounds and for the sake of the raw materials without which Japan could neither fight nor live. At the same time China must be induced to accept her role as a vassal State, and a strong force must be kept in Manchuria to discourage the Russians from throwing in their lot with the Americans. Too late, the Japanese also decided that henceforth their merchant shipping must move in convoy.

The Japanese offensives in Burma and China in 1944 followed logically from these conclusions. Both reflected an outlook which had become essentially defensive; for the first was intended to make Burma easier to hold, the second to prevent the Americans from using China as a base for attacks on

TABLE 17

THE JAPANESE MERCHANT FLEET: TONNAGE LOST AND TONNAGE ADDED, DECEMBER 1941 TO AUGUST 1945[2]
(Ships under 500 tons excluded)

Tonnage available December 7, 1941		5,996,607
Tonnage lost December 7, 1941—December 31, 1942	1,123,156	
less additions	945,374	177,782
Tonnage available December 31, 1942		5,818,825
Tonnage lost 1943	1,820,919	
less additions	878,113	942,806
Tonnage available December 31, 1943		4,876,019
Tonnage lost 1944	3,891,019	
less additions	1,734,847	2,156,172
Tonnage available December 31, 1944		2,719,847
Tonnage lost January to August, 1945	1,782,140	
less additions	565,443	1,216,697
Tonnage available at end of war		1,503,150

Gross losses in the first eight months of 1943 came to just under a million tons.

Japan and to secure interior lines of communications with territories which might otherwise become increasingly hard to reach as the Western Allies tightened their grip at sea and in the air.

Even so, the Japanese did not despair of a great naval battle which might put the clock back to Pearl Harbor. They were prepared to take risks in order to bring on such an encounter, and to give up outposts in the Gilbert and Marshall Islands and the Solomons, even at the cost of sacrificing their garrisons, in the belief that the enemy would be thrown back when he reached the strong system of deep defences which they counted on buying time to build in the Marianas, the Ryukyus and the Bonins. When the Western Allies decided in 1943 that the main effort against Japan should be made in the Pacific they committed themselves, therefore, to the kind of war which the Japanese still believed that they could win.

But the Americans, not uncharacteristically, prepared themselves for an uphill struggle with a promptitude and ingenuity which the Japanese did not expect of them. Often at a loss in a land campaign which posed the problem of advancing seven hundred miles from Cherbourg to the heart of Germany, their strategists were much more at home when all that was asked of them was that they should bridge the five thousand miles of blue water which divided Tokyo from Brisbane and Pearl Harbor. They had the benefit of accurate foreknowledge derived from the breaking of the Japanese naval cypher, and their Joint Chiefs of Staff Committee was particularly strong on the naval side.*

Moreover, in Admiral Nimitz and General MacArthur the Americans had in the Pacific theatre two commanders of outstanding ability and strength of will.[3] Nimitz was a comparative newcomer to high command; but he had made his mark at an early age, and as a submarine specialist he found it easier than many of his generation to adapt himself to a new kind of naval warfare in which the aircraft carrier rather than the capital ship was the decisive weapon. MacArthur, on the other hand, was considerably senior to all his rivals, having retired in 1935 from the post of Chief of Staff to the United States Army. He had then entered the service of the govern-

*The Joint Chiefs of Staff Committee consisted of: Admiral (later Fleet Admiral) William P. Leahy, Chief of Staff to the President and Commander-in-Chief of the United States Armed Forces (Chairman); General (later General of the Army) George C. Marshall, Chief of Staff of the United States Army; Admiral (later Fleet Admiral) Ernest J. King, Commander-in-Chief of the United States Fleet and Chief of Naval Operations; General (later General of the Army) Henry H. Arnold, Commanding General, United States Army Air Forces.

ment of the Philippines, and on the outbreak of war with Japan he was doubling the posts of Commander of the United States land forces in the Far East and Field-Marshal of the Armed Forces of the Philippines. His father had been Military Governor of the Philippines and he was deeply conscious of his responsibilities towards the Filipinos. His high reputation, proconsular background and lack of sympathy with the Democratic Party in the United States did not make his relations with the Chiefs of Staff and the government particularly easy; but he was in the fortunate position of being irreplaceable.

The Americans also had the advantage of a large though not unlimited industrial potential. Moreover, they soon made it clear that they had no intention of sacrificing it by interpreting their adherence to the 'Germany first' strategy as an undertaking to fall in with the plans of their Allies at the cost of denuding the one theatre in which American interests were paramount. Their insistence on opening at least a limited offensive in the Pacific while Germany was still undefeated did not suit the British, who had knowingly restricted their output of certain classes of equipment, such as transport aircraft and assault shipping, in the belief that Anglo-American resources would be shared between the various theatres on an agreed basis. As things were, they were unable to check the flow of equipment to a theatre over which the Combined Chiefs of Staff had only a nominal control. Nor could they controvert the American argument that, even in 1943, offensive power in the Pacific theatre was indispensable unless the Japanese were to be allowed to carry all before them while their opponents did nothing but retreat.

The broad effect was that, although the Western Allies never had in any theatre as much of everything as they would have liked to possess, on the whole commanders and staff officers in the Pacific Ocean Areas could draw up plans with a freedom seldom enjoyed by their counterparts in other areas. While Allied strategists in the European, Mediterranean and South-East Asian theatres often had difficulty in planning even a single offensive without exceeding their probable quota of equipment and supplies, in the Pacific theatre the Americans were able to plan two distinct though complementary offensives.

In common with most American naval strategists, Nimitz favoured an approach to Japan from the Central Pacific through the Caroline Islands and the Marianas. His answer to the objection that this course would not enable him to meet and defeat the bulk of the enemy's land forces until a comparatively late stage was that it was desirable, and indeed essential, that the enemy should first be weakened by naval and air action. On the other hand MacArthur, supported with reservations by his fellow-soldiers, pressed for the recapture of the Philippines and a subsequent landing in Formosa, or alternatively in the Netherlands East Indies or on the mainland of Asia. The Joint Chiefs of Staff agreed that both lines of approach should be followed, but were inclined to give priority to Nimitz.

Nimitz saw, however, that his strategy could not succeed unless he began by seizing bases closer to his starting-point than the Caroline Islands, and that even then the vast distances he had to cover would confront him with insoluble administrative problems unless he increased the mobility of his fleet to a point at which it became virtually self-supporting. Backed by King, he built up an elaborate fleet train of supply and repair ships which made it possible for his fighting ships to keep the sea for months on end, as their forerunners had done in the days of sail. Admiral Raymond A. Spruance, who commanded the main fleet under Nimitz, then divided his ships into a fast carrier force of fleet carriers, light carriers fast new battleships, cruisers and destroyers; an assault force designed for opposed landings, with older battleships, cruisers destroyers and escort carriers to give support and covering fire; and a fleet train whose commander also controlled any land-based aircraft in the area of operations. Thus equipped Spruance would begin his advance in the Central Pacific by seizing the Gilbert Islands. Meanwhile in the South-West Pacific MacArthur, supported on his right by the forces of the South Pacific Area under Admiral William F. Halsey, would follow his own line towards the Philippines, with the Admiralty Islands as his immediate objective.*

Accordingly, in the latter part of 1943 and the early months of 1944 MacArthur's Australian troops continued to advance by land and sea along the coast of New Guinea, while in the Northern Solomons and the Bismarck Archipelago the Americans assaulted Bougainville, overcame the Japanese garrison after a stiff fight, and established themselves in Western New Britain and on various islands of the Admiralty and St. Matthias groups.[4] The ultimate effect of this joint effort, to which New Zealand troops also contributed, was that the important naval and air base which the Japanese had established at Rabaul was encircled and that roughly 140,000 Japanese were cut off from all hope of relief. The immediate effect was that in the early stages of the assault on Bougainville Admiral Mineichi Koga, who had succeeded Yamamoto in command of the Japanese Combined Fleet when an aircraft carrying Yamamoto on a tour of inspection was shot down, made a desperate attempt to counter air attacks on Rabaul by sending carriers to disembark their aircraft there.

As a result of this unlucky stroke, which cost Koga three-quarters of his disembarked aircraft in one week, the Japanese were unable to give effect to a plan which they had made to defend the Gilbert Islands chiefly by naval means. When

*The division of responsibilities in the Pacific in August 1943 was that Nimitz was regarded, by virtue of his dual position as Commander-in-Chief, Pacific Fleet and Commander-in-Chief, Pacific Ocean Areas, as exercising direct command of all Allied forces in the Central and North Pacific, and indirect command through Halsey of all Allied forces in the South Pacific; while MacArthur, as Commander-in-Chief, South-West Pacific Area, was in operational command of all Allied land forces in that area, and issued orders by delegated authority to the United States Seventh Fleet under Vice-Admiral Arthur S. Carpender (succeeded in December 1943 by Admiral Thomas C. Kinkaid). Minor changes (in particular the transfer of the land forces in the South Pacific from Halsey's to MacArthur's command in December 1943) were made from time to time, and a radical change was made in April 1945, when MacArthur and Nimitz became respectively Commander-in-Chief, Army Forces in the Pacific, and Commander-in-Chief, Naval Forces in the Pacific.

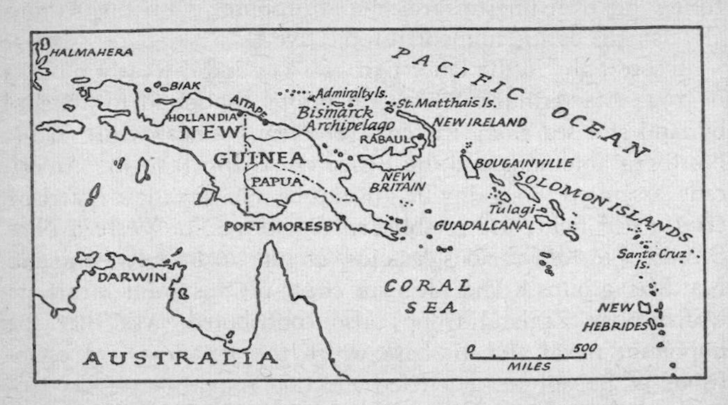

62 New Guinea, the Bismarck Archipelago and the Solomons

landing-forces from Pearl Harbor and the New Hebrides reached the principal islands of the group on November 20, Koga's carriers had withdrawn to home waters after parting with their aircraft at Rabaul. Without air cover for his six battleships and nine cruisers some 1,400 miles away at Truk, he was in no position to do more than send eight or nine submarines with orders to break up the landings, and to push forward a few land-based aircraft to Kwajalein, in the Marshall Islands. The Americans lost one escort carrier but no other ships, and the Japanese forces ashore were so heavily outnumbered that within four days nearly all of them died fighting.[5]

Thus the way was soon clear for the next stage of the American advance. In February Spruance captured as many islands of the Marshall group as he needed to give him command of the whole, at the same time using his fast carrier force to strike a deadly blow at Truk. Warned by a reconnaissance, Koga withdrew his fleet in time, and thereafter used Singapore as his main base outside home waters. But in twelve hours nearly 20,000 tons of Japanese merchant shipping, as well as 270 aircraft and a number of cruisers and destroyers, were destroyed or damaged.[8]

63 The Central Pacific

Encouraged by success, both Nimitz and MacArthur suggested in March that their progress should be speeded up, especially as experience had shown that command of the sea and air enabled them to by-pass even strongly-garrisoned Japanese bases without undue risk. The Joint Chiefs of Staff, who were drawing to the close of a long debate about future strategy when these proposals were received, then ordered Mac-

Arthur to push further west in New Guinea about the middle of April and establish air bases from which the Palaus and Halmahera Islands could be bombarded or controlled.[9] Nimitz was to occupy the Southern Marianas about the middle of June and the Palaus about the middle of September. He was then to establish a fleet and air base and a forward staging area in the Palaus as a step towards the occupation of Mindanao about the middle of November and of Formosa or Luzon in February 1945.

Almost simultaneously the Japanese came to the conclusion that the Marianas and the Palaus were likely to be attacked in the near future.[10] Leaving the remnant of their forces in Bougainville and Rabaul to hold on as best they could, they reinforced the Marianas, the Palaus and the Bonins. Between February and April the Japanese also set up a new organization to co-ordinate the defence of the islands as far south as Ponape in the east and the Palaus in the west. Their intention was to rely largely on land-based aircraft and on the Combined Fleet. Admiral Koga drew up a plan to bring the American fleet to action on favourable terms, but a flying-boat which was carrying him from Palau to Davao disappeared on March 31 and was believed to have crashed into the sea. A similar plan was afterwards adopted by his successor, Admiral Soemu Toyoda.

In accordance with the orders of the Joint Chiefs of Staff, MacArthur pushed further westwards in New Guinea and seized a number of Japanese airfields at Hollandia and Aitape and on the small island of Wakde, but found them unsuitable for the large force of heavy bombers needed for operations against the Palaus and the Halmaheras. Towards the end of May he decided, therefore to seize Biak Island, where the Japanese had built three airfields which seemed suitable. Recognizing that the loss of Biak might jeopardize their plans for a fleet action to be fought under cover of land-based aircraft, the Japanese then made two attempts to reinforce the garrison, but on each occasion their ships turned back under the threat of naval and air attack. They were about to make a third attempt, this time with the support of two of their giant battleships and two heavy cruisers, when on June 11 and 12 attacks on Guam and Saipan by aircraft of the American fast carrier force convinced them that the invasion of the Marianas was imminent. Thereupon Admiral Toyoda ordered his main fleet under Vice-Admiral Jisaburo Ozawa to leave its anchorage in the Philippines and make rendezvous in the Philippine Sea with the force under Vice-Admiral M. Ugaki which was to have covered the running of reinforcements to Biak.

When American landing-forces went ashore on Saipan on June 15, the stage was thus set for a naval battle on which the Japanese relied to restore their hold on the Central Pacific and the approaches to Japan.[11] After making rendezvous with Ugaki, Ozawa had at his disposal five battleships, five fleet carriers, four light carriers, thirteen cruisers and twenty-eight destroyers. The Americans were known to have many more carriers than this; but Ozawa counted on land-based aircraft, working from Guam and Rota in the Western Marianas, to redress the balance. Other factors in his favour were that his carrier-borne aircraft, unencumbered by armour and without self-sealing tanks, had a greater radius of action than the enemy's; that if all went well they would be able to save time by refuelling and rearming in the Western Marianas; and that the prevailing wind blew from east to west. This meant that, whereas Ozawa would be able to launch and recover his aircraftt while closing with the enemy, his opponent would be obliged to turn away in order to do so.

Ozawa was determined to make the most of these advantages. On June 18 he learned, after several days of inconclusive scouting by both sides, that the American fast carrier force was roughly 160 miles west of Saipan and therefore the best part of 300 miles to the east of him. He then decided to stand well away with his five fleet carriers and attack at extreme range on the following day. That evening he broke wireless silence in order to ensure that the commander of the land-based aircraft knew what was expected of him, and at 9 p.m. he sent a vanguard of battleships and light carriers towards the Americans while he himself maintained a course which would tend to keep him out of reach of United States reconnaissance aircraft and carrier-borne bombers.

Ozawa's signal was intercepted by the Americans, who were thus able to fix his position with fair accuracy. Thereupon Vice-Admiral Marc A. Mitscher, commanding the fast carrier force, asked permission to close the range and attack at daybreak. But Admiral Spruance, who had joined Mitscher with a number of ships which brought the strength of the force to fifteen carriers, seven battleships, twenty escort carriers, and sixty-seven destroyers, was unwilling to jeopardize the landings by uncovering Saipan while there was any risk that part of Ozawa's force might slip past him in the night. As he insisted for that reason on holding a course towards the Marianas until morning, the situation at first light on June 19 was that Ozawa was still at extreme range, as he wished to be, and that Spruance and Mitscher had no better guide to his whereabouts than the fix made some ten hours earlier.

Nevertheless June 19 proved a disastrous day for the Japanese. Between 8.30 a.m. and 11.30 a.m. Ozawa's carrier-borne aircraft struck four times at the American carriers. The range was so great that on each occasion Mitscher received ample warning from his radar, and had his fighters airborne in good time. Meanwhile part of his own carrier-borne force was attacking the Japanese airfields on Guam, only seventy miles away. The consequences were that roughly two-thirds of Ozawa's carrier-borne aircraft were lost within the first few hours, and that the land-based air force on which he relied was crippled before most of its aircraft were able to go into action. In addition two of his fleet carriers, the newly-commissioned *Taiho* and the veteran *Shokaku*, were torpedoed by American submarines and sank after remaining afloat for several hours.

But the full extent of the disaster was not known to Ozawa, who supposed that at least a fair proportion of his missing aircraft had landed safely in the Western Marianas and that probably they had done a good deal of damage to the American fleet. After delivering his fourth attack he made off to the north-west with the intention of refuelling and renewing the engagement within the next forty-eight hours. Meanwhile Mitscher was held back by the need to turn into the wind in order to fly his aircraft off and on, with the result that it was not until nearly 4 p.m. on June 20 that he found himself in a position to strike at Ozawa's fleet. Recognizing that to launch his aircraft against a distant target so late in the day would mean recovering them in darkness but that it was now or never, he decided to take the plunge. Despatched about two hours before nightfall, his bombers and torpedo-bombers came up with the enemy just as the sun was touching the horizon. In a twenty-minute engagement they sank the fleet carrier *Hiyo* and damaged two other fleet carriers, two light carriers, one battleship and one heavy cruiser at the cost of 20 American aircraft lost in action and 80 which failed to make safe landings in the darkness.* With only 35 of his carrier-borne aircraft still fit to fly, Ozawa withdrew on Toyoda's orders to Okinawa in the Ryukyu Islands.

Deprived of naval support and with only a handful of land-based aircraft left on Guam, the 32,000 Japanese troops on Saipan were bound to succumb to attacks by three American divisions. On July 6, when all but a small part of the island in the extreme north had been lost, the leading representatives of the army and the navy committed suicide in order to set an example of self-sacrifice to the troops, and two days later resistance ceased after a death-or-glory charge by the 3,000 survivors of the garrison.[12] With Guam and Tinian still to fall but clearly doomed, the Americans thus gained, at the cost of some 17,500 casualties, a secure base from which Japan could be attacked by very-long-range bombers.

The loss of Saipan, coinciding with the failure of the Japanese offensive in Central Burma and following closely on the

*Eventually all but 16 pilots and 33 other aircrew were rescued. Altogether the Americans lost 130 aircraft and 76 aircrew on the two days. Apart from the sinking of three fleet carriers out of five, Japanese losses in aircraft alone were at least three times as heavy.

first attack on the Japanese homeland by B29s from China, made a profound impression in Japan. On July 18 General Tojo, who had been Prime Minister since the beginning of the war and earlier, resigned with his entire Cabinet, and after four days of uncertainty a new Cabinet was formed on the advice of a council of elder statesmen. Its leaders were General K. Koiso, who had been Governor-General of Korea, and Admiral M. Yonai, who was urged to become Prime Minister but declined to do so.[13]

The conclusion drawn by the rulers of Japan from these events was not however, that the time had come to end the war, but that everything must be done to win the next battle, which seemed likely to take place in the Philippines. It was also agreed that attempts should be made to improve relations with Soviet Russia and to induce Russia and Germany to come to terms. At the same time the offensive in China should be maintained with the object of preventing the Americans from continuing to bomb Japan from bases in that country.

Accordingly, steps were taken during the next few weeks to strengthen the inner line of defences from the Kurile Islands through Japan and the Ryukyu Islands to the Philippines. By August roughly a third of the major formations of the Japanese Army were deployed along that line. The main effort would, however, be made by the navy and by land-based aircraft. Since most of the navy's carrier-borne formations had been knocked out in the battle of the Philippine Sea, and as it was doubtful whether new crews could be ready in time, the essence of the naval plan was that the coming battle should be an encounter between battleships.[14] A skeleton carrier force, coming south from Japan, would try to lure the American fast carrier force away while the main fleet from Singapore, working under cover of land-based aircraft, matched its guns against those of the rest of the United States Pacific Fleet. Toyoda believed that it would then be possible to deal with the American carriers by a combination of naval gunfire and attacks by land-based aircraft.

On the Allied side, the Joint Chiefs of Staff directed MacArthur on September 8 to occupy Leyte, in the Central Philip-

TABLE 18

DISTRIBUTION OF THE JAPANESE ARMY, AUGUST 1944[15]
(Major formations only)

	Divisions	*Army Air Divisions*
Japan, Sakhalin, and Kurile Islands	15	4
Ryukyu Islands and Formosa	7	1
Philippines	10	2
	32	7
Manchuria and Korea	12	—
China	26	1
Indo-China, Siam, Malaya and Sumatra	4	1
Burma	10	1
Celebes, Amboina and Timor	6	1
Central Pacific	5	—
South Pacific	6	—
	101	11

pines, by December 20, six weeks after the target-date for the invasion of Mindanao.[16] However, they did not commit themselves as to whether the next step after Leyte should be Formosa or Luzon. Although MacArthur pressed strongly for Luzon on political as well as strategic grounds, it was not until October 3, when events had transformed the outlook, that the question was decided in his favour.

Meanwhile Admiral Halsey, using the fast carriers which Nimitz put at his disposal to pave the way for MacArthur's advance to Mindanao and Nimitz's own projected seizure of the Palaus, made a series of attacks on Yap, the Palaus and Mindanao. Finding the opposition weak, he shifted the focus of his attention to the Central Philippines, but found that there, too, he was not much troubled by the enemy. Concluding that there were few Japanese aircraft in that neighbourhood he suggested to Nimitz on September 13 that MacArthur might speed up his advance by going straight to Leyte and leaving Mindanao to be mopped up later. Nimitz and MacArthur agreed, the proposal was discussed at the 'Octagon' Conference held at Quebec between September 12 and 16, and the Combined Chiefs of Staff gave their approval within an hour and a half of their first sight of the plan.[17]

Partly because the Americans were able to modify their programme with a promptness which would have been out of the question in any theatre less well stocked than the Pacific, but also for other reasons, the defence of the Philippines was a good deal less effective than the Japanese meant to make it. In the second week of October Admiral Halsey, with fifteen fast carriers, made a series of concentrated attacks on Formosa for the purpose of reducing Japanese air strength on the eve of MacArthur's assault on Leyte in the following week. The Japanese, concluding that the moment had come to strike a crushing blow at the much-feared fast carrier force, threw in every available aircraft but succeeded only in putting one American and one Australian heavy cruiser out of action and inflicting minor damage on three carriers. At the time, however, they believed that they had sunk two battleships and eleven carriers, and the mistake was not corrected until after the army section of the Imperial General Headquarters had reversed its policy of not committing the major part of its land forces until Luzon was invaded, and had issued orders to that effect.[18] Moreover, in two days of heavy fighting off Formosa the Japanese lost more than ten times as many aircraft as the Americans, whose pilots and air gunners were much better trained. As a result of the exaggerated claims made by Japanese airmen on those two days, and of the credence at first given to them, the Japanese Army was thus compelled, against its better judgment, to fight the decisive battle for the Philippines not in Luzon but on the cramped island of Leyte, and to do so at a moment when the land-based air forces on which it relied had just suffered a severe setback.

For his assault on Leyte, which marked the convergence of the two main thrusts in the Pacific, MacArthur was backed not only by his own Seventh Fleet under Admiral Kinkaid, but also by the fast carrier force, organized in four fast carrier groups which together formed, for the time being, the Third Fleet under Admiral Halsey. On land MacArthur had two corps of the United States Sixth Army under Lieutenant-General Walter Krueger. The Australian troops which had hitherto borne the brunt of the fighting in the South-West Pacific were to mop up the powerful remnant of the five or six Japanese divisions cut off in New Guinea, New Britain and the Solomons.

To defend the Philippines, the Japanese Army had ten divisions under Lieutenant-General T. Yamashita, who had been specially chosen for the task on the strength of his reputation as the conqueror of Malaya.[19] On the eve of the American landings on October 20, three of Yamashita's divisions were in Luzon and three in reserve. As Yamashita challenged the decision to fight the crucial battle on Leyte, and continued to challenge it until two days after the enemy began to come ashore, his remaining four divisions were not concentrated there but divided between Leyte, Mindanao, and the smaller islands of Panay, Negros and Cebu. Hence it was important that naval and air action should purchase a respite which might enable Yamashita to concentrate his forces and bring up his reserves. The chances of his gaining such a respite were not, however, very good. The greater part of the Combined Fleet, which had to come all the way from Singapore, did not start until October 18, and was not due to arrive until the early hours of October 25.

In its final form, the naval plan envisaged a series of all-out attacks by land-based aircraft on the American fleet and transports on October 24, followed on the next day by a major fleet action in the Leyte Gulf.[20] The First Striking Force from Singapore was to refuel at Brunei Bay, in North Borneo, on October 20, and would then split into two forces. The Centre Force, with five battleships, a dozen cruisers and fifteen destroyers under Vice-Admiral T. Kurita, was to enter the Leyte Gulf from the north at first light on October 25 after passing through the San Bernardino Strait, between Luzon and Samar.

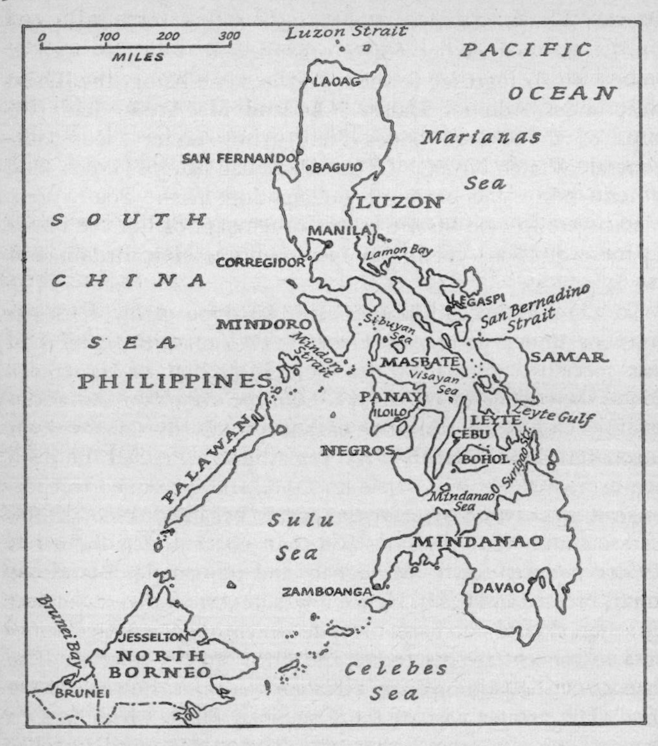

64 Leyte and the Battle of Leyte Gulf, October 1944

At the same moment the Southern Force, with two battleships, one heavy cruiser and four destroyers under Vice-Admiral S. Nishimura, was to enter the Leyte Gulf from the south after passing through the Surigao Strait, between Leyte and Mindanoa. In order to take advantage of the confusion which simultaneous attacks from opposite directions might be expected to produce, the weak Second Striking Force under Vice-Admiral K. Shima, with three cruisers and four destroyers, would then follow Nishimura through the Surigao Strait and make the most of its opportunities. Meanwhile Admiral

Ozawa's Northern Force, consisting of four carriers with 106 aircraft manned by half-trained crews, two converted carrier-battleships with no aircraft, and a screen of three light cruisers and eight destroyers, was to come south from Japan for the purpose of luring Halsey's fleet to the north while Kurita, Nishimura and Shima dealt with Kinkaid's fleet and with any American transports which they might find.

In the outcome, the attacks by land-based aircraft on October 24 failed disastrously. About two hundred naval aircraft from Luzon attacked Halsey's fast carrier groups; but most of them were intercepted, sixty-seven were destroyed, and apart from crippling one light carrier they achieved nothing. Most of Ozawa's carrier-borne aircraft also went into action against American carriers on that day. However, they sank no ships, and as nearly all of them were either shot down or went on to Luzon to refuel, the effect was to leave Ozawa with only thirty aircraft between his four carriers.

Meanwhile two American submarines had sighted the Centre Force north-west of Brunei Bay and had sunk two of its heavy cruisers and damaged a third so severely that it had to put back to Singapore. On receiving news of this occurrence Halsey sent three of his fast carrier groups to look for the rest of Kurita's force. The result was that Kurita was attacked throughout October 24 by Halsey's aircraft, lost one battleship sunk and one cruiser crippled, and was so much delayed that he had to warn Nishimura that he expected to reach the Leyte Gulf about seven hours late. Suspecting that Kurita might try to pass through the San Bernardino Strait that evening, Halsey expressed the intention of forming a task force of battleships and heavy cruisers to engage him at long range and destroy him.

At that point the luck changed. Misled by exaggerated reports from his airmen of the damage done to the Centre Force, Halsey came to the conclusion that, even if it did pass through the Strait, it would be far less dangerous to Kinkaid's ships than the Japanese carrier force, of which he had yet to receive news. When he sighted the Northern Force about four o'clock that afternoon, he swallowed the bait. Without pausing to form a task force to destroy Kurita, he made off with his whole fleet in pursuit of Ozawa's harmless carriers, leaving the San Bernardino Strait unguarded.

In the meantime some of Halsey's aircraft had engaged Nishimura's Southern Force on its way to the Surigao Strait, and Shima's Second Striking Force had also been seen heading more or less in that direction. Concluding that both forces were likely to attempt the passage of the Strait under cover of darkness, Kinkaid threw a screen of destroyers and light craft round his transports in the Leyte Gulf, and brought up six battleships, eight cruisers and twenty-eight destroyers of his bombardment and close support forces in addition to thirty-nine motor torpedo-boats. In the early hours of October 25 he took such heavy toll of the Southern Force that only one of its ships returned to base. Shima, following forty miles astern of the gallant but doomed Nishimura, held on for a while, but eventually turned back and escaped with the loss of one light cruiser.

Meanwhile in the north the departure of Halsey's fleet allowed Kurita, with four battleships, eight cruisers and eleven destroyers still intact, to pass unhindered through the San Bernardino Strait and turn towards the Leyte Gulf. Apart from destroyers and light craft, nothing barred his passage to the American transport anchorage except sixteen escort carriers disposed in three groups some thirty to fifty miles apart. Nevertheless he did not reach his destination. To all appearances hopelessly outmatched, the tiny carriers made such good use of their aircraft, and were so well served by their attendant destroyers, that after engaging them for two hours and sinking one carrier and three destroyers at the cost of two heavy cruisers so badly damaged that he had to sink them, Kurita turned away to reform his scattered fleet. Having done so, he resumed his course towards the Leyte Gulf, but three-quarters of an hour later changed his mind and made off to the north. In the meantime Halsey had sunk all four of Ozawa's almost defenceless carriers. Within a few hours all the surviving Japanese ships were homeward bound.

So ended the series of engagements which made up the

Battle of Leyte Gulf. All told, the Americans lost one light carrier, two escort carriers and three destroyers. The Japanese lost three battleships, four carriers, six heavy cruisers, three light cruisers and eight destroyers. With six battleships left but without a carrier force, their surface fleet was never again able to offer a serious challenge to the American fleet.

After their naval defeat the Japanese considered abandoning Leyte and concentrating on the defence of Luzon, but eventually decided to hold on.[21] They were able, at a heavy cost in transports and light naval craft, to raise the strength of the garrison from the original 15,000 to some 60,000 of all ranks. But by the beginning of November the United States Sixth Army had roughly 183,000 men ashore, so that the Japanese were still outnumbered by more than three to one. Making an unopposed landing on the west coast of the island, General Krueger succeeded on December 10 in capturing their chief port of supply at Ormoc, went on to take their only other port of any importance at Palompon, and by the end of the year was in possession of the whole island.

Weakened by his losses, Yamashita could spare only a handful of troops for the defence of Mindoro, which MacArthur captured with ease on December 15. Although driven to modify the organization of their carrier force and embark a higher proportion of fighters in order to reduce the danger from *Kamikaze* aircraft piloted by airmen willing to give their lives for a hit, the Americans went on to land the assault forces of two corps in Luzon on January 9.* By early February they were approaching the outskirts of Manila. In the meantime B29 bombers had begun to attack industrial targets in Japan from bases in the Marianas, and the Japanese merchant fleet was down to less than half its tonnage at the beginning of the war.

When the Yalta Conference assembled on February 4, 1945, Soviet participation in the war with Japan had become, therefore, less necessary from the point of view of the West-

**Kami Kaze* means 'Divine Wind'. The name appears to commemorate an incident in 1281, when a fleet sent by Khubilai Khan to invade the Japanese homeland was dispersed by a typhoon.

ern Allies than when Stalin's offer was first made in 1943. On the other hand, the Americans had yet to meet the major part of the Japanese Army, and the fanaticism with which the Japanese had defended their outlying possessions suggested that the cost of invading the Japanese homeland was likely to be very heavy. Concluding that, on balance, Soviet participation was still desirable and might save many lives, the Americans had already put a number of specific questions to the Russians, and at Yalta they went on to discuss terms. After a confidential interview between Roosevelt and Stalin, in which the British took no part, the American, British and Soviet leaders agreed that two or three months after the defeat of Germany the Soviet Union should enter the war against Japan on the side of the Allies.[22] In return she would receive substantial concessions at the expense of Japan and China. It was also agreed that the Chinese should not be consulted until after the agreement was signed. The strategic plan outlined by the Russians in the previous October and confirmed at Yalta was to attack with about sixty divisions, put pressure on the Japanese along the northern and eastern frontiers of Manchuria, and sweep down with a highly mobile force from Lake Baikal through Outer and Inner Mongolia to Peking and Tientsin.[23] A wedge would thus be driven between the Japanese forces in Manchuria and those in China.

The part which Britain should play in the last phase of the Far Eastern War was also discussed at some length on the eve of Yalta. Apart from the contribution made by Commonwealth forces in the South-West Pacific, the British were engaging in Burma many more divisions than the enemy could concentrate for the defence of any one of the islands attacked by Nimitz or MacArthur. But the American thrusts in the Pacific were, by definition and in fact, the main Allied effort against Japan, and the British government were not content that forces from the United Kingdom should make no substantial contribution to it. Churchill proposed at Quebec in September that a British fleet should be sent to the Pacific, and his offer was accepted in spite of objections from Admiral King, who feared that foreign warships would become a drag on his fleet train.[24]

Hoping to overcome the difficulty by devoting more than 300,000 tons of shipping to a vast fleet train of their own, the British planned to send ten carriers and four battleships to the Pacific by the following June, and the Australian government undertook to spend large sums on the development of Port Darwin as a naval base and on the dredging of its seaward approaches.[25] In addition the British proposed to station in the Pacific, when the war with Germany was over, a strategic bomber force of roughly a thousand heavy bombers and long-range fighters.

As a first instalment four fleet carriers, two battleships, three cruisers and ten destroyers reached Australian waters early in February 1945 after pausing on the way to attack Japanese oil refineries in Sumatra. By the end of the month most of the ships had arrived at a temporary base at Manus, in the Admiralty Islands. In March they took part, as an element of the United States Fifth Fleet, in attacks on the Ryukyu Islands as the prelude to American landings on Okinawa.

Like Iwojima in the Bonin Islands, which the Americans assaulted on February 19, Okinawa proved a hard nut to crack.[26] On both islands the Japanese had set up deep defensive systems, using dug-out positions as well as caves and tunnels where they came to hand, and were ready to die to the last man rather than give up. But Iwojima fell in March after a month-long struggle of extraordinary ferocity, and between April 1 and midsummer the Americans battered their way to victory on Okinawa at the cost of roughly 50,000 casualties. In the meantime the British were pushing forward in Burma, and at the beginning of May they took Rangoon.

Meanwhile the Japanese had reviewed their strategy in the light of their failure in the Philippines.[27] Other matters which caused them grave concern included a rising scale of air attack on their cities and centres of production, and an alarming shrinkage of their reserves of oil and other commodities. The last was an inevitable consequence of the attrition of their merchant fleet and the growing precariousness of their communications with sources of supply outside the homeland. Koiso and his colleagues concluded in January that they must prepare for a last-ditch stand in the hope that the Western Allies would offer reasonable terms rather than endure heavy losses. Such a stand would, however, be possible only if they found additional troops for home defence by calling up reservists and withdrawing officers and specialists from territories not immediately threatened. Besides accepting the need for such sacrifices, the government agreed to give exceptional priority to air defence.

The next few months brought some progress along these lines; but they also brought much else. Wherever Japanese troops were fighting the situation went from bad to worse; shipping losses mounted; air attacks grew heavier and the outlook on the home front gloomier. Discredited by the loss of Iwojima, the Koiso government resigned and was succeeded by a government headed by the veteran Admiral Kantara Suzuki, who adopted and extended his predecessor's policy of lessening the influence of the militarist party by concentrating effective power in the hands of a small Supreme War Council.[28] This consisted of the Prime Minister, the Foreign Minister, the Ministers of the Navy and the Army, and the Chiefs of Staff of the two armed services. At a secret meeting on June 18 the Supreme War Council agreed that, although they had no choice but to continue the war as long as the enemy insisted upon unconditional surrender, they should propose peace to the Western Allies through neutral Powers, especially the Soviet Union, and should try to obtain terms which would ensure the preservation of the monarchy.[29] Four days later the Emperor urged them in secret to find a way of ending the war.[30]

Meanwhile the Western Allies had learned from their experts that by the late summer they would almost certainly be in a position to use a few atomic bombs against Japan if they wished to do so.[31]

The atomic bomb was not an American invention, and the nuclear weapons produced during the Second World War were not unrestrictedly at the disposal of any one of the Allies. American-born scientists contributed to the researches which nade production of these weapons feasible, but their share s generally acknowledged to have been less important than he contributions made by scientists from Continental Eur- pe and the British Commonwealth. On the other hand, it is nore than probable that without American productive cap- city and technical skill, the Allies would not have succeeded n making an atomic bomb before the war was over. As it was, he United States government spent huge sums on the project. These sums were indeed so vast that, according to some well- laced commentators, the views of influential Americans as to vhether the atomic bomb should be used against Japan may vell have been coloured by the belief that awkward ques- ions might be asked by Congress if the American taxpayer aw no return for his involuntary investment.[32]

Before the war, scientists throughout the world knew that vork done in England by the New Zealander Ernest Ruther- ford suggested that one day nuclear energy might be harnessed or either peaceful or warlike purposes. They also knew that iis disciples J. D. Cockcroft and E. T. S. Walton had 'split he atom' experimentally in 1932, and that interesting con- ributions to the theory of nuclear physics had been made by hysicists and mathematicians in a number of European coun- ries. During the second and third decades of the twentieth entury much thought was given to the problem of pro- lucing a chain reaction; but until the eve of the war the pro- luction of nuclear weapons was widely regarded as a remote nd unattractive aim to which no scientist of repute would villingly lend himself. After Hitler's rise to power, how- ver, it was felt in Britain, and to some extent in Germany, hat German scientists might be induced by pressure of one ind or another to develop such weapons on his behalf, and hat the British would do well to forestall him even though hey had no intention of themselves using nuclear weapons nless the Germans used them or were known to be about o do so. Similar proposals were made to the United States overnment by refugee scientists, and eventually the British nd United States governments agreed to pool their resources n the understanding that neither country would use nuclear weapons against a third party without the consent of the other.[33] The two governments also agreed that they should draw on Canadian resources, and that, in the interests of security and because the Americans were willing to spend large sums on the venture, the development of nuclear devices for warlike purposes should be carried out largely in North America.

As time went on it became apparent that Germany was likely to be out of the war before nuclear bombing became a practical possibility. It followed that, if the atomic bombs which the Western Allies were developing ever came into service, they would be used not against Germany but against Japan, and would be dropped by very-long-range aircraft working from bases in the Pacific theatre. As the Pacific theatre was an American theatre, the decision to use atomic bombs on operational grounds would rest with the Americans, although the British would still have to be consulted in accordance with the undertaking given by the United States government in 1942 and reaffirmed at Quebec in 1943.[34]

As early as November 1944 Mr. Henry Stimson, the United States Secretary of War, set up a study group to consider how atomic bombs could best be used against Japan if the decision to use them were ever taken.[35] The training of American air-crew to drop such bombs began even earlier.[36] A British scientist, Dr. W. G. Penney, joined the study group as sole representative of the scientists who were working on the nuclear project at Los Alamos, in New Mexico. However, he was appointed not on account of his nationality, but because he happened to be the only scientist at Los Alamos who had studied the intelligence files relating to the layout of Japanese industry and its susceptibility to bomb-damage. In due course the group chose ten targets in Japan which seemed suitable and many months later their list was accepted, with modifications, by President Truman as Commander-in-Chief of the United States Armed Forces

It was not, however, until late in March that the scientists were able to say with any approach to certainty when the weapon was likely to be available for testing or operational use. The authorities on both sides of the Atlantic then learned that a few bombs would almost certainly be ready by the late summer. On April 30 Field-Marshal Maitland Wilson, Head of the British Joint Staff Mission in Washington, reported to London that the Americans were thinking of dropping a bomb some time in August, and asked for guidance as to how formal consent should be given.[37] In accordance with the British policy of leaving the management of the war in the Pacific to the Americans, the authorities in London appear not to have questioned Wilson's assumption that their response would be favourable and that all that remained to be done was to choose the right method of conveying it to the proper authority in Washington. On July 2 Wilson was instructed to record the concurrence of the British government at the next meeting of the Anglo-American Combined Policy Committee, and to add that the Prime Minister would doubtless wish to discuss the matter with the President at the conference due to begin at Potsdam on July 17.[38] The delay in answering Wilson's question about procedure seems to have been due to pressure of business arising from the German surrender rather than to doubts as to the wisdom of allowing the Americans to drop atomic bombs on Japan if they wished to do so.[39]

However, the Americans were not yet sure that they did wish to do so.[40] By July their aircraft were raining 40,000 tons of bombs a month on Japan;[41] the output of the Japanese aircraft industry was believed to have fallen to little more than half the peak attained in 1944;[42] and the two or three atomic bombs which the Western Allies might be able to drop in the late summer were thought unlikely to do as much damage as would result from another three or four months of orthodox bombing.[43] At the same time the Americans wished to avoid the heavy casualties which they must expect if they invaded the Japanese homeland. They were therefore anxious that the Japanese should surrender before November 1, which was the date fixed for the invasion.[44] On the assumption that she might surrender on terms but would not surrender unconditionally unless she had no choice, it seemed to follow that either the Japanese must be made to recognize before November 1 that their situation was hopeless, or the Western Allies must relax their demand for unconditional surrender.

At the beginning of July there were believed to be two ways, short of invasion, by which the Japanese might be brought to such a state of mind. One was the use of the atomic bomb as a 'psychological weapon'; the other was the entry of Soviet Russia into the war, which the Anglo-American Combined Intelligence Committee thought would be decisive.[45] As the State Department no longer wished the Russians to enter the war,[46] there was thus a strong, if superficial, case for the employment of the bomb as a means of inducing the Japanese to surrender quickly, and if possible before the Soviet Union declared war.

On the other hand, if the Allies were prepared to modify the unconditional surrender formula, there might be no need for either the atomic bomb or Russian intervention. The case for such a relaxation was forcefully put by Mr. Stimson on July 2. In a memorandum written after consultation with the Secretary of the Navy and the Acting Secretary of State, he recommended that the Japanese should be warned of the destruction which a fight to a finish would entail, but at the same time should be told that the Allies had no intention of depriving them of the means of existence or of permanently occupying their country. In addition, they might be told that there would be no objection to their continuing to live under a constitutional monarchy headed by the existing dynasty.[47]

However, in spite of the moderate and sensible tone of these proposals, it was implicit in Stimson's case that the bomb would be used if the warning were disregarded. An all-American Interim Policy Committee, set up with Stimson himself as Chairman to consider the political consequences of using the bomb, had recommended on June 1 that the bomb should be used against Japan 'as soon as possible' and that it should be aimed at a military objective surrounded by, or adjacent to, houses or other buildings.[48] The Committee also recommended that no prior warning of the nature of the weapon should be given, on the grounds that any such warning was unlikely to induce the Japanese to surrender, and would be inexpedient if the first bomb failed to explode.

Thus the gist of the advice which President Truman received up to July 16, when a test bomb was successfully exploded in New Mexico, was that nuclear bombing should be tried if the Japanese failed to surrender, but that first they should be given a chance of surrendering in the light of an assurance that surrender would not entail enslavement or oppression.

In the meantime the United States government had become aware that the unconditional surrender formula was regarded in high circles in Tokyo as practically the only obstacle to peace. While the President was on his way to Potsdam the authorities in Washington intercepted a signal from the Japanese Foreign Office to the Ambassador in Moscow, dated July 12, in which the Foreign Minister made it clear that he and the Emperor earnestly wished to end the war.[49] Further signals followed in the course of the next ten days or so. The Ambassador in Moscow did his best to persuade the Russians to act as mediators between Japan and the Western Allies, and at Potsdam Stalin spoke to Truman of the Japanese proposals, adding that the Soviet Foreign Office had given the Japanese Ambassador an evasive reply.[50]

In the light of this evidence of the state of mind of the Japanese government, and in the knowledge that Stalin expected to be ready to make war on Japan within the next few weeks, the Western Allies proceeded to draft the message of mingled warning and reassurance which Stimson had proposed to the President that they should send. They made it clear that their intention was not to enslave or destroy the Japanese nation, but that Japan would have to relinquish all her possessions except the homeland and such minor islands as they might allow her to keep; that she would be granted access to raw materials and eventually to world markets; and that unconditional surrender was to be taken as applying to the armed forces rather than the whole country.

However, after going to all the trouble of drawing up this

statement and sending it to Chungking for Chiang Kai-shek's approval,[51] the Allies did not wait to communicate it to the Japanese through a neutral intermediary in accordance with established procedure, but broadcast it by radio on the evening of July 26,[52] thus giving it the air of a mere declaration of war aims. The Japanese, who were hoping in spite of the unpromising attitude of the Soviet Foreign Office for a response to their Moscow proposals, received the text through their monitoring service,[53] studied it with interest, but came to the conclusion that they had better wait until they heard from the Allies before taking any action. When asked at a press conference on July 28 what the government meant to do about the Potsdam Declaration, Suzuki was understood to say that the government proposed to disregard it, although according to another interpretation his answer was that the government proposed to make no comment. The journalists reported him in the first sense, and the Allies heard nothing more before the Potsdam Conference broke up on August 2. On that day President Truman sanctioned the dropping of the two atomic bombs which had been delivered to the Twenty-first United States Army Air Force in the Central Pacific.[54] The first target on the list was Hiroshima, a major port and administrative centre with a population of rather more than a quarter of a million.

For some days the weather over Honshu was unsuitable for visual bombing; but on August 5 favourable forecasts were received. That evening the B29 chosen to carry the first bomb left Tinian in the Marianas to make rendezvous south of Kyushu with two similar aircraft carrying instruments and cameras before continuing its long flight to the target. The bomb was dropped at 8.15 a.m. on August 6, killed about 70,000 people,[55] and flattened buildings over a wide area.

The nature of the disaster at Hiroshima did not become clear to the Japanese government until August 7. The Emperor, the Prime Minister, the Foreign Minister and the Minister of the Navy then proposed immediate surrender, but could make no impression on the die-hard section of the government.[56] Meanwhile the Japanese Ambassador in Moscow was asked to

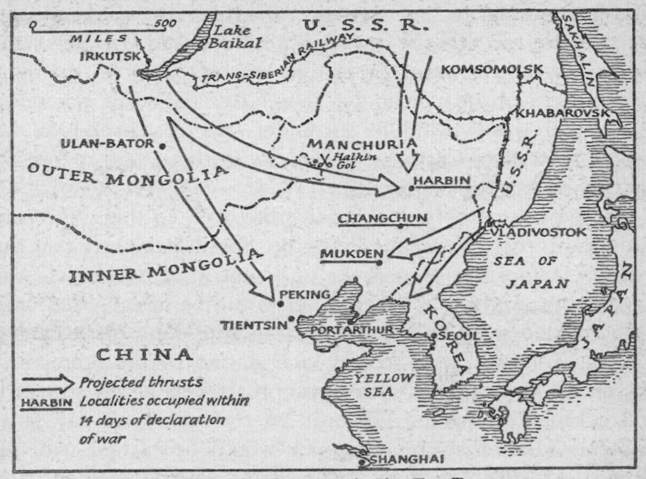

65 Soviet Strategy in the Far East

call on Molotov on the following day.[57] Receiving him at 5 p.m. on August 8, Molotov announced that Russia would be at war with Japan with effect from August 9. As it was already nearly midnight by Far Eastern time when the interview was over, only a few more hours elapsed before the Soviet forces in the Far East went into action on the lines discussed with the Americans.

About 9.15 a.m. on August 9 a B29 carrying the second and only remaining atomic bomb reached Kokura on the coast of Kyushu, made three unsuccessful runs over the target, and then went on to Nagasaki. After another bad run the crew dropped their bomb about four miles from the aiming-point, but scored a random hit on a built-up area.

For Suzuki August 9 began with a meeting of the Supreme War Council, continued with a meeting of the full Cabinet, and ended with an enlarged Supreme War Council still in session.[58] At all three meetings he urged his colleagues to accept the Potsdam Declaration without reservations, but found them unwilling to commit themselves. About 3 a.m. on August

10 he appealed to the Emperor to state his opinion. The Emperor replied that the war must end. The full Cabinet, summoned soon afterwards, approved unanimously of the Emperor's decision. Accordingly, soon after daybreak the news that Japan was willing to surrender was despatched to the United States and China by way of Switzerland, and to Britain and Russia by way of Sweden.

But even then the war was not quite over. In their reply the Americans insisted that the Emperor should make sure that the military authorities signed the instrument of surrender, but gave no guarantee that his position would be safeguarded once he had done so.[59] The sequel was another long tussle in the Cabinet, followed by a second intervention by the Emperor[60] But on August 14 the American proposals were at last accepted, and a broadcast by the Emperor on the following day satisfied the Allies that the surrender would be carried out. On August 27 ships of the United States Third Fleet and the British Pacific Fleet cast anchor in Tokyo Bay; on September 2 representatives of the Japanese government and armed services boarded the United States battleship *Missouri* to sign the instrument of surrender in the presence of Generals Wainwright and Percival, who had surrendered the Philippines and Singapore in 1942. As MacArthur insisted that the British should not land at Singapore or on the mainland of Malaya until the ceremony in Tokyo Bay was over, a formal close to hostilities in South-East Asia had to wait until September 12, when Mountbatten accepted at Singapore the surrender of all Japanese forces in his theatre.[61]

Thus ended the last phase of a world-wide struggle which brought death by violence to some twenty million people,[62] marked the eclipse of British naval and mercantile supremacy, and saw the emergence of the United States and Soviet Russia as two great arbiters of human destiny whose rivalries threatened to engulf mankind.

Appendices
Bibliography
Source Notes
Index

APPENDIX I

REPARATIONS, THE DAWES PLAN AND THE LOCARNO PACTS

Reparations and the Dawes Plan

The First World War left a massive legacy of internationl debts. At the end of the war Britain owed the United States about 4,500,000,000 dollars (or roughly £900,000,000 at par), and was owed more than twice as much by her European Allies. The British offered to forego the sums due to them if the Americans would do likewise; but the Americans rejected this proposal. Britain's financial relations with her European Allies and British indebtedness to the United States were, in the American view, two separate issues. The United States, it was pointed out, had entered the war not as an ally of France and Britain, but as an 'associated Power'.

The British then agreed to pay the United States £34,000,000 per annum for 62 years. About the same time they announced their intention of claiming no more from their European debtors than was needed to meet their obligations to the Americans. This announcement was deeply resented in the United States, where it was interpreted as an attempt to cast Uncle Sam for the role of Uncle Shylock.

There remained the problem of extracting from Germany the large sums which the Allies, and especially France, expected to receive by way of reparations. Towards the £6,600,000,000 which the Germans were asked in 1921 to pay in annual instalments of £100,000,000, they had paid by the end of 1922 only one instalment of £50,000,000, which they raised not from their own resources but by borrowing in London. They had, however, made a number of payments in kind by delivering coal from the Ruhr to France. This was uneconomic, for in normal circumstances it was cheaper to send French iron ore from Lorraine to the Ruhr to be smelted than to send German coal from the Ruhr to Lorraine.

At that stage the French decided, against British advice, to occupy the Ruhr in the hope of obtaining payment by establishing a lien on mines and factories. Early in 1923 French troops, accompanied by a small Belgian contingent and a number of Italian technicians, marched into the Ruhr. The Germans declared a general strike, and for some months not only refused to part with any of their gold but suspended deliveries of coal. Meanwhile the British condemned the action of the French government as a violation of the rights of Germany's creditors. Their policy was to restore good relations between France and Germany by encouraging the Germans to regain their self-respect and by urging them to make concessions which would enable the French to withdraw their troops without too much loss of self-esteem.

The outcome was that in the late summer of 1923 the Germans agreed, on British advice, to call off the strike and resume deliveries of coal as the prelude to withdrawal of the French and Belgian occupation forces. But meanwhile a headlong flight from the mark had eaten up the savings of small investors in Germany, and the franc had also suffered a setback in the world's money-markets. From one point of view the fall of the mark was, however not an unmixed disaster, since it wiped out Germany's internal debt and gave the German government a fresh start with a revalued currency.

Largely on the initiative of a group of British and American bankers and financiers, a committee under General Charles G. Dawes, a distinguished American soldier, was appointed in the following year to study the problem of reparations in the light of the new situation. As a result the Germans agreed to make annual payments on a scale rising from £50,000,000 in 1924 to £125,000,000 in 1929. Provision was, however, made to vary the instalments in accordance with Germany's capacity to pay, and to suspend payment if in any year the Germans could not find the money without risking a second inflation. Thus it became difficult to predict the date when the debt would be extinguished.

At the same time Germany raised in London and New York huge loans which were followed by an influx of capital from private investors. Some of the money went to provide backing for the new currency or was used to pay instalments under the Dawes Plan. The rest provided German industrialists with the means of raising their output well above the pre-war level in spite of the surrender of important centres of production under the Treaty of Versailles.

As the result of a marked improvement in Germany's relations with her former enemies during the next few years, the veteran statesman Gustav Stresemann was able to obtain substantial concessions from the Allies, particularly in regard to the occupation of the Rhineland. In 1929 he extracted from them a promise to start withdrawing their armies of occupation about five years ahead of the date contemplated in the Versailles Treaty. In return, he agreed that the Dawes Plan should be replaced by a new arrangement whose details were settled by a committee headed by another American, Owen Young. Under the Young Plan Germany's liability for reparations was reduced to £2,000,000,000, and provision was made to extinguish the debt in 59 years. These terms were not particularly onerous in comparison with those accepted by other nations which owed money; but one effect of the negotiations was that some Germans became aware for the first time that the generation which had plunged Europe into war in 1914 would have passed away before the account was settled. Consequently the Nationalist Alfred Hugenberg and the National Socialist Adolf Hitler, who joined forces to oppose the Young Plan, were able to whip up a good deal of popular indignation in Germany, although they could not prevent the Reichstag from endorsing Stresemann's acceptance of the plan.

However, a few years later it became clear that the world-wide slump which followed the collapse of the New York stock-market in 1929 had made the settlement of international debts on a large scale virtually impossible. In 1931 the American President Herbert Hoover suggested that all such payments should be suspended for twelve months. In the following year the Allies agreed to waive their claims under the Young Plan in return for a final token payment. The token payment was never made, but the Allies did not press the matter. Thus reparations lapsed after the Allies had received only a fraction of the sum which they had once counted on receiving.

The Locarno Pacts

One effect of the failure of the French to settle the reparations problem by occupying the Ruhr in 1923 was that in 1924 Raymond Poincaré, the chauvinistic Prime Minister who stood for a policy of relentless pressure on Germany, fell from office. This was satisfactory to the British, who aimed at a reconciliation between France and Germany as the first step towards a general European settlement.

Between 1923 and 1925 a policy of friendship with France was strongly recommended to the Germans at first by Ramsay MacDonald, who doubled the post of Prime Minister and Foreign Secretary in the first Socialist government to rule in Britain, and later by Sir Austen Chamberlain, Foreign Secretary in the Conservative government which succeeded MacDonald's. Gustav Stresemann, at times Foreign Minister and at times Chancellor, showed every sign of regarding this advice as sound, though his motives in seeking agreement with France were questioned in some quarters after his death in 1929.

At first the French, suspecting that Stresemann's aim was to detach them from their European allies, were unresponsive. But they found in Aristide Briand a Foreign Minister who believed that agreement with Germany was possible. The outcome was that in the autumn of 1925 Briand, Chamberlain and Stresemann, accompanied by representatives of Belgium, Czechoslovakia, Italy and Poland, met by the waters of a Swiss lake to conclude the 'peace of understanding' which had eluded the peacemakers of 1919. After a series of conferences it was agreed that the existing frontier between France and Germany should be regarded as permanent, and that its integrity should be guaranteed by an undertaking which pledged Britain and Italy (but not the British Dominions) to go to the aid of a victim of aggression. On the other hand Germany did not bind herself to seek no adjustment of her eastern frontiers. She did, however, agree not to seek any such adjustment by recourse to war, and to refer to arbitration any dispute between herself and Czechoslovakia or Poland.

In marked contrast to the ill-fated proceedings at Versailles some six years earlier, the negotiations which led to these conclusions were conducted in an atmosphere of great cordiality. At Locarno French and German delegates met without embarrassment for almost the first time since the war. They shook hands or embraced each other; compliments were paid and visits exchanged. Impartial commentators noticed, too, that at Locarno German journalists were no longer cold-shouldered by French colleagues, and that some friendships sundered in 1914 were renewed. Even if Stresemann's motives were mixed, there was evidence at Locarno of a sincere desire on both sides to bury the hatchet of Franco-German discord.

The Locarno pacts, which included formal treaties between France and Germany, Czechoslovakia and Germany, and Germany and Poland, were followed by renewed ties between the coal-owners of the Ruhr and the iron-masters of Lorraine, and after an interval by Germany's admission to the League of Nations. A chastened Poincaré returned to power in 1926, but Briand remained Foreign Minister and continued to work for good relations between France and Germany.

However, the goodwill engendered at Locarno did not last. In 1927 the French, alarmed by Germany's growing industrial potential and not content to rely for their security on British and Italian guarantees, began building the Maginot Line along their frontier from Switzerland to Belgium. At a moment of crisis in 1931 they refused to waive the clause in the Versailles Treaty which forbade Germany to seek a way out of her economic troubles by forming a customs union with Austria, or to back the threatened mark except on their own terms. In 1934 the Germans, who had already made it clear that they meant to rearm, withdrew from the Disarmament Conference and the League of Nations. Finally, in 1936 Hitler pulled down the cornerstone of the Locarno pacts by sending troops into the demilitarized Rhineland zone. This move was represented in Germany as a protest against harsh terms imposed by the Allies on a beaten enemy in 1919. In fact it was a flagrant breach of the freely-negotiated Franco-German Treaty of 1925, which Hitler denounced as his troops were entering the Rhineland. The ban on remilitarization of the zone had been reaffirmed at Locarno without dissent from the German delegates, who indeed had welcomed the renewed ban because it gave Germany an indisputable right to invoke the British and Italian guarantees if the French crossed the frontier without provocation.

APPENDIX II

THE WASHINGTON TREATIES AND THEIR BACKGROUND

In the second half of the nineteenth century Japan was forced by pressure from more powerfully armed countries, and especially the United States, to open her ports to foreign ships and enter into relations with the leading mercantile nations. She responded by reforming her system of government and providing herself with a conscript army and a navy organized on European lines. At a time when the need to feed and clothe an expanding population might in any case have compelled her to look abroad for markets and raw materials, she thus became well placed to succeed China as the dominant Power in the Far East.

In 1894 an insurrection broke out in Korea. The Chinese, who had agreed in 1885 that neither they nor the Japanese should intervene in Korea without prior consultation, sent a small force to help the government to restore order. The Japanese, alleging that the Chinese had broken the agreement of 1885 and seemed determined to treat Korea as a vassal State, thereupon declared war on China and soundly defeated her in a series of battles on land and sea.

Under the Treaty of Shimonoseki, which ended the Korean war, Japan received Formosa, the Pescadores, and a large indemnity. She was also to have received a tract of territory in Southern Manchuria, but Russia, backed by France and Germany, compelled her by diplomatic pressure to renounce it, and herself obtained from China substantial concessions in Manchuria, including a lease of the south-western extremity of the Liaotung Peninsula and the right to use Port Arthur as a base for her Far Eastern fleet.

Thus an important consequence of the Korean war was that the Russians, although not parties to the Sino-Japanese dispute, were able to extend their power and influence in the Far East without firing a shot, while the Japanese gained fewer benefits from their victory than they expected. Furthermore, not only Russia but also France, Germany and Britain succeeded after the Korean war in improving their positions in the Far East by exerting pressure on the moribund Chinese Empire. At the same time the United States, by vigorously upholding a British proposal that relations with China should be governed by the principle of equal treatment for all, implicitly rejected the Japanese claim to a special position on the Asiatic mainland.

In 1902 Japan, fearing that Russia's next step might be to annex Korea, concluded with Britain a pact of mutual assistance which was to take effect if either country became involved in a war to protect Chinese or Korean interests and was attacked by an outside party. In 1905 the pact was replaced by an alliance which provided for immediate co-operation in the event of an unprovoked threat to British or Japanese interests in India or Eastern Asia; and in 1911 the alliance was renewed with the addition of a clause intended by the British to ensure that Britain would never be called upon to support Japan by fighting the United States. The British intention was, however, defeated by the unexpected refusal of the United States to conclude the treaty or arbitration which would have made the saving clause effective. From the European point of view, the most important consequence of the Anglo-Japanese alliance was that it enabled the British to reduce their naval strength in the Far East to a cruiser force, and that this helped them to concentrate in home waters the strong fleet needed to offset the growth of the German Navy.

Meanwhile the Japanese pressed the Russians for an undertaking not to exclude them from markets in Manchuria, but could obtain no satisfaction. In 1904 they broke off negotiations, blockaded the greater part of the Russian Far Eastern fleet at Port Arthur, and went on to take Port Arthur from the landward side and drive the Russians from Mukden with heavy losses. Largely on American advice, they then concluded at Portsmouth, in New Hampshire, a peace treaty which pledged Japan and Russia to respect Chinese sovereignty in Manchuria, and which compelled the Russians to renounce their claims to Port Arthur, the Kurile Islands and Southern Sakhalin. Korea became a Japanese protectorate and was afterwards annexed by Japan.

Thereafter alarmists predicted that the Japanese, elated by success, would one day conquer the West by infiltration. In the meantime a number of Japanese had settled in California, and for a time relations between Japan and the United States became uneasy as the result of a decision by the American authorities to segregate the children of such settlers in special schools. In 1908, however, President Theodore Roosevelt obtained from Japan an informal promise not to flood the United States with immigrants. This understanding remained in force until, some seventeen years later, the United States put the matter on a different footing by closing the door to settlers of Asiatic origin.

Japan entered the First World War on the side of the Anglo-

French alliance, seized German possessions and concessions in the Far East and the Pacific, and made useful contributions to the defence of ocean trade. However, at the end of 1914 and early in 1915 she alarmed the Great Powers by presenting the insecure Chinese Republic with demands which, had they been fully met, would have given Japan a commanding position in China. Diplomatic representations induced the Japanese to modify some of their demands and couch others in terms less obnoxious to China; but Japan did not disguise her intention of claiming a substantial reward for her help to the Western Powers, and in due course the Treaty of Versailles awarded her the former German concession in Shantung. This decision was unfavourably received in the United States, and President Woodrow Wilson's acquiescence in it was partly responsible for his fall from power.

In addition, Japan received League of Nations mandates which gave her administrative control of the former German possessions in the Caroline and Marshall Islands and the islands of the Mariana group other than Guam. Similar mandates gave New Guinea and the Bismarck Archipelago to Australia; Samoa to New Zealand; and Nauru to the United Kingdom, Australia and New Zealand as joint trustees. The United States accepted no mandates, but retained her possessions in the Philippines, the Hawaiian Islands and the islands of Guam and Wake.

In the meantime the United States, alarmed by the growing power of Japan and her own dependence on the Royal Navy to safeguard her ocean trade, had begun a programme of naval construction which challenged Britain's worldwide supremacy at sea. Before entering the war she pressed for a definition of contraband which would allow neutrals to supply belligerents with almost everything except arms and ammunition; and even when taking part in a rigorous blockade of Germany she urged the nations to adopt the principle of the Freedom of the Seas. During the pre-armistice negotiations in 1918 the British insisted, however, that consideration of any such formula must await a full discussion of its implications, and a reservation to that effect was written into the pre-armistice agreement between Germany and the Allied and Associated Powers. When American spokesmen revived the issue at the Paris Conference, the British again succeeded in postponing it. They recognized, however, that the United States was no longer content that Britannia should rule the waves.

Against this background, and in the light of indications that within three or four years the United States would become the world's strongest naval power unless British programmes were accelerated, the

British government proceeded in the winter of 1920-21 to frame a new naval policy. Not wishing to embark on a crippling armaments race but unwilling to surrender the maritime supremacy without which the country would have suffered starvation and defeat in the recent war, they appointed a Capital Ship Sub-Committee of the Committee of Imperial Defence to consider whether control of the trade routes on which the British Isles depended for their livelihood could be secured by means short of an expensive programme of capital-ship construction which would compete directly with the American programme. When the Sub-Committee reported that such relatively cheap weapons as submarines and aircraft were not effective substitutes for battleships and battlecruisers, they came to the conclusion that the United Kingdom, with half the population of the United States, could not hope to match the American effort, and that their best course was to purchase American goodwill, if necessary by sacrificing the Japanese alliance. At the same time they recognized that the Japanese had proved valuable allies, and at least some members of the government believed that Britain might be able to remain on good terms with both countries.

The sequel was that Britain accepted an invitation to attend a disarmament conference at Washington in November 1921, and that a naval treaty between the British Commonwealth, the United States, Japan, France and Italy was signed on February 6, 1922. Its main provisions were:

Capital ships

a Total tonnage not to exceed:

Great Britain	525,000 tons
United States	525,000 tons
Japan	315,000 tons
France	175,000 tons
Italy	175,000 tons

b No ship built as a replacement to exceed 35,000 tons.

Aircraft Carriers

a Totals in roughly the same proportions as for capital ships.

b No ship built as a replacement to exceed 27,000 tons.

Other Warships

a No restrictions on numbers or total tonnage.

b No ship to exceed 10,000 tons.

c No ship to carry guns of a greater calibre than eight inches.

Fortifications and Bases

a Great Britain to establish no new fortifications or naval bases, or extend existing facilities, in Hong Kong or any of her insular possessions east of a line through Hainan and the western tip of Borneo, except in the neighbourhood of the coasts of Canada, Australia and New Zealand.

b The United States to establish no new fortifications or naval bases, or extend existing facilities, in her insular possessions in the Pacific, except in the neighbourhood of the coasts of the United States, Alaska (but not the Aleutians), the Panama Canal Zone and Hawaii.

c Japan to establish no new fortifications or naval bases, or extend existing facilities, in her insular territories and possessions in the Pacific.

The last provision debarred Japan from building or extending bases in the Kurile and Bonin Islands, the Ryukyu Islands, Formosa and the Pescadores, but did not apply to the Japanese homeland in the islands of Kyushu, Shikoku, Honshu and Hokkaido and the small islands immediately adjacent to them. Fortification of mandated territories was not expressly forbidden by the treaty since it was in any case ruled out by the terms of the mandates. Nothing in the treaty, however, deprived signatories of the right to maintain existing facilities in a reasonable state of efficiency by replacing worn-out equipment.

The Washington Naval Treaty was accompanied by a Four-Power Treaty in which the British Commonwealth, the United States, Japan and France agreed to preserve the *status quo* in the Pacific, refer any dispute between them to a joint conference, and make common cause should any of them be threatened by an outside Power; and by a Nine-Power Treaty in which Belgium, the British Commonwealth, France, Holland, Italy, Japan, Portugal and the United States undertook to respect the sovereignty, rights, interests and integrity of China.

Thus Japan accepted a position of marked naval inferiority in relation to the English-speaking Powers, while Britain agreed, in effect, to share command of the sea with the United States. Japan also relinquished her special position in Shantung and agreed, after some debate, that China should buy the Shantung Railway on equitable terms. On the other hand, Britain received an assurance that the United States would not build against her as long as the naval treaty remained in force, while Japan retained her hold on islands which lay astride American communications with the Philippines, although she could not fortify them without openly challenging the rule of international law.

In the outcome a tacit agreement between Britain and the United States to share command of the sea did not prove an effective substitute for the *Pax Britannica.* No machinery was set up by which the two countries could co-ordinate their naval strategies, and no provision was made to enforce the Four-Power Treaty by recourse to war or the threat of war. The United States did not follow up her moral victory at Washington by joining the League of Nations, her diplomatic success did nothing to lessen her distrust of the Old World, and within a few years her foreign and economic policies became more isolationist than ever. As for the Nine-Power Treaty, its cardinal weakness was that the signatories, no matter how sincere they were or how good their intentions may have been, were not in a position to provide China with the strong, stable, and independent government which would, in the long run, alone have been capable of securing the benefits promised in the treaty.

APPENDIX III

MUNICH: THE MILITARY ASPECT

The Naval Situation

A *Germany.* In the autumn of 1938 Germany had very few heavy ships, no aircraft carriers, and only the rudiments of an air striking force trained and equipped for maritime war. The plans of the German Naval Staff were based on the assumption that the country would not be involved in a major war much before 1944.

Under the terms of the Anglo-German Naval Agreement, Germany was entitled to build up to 35 per cent of British tonnage in surface ships and, in certain circumstances, up to 100 per cent in submarines.

B *Italy.* The Italian Navy was in good shape, was fairly well supplied with fuel, and was capable of presenting a substantial threat to British and French interests in the Mediterranean. In other respects, however, Italy was in no state to go to war.

C *Germany's potential enemies.* When orders were given to the Royal Navy to mobilize at the height of the Godesberg crisis in September 1938, the British and French fleets in European waters were numerically superior to the German Navy in warships of every category from the largest to the smallest, submarines included.

In general, the French Navy was in a high state of readiness and had excellent bases. British ports and harbours needed some preparation for war, such as the laying of anti-submarine and anti-boat booms, and the state of the fixed defences at most defended ports at home and abroad was unsatisfactory. In addition, time was needed to prepare trawlers for minesweeping, and the naval harbours at Dover and Harwich, as well as much of the berthing-space at Rosyth, were silted up. Even so, on balance the British and French navies were in a better state to go to war with Germany than the German Navy was to go to war with France and Britain.

The Situation on Land

A *Germany.* According to plans current about the middle of September 1938 the German Army would, in the event of war with Czechoslovakia, have attacked the Czechs with some 39 divisions out of a total of 55 divisions expected to be available on mobilization. Hitler was said by the Italian Foreign Minister, Count Ciano, to have told Mussolini on the way to the Munich Conference that 40 German divisions were 'immobilized' by the need to watch the Czechs, but to have added that, if war did come, he would be able to defeat Czechoslovakia in a lightning campaign and then move divisions to the West. The German General Staff, on the other hand, believed that the conquest of Czechoslovakia would take at least three months and that their 15 to 16 divisions in the West might well crumble in three weeks if the French attacked them in the meantime.

B *Italy.* The Italian Army was in no position to make a substantial contribution to an attack on Czechoslovakia or to do more in the West than defend the frontier.

C *Germany's potential enemies.* The mobilizable strength of the Czechoslovakian Army in September 1938 was estimated at 1,500,000 officers and men organized in some 30 to 40 divisions or their equivalent in fortress formations.

The French were believed to be capable of mobilizing at least sixty divisions.

The number of divisions which the British Army could send across the Channel within thirty to forty days of mobilization would not have exceeded two.

The Air Situation

A *Germany.* The strength of the Luftwaffe on September 26, 1938, was as follows:

	AIRCRAFT			OPERATIONAL CREWS		
	Establishment	*Strength*	*Serviceable*	*Total*	*Fully Trained*	*Partly Trained*
Bombers	1,220	1,128	1,040	1,171	744	427
Dive-bombers	235	226	220	251	118	133
Ground-attack	195	195	182	192	185	7
Fighters	985	773	738	883	705	178

Long-range reconnaissance	228	222	206	212	145	61
Short-range reconnaissance	303	291	270	311	184	127
Coastal	180	164	149	138	74	64
	3,346	2,999	2,805	3,158	2,155	997
Transport	362	308	299	357	289	67

Nothing is known of any plans to use these machines for attacks on France or Britain. The general intention of the Supreme Command was that, in the event of war with Czechoslovakia, the Luftwaffe should co-operate with the army by attacking both tactical and strategic objectives.

On the defensive side, the tendency in Germany was to rely on anti-aircraft guns for home defence and to regard fighter aircraft chiefly as a means of gaining ascendancy over the battlefield. Partly for that reason, partly because the long-term plans to which the Luftwaffe was working in 1938 did not envisage a general war before 1942, Germany had no system of air defence comparable with that which existed in Britain.

Germany's output of military aircraft of all types and categories was of the order of 400 to 500 a month, as compared with roughly 700 a month in the autumn of 1939.

B *Italy.* In the event of war with France and Britain, the Regi[illegible] Aeronautica would have been in a position to undertake small-scal[illegible] attacks on British and French bases in the Central and Eastern Medi[illegible]terranean and perhaps on objectives in France; but the Italians had los[illegible] their technical lead by 1938, and Italy was herself vulnerable to ai[illegible] attack.

C *Germany's potential enemies.* Britain, Czechoslovakia and Franc[illegible] all had small air striking forces, generally inferior in organization an[illegible] readiness for war to Germany's. In Britain there was some confusion a[illegible] to the true role of the bomber, and arrangements for the interpretatio[illegible] of air photographs were rudimentary.

On the defensive side, Czechoslovakia was vulnerable because he[illegible] vital centres were within easy reach of the frontier and because th[illegible] Czechs had no radar. France had few fighters, few anti-aircraft gun[illegible] and a poor early-warning system. Britain had an air defence system which was potentially strong, but incomplete. The following were some of the deficiencies revealed by the crisis:

Early-Warning System: a chain of about twenty radar stations was intended to cover the approaches to the United Kingdom between the Firth of Forth and the Isle of Wight. The stations in service in 1938 covered only the stretch between the Wash and Dungeness, and even there modifications were needed to fill gaps. Special equipment to detect low-flying aircraft had yet to be installed.

Control System: communication between ground and air was by high-frequency radio, much inferior to the very-high-frequency radio installed in 1939 and the early part of 1940. Landline communications between the various components of the air defence system were incomplete and had to be supplemented by overhead cables which were insecure and liable to severance by sabotage or bombing.

Fighter Aircraft: in the summer of 1937 the Committee of Imperial Defence had agreed that not less than 45 fighter squadrons were needed for home defence. The number of squadrons that could be mobilized in September 1938 was 29. Twenty-four of these were equipped with obsolete or obsolescent aircraft, only five with Hurricanes and none with Spitfires. The Hurricanes were armed with guns which, until modified, could not be relied upon to work properly at altitudes above 15,000 feet. There were no stored reserves of fighter aircraft; immediate reserves with squadrons or in workshops amounted to roughly two-fifths of first-line strength.

Anti-Aircraft Artillery and Searchlights: in 1937 the Committee of Imperial Defence had agreed that, in addition to a number of light anti-aircraft weapons still to be determined, 1,264 heavy guns and 4,700 searchlights would be needed in time of war to defend London, the industrial North and Midlands, and such outlying areas as the Clyde, the Forth and Bristol. About four hundred guns and rather more than a thousand searchlights were available in September 1938, but most of the guns were modified examples of a 3-inch gun which had been in service since the end of the First World War. They were due for replacement by 3.7-inch and 4.5-inch guns of recent design, but only about fifty 3.7-inch and no 4.5-inch guns were ready.

The Balloon Barrage: the London Balloon Barrage was intended as a deterrent to low-flying aircraft. It had an establishment of 450 balloons, but only 142 balloons were ready for deployment at the time of the crisis. The provision of barrages elsewhere was under consideration.

Passive Air Defence: more thought had been given to passive air defence in Britain than in any Continental country, Germany not excepted. An Air Raid Precautions Sub-Committee of the Committee of Imperial Defence had held its first meeting in 1924; the foundations of a highly-efficient emergency fire service had been laid in 1937; and close attention had been paid to the problem of removing children and 'useless mouths' from densely-populated areas. At the time of the Godesberg crisis thirty-five million gas-masks were distributed to the public, a far-reaching system of public warnings was brought to readiness, and trenches were dug in parks and other open spaces to provide blast-proof and splinter-proof shelter for people caught away from their homes or places of work. In addition public authorities, employers and householders were shown how parts of buildings could be transformed into refuges reasonably secure against anything short of a direct hit or a near miss.

At the time the value of these precautions was widely underestimated. Members of the public, unaware that the measures proposed by the authorities were the fruit of many years of patient work behind the scenes, were inclined to regard them as improvisations designed to save the government's face, and in some cases they were encouraged to do so by publicists eager to discredit political opponents by asserting that deep shelters ought to have been provided for the entire population. Airmen concerned to further a particular view of strategy also tended to undermine confidence in defensive measures by overstating the case for the bomber arm. The result was that, in the absence of reliable objective data regarding the effectiveness of bombing, neither ordinary members of the public nor supposedly well-informed statesmen had the means of forming a true estimate of the dangers of air attack.

The General Situation

In the autumn of 1938 the British and French governments had no reason to suppose that, in the event of war with Germany and Italy their forces on land and sea would prove weaker than the enemy's. Indeed, it is now clear that, if they had fulfilled their obligations to the Czechs and had been able to mobilize before Czechoslovakia was defeated, they would have had a big margin of superiority in the West as long as the Czechs held out. Even without Czechoslovakia, the would have had approximate numerical equality on land and a substantial measure of superiority at sea.

On the other hand, the Axis Powers were known to possess substantial air forces, and Germany and Italy were governed by men who made a parade of ruthlessness. In the absence of any reliable forecast of the part which air power would play in a future war, this factor made it difficult for British and French statesmen to assess the consequences of challenging Hitler to do his worst. Estimates made by their air advisers were largely conjectural, but they had to be taken at their face value since no one was in a position to assert that the Air Staffs did not know their business.

We now know that some of these estimates were ludicrously wrong. In Britain a good deal of planning about the time of Munich was based on the assumption that the Luftwaffe, working from bases in Germany and presumably under the stress of simultaneous war with Britain, Czechoslovakia and France, might be able to drop 600 tons of bombs a day on the United Kingdom for weeks on end. This was about three times the daily weight of bombs which German airmen were in fact able to drop in the autumn and early winter of 1940, when they were working from aerodromes only just across the Channel. Moreover, Britain had become in 1940 Germany's only active enemy, and the Luftwaffe was much stronger than in 1938.

Again, it was believed in 1938 that the Germans might be able to kill nearly sixty thousand people in the first twenty-four hours of an all-out air offensive by dropping 3,500 tons of bombs on London within that brief period. Yet, when they did launch an all-out air offensive on London on September 7, 1940, admittedly after many weeks of strain, they dropped less than 700 tons in the first twenty-four hours and killed fewer than a thousand people. To drop 3,500 tons of bombs on the United Kingdom within twenty-four hours in the autumn of 1938, the whole of the German long-range bomber force, with all its crews both fully trained and partly trained, would have had to make the round trip three times in swift succession. Moreover, they would have had to do so at a time when 39 German divisions on the Czechoslovakian front would presumably have been clamouring for air support to enable them to defeat some 30 to 40 Czech divisions and break through the strong Czechoslovakian fortress line.

APPENDIX IV

GERMAN, FRENCH AND BRITISH MILITARY RESOURCES ON THE OUTBREAK OF WAR

Land Forces

German. The German Army, with 52 divisions of Regular troops, mobilized 88 infantry, 6 armoured, 4 light mechanized, 4 motorized and 3 mountain divisions, besides fortress and frontier troops. Of the total of 105 divisions, 33 were on the Western Front when France and Britain declared war, but the figure rose to 46 or 47 by the end of the third week in September.

The armoured, light and motorized divisions were highly mobile, the remainder largely dependent on horse-drawn or mule-drawn transport.

In general, the German Army of 1939 was somewhat deficient in artillery, but it had the compensating benefit of powerful and well-organized air support.

The German tanks in service on the outbreak of war were lightly armed and poorly armoured, but could go comparatively long distances without refuelling and were fairly fast.

French. Starting with 45 'active' divisions, the French mobilized 81 infantry, 3 cavalry and 2 light mechanized divisions, in addition to 7 cavalry brigades, 2 armoured brigades and the equivalent of 13 or more divisions of garrison troops. A force equivalent to about 60 divisions was available for the main front after provision had been made for overseas territories and for the risk of a surprise attack by the Italians.

In general, the French Army was organized and equipped for a defensive role. It relied for its mobility largely on a widespread and well-organized network of railways.

The French were well supplied with field and siege artillery, but were deficient in air support. Partly because of a lag in production which had its source in political and industrial unrest, their air force was rather small and not very well equipped. Their air defences were meagre, their system of allocating air support to formations in the field proved unsatisfactory, and they were unable, for reasons discussed elsewhere, to obtain from the British as much help in the air as they hoped to get.

The French tanks were slow and had a limited radius of action, but were well armed and thickly armoured.

British. The British had expected until the spring of 1939 that their main contributions to a war in Europe would be made at sea and in the air. Nominally the British Army had a mobilizable strength of 6 Regular and 26 Territorial divisions, apart from garrisons overseas; but only 4 Regular and no Territorial divisions were expected to be ready (and in fact were ready) for despatch to France within the first five weeks. These divisions, and others which followed later, were well equipped with transport and artillery at the expense of the forces left at home.

In the Middle East the British had 1 incomplete armoured division, the headquarters of 2 infantry divisions, and about 20 battalions of combatant troops with supporing arms.

The Indian Army, consisting of long-term professional soldiers under British and Indian officers, provided a valuable reserve of trained troops for service in the Middle and Far East.

Naval Forces

German. The most powerful ships in the German Navy on the outbreak of war were the *Scharnhorst* and *Gneisenau*, classed by the Germans as battleships but regarded by the British as battlecruisers because of their high speed and relatively light armament. They were capable of 31 knots in favourable conditions, were armed with 11-inch guns, and displaced about 32,000 tons.

In addition the Germans had the two old battleships *Schleswig-Holstein* and *Schlesien*; but these were unsuitable for use outside the Baltic and were not effective fighting ships for the purpose of the present comparison.

The pocket battleships *Deutschland*, *Admiral Graf Spee* and *Admiral Scheer* were essentially commerce-raiders.

Besides these the Germans had the heavy cruiser *Admiral Hipper*, 5 light cruisers, 17 destroyers and 56 submarines. Ten of the submarines were, however, not fully operational when the war began.

Ships under construction or refitting included the battleships *Bismarck* and *Tirpitz*, the aircraft carrier *Graf Zeppelin*, the heavy cruisers

Blücher, Prinz Eugen and *Seydlitz*, and the light cruiser *Karlsruhe*. A further heavy cruiser was under construction, but was delivered to the Russian Navy in 1940 under the terms of the Moscow Pact.

French. French warships fully effective and in commission on the outbreak of war included the modern battlecruisers *Dunkerque* and *Strasbourg* and three older battleships; 1 aircraft carrier; 15 cruisers; 32 large and 43 or 44 smaller destroyers; and 59 submarines. Two modern battleships, the *Jean Bart* and *Richelieu*, were approaching completion and were expected to go into service in 1940.

British. The British began the war with 2 modern and 8 older battleships; 1 modern and 1 older battlecruiser; 6 aircraft carriers; 58 cruisers; 100 fleet destroyers and 101 escort destroyers and sloops; and 38 submarines. Two battleships were refitting, a third battlecruiser was refitting but about to return to service, and 5 battleships, 6 aircraft carriers and 19 cruisers were under construction. British naval forces in Home Waters on the eve of the war included 9 capital ships, 4 aircraft carriers, 19 cruisers and 96 destroyers.

Summary

The following table summarizes the foregoing figures.

GERMAN, FRENCH, BRITISH AND TOTAL ALLIED NAVAL FORCES ON THE OUTBREAK OF WAR

(Ships fully effective and in commission only)

	German	*French*	*British*	*Allied totals*
Battleships	—	3	10	13
Battlecruisers	2	2	2	4
Pocket Battleships	3	—	—	—
Aircraft carriers	—	1	6	7
Cruisers	6	15	58	73
Destroyers and sloops	17	75	201	276
Submarines	46	59	38	97

AIR FORCES

German, French and British

The first-line strengths of the Luftwaffe and the French and British metropolitan air forces on the outbreak of war were as follows:

	Luftwaffe	*French MAF*	*British MAF*
Bombers	1,180	186	536
Dive-bombers	366	—	—
Ground-attack aircraft	40	—	—
Fighters	1,179	549	608
Reconnaissance aircraft	844	377	516
Totals	3,609	1,112	1,660

Of the Luftwaffe's 3,609 first-line aircraft, about 1,600 were committed to the campaign in Poland, so that roughly 2,000 remained for other purposes. The British had, in addition to their 1,660 first-line aircraft at home, 415 overseas, giving a grand total of 2,075 aircraft. The French, too, had a number of squadrons overseas, but these were equipped largely with obsolete or obsolescent aircraft.

In point of equipment there was little to choose between the Luftwaffe and the Royal Air Force; but the Luftwaffe was organized as an army support weapon, and the British metropolitan air force was not. The French metropolitan air force had always been intended to support an army in the field, but in 1939 it was weak in numbers, organization and equipment.

APPENDIX V

JAPAN'S LAST ATTEMPT TO AVERT WAR IN 1941

I. *Summary of Japanese Proposals for Interim Agreement*

(Plan 'B' as modified on November 20, 1941)

1 Japan and United States to make no armed advance in South-East Asia or Pacific area outside Indo-China.
2 Japan to withdraw troops from South Indo-China to North Indo-China on conclusion of interim agreement, and from whole of Indo-China on conclusion of peace with China or other equitable settlement.
3 Japan and United States to co-operate in obtaining from Netherlands East Indies such commodities as each might need.
4 United States to remove embargo on trade with Japan and supply required quantity of oil.
5 United States not to put obstacles in way of peace between Japan and China.

II. *Summary of American Draft Proposals for Interim Agreement*

(The *Modus vivendi* proposals as shown to Australian, Chinese, Dutch and United Kingdom representatives on November 22, 1941)

1 Japanese and United States forces not to cross any international frontier unless attacked.
2 Japan to withdraw armed forces from South Indo-China and reduce forces in Indo-China as a whole to 25,000 men.
3 United States to receive all Japanese imports, with proviso that two-thirds of total in any month should be raw silk, and to export goods to Japan, including food, medical supplies, raw cotton, and oil for civilian use.
4 United States to invite Australian, Dutch and United Kingdom governments to make similar concessions.
5 United States not to oppose negotiated peace between Japan and China, and to provide facilities for peace conference in Philippines if asked to do so.

6 Interim agreement to remain in force for three months unless extended.

III. *The Course of the Negotiations.*

1 On November 20 Admiral Nomura and M. Kurusu, having advised the Japanese government that their proposals for a permanent settlement (Plan 'A') were not likely to be accepted, were instructed to put forward proposals for an interim settlement (Plan 'B'), with modifications in favour of the United States which the civil government and the military authorities had agreed earlier in the month to make if the need arose.

2 On November 22 the American Secretary of State, Mr. Cordell Hull, communicated the Japanese proposals for an interim settlement to the British and Chinese Ambassadors and the Australian and Dutch Ministers. He also showed them the draft of a reply which embodied the *Modus vivendi* proposals. They undertook to ask for instructions from their respective governments.

3 On November 24 President Roosevelt incorporated the substance of both the modified Plan 'B' proposals and the *Modus vivendi* proposals in a private message to Mr. Churchill, adding that the American draft seemed a fair proposition for the Japanese but that its acceptance or rejection was likely to be a matter of Japanese internal politics, and that he was not very hopeful.

4 On the same day Mr. Cordell Hull summoned the Australian, Chinese, Dutch and United Kingdom representatives to a further meeting. The Dutch Minister thereupon approved of the *Modus vivendi* proposals; the Chinese Ambassador thought that his government was unlikely to accept them; the Australian and United representatives were still awaiting instructions.

5 On November 25, or at the latest by the early hours of November 26, the United States government received, in addition to the expected message of dissent from the Chinese government, both a communication from the British Foreign Office and Churchill's answer to President Roosevelt's message of November 24. The substance of the British messages was that the Prime Minister and his colleagues were reluctant to see Japan appeased at the expense of China but wished to avoid war with Japan and trusted the President and State Department to conduct the negotiations in their own way.

6 On November 26 Mr. Cordell Hull handed the President a memorandum in which he recorded the opposition of the Chinese gov-

ernment to the *Modus vivendi* proposals and stated that the Australian, Dutch and United Kingdom governments, apparently not understanding the vast importance and value of the proposals, were either actively opposed to them or luke-warm about them. He added that, in his view, all proposals for an interim agreement with Japan should now be dropped.

7 That afternoon the United States government presented to the Japanese envoys a ten-point programme for a final settlement. Among the terms proposed were the withdrawal of all Japanese forces from China and Indo-China.

8 On November 27 a Japanese Liaison Conference, composed of representatives of Imperial General Headquarters and the civil government, agreed that, in view of the unrelenting attitude of the United States, Japan had no choice but to fight. Nevertheless discussions continued on November 28 and 29.

9 On December 1 the Japanese Imperial Conference, attended by the Emperor, formally ratified the decision reached on November 27.

10 On December 7 the Japanese Embassy in Washington received the last instalment of a long message from Tokyo rehearsing the Japanese case and breaking off negotiations with the United States. Admiral Nomura and M. Kurusu were instructed to deliver the message at 1 p.m., but were unable to hand the text to the Secretary of State until 2.30 p.m. By that time the American authorities had intercepted and decoded the message, and hostilities had begun in Malaya and at Pearl Harbor.

APPENDIX VI

THE ORGANIZATION AND COMPOSITION OF LAND FORCES

Higher Organization

During the Second World War the land forces of the Western Powers, in theatres where major campaigns were in progress on land, were organized in army groups, each comprising two or more armies and General Headquarters troops or their equivalent. Each army consisted of army troops and two or more corps, each corps of corps troops and two or more divisions. To these were added troops under the direct control of the force commander, or of higher authorities such as the German Supreme Command of the Armed Forces (OKW).

In the Japanese Army there was no corps organization. Armies, generally of not less than two and not more than five divisions, were grouped in area armies subordinated in most cases to regional commands. For example, at the height of the Far Eastern war Lieutenant-General R. Mutaguchi, commanding the Fifteenth Army in Burma, was responsible to the Burma Area Army (Lieutenant-General M. Kawabe), which received its orders from a command known to Allied intelligence officers as the Southern Army (Field-Marshal Count H. Terauchi).

In the Red Army, army groups were known as 'fronts', and the term 'corps' was applied to armoured and mechanized formations of approximately divisional strength.

The 'Administrative Tail'

The strength of land forces was commonly assessed in terms of divisions. However, in practice all self-contained expeditionary and field forces in theatres where large-scale land operations were in progress consisted partly of troops organized in divisions, partly of troops not organized in divisions. Furthermore, every such force included a substantial number of units whose function in normal circumstances was not to fight, but to provide services or perform administrative tasks. A low ratio of fighting troops to total strength was sometimes frowned upon by statesmen preoccupied with manpower problems, but was not necessarily a sign of inefficiency or a source of weakness. A force with relatively few troops in the line and a big administrative tail might well be superior in fighting value to one with more fighting troops but with poor base facilities, a weak staff and inadequate arrangements for supply and maintenance.

A further complication arises from the fact that every division which formed part of an expeditionary force carried both a visible tail in the shape of its own non-fighting units, and a hidden tail consisting of its share of the non-divisional troops needed to maintain the force in the field. It will be seen below that in 1944 and 1945 the ration strengths of British divisions in the North-West European theatre were higher in each case than those of corresponding American formations, although an American infantry division was built, like a British infantry division, round a core of nine infantry battalions. But the number of troops which had to be transported to North-West Europe for each division of the Allied Expeditionary Forces sent there in 1944 and 1945 was much the same in the American component of the land forces as in the British one.

In the British Army the term 'divisional slice' was used to denote the number of troops ultimately present in a theatre for each division sent there. In the case just cited the figure for both the American and British components was of the order of 40,000 of all ranks. This was more than twice the average strength of a division.

Strength and Composition of Major Formations

As we have seen, army groups, armies and corps (in the Western sense) were of no fixed size. Divisions, on the other hand, conformed as a rule with fixed establishments; but these establishments differed not only from belligerent to belligerent and from one kind of division to another, but also from time to time. The following generalizations apply, except where the contrary is stated or implied, to the last two years of the war.

1. *Infantry Divisions.* In all armies an infantry division was built, as the name implies, round a substantial body of infantry, often organized in three brigades or regiments. For example, in 1944 the core of a British infantry division consisted of three infantry brigades, each of three battalions about 900 strong, in addition to a reconnaissance

regiment and a machine-gun battalion. Similarly, an American infantry division contained three infantry regiments, also of three battalions each. Again, most German infantry divisions contained three infantry regiments, although in 1944 these usually contributed only two battalions each instead of the orthodox three.

The addition of artillery, engineer, signals, supply and transport, medical, ordnance, workshop and provost units brought the total strength of a British infantry division to approximately 18,000 of all ranks. The corresponding figures in other armies were:

German infantry division (1944)	12,500
Russian rifle division	14,000
United States infantry division	14,000

The establishments of Japanese field divisions varied, but again three regiments of infantry was the standard number, and roughly 18,000 of all ranks seems to have been regarded as the optimum size for a division serving overseas.

The establishment of a Chinese division was approximately 12,000 officers and other ranks; but in practice few Chinese divisions, other than those trained and equipped by the Western Allies in India, had much more than half their nominal strength.

When Italy entered the war Italian divisions, although not very well equipped, were comparable in size with those of the other leading belligerents. After the early part of 1941, however, the Italian forces in North Africa were usually so short of troops that establishment figures became almost meaningless. In January 1942 the average strength of five infantry divisions and two armoured or mechanized divisions in Tripolitania was only about 3,600 officers and other ranks.

Scales of equipment differed widely, not only with respect to such items as rifles, carbines, machine-guns, mortars, field guns, anti-tank guns and anti-aircraft guns, but still more with respect to transport. Broadly, the situation in Europe in 1944 and 1945 was that British and United States infantry divisions, each with upwards of three thousand mechanically-propelled vehicles, were either fully mobile or able to move in one lift with assistance from corps transport; that Russian rifle divisions employed in an offensive role were also well supplied with cars and lorries; but that German infantry divisions, each with about 600 motor vehicles and tractors and some 1,450 horse-drawn vehicles, could scarcely hope to extricate themselves from awkward situations unless their retreat was covered by armoured or mechanized formations. In South-East Asia and the Pacific Japanese divisions, operating largely in territories with poor communications, were equipped not on fixed scales but according to needs and the weapons and vehicles available.

When divisional establishments are compared it must, however, be remembered that there were marked differences, as between one belligerent and another, in the extent to which divisions could count on support from air forces and from artillery not borne on divisional strengths. Even towards the end of the war German infantry divisions were not hopelessly inferior in firepower to their Russian counterparts; but by 1943 the Soviet Supreme Command had accumulated, outside divisions, such large reserves of medium and heavy guns that Russian army commanders were able to dominate the sectors chosen for attack. Similarly, the Anglo-American landings and breakout in Normandy in 1944 would have been extremely difficult without air superiority.

11. *Armoured Divisions.* Experience in North-West Europe and North Africa early in the war showed conclusively that an armoured division or equivalent formation needed not only an adequate number of well-armed, well-armoured and mechanically reliable tanks to enable it to take possession of the battlefield, but also a strong infantry component and a powerful array of artillery to enable it to consolidate gains and withstand counter-attack.

Accordingly, attempts were made by all the leading belligerents to attain what each judged to be the optimum balance between armour, infantry and supporting arms.

In 1944 the armoured component of a British armoured division consisted of an armoured reconnaissance regiment and an armoured brigade of three armoured regiments and one motor battalion, with 246 cruiser and 44 light tanks. These were complemented by an infantry brigade of three battalions, an independent machine-gun company, and four artillery regiments, the whole with 1,398 machine-guns, 468 mortars and anti-tank projectors, 48 field guns, 78 anti-tank guns and 141 anti-aircraft guns. Ancillary units, including engineers, gave a total strength of roughly 15,000 of all ranks.

An American armoured division, with 270 tanks, 36 field guns and approximately 11,000 officers and other ranks, was constructed according to the same principle of balance, although it was smaller.

The establishment of German armoured divisions was not standardized. However, in 1944 a typical Panzer division contained two armoured battalions and four infantry battalions, with roughly 160 to 180 tanks, upwards of 200 guns of all types and calibres, and approximately 14,750 officers and other ranks. SS Panzer divisions were larger, with six or more infantry battalions but approximately the same number of tanks.

A Russian tank corps comprised three tank brigades and one motorized rifle brigade, with about 230 armoured fighting vehicles, including self-propelled guns designed as tank-destroyers.

There were no Chinese or Japanese armoured divisions, and the Italian armoured division of 1940 to 1943 were not comparable with the Allied and German armoured divisions of 1944 and 1945.

III. *Other Major Formations.* In the early stages of the war the Germans made considerable use of mechanized divisions consisting essentially of lorried infantry with supporting arms. Later, Panzer Grenadier divisions were introduced. These had no tanks, but each was equipped with 45 self-propelled guns in addition to some 2,800 other mechanically-propelled vehicles. Strengths were about the same as for armoured divisions.

A Russian mechanized corps comprised three motor brigades and one tank brigade, with supporting arms. Its allotment of armoured fighting vehicles was roughly the same as that of a tank corps, but the proportion of tanks to self-propelled guns was reversed.

A mountain division consisted essentially of infantry supported by pack-artillery suitable for employment in difficult country with few roads and steep gradients. In theory, such divisions were composed of troops recruited in mountainous districts and trained to move across snow, ice, or broken ground. In practice, such rigid selection was not always possible.

Airborne divisions figured, at one time or another, in the plans of most of the leading belligerents. The Germans, however, made no use of large airborne formations after narrowly escaping disaster at Crete in 1941, and the Russians seem not to have used airborne formations larger than brigades, although they gave much thought to the problem of grouping their brigades in divisions or equivalent formations. The Americans and the British, on the other hand, not only formed airborne divisions but used them in their intended role in 1944.

A British airborne division was composed of two parachute brigades and an air-landing brigade, each of three battalions, in addition to an airborne reconnaissance regiment and airborne artillery, engineer and other ancillary units. It had an establishment of slightly more than 12,000 officers and other ranks, with more than 1,700 vehicles and a wide assortment of infantry and artillery weapons, including anti-tank guns and anti-aircraft guns. American airborne divisions were broadly similar, but their strength was rather less than 9,000 of all ranks.

The German airborne corps which took Crete was about 13,000 strong and comprised an assault regiment and three parachute regiments, each of three battalions, in addition to supporting and ancillary units. It was supplemented by elements of a mountain division carried in transport aircraft.

Minor Formations of All Arms

Practically all the belligerents made use, from time to time, of self-contained formations of less than divisional strength. Examples were the British brigade group, consisting of an armoured or infantry brigade with supporting arms, and the *ad hoc* groups formed by the Germans on various fronts to meet special situations. As part of the artillery in an American infantry division was borne on regimental strengths, the American system readily lent itself to the creation of regimental combat teams which filled a similar role.

BIBLIOGRAPHY

A comprehensive list of books about the Second World War would fill a volume. The short list given here includes only (a) books cited as sources in footnotes or the notes below; (b) a selection of books consulted for background or corroborative detail; (c) a few books somewhat arbitrarily chosen from the many to which readers may refer for additional detail or a different outlook or interpretation.

AMRINE, MICHAEL. *The Great Decision.* London, 1960.

ANDERS, GENERAL W. *Katyn.* Paris, 1949.

ANDERSON, O. E. See Hewlett, R. G.

ASSMAN, (VICE-ADMIRAL) KURT. *Deutsche Schicksalsjahre.* Wiesbaden, 1950.

AVON, THE EARL OF. *The Eden Memoirs: Facing the Dictators.* London, 1962.

BARNETT, CORRELLI. *The Desert Generals.* London, 1960.

BEHRENS, (MISS) C. B. A. *Merchant Shipping and the Demands of War* (History of the Second World War, United Kingdom Civil Series). London, 1955.

BELOFF, MAX. *The Foreign Policy of Soviet Russia, 1929-1941.* 2 vols. London, 1947-1949.

Soviet Policy in the Far East,1944-1951. London, 1953.

BENNET, H. G. *Why Singapore Fell.* Sydney, 1944.

BLACKETT, P. M. S. *The Military and Political Consequences of Atomic Energy.* London, 1952.

BLAKE, ROBERT. *The Unknown Prime Minister.* London, 1955.

BLUMENTRITT, (GENERAL) GUENTHER. *von Rundstedt, The Soldier and the Man.* London, 1952.

BRADLEY, GENERAL OMAR H. *A Soldier's Story.* London, 1951.

BROCH, THEODOR. *The Mountains Wait.* London, 1943.

BROOK-SHEPHERD, GORDON. *Anschluss, The Rape of Austria.* London, 1963.

BRYANT, ARTHUR. *The Turn of the Tide.* London, 1957.

Triumph in the West. London, 1959.

BUCKLEY, CHRISTOPHER. *Norway—The Commandos—Dieppe.* London, 1952.

BULLITT, WILLIAM C. *The Great Globe Itself*. New York, 1947.

BULLOCK, ALAN. *Hitler, A study in Tyranny*. London, 1952.

BUNDY, MCGEORGE. See Stimson, H. L.

BUTCHER, CAPTAIN HARRY C. *My Three Years with Eisenhower*. London, 1946.

BUTLER, J. R. M. *Grand Strategy Volume II* (History of the Second World War, United Kingdom Military Series). London, 1957.

Grand Strategy Volume III Part II (History of the Second World War, United Kingdom Military Series). London, 1964.

BUTOW, ROBERT J. C. *Japan's Decision to Surrender*. Stanford University Press, 1954.

BYRNES, JAMES F. *Speaking Frankly*. London, 1947.

CARELL, PAUL. *Hitler's War on Russia*. London, 1964.

CARTON DE WIART, (MAJOR-GENERAL) A. *Happy Odyssey*. London, 1950.

CHENNAULT, (MAJOR-GENERAL) C. L. *The Way of a Fighter*. New York, 1949.

CHURCHILL, WINSTON S. *The Second World War*. 6 vols. London, 1948-1954.

CLARK, ALAN. *Barbarossa: the Russian-German Conflict, 1941-1945*. London, 1965.

CLARK, R.W. *The Birth of the Bomb*. London, 1961.

CLARKE, BRIGADIER DUDLEY. *Seven Assignments*. London, 1948.

COAKLEY, R. W. See Leighton, R.M.

COLE, HUBERT. *Laval, a Biography*. London, 1963.

COLLIER, BASIL. *The Defence of the United Kingdom* (History of the Second World War, United Kingdom Military Series). London, 1957.

The Battle of Britain. London, 1962.

The Battle of the V-Weapons, 1944-1945. London, 1964.

COLVIN, IAN. *Chief of Intelligence*. London, 1951.

CONNELL, JOHN. *Auchinleck*. London, 1959.

CONRAD, R. *Kampf um den Kaukasus*. Munich, 1955.

CUNNINGHAM OF HYNDHOPE, THE VISCOUNT. *A Sailor's Odyssey*. London, 1951.

DALLIN, A. *German Rule in Russia, 1941-1945*. London, 1957.

DAVIES, J. *Mission to Moscow*. London, 1942.

DAVIN, D. M. *Crete*. Wellington, 1953.

DEAKIN, F. W. *The Brutal Friendship*. London, 1962.

DEANE, (MAJOR-GENERAL) JOHN R. *The Strange Alliance*. New York, 1947.

DEMPSTER, DEREK. See Wood, Derek.

DERRY, T. K. *The Campaign in Norway* (History of the Second World War, United Kingdom Military Series). London, 1952.

DEXTER, DAVID. *The New Guinea Offensives.* Canberra, 1961.

DIBOLD, HANS. *Doctor at Stalingrad.* London, 1958.

DONITZ, ADMIRAL KARL. *Memoirs.* London, 1959.

DULLES, ALLEN W. *Germany's Underground.* New York, 1947.

DUROSELLE, JEAN-BAPTISTE. *From Wilson to Roosevelt: Foreign Policy of the United States, 1913-1945.* London, 1964.

EHRMAN, JOHN. *Grand Strategy Volume V* and *Grand Strategy Volume VI* (History of the Second World War, United Kingdom Military Series). Both London, 1956.

EISENHOWER, GENERAL OF THE ARMY DWIGHT D. *Crusade in Europe.* London, 1958.

ELLIS, MAJOR L. F. *The War in France and Flanders, 1939-1940* (History of the Second World War, United Kingdom Military Series). London, 1954.

Victory in the West (History of the Second World War, United Kingdom Military Series). 2 vols. Volume I, London, 1962.

ERICKSON, J. *The Soviet High Command, 1918-1945.* London, 1962.

FEILING, KEITH. *The Life of Neville Chamberlain.* London, 1947.

FEIS, H. *The Road to Pearl Harbor.* Princeton, 1950.

The China Tangle. Princeton, 1953.

Churchill, Roosevelt, Stalin. Princeton, 1957.

FERGUSSON, BERNARD. *Beyond the Chindwin.* London, 1945.

FLANDIN, PIERRE-ÉTIENNE. *Politique française, 1919-1940.* Paris, 1948.

FLEMING, PETER. *Invasion 1940.* London, 1957.

FRANCOIS-PONCET, ANDRÉ. *The Fateful Years.* London, 1949.

FRANKLAND, N. See Webster, Sir Charles.

FULLER, GENERAL J. F. C. *The Second World War.* London, 1948.

GAFENCU, GRIGORE. *The Last Days of Europe.* London, 1947.

GALLAND, (LIEUTENANT-GENERAL) ADOLF. *The First and the Last.* London, 1955.

GAMELIN, GENERAL MAURICE. *Servir.* Paris, 1946.

GAULLE, (GENERAL) CHARLES DE. *War Memoirs.* London, 1954.

AVIN, LIEUTENANT-GENERAL JAMES M. *War and Peace in the Space Age.* London, 1959.

EORGE, DAVID LLOYD. *The Truth about Reparations and War Debts.* London, 1932.

ILBERT, MARTIN, AND GOTT, RICHARD. *The Appeasers.* London, 1963.

GLEASON, S. E. See Langer, W. L.

GORLITZ, WALTER. *Der Zweite Weltkrieg.* Stuttgart, 1951.
Paulus and Stalingrad. London, 1963.
The Memoirs of Field-Marshal Keitel. London, 1965.
GOTT, RICHARD. See Gilbert, Martin.
GOUTARD, COLONEL A. *The Battle of France, 1940.* London, 1958.
GOWING, M. M. See Hancock, W. K.
GREINER, HELMUTH. *Die Oberste Wehrmachtführung.* Wiesbaden, 1951.
GREW, J. C. *Ten Years in Japan.* New York, 1964.
GRINNELL-MILNE, DUNCAN. *The Silent Victory.* London, 1958.
GROVES, LIEUTENANT-GENERAL LESLIE R. *Now It Can Be Told.* New York, 1962.
GUDERIAN, (GENERAL) H. *Panzer Leader.* London, 1952.
GUINGAND, MAJOR-GENERAL F. DE. *Operation Victory.* London, 1947.
GWYER, J. M. A. *Grand Strategy Volume III Part I* (History of the Second World War, United Kingdom Military Series). London, 1964.
HALDER, (GENERAL) FRANZ. *Hitler als Feldherr.* Munich, 1949.
HALIFAX, THE EARL OF. *Fullness of Days.* London, 1957.
HALL, H. DUNCAN. *North American Supply* (History of the Second World War, United Kingdom Civil Series). London, 1955.
HANCOCK, W. K., AND GOWING, M. M. *British War Economy* (History of the Second World War, United Kingdom Civil Series). London, 1949.
HARRIS, MARSHAL OF THE R.A.F. SIR ARTHUR. *Bomber Offensive.* London, 1947.
HART, CAPTAIN B. H. LIDDELL. *The Other Side of the Hill.* London, 1951.
(Editor) *The Rommel Papers.* London, 1953.
HASSELL, U. VON. *The von Hassell Diaries.* London, 1948.
HEIM, F. See Philippi, A.
HENDERSON, SIR NEVILE. *Failure of a Mission.* London, 1940.
HERRIOT, EDOUARD. *Jadis.* Paris, 1952.
HEWLETT, A. G., AND ANDERSON, O. E. *The New World, 1939-1943* Pennsylvania State University Press, 1962.
HEYDTE, BARON VON DER. *Daedalus Returned.* London, 1958.
HINSLEY, F. H. *Hitler's Strategy.* London, 1951.
HITLER, ADOLF. *My Struggle (Mein Kampf).* London, 1939.
HOARE, SIR SAMUEL. See Templewood, Viscount.
HOUSE, EDWARD MANDELL, AND SEYMOUR, CHARLES (Editors). *What Really Happened at Paris.* London, 1921.

HULL, CORDELL. *The Memoirs of Cordell Hull.* 2 vols. London, 1948.

ISMAY, LORD. *The Memoirs of Lord Ismay.* London, 1960.

JACOBSEN, H.-A., AND ROHWER, J. (Editors). *Decisive Battles of World War II: the German View.* London, 1965.

JONES, F. C. *Japan's New Order in East Asia.* London, 1954.

JOUBERT DE LA FERTÉ, AIR CHIEF MARSHAL SIR PHILIP. *Birds and Fishes: The story of Coastal Command.* London, 1960.

JUNGK, ROBERT. *Brighter than a Thousand Suns.* London, 1958.

KASE, TOSHIKAZU. *Eclipse of the Rising Sun.* London, 1951.
(Also published as *Journey to the Missouri.* New Haven, 1950.)

KEITEL, FIELD-MARSHAL WILHELM. See Görlitz, Walter.

KENNEDY, GENERAL SIR JOHN. *The Business of War.* London, 1957.

KENNEY, GEORGE C. *General Kenney Reports.* New York, 1949.

KEYNES, J. M. *The Economic Consequences of the Peace.* London, 1919.

KIRBY, MAJOR-GENERAL S. WOODBURN. *The War Against Japan* (History of the Second World War, United Kingdom Military Series). 5 vols., 4 published. London, 1957-65.

KIRKPATRICK, SIR IVONE. *The Inner Circle.* London, 1959.

KNATCHBULL-HUGESSEN, SIR HUGHE. *Diplomat in Peace and War.* London, 1949.

LANGER, W. L. *Our Vichy Gamble.* New York, 1947.

LANGER, W. L. AND GLEASON, S. E. *The Challenge to Isolation, 1937-1940.* New York, 1952.
The Undeclared War, 1940-1941. London, 1953.

LEAHY, FLEET ADMIRAL W. D. *I Was There.* New York, 1950.

LEIGHTON, R. M. AND COAKLEY, R. W. *Global Logistics and Strategy, 1940-1943.* Washington, 1955.

LONG, GAVIN. *To Benghazi.* Canberra, 1952.
Greece, Crete and Syria. Canberra, 1953.

LOSSBERG, GENERALMAJOR BERNHARD VON. *Im Wehrmachtführungsstab.* Hamburg, 1949.

LYTTELTON, OLIVER (VISCOUNT CHANDOS). *The Memoirs of Lord Chandos.* London, 1962.

MCCARTHY, D. *South-West Pacific Area, First Year.* Canberra, 1959.

MCKEE, ALEXANDER. *Strike from the Sky.* London, 1960.

MACKIEWICZ, JOSEPH. *The Katyn Wood Murders.* London, 1951.

MACLEOD, IAIN. *Neville Chamberlain.* London, 1961.

MACLEOD, RODERICK, AND KELLY, DENIS (Editors). *The Ironside Diaries.* London, 1962.

MAJDALANY, FRED. *Cassino: Portrait of a Battle.* London, 1959.

MAISKY, I. *Who Helped Hitler?* London, 1964.
MANNERHEIM, MARSHAL. *The Memoirs of Marshal Mannerheim.* London, 1953.
MANSTEIN, FIELD-MARSHAL ERICH VON. *Lost Victories.* London, 1958.
MARTIENSSEN, ANTHONY. *Hitler and His Admirals.* London, 1948.
MATLOFF, MAURICE, AND SNELL, E. M. *Strategic Planning for Coalition Warfare.* Washington, 1953.
MAUND, (REAR-ADMIRAL) L. E. H. *Assault from the Sea.* London, 1949.
MEDLICOTT, W. N. *The Economic Blockade.* (History of the Second World War, United Kingdom Civil Series). London, 1959.
MERRIAM, ROBERT E. *The Battle of the Ardennes.* London, 1958.
MIDDLETON, DREW. *The Sky Suspended.* London, 1960.
MILLIS, WALTER (Editor). *The Forrestal Diaries.* London, 1952.
MILNER, S. *Victory in Papua.* Washington, 1947.
MONTGOMERY OF ALAMEIN, FIELD-MARSHAL THE VISCOUNT. *Normandy to the Baltic.* London, 1947.
El Alamein to the River Sangro. London, 1948.
The Memoirs of Field-Marshal the Viscount Montgomery of Alamein, K.G. London, 1958.
MOOREHEAD, ALAN. *African Trilogy.* London, 1944.
MORISON, SAMUEL ELIOT. *The Battle of the Atlantic.* Boston, 1946.
The History of United States Naval Operations in World War II. 15 vols. Boston, 1947-1962.
The Two-Ocean War. Boston, 1963.
MORTON, LOUIS. *The Fall of the Philippines.* Washington, 1953.
MUGGERIDGE, MALCOLM (Editor). *Ciano's Diary.* London, 1947.
Ciano's Diplomatic Papers. London, 1948.
NAMIER, L. B. *Diplomatic Prelude, 1938-1939.* London, 1948.
Europe in Decay. London, 1950.
In the Nazi Era. London, 1952.
NICOLSON, HAROLD. *Peacemaking, 1919.* London, 1933.
Curzon, The Last Phase. London, 1934.
NORWICH, VISCOUNT. *Old Men Forget.* London, 1953.
O'BRIEN, TERENCE H. *Civil Defence* (History of the Second World War, United Kingdom Civil Series). London, 1955.
PAPAGOS, GENERAL ALEXANDROS. *The Battle of Greece, 1940-1941.* In English, Athens, 1949.
PAPEN, F. VON. *Memoirs.* London, 1952.
PERCIVAL, LIEUTENANT-GENERAL A. E. *The War in Malaya.* London, 1949.

PHILIPPI, A., UND HEIM, F. *Der Feldzug gegen Sowjetrussland.* Stuttgart, 1962.
PLAYFAIR, MAJOR-GENERAL I. S. O. *The Mediterranean and Middle East* (History of the Second World War, United Kingdom Military Series). 6 vols., 4 published. London, 1956-.
POSTAN, M. M. *British War Production* (History of the Second World War, United Kingdom Civil Series). London, 1952.
PRITTIE, TERENCE. *Germans against Hitler.* London, 1964.
RENTZ, JOHN N. *Bougainville and the Northern Solomons.* Washington, 1948.
Marines in the Central Solomons. Washington, 1952.
REYNAUD, PAUL. *La France a sauvé l'Europe.* Paris, 1947.
RITTER, GERHARD. *The German Resistance.* London, 1958.
ROHWER, J. See Jacobsen, H.-A.
ROOSEVELT, ELLIOT. *As He Saw It.* New York, 1946.
ROSKILL, CAPTAIN S. W. *The War at Sea* (History of the Second World War, United Kingdom Military Series). 3 vols. in 4 parts. London, 1956-1961.
The Navy at War, 1939-1945. London, 1960.
ROTHFELS, HANS. *The German Opposition to Hitler: an Assessment.* London, 1961.
ROWSE, A. L. *All Souls and Appeasement.* London, 1961.
SAUNDBY, AIR MARSHAL SIR ROBERT. *Air Bombardment.* London, 1961.
SCHACHT, HJALMAR. *Account Settled.* London, 1949.
SCHELLENBERG, WALTER. *The Schellenberg Memoirs.* London, 1956.
SCHLABRENDORFF, FABIAN VON. *The Secret War against Hitler.* London, 1966.
SCHRAMM, WILHELM VON. *Conspiracy Among Generals.* London, 1957.
SCHROTER, HEINZ. *Stalingrad.* London, 1958.
SEYMOUR, CHARLES. *The Intimate Papers of Colonel House.* 2 vols. London, 1926-1928.
SHERWOOD, ROBERT E. *Roosevelt and Hopkins, an Intimate History.* New York, 1948.
(Also published as *The White House Papers of Harry L. Hopkins.* 2 vols. London, 1948.)
SHIRER, W. *The Rise and Fall of the Third Reich.* London, 1960.
SHULMAN, MILTON. *Defeat in the West.* London, 1947.
SIMONDS, FRANK H. *How Europe Made Peace without America.* London, 1927.

SLESSOR, MARSHAL OF THE R. A. F. SIR JOHN. *The Great Deterrent.* London, 1957.

SLIM, FIELD-MARSHAL LORD. *Defeat into Victory.* London, 1956.

SNELL, E. M. See Matloff, Maurice.

SPEARS, MAJOR-GENERAL SIR EDWARD. *Assignment to Catastrophe.* 2 vols. London, 1954.

SPEIDEL, HANS. *We Defended Normandy.* London, 1951.

STACEY, C. P. *The Canadian Army, 1939-1945.* Ottawa, 1948.

STETTINIUS, EDWARD R. *Roosevelt and the Russians.* New York, 1950.

STIMSON, H. L., AND BUNDY, MCGEORGE. *On Active Service in Peace and War.* London, 1948.

TANNER, V. *The Winter War.* New York, 1955.

TAYLOR, A. J. P. *The Origins of the Second World War.* London, 1961.

TEMPERLEY, H. W. V. *A History of the Peace Conference of Paris.* 6 vols. London, 1920-1924.

TEMPLEWOOD, VISCOUNT. *Ambassador on Special Mission.* London, 1946.

Nine Troubled Years. London, 1954.

TREVOR-ROPER, H. R. *The Last Days of Hitler.* London, 1956.

TRUMAN, HARRY S. *Year of Decisions, 1945.* New York, 1955.

VAETH, J. GORDON. *Graf Zeppelin.* London, 1959.

WALDECK, R. G. *Excellenz X.* London, 1944.

WALLACE, GRAHAM. *R.A.F. Biggin Hill.* London, 1957.

WARLIMONT, WALTER. *Inside Hitler's Headquarters, 1939-1945.* London, 1964.

WATSON, MARK S. *Chief of Staff: Pre-War Plans and Preparations.* Washington, 1950.

WEBSTER, SIR CHARLES, AND FRANKLAND, N. *The Strategic Air Offensive against Germany* (History of the Second World War, United Kingdom Military Series). 4 vols. London, 1961.

WELLES, SUMNER. *The Time for Decision.* London, 1944.

Seven Decisions that Shaped History. New York, 1950.

(Also published as *Seven Major Decisions.* London, 1951.)

WERTH, ALEXANDER. *Russia at War, 1941-1945.* London, 1964.

WESTPHAL, (GENERAL) SIEGFRIED. *The German Army in the West.* London, 1950.

WEYGAND, (GENERAL) MAXIME. *Rappelé au Service.* Paris, 1950.

WHEATLEY, RONALD. *Operation Sea Lion.* London, 1958.

WHEELER-BENNETT, J. W. *The Nemesis of Power; the German Army in Politics, 1918-1945.* London, 1953.

WIGMORE, L. *The Japanese Thrust.* Canberra, 1957.

WILLIAMS, W. A. *The Tragedy of American Diplomacy.* New York, 1962.

WILMOT, CHESTER. *The Struggle for Europe.* London, 1952 and 1965.

WILSON OF LIBYA, LORD. *Eight Years Overseas, 1939-1947.* London, 1948.

WOOD, DEREK, AND DEMPSTER, DEREK. *The Narrow Margin.* London, 1961.

WOODWARD, E. L. *British Foreign Policy during the Second World War.* London, 1962.

WYKEHAM, PETER. *Fighter Command.* London, 1960.

YANAGA, C. *Japan Since Perry.* New York, 1949.

YOUNG, DESMOND. *Rommel.* London, 1950.

YOUNG, G. M. *Stanley Baldwin.* London, 1952.

ZBYSZEWSKI, KAROL. *The Fight for Narvik.* London, 1940.

SOURCE NOTES

1. Prelude (1918-1934)

1. For the pre-armistice negotiations and the Versailles Treaty, see Temperley, *A History of the Peace Conference of Paris;* Seymour, *The Intimate Papers of Colonel House.* For a cross-section of contemporary opinion see House and Seymour, *What Really Happened at Paris;* Keynes, *The Economic Consequences of the Peace;* Nicolson, *Peace-making, 1919.* Duroselle, *From Wilson to Roosevelt,* p. 86, refers briefly to the exchanges between House and the European Allies.
2. The draft treaty was formally presented to the German delegates at Versailles on May 7, 1919; a version amended in the light of written comments was signed on June 28. On the first occasion Count Brockdorff-Rantzau offended President Wilson and others by making an oral protest without rising. However, by remaining seated when offering his opinion Brockdorff-Rantzau (an experienced professional diplomat) merely observed the usual practice at international conferences.
3. The Germans were promised a conference to discuss the detailed application of the Fourteen Points. (Pre-armistice telegrams, text in Temperley, *op. cit.*). No such conference was held. The Paris Conference (officially styled the Preliminary Peace Conference of Paris) was a conference between the Allied and Associated Powers, from which the Germans were excluded. On the two occasions when the Germans met the Allied and Associated Powers face-to-face at Versailles the proceedings (apart from Brockdorff-Rantzau's outburst) were purely formal.
4. Quoted by Symonds, *How Europe Made Peace without America.*
5. For the decision to build the Maginot Line see Namier, *Europe in Decay,* p. 37.
6. The book was Oberth, *Wege Zur Raumschiffahrt* (Munich, 1929). For a reference to its supposed influence on German military thought see Collier, *The Defence of the United Kingdom,* p. 334.
7. For the background of Western strategy in the Far East see Feis, *The Road to Pearl Harbor;* Kirby, *The War Against Japan,* volume 1. For references to a number of books on relations between Japan and the West see notes to Chapters 12, 20, 21.
8. Collier, *Defence of the United Kingdom,* p. 24.

9. For Hitler's rise to power see Bullock, *Hitler: A Study in Tyranny;* Hitler, *My Struggle (Mein Kampf);* Papen, *Memoirs;* Schacht, *Account Settled;* Shirer, *The Rise and Fall of the Third Reich;* Wheeler-Bennett, *The Nemesis of Power.*

2. Breakdown in Europe (1931-1936)

1. Avon, *Facing the Dictators*, pp. 24ff.
2. Collier, *Defence of the United Kingdom*, pp. 25-48.
3. No one knows precisely what Laval said to Mussolini. See, however, Avon, p. 123; Namier, *Europe in Decay*, pp. 16-17.
4. Avon, p. 179.
5. *ibid.*, pp. 133-41; Collier, p. 30.
6. Collier, pp. 28-30 .
7. Avon, p. 230.
8. *ibid.*, pp. 332-3; Namier, pp. 10-11, 17-18.
9. Avon, p. 134.
10. For French indecision and unpreparedness see Namier, pp. 5-6, 11-25. For Flandin's account see *Politique française, 1919-40.*

3. On the Eve (1936-1939)

1. Avon, *Facing the Dictators*, pp. 485, 490.
2. Collier, *Defence of the United Kingdom*, pp. 46-8.
3. *ibid.*, p. 42 (footnote).
4. *ibid.*, p. 66 (footnote).
5. For Right Wing opposition to Hitler, see Colvin, *Chief of Intelligence;* Hassel, *The von Hassel Diaries;* Prittie, *Germans Against Hitler;* Ritter, *The German Resistance;* Rothfels, *The German Opposition to Hitler;* Schlabrendorff, *The Secret War against Hitler;* Schramm, *Conspiracy among Generals;* Wheeler-Bennett, *The Nemesis of Power.* These are cited below by names of authors only.
6. Ritter, p. 95; Rothfels, p. 59; Schlabrendorff, pp. 91-2.
7. Ritter points out (p. 95) that Kleist was not aware of Jodl's views when he spoke of 'all the German generals.'
8. Schlabrendorff, p. 103; Ritter, pp. 113-14; Rothfels, p. 60.
9. Collier, pp. 67-8.
10. Ritter points out (p. 131) that the report did not reach London

until after Chamberlain and his colleagues had decided to announce their readiness to stand by Poland if the French agreed.

11. Warlimont, *Inside Hitler's Headquarters*, p. 20.
12. Collier, p. 72.
13. Warlimont, p. 22.
14. Collier, p. 73.
15. Vaeth, *Graf Zeppelin*, p. 231; Wood and Dempster, *The Narrow Margin*, pp. 17-20; Wykeham, *Fighter Command*, p. 148.
16. Schlabrendorff states (p. 96) that he told Lord Lloyd in the summer of 1939 that a German attack on Poland was imminent and that a treaty between Hitler and Stalin could be expected at any moment. Doubtless the government had other sources of information.
17. Most authorities (including Warlimont, who provided notes for Greiner's account of the proceedings in the OKW Operations Staff War Diary) give the date as August 22 (Warlimont, pp. 25, 590). Manstein (*Lost Victories*, pp. 28-30) says that the date was August 21 and that Ribbentrop took leave of the Führer while the conference was sitting. As Ribbentrop seems to have had time to make a telephone call to Ciano and spend a night in East Prussia before reaching Moscow about 1.30 p.m. on August 23, he must have travelled fast from the Berghof if both Manstein's account of his presence and the date given in the War Diary are correct.
18. Warlimont, p. 26.
19. Namier, *Diplomatic Prelude*, pp. 320-31.
20. *ibid.*, pp. 350-2.

4. *The Campaign in Poland and the Russo-Finnish War (1939-1940)*

1. Butler, *Grand Strategy Volume II*, p. 54; Namier, *Europe in Decay*, pp. 257-8, and *Diplomatic Prelude*, pp. 150, 171-2, 205-10
2. For an account of Polish strategy see Butler, pp. 54-5.
3. *ibid.*, p. 55.
4. *ibid.*, pp. 55-6; Goutard, *The Battle of France, 1940*, p. 65 Namier, *Europe in Decay*, p. 7; *Diplomatic Prelude*, pp. 457-62.
5. For German dispositions and plans see Butler, pp. 57-8; Manstein *Lost Victories*, pp. 34-40.
6. Warlimont, *Inside Hitler's Headquarters, 1939-1945*, pp. 32, 591
7. Manstein, p. 56.

8. Butler, p. 58.
9. Manstein, p. 58.
0. *ibid.*, p. 60.
1. Speech by Molotov, reported by Werth, *Russia at War, 1941-1945*, p. 63.
2. Werth, pp. 64, 66.
3. *ibid.*, p. 74 (quoting Soviet official history).
4. *ibid.*, p. 75 (footnote).
5. Butler, pp. 107-9.
6. Werth, pp. 70 and 72 (quoting Stalin and others).

. War in the West: the Saar to Narvik (1939-1940)

1. For Allied and German plans and dispositions see Butler, *Grand Strategy Volume II;* Roskill, *The War at Sea,* volume 1; Ellis, *The War in France and Flanders, 1939-1940.* See also Goutard, *The Battle of France, 1940*; Warlimont, *Inside Hitler's Headquarters, 1939-1945.*
2. Goutard, pp. 66-71.
3. Roskill, p. 103; Collier, *Defence of the United Kingdom,* p. 81.
4. For magnetic mines see Roskill, pp. 98ff; Collier, pp. 85-8.
5. Roskill, pp. 63-90, 111ff.
6. Saundby, *Air Bombardment,* pp. 82-3.
7. For facts and figures relating to the Scandinavian campaign see Derry, *The Campaign in Norway.* For high-level discussions and decisions see Butler, *Grand Strategy Volume II,* and Warlimont, *Inside Hitler's Headquarters, 1939-1945;* for the naval aspect see Roskill, *The War at Sea.* For background and corroborative detail see Broch, *The Mountains Wait;* Buckley, *Norway—The Commandos—Dieppe;* Carton de Wiart, *Happy Odyssey;* Churchill, *The Second World War;* Maund, *Assault from the Sea;* Zbyszewski, *The Fight for Narvik.*
8. Warlimont, pp. 76-9.
9. Major-General A. Carton de Wiart, V.C. He tells his story in *Happy Odyssey.*
0. For Churchill's shortcomings compare Roskill, pp. 201-5.

6. War in the West: the Climax (I) (1939-1940).

1. Manstein, *Lost Victories*, pp. 85-7; Ritter, *The German Resistance*, p. 149; Warlimont, *Inside Hitler's Headquarters*, pp. 58, 594.
2. Goutard, *The Battle of France, 1939-1940*, pp. 75-76 (citing German sources).
3. *ibid.*, p. 27 (citing Guderian).
4. Butler, *Grand Strategy Volume II*, p. 177; Goutard, p. 24, says 135.
5. Butler, p. 178.
6. Goutard, pp. 76-7.
7. Butler, p. 177; Goutard, p. 24; For French tanks see Goutard, pp. 27-8.
8. Goutard, p. 37.
9. *ibid.*, p. 32.
10. Saundby, *Air Bombardment*, p. 98; Collier, *Defence of the United Kingdom*, p. 108.
11. Butler, p. 178; Goutard, p. 32; Collier, pp. 88-9, 108-11.
12. Butler, p. 166; Ellis, *The War in France and Flanders*, p. 25; Goutard, pp. 35-7.
13. Ellis, pp. 335-44; Manstein, pp. 94-126.
14. According to Manstein (p. 118) Jodl also referred to it, less favourably, as 'a roundabout route on which the God of War might catch us.'
15. Ellis, p. 318.
16. For the bombing of Rotterdam see Butler, pp. 569-70.
17. *ibid.*, p. 182.
18. Goutard, pp. 97-102.
19. *ibid.*, pp. 110-11 (quoting General Prioux).
20. *ibid.*, pp. 121-2.
21. *ibid.*, pp. 111-12, 115, and *passim.*
22. *ibid.*, p. 122.
23. *ibid.*, p. 144.
24. *ibid.*, p. 185.
25. *ibid.*, pp. 168-9.

7. *War in the West; the Climax (II) (1940)*

1. According to Goutard (*The Battle of France, 1939-1940*, p. 183), on May 16 there were no troops at all between the Sambre and the Aisne.
2. *ibid.*, pp. 193, 199, 206-7, 246
3. *ibid.*, pp. 201-3 (quoting Rundstedt and citing Liddell Hart).
4. General Order No. 14 of May 16, quoted by Goutard, pp. 181-2.
5. Ellis, *The War in France and Flanders*, p. 61; Goutard, pp. 203-4.
6. Goutard, pp. 102-3.
7. *ibid.*, pp. 102, 208.
8. Ellis, pp. 106-8; Goutard, pp. 210-11.
9. Goutard, p. 213.
10. Ellis, pp. 68-9; Collier, *Defence of the United Kingdom*, p. 111.
11. Ellis, p. 95. See also *Rommel Papers*, pp. 32-3.
12. Ellis, pp. 101, 348-9.
13. Goutard, p. 222.
14. Ellis, pp. 347-8.
15. *ibid.*, pp. 349-53. For another view see Goutard, pp. 227-34.
16. Roskill, *The War at Sea*, 1, pp. 217-28; Collier, pp. 111-16.
17. Goutard, pp. 246-7.
18. Butler, *Grand Strategy Volume II*, p. 200; Namier, *Europe in Decay*, pp. 49-57.
19. Collier, pp. 119-25.
20. *ibid.*, p. 121 and footnote 2.
21. For German invasion plans and preparations see Wheatley, *Operation Sea Lion*. Collier, pp. 147, 159-60, 220-8, 241, 245, also refers. See also Grinnell-Milne, *The Silent Victory*.
22. Wheatley, pp. 35, 40; Collier, pp. 175-6.
23. Wheatley, pp. 58-9, 60, 87; Collier, p. 160.
24. For a detailed account see McKee, *Strike from the Sky*.
25. Wood and Dempster, *The Narrow Margin*, p. 204.
26. Squadrons available, from Collier, pp. 453-5; strength, from Wood and Dempster, p. 463.
27. Wood and Dempster, p. 464.
28. *ibid.*, p. 470.
29. Collier, p. 452. Slightly different figures in Wood and Dempster, p. 479, appear to reflect different treatment of fighter-bombers and units employed for local defence.

30. Collier, p. 452. Wood and Dempster (p. 479), have 261 serviceable dive bombers.
31. For the progress of the battle see Collier, *The Defence of the United Kingdom*, and *The Battle of Britain;* O'Brien, *Civil Defence* (for civilian casualties); Wheatley, *Operation Sea Lion* (for relation to invasion plans); Wood and Dempster, *The Narrow Margin* (especially for details of British actual strengths and reserves). For background and detail see also Galland, *The First and the Last;* McKee, *Strike from the Sky;* Middleton, *The Sky Suspended;* Wallace, *R.A.F. Biggin Hill;* Wykeham, *Fighter Command.*
32. Luftwaffe estimate, Collier, *Battle of Britain*, p. 93.
33. Wood and Dempster, pp. 463-4.
34. Collier, *Defence of the United Kingdom*, pp. 203-4.
35. Wood and Dempster, p. 463.
36. Collier, *Defence of the United Kingdom*, pp. 459-60; *Battle of Britain*, pp. 121-2.
37. Collier, *Defence of the United Kingdom*, pp. 463-7.
38. Wheatley, pp. 76-8, 86.
39. Collier, *Defence of the United Kingdom*, pp. 223-4.
40. O'Brien, p. 388.
41. Wheatley, p. 73.
42. *ibid.*, pp. 88-9.
43. Figures from Collier, *Defence of the United Kingdom*, pp. 456-60, 491-2.
44. Wheatley, p. 49.

8. The Crossroads (I) (1940-1941)

1. Butler, *Grand Strategy Volume II*, p. 296.
2. Roskill, *War at Sea*, I, pp. 593-7; Butler, p. 297.
3. Butler, pp. 299, 303.
4. Butler, pp. 219-27; Roskill, *War at Sea*, I, pp. 241-5.
5. Butler, pp. 436-7, 516-23.
6. *ibid.*, pp. 341-5, 423-7.
7. Roskill, *War at Sea*, I, pp. 300-1. Some aircraft from the *Eagle*, with their crews, were transferred to the *Illustrious*.
8. Playfair, *The Mediterranean and Middle East*, volume I.
9. Collier, *Defence of the United Kingdom*, pp. 251-81, 494-8, 503-5; O'Brien, *Civil Defence*, pp. 386ff

10. Collier, p. 258.
11. *ibid.*, p. 265.
12. Butler, p. 408.
13. *ibid.*, p. 412.
14. *ibid.*, p. 485.
15. *ibid.*, p. 466.
16. This term seems to have come into general use after the issue of Churchill's 'Battle of the Atlantic' directive of March 6, 1941. The battle itself began much earlier. Captain Roskill, whose *War at Sea*, 1, and *The Royal Navy at War, 1939-1945* are the chief sources for the account given in this chapter, regards the struggle to protect the Atlantic convoy routes as having assumed a separate identity soon after the fall of France. Hitler's directive of February 6 has been taken as a convenient starting point for the phase considered here.
17. Roskill, *War at Sea*, 1, p. 346.
18. *ibid.*, pp. 617-18.
19. Butler, p. 472.
20. Collier, p. 289 and footnote; Roskill, *War at Sea*, 1, p. 477.
21. Roskill, pp. 617-18.
22. Figures adapted from Roskill, *War at Sea*, 1, pp. 617-18.
23. Collier, pp. 279ff, 615-16.
24. *ibid.*, pp. 287-92.
25. *ibid.*, pp. 373-8, 393.
26. *ibid.*, pp. 394-415; Joubert, *Birds and Fishes*, p. 142. See also Roskill, *The Royal Navy at War, 1939-1945*.

The Crossroads (II) (1940-1941)

Facts and figures in this chapter are from Playfair, *The Mediterranean and the Middle East*, and Butler, *Grand Strategy Volume II*, except where a different authority is cited below. See also Barnett, *The Desert Generals;* Bayerlein, *The Rommel Papers;* Davin, *Crete;* Heydte, *Daedalus Returned;* Long, *Greece, Crete and Syria;* Roskill, *The War at Sea* and *The Royal Navy at War, 1939-1948;* Young (Desmond), *Rommel.*

1. For an estimate of General O'Connor's contribution see Barnett, *The Desert Generals.*
2. For a British view of Rommel see Young (Desmond), *Rommel.*
3. Roskill, *War at Sea*, 1, p. 421.

4. *ibid.*, p. 437, gives (for the period after the arrival of reinforcements) 62 German and 15 Italian aircraft destroyed for the loss of 32 British fighters in the air and nearly as many on the ground.
5. The figure of 100,000 tons is for the Central Mediterranean alone. Roskill, *War at Sea*, I, p. 439, gives 233,440 tons of Italian shipping sunk in all areas, and 53,119 tons of German and German-controlled shipping sunk in all parts of the Mediterranean.
6. Photographs reproduced in Playfair, I, give some idea of the territories in which these offensives were launched. Even today it is something of an adventure to *travel* in parts of Abyssinia, let alone move supplies and equipment for an army.
7. The loss of O'Connor and of Lieutenant-General Philip Neame, V.C., who together took a wrong turning in the darkness and fell into Axis hands, was also a severe blow to the British.
8. Desmond Young (*Rommel*, p. 83 and *passim*) stresses the veiled hostility between Rommel and OKH. See also Playfair *passim* on differences of outlook between Rommel and his German and Italian superiors.
9. Roskill, *War at Sea*, I, pp. 427-30.
10. For an Australian view see Long, *Greece, Crete and Syria.*
11. Papagos, *The Battle of Greece* (Athens, 1949, in English) gives the Commander-in-Chief's retrospective view. The account given here follows the British official histories.
12. For a New Zealand view of the Campaign in Crete see Davin, *Crete.*
13. Heydte, *Daedalus Returned*, pp. 39-43.
14. *ibid.*, pp. 101, 118, 127, 132, 166-7, 171.

10. *Germany and Russia (October 1939-March 1942)*

1. Werth, *Russia at War,1941-1945*, pp. 141, 142.
2. *ibid.*, pp. 133-4 (quoting Draft Field Regulations and official history).
3. *ibid.*, pp. 83, 87, 90.
4. *ibid.*, pp. 137-8.
5. *ibid.*, p. 138.
6. Gwyer, *Grand Strategy Volume III Part I*, p. 75; Werth, p. 113.
7. Gwyer, p. 63.
8. *ibid.*, p. 92.
9. According to the Soviet official history, the General Staff assumed

that a surprise attack was out of the question. A German offensive 'would be preceded by a declaration of war, or by small-scale military operations, after which the Soviet troops could take up their defensive positions.' Werth, p. 139 (quoting Soviet official history).

10. Soviet official history, quoted by Werth, p. 137.
11. Soviet official history, quoted by Werth, p. 141.
12. A first-line strength of fewer than 3,000 aircraft, as compared with about 3,500.
13. Gwyer, p. 90.
14. Gwyer, p. 90; Sherwood, *The White House Papers of Harry L. Hopkins*, volume 1, pp. 303-4.
15. Gwyer, p. 92, has 10,000 prisoners and 800 aircraft. Werth, p. 156, has 1,200 aircraft before noon on the first day.
16. Werth, p. 156 (citing Soviet official history).
17. *ibid.*, pp. 159-61.
18. For German progress see Gwyer, Werth. See also Alan Clark, *Barbarossa;* Philippi und Heim, *Der Feldzug gegen Sowjetrussland.* For National Socialist policy and conduct in occupied territory see Dallin, *German Rule in Russia, 1941-1945.*
19. Gwyer, pp. 95-6.
20. Werth, pp. 162-7.
21. *ibid.*, pp. 213-23.
22. *ibid.*, p. 222 (quoting Soviet official history).
23. Sherwood, *The White House Papers of Harry L. Hopkins*, volume 1, pp. 332ff; Gwyer, pp. 96, 109.
24. Roskill, *The Royal Navy at War, 1939-1945; War at Sea*, 1, pp. 489, 492ff.
25. Gwyer, pp. 146-8.
26. *ibid.*, pp. 151-5.
27. *ibid.*, pp. 155-61.
28. *ibid.*, pp. 98-100.
29. For operations on the Leningrad front in 1941 see Gwyer, pp. 92-3; Werth, pp. 297-362; Manstein, *Lost Victories*, pp. 178-203. See also Alan Clark, *Barbarossa:* Philippi und Heim, *Der Feldzug gegen Sowjetrussland.*
30. For operations in the central sector see Gwyer; Werth; Clark. Philippi und Heim also refer.
31. Clark; Werth. See also Philippi und Heim.
32. Werth, pp. 310, 324.
33. Clark; Gwyer; Werth. See also Philippi und Heim.

34. Werth, pp. 231-42.
35. Clark, pp. 144-5; Werth, p. 230.
36. Werth, pp. 175, 182, 254.
37. Werth, pp. 256-7 (quoting account by Soviet commander on the spot).
38. For Zhukov's counter-offensive see Clark; Philippi und Heim; Werth.
39. Werth, pp. 259-60 (citing Soviet and German sources).

11. The Desert War (May 1941-February 1942)

Facts and figures in this chapter are from Playfair, *The Mediterranean and Middle East*, and the British *Grand Strategy* volumes, except where a different authority is cited. See also Barnett, *The Desert Generals*, Churchill, *The Second World War;* Connell, *Auchinleck;* Liddell Hart *The Rommel Papers;* Roskill, *The War at Sea;* Young (Desmond), *Rommel.*

1. Gwyer, *Grand Strategy Volume III Part I*, p. 90.
2. General Cunningham was a brother of Admiral Sir Andrew Cunningham. For an estimate of his character and achievement see Barnett, *The Desert Generals.*

12. The Far East (December 1935-May 1942)

1. Avon, *Facing the Dictators*, p. 524; Jones, *Japan's New Order in East Asia*, p. 23; Kirby, *The War Against Japan*, volume 1, p. 13
2. Avon, pp. 530ff; Jones, pp. 30-70; Kirby, 1, pp. 18-19. For the British and American response see Avon, pp. 531-5; Duroselle *From Wilson to Roosevelt*, pp. 300-1; Jones, pp. 38ff.
3. Jones, pp. 172-90; Werth, *Russia at War, 1939-1945*, pp. 9, 135
4. For British and American policy and strategy see Duroselle, pp. 300ff; Jones, pp. 153-70; Kirby, 1, pp. 21-33. See also Butler *Grand Strategy Volume II;* Feis, *The Road to Pearl Harbor* Morison, *The Rising Sun in the Pacific;* Woodward, *British Foreign Policy during the Second World War.*
5. Morison, *The History of United States Naval Operations in World War II*, volume III, p. 4.
6. Jones, pp. 165-71; Kirby, 1, pp. 45-6.
7. Jones, pp. 221-31; Kirby, 1, p. 44.

8. Jones, pp. 196-200; Kirby, I, p. 46.
9. Butler, pp. 423-7, 504-5.
10. Kirby, I, p. 63.
11. *ibid.*, p. 64. For a discussion of Matsuoka's views see Jones, pp. 250-6.
12. Jones, pp. 273-8; Kirby, I, pp. 64-5.
13. Jones, pp. 278, 280; Kirby, I, pp. 66, 69.
14. Jones, p. 263; Kirby, I, p. 69.
15. Gwyer, *Grand Strategy Volume III Part I*, p. 131; Kirby, I, p. 70.
16. Jones, pp. 281-2; Kirby, I, pp. 71-2, 73-4.
17. Gwyer, pp. 130-7; Jones, pp. 282-3; Kirby, I, pp. 72-3.
18. Jones, p. 284; Kirby, I, p. 74.
19. Gwyer, p. 256.
20. For the subsequent course of the negotiations see Gwyer, pp. 256-65; Jones, pp. 307-20; Kirby, I, pp. 84, 86-8.
21. Kirby, I, p. 90.
22. Kirby, I, pp. 491-2, 418-20; Roskill, *The War at Sea*, I, pp. 559-60.
23. For the Japanese strategic plan see Kirby, I, pp. 90-6.
24. *ibid.*, pp. 90-6.
25. *ibid.*, p. 97.
26. For details of the Pearl Harbor attack see Morison, *The History of United States Naval Operations in World War II*, volume III. See also Kirby, I, pp. 98-9; Roskill, *War at Sea*, I, pp. 562-3.
27. Morton, *The Fall of the Philippines*. See also Kirby, I, pp. 100-3.
28. Morison; Wigmore, *The Japanese Thrust*. See also Kirby, I, pp. 103-5.
29. Kirby, I, pp. 107-51.
30. For operations in Malaya see Kirby, I. See also *War at Sea*, I, pp. 563-7.
31. Kirby, I, pp. 14-15.
32. *ibid.*, p. 35.
33. *ibid.*, pp. 41, 55, 459-60.
34. Roskill, *War at Sea*, I, pp. 555-9.
35. Kirby, I, pp. 77, 163.
36. *ibid.*, pp. 169-70.
37. *ibid.*, pp. 76-7, 170.
38. *ibid.*, pp 173-5. See also Gwyer, pp. 292-3.
39. Kirby, I, p. 180; Gwyer, p. 303.
40. Kirby, I, p. 182; Gwyer, p. 303.
41. Kirby, I, p. 183.

42. *ibid.*, .pp. 186-7.
43. For details see Roskill, *War at Sea*, I, pp. 564-7.
44. Gwyer, p. 370.
45. Kirby, I, p. 369.
46. *ibid.*, pp. 283-4, 296.
47. *ibid.*, p. 362. In addition there were about 15,000 non-combatant troops.
48. *ibid.*, p. 375.
49. Kirby estimates (I, p. 409) that by February 13 there were about a million civilians within a three-mile radius of the waterfront at Singapore town.
50. *ibid.*, pp. 409-15.
51. Butler, *Grand Strategy Volume III Part II*, pp. 471-4.
52. *ibid.*, p. 475.
53. Roskill, *War at Sea*, II, pp. 13-18. See also Morison.
54. Butler, p. 468.
55. *ibid.*, p. 469.
56. Roskill, *War at Sea*, II, p. 28.
57. *ibid.*, pp. 28-30.
58. *ibid.*, p. 191; Butler, pp. 489-92.

13. A Ring Round Germany: the North and West (December 1941-August 1943)

Part I (Gwyer) and Part II (Butler) of *Grand Strategy Volume III* are cited below as *Grand Strategy III*.

1. *Grand Strategy III*, pp. 669-72.
2. *ibid.*, pp. 572-81.
3. *ibid.*, p. 622.
4. Roskill, *War at Sea*, I, pp. 513-14; II, pp. 168-73; Collier, *Defence of the United Kingdom*, p. 331.
5. Roskill, *War at Sea*, II, pp. 240-52. See also Buckley, *Narvik—The Commandos—Dieppe;* Stacey, *The Canadian Army, 1939-1945*.
6. For the origin of 'Torch' see *Grand Strategy III*, pp. 16-17, 157, 326-9, 334, 337, 353-6, 360-5, 626-8, 631-4, 671. See also Morison, *The Two-Ocean War*.
7. *Grand Strategy III*, p. 645.
8. Roskill, *War at Sea*, II, pp. 115, 475.
9. For the move of the *Scharnhorst and Gneisenau* see Roskill, *War.*

at Sea, II, pp. 149-58. See also *The Royal Navy at War, 1939-1945*.

10. Roskill, *War at Sea*, II, pp. 115-46, 277-99. See also *The Royal Navy at War, 1939-1945*.
11. Morison, *The History of United States Naval Operations in World War II*, volume I, pp. 125ff; Roskill, *War at Sea*, II, p. 96.
12. *Grand Strategy III*, p. 509.
13. Webster and Frankland, *The Strategic Air Offensive against Germany*, volume I, pp. 473-92.
14. For an account of the Baedeker raids see Collier, *Defence of the United Kingdom*, pp. 305ff, 512-14.
15. Roskill, *War at Sea*, II, pp. 485-6.
16. The true figures appear to have been 436 all told and 168 fit for sea (Roskill, *War at Sea*, III, I, p. 364).
17. Roskill, II, p. 351.
18. *ibid.*, pp. 352-3.
19. *ibid.*, pp. 362-4; *Grand Strategy III*, pp. 534-40.
20. Roskill, *War at Sea*, II, pp. 358-9. See also *The Royal Navy at War, 1939-1945*.

14. *A Ring Round Germany: the East (March 1942-September 1945)*

1. Manstein, *Lost Victories*, p. 263.
2. *Grand Strategy III*, p. 594.
3. *ibid.*, p. 513.
4. Manstein, pp. 231-59; Werth, *Russia at War, 1941-1945*, pp. 388-9, 393-400.
5. Werth, pp. 389-93 (quoting Soviet official history and Khrushchev's speech).
6. Werth, p. 406.
7. *ibid.*, pp. 407-8.
8. Clark, *Barbarossa*, p. 184
9. Manstein, pp. 291-4; Werth, pp. 566-7.
10. Manstein, p. 293.
11. Werth, pp. 564-81; Conrad, *Kampf um den Kaukasus*.
12. For events at Stalingrad see Manstein, pp. 289-366; Schröter, *Stalingrad;* Werth, pp. 441-72, 493-563. See also Clark, *Barbarossa*; Philippi und Heim, *Der Feldzug gegen Sowjetrussland*.
13. Werth, p. 495.
14. Schröter, pp. 52-3.

15. For a discussion of this figure see Manstein, p. 296.
16. Schröter, pp. 107, 163; Manstein, pp. 309, 316-18.
17. Manstein, pp. 311, 557.
18. *ibid.*, p. 557. See also Schröter, pp. 163-4.
19. Manstein, pp. 332-4.
20. *ibid.*, 336-7, 560-3.
21. *ibid.*, pp. 338-42.
22. *ibid.*, pp. 347-50.
23. *ibid.*, p. 365. Dibold, *Doctor at Stalingrad*, p. 191, says that 45,000 were flown out.
24. Schröter, pp. 225-6, 242-4.
25. Schröter, p. 225.
26. Manstein, p. 358.
27. Schröter, p. 261.
28. Manstein, p. 372.
29. Werth, p. 595.
30. Manstein, pp. 392, 404, 408-9, 412; Warlimont, *Inside Hitler's Headquarters*, p. 286.
31. Manstein, pp. 412-13.
32. *ibid.*, p. 426.
33. *ibid.*, pp. 423, 428, 431.
34. *ibid.*, pp. 431-7; Werth, p. 632.
35. Ehrman, *Grand Strategy Volume VI*, pp. 4-6.
36. Schlabrendorff, *The Secret War against Hitler*, pp. 230-8.
37. Clark, pp. 284-8, 291-3; Manstein, pp. 447-8.
38. Clark, pp. 288-91; Werth, p. 681.
39. Clark, pp. 294-7.
40. Werth, pp. 682-3 (quoting communiqué).
41. Clark, p. 300; Manstein, p. 448.
42. Clark, p. 300.

15. A Ring Round Germany: the South (I) (February-September 1942)

Facts and figures in this chapter are from Playfair, *The Mediterranean and Middle East*, volume III, except where a different authority is cited.

1. Roskill, *War at Sea*, II, pp. 47-8.
2. *ibid.*, pp. 51-5.
3. *Grand Strategy III*, p. 460.

4. *ibid.*, *loc. cit.*
5. The reference to artillery is based on information communicated by General Corbett.
6. *Grand Strategy III*, pp. 606-7.
7. *ibid.*, p. 629.
8. *ibid.*, p. 607.
9. Barnett, *The Desert Generals*, pp. 216-19, 303; Connell, *Auchinleck*, pp. 717-18, 941-3.
10. *Grand Strategy III*, p. 607.
11. According to General Corbett, the immediate occasion (though not necessarily the sole cause) of Churchill's anger was the disclosure that the tanks which Churchill had persuaded the Americans to send could not be used in battle for at least a fortnight after their arrival.
12. Or according to Rommel's subsequent account, because the British tanks were again assembled ready for immediate action (Young, *Rommel*, p. 272).

16. A Ring Round Germany: the South (II) (July 1942-June 1944)

1. For the evolution of plans for 'Torch' see Morison, *The History of United States Naval Operations in World War II*, volume II; Playfair, *The Mediterranean and Middle East*, volume IV; Roskill, *The War at Sea*, volume II.
2. Figures from Playfair, pp. 126-7. These do not include follow-up formations.
3. *ibid.*, p. 2.
4. *ibid.*, p. 30, gives a tentative figure of 104,000.
5. *ibid.*, pp. 9-10.
6. *ibid.*, p. 28.
7. Stumme told his subordinate commanders on October 20 that the attack might come at any point (Playfair, p. 27).
8. Playfair, p. 27.
9. *ibid.*, pp. 7-10, 30.
10. Barnett, *The Desert Generals*, p. 255. Compare Playfair, pp. 4-5, 6-7, 34, 35.
11. Playfair, pp. 38-40.
12. *ibid.*, p. 44.
13. *ibid.*, pp. 45-6.

14. *ibid.*, pp. 46, 47, 51, 52, 53, 54, 56-7.
15. *ibid.*, pp. 52, 78, gives 6,140 casualties in the first 60 hours, and a total of 13,560 by dawn on November 4.
16. *ibid.*, p. 52, gives an approximate figure of 300 knocked out by October 26.
17. Churchill, *The Second World War*, volume IV, p. 534.
18. *ibid.*, pp. 534-5.
19. Axis losses in killed and wounded during the fighting at El Alamein are not precisely known; but General Bayerlein gives a tentative estimate of 7,800 for the battle and the subsequent retreat to Mersa Brega (*Rommel Papers*, p. 358). In addition about 7,000 prisoners were taken during the battle (Playfair, p. 79). If these figures are even approximately correct, and if the Axis forces started with 104,000 fighting troops, there cannot have been less than about 90,000 survivors, non-combatants included. As the Eighth Army took only about 23,000 prisoners in the round-up immediately after the battle, it follows that the number who escaped must greatly have exceeded the number left behind.
20. Barnett, p. 271.
21. For the execution of 'Torch' see Morison, *The History of United States Naval Operations in World War II*, volume II; Playfair, *The Mediterranean and Middle East*, volume IV; Roskill, *The War at Sea*, volume II. See also Churchill, *The Second World War*, volume IV; Moorehead, *African Trilogy*.
22. Playfair, p. 172.
23. *ibid.*, pp. 289-90.
24. On February 20 Alexander ordered Anderson to cover four localities to the north of the main axis of the enemy's advance, and one locality immediately to the west, where there was an important group of landing grounds (Playfair, p. 305).
25. Playfair, p. 321.
26. *ibid.*, p. 320.
27. *ibid.*, pp. 397-8.
28. Churchill, p. 734.
29. Ehrman, *Grand Strategy Volume V*, pp. 112-13.
30. *ibid.*, p. 288. The figure has been taken, by permission, from an unpublished source.
31. *ibid.*, p. 61.
32. *ibid.*, pp. 63-4.
33. *ibid.*, pp. 64-5.

34. *ibid.*, p. 65.
35. For the invasion of Italy and the advance to Rome see Ehrman; Roskill, *The War at Sea*, volume III, Part I. See also Majdalany, *Cassino: Portrait of a Battle.*
36. Ehrman, pp. 106-21.
37. *ibid.*, pp. 94-8.
38. *ibid.*, pp. 61-2, 68.
39. *ibid.*, p. 69.
40. *ibid.*, p. 71.
41. Roughly 18,500 assault vessels of all categories were produced in 1943. (Ehrman, pp. 37-8.)
42. For the 'Anvil' controversy see *ibid.*, pp. 233ff.
43. *ibid.*, p. 264.
44. *ibid.*, pp. 256, 264.

17. The Conquest of Germany (I) (August 1943-August 1944)

1. Manstein, *Lost Victories*, pp. 474-5.
2. *ibid.*, p. 472.
3. *ibid.*, p. 473.
4. Werth, *Russia at War, 1941-1945*, pp. 625-6.
5. Manstein, pp. 487, 495.
6. Werth, p. 759.
7. *ibid.*, pp. 700-9. See also Dallin, *German Rule in Russia, 1941-1945*
8. Werth, pp. 635-67.
9. For the proceedings at Teheran see Ehrman, *Grand Strategy Volume V*, pp, 173-83.
10. Werth, pp. 765, 776, 777-85.
11. *ibid.*, pp. 832-3.
12. Figures from Ehrman, p. 279.
13. Ellis, *Victory in the West*, volume I, p. 10.
14. *ibid.*, p. 17.
15. Ehrman, p. 200.
16. *ibid.*, pp. 179, 180.
17. Ellis, p. 34.
18. Figures from Ellis, pp. 72, 79, 80, 507.
19. *ibid.*, pp. 128-9.
20. *ibid.*, p. 128.

21. *ibid.*, pp. 119-20.
22. *ibid.*, p. 129.
23. *ibid.*, p. 130.
24. *ibid.*, pp. 139-44.
25. Figures from Ellis, pp. 57, 120, 519-20.
26. Figures from Ellis, p. 223.
26. Figures from Ellis, p. 223.
27. *ibid.*, p. 198.
28. Facts and figures in the rest of the chapter are from Ellis, except where a different authority is cited.
29. Collier, *Defence of the United Kingdom*, p. 359.
30. *ibid.*, pp. 360-1, 362.
31. *ibid.*, pp. 376-9, 385-9.
32. Figures from Collier, pp. 523, 524, and *passim.*
33. Figures from Werth, pp. 625-6.
34. Ehrman, p. 368.
35. Werth, p. 860.
36. *ibid.*, pp. 864-5.
37. *ibid.*, pp. 867-9.
38. *ibid.*, pp. 869-83; Ehrman, p. 369-76.
39. Werth, p. 872.
40. Ehrman, p. 376.
41. *ibid.*, p. 384.
42. For details of Stauffenberg's attempt see Schlabrendorff, *The Secret War against Hitler*, pp. 276-302; Ritter, *The German Resistance*, pp. 257-87.

18. The Conquest of Germany (II) (July-November 1944)

1. Ellis, *Victory in the West*, volume 1, pp. 398-9.
2. Ehrman, *Grand Strategy Volume V*, p. 347.
3. Ehrman, *Grand Strategy Volume VI*, p. 10.
4. Ellis, pp. 395-8.
5. Ehrman, v, p. 354.
6. Facts and figures relating to Allied progress on the Western front are from Ellis, except where a different authority is cited.
7. Collier, p. 390.
8. Ehrman, v, p. 401.
9. Tables 13 and 14 based on Collier, pp. 392-7, 406-20, 523-8.
10. Ehrman, v, p. 530.

11. Ehrman, VI, p. 6.
12. Collier, p. 410.
13. Ehrman, V, pp. 532-3.

19. *The Conquest of Germany (III) (December 1944-May 1945)*

1. Ehrman, *Grand Strategy Volume VI*, pp. 36-7.
2. Ellis, *Victory in the West*, volume 1, p. 444 (footnote).
3. For the German plan and its execution see Merriam, *The Battle of the Ardennes;* Wilmot, *The Struggle for Europe.*
4. Ehrman, pp. 67-8; Merriam, p. 117.
5. Merriam, p. 152.
6. *ibid.*, pp. 199, 200.
7. *ibid., loc. cit.*
8. Wilmot, p. 693.
9. *ibid.*, p. 694.
10. Ehrman, pp. 69-95.
11. *ibid.*, p. 72.
12. *ibid.*, p. 80.
13. *ibid.*, pp. 80-1.
14. *ibid.*, pp. 72-6.
15. *ibid.*, pp. 89-91.
16. *ibid.*, p. 89.
17. Bryant, *Triumph in the West*, pp. 393-4.
18. Ehrman, pp. 81-2; Werth, *Russia at War, 1941-1945*, p. 953.
19. Wilmot, pp. 692-3. For importance attached to U-boats, see also Ehrman, p. 16.
20. Wilmot, p. 695.
21. Werth, p. 955.
22. Ehrman, pp. 96, 111.
23. *ibid.*, p. 103.
24. *ibid.*, pp. 137-8.
25. *ibid.*, p. 138.
26. *ibid.*, pp. 92, 113.
27. *ibid.*, p. 115.
28. *ibid.*, p. 132.
29. *ibid.*, p. 133.
30. *ibid.*, p. 137.
31. *ibid.*, p. 149.

32. *ibid., loc. cit.*
33. *ibid.*, p. 144.
34. *ibid.*, p. 145.
35. *ibid.*, pp. 147-8.
36. *ibid.*, p. 156.
37. *ibid.*, p. 151.
38. *ibid.*, p. 153.
39. *ibid.*, pp. 155-6.
40. Werth, pp. 964-7.
41. Clark, *Barbarossa*, pp. 360-402; Trevor-Roper, *The Last Days of Hitler*.

20. *The Conquest of Japan (I) (April 1942-January 1945)*

Throughout this chapter accounts of naval actions are based on Morison, *The History of United States Naval Operations in World War II* and *The Two-Ocean War*. Reference has also been made to Kirby, *The War against Japan*, and Roskill, *The War at Sea* and *The Royal Navy at War*.

1. Kirby, *The War against Japan*, volume II, p. 226.
2. Figures from Kirby, III, p. 518.
3. Kirby, II, p. 271.
4. Kirby, II; Morison, *History*, V, Roskill, *War at Sea*, II.
5. Kirby, II; McCarthy, *South-West Pacific Area, First Year*.
6. Kirby, III, p. 83; Ehrman, *Grand Strategy Volume V*, p. 124.
7. Figures from Kirby, III, pp. 472-3.
8. Ehrman, V, p. 124; VI, pp. 203-11.
9. Beloff, *Soviet Policy in the Far East, 1944-1951*, pp. 20-7.
10. For very long-range bombers in China see Kirby, III, pp. 11, 57-8, 231, 232, 391-3; IV, pp. 37, 70, 89-91, 131-3.
11. *ibid.*, p. 394.
12. *ibid.*, p. 21.
13. Ehrman, V, p. 137.
14. *ibid.*, p. 138.
15. *ibid.*, p. 136.
16. *ibid.*, pp. 13-14; Kirby, III, p. 3-4.
17. Kirby, III, pp. 217-22.
18. Ehrman, V, pp. 163-7, 184-92.
19. *ibid.*, p. 427.
20. Kirby, III, p. 73.

21. *ibid*, p. 66.
22. *ibid*., p. 127.
23. *ibid*., pp. 133-52.
24. *ibid*., p. 45; Ehrman, v, p. 407.
25. Kirby, III, p. 189.
26. *ibid*., pp. 190-1.
27. *ibid*., p. 194.
28. *ibid*., pp. 197-200.
29. *ibid*., p. 372.
30. *ibid*., p. 226.
31. *ibid*., pp. 230-1.
32. For Stilwell's relations with Lentaigne and Mountbatten see Kirby, III, pp. 282-3, 402-15.
33. *ibid*., p. 295.
34. Kirby, IV, p. 108.
35. *ibid*., p. 193.

21. *The Conquest of Japan (II) (September 1943-September 1945)*

1. Kirby, *The War against Japan*, III, pp. 72-3.
2. Figures adapted from Kirby, III, pp. 474-5.
3. For a British view of Nimitz and MacArthur see Ehrman, *Grand Strategy Volume V*, pp. 431-3.
4. For the land fighting in New Guinea and the Bismarck Archipelago see Milner, *The New Guinea Offensives;* Rentz, *Bougainville and the Northern Solomons*. For the naval aspect see Morison, *History of U.S. Naval Operations,* volume VI; Roskill, *War at Sea*, volume III, Part I.
5. Kirby, III, p. 87.
6. For the assault on the Gilbert Islands see Morison, *History of U.S. Naval Operations*, volume VII; Roskill, *War at Sea*, volume III, Part I.
7. For the capture of the Marshall Islands see Morison, *History*, VII; Roskill, *War at Sea*, III, I.
8. Kirby, III, p. 109. Many more ships were destroyed in the next thiry-six hours.
9. *ibid*., p. 112.
10. *ibid*., pp. 425-7, 430, 432.
11. For the Battle of the Philippine Sea see Morison, *History*, VIII; Roskill, *War at Sea*, III. See also Kirby, III, pp. 443-6.

12. Kirby, III, p. 436.
13. Kirby, IV, pp. 53-4; Jones, *Japan's New Order in East Asia*, pp. 424-5.
14. *ibid.*, pp. 66-7.
15. Figures from Kirby, IV, pp. 448-51.
16. *ibid.*, p. 63.
17. *ibid.*, p. 64.
18. *ibid.*, pp. 70-1.
19. *ibid.*, p. 68.
20. For the ensuing naval battles for command of Leyte Gulf see Morison, *History*, XII; Roskill, *War at Sea*, III, II; *Kirby*, IV, *pp.* 73-83.
21. For operations on land see Kirby, IV, pp. 83-7.
22. Beloff, *Soviet Policy in the Far East, 1944-1951*, p. 25; Ehrman, VI, pp. 212-9.
23. Ehrman, p. 216; Beloff, p. 23. Deane, *The Strange Alliance*, pp. 247-8.
24. Ehrman, V, p. 518.
25. Ehrman, VI, pp. 221-2.
26. Morison, *History*, XII; Roskill, *War at Sea*, III, II.
27. Kirby, IV, pp. 225-33.
28. Jones, pp. 430-3.
29. *ibid.*, p. 436; Ehrman, VI, pp. 284-5. See also Kase, *Eclipse of the Rising Sun*, p. 184.
30. Ehrman, VI, p. 285; Jones, p. 436.
31. Ehrman, VI, p. 275.
32. Leahy, *I Was There*, p. 514.
33. Agreement was reached on June 20, 1942 (Butler, *Grand Strategy Volume III Part II*, p. 625).
34. Ehrman, VI, p. 276.
35. *ibid.*, p. 295.
36. *ibid.*, p. 296; Amrine, *The Great Decision*, pp. 59-60.
37. Ehrman, VI, pp. 275-6, 296.
38. *ibid.*, p. 298.
39. *ibid.*, p. 297.
40. *ibid.*, pp. 285-95.
41. *ibid.*, p. 279.
42. *ibid.*, p. 280.
43. *ibid.*, p. 289 (quoting article by Henry L. Stimson in *Harper's Magazine*, February 1947).
44. *ibid.*, p. 281.

45. *ibid.*, p. 290.
46. *ibid.*, p. 292.
47. Memorandum dated July 2, 1945 (text in Ehrman, VI, pp. 286-8).
48. Ehrman, pp. 277-8.
49. Millis, *The Forrestal Diaries*, pp. 86-7; Ehrman, VI, p. 304.
50. Byrnes, *Speaking Frankly*, pp. 205, 262; Ehrman, VI, pp. 301-3; Jones, p. 438.
51. Ehrman, VI, p. 306. See also Jones, p. 439.
52. Byrnes, p. 206.
53. Kase, p. 210.
54. Ehrman, VI, p. 310.
55. Saundby, *Air Bombardment*, p. 220.
56. Butow, *Japan's Decision to Surrender*, pp. 50ff; Ehrman, VI, p. 310; Jones, p. 442.
57. Jones, p. 442.
58. Ehrman, pp. 311-12; Jones, pp. 444-5.
59. Ehrman, VI, p. 312; Jones, p. 446.
60. Ehrman, VI, pp. 312-13; Jones, p. 448.
61. Roskill, *War at Sea*, volume III, Part II, pp. 382-3.
62. In a speech delivered on June 10, 1963, President John F. Kennedy estimated that not less than 20,000,000 people were killed in the Russo-German war alone (quoted by Werth, *Russia at War, 1941-1945*, p. xi).

INDEX